TOWARDS EMPOWERING INDIAN WOMEN

Mapping Specifics of Tasks in Crucial Sectors

TOWARDS EMPOWERING INDIAN WOMEN

Mapping Specifics of Tasks in Crucial Sectors

Edited by

R.B.S. VERMA

H.S. VERMA

NADEEM HASNAIN

Under the aegis of DSA and ASIHSS Programmes of U.G.C.
Department of Social Work
University of Lucknow
Lucknow

SERIALS PUBLICATIONS
NEW DELHI

© R.B.S. Verma, H.S. Verma & Nadeem Hasnain

First Published - 2007

ISBN : 978-81-8387-118-1

All rights reserved with the Publisher, including the right to translate or reproduce this book or parts thereof except for brief quotations in critical articles or reviews.

Published by

SERIALS PUBLICATIONS
4830/24, Ansari Road, Darya Ganj
New Delhi-110002 (India)
Phone : 91-11-23245225
Fax : 91-11-23272135
E-mail: serials@satyam.net.in,
serialspublications@vsnl.net
Website: www.seriealspub.com

Contents

PART - III
Education: Issues in Access, Choice and Substance

PART - IV
Women in Traditional Economic Activities: Presence, Agency and Control

PART - V
Space, Voice and Turbulence in the Newer Sectors of Economy

Preface

This collection of essays grew out of dissatisfaction with the tone and tenor of public discourse on the women's problematic in India, in particular by the feminists leading the women's movement. While this long drawn out debate has been critical of society and the state in general and entrenched culture of patriarchy in particular, it has not directly addressed the basic question: how have some sections of the women's movement itself collaborated with the state apparatus, and been responsible for introducing 'welfare', 'development', 'empowerment', and 'participation' programmes for the Indian women that have, instead of genuinely promoting gender balancing, tended to reinforce patriarchy and reproduce the unequal gender and class relations? Similarly, while there has been tremendous change in the nature and intensity of the problems being encountered by different segments of women—some older ones have been transformed and newer ones have emerged on the horizon—, the delineation by the mainstream of the women's/gender studies, with some honourable exceptions, continues to treat them homogeneous, unilinear and more or less stationary. Undertaking fresh research to fill all these gaping holes is beyond the capacity of a single set of professionals howsoever gifted, dedicated and resourceful they are. Fortunately, quite a few of the researchers had indeed recognized these drawbacks and had launched their individual/institutional initiatives to correct the anomalies piecemeal. What remained to be accomplished was piecing together of these scattered efforts blazing new trails and putting them in a well weaved out analytical framework. This endeavour to paint the picture that is nearer the lived and experienced empirical reality is a modest exercise in this direction.

When we embarked on this series, several surprises lay in store for us. The first and foremost among these was the fact that editing books –that too of the lengths exceeding 500 pages—was a far more strenuous and demanding exercise than merely writing a book. This route involved, among other things, getting concurrences from a wide variety of high calibre professionals possessing a bewildering range of temperaments forcing us to deploy a slow 'handle with care approach'. Obviously, it also meant spending considerable time and efforts in coaxing, cajoling and, in some cases, even 'coercing' concurrence. While the exercise of getting green signals itself had only minor hiccups, procuring both hard and soft copies presented a large number of complications. While quite a few of our contributing colleagues provided us with the soft copies of their papers, some others had to be either totally retyped or scanned. Scanning/typing and copy editing the entire material was a very tedious and time-consuming exercise, and considerably delayed the finalization of the volumes. To our surprise we also discovered that receiving soft copies via the email has its own attendant problems: part of the material was either lost or, got distorted. In case one did not possess the hard copy, as was the case in a few instances, we had to procure the hard copy from alternate sources. Initially, we had a vague, blurred vision of this project. When we brainstormed the idea amongst the three of us, its thematic spread and scope became clearer. From the tentative selections of the possible pieces for inclusion in the resultant volumes, firming up of the sub-thematic alignment of the pieces, it became clear that we would be assembling three volumes, one each dealing with the concept, approach and methodology, shades of tasks of empowerment and the relationship of women's empowerment with the state. Eventual sequencing of the volumes was yet another surprise. While the material on the first two was more or less sufficient, there were some areas in which no updated published material was available for the third one. These gaps had to be filled either by those who were 'established' names in this area of research and had completed work of the nature desired by us or, alternately, by some one from amongst us. Our initial attempts to persuade some leading scholars brought in mixed responses. We had to first find out how many of the scholars, whose pieces we had short listed for inclusion in our collection, would be permitting us given the fact that we were somewhat new to this area of research and, inappropriately enough, were also males! We began the exercise of securing clearances from the identified scholars and their publishers in April 2006. What encouraged us was the very enthusiastic and overwhelming response we received from some of the celebrated colleagues once they had a close look at our outline and our resumes. Once these responses were in we became sure of the exact gaps in our schema. The identified gaps were in the sub-area of policy, programme, and organizational analysis, an area on which not much work has been done from the leading disciplines contributing to the women/ gender studies. Fortunately for us, at least one amongst us was fairly conversant with this area and was in a position to fill in the gaps to a great extent. We also approached some key area experts to fill some, if not all, of these gaps. Refusals come in many forms and we were to see some shades of these ourselves. While some were 'very busy', others, while agreeable, were offering time deadlines that did not suit us. We made our compromises and settled for a via media in which we got one contribution from an expert and filled the remaining gaps ourselves.

We had planned to bring the three volumes as one single series and in one go. We approached some of the leading publishers. However, while the three volumes themselves were deemed very attractive commercial proposition as single entities, even celebrated publishers were not too sure of its success as a single, composite series. Although thematically inter-linked, it was consequently decided to bring the volumes out as separate books. Because we had planned this venture as a three unit single product we had decided to devote our time to fill the gaps of the third volume first before copy editing all three volumes. Therefore, it so turned out that the third volume was readied first. Given the fact that each of the volumes came to be treated as separate product and relied on its own content for its viability, there was no point in waiting for the others to be finalized. The intended 'third' volume, *The Indian State and the Women's Problematic: Running with the Hare and Hunting with the Hounds,* covering the problematic nature of relationship between the Indian state and the women's question, was consequently published first.

This collection of 26 papers is second volume delineating the emergent contemporary tasks of women's empowerment. It covers this larger task space under five major sub-themes: Women, Masculinity and Violence; Survival, Reproduction and Protection from Lethal Threats; Issues in Access, Choice and Substance in Education; Presence, Agency and Control of Women in Traditional Economic Activities; and Space, Voice and Turbulence in the Newer Sectors of Economy. Eighteen of the papers included were first published in different journals. The details of these previously published pieces are as under:

Satish B. Agnihotri, Survival of the Girl Child: Tunneling out of *Chakravyuha*. *Economic and Political Weekly*: 38:41: 2003: 4351-60.

B. Akila, Reaching Global Goals in Primary Education: Some Gender Concerns for Tamil Nadu. *Economic and Political Weekly:* 40:11: 2004: 2617-2622.

Vineeta Bal: Women Scientists in India: Nowhere Near the Glass Ceiling, *Economic and Political Weekly*: 39:32: 2004: 3647-53.

Sunita Bandewar, Abortion Services and Providers' Perceptions: Gender Dimensions. *Economic and Political Weekly:* 38:21: 2003: 2075-81.

Deepika Chakraborty, Expansion of Markets and Women Workers: A Case Study of Indian Garment-Manufacturing: *Economic and Political Weekly*: 39:45: 2004: 4910-16.

Somen Charaborty, and Shalu Nigam.1999:Implications of Globalization: Culture of Workplace and Violence on Women: *Women's Link*: 5:4: 1999: 25-30.

Prem Chowdhry, Crisis of Masculinity in Haryana The Unmarried, the Unemployed and the Aged: *Economic and Political Weekly:* 40:49: 2005: 5189-99:

Molly Chattopadhyaya, and David Seddon. Life Histories and Long-Term Change: Rural Livelihoods and Gender Relations in a West Bengal Village: *Economic and Political Weekly*: 37:46: 2002: 4633-37.

Radhika Chopra, From Violence to Supportive Practice: Family, Gender and Masculinities, *Economic and Political Weekly*: 58:17: 2003: 1650-57.

Radhika Coomaraswamy, Human Security and Gender Violence*: Economic and Political Weekly:* 40:44-45: 2005: 4729-4736.

Maithreyi Krishnaraj.Food Security: How and for whom? *Economic and Political Weekly*: 40:25: 2005: 2508-12.

Nandini Manjrekar, Contemporary Challenges to Women's Education. *Economic and Political Weekly EPW*: 38:43: 2003:4577-82.

G. Rama Padma, Perceptions of Safe Motherhood: An Analysis, *Economic and Political Weekly:* 40:5: 2005: 465-73.

Saseedran Pallikadavath and R.William Stones.2003.Women's Reproductive Health Security and HIV/AIDS in India, *Economic and Political Weekly:* 38:39: 2003: 4173-81.

Susan Rankle, 2005: Broken Lines, Desperate Choices: The Political Economy of Global Trafficking. *Manushi*: 146: 2005: 16-21.

Ranjan Ray, Simultaneous Analysis of Child Labour and Child Schooling: Evidence From Nepal and Pakistan. *Economic and Political Weekly:* 37:52: 2003: 5215-24.

Debnarayan Sarkar, and Nimai Das: Women's Participation in Forestry: Some Theoretical Issues: *Economic and Political Weekly.*

J.P. Singh, Dowry in India: A Search for New Social Identity: *Eastern Anthropologist*: 58:2: 2005: 199-220.

Preeti Singh, and Anu Pandey. Women in Call Centres: *Economic and Political Weekly*: 40:7: 2005: 684-88.

Anil C. Shah: Women, Water, Irrigation: Respecting Women's Priorities: *Economic and Political Weekly*: 37:43: 2002: 4421-28.

Aruna Sitesh, Portrayal of Workingwomen in Indian Popular Literature-Changing Scenario: *Women's Link*: 5:4: 40-51.

Divya Vaid, Gendered Inequality in Educational Transformations: *Economic and Political Weekly: EPW*: 39:35: 2004. 3927-38.

We are grateful to Professors Satish B. Agnihotri, Sunita Bandewar, Maithreyi Krishnaraj, Radhika Coomaraswamy, Prem Chowdhry, G. Rama Padma, Saseedran Pallikadavath and R. William Stones, Ranjan Ray, B. Akila, Nandini Manjrekar, Molly Chattopadhyaya, and David Seddon, Debnarayan Sarkar, and Nimai Das, Anil C. Shah, Vineeta Bal, Preeti Singh, and Anu Pandey, Deepika Chakraborty, J.P. Singh, Aruna Sitesh, Somen Charaborty, and Shalu Nigam, Susan Runkle, and Mala Bhandari and Dr. Ram Manohar Reddy, Editor, *Economic and Political Weekly*, Professor Madhu Kishwar, Editor, *Manushi,* Alka Srivastava, Editor, *Women's Link*, and Professor Nadeem Hasnain, Editor, *The Eastern Anthropologist* for graciously permitting us to include their pieces in this collection. We are also grateful to Professor Mala Bhandari for finding time from her busy schedule to contribute a fresh piece for this volume.

Apart from this acknowledgement here, we have similarly expressed our gratitude at the end of each contribution in the text of the book.

We have received help and assistance of many more individuals in assembling and finalizing the manuscript. It is not possible to acknowledge all of them. Among those whom we must, two stand out. Supriyo Cahatterjee, who was holding a full time job in as demanding a profession as a call centre-and that too on a permanent night shift—, shared the load of typing/scanning part of the manuscript. Shashi Kant Srivastava is the second professional who shouldered the main burden. Along with the main—and very heavy—responsibilities of the Department of Social Work, University of Lucknow, Lucknow he handled the entire email and postal correspondence for this volume, procurement of hard and soft copies of different pieces, typing /scanning, correction of various versions of the drafts, formating the manuscript and putting it on the CD very promptly and always cheerfully. He handled the task space of a programme officer and a research associate and it is our view that he has contributed as much to the finalization of this volume as the three of us. Apart from recording our deep appreciation of his dedication and commitment, we wish we could recommend his case for a better position in the University set up.

The personal libraries of all three of us were used extensively for this volume and the longer absence of this material from our own stacks deprived their use to other students and colleagues who normally do so to pursue their research exercises. Reposing considerable faith on us and the commercial potential of our volumes, S.K. Jha and Serials Publications, New Delhi published *The Indian State and the Women's Problematic: Running with the Hare and Hunting with the Hounds*, the first volume in this series on women's empowerment in record time. They have repeated the feat once again in this case. We record our appreciation of their efforts. Our first volume received widespread appreciation from a wide variety of professionals from the academaic, research, planning and execution, and consulting communities. Similar effort has gone in bringing out this collection .We are reasonably confidant that this offering too would receive enthusiastic response from diverse user communities.

R.B.S. Verma
H.S. Verma
Nadeem Hasnain

Chapter - One

Towards Empowering Indian Women: Mapping Specifics of Tasks in Crucial Sectors

R.B.S. Verma, H.S. Verma and Nadeem Hasnain

I

Changing Status of Women's Subordination

Thanks to the process we loosely call "globalization", women are on the move as never before in history. This also applies to the developing countries of the 'Third World', which are trying to confront the forces of tradition through the tools unleashed by the process of social change. But their position in the global as well as in Indian contexts may not be separated by the existing great divides– of nations, wealth, race, religion, education, class, gender and sexuality-all constructs created by human agency. As Cynthia Epstein (2007) in her brilliant analysis points out, "today, as in the past, these constructs not only order social existence, but they also hold the capacity to create serious inequalities, generate conflicts and promote human sufferings.... I argue that the boundary based on sex creates the most fundamental social divide-a divide that should be a root issue in all sociological analysis. I consider *gender* to be the most basic and prevalent category in social life throughout the world". "The great divides of society are enforced by persuasion, barter force, and the threat of force. Of all the socially created divides, the gender divide is the most basic and the one most resistant to social change". Obviously, this divide constitutes a marker around which all major institutions of society are organized. Therefore, we can conclude that all social statuses and the roles attached to them are socially prescribed. She further suggests that:

- Actual and symbolic roles of the females and males in the social structure are a seedbed for group formation and group boundary maintenance;

- All societies and large institutions are rooted in the differentiation and subordination of females;
- The more group solidarities are in question in a society, the stronger the differentiation between males and females and the more severe is women's subjugation (ibid).

Before taking up the changed context and changing tasks of women's empowerment with special reference to India, let us *see what has changed or is changing vis-à-vis women's subordination.* All empirical studies tell us that female subordination is not a static process. The extent and severity of it varies from region to region and from society to society. Interestingly, most of the times, the idea of protection camouflages this subordination. In the entire South Asia, because Hinduism is India's dominant religion, women are ascribed a reduced and inferior status through which they are seen to need 'protection' of men throughout their life-cycle- first their fathers, still later their husbands and then their sons. In India only a microscopic section of women may cross gender barriers and enter into the elite professions without the 'protection' of males.

Generally, the females have been regarded as a commodity everywhere. In a number of societies they have been-and still are being-treated as a form of compensation or repayment of debt and in a variety of other similar situations. The brutal practice of honour killing of females is another case in point. They are designated as carriers of honour in many societies including India. In a remarkable study, Mary Douglas (1966) says that we can think about any social practice in terms of purity and danger. Females are expected to conform to norms violation of which is considered as an act of dishonour. In order to retrieve the lost 'honour' she is disfigured and killed while the males have much greater latitude to engage in deviant behaviour. As Epstein (ibid) forcefully asserts, the idea that girls must remain virgin until they marry or their entire family will suffer dishonour is used as a mechanism for women's segregation and subordination all over the world. Such murders are barely noted by the police or no serious efforts are made by the male dominated law enforcing agencies to seek the successful conviction of the culprit. Conferring the symbolism of sexual purity on women as a basis of honour contributes to their vulnerability. Social harmony is thus 'equilibrated' through the bodies of females.

In most parts of the world women rise earlier than do men and go to bed later than men. In an outstanding work, *Deceptive Distinctions* (1988), Cynthia Epstein proposes the theory that the division of labour in society assigns the women the most important survival tasks-reproduction and gathering and preparation of fuel and food. All over the world, women do much of the reproductive work, ensuring the continuity of society. They do so through childbirth and childcare. They do much of the daily work that any social group needs for survival. For example, women produced half of the world's food, and up to 80 per cent in developing countries (Food and Agriculture Organisation: 2006). They also prepare the food at home and in commercial units. In their homes and in schools, they prepare most pre-school and primary school children for education. They take care of the elderly and the infirm. They socialize their children in the social skills that make inter-personal communication possible. This is a good deal, indeed a great deal for the men. Men tend to legitimize their behaviour through ideological and theological constructs that justify their domination. Social institutions reinforce this assiduously. Controlling women's labour and behaviour is a mechanism for male governance. As women's lives within the family and household do not exist in a vacuum, it is not surprising that power relations experienced at home or thought to be carried through other spheres.

Changing Perception of Women's Empowerment

In traditional societies such as India, the promotion of women's empowerment is often viewed as a western cultural import that threatens to demolish the male dominated power structure. Perhaps that is why, a number of sociologists and anthropologists, especially the later, call for women's indigenous strategies for empowerment that could transform unfavourable power relations. But ironically, as Amartya Sen (1990) rightly points out, "there is much evidence in history that acute inequalities often survive precisely by making allies out of the deprived. The underdog comes to accept the legitimacy of the unequal order and becomes an implicit accomplice".

Without going into the rhetoric and polemics of the concept of women's empowerment let us see how the development agencies, human rights activists/ organizations and academics look at women's empowerment. Experience has shown that addressing gender equality and women's empowerment require strategic interventions at all levels of programming and policy making.

The 1990s have seen increasing recognition of the centrality of women's empowerment to the success of development programmes. The document prepared by the United Nations Agency Task Force on the implementation of the ICPD Programme of Action gives five components in women's empowerment:

(i) Women's sense of self worth;

(ii) Their right to have and to determine choices;

(iii) Their right to have access to opportunities and resources

(iv) Their right to have power to control their own lives, both within and outside the home; and

(v) Their ability to influence the direction of social change to create a more just social and economic order, nationally and internationally.

United Nations International Research and Training Institute for the Advancement of Women (2006) describes empowerment in terms of choice and social transformation. It argues that if women's disempowerment is primarily about social norms legitimizing "differential entitlements" that work to place limits on what women can or can not do, then empowerment should be about expanding women's entitlements and increasing their choices so that they are better enabled to bring about social change. Empowerment is about women having the power to make strategic decisions in their lives, such as selecting a spouse, a livelihood or whether and when to have children. These choices then help to frame secondary choices in women's lives. In order for women to be able to make these choices, they need access to material, economic, human, and social resources such as land, equipments, financing, skills, and networks. Naila Kabeer (2003) adds an important dimension to women's empowerment when she says that empowerment is not just an outcome but also a process. For example, if woman gains an income but still has to carry out all her domestic duties, her so called economic empowerment may have actually increased her work burden. If she asks a female relative to help, empowerment has not taken place because women are still primarily responsible for domestic work. If the woman continues to work but persuades her husband to help out at home, then some degree of empowerment has taken place because the woman has gained some negotiating power. In another instance as a mother in law, the women gained the ability to exercise agency (in the form of power over another person) in a way that she could not when she was a young woman herself. But is it empowerment? The mother in law is acting within an inequitable gender system that severely constraints her ability to make strategic life choices. The system lets her exercise power, but only in ways that reinforce the system. This sort of agency is similar to what Kabeer (1999) describes as choices that reflect *women's consent and complicity in their own subordination.* When they lack agency in a broader sense, women should not be considered to be making empowered choices. Some of the most popular soap operas currently on the Indian TV channels (such as *Kyonki Saas Bhi Kabhi Bahoo Thi*) are cases in point. The ideal daughter in law is one who does not revolt against the system but gets composed to help perpetuate the system.

Among the commonly used dimension of empowerment, the economic, socio-cultural, familial/interpersonal, legal, political and psychological may be seen as ready reference points. The economic dimension at the household level includes women's control over income, relative contribution to family support and access to and control of family resources. At the community level women's access to employment, ownerships of assets and land, access to credit, involvement and/or representation in local trade associations and access to markets are considered as important markers, while at the broader macro level women's representation in high paying jobs, women CEOs, representation of women's economic interests in macro-economic policies and state and Central/ Federal budgets are considered important from the point of view of development administration.

The socio-cultural dimension at the household level includes women's freedom of movement, lack of discrimination against daughters and commitment to educating daughters. At the community level women's visibility in and access to social spaces, participation in extra-familial groups and social networks and shift in patriarchal norms such as son preference may be taken as important markers while in the broader arenas women's literacy and access to a broad range of educational options and positive media images of women, their roles and contributions are important.

The familial or interpersonal dimension at the household level may include participation in domestic decision making, control over sexual relations, ability to make child-bearing decisions, use of contraception, control over spouse selection and timing marriage and freedom from domestic violence. At the community level shifts in marriage and kinship system indicating greater value and autonomy for women, elimination practice of dowry and acceptability of divorce are important factors and these must get reflected at the broader micro level.

The psychological dimension is also very important and it may include self-esteem, self-efficacy, and psychological well being at the individual level while collective awareness of injustice, potential of mobilization and systematic acceptance of women's entitlement and inclusion at the community and broader level may be very important factors.

Thus, four of the main processes that could lead to women's empowerment have been identified as:

- Changes in women's mobility and social interactions.
- Changes in women's labour patterns.
- Changes in women's access to and control over resources.
- Changes in women's control over decision-making.

This is not possible without identifying and attacking the disempowering structures.

Anthropological studies, which are better recognized for their qualitative flavour, can successfully blend individual or household situations with the meso level institutional structures. Needless to say empirical research done by anthropologists and sociologists shall go a long way in providing the much needed cutting edge to the development regimen the way time ethnography helped development administration devise schemes for tribal development.

The same task force of the United Nations, cited earlier, also calls for intervention in a human rights framework based on several key principles:

- Women have the right to autonomy and reproductive choice.
- Women have the right and social responsibility to decide whether, how and when to have children and how many to have; no women can be compelled to bear a child or prevented from doing so against her will.
- Men also have a personal and social responsibility for their own sexual behaviour and fertility and for the effects of that behaviour on the health and well-being of their partners and children.
- Reproductive health issues should be addressed in the way women and men experience them; not as isolated, bio-medical phenomenon or matters of public policy, but as an integrated part of everyday life.
- The fundamental sexual and reproductive rights of women cannot be subordinated against women's will to the interest of partners, family members, policy makers, or any other set of actors.

- Women must be respected to make their own reproductive decisions; they must have both the information and the authority to make decisions about reproduction and the services that will enable them to satisfy their reproductive health needs.

Sociologists and anthropologists have contributed substantially and meaningfully to conceptual discussion of power and modes of empowerment. They have written on aspects of tradition and culture that are so taken for granted that they have become naturalized. They have come out with a number of empirical studies that prove that violence against women exists in a continuum, from domestic violence in the privacy of the house, to violence as a weapon of war, where rape and other forms of sexual exploitation committed against women are now acknowledged as a crime against humanity. Family and kinship systems are corporate in nature. Traditionally, a male heads the domestic unit or household. Money, property and assets are handed down to sons despite the presence of the so called inheritance laws further restricting women's economic freedom and perpetuating their dependence on male support. Classic patriarchy plays a vital role not only in North Africa and Muslim Middle East but also in South and South East Asia. Almost the same situation prevails in the Indian society and culture. Indian society, rooted in caste ideology, makes the life harsher to the *dalit* and other disadvantaged groups while it is highly 'religionised' in the context of Muslim women. *Empowerment is rooted in how people see themselves-their sense of self worth. The way religions are being interpreted and practiced and the way socialization of girls is conducted under the umbrella of patriarchy there seems to be no hope for the emancipation of women until they demolish the organized religions. This may be a part of their survival strategy to develop a 'liberation theology'.*

Changing Status of Women's Empowerment

The status and empowerment of women is not a static condition. Women in the Western world have certainly moved upwards in the continuum toward equality and women in India also seem to be gradually waking up from slumber of social inertia. If the violence against women has increased it is largely due to the increasing mobility of women.

Creating spaces for change may be a harbinger of social transformation. Social transformation may involve changes in social structure, labour relations, urbanization, attitudes, beliefs and values, freedom and rights, the quality of education, competitive and comparative advantages and effective governance. Though uneven yet there have been significant advances for women in relation to health, education and employment for the past two decades. Socio-cultural boundaries are being pushed in a number of ways. Studies indicate that not only in cities, but also even in towns and villages husbands in increasing number now consult the women on various issues. Women in many places have gained new prestige in the community as office bearers of civic bodies.

But the foregoing changes must not conceal the fact *that empowerment is context specific*. For example, a shift in women's ability to visit a primary health centre unescorted by husband or without seeking permission of husband may be a sign of empowerment in rural India, not for any South American country which may be only a little better than India in terms of economic prosperity.

Education is looked at as a crucial route to empowerment. It may also be deceptive when one tries to evaluate empowerment and seeks to do some generalization. Education also has a context. Neila Kabeer (ibid) writes that there are studies that suggest that the changes associated with education are likely to be conditioned by the context in which they are provided and the social relationships that they embody and promote. In societies that are characterized by extreme forms of gender inequality, not only is women's access to education curtailed by various restrictions on their mobility and their limited role in the wonder economy, but its effects may also be more limited. Where women's role in the society is defined purely in reproductive terms, education is seen in terms of equipping girls to be better wives and mothers, or increasing their chances of getting a suitable husband. Given the realities of the society, these are legitimate aspirations. However, they do little to equip girls and women to question the world around them, and the subordinate status assigned to them. Nothing will change radically through education unless it provides them with the analytical capacity and courage to question unjust practices.

Discrimination and disempowerment of women is accepted as a norm- a private business, a normal occurrence in the relationships between men and women where the state, community or family should not interfere. This mindset of an average Indian male, product of a strong patriarchal society, leads him to protest that the efforts for gender equality and women's empowerment constitute undue interference in the culture, religion or traditional practices of the country.

While the empowerment of women has advanced in some respects in the past two decades, progress has been uneven. Empowering women is essential for achieving goals of sustainable development. Restructuring of work patterns and sharing of family responsibilities should also be major goals.

The ability of women to control their own fertility is absolutely fundamental to women's empowerment and equality. It has been observed that given a choice women go for smaller family. Moreover, when a woman can plan her family, she can plan the rest of her life. When she is healthy, she would be more productive. With this freedom she can participate fully and equally in society. Socio-cultural change can hasten giving increased economic opportunities to the women. To get control of her income is one significant step forward. Investing in education of the girls is the single best investment in women's empowerment because it also results in drop in fertility rate and hence increased income.

In this fast changing world multi-tasking capability is a very important asset. Women have uncanny ability to perform varied tasks and responsibilities, much better than males. Women lead by example. Change is in the air. It is palpable. They have to challenge the caste system, religious customs and traditions and the deeply entrenched patriarchal values in a forceful and organized way because legal and constitutional rights in themselves do not change social attitudes. The forces of *Hindutva* and Muslim obscurantism will not accept an empowered woman easily.

The points set out here need to be fully incorporated or 'mainstreamed' into tasks and responsibilities into the policy and action by the state and the civil society. Small sections of men may prosper by stifling women's potential, but prosperous societies benefit from women's full participation and productivity.

II

Organization of the book

This collection consists of a total of 26 very carefully selected papers. These have been organized into five parts. Containg five papers, Part One examines women, masculinity and violence. These adeal with tasks that have gone from bad to worse. The Second Part too contains five papers. These deal with survival and nurturing. These are areas where steady progress has certainly been made; yet, there are miles to traverse. The five papers in Part Three take a critical look at education. Six papers in Part IV present the changing perceptions of women and work in diverse economic activities. There are four papers in Part V that examine the implications of increased presence of women in the knowledge economy sectors of the Indian economy.

Women, Masculinity and Violence: Addressing forms old and new

Despite the fact that dowry is widely regarded as an 'evil' and outlawed practice, it is clearly in vogue all over the country irrespective of caste, community, religion and region. In fact, it has become more effervescent than ever before. J.P. Singh examines how different factors and forces have been at work, though not concurrently, to tempt various sections of the Indian society characterized by varying marital practices to come under the spell of dowry as a crucial consideration for marriage. The system of *stridhanam* in South India, strict endogamy coupled with the lack of right of inheritance for females in various parts of the country, *sanskritization* in the case of backward castes (both OBCs and *dalits)* and scheduled tribes, and urbanization and acculturation in the case of non-Hindu communities have been possibly the most predominant factors behind universalization of the practice of dowry. In a social setting marked by endogamy and gender differentials in inheritance rights, Europeanization, rise in the level of education, spread of mass communication media and modernization in general have distorted the indigenous marital practices enough to transform them into a uniform dowry practice in course of time.

With the rise in the level of education, urbanization and modernization, increasing occupational differentiations with greater opportunities for personal advancements and greater consciousness of one's special identity, far-reaching changes have occurred in marital practices. Despite being outlawed, the rising achievement motivation of individuals in an open environment has indirectly exacerbated dowry practices. The practice of dowry is one of the unintended costs of modernization and development that the Indians have to bear willingly or unwillingly. The Indian society has progressively become more and more unwrapped and competitive. It is an established fact that with new career openings and greater opportunities to accumulate wealth, every one is in the quest of higher and higher goals of life no matter what means or course they have to adopt to accomplish them. In the process, countless people tend to pass through the dilemma of identity crisis under the new state of affairs. It is because of this reason that scores of dowry takers as well as dowry givers tend to exaggerate the amount of cash or property they have taken or given in the form of dowry in a common tête-à-tête with kinsmen, friends and even people with nodding acquaintances. Since dowry has become a status symbol, it is not going to evaporate into thin air so readily. The system of caste or sub-caste endogamy, the system of arranged marriage and the lower incidence of divorce rate from the women's side promote and sustain dowry practices in the country. Until and unless the sub-caste endogamy is not replaced by exogamy and arranged marriage by so-called 'romantic' or civil marriage, the Indians would have to bear with the cultural crime of dowry in days to come too. In an ultimate analysis exogamy may serve as a panacea for many of the societal challenges that India has to cope with as a nation state. The practice of exogamy would not only solve the problems of dowry, but also diminish social distance and differentiations across castes and communities through social and cultural amalgamation and integration.

Prem Chowdhry's article engages with the complexity of masculinities in present Haryana, generated by increasing numbers of unmarried, unemployed men as well as elderly men, and the relation this bears to power by uncovering those aspects of political economy in contemporary Haryana that shape these complexities. Operating in the era of new technologies, globalization and consumerism, this combination is leading to greater aggression and violence, worsening gender equations and encouraging a greater exploitation of other subordinate categories, consolidating repressive social forces and strengthening casteism. Such masculinities also afford an unprecedented role to illegal and unconstitutional bodies like caste *panchayats* and thereby also strengthen highly regressive trends in society.

The construction of masculinity is in itself a historical process, full of tension and contradiction. Implicated in historical change, the status of being unmarried and/or unemployment is linked in a major way with masculinity, which remains a primary way of signifying relationship of power. Its shifting and changing contours have redefined social relations between men and produced subordinate and marginal masculinities.

The female sex ratio, as recorded in the decennial census operations, has been declining since the colonial period. In the post-colonial period, introduction of new technologies has wrecked havoc in this ratio. The recent and rampant use of sex determination tests and sex-selective abortions has put the very existence of females at stake. Admittedly, a one to one relationship cannot be made between adverse sex ratio and the number of unmarried men or women. Yet, this link is accepted at the local level. In a situation where status hypergamous marriages are the norm, such an equation leaves a surplus of brides at the top but a pronounced deficit at the bottom. The size of the dowry is considered relative to the "worth" of the groom. Consequently, the ranks of "suitable boys" register a different kind of masculinity, at once self-assured, aggressive and more importantly, manipulative of market forces. However, it can be observed that the unemployed either settle for lesser matches or do not get married at all. Generally, most political commentators agree that low educational and training accomplishments of prospective rural job aspirants stand in their way of getting jobs in the private sector.

The educated have also been known to be averse to going into agriculture. The income generation in the green revolution areas has driven away rather than attracted the younger generation to agriculture. This suggests a subtle shift of preference away from agricultural work associated with an aspect of masculinity such as muscle power or the body, as has been argued by a recent analyses. The male population forms a major chunk of the unemployed. In the absence of employment opportunities in the secondary and tertiary sectors, unemployed youth, educated or uneducated, are compelled to fall back on agriculture. Over time the capacity of agriculture to absorb labour forces has also come down drastically; therefore unemployment is growing day by day.

The unemployed youth of Haryana provide raw material for all the agitations in the state. Although the role of employed males cannot be discounted, the unemployed sections are known to take a lead in whatever violence that occurs. As popularly acknowledged there is also a connection between unemployment and crime. Certain villages in Haryana have become so notorious for crime that people do not wish to marry their daughters into those villages, notwithstanding the "employment status" of individuals. Though still unexplored, there appears to be a strong connection among unemployment, unmarried status and growing incidents of suicides in Haryana. This is primarily because masculinity is popularly located in the 'working' men whether involved in agricultural or non-agricultural work. Unemployment has been accepted as one of the major challenges to masculinity. The halo of masculinity rests on his fulfilling the idealized norm of an earner. Even after marriage, a man is still not fully considered a "man" till he has had an offspring, specially a son. On the other hand, if married and with a child, but unemployed, he is still not masculine enough. In the rural cultural milieu, masculinity is linked to the ability of a man to protect and materially support a family. Men prove their manhood in the eyes of other men not necessarily through demonstration of wealth and other accomplishments, but by supporting/participating and implementing the decisions of the male leadership of dominant caste which calls the shots in the traditional *panchayat.* Masculinity is established not only in relation to femininity but also in relation to the evaluation of male peers and male authority. Subaltern men become a casualty of dominant masculinities, with caste emerging as an integral part of the dynamic between masculinities.

Infliction of violence gives an opportunity to present "masculinity" before different audiences. Exercise of power is equated with manhood. Both older and younger men want to be seen exercising it as much against women as against other men. In this violence they have the full support and backing of the traditional caste leaders. There exists a workable bond between the two male segments: the unemployed/unmarried men and the traditional leadership drawn from the elderly male members of the village. What is it that brings the elderly and the youth, especially among the unmarried/unemployed, together? The answer lies in marginalisation and diminished masculinity experienced by these male segments. With the gradual decline of the provider's role, ageing and later life has also come to be associated with a subordinate form of masculinity. Importantly, post-colonial India has witnessed a considerable erosion of the traditional power base of the caste leadership due to the introduction of different state structures, such as the elected statutory *panchayat* (since 1950) and election mechanism, based upon equal citizenship and adult franchise but the moot point is that age, which was an important factor of dominance in the past, is losing its significance as a criterion for selection of village leadership. Checkmated in certain spheres, this generation wants to retain its hold over certain matters-marriage and morality is one such domain. Thus, tightening controls over marriage is a popular "masculine matter", worthy of support-an issue over which all men, notwithstanding differences of caste, class, creed and age, are united. In matters other than those related to village culture and tradition, the traditional *panchayat* may or may not be effective. These two segments, with doubts around their masculinity and value to society, join hands to empower each other, the former by giving decisive though biased leadership and the latter by supporting and implementing their illegal decisions. It represents a direct attempt at shrugging off their diminished and devalued masculinity and assertion of power by both the segments. Unemployed men have lately shown the tendency of bringing in women from other castes. Not incorporated fully into the rural household, the "married" status of these women remains highly ambiguous. Such dubious marriages can hardly afford a 'status' to the men concerned or resolve the contradictions faced by men in relation to their masculinity. Yet, this social solution to the problem faced by the growing numbers of single status men in Haryana has widespread approval. It is ironic that a society given to inflicting extreme violence upon their own youth who breach customary norms of marriage by bringing in local women of other caste groups "permit" women from different regions and castes. Also it may be remembered that it is the men, not women, who are breaking the norms. Women are not given in marriage to men of other caste groups. However, even for men such an arrangement has limited and uncertain validity. Such men are not held at par with other married men. The legal status of such marriages is suspect. Such men remain with devalued masculinity for seeking an association with a woman of uncertain origins and caste. It is doubtful if these women or their children would be able to prove that the marriage had taken place. In the years to come, the children born of such liaisons are going to be a major source of tension and conflict when the question of their inheritance rights comes up. Apart from accentuating dominant and subordinate masculinities in the private and public spheres, it also has singularly negative effect on gender relations. But the fact that it is crucially linked up with the demographic pressure and the wider political economy remains to be officially acknowledged or recognized. The societal attempt at solving this problem by entering into highly dubious marriages by purchasing women is wrecking widespread havoc and unimaginable levels of violence and exploitation in rural areas. Despite wooing by different political parties, the basic problems of all these categories of people are not being addressed. Consequently, all of them continue to experience diminished masculinity, powerlessness and marginalisation. Despite their devalued masculinities, such men are in a continuous process of strategizing to shape their relations with others. Their united attempts to assert themselves through the exclusive male preserve of the caste *panchayats*, in crucial social matters relating to village and caste customs, has led to the strengthening of highly regressive and illegal trends in society. Although their actions have challenged and subverted the authority of the state, the latter and its functionaries stand as mute onlookers, unable and unwilling to intervene. In their success and failure these marginalized categories despite the question mark around their masculinities, constitute a highly combustive material in society.

The politics of gender, and feminist research have outlined the deprivations and unequal entitlements in the lives of women. This frame has also produced the view that understanding women's lives is incomplete without looking at their everyday location within families that must include relations with men. Research by Radhika Chopra has tried to bring into focus the way that men's support can be outlined and reflected upon in the context of gender equality and domestic democracy. Supportive practices are more than and 'alternative' frame within which to place men. They enable us to hear an aspect of men's lives and expressions of their subjective positions in ways that have not so far been addressed.

Gender studies, gender theory and gendered interventions have always been arenas inhabited by women. It is lives and the contexts of women's material and social conditions that provide key issues for research and interventions. One of the critical concerns of gender studies is the issue of women's agency and autonomy. While feminist writing and research has established the fact that women are not passive subjects, but are agents and subjects in their own lives, their agency and subjectivities are not fixed or absolute. Neither is women's agency wholly recognized. A great deal of attention has been paid to the unacknowledged nature and 'subterranean' existence of women's subjective agency, as well as to the way that these subjectivities need to 'surface' through a discourse of rights, claims and entitlements. Some feminist theorists have insisted that agency cannot only be understood as an exercise of volition in the abstract. Thus, agency as an issue has to address the horizons within which it is articulated and realized as a political and substantive position. It is precisely this frame of women's agentic positions located within material conditions of existence that has also produced the view that understanding women's lives is incomplete without looking at their everyday locations within families that must, of necessity, include relations with men. There is enough evidence to demonstrate the unequal gendered distribution of critical resources, an inequality that is weighted against women. When gender is combined with age, or with caste, then the question of entitlements and deprivation becomes part of a politics of distribution, a relational politics shaped and sustained by cultures of deprivation.

It is clear that entitlement and deprivation are related to each other. The next question therefore is whether all conditions of entitlement and therefore *all entitlements* translate equally and exactly across all cultural and political locations. If we take the social and cultural unit of the household as an object of analysis, it has been adequately demonstrated that men have greater entitlements to household resources, like food. Aspects of class enter to divide a household and family along lines of entitlement and deprivation. The household is an arena of political divisions along fractured lines of deprivation. However, the fact that households are part of different social, cultural and class locations impels us to reopen the issue of how men's entitlements are to be understood and evaluated. The *experience* of being male needs to be placed within these questions and masculinity as an identity has to be understood as a complex negotiation between gender, class and power. Outlining deprivation has produced another dynamic: the need to redress unequal distribution. This redressal is part of a politics that seeks to 'enter' households and rework inequality and gender imbalances through what has been termed gender intervention and gender sensitization. The interesting point about this politics of entry is that it moves along a terrain of materiality. In part the politics of entry seeks to change material conditions within households. Simultaneously it seeks to encourage the emergence of a form of domestic democracy. Men-as-supportive-partners campaigns focus primarily on involving men in reproductive healthcare. Such interventions shift the 'target' from women to men. Unlike micro-credit schemes that focus on provisioning women with the means to sustain themselves and their families, and in the process expand the number of breadwinners within a family or a household, newer policies of reproductive health strategise ways and means of getting men involved in the work of pre and post-natal care. The outcome of including men in reproductive health reworks the division of labour within the household, and locates men directly into the domestic work of care and reproduction. Further, the data in these and other studies demonstrates that violence is also framed and formed by cultures of power and deprivation.

Violence within a household does not remain untouched by political ideologies of violence and valour or cultural dimensions of caste. Histories of Rajput celebrations of violence against the self, for example, enter the household not only through men's violence against women, but women's violence against themselves through their understandings of '*sati*'. The question of violence and men demands that we rethink the ways in which men inhabit particular subject positions in relation to violence. An analysis of men's everyday speech will allow us to tease out another dimension of gender relations that has remained muted, the support that men extend towards their families. We need to address ourselves to the forms and dimensions of support as a substantive set of practices. In these campaigns the position and role of men is restricted to a single dimension of their subject positions within households as husbands, but not as fathers or sons. At the very least, existing practices of support may be an *ideology* that might be drawn upon and elaborated when the whole question of domestic democracy and gender equality are sought to be addressed. In other words, we need to address a dimension of relationships that patriarchal *structure* often hides or mutes and look more closely at the everyday *practices* of men. There is a need to explore men's perceptions of supportive practices. Through this research, an endeavour was made to make visible the 'doing of support' by men. Understanding masculinities is an exercise that must address itself to key institutional locations like the family and not confine itself to 'public' spaces like streets or factories. Thus the site of the family was an important starting point for the exploration of masculinity and maleness. The second choice was to demarcate the kinds of contexts within which to explore masculinities and male supportive practices within families. The research enabled a view of the father-son relationship within the domestic domain as well as the expansion of the family ideology beyond the immediate boundaries of the home. To explore the manner in which the question of hegemony and dependence work in male relations within the domestic and family domain, the second field site was the lives and histories of male domestic workers. Any analysis of men and work must therefore focus on work that is 'unconventional' in the way it lies outside the accepted division of labour. The primary methodological focus of the research was not to 'change' the way people think. Rather it was to track the way people think differently with the horizons and limits of their cultural and social positions. The fact of doing work that flew in the face of their entitlements made the entire research team recognize and acknowledge the extraordinary choices that ordinary men make to support key people in their lives. Such a frame enabled the researchers to look at the modes and styles of male-male relations within workspaces, as well as examine the way that these relations subvert hegemonic convention. Thus, the deliberate choice of a non-family field like the beauty parlour enabled an exploration of the ideology of the family and the ways it is elaborated and given substance. A site like the boys' club in Kolkata, the fourth field work site, provided an opportunity to explore formations of masculinity in the public, or non-domestic, domain. While each research was distinctive in the issues and questions it raised, all four-research sites also crosscut and interlinked with each other in terms of the way in which family, masculinity and gender identity are framed in south Asia. The analysis of family businesses highlighted the material substance of supportive practices and the affirmation of the ideology and ethos of the family when extended towards the economic institution of the shop or business. The ethos of the family shapes the outlines of the business, and in turn, is forged and changed by the support structures that develop over the life cycle of the business.

Living between two families in two startlingly contradictory positions-as a fully entitled male member in one family context, and as a partial member in the other-the subjective position of the man is 'split' between the two contexts in which power dynamics play out very differently. The methodological imperative of doing fieldwork has also raised a number of other questions and highlighted some issues that do not relate directly to support. But they do point our attention toward the subject positions of men, the cultures of male existence, and the formations of masculinity. Three among them are: hierarchies between men, forms of egalitarianism and impositions of control and regulation. These all-male institutions are accorded an authorised existence; in turn their young members contribute to the collective life of the neighbourhood. The point that this study highlighted was the value placed on friendship by men, who nurtured, enabled, and supported the bonds. It was friends who 'taught' them the skills necessary for beauty work and passed on valuable knowledge and skills in a spirit of friendship. It is this 'spirit' that translates substantively into supportive practices between men, and if extended and elaborated, by men 'for the sake of their friends families'. Thus men's supportive practices may not only orient themselves towards their own families, but to other families as well. This expansion of the role of fathering undertaken by a variety of men is not unusual in south Asian contexts. The expansion allows us to view the whole context of the authority of the father as both re-enforced and simultaneously dissolving as it expands beyond the single person of the genitor. The two field sites 'outside' the family provided a contrast for the research within the family. In addition, these two sites simultaneously enabled the possibility of understanding how work and non-work were key issues in the formations of masculine identities in the lives of men. Unfortunately, biographies of ordinary men often disappear from the pages of histories, even though they are a rich source for understanding changing social contexts within which lives are lived and choices made. We thought of these men as extraordinary because in their own small way their lives are 'models' for others to rework how gender identity is made, fixed and remade, within the limits and horizons of social and economic conditions. Labouring bodies confront the issue of male identity and effeminacy in extremely complex ways that complicate the relationship between sexual identity and effeminate bodies. The work in beauty parlours yielded important insights and allowed us to explore both the subversions of masculinities and the re-assertions of the male self through the performance of work. The point that is important for this research is the way that initiation rituals produce masculinity through transactions between men. Male friends worked 'like family' to enable their friends to work and earn 'for the sake of the family'. Friendship networks were critical at significant junctures of men's lives. On the one hand, they enabled entry into working lives and the reproduction of necessary skills. On the other hand, friendship networks were the context for men to re-articulate autonomy, a sense of male self 'lost' through the performance of 'women's work'. Friendship groups enabled the emergence and the re-articulation of agency and autonomous subjectivities. It seemed clear, therefore, that the entire community recognised the club as a significant institution and were willing to donate valuable resources, like land and money, to establish the club and keep it going. The all-male friendship clubs are spaces and sites for the articulation of formations of masculinities 'outside' the home. The egalitarian mode or the idiom of fraternity was most apparent in the boys' clubs, but emerged in nascent and overt ways in narratives of male domestic workers and beauty parlour workers as well. Fathering is a role centred on more than one single man. Fathering as an ideology extends beyond the single man, the father, and is taken on, as it were, by men other than the genitor or the 'biological' father. By looping inheritance outwards on to tangential lines of affinal and collateral kin, a key relationship within the family, the father—son relation is protected from disruptions. The doing of fathering as a supportive practice that is not done by the genitor alone, but by a whole group of men who stand in place of the father. It draws attention to the fact that just as there might be a proliferation of businesses that make up 'the family business', there is the equal possibility of a proliferation of fathers who play a critical role in the lives of younger men, not necessarily their sons. The question of fathering as a wider set of practices done by a group of people highlights the material and the ideological existence of support. The social networks of support are those that are drawn upon during times of need and times when a family affirms and celebrates itself. Certain individuals exemplify this aspect of institutionalized support networks. In the life histories of such individual men, support might be extended along lines of hierarchy in the beginning, but may translate into friendship or egalitarian forms of support at subsequent periods of time. Research such as the kind described above engages with the social worlds and the narratives of individual people in their different locations or contexts and begins from a stance that is critically different from the stance adopted by intervention research. The problem with intervention research is that it is not always self-conscious of own power position in relation to target groups. Both penetration and intervention involve notions of active bodies, influential points of view and powerful subject positions directed towards those who need to be altered, changed and transformed, as passive recipients of new knowledges, different roles and good practices. It is an exercise in engagement that we need to strive towards, not the politics that underlies intervention.

A few issues emerge when thinking about practices of support. First, it is quite clear from the field research and analysis that support has a material and a non-material aspect. Second, support practices are diverse in terms of the cultural contexts within which they are articulated. Supportive practices are distinguished between those that already exist and those that come into existence or are created when people find themselves in situations of deprivation and a perceived loss of autonomy. In the latter instance, supportive practices have a transformative potential. Neither is support at least among men-taken for granted. It is cultivated with care and time (a thing of value) is freely spent in the cultivation of support networks. Strategies are developed to enhance support and deflect conflict within the family especially where the reproduction of family fortunes depends on the continuance of the family. This research has tried to bring into focus the way that men's support can be outlined and reflected upon. Men's friendship groups may become an enabling site within which issues of domestic democracy can be parleyed into a discursive context. Drawing from these instances it may be possible to argue that in the case of women's reproductive health, the husband (the most direct partner) may not necessarily be the most supportive partner. Asserting support as a frame enables us to engage with a particular language and practice of masculinity. In talking about themselves and their lives, men did not have a very articulate vocabulary to speak about themselves, except when they were narrating the support they received or had given. Supportive practices are therefore more than and 'alternative' frame within which to place men. They enable us to hear an aspect of men's lives and expressions of their subjective positions in ways that have not so far been addressed. Supportive practices are an idiom that explicate agentic subjectivities and provide a language of engagement with the lives and cultural locations of men.

Recognizing the important role that states can play in transforming legislative, administrative and judicial practices, UN report points out that states are nevertheless also perpetrators of violence against women (VAW) whether in prisons, jails or during armed conflict and when turning a blind eye to violence against women that takes place in their society. Radhika Coomarswamy argues that economic and social exploitation of women and their labour also contributes to violence against women. Violence against women also takes place in the most intimate of places, the family. Women are socialized to accept their inferiority and vulnerability. It is the family that often first teaches women to have negative, disempowering self-images and it is in the family that young men first learn about female subordination. It is also men who control the knowledge systems of the world. Whether it is science and modern technology or religion and its edicts, women are often excluded from creating symbolic systems or analyzing and transmitting knowledge. The public private distinction relegates women to the sphere of domestic activity, immune from scrutiny and activism, while men control and determine public power and the priorities of a society as a whole. These newly emerging international norms and standards are still very aspirational in content. The reality on the ground has not changed dramatically.

South Asia has particular cultural and religious practices that also accentuate the problem of VAW in the region. The general low status of women in the region and the entrenched nature of discriminatory structures have led to what is seen as a "Lifecycle of VAW". The vulnerability to violence at every stage of the life-cycle makes VAW a terrible south Asian legacy that requires concerted regional national and local level action. Women are affected by armed conflict in different ways. First, they are often the victims of direct violence especially sexual violence by armed soldiers or militants. Another way in which women are affected during wartime is as internally displaced persons (IDP). Women and children put in these camps continue to have psychosocial and long-term adjustment problems. In the post-conflict situation, many obstacles are put in the reintegration of women cadres into civilian life especially in patriarchal societies. Women as warriors, though exciting because of the transgressing of gender roles, raise other issues relating to the realization of women's rights within the framework of military imperatives and war. Trafficking of women and girls, especially into the big cities of India, remains a serious problem in the south Asian region. Sometimes trafficking is linked to traditional contexts and practices. Trafficking is also complicated by the legal regimes that are in place for the regulation of prostitution. However, trafficking is perhaps most complicated by its link to migration. Research clearly shows that most of the women who are trafficked have a strong desire to migrate and are thereby abused in the process. State inaction against perpetrators of violence helps perpetuate an ideological belief that violence may even be justified and even if it is not, it is not a terrible matter that requires concerted action. Rape and sexual harassment continue to be important issues in the south Asian context. 50 per cent of all workingwomen claimed that they were sexually harassed in the workplace. Marital rape and sexual violence as a means of initiation are also reported in some of these surveys, a factor that will influence the marriage relationship for years to come. This is the case even though marital rape is not a crime in all the countries of south Asia. Even when judgments convict, the rape survivor emerges brutalized and sometimes a "scandal figure" in a still very patriarchal society. For this reason most women continue to be silent when they are victims of sexual violence. The failure of the law is particularly relevant when it comes to customary practices in a region that is violent toward women. The question of culture seems primarily relevant only to the subordinate position of women. Another customary practice that is associated with south Asia is the practice of bride burning, practice of sati. The practice of *sati* reminds us that violence and discrimination against widows is a common cultural practice in south Asia. Peculiar forms of masculinity cause violence against women. Violence against women is generally treated as normal both by the societies as well as their judicial systems. This normalization of violence shows the interlinkage between ideology and violence against women. Women's lack of economic security forces them to put up with extreme acts of violence for the sake of survival. Inheritance laws and practices, the lack of access to land, the lack of education and the denial of mobility contribute to keeping women locked into situations from which there is no escape. The basic economic dependence of women, their propertylessness and resourcelessness renders them fearfully weak in standing up and challenging the violence and power that is used against them in society. Models of masculinity in the south Asian region also contribute to violence against women. The emergence of this masculine category in post independent south Asia as a dominant paradigm has worrisome implications for violence against women. Linked to notions of masculinity is also a belief in the proper emotional and sexual behaviour of women. A great part of violence against women has to deal with female sexuality. For this reason it is important that the protection of women from violence must be accompanied by the recognition of the reproductive rights and freedoms of women. This linkage is extremely important if we are to create conditions for women to be free from the fear of violence.

Violence against women has costs for the individual victims as well for the society at large. These include: damage to the health of women (physical consequences, sexual and reproductive consequences, psychological and behavioural consequences). Violence against women also exacts economic costs for the women concerned and therefore for the society. Violence against women also has a profound effect on the children in the family. Perhaps the greatest consequence of violence against women is fear and the chilling effect it has on women's empowerment and mobility. Living in anticipation of violence curtails their priorities and the choices they make for the future. It makes women search out men for protection rather than companionship and makes women dependent and vulnerable. Fear then socializes women to conform to the very ideological norms that ensure their subordination. Research from around the world points to the fact that violence against women can only be combated if there is a healthy partnership between women's groups and the state apparatus. While women's groups must protect their independence, on certain issues they have to work effectively with the criminal justice system, joining forces to protect the rights of women victims. However, this also poses a major dilemma. The decade ends with the triumph of a certain "law and order feminism" which aims at punishing the perpetrator, using draconian provisions in the law. Fighting violence against women will only succeed if it is done through the lens of human rights, protecting the rights and dignity of the woman survivor while ensuring a fair trial for the perpetrator. Any other course of action will not stand the test of time and important legislation will fall into disuse. Fairness must be a central concern for women even when they are dealing with abusers. Moreover, the law is an important tool but it is one of the many strategies available to women.

While fighting for justice through the legal system, there should also be attempts to put in place education policies, health strategies and community level programmes that promote equality between men and women and teach non-violent methods of resolving conflict. A multipronged approach to violence against women will result in far-reaching changes, transforming attitudes and practices so that women and men can live in equality and dignity.

All countries comprising the south Asian region have responded in some measure to the challenges posed by violence against women in the region. However, what remains a matter of concern is the fact that apart from India, none of the other south Asian countries have adopted domestic violence legislation or made the necessary changes to anti-trafficking legislation. Progress to ensure security and a world without violence for women has been slow but its pace especially in the last decade has been heartening. Violence against women, as borne out by research from around the world, can be effectively combated if a healthy partnership prevails between women's groups and the 'state apparatus.

Susan Runkle's paper, based on her field and archival research under very dangerous conditions in Armenia, examines the political economy of global sex trafficking In recent years, the Indian media has done several exposes on how global sex trafficking mafias have set up shop in India and how the women they bring from the former Soviet bloc countries and the collapsed regimes of Eastern Europe as sex workers are hot favourites with the nouveau riche Indian men because of their fair skin and western appearance. This article provides a glimpse into the factors and conditions that force women from these countries to be sucked into sex trade. Comparatively privileged men buy the bodies of poor women, because they can. Politico-economic analyses (e.g. Bishop: 1998) have been particularly enlightening, as they allow for an analysis of the root causes of sex trafficking in specific historical and cultural locations. The existence of trafficking as transcending poverty, noting that it represents a macro-level view of the distorted power relations between men and women, the wealthy and the poor and those who have access to resources and those who do not. Women who are victims of sex trafficking face a special set of issues that migrants do not, not least of which is the lack of option to return to their place of origin of their own free will. Factors that facilitate trafficking in Armenia include political and economic instability combined with natural calamities, like the earthquake of 1998, to make a large proportion of the population internally displaced persons (IDPs) or migrants to neighbouring states like Russia. This added to the trend of seasonal migration of labour that has prevailed since the 1960s. Social structures which would have formerly served to support women have been fundamentally destabilized following the breakup of the Soviet bloc, and the privatization initiatives of the Government of Armenia between 1998 and 2000 only further served to marginalize women, who cross culturally form the bulk of the poor. These inequalities make young, divorced or abandoned women particularly vulnerable to being trafficked. An unstable economic situation, limited opportunities for employment, coupled with gender norms which consider divorced women and single mothers abnormal and even "anti-family", positions such women as social outcasts who have to negotiate a larger social structure which effectively works against them at every turn. Migration is often seen as the only source of income with which to support themselves and their families. While their choice to leave their place of origin is definitely risky, it is also the result of a life situation in which there are often no other choices to be considered. As such, it is imperative that analyses of trafficking be sensitive to the fact that women who migrate are not making unintelligent decisions, *but rather desperate ones*. Sex trafficking can often be masked via the construction of false fronts such as employment agencies and marriage bureaus, enabling traffickers to justify the movement of women across borders without much interference at the state level. Traffickers are criminal elements that thrive in situations of instability, war and economic hardship, exploiting human suffering to their own advantage. The primary source of their power lies in the system of debt bondage, in which women are forced to perform sex work without pay, sometimes for years, in order to "repay" the cost of being trafficked, including their plane fare and dubious fees which are more often than not fabrications. Traffickers also maintain control over women through physical and linguistic isolation. The problem of sex trafficking is not just about changes in an economic system, but something much more profound: a view of women that perceives them as items available for male consumption. Were it not for the existence of pre-existing gendered social structures such as sex work itself, sex trafficking could not exist. In looking for solutions it follows that broader understandings of what it means for women to survive in a gendered world need to be incorporated into the formulation of recommendations to ameliorate what is clearly a mere symptom of the greater disease of gender inequality.

Survival , Reproduction and Protection from Lethal Threats

In a very hard-hitting paper, Satish Agnihotri discusses the vital question of the survival of the girl child. Results of the first population census of the millennium reveal a number of significant changes in the sex ratio patterns in the country. Firstly, the sex ratio decline among children in the 0-6 age group turns out to be sharper in the urban areas (32 points) than in the rural. Second, the traditional north-south divide stands significantly modified and the 'northernisation' of sex ratios is rapidly taking the urban route. The sharp decline in urban female/male (f/m) ratios among children cannot be explained away by any of the three popular escape hatches of yesteryears, i.e., migration, undercount or biologically ordained high sex ratios at birth. This decline clearly points to one factor, sex selective abortion or female foeticide that has gained currency during the 1980s and more sharply in the 1990s.

It is important to debate here the ethical dimension of sex-based elimination of a segment of population. Once this is sanctified, it could well be a thin wedge that provides in its wake currency to eliminate other segments of population based on other criterion whether religion or, caste or the colour of the skin or shape of the nose!

Development, frankly, cannot be viewed in isolation; it is important to know how it combines with discrimination, gender based in particular. If we remain underdeveloped and yet aggravate discrimination, that is the worst-case scenario. If underdevelopment co-exists with lack of discrimination, life gets tolerated but not enjoyed. But highly developed society with high discrimination levels as in our 'epicenters' is not a great goal for women either. We must, therefore, strive to become a society where development goes hand in hand with absence of discrimination against women.

We must, therefore, question current models of development where discrimination necessarily appears to accompany development. It is not that success stories of alternative 'development' do not exist; Kerala, Goa or Manipur provide examples where social indicators have developed, but not at the cost of gender equity. This is role model that the society has to follow and not the model of Punjab, Haryana and western UP where discrimination appears as 'inevitable'.

But that necessitates that the fight against gender-based discrimination has to become part of a larger fight against all other discriminations. In fact gender based discrimination gets aggravated when combined with other inequalities. It becomes necessary therefore to identify the most unreached and the most unserved, within the gender domain and advocate strongly for improving their lot. Just as different inequalities multiply the misery of the affected, reducing these together also gives multiple benefits. Willy-nilly we are talking here of eliminating the *chakravyuha* of discrimination altogether rather than its specific manifestation we began with, so that no child dies an avoidable death, let alone a girl child.

In her review of several important studies, Maithreyi Krishnaraj examines the critical issue of food security, in particular how and for whom? Food security (FS) is contingent on three parameters-availability, accessibility and affordability. While availability and accessibility relate to production and distribution, the question of affordability is linked to Amartya Sen's concepts of 'endowment' and 'exchange entitlements', that is, the resources at one's disposal that determines one's capacity to buy food. The papers in this collection on gender and food security deal precisely with this problem of endowment and exchange entitlement, especially with regard to women. They seek to draw attention to the resources, mainly employment, available to women for procuring food. However, apart from inadequate opportunities for wage labour, lack of command over productive resources acts as a major constraint on those women who do undertake farming for the household. Participation in the production of food, moreover, does not guarantee commensurate returns. The papers are however illustrative of the general situation regarding food insecurity among poor women and point to the urgency of public measures for protection of this vulnerable section.

All the papers deal with rice farming, but they are illustrative of the general situation regarding food security among poor women and point to the urgency of public measures for the protection of this vulnerable section. After overviewing developments on food security, Maithreyi argues that production and productivity have been deeply affected by macro policies. Secondly, market-oriented production can pose risks to household food security. Recent farmer suicides show how relying on fickle export markets can bring disaster. The risks are too heavy for farmers who rely on debt to take advantage of commercial opportunities. Development projects that promote market-oriented production should ensure some buffer for poor households with a minimum basic level of food, as those facing the greatest risk are those with limited land and labour and insufficient financial resources to carry them through the transition. The singular neglect of dry land farming and cereals other than wheat and rice in policy has led to deterioration in the nutritional level of the poor. Distortions in the distribution system include uneven distribution and the failure of Public Distribution System (PDS) to reach the needy, its patently urban bias and poor quality and unreliable supply in the ration shops. What really went wrong with the system of Food Corporation of India (FCI) is that the minimum support price assured to surplus farmers through procurement kept rising under pressure from the farm lobby and the issue price of the grain began to be closer to the market price.

FS is not just a matter of food-quality, of food that ensures nutrition, and healthcare that protects people from debilitating diseases or intestinal parasites that leak nutrition are all part of it. Public expenditure on safe water, sanitation, health care, and public assistance for affordable food are all part of ensuring FS. The papers reviewed draw attention to the resources available to women for procuring food mainly through employment. They focus on exchange entitlements and narrate trends that they find disquieting. One of the things, feminist discourse, concerned with domestic violence and subordination of women in the family, forgets is that households undertake many cooperative tasks and women as members of households have high stakes in its stability and social esteem. They derive their basic identity from the family-household. Nitya Rao and Praveena Kodoth address the issue of land rights but from different angles. Rao questions the premise underlying policy and discourse that independent land rights for women will reduce poverty. Kodoth examines the effect of progressive land reforms in West Bengal and Kerala and concludes that they resulted in regressive effects on women. Rao sees no evidence that land ownership reduces poverty given that land sizes are so small and agriculture has become a sinking ship for the majority of poor farmers who constitute the bulk of our rural population. With the drastic reduction of the role of agriculture in supplementing household income, work burden on women and girls has increased greatly. In a situation of restricted mobility and restricted choices, women prefer the security of marriage, as Rao says. It is the socially embedded nature of kinship and marriage systems, its strong association with cultural identity and symbolism that makes it different from other aspects of gender relations such as sexual harassment, violence, etc. Rao advocates diversification of employment for women. This was also the conclusion arrived at by Krishnaraj and Shah (2004). Kodoth's paper deals with both the Left Front states of West Bengal and Kerala. While in both states, the proportion of women in non-farm activities increased, in Kerala it was more in household industry. This diversification of women's employment was intertwined with gender conservatism. The net result has been women's livelihood security has been anchored in marriage. In this scenario, widows, divorced or single women are at a disadvantage. Thelma Paris, Abha Singh, Joyce Luis and Mahabub Hossain in their paper on impact of male labour migration on women in rice farms in eastern Uttar Pradesh document the high responsibility for keeping the family farm imposed on women left behind. Their findings drive home the point that responsibility on women does not make for more equitable gender relations. While family farm management does provide for a measure of food security, it is laid unilaterally on the shoulders of women. No one can deny the fact that women continue to be immersed in agriculture and bear a heavy burden of farming tasks with less access to non-farm work than men. Sumi Krishna captures this reality that the price of rice is gendered-in other words the cost of food security is borne by women. The paper by Barbara Harris is quite complicated. However, the Harris saga ends on a sadder note-while women's employment expanded, real wages increased, actualisation and insecurity were attendant features. Self provisioning which gave women direct control over food supply is now replaced by the need to look for non-farm work with poor returns relative to labour.

Analyzing results of a study from rural Andhra Pradesh, Rama Padma examines perceptions on safe motherhood. Complications of pregnancy and childbirth in developing countries often result in illnesses or permanent disability for the mother or child. While the tragedy of maternal mortality affects mainly the poorer sections, it is only very recently that serious attention has focused on the issue of 'safe motherhood'. Her paper analyses the levels of safe motherhood in rural areas of

Andhra Pradesh vis-a-vis other southern states; it also seeks to understand the perceptions and limiting causes that come in the way of safe motherhood.

A changed attitude to belief that 'Pregnancy is Special', safe motherhood initiative was launched at the safe motherhood conference that took place in Nairobi, Kenya in February 1987. Safe motherhood initiatives have clearly defined these as its four pillars. These are family planning practice, antenatal care, clean/safe delivery, and essential obstetric care.

Actual utilization of health services occurs when this generated demand connects with availability. In the Indian context, the situation is further complicated by women's perceptions of illness, which are affected by women's cultural conditioning to tolerate suffering. Because of this tolerance, which varies considerably across regions of India, even when the actual need is great the perceived need for health services can be small. It is argued that women's health seeking behaviour, especially related to pregnancy and childbirth, is considered a natural state of being for a woman rather than a condition requiring medical attention and care. The government's policy to promote sterilization to lower number of children per woman in the larger interest of controlling population growth needs to be reassessed from the overall reproductive health perspective.

The data from two consecutive National Family Health Surveys (NFHSs) reveal that the unmet need for spacing methods still continues at the same levels, whereas there is an overall decrease in the total unmet need. Further, an analysis of the non--users of any contraceptive method reveals that a substantial percentage of women are not using it because of either some method-related problems or they are opposed to using any method.

At a glance, the NFHS-2 data suggest that the rural women in rural Andhra Pradesh are experiencing safe motherhood. However, social and group perspectives reveal that many women are exposed to unsafe motherhood and often non-biomedical causes influence the medical determinants of safe motherhood. Rama Padma's paper brings out the differences in perceptions in a backward district (Mahabubnagar), and a developed district (Guntur).

Age at marriage and age at first pregnancy in Andhra Pradesh are the lowest in the country. Early age at marriage is mainly related to social problems like dowry and fear of fathers about social disgrace attached to their inability to get daughters married. Thus it requires to be handled at a broader level, not merely by enacting laws. If early marriages cannot be discour-aged, all efforts must be made to delay the occurrence of an early pregnancy. Information should be given on the benefits of delaying pregnancy by providing adequate knowledge on temporary methods. Low usage of temporary methods and the un-met need for them is a reflection of gaps in implementing the need-based approach. The desire of the younger couples to postpone first pregnancy vis-a-vis fears related to infertility and health problems caused by using some temporary methods has to be talked off by spreading correct reproductive health knowledge and persuasion. Availability and accessibility of contraceptives has also to be reviewed periodically. Apart from targeting younger couples, educating older members of the family, both men and women to develop a favourable attitude towards temporary methods has to be considered for effective implementation of safe motherhood practices.

Women perceive that motherhood confers on them a relatively a higher 'status' within the family. Across all socio-economic classes, the stages of pregnancy are still celebrated in traditional ways. However, the real care and protection in ensuring safe motherhood has not reached desired levels. The main problem in these rural areas is the lack of awareness about the need for maternal health care. Especially in the backward district, women perceive pregnancy and the problems associated with it as a natural process. Even when women realize the need for health care, their inability to convince family members leave them to unsafe motherhood practices. In addition, unfriendly attitude of the governmental health staff does not encourage women to utilise antenatal care facilities at public health centres. A few ANMs in backward district also find it difficult to cover all the assigned villages because of a large geographical area allocated to them and poor transportation facilities. Because of their poor financial status, most of the rural women in Mahabubnagar district, unlike those in Guntur district, do not go to private health facilities for antenatal care. In the backward district, the women frequently go to untrained health care providers, viz, RMPs, *dais,* and traditional healers. The most commonly received antenatal care in both the districts is the supply of IFA tablets and TT injections. Among the women who receive the IFA tablets, all do not consume them in backward areas due to misconceptions.

Depending on one's own financial position, the male elderly members of a family decide the place for a delivery. The role played by local non-institutional health care providers is detrimental to the health of the women. Most of these providers are inadequate in their own knowledge levels on maternal risk factors. Comparatively, *dais* are better aware than RMPs. For want of meagre fee *dais* do not refer a serious case at an early stage. RMPs on the other hand would want to refer to a private hospital for their own benefit. At the same time villagers trust them. It is, therefore, necessary to acknowledge their role and design methods to co-opt their services in providing better maternal health care. Unfriendly behaviour of some of the governmental health staff and the uncontrolled levels of fee charged by private health centres, and fears of unnecessary caesarean sections imposed by private hospitals are forcing the lower economic sections to opt for home deliveries. People in the backward district are experiencing more of such problems. Even in places where governmental health staff is willing to extend sincere services, the already existing notions against them induce people to take decisions against utilisation of services from public health centres. Concerted efforts are urgently needed to remove such notions in these areas.

Maternal care includes not only care during pregnancy and delivery but also during post-partum period. Care after delivery is highly neglected by both women as well as health care providers. The health workers in rural areas appear to be burdened with multiple tasks. Thus, they divert their efforts more towards immunization programmes and meeting the sterilization targets rather than on post-partum care. Women's knowledge levels are also very poor with respect to delivery and post-partum care. They wrongly perceive that many a problems could occur only during pregnancy rather than during delivery or post-partum period.

Sunita Bandewar's paper explores the gender dimensions of abortion-service providers' perceptions of women who access such care. A study in two districts of Maharashtra indicates that providers' responses to abortion situations are shaped largely by their attitude towards women, to women's health care and especially to abortion care. These attitudes in turn influence women's access to abortion and to the quality of service.

In this paper, Bandewar examines perceptions of the providers on women's abortion needs in terms of whether these perceptions reinforce the gender based value system victimizing women or facilitate a gender sensitive (and not a gender neutral) value system empowering women. The information discussed in this paper was collected as part of a larger initiative entitled 'Research and advocacy programme for improving access to abortion' taken up by CERAT, a non-governmental research and advocacy organization. Research under this larger initiative was conducted primarily to assess the quality of institution based abortion care services. Providers' perception about women's abortion needs was studied because the researchers believed that this would have an important influence on the quality of services provided. According to the providers, sex selection, social sanctions against seeking abortions by certain groups of women, women's own gender-related constraints and lack of access to safe abortion services contribute to second trimester abortion situations. In addition, malpractices by the medical community also contributed to second trimester abortions.

Thus, the views oscillated between 'opposition to' and 'in support of sex selective abortions', between those who were willing to forgo their practice by not engaging themselves in unethical medical care and those who were capitalizing on demand for sex selective abortions by indulging themselves in unethical practices. Once again social compulsions and population control concerns featured prominently. Women have been able to exercise their right to abortion and had their own ways to translate the abstract concepts in to reality. Their articulation was different than the feminists' understanding of abortion as woman's right. The latter looked at abortion as one of the important means to have control over the matters related to one's own body and articulate this in the context of women's human and political rights.

Providers' perspective about reasons for non-utilization of contraception is devoid of analysis of larger health care system and lacks understanding of gender biased policies/programmes. People's ignorance about and apathy towards contraception cannot be seen in isolation without looking at the way the 60 year old family welfare programme is being implemented; it has underlying anti-people philosophy-population control obsessions, and gender biased approach, over emphasis on female contraceptives and sterilsation; commercialized and unregulated private sector; dynamics between public and private health care sector; and the larger development paradigm, which is not able to create equitable access to resources. Besides, providers seem to have side tracked the critical fact that in addition to having knowledge about contraceptives, they should be available and accessible for people to make use of them.

Providers have a significant role to play in this sphere. This is because they have the necessary knowledge and potential opportunities to interact with the people on this. Also, most importantly people's trust of the medical community could be utilised for the benefit of people. However, the providers have not articulated much about their role in addressing the issue of people's ignorance about and apathy towards contraceptives. Women were blamed and held responsible for abortion situations in two diametrically opposite contexts-one, various situations within marriage, and two, various situations outside marriage, including single women's pregnancies. However, holding women alone responsible for this seems to be naive and fragmented analysis. Providers expected women to be firm and determined to exercise their rights in these matters. Internal contradictions in positions of providers about women's responsibility for their abortion situations/needs are revealed by aggregate response. These are the misplaced contemplation of providers about women's knowledge about contraceptive methods and their power to negotiate be it sexual encounters or otherwise-with their partners/husbands. Contradictions also arise when providers hold women entirely responsible by saying that it depends upon women to avail of opportunities for education and to be able to have voice in family matters. It appears that somewhere providers have missed out on the fact that women are part of the larger social system, which is patriarchal and gender biased. It reflects on prevailing tendencies among providers to think of women in isolation and not as an integral part of the social system. These one-sided views, disjoined from social realities, will have mostly negative implications for quality of care. It is baffling to see the contradictions in this context. Participation of a powerful and respected community like medical professionals in such anti-women practices has potential to legitimize them.

This pattern of practice once again indicates that perceptions and concerns for women's health in the context of their abortion needs do not go with their abortion care service pattern. In general, their commercial interest in abortion care service provision seems to overpower their understanding of women's abortion needs, which is swamped with gaps and contradictions. These gaps between perceptions and practices could be better explained with the help of forces at work that are pushing medical care service sector towards its commodification. Commercial interests of the medical community in abortion service provision in particular can further explain these gaps. The gap between the perceptions and abortion care practices perhaps forms a solid case to look into the health care delivery system, which is paralyzed with the obsession of commercial interests of the medical community. This is complemented by the convenient patriarchal attitudes towards women specific health care needs, such as abortion care needs. One concrete strategy to repair the damage and bring back the humanitarian and ethical spirit in health care service provision is to revamp the entire health/medical education system in which ethics and gender are integrated and an organic link is established between health care practices and users of health care services. Number of interim strategies-organizing gender sensitization workshops for members of the medical community, improving regulatory mechanisms, motivating bodies like IMA to playa proactive role-could be designed for actually making the services gender sensitive and ethically sound.

The study conducted by Saseendran Pallikadavath and R. William Stones discusses reproductive health security of women and HIV/AIDS in India. The rate of infection with HIV among women is increasing. This has significant implications for the reproductive health of women in India. The present configuration of national family planning services is not likely to bring about widespread condom use, which would protect women from HIV. Limited access by women, especially the poor, to health care in general means that women who are HIV positive are at an additional disadvantage. Absence of accessible voluntary counselling and testing (VCT) services will impair the effectiveness of HIV control programme in India. HIV positive women in India face serious problems with respect to marriage, sexuality, and childbearing and as the epidemic spreads these will impact on the wider society. Research studies are required in the field of mother to child transmission (MTCT) of HIV, particularly through breastfeeding, in the Indian context. While social initiatives such as the empowerment of women are required to provide reproductive health security to women, a comprehensive confidential voluntary counselling and testing programme is urgently needed.

The increasing proportion of HIV and the higher HIV/AIDS death rate in women is a serious cause for concern. Pallikadavth and Stone focus on India in this paper for the following reasons. Firstly, in India the number of women with HIV infection is already high and is most likely to increase in the future. Secondly, there is a higher mortality of HIV/AIDS infected women than men. Furthermore, death of an infant is often associated with the death of her/his mother-infants are more likely to die if their mother has already died. The number of orphans due to HIV/AIDS related death of parents is on the rise for the reason that if the wife is HIV infected, it is more likely that the husband too is HIV infected. Thirdly, women in India possess relatively low status, economic and social, in the family leading to discrimination in access to food and nutrition, health care, and education. This dimension of discrimination could further increase if they have HIV/AIDS resulting in poor health, becoming destitute, and possibly an early demise. Fourthly, Indian women traditionally take care of the children and family, hence their survival is essential for the welfare of the traditional Indian family. This is more important in the context of demographic transition leading to nuclear as well as to small families. Fifthly, since India is currently undergoing economic reforms, public spending on health is unlikely to be enhanced further. This implies that there will be no additional funding from the government to meet the needs of the generally weak public health system in India, or to meet the new challenges posed by the HIV/AIDS. Thus, if women, particularly some of the vulnerable groups among the population, are not targeted for protection from HIV infection it is most likely that they would become victims of the HIV epidemic in India.

In sum, very little is known about the HIV infection dynamics in India.Thus, the crucial issue, much to do with policy, is the shift required in the family planning programme of India. As is well known the family planning programme in India is predominantly a sterilization programme, although it does not officially favour any particular method explicitly. If condom use is to be increased as a part of the family planning programme, there is definitely a need for a sincere departure from the implicit emphasis on the sterilization programme. This needs to happen at all levels, from top management to the grass roots level workers at the sub-primary health centre (sub-PHC) level of the public health system in India.

In sum, Pallikadavath and Stones argue that sexual behaviour, emphasis on sterilization in the family planning programme, and the enormous funding required to make condom available in the public health system together make women vulnerable to HIV infection. Alternative strategies are to be identified in order to guard women from HIV infections. Access to health care is an important issue for those infected with HIV as well as those not infected with HIV. However, access to health care is more important for women infected with HIV because of their specific health needs. The status of women is an important variable influencing the risk of HIV infection. There is great resistance in providing health care to HIV infected women. This could be even more serious in rural areas where correct information about HIV/AIDS is limited. If adequate steps are not taken, reproductive health security of women may be negated under the wave of economic reforms in India. Health care support needed for preventing HIV infection and treating HIV infection in India is far from adequate. Under the current situation, it is highly likely that HIV epidemic in India would further aggravate the already poor reproductive health status of women. The social status of an HIV/AIDS infected person could very well compare with that of a leper in India. Thus, HIV infection of an unmarried woman is very likely to influence the social and psychological aspects of her reproductive health. Since most of the people in India do not have easy access to HIV testing it is not possible to know who is HIV infected and who is not. Thus, while knowing the HIV status of an unmarried girl can push her to remain unmarried, not knowing about it can spread the virus to her husband (if not already infected) and possibly to her children. Some of the pertinent issues in this regard, associated with status of women, are a woman's control over sexual relations and her ability to refuse sex without a condom. The policy also states that in order to stop effectively the spread of HIV from mother to child while at the same time protecting the health of infants the following steps are necessary. First, voluntary and confidential HIV testing be made available to all people; second, HIV positive women be provided with sound antenatal care and they be offered anti-retroviral drugs that lessen the risk of HIV transmission to their infants; third, they be counselled on the benefits and risks of all available feeding options, based on the best available information; fourth, the choice of feeding option is that of the woman's by right; fifth, once a woman make a choice, she be fully supported in that choice; and sixth, when an HIV positive woman chooses to breastfeed, she be counselled on the means of doing it most safely.

Research on the issue of mother to child transmission and its relation with breastfeeding is almost non-existent in published work.

Education: Issues in Access, Choice and Substance

In a study primarily focusing on primary education in Tamil Nadu, Akila discusses the current status in Tamil Nadu, and highlights certain issues for attention regarding access to and completion of primary education among girls. While at all-India levels, discontinuation is only 6 per cent among children enrolled in a primary class in a rural area, the same is 11 per cent for Tamil Nadu. Further, Tamil Nadu also displays a high incidence of discontinuation among children in the 12-14 age categories, often girls, probably owing to the demands of domestic and remunerative labour on them. Factors causing poor retention or high discontinuation are either supply related (such as school-based difficulties), demand based (need to work) or customary, such as the need for girl children for sibling care at home. In Tamil Nadu, customary factors are more prevalent. It shows that discontinuation is increasing rather than decreasing in Tamil Nadu, and is especially high among girls. This suggests the need to focus more attention on the regular attendance of girls, especially in backward districts. Repetition rates of Tamil Nadu, both for boys and girls, are considerably higher than the corresponding national average. Further, its repetition rates are slightly higher for boys than girls, not only in class one but also in classes four and five. This indicates that girls get lesser chance to repeat, and that in cases of failure to study, migration, demands for child labour and the like, girls may greatly lose their access to schooling rather than win chances to repeat. That girls suffer more denial of schooling than boys do probably reflects in their differential dropout status.

If primary education and completion for all has to be a reality, effective tackling of dropout among girls should be immediately prioritized. While it is true that children who drop out of the system fail to gain from it, not all those who continue in the system actually do gain either. The attainment level reached was quite low. Children's poor achievement, probable elsewhere in the state too, raises concerns related to the burden of non-comprehension in schools, which was highlighted in the government of India report titled, 'Learning without Burden'. In sum, primary-level enrolment, retention and attainment need greater attention in Tamil Nadu. They are currently suffering due to several reasons, some of them home related, and some school related. While home-related factors may either be generational and indicative of cumulative backwardness (such as a tradition of illiteracy), or may be contemporary (such as the economic demands on children in poor families), they are nevertheless more complex to solve than school-related factors. But it is increasingly recognized that many of the home-related difficulties could be effectively tackled by appropriate school-related developments. In this context, it may be useful to assess the role of the state in terms of its supply provisions for universal primary education in Tamil Nadu.

Currently, awareness for primary education is being created across all districts and there is hope that parental motivation for enrolment is likely to improve further in the light of education becoming a fundamental right of all citizens. In this context, the state needs to be equipped better for both sufficient and qualitative supply. However, while the probable impact of these measures on enrolment has been shown by some studies, field-based evidence on its role in reducing gender gaps in primary education is wanting. It should be recognized that the quality of schooling offered with currently available funds should become a central concern. The need to bridge lower and upper primary schooling in Tamil Nadu is vital, given the high discontinuation rates in classes four and five, and that especially among girls. The improvement in meeting the need for classrooms does not seem significant. PTAs, village education councils (VECs), and community participation in general are expanding in rural Tamil Nadu, and have the scope to ensure local monitoring as an effective strategy, although resources in poor and illiterate areas may need greater attention. In any case, unless the parents of girls are satisfied with the quality of schools that their children may attend, targeting all girls will remain a distant dream. Schooling infrastructure is an important criterion in this regard. Random field visits do show that the problem continues in many villages across districts. Two major issues regarding teachers are even more crucial. One is their availability, which can be gauged in terms of the teacher-school ratio, and teacher-pupil ratio. The other is their efficiency in terms of creating and sustaining interest in learning and thus producing greater attainment levels among children. It is true that many teachers have greater responsibilities than they can handle. The low motivation levels among teachers translate into indifferent classroom practices, teacher absenteeism, and low turnout of students in terms of both numbers and attainment levels. The state's strategy to have more male teachers and to encourage monitoring by the parent community and *panchayats* offers some promise for targeting more girls. In a number of cases, sensitized and motivated community participation seems to hold the key to ensuring that all children are in school. As mobilization of additional resources becomes difficult, restructuring of the available educational budget is becoming the solution. Similarly, the inter-functional allocation of resources is also vital. The government has been encouraging private contributions to primary education. But this needs careful consideration in terms of not only quality but also certain gender concerns. This indicates parental preference for educating boys rather than girls when educational expenditure becomes higher. Hence the state must shoulder more responsibility both for quantity and quality rather than depend on private schooling that may adversely affect female education. To meet elusive EFA goals, Akila recommends reduction of both rural-urban and OBC-SC/ST factors, bridging the gap between availability and access at lower and upper primary schooling, curtailing the increasing wastages, paying attention to repetition, integrating gender perspectives in all functional areas and increasing the spending on education.

Chetna Gala Sinha and Michelle Rosenthal analyse education of girls in Maharashtra. Contrary to the opinion of many, school drop out does not result from a lack of desire on the part of the girls or a lack of support from their families. Rather, girls drop out of school due to a lack of resources, and the financial constraints, in actual and opportunity costs, of education. The lack of educational opportunity results in part because of the low quality of education provided by government schools, and in part because most rural girls will not be able to afford to continue their education through the university level. Thus, while a junior college degree has the positive affect of postponing marriage, it rarely provides the professional training necessary to earn an income outside of the fields. Wider access to vocational training for women is an important intermediate step on the road to improving girls' education. Vocational skills, such as tailoring or salon skills, allow women to become financially independent. Research has shown that these women are more likely to support their own daughters' education in the future because as income increases, opportunity and commitment to education do as well. There are two primary difficulties they face when trying to educate rural children. The first is *parental illiteracy*. Despite supporting their children's education, rural parents who have not been educated themselves cannot adequately assist their children with homework or ensure that they spend sufficient time studying. Because the education of parents directly impacts the ability of their children to succeed in school, it is an urgent necessity that this generation of Indian youth is properly educated. The second pressing issue is the need to make education more employment oriented. Students and their families are loath to sacrifice for the sake of an education that cannot supply them with a job and additional income in the future. These issues must be addressed on a broad scale if education in India is to improve. Thus, the burden no longer rests with the rural families of India, or even with individual village schools. They have shown a commitment to educating their girls and have sacrificed immensely on their behalf. It is now time for the educational system to reform its half of the deal. Girls deserve an education that will benefit them in the future and a government that is committed to supporting their future with viable and honest policies and officials. The government should provide uniforms to families, rather than wasting money preparing inedible rice for primary school students. The practical reforms that should be undertaken to facilitate education of the rural girls include: making sure that the educational facilities are equipped to actually educate students. Schools should have clean water for their students. They should also own computers and provide classes that teach students how to use them with proficiency; schools should also offer professional and vocational training for students, especially those girls who will otherwise drop out to work in the fields; teachers should be held accountable to parents and students, and censured or removed if they prove inadequate. These are not the ideas of an outsider, critiquing a system only briefly examined. These are the words of the parents and girls themselves, eager to avail themselves of an education they can use. The passion for education exists in abundance in rural India. It is now a matter of harnessing that energy with an effective system, designed to maximize the benefit of educating girls. As the experiment of Satara district in Maharashtra demonstrates a system of this sort would benefit an eager and enthusiastic young girl like Savitra from Waghmodewadi, and despite all the obstacles in her path, when she and her family heard about the Girls' Education

Competition, it served as the final catalyst necessary to encourage her to go back to school. With a loan from the *Mann Deshi Mahila Sahakari Bank*, she has now enrolled in a vocational school in Gondavle and will earn her tailoring degree in a few months. Eager to support their daughter's education, but also intent on helping their village improve its school by winning the award, her family serves as an example of how this programme can truly have an impact on individual girls, village pride and the rural educational system. As Savitra has demonstrated, educating girls in rural India is not a hopeless task: rather it requires a commitment from the government to follow the lead of its citizens and provide the requisite resources for good quality schooling to village children.

Ranjan Ray's study investigates the key determinants of child labour hours and child schooling experience, paying special attention to the interaction between the two. A significant methodological feature that distinguishes his study from previous investigations is that this analysis recognizes the joint endogeneity of child labour, child schooling and child poverty. The study was conducted on Nepalese and Pakistani data, and the results are compared. A key empirical finding, with significant policy implications, is the sharp trade-off between child labour and child schooling. Another common feature of both countries is the gender bias in favour of boys' schooling, though the bias is much larger in case of Pakistan.

While there is universal agreement about the harmful effects of child labour, there is not much consensus on effective ways of dealing this phenomenon. Proposed action plans range from legislative measures that ban child labour to concerted international trade sanctions by developed countries against the import of products made by underage children in developing countries. The linkage of child labour, under the guise of 'labour standards', with trade has led to the hijacking of this issue by the WTO from child welfare agencies such as the UNICEF and the ILO. The recent international outcry over child labour has provoked talk of measures designed to satisfy several lobby groups, not all of whom are directly interested in the welfare of the working children in third world countries. There has not been much attempt, until recently, to examine systematically the causes of child labour with a view to identifying factors that could lead to its reduction and eventual elimination. That is now changing with a proliferation of empirical studies on child labour. These have either taken the form of case studies of a particular region inside a country with high incidence of child labour or they involve econometric investigations based on sample survey data containing information on child labour and child schooling. The present study, which belongs to the latter tradition, compares the results of two countries (Nepal and Pakistan) from one of the poorest regions (south Asia), which accounts for a significant proportion of child labour in the world.

Ray's study has some special features that distinguish it from previous investigations. First, he distinguishes between household level and cluster-level poverty in examining the importance of poverty as a determinant of child labour. The significance of this distinction is evident from the fact that the two poverty variables do not always agree on the nature of their impact on child labour or child schooling. Second, he provides evidence on the impact of inequality on child labour and child schooling, and examines the relative importance of inequality vis-à-vis poverty as a determinant. Third, the study examines the impact of borrowings, both at household and cluster levels, on child labour and child schooling. While there has been much analytical work and related discussion of the inequality and credit variables in the context of child labour, there has not been much empirical evidence to guide policy action in this regard. Finally, and quite crucially, he reports the results of simultaneous estimation of child labour hours, years of child schooling and the child's poverty status using a framework that recognizes their joint endogeneity. The endogeneity of child poverty marks a significant point of departure from previous studies.

An important finding of this paper, arising out of the joint estimation of child labour hours and child schooling experience equations, is the significant role that a girl child's current school attendance plays in sharply diminishing her labour hours. Alternatively, long hours spent in work by the child have a detrimental effect on her schooling. Notwithstanding the rhetoric in public statements, the record on primary schooling in south Asian countries is quite disappointing, leaving the children prone to long labour hours. Rising education levels of the adult members in the household and increased public awareness have a highly significant, positive impact on child schooling and, consequently, can play an important part in reducing the child's long labour hours. Improvements in the schooling infrastructure, by making them more relevant to the child's needs as viewed by the parent, and locating them near places of child employment will be conducive to shorter working hours and encourage combination of child labour with child schooling to a greater extent than has happened in countries such as Pakistan in relation to Latin American countries such as Peru. A common feature of the Nepalese and Pakistani results is the sharp gender bias in favour of boys' schooling in both countries. However, the extent of the bias is much larger in Pakistan. Government assisted programmes such as the district primary education projects and the integrated children development schemes (ICDS) in India can play a useful role in promoting schooling. The role of household credit that is tied to its use in keeping the child in school and to compensate the household from its consequent loss of child earnings can also be very useful in this regard. The results obtained in this study warn that untied lending to the household may be misused and can make matters worse by increasing child labour. Since tying is administratively costly and loan is fungible, a more effective strategy could be the use of mid-day school meals and enrolment subsidy that will encourage parents to keep their children in school and out of employment.

Divya Vaid highlights the causes for the inequality in educational transitions in India. Where education is concerned, not only do girls lag behind, but also certain communities and classes fare worse than the others. The aim of her paper is twofold. Firstly, to highlight the factors responsible for this inequality for both boys and girls from socially deprived origins, and secondly, to highlight in particular the inequality faced by girls at each educational transition stage. In other words the aim was not only to see how social background variables affect children's schooling, but keeping all else equal to study how girls from a particular community or class fared as compared to boys from the same community. This was achieved through interaction effects between gender and all the background variables. Logistic regression was considered the most appropriate method to conduct the present analysis.

The paper uses a unique National Election Study (1996) data set that contains information on the respondent and the respondent's parent's caste, class, religion and locality. The major results of this study are only partly consistent with previous research. There was weak support for the effect of caste, but class on the other hand emerged as a strong determinant of the relative chance of a child continuing in school. No support was found for an additional class effect where the education of girls is concerned, thus refuting the notion of a more egalitarian Indian middle class.

Adding caste to the analysis did not appreciably lead to a decline in the parameters of class, and it then emerges that given caste and class together, class seems to have a greater impact on the education that a child receives. This is not to deny the fact that caste has an important part to play in social interaction, especially in blocking certain avenues of education to the minority backward community. But what it does really is to highlight the fact that for better or for worse class appears to be an important determinant of who gets ahead and who lags behind.

The effects of other background characteristics like parental education, religion and region were found to be important determinants of the likelihood of an educational transition for a child. Parental literacy (especially father's literacy), state (especially the state of Rajasthan), and religion (belonging to the 'other' religion category) had strong interactions with gender. The decrease of gender inequality as seen in the west has not yet come into play in India, where the education of girls is still not considered a necessity. This could well be due to the dynamics of an agricultural society, where children are an asset on the farms and the opportunity cost of educating them (and doing without their labour) is quite high.

While interpreting the results of the present analysis one must bear in mind that the method of logistic regression is not without its drawbacks. According to Mare 'the more that unobservable factors affect school continuation and the greater the degree of selectivity, the more difficult it is to estimate social background effects, and the more important to compare background effects across social contexts.' This problem of unmeasured heterogeneity could be overcome in subsequent studies by the introduction of additional control variables, which are conceptually believed to affect the schooling of girls. These could be the availability of schools, the availability of female teachers, the quality of schools available, the distance of the schools from the village and girls labour force participation. Even though the present data do not include information on these variables, nevertheless, the data do help to shed light on gender inequality where education is concerned and is a step in the right direction to understand this inequality. A future qualitative field study could also complement the current research and would provide a clearer picture of factors that affect the schooling of girls and boys.

Keeping in mind the results of this study, many avenues for further research emerge. It would be interesting to study if and how caste and class mediate with education to affect the job opportunities for women and men. This could be a good test of the human capital approach which posits that the job opportunity structure could be biased against women, and parents knowing well that their daughters will not get good enough jobs in the labour market, prefer to invest in the education of their sons instead. This research is a first step albeit a small one to analyze some of the determinants of inequality in educational transitions in India with particular emphasis on gender inequality.

Nandini Manjrekar discusses contemporary challenges to women's education. Given the legacy of struggle by women to establish their right to education why has education been peripheral to the concerns of the contemporary women's movement in India? How can the women's movement re-engage with questions of education? Part of the challenge in thinking through concerns about gender and education lies in uncovering the dialectical linkages between the formal education system and larger social and economic processes and their influence on girls' and women's lives.

The findings of the Committee on the Status of Women in India should have alerted the women's movement to the need to interrogate the social character of formal education in India, which has acted to divide women by class, caste and ethnicity. Larger feminist critiques of development policies and paradigms have unfortunately overlooked the ways in which formal education, in its organization and processes, offers a narrow range of subject positions for girls and women, locating and even objectifying them as mere instruments in the narrative of national progress. Forms and representation of knowledge in school curricula reflect the discourses of formal education and the pattern of social relations in society-framing, normalizing and legitimizing social inequalities, processes in which the state plays a critical regulatory role.

We need to critically analyze why education has been peripheral to the concerns of the contemporary women's movement in India, given the legacy of struggle by women to establish their right to education. It is worth considering whether the assumed instrumentalist nature of formal education, particularly in the post independence era, has not inhibited more radical interpretations of what formal education means for girls, both in terms of self perceptions as well as materially. Part of the challenge in thinking through our concerns about gender and education lies in uncovering the dialectical linkages between the formal education system and larger social and economic processes, and their influence on girls' and women's lives. In the present context, we are now seeing how an education system already fragile and alienated from its objectives is increasingly facing the combined onslaught of rightwing reaction and the market. Both portend the deepening of social divisions and inequalities.

The child, in the vision of the National Curriculum Framework (NCF), is to be immersed in an environment where values, not derived from rules of citizenship in a democratic polity, but from religion, will predominate. Value education and education about religions would not form a separate subject of study or examination at any stage. These would be so judiciously integrated with all the subjects of study in the scholastic areas and all the activities and programmes in the co-scholastic areas that the objectives thereof would be directly and indirectly achieved in the classrooms, at the school assembly places, play-grounds, cultural centres and such other places. Quite apart from the dreary drive it contains, the framework is an enormous setback to the women's movement. It portends a future for women's education that is deeply disempowering. The lack of seriousness with which the NCF approaches social disadvantage can be seen in the manner in which a range of citizens is subsumed within a single disadvantaged category: women, *dalits, adivasis*, along with children with impairments. Valorization of religious tradition, the leitmotif of the document, negates the essentially oppressive role tradition plays in women's lives to curb and control their sexuality, labour and individuality. Ironically, moreover, the anti-modernity of the NCF's vision of education is entirely compatible with the processes of globalization. 'Indianising' and 'spiritualizing' the curriculum is not antithetical in the least to orienting education to the market. Vocationalisation, a recommendation of the NCF, was originally envisaged as an alternative to college education, which students could opt for after Class XII. It has been a non-starter in Indian education, with less than 5 per cent of students opting for vocational courses. Vocational courses for girls are highly gendered-typing, tailoring, etc, which only allow them entry, if at all, into low-paying jobs in the unorganized sector. The NCF now recommends vocational streaming after Class X. This will only serve to heighten inequalities by caste, class and gender, by further restricting the access of poor girls, *dalits* and other marginal groups to higher education, and decreasing their representation at this level.

There was planned saffronisation of education, with emphasis on 'value education' derived from religion and 'tradition' replaces that on social justice, tolerance and plurality. The idea of 'unity in diversity', an educational slogan of the post-independence era, which had some pedagogic value despite its problems, has been given a quiet burial. This new thrust is of a piece with efforts in other spheres to manufacture a majoritarian view of society in which the cultural and political space for all marginalized sections, especially minorities, will progressively shrink. Undoubtedly, the Indian state must bear the responsibility for its lack of commitment to constitutional directives that mandate that all children must be healthy and educated in independent India. However, we need to consider whether privatization in the education sector is an adequate answer to the government's lack of performance. There is increasing evidence that privatization is likely to exacerbate existing gender inequalities in education.

This report explicitly argues the necessity of opening up the secondary sector to private initiatives, while maintaining that the primary sector needs the full support of the government in order to meet the requirement of Article 45 of the Constitution.

Several contentious issues in the report need to be debated. Firstly, we must ask ourselves how is it that industry is dictating what national educational priorities must be. It is clear that the logic of market intervention in education is related to so-called 'efficiency' and the generation of profit, in the context of education supposedly emerging as a new sector of the global economy. What is frightening, however, is that any educational vision or perspective will be surrendered to this logic.

The government's withdrawal from the education sector and the entry of private enterprise is by design, not by default. The failure of the state to provide basic education to all children takes on a different dimension in the context of structural reform of economies. The experiences of other countries attempting such reforms in the name of efficiency tell us that they serve to further marginalize communities who already find themselves on the periphery of formal education. Justified on the basis of returns through employment, increased household expenditure on education will inevitably be discriminatory: boys' education will be favoured over that of girls. Recent developments indicate that policies are becoming increasingly gender-blind. One may even venture to say that they are erasing whatever gains have been made towards girls' well being. Class, caste and gender inequalities in education are only going to increase without strong state commitment to equality. That the Indian state has failed to stem these inequalities is not in doubt. However, we should recognize that entrenched privileges of the elites functioning within Indian patriarchal society have contributed to this failure. These interests will continue to influence privatization as well. 25 years ago, J.P. Naik said that equal opportunity in education cannot be seen in isolation from enhancing opportunity on the political and economic fronts to 'destroy privilege itself'.

Given the foregoing scenario, what is to be done? Where democratic spaces are increasingly shrinking under the weight of a majoritarian state and the forces of the market, how can the women's movement re-engage with questions of education? In this paper, Manjrekar has tried to raise a few issues that could be addressed as a tentative beginning to this re-engagement. To her mind, there is need for intensive monitoring of new developments that are likely to impact girls' education. Women are central to the contemporary politics of culture embodied in the NCF. The struggle for an egalitarian and democratic culture should be extended to a struggle for an education that is critical of received ideologies and can promote such a culture. For this we may have to work to mainstream gender concerns into alternative educational discourse. Unfortunately, there is a gap between those who are part of the more radical debates on education, most of whom are sensitive but hesitant to address gender issues, and women's studies scholars and activists who do not direct their analysis of gender and society towards questions of educational theory, pedagogy and curriculum. Many women's activists and organizations participate in sessions with teachers where gender issues are discussed. Teacher training is an important area of intervention, but we should be a little wary of training in isolation from the experience of teachers in schools.

Privatization is another area we must keep monitoring. Finally, in the face of multiple pressures, can we debate our feminist understanding of what it means to be educated as a girl/woman in contemporary India? Can we put forward an alternate perception of girls' education? Young girls today are facing newer, more complex, forms of regulation. Questions of physical insecurity loom large in these discussions, as can be expected after the trauma that Muslim women and the community as a whole have been through, and the insecurity that continues to loom large over their lives. Can education engender such resistance? Is this the alternate, critical consciousness we have been hoping to articulate as an aim for girls' education? And does it necessarily have to come at so heavy a price?

Women in Traditional Economic Activities: Presence, Agency and Control

Through an overview of Indian popular literature, Aruna Sitesh analyses the portrayal of workingwomen in India. With the spread of education and the changing social ethos, there has been a marked change and departure from tradition in our society creating new pressures, new situations and new attitudes. The new crossing to a technological-metropolitan society has altered the spectrum of choices available to the Indian woman. Workingwomen are no longer seen as a stigma on the family-as the inability of the patriarchal head to provide for the family. The power structures of the nuclear families have also changed creating new roles and responsibilities. It has become an accepted pattern to expect the daughter, especially the eldest daughter, to take up a job and help settle her younger brothers and sisters. The trend is very explicit in our literature also which is regarded as a major tool to gauge the true image of the society. Reviewing the literature, mostly Hindi but not entirely, this paper examines the portrayal of working women by eminent women writers during the last few decades. To the extent the characters in the Indian popular literature are actually representing the society, its analysis clearly reflects the attitudinal changes registered in the society in context of working women.

Economically independent, so-called 'free women' are not really free;they still cannot lead their lives the way they want to. They internalize the self-sacrificing values and decide that they live only for their parents and siblings. Exploited thus by their families both economically and emotionally, these women remain on tenterhooks constantly balancing their home needs and career.

Yet another paradox of our times is that young women can work if their parents or parents-in-law permit them to. Where they should work, how they should work, when they should resign-these crucial questions which would determine the quality and direction of their lives would also be decided by parents or parents-in-laws without paying the slightest heed to the likes or dislikes of the girls concerned. The majority of women themselves don't think that after marriage, personal fulfillment for a woman in her career or having her own life is justified if the husband does not approve of it. It is for the woman to make the major adjustment in a marriage even if it means giving up her career. Perhaps a workingwoman clashes with the bourgeois conventional image of a dutifully passive wife. They perhaps see it as a reflection on their role as a provider of the family. Also fear that if she becomes economically independent, their sole authority would be eroded. A large number of Indian men, fortunately not all, have not been able to internalize breaking away of every male bastion by the Indian women. Especially if financially comfortable, they expect an extra pat for being so condescending! So liberal, so accommodating as to let their wives work. They feel that their responsibility ends there. The idea of sharing some of the domestic chores with her is quite alien to them. She, therefore, finds herself in the demanding dual role of a housewife and a workingwoman. Successful women very often find themselves dealing with the remnants of a broken marriage. The apparent reversal of traditional gender roles and subsequent power equations constantly threatens the tenuous fragility of their marriage. It is an acceptance of their innate need to love and be loved that makes the Indian workingwomen to shun divorce and try to reconcile. While looking for new possibilities of choice, personal control, personal growth, these women don't want to sacrifice the vital human satisfaction of warm loving relationships some of which exist only in a family context. This dualism, best explained in terms of individualism and with conformity in the desire to want to belong and to being dependent explains why these women suffer indignities and tyranny of the family. In modern society money and social esteem go together. Those without money are also denied esteem. Most husbands and housewives blame the working mother for her child's delinquency. This is another striking anomaly of our times. There is a visible and rapidly rising decline in work ethic: this needs to be set right before irreparable damage is done to the image of women as a conscientious, industrious and responsible work turf. However, not all have fallen into the rut. Some among them decide to be freelancers so that they can retain their freedom and dignity. Some women work not because of family compulsions but because of their own inner compulsions to carve a niche for themselves as individuals and simultaneously forge a new consciousness in their society. While the majority of the novels of the 60s and 70s had portrayed working young women as victims-turned-martyrs, the novels of the last decade, in particular, have depicted women attempting, often successfully, to get out of the social shackles and familial fetters to take their own decisions and even pave the way for a dignified life.

From her analysis, Sitesh outlines certain 'factual' situations of workingwomen: women who have to work to support themselves and their families; women who work while waiting to get married; women who work to supplement husband's income and raise the economic status of the family; women who work for a label; women who work because they want to feel they are more than breeders and caretakers; women who work because they have a vision, an idea of what they want or don't want in life. They can work towards it only if economically independent. Whatever be the motive, workingwomen have no proper support system that can help them cope simultaneously with their professional and personal responsibilities without losing their reason. In the final analysis, economic independence does give you the freedom to make your own choices though the price you pay for making a particular choice may at times be very high. Let us hope the women of the 21st century are not called upon to pay such a heavy price, are not called upon to make these hard choices in life.

The paper by Sarkar and Das is in an attempt to examine the extent of women's involvement in forestry and their role in Joint Forest Management (JFM) in West Bengal, a key precursor to the JFM concept for India. It observes that despite women's greater involvement in forestry, State JFM resolution has proved inadequate for ensuring their participation in community institutions. But the setting up of female FPC in some areas of West Bengal by recent policy provisions has extended the scope of women's active participation in Forest Management.

In SC and ST households where women retain their earnings, their husbands actually hand over their own earnings, besides what they keep for personal expenses, to their wives for managing their household. But does that constitute autonomy? Given that there are households living always at the edge of poverty even if they are not actually suffering from starvation, it is clear that there is very little that the women can do with their earnings apart from buying food and other essentials. It can be confidently said about ST households that they enjoy autonomy to a greater extent than the other groups. ST women can take decision of marriage, separation, divorce and remarriage.

All of this leads to a general discussion of women as earners and the extent to which this affects their status in the household. In spite of being an essential economic contributor, there are social constraints, which work against the woman to improve her status and position within the household. Though their paper lacks any concrete data, it is their strong impression that when a woman is more or as well educated than her husband she tends to be better positioned than otherwise.

Women's control of the product of their labour depends on many factors. Females who work as agricultural labourers do not automatically enjoy same rights. It is again dependent upon caste hierarchy and the probability of her having a better education than their husbands. A variety of cultural and socio-psychological factors also play a part in how much autonomy a woman has. Some women early in life are able to earn a reputation for being able to handle people and being able to manage things well. Such women are often able to gain considerable autonomy in their households, and even in the community at large. A man who is very family -oriented and understanding can see to it that even a woman who is not exceptionally efficient or good at human relations has more autonomy. Thus, within the social, economic and cultural parameters mentioned above there is still room for significant individual variation among households.

Anil Shah attempts to sketch the priorities of women in using water for domestic and irrigation purposes in Gujarat.Transferring irrigation management to water users' associations is considered essential for improving the canal management. Those, particularly NGOs committed to gender priority, would like women to be brought in the 'mainstream' of irrigation management by encouraging them to participate actively in the affairs of water users' associations. The paper seeks to examine such an approach. It begins with reporting on the interaction with women groups in six villages that had different sources of water for domestic use but one common feature they all possessed was that a canal served them all. Participatory rural appraisal conducted in these villages brought out that women's priority concern was very largely for water for domestic use. These women had hardly any interest in canal waters as they were perceived to be meant for agriculture, not for meeting 'their' priority requirements. How can canals serve petter the women priority needs for domestic use of water? What can women do for improving the canal management and better functioning of water users' associations?

The Secretary to the Government of India, Ministry of Irrigation identified the following ailments of public irrigation management in India: (a) unreliability of water delivery; (b) almost universal inequitable and tail end deprivation in water distribution; (c) small farmers suffer more deprivation of water; (d) very inefficient use of water leading to over irrigation in part of the command that leads to wastage of water; (e) no group/individual incentive for farmers to conserve water and economize its use; (f) poor service to farmers marked by insensitivity; (g) no relation between levy of water rates and the recovery with the actual cost of water; and (h) widespread deterioration of infrastructure. On the basis of a critical analysis of the performance of 24 irrigation projects carried out by the Central Groundwater Board, India, it is possible to add a few more deficiencies to the foregoing list: (i) excessive canal seepage; (j) inefficient drainage and water logging; (k) main system's deficiencies; and (i) mismatched cropping pattern and water supply calendar. The approach in the present system is top-down. The prescriptions are handed from the top and irrigation is managed more according to standard administrative procedures than by local variable needs.

Left to itself the irrigation establishments will only tinker with these problems. It has a built-in incapacity to undertake bold reforms that are necessary for improving the performance of the vital irrigation sector. There is therefore need for influencing and supporting irrigation reforms by those who have wider understanding of development, particularly rural development and who can look at the issues from variety of perspectives required for serving the cause of improving performance of irrigation sector. Since the irrigation engineers would not take initiative for reforming the system they are managing, pressure has to be brought from outside by those who value the significance of irrigation in economy, particularly rural economy of the country and ensure its benefits for the people including the poor.

Irrigation engineers would implement orders about participatory irrigation management more as a formality to reach targets given to them. Few NGOs that have taken to Participatory Irrigation Management (PIM) are facing resistance from irrigation establishment and hurdles in implementing changes in irrigation management. Even the farmers, the highest stakeholders to benefit from PIM, do not show keenness and initiative in availing of the enabling orders. Farmers have settled down in their apathy and passively use the irrigation waters as and when available. Making a success of PIM is indeed a difficult task, involving motivating and organizing farmers into Water User Associations (WUAs), guide them to get their organization registered and contribute share capital; take responsibility for planning of water supply in every season for which applications have to be collected from individual members; managing water distribution to the satisfaction of farmers particularly tail enders against unreliable release of water by the irrigation authorities and out of turn drawl of water by the head reach and other head strong farmers; fixing and collection of fees and paying government charges; maintenance of the system; maintaining accounts, resolving inevitable conflicts and so on. This requires a shake up of the system, which is in the state of a malignant equilibrium.

So far as government irrigation agencies promoting PIM are concerned it will be useful to (a) develop in them gender awareness programmes and (b) PR techniques to understand and appreciate women's perception, need priorities with respect to water. It should be therefore considered an achievement if they (c) formulate systems and accept as their responsibility to incorporate in irrigation planning and, management the special requirements of women as listed earlier in designing canal system, in redesigning water supply scheduling, and management of water delivery. The NGOs, which are committed to efficiency and equity, should ensure that (a) the agenda for reforms should include securing government orders to give importance to meeting the 'domestic' need of water as listed earlier in designing and redesigning canals, in scheduling, in planning water supply rotation; and (b) securing orders will be only the first step. Operating them satisfactorily will be the major task requiring NGOs to orient the irrigation bureaucracy and induce implementation; (c) they should also strive for creating enough space and scope for women to present their special requirements and contribute their strengths to successful working of WUAs. Besides reservation of some positions for women in the executive committee, it is important (d) to help the WUA members to elect such women who can conveniently attend meetings and other duties. Elena P Bastidas has found in her studies that participation of women depends upon their household composition and life stage. She classifies households into four types: (i) young couples with small children; (ii) couples with grown-up children (iii) women headed house households, and (iv) old couples. She found that old couples participate more fully. For those women, who can conveniently spare time, may be encouraged to participate if they exhibit potential for leadership qualities such as education, and "urge to do something for the community". For women to contribute to better working of WUA, it is not necessary to prove that women are farmers and women are irrigators. Even a non-farming educated woman can help WUA in better record keeping. In fact, similar criteria are applicable when electing male members: leadership quality and availability of other adult males in the family to look after family business; (e) They may also organize women's group separately so that the women can collectively present their requirements through the women members of the executive committee. Such members in turn can keep the women informed about the discussions and decisions in the executive committee meetings. The NGOs can also provide encouragement to the women through training and exposure visit to WUAs where women are more actively participating and contributing to that success of PIM. Elena has found out that appointing women staff members helps and trains women to gain confidence and overcome the initial resistance.

The NGOs that are gender equity committed, working for women's empowerment, can contribute by (a) demonstrating through examples in diverse cultural situations how women could shoulder responsibility and through leadership qualities ensure better performance of WUAs-tribal and non-tribal, good rainfall and low rainfall areas, etc. The NGO, AKRSP has promoted a unique project of Kevdi in Bharuch district, Gujarat where 50 per cent of WUA members are women as also in its executive committee. Experience of irrigation management on the basis of equality between men and women would yield valuable lessons. Though 'island of excellence' has its own value, it is considerably enhanced when its feasibility is demonstrated in good number of cases. (b) Detailed documentation of the process, positive gains and problems resolved and unresolved will further add to the value of such examples. (c) For creating an impact on the 'mainstream' PIM, such gender priority organizations should also get the experience of promoting gender-equity approach in new as well as existing WUAs. They can then develop suggestive approaches of introducing gender equity in different stages of WUAs. It may be useful to keep in view Christine Van Wijk's counsel, "Kwaule points out that shifting the balance from men to women is no solution either because it caused men to oppose women's role qr even withdraw from the project". To avoid such a backlash, reforms towards desirable have to be pushed with circumspection. (d) Such organization could also take up the change and get changed that only men are considered as heads of family and therefore entitled to represent family in the WUAs. (e) They would require working for removing administrative and legal hurdles in women's full membership of WUA. (f) While 'mainstreaming women', they would be well advised not to neglect the mainstream issues of canal irrigation reforms. Unlike other women centred activities like micro-finance, PIM cannot be conducted in isolation at micro level. It is not possible to ignore other requirements of irrigation reforms, many of which are gender neutral, but impact the gender sensitive micro management. (g) Again securing administrative and legal entitlement for women to participate fully in WUA would not be enough. Such organizations will have to work for translating such orders into reality on the ground. This has been found necessary, for example, in the case of legal rights conferred on daughters to equal share of ancestral property. This has yet to be translated into reality. Traditional mindset has to be changed to translate legal provisions into reality. A strong case has to be made out not only about the desirability but also about feasibility. These subsequent steps of creating awareness and demonstrating feasibility can be accomplished by promoting actual cases.

Meanwhile the development agencies may better respect women's priorities in water for domestic purpose and see what irrigation can do to meet this requirement. Simultaneously, they should be creating scope and space for their contribution to irrigation sector reform, particularly through PIM. They should hold on to the faith and reality that society is changing towards more gender equity. As is happening in the developed countries, including in the Indian households, the gender roles would change, giving women much more freedom to contribute their strength to the 'mainstream' activities in economic, social and political spheres.

This approach demands combination of innovative work and patience, all the time respecting women's 'reproductive' and domestic responsibilities as well as their present perceptions and priorities.

Deepita Chakravarty examines the expansion of markets and its impact on the women workers in the garment manufacturing industry. The literature on the gendered implications of expansion of markets for employment often looks at women workers as the victims of the trade liberalization process resulting from discrimination in the labour market. However, discrimination is a complex process taking different forms in different contexts leading to different outcomes. This study suggests that in the context of a dynamic industrial activity of a poor labour surplus economy, discrimination against women can take place outside the labour market. For example, employment depends on education and skills to which women have unequal accesses. The study is based on selected firms of Indian garment-manufacturing industry in and near the city of Hyderabad. Data indicate that the differences in earnings and wage rates between the male and female workers occur because of the existence of piece rate work at times of necessity. The firms that work for three shifts in a day do not practice the piece rate system. Chakravarty emphasizes this fact not to contest the usual feminist understanding but to highlight the importance of context. She believes that for the greater part the reason lies in the generally low economic conditions of the country where men are also ready to work at very low wages. The discussion of similar experiences in other developing countries suggests that it is not the labour market discrimination that leads to lower earnings for the female workers. On the contrary, it is the general social constraints (sometimes in the form of legal constraints), which prohibit women to work and earn at par with their male counterparts in the labour market. Chakravarty argues that the discrimination against women is not taking place within the labour market. It is the lack of education in general and lack of technical education in particular which makes a woman less endowed and bars her entry into the industrial labour market as such. A similar situation of difficulty in getting female supervisors is reported in the case of Bangladesh garment manufacturing industry. Chakravarty finds that there is a general decline in the percentage of women workers in the total workforce of the sample firms, while in almost every case total employment has increased. In the context of strong preferences for female workers, this is apparently contradictory. Apart from social constraints pointed out earlier, however, managements say that the shortage of educated female workers is the main reason behind this.

Space, Voice and Turbulence in the Newer Sectors of Economy

The papers in this section are far more important in as much as they highlight the emerging concerns for the women in the knowledge economy. Using data on enrolment in engineering colleges, out-turn job opportunities, career status and other factors, and also analyzing responses of women engineers and employers on perceptions and barriers, Parikh and Sukhatme's paper discusses the findings of two extensive studies on women engineers in India.

In India, the participation of women in engineering was negligible till the early 1980s. It is only in the past 15 years that their enrolment has shown an increasing trend. However, with the increase in numbers, women engineers are facing many problems in their careers. These problems need to be understood and analyzed. Keeping these issues in view, two extensive studies on women engineers were taken up at IIT Bombay. The Department of Science and Technology sponsored both studies. This paper presents the salient findings of the two studies. The data on enrolment and out-turn of women engineers over the years has been presented to evolve a feel for the numbers involved. This is followed by analysis of the data obtained through the two studies in regards to job status, nature of work and career problems of women engineers. Following this, a summary of the reactions obtained from employers and then some recommendations for action based on the results of both studies are presented.

From Study I to Study II, the employed percentage has decreased by 13.8 per cent, while the unemployed percentage has increased from 26.1 per cent to 30.6 per cent. This is not a happy situation. Although comparable data for men is not readily available, it is likely that the unemployment percentage is much less. A good guess would be 15-20 per cent.

Finding the first job after graduation is a major hurdle in the career path of women engineers. This is duly reflected by a higher percentage of unemployment amongst younger members and the fact that the unemployed were without a job for over a year at the time of data collection.

On a branch wise basis, the percentage unemployment amongst electronics (37.3 per cent) and electrical (36.4 per cent) engineering graduates has increased significantly, surpassing the unemployment amongst civil engineers, which is 30.9 per cent. This scenario is not quite in tune with the general belief that electronics is a good area for women engineers. It seems that there is now a big imbalance between the demand and supply of graduates in electronics engineering. It is necessary to verify whether the increased unemployment is generally applicable to all the graduates in electronics engineering, both men and women, or is true only for women engineers.

Employment in the large-scale private sector industry has increased from 12.7 per cent in Study I to 18.4 per cent in Study II. Data indicate that technical educational institutions (TEIs) provide the largest avenue for employment of women engineers. In an overall sense, limited job opportunities in terms of sector of employment are reflected by the data of both studies. Although some changes have taken place since the first study, the situation is still far from satisfactory. What the data does not reflect is that even today there are industrial organizations that have policies against hiring women engineers and that they have no hesitation in making statements to such an effect. It is interesting to note that only 20 per cent of the graduates of 1975 and 1976 belonged to the upper management and that this figure fell to less than 5 per cent for graduates of later years. This can be referred to as the 'glass ceiling' that women rarely cross. It is even more disheartening to note that a quarter of those who passed in 1975 and 1976 had 'no management responsibilities' at all, even after 15 years. There are no campus interviews in some of the new colleges. In fact, getting the first job after graduation emerges as the major hurdle women engineers face during their professional career. A significant number of those who do not secure jobs opt for further studies. Lack of opportunities, reluctance of the employers and requirement of experience are prominent factors responsible for such a situation. The need to have contacts to get a job has been clearly expressed by the respondents. An overall scarcity of jobs and abundance of engineers is reflected in the responses. The respondents strongly expressed the view that they do not get what they deserve in terms of jobs, promotions, salaries as well as professional recognition. 'Unsatisfactory work opportunities and environment' is the most frequently stated factor affecting their career. 'Low financial incentives' has also figured as a career problem. The employment data show that women engineers constitute about 21 per cent of the engineering staff of TEIs, whereas in industries, the percentage is only 3.5 per cent. On the whole, the percentage of women engineers works out to 6.1 per cent. Participation of women engineers in management is low. It decreases with increase in the level of management. Among all types of organizations, industries rank the lowest as far as participation of women engineers in management is concerned. A majority of the responding executives felt that opportunity for advancement of women engineers was the same as for men engineers at the middle and lower management levels. However, at the upper management level, they felt that the opportunity for advancement was less. Regarding the possibility of giving preference in selection to a woman in the event of having an equally qualified and experienced man and woman, a larger number of respondents have expressed their preference for a woman engineer. Discipline, punctuality, hard work and obedience are stated to be the qualities of women engineers, because of which respondents would like to exercise a preference in their favour.

Based on the results and viewpoints presented, Parikh and Sukhatme make a number of suggestions in the form of recommendations for action. Implementation of these recommendations should alleviate existing problems and smoothen the entry of women engineers into the mainstream. At present, the work format does not accommodate the needs of a woman professional. Although there has been a significant increase in out-turns of women engineers, their prospects of employment and career advancement profiles remain matters of concern. However, the increase in out-turn has created many problems. There is considerable unemployment and underemployment of women graduates. They have difficulty in being accepted as equals in a male-dominated profession and they have difficulty in rising to the top. There are no easy solutions to these probiems. A number of approaches have to be tried and many recommendations have been made in this regard. The recommendations are largely based on the suggestions of the respondents-the women graduates and their employers. Their implementation will help in alleviating the situation.

As far as the employers are concerned, their viewpoints are generally positive. Replies to the formal questions suggest a positive attitude towards hiring of women engineers. Women engineers are perceived as capable professionals with high potential. Such a response could be because of the general acceptance of 'women in engineering' as a ground reality. It could also be due to the anxiety of the executive respondents to be correct in responding to the questions. The opinions coming through the replies to certain other questions, however, indicate that many employers have some reservations about the concept of women participating in the engineering profession. This is to be expected. Any change in social values is a complex phenomenon and takes time. The studies show that changes are in the offing. It is now a matter of time.

In a pioneering study, Vineeta Bal examines the status of women scientists in India. Despite the increase in the number of women scientists in biology, gender-based disadvantages in a patriarchal Indian culture continue to be the order of the day. Are there any unique circumstances in this context in the workplace situation of women biologists? Being experimentalists, biologists work as part of a team in their professional careers. They may be leaders, or junior or not-so-junior partners in the team. For optimal work output it is necessary for experimentalists to form a team with overlapping interests and individual specialized skills. Both for getting adequate funding to carry out the research and publishing in reputed journals, it is necessary that the teamwork be optimal. Cultural upbringing often makes it difficult for a man to work under a woman or take orders from a woman, causing problems. Such a situation for women biologists may thus be different from, say, that of theoretical physicists or mathematicians who can work as individuals and achieve professional stature. Even women science teachers or doctors may have to depend less on their colleagues in this sense for survival in their fields.

A factor common to many professions affecting women adversely is long working hours. While keeping strictly to standard working hours is possible in some kinds of jobs, academic research in biology needs longer hours beyond 9 to 5 if success is to be achieved. With family responsibilities being culturally their burden, it becomes very difficult for women faculty to spend such long hours at work. In fact, this issue affects the ability of women both to find and keep faculty positions. Women who complete their Ph.D in their late twenties are usually likely to be under pressure to get married during the course of their doctoral work, or immediately after. They also end up taking career breaks of a few months to a few years for childbearing and child rearing. Taking time off always affects careers adversely, but even more so where the work needs a lot of infrastructure and teamwork, as for biologists. If a working scientist loses touch completely for a couple of years, coming back becomes that much more difficult. Employment rules frequently tend to have upper age limits for positions. Many institutions have a convention of not offering jobs to husbands and wives together, and inevitably, women suffer more from these practices than men do. Gaps in careers can haunt women for the rest of their professional lives even if they manage to make a comeback into their careers.

Thus, in a patriarchal culture, even those women who try to break weak gender barriers in order to provide better living conditions for their families while pursuing their interest in the field are faced with many career difficulties. Many of them lose out in the pursuit of their profession in the early phases. Even for those who cross this hurdle successfully, the profession can make them invisible-not rising far enough to step into leadership roles, and not getting recognition. Rumbler strips on the road function as more efficient controllers of speed than a single speed breaker bump, a situation depressingly familiar to women biologists. Vineeta Bal argues that establishment of gender-unbiased, transparent criteria for approval of project proposals, selection of candidates for jobs, and nomination to decision-making positions may go a long way towards correcting the situation.

Preeti Singh and Anu Pandey explore the value of women at work in call centers and at home. It analyses their perceptions and constraints and how they balance their family life with their work. The study is mainly at an exploratory level to determine the quantum and quality of women employed in call centres in India. It throws light on issues such as family background, education, job level, motivation and commitment, attitudes, decision-making power and health. This study has in a small measure conducted an analysis of women from middle class families in their new area of employment. Indian women have taken up professional roles to create an identity for themselves or out of economic necessity.

The advantage of the time factor has provided employment but is also the source of most of women's family problems. It is expected that such employment would have an effect on her physical and mental health as well. This study deals with the problems occurring due to the unusual hours of work. It looks into the changes in the urban outlook, where it was once taboo for girls to travel alone out of the house after dark, and where now they are encouraged to work and do night shifts at call centres.

Call centres are increasingly interested in keeping their employees fit, relaxed and less stressed, by providing gyms and yoga classes. The company canteen provides tea, coffee, refreshments and meals. Recreational facilities such as 'carrom boards' and table tennis are available in large call centres that have many employees. The environment is a positive aspect of the job in a call centre, a view that was supported by the employees. One of the questions in the questionnaires was: 'What do you like about your job?' Seventy-five per cent of the respondents answered 'Good Environment'. The call centres did not require any major degrees for the jobs. A graduate with good communication skills was acceptable. Undergraduates and housewives were also attracted to such jobs. Since call centre jobs have night duties and long hours of work, few women in the reproductive age are employed here. Married women with small children find it inconvenient to pursue a career in such places. There is no discrimination in male or female jobs at the lower levels. Female executives say that being a woman is their major career obstacle because they have multiple roles to play. Women occupy mid-level positions and men tend to move into higher positions. This inhibited rise of women in the corporate ladder in call centres. It is largely due to the fact that they move out of the employment structure due to the demands of marriage, children and household responsibilities. Women are represented more in the lower paid jobs. There appears to be no other area of employment in India that gives its employees an attractive pay package at such a young age and with minimum qualifications.

Call centres are one of the most sought after workplaces for young graduates and undergraduates as it provides them with a good environment to work in, decent emoluments and financial incentives, transportation both during day and night, and meals and refreshments. No other job allows the entry of employees with minimum education (school pass) at such attractive perks. There is a change in the acceptability of women working in call centres having night duties, both in nuclear and joint families. There are also some negative aspects about this job, which includes risks such as the difficulty of travelling at night, health hazards and social stigma. But the major problem is the health hazard from doing night duty. They suffer from problems like sleep disorder and indigestion. Health problems that employees from call centres suffer including backache, spondylitis, eyestrain, headache and pressure because of the headsets and constant calls. In the changing socio-economic scenario a large number of families have started accepting the idea of women working in non-traditional spheres like call centres. 90 per cent of the respondents did not balance work and family life. The respondents had no social life or interaction with people in the family. This job restricted their social life. Major household chores of most unmarried respondents were left to be performed by their parents. Among married women, some were stressed because husbands did not alter their domestic roles.

Other married women who shared the provider's role negotiated for a greater share in family power and authority. Such women were able to alter attitudes of their families and the men did an equal amount of work at home to allow them to continue working in call centres. That means that certain changes are evident even in India's patriarchal society. 41 respondents also stated that one person did not take the decisions but that themselves made them mutually on matters regarding the family and, at work.

Mala Bhandari's paper analyzes the contemporary demographic changes in the labour force within the context of work-life balance and other issues related to women working at executive positions in the corporate sector. She undertook her study with the hypothesis that the role conflict theory cannot adequately explain all the intricate social realities in a woman's life. Consequently the present study was undertaken with an alternate approach, the quality of life (QOL) approach. This emphasizes that work and family are two interacting structures or social systems that most profoundly impact women's lives. Therefore, this study focuses on inter-linkages between family/household and women's work life as it has altered with macro-economic changes and analyzes all aspects of women's lives, viewing home, work and family as one integrated whole with relations of interdependence and inter-reliance. The home and office lives of women executives were studied through following indicators: economic autonomy and empowerment through achieved status of an earner; intra-household decision-making through management and control over money resources; and the traditional division of labour within the household. These indicators included the objective conditions of life as well as subjective interpretations by women of their lives that were influenced by social and cultural forces affecting the household.

This paper is based on an empirical study of women executives, undertaken by the author with support from the University Grants Commission. This was an in-depth study of the home and office lives of women working in corporate executive positions in Pune city in Maharashtra, India. The sample of the study comprised 40 married women executives in the age group of 30 to 40 years. They worked at executive positions in the manufacturing, information technology, and banking and hospitality areas of the service sector. They held independent charge of operations, marketing, management, sales and public relations departments of their respective industrial units and companies. They lived in nuclear and extended households and were selected through a random sampling procedure. The information was collected by the standard interview method using an interview guide. A preliminary survey among women executives in the city showed their preference for working in the corporate sector for higher monetary gains and perks, greater opportunities for professional growth, a competitive work environment and respect for acquired status in the society. They emerged as a common group with similarities in socio-economic backgrounds, educational qualifications, familial and household patterns and work and family related stresses and anxieties.

A woman's employment may not provide the sufficient context for renegotiation of a domestic division of labour. Research shows the lack of sharing in household activities between husbands and working wives. This may clearly mean that women's economic status may not be necessarily accompanied by the increasing willingness of male partners to take on domestic labour. This observation has another dimension that emerged from a study of women professionals, which showed that women who felt equal to their husbands in ability and intelligence, still perceived housework and child care as their responsibilities and spent much more time in doing these tasks than did their husbands. This may suggest that egalitarian concepts about the self with unequal division of labour may be a temporary compromise in the process of role definition for both spouses.

Women's work profiles are affected by the following stages in their life cycles: marriage, childbirth and re-entry. However, the present study showed that the pattern of the respondents' labour force participation was indistinguishable from that of their husbands. They had continuous uninterrupted work profiles. The processes of reproduction interrupted their work profiles but it was neither unprecedented in duration nor permanent in nature.

The respondents' contribution to the household economy was in the form of: raising the total cash inflow in the household; asset-making (movable and immovable) with a long-term perspective; savings for future needs of the family through investments; helping in occupational mobility of husbands by shouldering the burden of the household economy The respondents' incomes contributed significantly to the upward mobility of the sample households. The findings reaffirmed that financial resources contributed by women enhanced their familial living standards and social class position. However, potent ideological forces downgrade women's financial role and reaffirm their domesticity. One such attempt is cultural definition of the man as a 'breadwinner'. The present study observes the 'supplementary' nature of respondents' salaries as these amounts were used for certain extras, while the basic necessities of the household were born out of the husbands' salaries. This connotes an unequally gendered form or differentiated nature of the husbands and wives' earnings within their households. This defines the man as the 'primary breadwinner' and the woman as the supplementary earner, completely ignoring the fact that both contributed fairly comparable incomes to their households. Related to the gender differentiation in incomes in the households was the issue of control over income and autonomy in spending it. In the light of these gender differences regarding their incomes, evidently women worked for their families rather than themselves, more so than their husbands.

The data on intra-household decision-making illustrated the dominant role of husbands. While the respondents played an important role in deciding about the basic issues relating to expenditure, the final say and decisions remained with their husbands. The respondents' participation was more evident in decisions relating to food and entertainment than to savings for the household. In traditional setups, women were considered weak in money matters, therefore, the men as breadwinners of the family held the reins over their monetary resources. In the contemporary setup, although the economic meaning of breadwinner has changed, particularly in dual earner households, the socio-cultural locus of control over money management and related decision-making remains unchanged. The men still control the reins over the cash flow and resource disbursement in the household. This is evident from the fact that my respondents' salary details and personal bank accounts were clearly known to their husbands, but not vice versa. The practice of maintaining common funds or joint accounts was adopted more for reasons of convenience and other benefits, rather than to facilitate and encourage joint decision-making. The respondents did reportedly feel the stranglehold of socio-cultural factors with respect to money matters but called it a voluntary give up in the name of 'trust' or 'faith' in husbands. These observations may be well understood in the context of patriarchy: historical, material and psychoanalytic.

The emergence of patriarchy may be traced in the Engel's work, whereby women lost power during the shift in importance of reproduction to production. It was a shift of patriarchal structures in the 19th century from the private forms 'based upon household production' to their more public forms in the 20th century, 'employment and state'. In material sense, patriarchy originated and practiced by means of control over modes of production; by means of which men exploited the productive and reproductive activities of women in the context of family relations. In psychoanalytic sense, patriarchy formed sexual identities, which were internalized by individual psyche through conscious and unconscious processes.

With regard to household work routines, there was no change in the division of labour among the family members. The respondents were responsible for work at home and the household tasks were gendered. While they added work role demands to their traditional family roles and responsibilities, their husbands had not been quick to add new family tasks to their traditional work responsibilities. The lack of interchangeability between the respondents and their husbands for household and work roles led to a 'double burden' for respondents who were trying to simultaneously perform home and market work. The husbands' participation in household tasks was not only selective and occasional but was often extended in the way of doing a 'favour' to their wives. These women's work at home created their husbands' leisure. At home, the respondents not only had less leisure time than their husbands but also were constantly 'on call' by other family members. Their time was a resource, which could be drawn anytime by the family members. This was due to an asymmetrically permeable boundary between work roles and family roles for men and women. While the demands of the family role restricted by respondents' work roles, the men's demands and work roles could intrude into family time.

Economic changes at a global level have had their impact upon the institutions of social system. However, this study indicates that micro-level institutions such as family and household have not shown much change in their traditional orientations in the Indian context. As discussed before, women's role in the workforce has changed but no corresponding change has taken place in the home. The dominant role of husbands in controlling the household resources remains the same. The norms of patriarchy over economic resources and division of labour among the household members are still predominantly evident. These women's status in the workplace has not changed the traditional orientation of the family.

In today's globalised world, women's liberation and equality require a radical transformation of imperialism, capitalism and patriarchy. A beginning has to be made at the household level, whereby a more egalitarian one replaces a gendered division of labour so that men take up a larger share of responsibilities. These changes would be possible only when women's work issues are considered as family issues, which would imply an approach based on an equitable distribution of work between the spheres of home and office. Another important approach in this context is the renegotiation of the gendered division of labour by both men and women in the private as well as public spheres, and reassessment of the relative worth of women's and men's work in both. The social connotations of money, income, roles and work require restructuring in line with contemporary economic changes. The study of quality of life of women executives cannot remain independent of such issues, as they reflect the social conditions under which women work in their professional careers.

III

Revisiting Diagnosis and Prescriptions on Women's Empowerment in India

Undertaking a second and better-informed diagnosis of women's empowerment tasks

In ways more than one, *The Towards Equality Report* was just about the only generalized diagnosis of the problems faced by the Indian women. All subsequent efforts have generally addressed themselves to only fractional problems or specific problems of the women or specific segments of women. A critical analysis of this Report (see H.S. Verma: 2007A) has indicated that the Report lacked quite a few things. The Report offered basically an urban, middleclass perspective of women's problematic in India. Also, its coverage certainly lacked many details. For instance, the problems of rural, tribal and agrarian women, and women with special problems, which form the bulk of womenfolk in the country, belong to the somewhat neglected category. Similarly, women and domestic violence that has been present all along in the Indian society, is another area that did not receive commensurate attention. Thus, the inadequacy in the diagnosis part lay in not so much in what it succeeded to present but in what the Report failed to cover. From the footage that was devoted, it appeared as though the Committee was very much convinced of the effectiveness of legal measures for removing the obstacles in empowering the women. That was one major reason why the vast majority of recommendations made by the Committee focused just on either making new laws or amending the existing ones. As the history of initiatives undertaken during the last twenty-three years indicates, the ruling politico-administrative class was more than happy to bring almost the entire recommended legal package of the Committee on the statute book without ever facilitating its efficient implementation. Thus, it can justifiably claim that it had complied with the wishes of the Committee and met the demands put up by the women's movement. If there was no appreciable improvement in the socio-economic, educational, and political status of the Indian women, which apparently happens to be the case, at least some part of the blame has to be laid at the door of the women's organizations themselves.

Technically, on quite a few points the diagnosis and the prescriptions of the Committee did not attain a very good fit with each other. Designing new organizations or redesigning existing organizations to promote cause of women's empowerment was not exactly an area in which the Committee had much expertise. Thus, if one examined the task identified by the Committee for intervention and then juxtaposed it with the organization that it ended up in recommending to deliver the expected impact, it became obvious that the two do not gel well. The Committee was convinced that a change in the status of the Indian women had to be brought about by deliberate and planed efforts; that the responsibility for this acceleration had to be shared by the State and the community, particularly that section of the community, which believed in the equality of women. It, therefore, urged that community organizations, particularly women's organizations, should mobilize public opinion and strengthen social efforts against oppressive institutions like polygamy, dowry, ostentatious expenditure on wedding and child marriage, and mount a campaign for the dissemination of information about the legal rights of women to increase their awareness. In the opinion of the Committee, this was a joint responsibility that had to be shared by community organizations, legislators who had helped to frame these laws and the Government that was responsible for implementing them. There was a contradiction involved in the assignment of the agency to discharge this task. Certainly, it should have been quite clear to the Committee that major states where the women's status was quite dismal were also the states that lacked good and committed community organizations. To compound the problem further, the legislators were—and continue to be—the one fraction of the ruling class in India that was—and continues to be—perhaps more inclined to perpetuate the problems rather than quickly solving them. A second and better-informed diagnosis of women's empowerment tasks must be undertaken as quickly as possible.

Professionalized Policy Formulation, Programme and Organization Design

In a very incisive analysis, it was concluded that the commitments of the ruling elites to the cause of women's empowerment reflected very *high level of "commitment" on paper* (i.e., in the provisions of the Constitution, revisions of various laws, text of the NPEW, National Plan of Action, endorsement of various UN and international covenants, international declarations, Five Year Plans and similar other official documents): the genuineness, sincerity and integrity of translation of these commitments on paper into operative processes of diagnosis and situation analysis, policy and programme formulation, organization and process design, resource allocation, execution of programmes and monitoring and evaluation, was hopelessly doubtful (H.S. Verma: 2007B). The study argued that proper handling of the women's problematic has suffered in India because of absence of an appropriate organizational set up. An organizational analysis of institutions dealing with women's empowerment discovered an overlap of boundaries in the tasks of the Department of Women and Child Development (DWCD) and National Commission of Women (NCW). Whereas the legal/constitutional position is that the Department of WCD lays down the policies and designs the programmes, allocates resources, monitors and evaluates the programmes, sometimes, the NCW tends to tread on these territorial paths. The DWCD on the other hand ignores well-intentioned advice and recommendations of the NCW.The visualized quasi-judicial role of the NCW keeps it in constant confrontational mode with the Central as well as the state governments. The contribution of the area experts is some thing that should have been most welcome input at all levels of planning and execution.

The National Policy on Empowerment of Women (NPEW) contains very impressive, and hyperbole verbal commitment of the government. It lacks specificity on almost on all dimensions. The commitment is quite slippery and that explains why the NPEW does not contain measurable objectives and specific steps to be taken. Analyzing the characteristics of the programmes formulated, the study indicated that, with some exceptions, there was the lack of much effort in planning or policy formulation for women in the states; that there was almost no conceptualization about the needs of women and what should be done to give them a bigger share of development; that schemes for women's development, prepared by some of the states were extremely inadequate and did not meet the needs of the women; and that initiatives had mainly come through the Central government. The study found the approach of the state to women's issues was very limited in focus and highly biased in its approach and methodology. It did not take into account systemic relations of inequality, involving the relations between both men and women. The emphasis in the women development and empowerment programmes has mainly been to improve mainly the material conditions and much less to change gender relations in their social context and ideological dimensions. In the globalized context, there is no longer talk of eradication of poverty: it has to be endured, but situation can be made a little better by efficiently managing it. The main message still is that women must have greater entry in market economy, but the question that women are being inducted in market economy on discriminatory terms is not being genuinely addressed. There is a basic contradiction in the policies set and the programmes designed to achieve them. Emphasis on women's increased economic participation is equated with equity for women while the actual policies seek to rely on women's role as mothers, house-managers and workers, as also on an elastic concept of women's time. Thus, the commitment of the government of India to ensure women's empowerment is not effectively reflected in the policy it has framed, the organization structures it has put in place, the resources it has allocated and overall the efforts it has made to translate its commitment into a live reality.

An analysis of the character of women development programmes in India during the crucial periods of 1970s and 1990s (Sadhna Arya: 2007) makes it clear that the Indian state has not genuinely addressed the issues of reproduction and household work, and thus the issues of sexual division of labour. Similarly, sexual stereotypes have been neglected. Programmes addressing the various specific facets of women's problematic have remained outside mainstream development process and these have remained only at rhetorical level. The concern for women's productive roles was also incorporated as part of women in development (WID) approach by recognizing that these responsibilities had an economic component and therefore, required income-enhancing measures. This actually reassured continuity with earlier welfare approaches in that it focused on women's responsibilities for the family and child welfare and therefore, carried little prospects for changing women's position in society and economy. The approach had within itself the potential to negate its own objectives and was intended to continue the *status quo.* This was because women's needs were defined in terms of family's basic needs rather than in terms of their unequal access to productive resources and changing the institutionalized discrimination against them. This tactic was intended by the decision-makers to be more acceptable both to male-dominated implementing agencies as well as to entrenched patriarchal interests. The manner in which programmes for women have been conceived by the state point to the fact that state views men and women in terms of their certain specific roles in family and community. Thus, it is found that the dominant presumption in development programmes for women is that women are first and foremost homemakers, and they are only secondary productive workers. One of the important objectives of these programmes is to enable women to combine both the functions in an efficient manner. Therefore, women needed to be integrated into the development process and work like men. The concept of domestic work as primary women's work remains unchallenged. Though the income generation and other programmes of the state helped in supplementing the day-to-day needs of the poor families, they failed to help women for many important reasons. Firstly, these programmes ignored the fact that women are already productive workers. State planners projected these economic projects as supplementors to family resources, without touching the power imbalance between men and women in the family. The result was that the existing inequalities between men and women, i.e., the unequal access to productive resources, credit, technical assistance, training programmes and income earning opportunities and the unequal burdens of reproductive and productive work remained intact and sometimes even exacerbated. Secondly, the emphasis of integration approach on increasing productivity without taking into account the reproductive work of women tends to conceal the contradictory relationship between two spheres of women's work. Thirdly, these programmes include essentially low-income, and low productivity activities as a result of which the subordination of women in the development process continued. Thus, such programmes also seemed to facilitate inequality-generating processes and in so doing reinforced gender hierarchies and the sexual division of labour. They actually served to isolate women further from the mainstream of economic activities and lock them into a subordinate position.

These programmes were based on two faulty assumptions: first, they negated domestic and subsistence work and also their work as unorganized and agricultural workers; second they considered paid or public production process (as different from domestic reproduction) as a panacea for women's economic and social subordination. Both macro and women specific policies are reinforcing the trends of marginalisation and actualization of women in employment. *The approach also fails to recognize the enforced but asymmetric participation of women in development process by which they bear the costs but are excluded from the benefits.* The concentration of means of production and control of wealth and resources and even better paying technical knowledge remains undisturbed in the hands of men. These women-only-projects become marginal as they are small and under-funded and are widely perceived as welfare oriented and hence remain outside the mainstream of national policies. *These serve to create a confusion of their being part of development efforts when they are essentially welfare services.* In fact, the welfare component of the programmes helps to garner support from family and community. But in the process it simply serves to reinforce the stereotypes of work and dependent women with children and home to look after. *As welfare services serve to forestall people's unrest, these activities too serve the same purpose and while helping women and their families in the same manner continue to maintain unequal power and gender structures.* Mainstream development efforts needed to be reconstructed from a women's perspective. But this has not happened. In fact, the major criticism of present liberalization policies is their gender-neutral nature with the result that the state has been unable to check the trend towards marginalisation of women in the economy and majority of women continue to work in the informal sector. Women enter public production process to augment family income, and do non-market work for the same purpose and in addition to undertaking the care and nurturing of children and other family members. Large part of this activity remains invisible and, thus, is not valued or undervalued. Macro-level state policy and planning does not take this into any calculations of employment, saving, investment or consumption. In addition, as they are concentrated in low paying sectors, a lot of work that women do fetches them poor returns.

Two things need to be noted in this context. One is that unequal gender relations, wherein the stronger gender controls the labour and sexuality and the other social arrangements that are made for reproduction of human beings, inform all productive and reproductive activity. This results in man's control over women's sexuality, and reproduction and labour power. In this manner, gender relations are expressed in power relations between men and women. This means that gender equality cannot be attained unless power relations between genders change. *The development process that emphasizes on 'growth' and 'production' without removing existing inequalities can only result in reproducing and many times accentuating some inequalities.*

Participation and empowerment approaches, though radical in vocabulary, were founded on faulty assumptions over the nature of the state and state apparatus. Their objective did not include restructuring of gender relations within family and society at large. They overlook the role played by state structures, discriminatory laws, and market forces and interplay of these with gender biases prevailing at the level of society. Empowerment requires transformation of structures of subordination through radical changes in the legal system, property rights, ownership patterns and other institutions that reinforce and perpetuate male domination. *The concept of empowerment does not capture this as it fails to see that the state itself is a power structure and, therefore, has inherent limitations in supporting 'empowerment' of the poor and deprived. The concept also promotes a type of politics wherein it shifts the focus from politics of struggle to NGO activity. Thus, instead of enabling, this process of empowerment disables the weak and oppressed.* Given the present discourse of liberalization, the state has been advocating and pursuing authoritarian measures to maintain law and order with a view to curb trade union activity and provide stable environment for economic growth. In such a situation the idea of empowerment as promoted through various state policies and programmes contradicts the actual objectives of the state. Consequently, NGO activity works towards limiting the capacity of the oppressed by co-opting their movements and activists. The programmes safely adopted the strategy of raising non-controversial issues, in which women face least opposition from men in family and community and do not come in direct confrontation with existing structures. It is hard to understand that if empowerment implies a fundamental redistribution of power it can only be achieved through disempowering some structures, processes, institutions, individuals, etc. Despite ideas of flexibility and decentralization, top down approach and centralization of authority in decision-making is evident. Though programmes are meant to strengthen the capacities of women, they do not provide any space for redressal of grievances to grass-root level functionaries of the programmes. This highlights a basic contradiction of these programmes. The programmes view the work of grass-root level workers as 'voluntary' that justifies the meagre payment of Rs. 200 or Rs. 250 per month to them. This work is an extension to rural women's domestic responsibilities and their income generation work. It is strange that through these programmes the state is asking the poor, deprived and the marginalized to contribute to voluntary work. It also speaks of the manner in which poor women's labour is being treated by the state. Viewed in this context, the programmes have no mechanisms to reduce the drudgery and domestic responsibilities of the grass-root workers as also to improve their earning capacities. Even in the absence of the above, rather the emphasis is to change their own and society's social perceptions, thus, playing the role of social reformer. *The state is, thus, trying to optimize the use of women's labour at less and less cost. It has no component to tackle the gender biased, corrupt, insensitive state machinery and discriminatory legal system. It assumes that all is well at that level, the problem of disempowerment and subordination is only at the level of society.* Thus, organization and awareness generation are presented as a panacea for women's problems, without any substantive change at other socio-economic and political levels. *This omission, insensitivity and unwillingness to change conditions so as to favour women become even more significant when programmes are specially designed for the development of women. These contradictions of the state approach to women issues have also led to a lot of tension between voluntary women's organizations associated with the programmes and the Government staff because of two different cultures they are associated with.* There has been unpleasantness and conflict over the fact that the functioning of the administrative staff at top levels did not match with the spirit of the programme. The programmes, thus, have contributed to sharpening of conflict between women's group/ and the State This means that the programmes did not help in strengthening the organizational potentials of women and their politics as well as conceptualizing state in a different manner. Rather the conceptualization and organization was the result of the inability of a women's programme to address women's issues.

Experience in India and other third world countries has shown that adjustment packages and liberalization process is accompanied by policies which favour relatively well-off sections of society. Cheap and unorganized labour is the main attraction of multinational corporations and export-oriented industries in third world countries. And women who constitute the bulk of the employment in the unorganized sector are bound to be the worst sufferers. The argument is that the present development thought and process does not place value on women's subsistence activities. Neither does it treat them as productive activities, since any activity that does not bring with it monetary gains is seen as non-or unproductive work. Productivity as a measure of producing life and sustenance has been rendered invisible and thus finds no place of support in the state policies. The new ideological legitimacy that has been accorded to the market means that issues of equality and distributive justice have been pushed to the background. There is no longer talk of eradication of poverty; it has to be endured, but situation can be made a little better by *efficiently managing* it. *The main message still is that women must have greater entry in market economy, but the question that women are being inducted in market economy on discriminatory terms is not being genuinely addressed.*

The post-independence period has witnessed a number of shifts in the perception of the nature of women's problems as well as solutions in the state policies with regard to women's role in development. Emphasis on women's increased economic participation is equated with equity for women while the actual policies seek to rely on women's role as mothers, house-managers and workers, as also on an elastic concept of women's time. Women have been viewed as more reliable and efficient in all these three roles than men. Thus, we find that from welfare to development, participation, empowerment to efficiency solutions have shifted but these changing perceptions have been in tune with the mainstream development thinking and not against it. The emphasis has mainly been to improve mainly the material conditions and much less to change gender relations in their social context and ideological dimensions.

Legal reforms, instead of reconstituting identities of women, which are liberating and based on equality, have served to reinscribe the assumptions of women's dependency in family, women as primarily mothers and wives adhering to the norms and standards set by family and society and in sustaining public/ private distinction. Such a view of women not only assumes the homogeneity of women's experience but also assumes the sexual division of labour as natural and universal. Both the assumptions of law fail to acknowledge diversity of women's experience beyond their wifely and motherly roles and are faulty because women's lives are not based neatly on sexual division of labour. *An important aspect of law-reform in India has been with regard to women's rights within religious personal laws of various communities. The personal laws of other minority communities have been left virtually untouched. This is, ostensibly because the leaders of these communities claim that since the personal laws of any community derive their authority from religion, any change in the personal law of any community would amount to threat to its religious identity, as also to its religious freedom. The state's position has been not to change any personal law till the demand comes from the community concerned, as this would amount to interfering with their religious freedom.* Such a situation raises two important questions: can the right to religious freedom of any community become the basis of continued denial of certain rights to women in a democratic and secular state? Similarly, can the argument of absence of demand from the community for change become the reason for the state not to modify an unequal law? The increasing communalization of politics and the state's treatment of purely women's rights issue in religious terms have resulted in increasing the powers of religious leaders of both the majority and minority communities. Since the issue of religious identity is so closely tied with regulation of relations between men and women, i.e., family and society, *the state can only be seen to be acting as an ally in perpetuating a patriarchal system.* One finds that the state at times has used its legislative powers to lessen the significance of religions, but on many other occasions, it has also enhanced the role of religion in determining the civil rights of people and this has been done irrespective of their consequences for women. Thus, engagement with law and legal process has challenged the belief that law is neutral or objective. It has also been argued that actual change in behaviour does not come with a mere change in law, in the absence of which law has only a symbolic and no real value.

Despite these limitations, law is going to remain a major focus of women's concerns. By changing the law in favour of women' rights, an alternative view about women, their contributions and rights in society is promoted, which by challenging the existing norms generates the possibilities of changing the position of women. Secondly, there is a clear link between women's unequal access to resources and their access to social and political power. The attainment of laws, which accepts women's right on an equal basis with men in family is important in so far as it would unleash a process which would eventually pave the way for achieving the ultimate objective of equality. The women's movement has to continue confronting the law for the inequalities that it sustains and the oppressive norms and values that it upholds. Thus, law reform has to continue to be an important part of women's struggle and has to be used to mobilize women and provide them with a language that challenges discriminatory laws and practices.

The inability of the state to effectively address the issue of equality between men and women, the manner of approaching women's issues within them and the gap in the implementation, *raises doubts about the state's intentions to actually improve the status of women. This also points to the problematic nature of relationship between women's movement and the state. The state has resorted to symbolic policy-making and in the process has co-opted women's movement vocabulary, terminology and agenda without bringing in any real changes in the lives of women. While this has provided the state with a pro-women image, it has had a de-politicizing effect on the movement.* It is also true that the process has also helped in putting the issues on public and political agenda and has also contributed to establishing them as issues of legitimate public concern. This can be treated as positive outcome of pressure of women's movement. But the fact of continuing gap between state rhetoric and actual state policy cannot be overlooked and that calls for more struggles to bridge this gap. There is a need to go deeper into analyzing the state policies and actions with a view to uncover the nature and approach of the state towards women issues, by laying bare the inconsistencies, contradictions and premises of the state policies. There is also the crucial question of mobilizing and organizing women in both political and economic arenas of life. This is a plea for greater participation and integration of women in the administrative, political and economic decision-making institutions of the state. But again these handicaps, though real in many cases, actually call for greater support from active women's and other progressive organizations to help women overcome these obstacles. This also calls for a need to change the nature of political decision making with a view to make it more decentralized and participatory. The state has to take full account of gender inequality and to reorient itself from within- as the embodiment of male dominance. It needs to revise its categories of family, household, production and reproduction and take account of the diversity and complexity of activities, to see society in detail and not in aggregates while framing policies. The question of reproduction in terms of rearing of children, caring for old and sick in the family and responsibility of carrying on all the domestic and household tasks is a very real one for women. And this is an area, which has not been genuinely addressed by the state in its policies. The issue is not limited to changing perspectives. *State accountability has to be stressed.* The withdrawal of the state being emphasized by privatization sloganeering actually means withdrawal from its welfare functions. In sum, *every action of the state affects women and as long as it affects them adversely, women have to get together collectively and raise their voice to fix the accountability of the state to act in their favour.*

From the foregoing analysis it emerges that in system maintenance and furthering its interests, the ruling class quite often works out a deal with its adversaries through a process of legitimization of charter of demands through the mechanisms of Working Groups/Committees/Commissions/Consultations/Round Tables, etc.in which key members of the adversary groups are 'accommodated' in these bodies and even the report that such mechanisms produce appear quite often 'radical' from the ruling class perspective. However, when the stage comes to take vital decisions concerning their recommendations, in shaping the policies, programmes and implementation organizational structures, the class interests of ruling elites are very routinely protected. Thus, the policy and programme planning, and organization designs of women development/empowerment programmes have tended to end up in furthering and maintaining its class interests of the ruling classes rather than alleviating the women, creating spaces for them in social, economic and political spheres. These exercises have to be undertaken from a perspective that is genuine, involves significant participation of the women, from different life situations and representing divergent backgrounds of women's movement groups, and have to move from generalized to specific solutions addressed to specific women living and working in specific contexts.

Correcting a false history of women's empowerment

In a very scintillating analysis, Verma (2007C) nails the diabolical duplicity of the ruling fractions in translating its 'commitment' to empowerment of the women, seen in many notable documents into concrete action to realize the objectives set forth. His objective is to show the true colours of the conduct of the politico-administrative fraction of the ruling class in making concerted moves that give the illusion of addressing themselves to different aspects of the women's problematic but are immensely successful in ensuring that the stranglehold of patriarchy continues to flourish. His analysis reveals the not so hidden methodology used by the Indian politico-administrative class to write the CEDAW history in the manner it has. From its gleaning it emerges that there is a definite method in chronicling this peculiar version of history. From a rigorous programme planning audit it emerges that *there is quite often a mismatch between what the objective is set and what delivery mechanism is planned and able to deliver on quite a few tasks.* Despite their bulky sizes both the CEDAW *documents quite often conceal more than what they reveal.* This is done very ingeniously. *The aspect that has not received attention of the government is quietly omitted*: at best, there might just be mere tit bits about it in the report.

The claims of achievement of goals, and objectives or the "commitments' made are quoted throughout along with figures that at best deal with the physical, and financial coverage targets: in some rare cases there are some figures of outputs also but *impact statistics are generally conspicuous by their absence.* The CEDAW reports *scrupulously avoid quoting their findings.* How can one assess the efficacy of a scheme/programme without impact analyses? *This tongue-in-cheek stance of the government is seen even in the new 'commitments' made (i.e., welfare of the aged) where diabolically the government promises to deliver every thing but also states at the same time that no fresh schemes/programmes shall be undertaken to realize this commitment; that these commitments shall be met with the existing programmes only.* The narratives in both the CEDAW documents provide ample evidence of routine bureaucratic tactics of delaying decisions on urgent issues by resorting to use of multiple institutional mechanisms of deliberation, some times the referrals coming one after another and taking years on decisions that could have been taken fairly quickly using just the area experts. The tactic appears to be well rehearsed one with one fraction of the ruling class trying to work out a quid-pro-quo with another and repeatedly testing the capacity of the emergent group(s) asserting their claims and demanding more space and voice for itself/themselves. These mechanisms buy time to the ruling—and dominant–fractions and keep the newer entrants on the periphery for as long as they are unable to force the former to accept their position. Thus, this history of CEDAW written by the Indian politico-administrative class is not exactly an exercise in *suppressio veri* and *suggestio falsi: however, without any trace of doubt it is not so hidden attempt of running with the hare and hunting with the hounds.* The women's movement that collaborated with the drafting of at least CEDAW-II and III need to do some serious introspection on being used as accessories to this manufactured history. Thus, this whole exercise is system maintenance of a different nature: not only has women's empowerment has received short shrift but its history is being seen through coloured glasses. Women's movement must see to it that a more accurate history of women's empowerment is re-written in the immediate future.

Reclibrating Women Empowerment

Papers included in each of the five sections of this collection have indicated the nature of transformation that has taken place in the problems being faced by the Indian women. One group that needs special mention is concerning the new woman. These include the masculanity and feminity interface, the newer situations of live-ins, sex with colleagues by already married males and females, very little time with kids, sharing of domestic chores, working from the home, coping with the stress and strains in the demanding knowledge based professions. That the empowerment of Indian women needs recalibration cannot be possibly denied. The crucial questions in this regard would be: What approach should be adopted in doing so? What role the women's movement, and its specific groups dealing with specific problems of women should play in debating the complexities involved, suggesting the remedial measures, helping their formulation, operationalization, execution and monitoring? Disturbing developments have been taking place in various locales and on various issues (i.e., Karnataka government's proposed ban on night employment of women on grounds of safety, enforcement of Talibani codes by Hindu militant organizations, changes proposed in the Anti-Dowry Act, etc). How these should be quickly and appropriately addressed?

References

Arya, Sadhna. 2000. 'Women and Development—1970s-1990s' pp. 250-272 in R.B.S. Verma, H.S. Verma and Nadeem Hasnain (eds.). *The Indian State and Women's Problematic: Running with the Hare and Hunting with the Hounds*. New Delhi: Serials Publications.

Douglas, Mary. 1966. *Purity and Danger: An Analysis of Concepts of Pollution and Taboo.* London: Routledge & Kegan Paul.

Epstein, Cynthia Fuchs. 1988. *Deceptive Distinction.* New Haven, CT & New York: Yale University Press & Russel Sage Foundation.

Epstein, Cynthia Fuchs. 2007. Great Divides: "The Cultural, Cognitive and Social Bases of the Global Subordination of Women" *American Sociological Review:* 72:1.

Kabeer, Naila. 1999. "Resources, Agency Achievement: Reflections on the Measure of Women's Empowerment", *Development and Change*: 30.

Kabeer, Naila. 2003. *Gender Mainstreaming in Poverty Eradication and the Millennium Development Goals" A Handbook for Policy makers and other Stakeholders.* London: Commonwealth Secretariat.

Sen, Amartya. 1990. "Gender and Cooperative Conflict" in Tinker, I. (ed.) *Persistent Inequalities*, London: Oxford University Press.

Verma, H.S. 2007A. 'Towards Equality: An Overview of a Milestone Report', pp. 193-221 in R.B.S. Verma, H.S. Verma and Nadeem Hasnain (eds.). *The Indian State and Women's Problematic: Running with the Hare and Hunting with the Hounds*, New Delhi: Serials Publications.

Verma, H.S. 2007B. 'Commitments and Their Operationalization: Asssesssing Policy Formulation, Programme and Organisation Design of Women Empowerment in India', pp. 222-249 in R.B.S. Verma, H.S. Verma and Nadeem Hasnain (eds.). *The Indian State and Women's Problematic: Running with the Hare and Hunting with the Hounds.* New Delhi: Serials Publications.

Verma, H.S. 2007C. 'India's Country Reports on CEDAW: Separating Facts from Fiction in the "History" of Women's Empowerment Written by the Indian Politico-Administrative Class', pp. 273-333 in R.B.S. Verma, H.S. Verma and Nadeem Hasnain (eds.). *The Indian State and Women's Problematic: Running with the Hare and Hunting with the Hounds*, New Delhi: Serials Publications.

PART - I

WOMEN, MASCULINITY AND VIOLENCE: ADDRESSING FORMS OLD AND NEW

CHAPTER - TWO

Dowry in India: A Search for New Social Identity

J.P. Singh

The practice that begun presumably as a gift to the daughter as a token of love and affection or as her right of inheritance on separation from the natal home following marriage has taken the form of dowry—an essential condition for marriage in contemporary India. It surfaced prominently in the late nineteenth and early twentieth centuries when there was poor economic safety for women in a setting where they always married outside their natal villages and where their rights in their natal home lapsed on joining the marital home. The system of village exogamy (a typical North Indian practice) and the virilocal system of residence have survived, but the essence of dowry, and not the practice itself, has largely faded away. The voluntary aspect of dowry has dissolved and so also its significance as a security blanket for the newly wed-women in case of any personal exigency.

There is a range of debates on what connotes or involves a dowry. For instance, Tambiah (1973: 64) has argued that 'dowry connotes female property or female rights to property which is transferred at a women's marriage as a sort of pre-mortem inheritance.' A similar view has been expressed by Goody (1973: 1). In Madan's (1975: 237) view, it is a 'substitute for women's lack of rights of inheritance equivalent to those of men.' Yet another view is that dowry is a 'moral claim... in lieu of the rights of maintenance she renounces at marriage' (Parry: 1979: 237). This paper has got no immediate concern to resolve such differences in perception about conceptualization of dowry, as it is primarily addressed to issues relating to reasons for spread and persistence of dowry in contemporary India. Nevertheless, it may incidentally be stated that the prevailing system of dowry does not fully correspond to any of these conceptions, as these scholars have in the main stressed the rationale behind the emergence of the practice of dowry. Reasons for the rise and development of dowry have not been uniform throughout the country. The existing reasons for its persistence appear to be different from the earlier basis for its emergence or relevance. The paper largely hinges around this theme.

Now the dowry, or the bridegroom price, has become a dreaded payment on demand that accompanies or/and follows the marriage of a daughter. The impact of money relations on dowry is underscored by the fact that the dowry could not wither away in India in the twenty first century; rather, it unexpectedly got further accentuated on a more massive scale than ever before. The dowry and its cognate problems have become so serious that the marriage of daughters tends to bring in nightmarish experiences for scores of parents these days. Dowry as a cultural crime on such a massive scale has been a bewildering issue for the social scientists as well as the concerned social activists particularly since the second half of the twentieth century. This has been a point of concern mainly because the country has been gradually attaining a higher level of literacy, industrial urbanization and so also modernization and social awareness, resulting from a faster pace of economic development. Legislative measures have also been initiated to do away with this practice, but they too have so far proved an ineffective exercise.

Considering these facts there is a strong necessity to explore whether there exists any relationship between the processes of development or modernization on the one hand and the rise in the practice of dowry and marital violence in India on the other. It has been argued that diverse factors had contributed to the rise and development of dowry at different points of time, but now it is getting sustenance essentially from a common societal belief that the amount of dowry and the marriage related gifts and extravagant expenses on the elaborate arrangements of wedding ceremony, which may be labeled as 'marital potlatch', determine *izzat* (social honour or prestige) of both dowry takers and dowry givers not only in their neighbourhood but also in the community as whole. Obviously, there is a widespread belief that higher the expenses higher the social image of the parties involved. Dowry tends to act as a crystallizer of one's social status in a transitory society like that of India. As the society has become more and more open and competitive under the new political and economic milieu, everyone vies with everyone else to attain greater *izzat*. The caste-based endogamy regulated by parents or the family elders, among other factors, help sustain in a large measure the practice of dowry in the society. In the past the consideration of dowry was based on the amount of property held by the parents or socio-economic standing and pedigree of the family, called *khandan*, but now the consideration has largely shifted to the social and economic standing or professional career of the groom himself.

Before we address the main theme of the paper, let us briefly dwell on the notion of dowry or *dahej* that is an indigenous term in its own right. The term 'dowry' has been used in a number of different ways in the literature. By dowry, or *dahej, hunda* or *daaj* as it is called in North India, we mean a groom-price, a payment in cash and/or kind directly made from a bride's family to a groom's before the performance of *kanyadan*–an act of giving away a maiden in marriage. We will call the reverse transaction a bride price. In the case of *kanyadan* and *varadakshina* also the bride's father or the bride is offered something, but compared to dowry *kanyadan* or *varadakshina* usually involves a much lesser amount of gift or/and money. All the three forms of transactions may take the form of immoveable property, ornaments, household effects, clothes and cash depending upon the economic position of prospective kin groups involved. *Kanyadan* is regarded as one of the most important Hindu nuptial rites.

As regards the word *'hunda'* it is believed to be derived from '*handa*', which means a pot. This could be due to the now extinct practice of offering dowry in a pot. The dowry is not to be confused with *stridhanam or stridhan* (a daughter's wedding settlement) as practiced relatively more widely in South India. *Stridhan* is completely owned by woman, not by her husband. It is a gift given to a woman by her natal kin or by her husband at or immediately following the marriage. Gift to brides in the form of jewellery and clothes at the time of her marriage from friends, in addition to those from kinsmen, also form a part of *stridhanam*.

Dowry is also not to be confused with demands, monetary or otherwise, made through the newly married women from time to time by their husbands or the members of their family. Dowry commonly includes only such money, property or gifts mutually agreed between two prospective kin groups at the time of marriage negotiations. In certain cases the dowry transactions go beyond the actual performance of marriage or consummation—commonly known as *gauna* in Hindi.[1] Any demand which was not stipulated at the time of negotiation but placed posterior to marriage either through the bride herself or the groom's family directly to bride's parents is a kind of emotional blackmail or extortion which has become a common occurrence these days. Several social analysts have used the word 'dowry' in a wider legal sense so as to include all sorts of transactions and coercive demands placed posterior to marriage (Oldenburg: 2003; Karlekar: 2003: 1142-1146). But the people in general use it in a very restricted sense to comprise only such transactions that form the basis of wedding settlements. Being an important prerequisite for marriage, now the process of dowry giving or taking commonly precedes the actual ceremonization of marriage and in rare cases dowry continues beyond the actual event of marriage ceremony. In brief, dowry or bridegroom price involves two distinct transactions:

> *First, it refers to a lump sum of money with or without some tangible assets constituting an essential part of the wedding settlement, which is transferred by the bride's household to that of her prospective spouse before the actual ceremonization of marriage. It does not go under the bride's control, as dowry is not a fixed share of a divisible estate. It is neither her inheritance nor women's wealth. It goes to parents of the prospective groom that may be further used for their daughter's marriage, if necessary, or some other purposes in larger familial interests such as construction of house and opening a new business.*
>
> *Secondly, it also refers to the traditional items, such as jewels, cooking vessels, clothes and other household goods that accompany a bride to her conjugal home. In general, these remain bride's property and form a part of the conjugal estate to be enjoyed by husband and wife in particular. Keeping apace with time these*

> *items have always kept on changing with the arrival of various modern consumer goods in the market. The legal definition of dowry has been given somewhat broader ambit possibly with intent to deter the bridegroom or his parents from making further post-marital demands. The Prohibition of Dowry Act of 1961 has defined dowry 'as any property or valuable security given either directly or indirectly at or before or after the marriage as consideration for the marriage'.*

Anyway, the daughter-in-law who brings in a hefty amount of dowry or bridal wealth or is an important earning member of the family is treated better than other female members of the family. In fact, it is this relative scale of comparison that might invite the additional demand for money after marriage. Those who have come with a lesser amount of dowry are often subjected to harassment by their mother-in-law on various pretexts such as the bride is poorly educated, inefficient in household chores or less obedient. The victim gets little succour or emotional support from other members of the family. In lots of cases the younger members of the family tend to disassociate themselves from her for fear of antagonizing the elders of the family or the parents. Although the practice of dowry exists in several societies, it has assumed the form of a challenge to the forces of modernity and change only in India. Many reasons are put forward to explain the rise and development of this practice and they are briefly dealt with here to underline the crux of dowry practices typical of the Indian society.

Roots or bases of dowry practices

As the analysis of origin of this practice may explain the basis of existence or pervasiveness of dowry, let us dwell on the roots of this practice that can deepen our understanding of dowry in contemporary times more holistically. Explanations based on historical and contemporary sources on dowry, however, offer glaring contradictions. The colonial finger pointed at Hindu culture, whereas the present-day Indian social analysts blame westernization, which increased materialism, greed and a desire for consumer goods and commercialization of human relationships. In the opinion of Oldenburg (2003: 4-5) dowry is an old practice but the dowry-related violence has got imperial origins in India. Imperial policies created 'masculine' economy that prepared the ground for a strong son preference, worsening gender inequality that, in turn, increased the vulnerability of women to violence. She has further observed that in Europe where the traditional dowry system has vanished, violence against women is still rampant. Modern industrial capitalism eroded the culture of dowry in the West, but did economic distortions peculiar to the colonial setting change it for the worse in India? Such an analysis, however, underplays the role of indigenous socio-cultural factors supporting the rise and development of the practice. Expressing a similar view in his seminal essay on the topic Tambiah (1973: 63) observed, "modernization may accentuate and distort a traditional arrangement...".

There is yet another explanation concerning the origin of dowry in India. It is believed to be linked with varied practices and institutions such as the nature of hierarchy and division of labour that characterize caste system, certain marriage practices like *stridhanam,* hypergamy and the system of caste endogamy and now the concerns for acquiring a higher social status, real or imaginary, under the influence of Western way of life. Historians may like to move backwards into antiquity in search of roots of dowry practices. But India's hoary past may not throw much light on this practice, since the ancient Hindu scriptures do not contain any explicit reference to dowry. The practice of dowry may have its origin in the less prevalent practice of bride price, which is in fact a reversal of dowry. Although it may not be possible to ascertain when and where both these practices came into being, it can be speculated that dowry and bride price are quite posterior to the emergence of monogamian form of marriage and family. This is the same as saying that dowry and bride price came into being after the practice of monogamous marriage became quite institutionalized in society.

For a long time humans lived in the stage of sexual promiscuity. Passing through various stages of social evolution promiscuity slowly gave way to polygamy (polygyny and polyandry), and after various permutations and combinations, monogamy became the predominant social order. Explicitly this fact is evident from the evolutionary theory of marriage and family as enunciated by ethnographer L.H. Morgan. So long as promiscuity existed, there was no question of dowry and bride price for obvious reasons. The origin of these two practices could be linked up with the discarding of promiscuity in favour of polygyny and polyandry. These two forms of marriage are themselves mutual opposites. But the existence of the diametrically opposite practices of dowry and bride price presumably owe their origin to polygyny and polyandry respectively. The emergence of polygynous and polyandrous forms of marriage could have been inevitable following changes in the demographic balance between the sexes. Preponderance of females as compared to that of males was probably a congenial situation for the development of polygyny. Singh (2003: 80) has reported that out of 4,653 communities covered under the survey there are 839 communities in India who still practice polygamy along with monogamy under varying conditions.

In the absence of polygyny in a society having a larger number of females than males, many females would have to be deprived of the institutionalized marital life. The obligation to get more than one female member into wedlock with one male member could have been the situation that gave rise to dowry as a price exacted by the male and his family from the female's family. The origin of bride price could have taken place in opposite circumstances where the sex ratio favoured males. A greater number of males than females could have been the central factor behind the emergence of polyandry and bride price. Such a view may be taken as speculative rather than a hard reality for want of definitive evidence. The prevalence of polygyny and polyandry cannot really offer a full account for the origin of dowry, as both forms of marriages were prevalent in India until the *Mahabharata* period, but neither dowry nor bride price appeared to be in vogue those days.

Explaining the contemporary situation several scholars have noted a strong association between class or status position and dowry in India (Goody: 1973: 19). It has been observed that groups at the top of the hierarchy tend to follow dowry customs, while those at the lower end tend to follow bride wealth practice. It is definitely noticeable that dowry is prevalent among the higher castes while the bride-price is customary among the lower OBCs, scheduled castes (*dalits*) and scheduled tribes (*adivasis*) in many parts of the country, as it is evident from the survey carried out under the auspices of the Anthropological Survey of India. Of 4,653 communities covered under the survey, 632 communities have reported to practice bride price (Singh: 2003: 81). We can only speculate as to why this curious combination could have come into being.

It is argued that dowry originated among upper castes, because the practice of wedding gift to the bride from her family first came into being among them, as the upper castes were generally affluent enough to give away something at the time of marriage as a token of love for their daughters. In the caste hierarchy it was the lower castes that did most of the manual and menial work. Therefore, various caste-based occupational divisions came to exist among them in course of time. The two upper castes at the national level, the *Brahmins and Kashatriyas*, had respectively priestly and martial duties assigned to them and hence no occupational sub-division existed among them. Among the lower castes, while the family from where the bride came suffered the loss of one earning member, the coming of a bride into the bridegroom's family meant an increase in the number of earning members who could work along with other members and become a source of sustenance or greater income for the family. Hence, a bride price was paid to the bride's parents to make up for the loss. Bride-price may involve the receipt of presents, in cash or kind, by the bride's family in return for giving away of the bride. Hence, bride price has the character of an exchange. Contrarily, among the higher castes to which no manual labour was assigned in the caste hierarchy, the reverse logic applied. A marriage meant an additional member who was to be supported and hence was a burden on the groom's family, as the bride did not go out to earn and contribute to the income of the family. Presumably, one reason for the origin of dowry could be that the groom and his family had to take up the onerous responsibility of supporting the bride for the rest of her life. Dowry and bride price payments were ultimately meant to economically equalize the two affinal families—either through sharing the burden or sharing the wealth.

One more explanation concerning the origin of dowry is that it originated from the system of *stridhanam* (woman's wealth) given in the form of money, property or gifts to the woman by her parents at the time of her marriage. As a woman had no right to inherit a share in the ancestral property, *stridhanam* was seen as a way by which the parents tended to ensure her against any future exigency or personal necessity in case of lack of support as was normally expected from her husband's family. Gradually, the practice of this custom declined and aborted the original meaningful function of *stridhanam* as a safety net for the woman and was corrupted to become a price tag for the groom. This is, however, not firmly known as to when the practice took the form of dowry. Some fragmentary studies have borne out that the practice of making cash offerings to the bridegroom's family came into being in the early part of the twentieth century. The consensus in the literature is that this practice is spreading and the amounts involved are increasing (Caplan: 1984: 218). It may be noted here that the customary practice of *stridhanam* was prevalent more in South than North India where dowry has been a very recent development. *Stridhan* was prevalent in North India in a very crude form particularly among the rich landed castes. In Bihar this is locally known as *tarka or khetari* in Hindi (a kind of personal bridal wealth) secretly given away to the women by their parents in addition to dowry. A high level of secrecy is maintained merely with view to denying the share to groom's coparceners in case of a joint or extended family. Sometimes bride's father tries to maintain secrecy with a view to concealing this fact to his coparcener, if any.

Along with these generalized views there could have been still some additional factors specific to different situations, giving rise to dowry and bride price. The term, 'dowry' as a quantifiable offering in a marriage may not necessarily have its roots solely in the Indian culture. Some historians believe that dowry was in practice in the early 12th century Europe and was often reflected in the European fairy tales and literature making such references to a woman's 'dowry' as offerings of a 'straw mattress', a 'wooden stool' or 'farm animals'. European monarchs and aristocrats were conspicuously extravagant at weddings, funerals and other ritual occasions, but they were resentful if their subjects acted in a similar manner (Oldenburg: 2003: 236). The exchange and amount of money for a dowry depended on the relative status of being a rich or poor woman. Monetary exchanges also had the function of preserving the aristocracy as a class and having marriages arranged as a means of cultural and economic determination. An interesting instance of dowry, symbolizing both marriage as well as a union of aristocracy and colonial dominance, was noticed in 1661 when Charles I of England was given the fishing villages of Bombay as a part of dowry for marrying Catherine of Braganza of Portugal (at that time Bombay was a Portuguese colony). Kaplan (1985) has observed that the custom of dowry was widely prevalent in pre-industrial Europe, and is still to be found in several southern European countries. In India's context, these practices can be seen to be a result of the dialectics of caste system under the influence of European culture. Such a practice was emulated by the Indian feudal lords to establish their distinctive status in society that in course of time trickled down to the lower stratum of society. This view seems to be more plausible than others.

In addition to the influence of European culture the age-old system of endogamous form of marriage has been no less accountable for the rise of dowry practices in India. The inherent conflict of opposing tendencies in the caste hierarchy, as we all know, led to the practice of caste endogamy, prohibiting marriages across different castes. While caste or sub-caste based arranged marriages always tended to restrict the people to a restricted choice of selection of life partners, the dowry seldom comes in the way of exogamous or civil marriages based on mutual consents of bride and groom. A strict adherence to the norms of caste or sub-caste endogamy under new circumstances characterized by rising economic aspirations for attaining higher social status and greater happiness in social life significantly reinforced the custom of dowry.

Hypergamy as a basis of dowry

Now let us come to the issue of regional variations in dowry practices in India. Evidence suggests that the custom of giving dowry has traditionally been more prevalent in north than in south India (Miller 1980; Srinivas 1984). Srinivas (1984) has tried to explain the regional variations in the practice of dowry with the help of hypergamy. To quote Srinivas (1984: 8), 'India to the north of the *Vindhyas* ... is broadly characterized by either hypergamy or a hypergamous ideology and dowry seems integral to hypergamy.' Explaining this fact he has further observed (Srinivas 1984: 8): 'Hypergamy refers to the custom of marrying a man from a superior grade or clan, within the same *jati.* Sometimes, the superior grade or clan may not be specified, but the general notion prevails that a girl should wed a superior male'.

Here Srinivas, like Kapadia (1972), has suggested that hypergamy is accountable for the commonness of dowry in North India. Such a view of Kapadia or Srinivas looks simplistic and over-generalized in view of certain contrary evidence. At least at caste or sub-caste levels hypergamy was never in vogue in modern India north of *Vindhyas.* South India did not have the system of dowry for long, because marriage was solemnized essentially between very close kins. In all places and in all ages every father tends to aspire that his daughters should be married with men of superior means or wealth, but that does not necessarily lead to dowry. Hypergamy is said to have existed partly in ancient as well as medieval periods in certain sections of the North Indian society, but dowry was not evidently associated with such marriages. There has been of course some evidence of hypergamy in case of certain tribes, but they did not practice dowry.

Even if we admit that hypergamy was the primary factor giving rise to the practice of dowry, it is hardly a factor now to explain the ever-increasing incidence of dowry in its present form across different segments of the Indian society. A new move for greater social recognition or a search for superior social identity under the changed socio-economic circumstances, surfacing in the wake of spread of modern education, spirit of individualism, secular occupations and fresh chances for upward mobility, appears to be the most potential factor behind the sustenance of dowry in the present day society despite being outlawed. Epstein (1973: 199) has attributed similar reasons for changeover from bride price to dowry among the Okkaligas in Karnataka. Some believe that the joint family system has engendered the menace of dowry, but again there is no concrete evidence of that either. Rising materialism and consumerism coupled with intent to acquire higher social image have dominated our value system so much so that dowry has steadily become one of the most essential conditions for nuptial bonds. Explanations based only on hypergamy or the joint families fail to explain the incidence of dowry. During the last four-five decades the incidence of joint family has perceptively declined, but not the dowry (Singh: 2003: 53-70).

To be capable to offer a huge dowry or meet bumper expenses on the marriage ceremony of one's daughter or to be worthy to demand a big dowry for the marriage of one's son is a matter of social prestige one might have acquired or claim to have acquired. Goody (1973: 19) has rightly observed a strong association between class or status position and dowry in India. These days dowry is taken as an important marker of the social honour of family in a given community. The dowry has become a status symbol in view of the rising economic prosperity of the people. It is because of this value system that dowry has steadily covered the whole of South India where the practices of bride price and consanguineous marriages had been the most common phenomenon for a fairly a long time. Srinivas (1984: 17) has observed that all the castes in South India, excluding Kerala, practiced bride price in the nineteenth century. Castes and communities that were not traditionally demanding and taking dowry are freely insisting on dowry now (Caldwell, *et al*:1983). The situation has come to such a stage that no marriage can really take place without dowry.

Rise in the practice of dowry has accounted for rise in non-consanguineous marriages in South India. Caldwell, *et al* (1982: 706-707) have observed that in rural South India marriages are moving from bride wealth to dowry, resulting in diminution of the proportion of marriages between relatives. This transition, however, first occurred in urban areas and gradually percolated to the rural areas. The system of dowry has also become popular among the Christians of urban Tamil Nadu (Caplan: 1984: 216-33). Persons practicing bride price is now looked down upon by dowry takers. They are dubbed 'backward' or 'primitive'. The main reason for such a feeling is that it was quite widespread among non-twice born castes and till recently among most Scheduled Tribes, both in pre-British India and British India till 19th century. In this context observation made in the Report of the National Committee on the Status of Woman in India seems relevant. 'Changing from bride-price to dowry is an attempt to improve the social status of family or group, because dowry is associated with the higher social groups' (ICSSR: 1975: 24). A high dowry, stated as above, is taken as one of the important indices of high status. Here it may be concluded that the practice of dowry is bound to perpetuate until society does not innovate its substitute as a determinant of status. As or when the Indian society achieves a higher level of development and modernization, dowry as a determinant of social status would steadily decline in its significance. Such a trend may be expected, as it has happened in case of upper class in our society in particular and the European society in general.

The widening horizon of dowry

It needs no stress that the process of acculturation has gradually intensified in the country as a result of massive spread of media of mass communication and internal migration. The practice of dowry, which remained restricted to the affluent caste Hindus of north of *Vindhyas* for long, has enveloped almost the whole country cutting across the age-old barriers of caste, class, community, region and religion. Dowry is widely prevalent among those who berated it and also among those who denounced it publicly as an evil practice.

What is generally still noticed among most tribal communities (535) is the practice of bride price in cash or kind or both (Singh: 1997b: 8). The bride price was popular also among the Scheduled Castes, but they have gradually drifted towards the practice of dowry. To quote Singh (1997a: 7), 'The incidence of bride-price is reported from 247 communities, while 303—a good number of communities (41 in cash, 129 in kind and 282 both in cash and kind)—have taken to dowry.' Compared to dowry, amount involved in bride price is quite meagre. Both Scheduled Castes and Scheduled Tribes, particularly those settled in towns and cities, have already moved away from bride price to dowry emulating the life style of affluent caste Hindus. Tribals settled in remote hilly terrains would not, however, remain free from the spell of such change for long. By and large, the practice of dowry has become popular among various other sections of society all over the country (Singh: 2003: 80; Singh: 2004).

A recent survey covering 10,000 respondents from 18 states conducted jointly by the AIDWA (All India Democratic Women's Association) and the ISWSD (Indian School of Women's Studies and Development) presents a disquieting state of affairs about the prevalence of dowry in different parts of the country. The survey report presents an alarming picture of how dowry has gained social legitimacy across all communities and regions.[2] According to the study done by the AIDWA dowry has become essential for marriage even among Scheduled Tribes. Over 1,000 tribal women interviewed in Assam, Tripura and Orissa have indicated that the traditional practice where the groom had to give a bride price has been completely reversed. Now the parents of the brides have to cough up heavy dowry in the form of cash and jewellery to the parents of the grooms. All the female respondents from Kamrup, Barpeta, Dibrugarh, Dhubri and Sonitpur districts in Assam responded saying that this appeared to be a distressing trend especially when the Assamese women had never been regarded as an economic liability for their parents (*Times of India*, 8 September 2002: 4).

In the same survey it has also been observed that all the SC, ST, OBC and Muslim female respondents from the northeastern State of Tripura unanimously reported that dowry which was once largely an upper caste phenomenon had now trickled down to all sections of their society. The poorer sections of society who own no land to sale or mortgage for the sake of money are being forced to take resort to moneylenders to borrow money at exorbitantly high rates of interest to get their daughters married. Not so long ago among the Tripura tribals, the grooms had to act as unpaid labourer in the bride's house for a stipulated period of time to compensate the economic loss to her parents resulting from marriage, which was known as *jamai pratha.* But now this practice has evaporated into thin air in the face of dowry system (Singh: 1984).

The AIDWA survey has further substantiated the fact that dowry has now become a common practice among the Muslim community as well. The survey has revealed that the majority of Muslim spinsters interviewed in Delhi insisted that they should be given dowry, as they would not have an opportunity to get a share in their parents' property once they are married. Muslim females interviewed elsewhere also expressed a similar view in favour of dowry. The dowry is learnt to have become an indispensable consideration like *meher* among Muslims in various parts of the country including Bihar, Jharkhand, Uttar Pradesh, Uttaranchal and other neighbouring states. The dowry was a highly uncommon practice in South India, as stated above, because of the system of *stridhanam* and cross cousin marriages. But the adoption of dowry has shattered the age-old practice of marriage between close relatives. The practice of dowry is reported to have covered up even remote rural areas of such states as Kerala and Tamil Nadu where it was possibly despised and discouraged for centuries.

At a time when India is enjoying unprecedented economic advancement and boasts of the world's fastest growing middle class, the country is experiencing a serous problem of dowry deaths and bride burnings. Hindu traditions seem to have been transformed as a means to escaping poverty, augmenting one's wealth or acquiring the modern conveniences that are now advertised daily through media. Dowry seems to have developed certain class characteristics. The upper class people have set the trend. The middle classes emulate them and the lower middle class kills itself trying to keep pace with the trend. The problem of dowry is reported to be particularly more serious with the middle class, as they are relatively more anxious about their social climbing. In search for a higher social status within the middle class itself, those at the lowest rung are particularly more serious about dowry. The quantum of dowry exchange may be greater among the upper middle class people, but 85 per cent of dowry deaths and 80 per cent of dowry harassment occur in the middle and lower strata. Statistics produced by *Vimochana* (a women's NGO in Bangalore) show that 90 per cent of the cases of dowry violence involve women from poorer families, who are unable to meet dowry demands. Similarly Sharma (1999: 348) has observed that now a days dowry is increasingly adopted by low castes and impoverished people who formerly paid bride price. Leave aside the scale of prevalence of dowry as evil or illegal practice for a while, *prima facie* it comes out from the prevailing scenario that with the rise in the level of development India has slowly moved from socio-cultural heterogeneity to socio-cultural homogeneity in the area of marital practices.

Marriage as a pecuniary venture

As the size of dowry and varieties of gifts have a lot to do with the economic status of family or *khandan,* marriage has been transformed into just another business deal. This is the era of direct talks where negotiations are conducted across the table between the two families. Post-marital demands or expectations for gifts in the form of household effects go on for years. Parents of brides are obliged or keenly expected to offer post-marital gifts to their daughter and son-in-law on the occasion of birth of first child, marriage of other siblings of their daughter, if any, and certain religious ceremonies performed at the daughter's marital home. Sometimes the construction of a new house or opening a business often becomes the occasion for further demands for money or household effects. The inability of the bride's family to meet these gifts or demands frequently leads to the daughter-in-law being treated as a pariah and subject to abuse or violence. Violence against bride is used as an instrument by the husband in the wider context of bargaining between the families of the husband and wife over the distribution of resources. In the Indian contexts marriage is to be viewed as the establishment of durable links between two families (rather than individuals) and usually implies transfers of resources from one family to another. In some cases, wives are simply killed to make the way for a new financial transaction—that is, another marriage.

There appears to be a definite market in India for brides and grooms these days. Newspapers are filled with pages of women seeking husbands and men advertising their eligibility and social prowess, usually using their caste as a bargaining chip. A 'good' marriage is often seen by the wife's family as a means to advance up the social ladder. But the catch is that there is a price to be paid in the form of dowry. If for any reason that dowry arrangements cannot be met then it is the young woman who suffers most. In recent years the price of the Indian groom has increased astronomically. Generally, it is based on his qualifications, professional career and income through salary or even possible bribes. Even prior to their graduation, doctors, engineers, business managers and chartered accountants expect a 'fat' dowry, as they are the most sought after cream of the graduating and educated dowry league. At the same time it is also true that the prospective bride's personal qualities and accomplishments adversely affect the amount of dowry. The more attractive, sophisticated and well educated she is, the less dowry her parents are obliged to pay (Caplan: 1984: 221). The beautiful (preferably fair skinned) and well-educated brides are most sought after and in fact their parents are found to be less worried about dowry since they would have a range of eligible mates from which to choose.

Dowry prices in today's India frequently increase proportionally to the groom's education, career prospects and professional position. The receiving family often uses the dowry for business purposes, education of family members, or the dowry to be given for the husband's sisters. In some cases dowries are used to help newly weds set up their new home. With a view to justifying the practice of dowry many people tend to treat it as a compensation for the expenses incurred on groom's education.

Dowry is one of those social practices that no educated Indian would own up with pride in public, although most of us still practice it. Even among educated sections of the metropolitan society, dowry continues to form an essential part of the negotiations that take place in an arranged marriage (Ross: 1961; Ramu: 1977; Caplan: 1984: 216-33). Marriage-negotiations tend to break down if there is no consensus between the contending families regarding the mode or amount of payment of dowry. During the marriage ceremony the articles comprising the dowry are proudly displayed before all the kins, friends and acquaintances present there. Dowry has become such an ostensible measure of social status that people tend to exaggerate what they have got. This is, however, true more of rural than urban areas because of the relatively limited scope for asserting one's position on a social ladder. Greed for dowry is on gradual rise. When expectations are not met or when they suddenly shoot up after the marriage, the woman is harassed, tortured or sometimes even killed for another marriage to get a higher amount of dowry from yet another marriage.

Among the employed, persons from Indian administrative, police and other central services, doctors, engineers and managers in multinational companies are the most sought after grooms in the matrimonial market. No matter how much demand they may place before the parents of prospective bride, chances are that this is more likely to be conceded. So far as I have observed the cases of dowry biddings in Hindi-speaking states it appears that no average man can aspire to have an IAS son-in-law. There is always a queue of ministers, top politicians, chief/principal secretary of the state in front of an eligible IAS officer. Since the politicians have got a special penchant for bureaucrat son-in-law, they are ready to sell out abominable sums of money to get their daughter an IAS groom.

In cases where there is enough freedom for mate selection, the matrimonial alliance is not determined by the size of dowry. However, the expectations of dowry/gift of the bridegroom may remain alive in the back of their mind. Bridegrooms and their parents always keep in their mind as to how much material benefits they can extract, or how much personal interest they may be able to serve in future through bride's family. In the age of naked consumerism the Hindu marriage, which was for long regarded as a sacrament, has now been transformed into a lucrative business.

Dowry, as stated earlier, has become such an essential consideration of marriage that rarely any marriage can take place without it. It may be regarded as a functional imperative for family formation in contemporary India. In very rare cases demands for dowry are eschewed. If the groom's parents, for instance, sense that they can reap greater economic or personal benefits than dowry from bride's parents, dowry is not demanded under the pretext that dowry is an evil of Indian society. Ramu (1977: 48) has observed in the Kolar Gold Field area of the State of Karnataka that the daughters of noted politicians are readily married without demanding dowry, because 'an influential father-in-law is worth a million rupees.'

There has been a strong preference for sons in India. The rising dowry practices have further intensified this preference resulting in a high incidence of gender-based abortions—almost two million female babies a year. In metropolises we often come across billboard advertisements encouraging pregnant women to spend Rs. 500 on unwanted pregnancy which is a clandestine way of doing outlawed gender test to evade huge expenses on the marriage of daughters (abortion is legalized in India). According to the report of the UN Population Fund for the year 2000, female infanticide has also increased dramatically over the past decade and infant mortality rates are substantially higher for female than male infants.[3]

Dowry and domestic violence

The practice of dowry in general may have a long historical record, but the incidence of dowry related violence against women does not probably stretch far beyond the later part of the colonial regime characterized by pinnacle of feudalism. As it appears from the evidence and arguments placed by Oldenburg (2003), the 'dowry murder', in particular, is more and more a post-colonial development. When the dowry amount is not considered sufficient or the expected demands are not met easily, the bride, as stated earlier, is often harassed, abused and tortured. 'Dowry violence' does not refer directly to marriage related payments made at the time of the wedding, but to additional payments demanded after the marriage by the groom's family where the husband systematically abuses the wife in order to extract larger transfers. The dissatisfied husband takes recourse to domestic violence to show his displeasures with the marriage in order to extract additional transfers from the wife's family by credibly threatening her with separation if no transfers are made.

Though dowry harassment most likely arises from complete lack of respect for the woman and avid greed for money, the incidence of violence against women is not to be assessed in terms of the status of women alone. The woman as a bride is subjected to humiliation and brutal behaviour not merely because they have been assigned a low status in the society but also because they are the softest and surest means of extracting maximum amount of money or property from their parents to enhance one's economic position in society. The bride is helpless in her new home and physically so powerless that she cannot retaliate against the coercive behaviour of others. Not many women have enough guts to divorce their husbands on the ground of frequent mental or physical torture, since they have nothing to fall back upon in a traditional and poorly developed country like India. Once the wedding is over and the newly married bride moves to her husband's home, she not only remains a bride but also a potential hostage. Since divorce is the toughest choice/option for her, under no circumstances can she move back permanently to her parent's home.

In the ghastly drama of endless greed for dowry, it is not just the man who is culpable; at times the parents of the girls who meet hefty dowry demands are also found partly liable. A careful observation has shown that the well-educated women tend to face greater harassment for bringing more and more money than illiterate or barely educated women. And the greed never seems to stop. The parents keep doling out the money hoping that everything will be all right, but unfortunately the demands keep increasing.[4] Dowry harassment is far more prevalent in extended and stem families than in nuclear or traditional joint family.

The dowry abuse can escalate to the point where the husband or his family burns the bride, often by pouring kerosene/petrol on her and lighting it, usually killing her in the process. Routinely the in-laws claim that what happened was simply an accident. When the evidence of foul play is too obvious to ignore, the story changes to suicide—the wife, it is said, could not adjust to new family life and subsequently killed herself. There is no doubt that dowry and its related problems lead to psychological torture, suicides and murder of married women, desertion by their husbands, widespread abortion of female foetuses, and poor families resorting to female infanticide for fear of not being able to provide dowry.

The disturbing fact about dowry related violence is that it is not confined to a particular group, social stratum, geographical region or even religion. Rather, it is regarded as a universal phenomenon, cutting across all sorts of boundaries, as it has already been stressed before. It is claimed to be on continuous increase in the country. It has been often reported that like clockwork every 12th hour a dowry related death claims to take place. Between 1990 and 1993, the lives of over 20,000 women were lost across the country. For instance, it has also been reported that at least three girls are burnt for dowry related demands every day in the State of Karnataka. From December 2002 to March 2003, over 150 women were admitted to the burn's ward in Victoria Hospital, Bangalore, with 80 to 100 per cent burns. In 2002, of the 632 women who sustained burns, 80 per cent cases were dowry related; 446 died (TOI ,May 18, 2003: 12). Some commentators have, however, wrongly stressed that the dowry related violence has progressively increased, resulting from ever-wider spread of the practices in the country.[5]

Table 1

Dowry deaths and other crimes against women in India, 1995-2000

Year	*No. of crimes against women*	*No. of dowry deaths*	*% of dowry deaths of all crimes against women*	*No of crimes under Dowry Prohibition Act*	*% of crimes under Dowry Prohibition Act of all crimes against women*	*% of dowry deaths to all cognisable crimes under Indian Penal Code*
1995	109259	5092	4.66	2814	2.58	0.27
1996	115723	5513	4.76	2647	2.29	0.32
1997	121265	6006	4.95	2685	2.21	0.35
1998	131338	6917	5.27	3578	2.72	0.39
1999	135771	6699	4.93	3064	2.26	0.38
2000	141373	6995	4.94	2876	2.03	0.39

Note: A cross-verification of figures, as available in different annual reports of the national crime records bureau, reveals minor variations in certain cases because of printing or editorial errors. Such errors have been fixed as far as possible. Data for period beyond 2000 are not yet available.

Sources: Based on the annual reports of national crime records bureau of the Union Government (GOI: 1996: 88; 1999: 156; 2002: 16, 196).

The statistics furnished by the National Crime Records Bureau of the Ministry of Home Affairs registered 5000 to 7000 cases of dowry deaths in the country annually during 1995-2000 (see Table 1). But in terms of the percentage distribution dowry deaths constituted merely 4 per cent to 5 per cent of all the crimes against women. Moreover, when this figure is viewed against the total population, it does not comprise even 0.001 per cent of the total population of married women (according to the 2001 census the married women (15-44) comprised about 175.5 million, which was 35.4 per cent of the total female population of India).[6] The incidence of dowry deaths varied merely between 3 and 4 women per one lakh (or 0.01 million) married women during 1991 and 2001 censuses which may not be regarded as alarming in terms of the number of married females at risk in the country. This, however, may be taken, as a matter of grave concern, for the incidence of dowry deaths is one of the typical problems of the Indian society.

The feminists and other social activists may consider official figures, as given in Table 1, as gross underreporting of the real situation, since they have often argued that a large number of cases are never reported and many of the reported cases are recorded as simple crimes. This fact is also partly recognized by the government that a sizable number of crimes against women go unreported due to social stigma attached to them (GOI: 2000: 197). On the contrary, it is also true that sometimes minor accidents are reported or recorded as dowry related crimes by the brides' parents. At times even maternal mortality is recorded as dowry death. By way of an example let me refer to a study that has proved how the women activists have overplayed the issue of dowry deaths through media. The incidence of death, particularly at younger ages, is usually so emotional that it is easy to be politicized and, therefore, it becomes quite tricky to ascertain the actual number of dowry deaths. *Vimochana*, a women's group in the city of Bangalore, had files of 800 married women who had been murdered, or had committed suicide or had died accidentally; 450 of whom had died of burns. With a view to making objective assessment of the cases of dowry deaths Celia Dugger of the New York Times came all the way to Bangalore and "studied 50 murder cases closely, and to her profound astonishment she found no 'typical bride-burning' on account of dowry. 'Not even one', she said. 'What did you find', I [Oldenburg] asked. Well, it seems to be drunken men who beat up on their wives and finally kill them" (Oldenburg: 2003: 228). The study is not cited to underplay the size of incidence of dowry death; rather, it is argued that all the violence against women is not necessarily dowry-related violence. Dowry death has been defined so liberally in the Indian Penal Code that any unnatural death or death due to personal negligence or accident within seven years of married life is prone to be classified as dowry death. Hence, it is very hard to ascertain the actual number of dowry related crimes against women. The proportion of dowry deaths, as stated above, forms a minuscule fraction of the number of married women in the country. Nevertheless the problem is a crucial one to investigate. It is definitely a matter of concern for one and all that in spite of the specific legal provisions, dowry deaths and bride-burnings become frequent headlines of the Indian dailies.

Parents usually remain emotionally so attached to their daughters that for the sake of happiness and safety of life of their daughters they readily succumb to the moneymaking pressure tactics employed by the family of their sons-in-law. The post-marital abusive behaviour is mostly triggered off by the incapacity or failure of the father of the newly wed girls to meet the stipulated amount of dowry or sometimes variety of usual gifts that commonly go with the wedding. At times violence is employed as a strategy to subordinate women to men and ensure obedience to behave in accordance with the set norms of the marital home. This may be a reflection of typical value system concerning the position of women as embedded in patriarchy. Sometimes women are also criminally assaulted by their husband on the ground of suspicion or the lack of sexual fidelity, but are reported to the police as dowry related violence by the parents of newly wed women. Violence is used as a mechanism to extract further transfers from the bride's family.

Dowry and law

The Prohibition of Dowry Act of 1961 explicitly stipulates that a person who gives or takes or helps in the giving or taking of dowry can be sentenced to jail for 5 years and fined Rs.15,000 or the amount of the value of dowry, whichever is more. The Act also prohibits the giving and taking, directly or indirectly, any property or valuable security, any amount either in cash or kind in respect of a marriage. The control is provided by stating a limit and names of gift givers and their relationship to the married couples to be signed by both sides of parents. With a view to preventing the offences of cruelty by husband or his relatives on the wife, Section 498-A was added in the Indian Penal Code and Section 198-A in the Criminal Procedure Code in 1983. In case of cruelty to bride by the husband or his affines there is a provision of imprisonment for three years under the Section 498-A of the IPC. Cruelty is harassment of the women with a view to coercing her or her affines to meet an unlawful demand for property or values. Cruelty also includes any conduct that is likely to drive the woman to commit suicide or cause grave injury or danger to her. Section 406 of the IPC stipulates imprisonment up to three years, or fine, or both for the husband and in-laws of girl, if they refuse to part with the *stridhan* in their safekeeping.

In view of the continuing problems of dowry and marital violence the Prohibition of Dowry Act of 1961 was amended in 1985 to give it more teeth. Provisions were made under Section 174 of the Cr PC for investigations of suspicious bridal deaths and punishment of seven years to life imprisonment and possibly death for those found guilty and convicted of bride burning. Dowry death falls under the Section 304-B of the IPC. If she dies due to burns or injuries or not under normal circumstances within seven years of her marriage and it is proved that before her death she was subjected to cruelty or harassment in connection with dowry, such death will be called 'dowry death.' The husband or relative shall be deemed to have caused her death. The punishment for dowry deaths involves imprisonment for not less than seven years that may be extended to life imprisonment.

The people have such a strong vested interest in dowry that they have discovered loopholes in the Act to dodge legal traps. The dowry takers are seldom scared of unlawful acts, because the state instruments do not enforce laws strictly. The Act has provided that presents made at the time of marriage in the form of cash, ornaments, cloths or articles should not be deemed to be 'dowry', unless they are made as consideration for the marriage. In addition to general slackness on the part of government to make effective implementation of any legislation, it is this clause that provides the legal loopholes allowing unabated continuation of dowry in India. Moreover, the custodians of law themselves are also found to indulge in the dowry practice when they are involved in marriage of their sons and daughters. There is a fair amount of slackness in handling the dowry related cases both by the police and the court. Regarding the failure of dowry prohibition legislation Mandelbaum (1972: 652) has rightly remarked, 'Nor is it likely to have great success unless many more people in India change their ideas about the central importance of family status and about the proper ways to maintain and raise that status.'

Anti-dowry movement

It was only in the middle of the 1970s that the women's movement and other human rights groups exposed the perniciousness of the system in India, when it was realized that there were an increased number of 'accidental kitchen deaths' of young married women. The first reports to the police were often registered as suicides or accidents. Initially, women's groups protested individual cases of dowry deaths. A national campaign focused on humiliating and socially boycotting the families in these cases. The campaign also demanded that mysterious deaths be presumed to be murders until investigated and proved otherwise by the police. The demand for special cells of women police officers to head investigations of dowry murders led to an amendment of the Prohibition of Dowry Act, which was later further amended so that all *stridhan* gifts (both movable and immovable) had to be registered in the wife's name at the time of the marriage. Unfortunately, in India basic attitudes to female life have remained unchanged, and the dowry is seen as a bribe to the son-in-law to keep the daughter, who after a certain age is totally unwanted in her natal home. Families often know that they are virtually signing a death warrant when they give their daughter in marriage, and yet, they do so.

The elimination of dowry abuse requires changing the mindset of the people. It is obvious now that the solutions that have been superimposed, like legal regulations, are not very successful. The dowry evil is in need of social agitation at the grassroots levels. It seems that women's groups are much less interested in campaign against dowry. Somehow the urgency of dealing with this type of rooted custom has now vanished. Women's groups are engaged on a range of issues. But the dowry issue, which brought together a diverse spectrum of groups in the late 1970s, has virtually fallen off their maps. Of course, it is possible that this issue is not a rallying point any more because women's groups have recognized that at root, it is not just one custom, but larger issues such as women's inheritance rights to property, equal rights and economic empowerment that must be taken on board simultaneously.

Social movements may be necessitated to impede injustices of dowry deaths, the killing and abandoning of female infants, the banishment of women who fail to produce sons and breakdown of the family due to dowry harassment. More importantly there is a strong necessity of cultural rethinking on the status of women that can occur only through education. The problem is compounded by the fact that 46.0 per cent of the female population in India is still illiterate (2001 census). Perhaps a good starting point is population control and compulsory education for boys and girls alike. A 'Say No to Dowry' campaign was launched at the Association for India's Development's (AID) Annual Conference 2002 at San Francisco on Saturday, May 25th. Over 200 Indians, both students and professionals, signed a dowry pledge that decrees 'I promise never to give or take dowry.' It is a particularly significant move as the non-resident Indian grooms are able to command the highest dowry rates in India. Such a movement is bound to influence the Indian psyche in days to come. The intelligentsia cannot remain silent spectators for long.

Educated people need to consider the following: In which other culture are girls expected to carry to their marital home all the equipments for a house—washing machine, fridge, oven, home theatre, digital video camera, furniture, cupboards, soft furnishings—as well as a car or scooter apart from loads of gold or diamond jewellery and clothes? In some customs, the bride is expected to carry with her not just her wedding trousseau but also an odd number of *saris*, 21 or 31 or 41 complete with separate blouses and petticoats—and sometimes even matching *chappals*! How can even this be considered 'reasonable'?

A girl's ability to say 'no' in our culture depends a great deal on the support she gets from her family. Parents have to decide that they will not marry their daughters if a dowry is demanded, directly or indirectly. If there is even a hint of this at any stage, they should have the courage to call off the arrangement. Unless enough parents do this, a change will not take place. Of course, we can hope for a day when boys grow up believing that it is a privilege if they get a bride and they should not ask her to pay for marriage. But such a day is some way off given the son-preference that continues to dominate our culture.

As the matter now stands, the anti-dowry activists need to work more closely and actively among the women-folk themselves for the reason that they are the real source of all the troubles for the newly married women. It is they who instigate and encourage their son, husband and daughter, if any, to fix up their daughters-in-law. It is very bizarre that such women completely fail to grasp that their daughters may have to encounter similar troubles or dilemmas elsewhere. The women activists are mistakenly accusing the male members of the family for all the acts of violence and humiliation against the women generally under the excessive influence of the theory of patriarchy and gender relations. The bride seldom countenances any problem of adjustment when she does not have to live with her mother-in-law. In scores of cases it has been noticed that in an extended family situation whenever the males come to defend their daughter-in-law, their wives, strangely enough, attempt to silence them by accusing them of having illicit relationships with their daughter-in-law.

Though the dowry has got numerous dysfunctions to perform in a society, as it tends to encourage a chain of evil practices such as corruption in public life and violence against women, it has also got some positive consequences in numerous cases. Many a people try their sons to achieve higher education or professions in an effort of securing a higher amount of dowry, delaying their marriage as far as possible. Delay in the age at marriage has adversely affected high fertility regime in India. However, it does not imply that dowry should persist for these very reasons. It is indeed tough to get rid of this practice, as once tradition becomes time-honoured, no matter how dysfunctional or evil it is in the larger interest of the system, it dies very hard. Simply by declaring it unlawful, it cannot disappear so readily in a country like India where the state of affairs with the rule of law is very awfully poor.

Reasons for persistence of dowry

In addition to the fact that the size of dowry helps in the process of status crystallization or status attainment, there are some other factors which help sustain the dowry practices in the Indian society. And in the process people seem to be prepared to put up with dowry-centric violence in society. The marriage of daughter is so essential in Indian society that all parents find themselves under extreme pressure to meet even the toughest demands to get their daughters married, no matter whether that money comes from money-lenders at a heavy interest rate, or through the sale of property or through some illegal means. Getting one's daughter married is considered a primary duty and to have an older unmarried daughter is a tremendous misfortune with huge social and economic costs. The bride's parents ruin themselves while hosting lavish wedding receptions, as weddings throughout the country are invariably performed in the bride's house. So groom's parents simply cannot understand why they should not ask for a bumper dowry. In fact, they owe him a living simply for having taken daughters off their hands.

So long as the choice is restricted to a few suitable men within the same *jati* or *upjati* (sub-caste) of same cultural region, search for superior or suitable grooms will go on perpetuating dowry. The people are only permitted to marry within a well-defined set of families who make up their sub-caste. Ross (1961: 263) and Vatuk (1972: 98) express a similar view. Boys having government jobs or being in the professions have a special image in the society and they are in short supply. Increasing unemployment and rising female education have further widened the gap between the number of well-placed boys and well-educated girls. Gradual decline in the number of eligible mates for girls, particularly belonging to middle and upper classes, have made the prospects of dowry still brighter at least for some time more. Other factors, which also contribute to the dowry practices, are that the Indians practice the patrilocal system of residence after marriage for women and parents arrange marriages. In addition, marriage is considered final and cases of separation and divorces are still not widespread.[7]

The process of giving or taking dowry is no doubt embroiled in a vicious circle. Nobody is prepared to give up the dowry, as there is no guarantee that others would forgo dowry in the case of marriage of his sister or daughter. Whenever or wherever I have questioned the prospective grooms or their parents about the rationale of dowry in Bihar, Jharkhand, Uttar Pradesh and other Hindi speaking states, instant was the reply that nobody would marry their sisters or daughters free of dowry. This was the most usual reaction from all those well-educated and well-placed persons who were demanding dowry. Some regard dowry as a compensation for bad-looking or poorly educated bride. A person opposing or demanding for a lesser amount of dowry than he normally deserves is often taken as a man of poor or suspicious social standing or the groom is suspected to suffer from certain physical or social disabilities.

Yet another, but equally important reason behind the persistence of dowry practice is the fact that parents have got a kind of vested interest in the proper upbringing and education of their son. They seek to derive maximum returns from their investment in the form of dowry, because upon marriage their son may not provide them the necessary care in the old age. In the age of individualism, people are generally uncertain about the help from their son in the case of certain exigency in the old age. The son generally gets so much engrossed in his own affairs concerning his wife and offspring that the gap between the personal interests of married son and those of parents get obviously widened in scores of cases. When the aged people eagerly expect help from their son or the state, they are often found struggling alone. Hence, most parents try to derive maximum benefits from their sons' marriage in the form of dowry to compensate their investment in upbringing and education of their sons.

Conclusions

Despite the fact that dowry is widely regarded as an 'evil' and outlawed practice, it is clearly in vogue all over the country irrespective of caste, community, religion and region. In fact, it has become more effervescent than ever before. Different factors and forces have been at work, though not concurrently, to tempt various sections of the Indian society characterized by varying marital practices to come under the spell of dowry as a crucial consideration for marriage. The system of *stridhanam* in South India, strict endogamy coupled with the lack of right of inheritance for females in various parts of the country, *sanskritization* in the case of low castes (both OBCs and *dalits)* and Scheduled Tribes, and urbanization and acculturation in the case of non-Hindu communities have been possibly the most predominant factors behind universalization of the dowry practice. In a social setting marked by endogamy and gender differentials in inheritance rights, Europeanization, rise in the level of education, spread of media of mass communication and modernization in general have distorted the indigenous marital practices enough to transform them into a uniform dowry practice in course of time.[8]

With the rise in the level of education, urbanization and modernization, increasing occupational differentiations with greater opportunities for personal advancements and greater consciousness of one's special identity, far-reaching changes have occurred in marital practices. The rising achievement motivation of individuals in an open environment has indirectly exacerbated dowry practices despite being outlawed. The practice of dowry is one of the unintended costs of modernization and development the Indians have to bear willingly or unwillingly. The Indian society has progressively become more and more unwrapped and competitive. It is an established fact that with the availability of new career openings and greater opportunities to accumulate wealth, every one is in the quest of higher and higher goals of life no matter what means or course they have to adopt to accomplish them. And in the process countless people tend to pass through the dilemma of identity crisis under the new state of affairs. It is because of this reason that scores of dowry takers as well as dowry givers tend to exaggerate the amount of cash or property they have taken or given in the form of dowry in a common tête-à-tête with kinsmen, friends and even people with nodding acquaintances.

Since dowry has become a status symbol, it is not going to evaporate into thin air so readily. The system of caste or sub-caste endogamy, the system of arranged marriage and the lower incidence of divorce rate from the women's side promote and sustain dowry practices in the country. Until and unless the sub-caste endogamy is not replaced by exogamy and arranged marriage by so-called 'romantic' or civil marriage, the Indians would have to bear with the cultural crime of dowry in days to come too. In an ultimate analysis exogamy may serve as a panacea for many of the societal challenges that India has to cope up with as a nation state. The practice of exogamy would not only solve the problems of dowry, but also diminish social distance and differentiations across castes and communities through social and cultural amalgamation and integration.

Notes

1. The latest survey on family has recorded that about 60 per cent of girls are married before the legal age of 18 and the average time gap between the median age at first marriage and the median age at first cohabitation is nearly a year (NFHS: 2000: 56). It is an old practice that after marriage the girl returns to her natal home and in the case of pre-puberty marriage she stays back with her family until the onset of puberty. On attaining puberty another ceremony known as *gauna* (consummation) is performed which marks her fitness to join her husband's family. As the age at marriage has gone up in the case of both sexes, *gauna* is usually performed just after *vivah* (marriage)—the same day or the next day, while in the past, when there was a practice of child marriage, the gap between marriage and *gauna* used to vary on the average from three to six years. This ceremony has always involved transactions of household effects and property, depending upon the economic condition of bride's parents.
2. See the abridged report of Rashme Segal (Dowry spreads its dragnet) in *Times News Network* (Sunday, September 08, 2002). http://timesofindia.indiatimes.com/cms.dll/articleshow.
3. An exhaustive discussion on the subject based on the latest data is available in one of the papers by Singh (1984b).
4. Let me cite an intimately known case that occurred in 2002 in my neighbourhood in Patna—the capital city of the State of Bihar. The grieving mother of a woman belonging to upper middle class family, whose husband shot her dead in front of her child, spoke of how she secretly managed for years single-handedly to fulfill her son-in-law's lust for more and more money. When it became clear that her son-in-law was not about to give up his demands, she advised her daughter to be prepared for death.
5. See the newspaper coverage done by the *Sunday Times of India* (New Delhi), 2002, 8 September, p. 4 and the *Sunday Times of India* (Patna, New Delhi), 2003, 18 May, p. 12.
6. The incidence of any event, methodologically speaking, should always be examined in terms of the number of people at risk for a scientific comparison across the state or within it longitudinally. While many of the social activists have wrongly insisted that the incidence of dowry-related deaths has increased over the years, ignoring the fact that the number of women in the age group 15-44 has also increased over the years.
7. The census reports of India have never recorded a divorce rate of more than two per cent at any census in the country so far.

8. Of 4635 Indian communities succession goes to the eldest son in cases of 4429 communities. While property is shared equally among sons in 3680 communities, there are only 570 communities that allow equal share in property for both son and daughter (Singh: 2003: 82).

References

Caplan, Lionel. 1984. 'Bridegroom price in urban India: Class, caste and 'dowry evil' among Christians in Madras', *Man*: 19:2: 216-233.

Caldwell, John C, *et al.* 1982. 'The causes of demographic change in rural South India: A micro approach', *Population and Development Review*: 8:4: 689-727.

Caldwell, John C. *et al* 1983. 'The causes of marriage change in south India', *Population Studies*: 37: 3: 343-361.

Epstein, Scarlett. 1973. *South India, Yesterday, Today and To-morrow*. London: Macmillan.

Goody, Jack. 1973. 'Bridewealth and dowry in Africa and Eurasia', pp. 1-58 in J. R. Goody and S. J. Tambiah (eds.), *Bridewealth and Dowry.* Cambridge: Cambridge University Press.

Indian Council of Social Sciences Research. 1975. *Report of the National Committee on the Status of Women in India.* Summary Report. New Delhi: Indian Council of Social Science Research.

Kapadia, K.M. 1972. *Marriage and Family in India.* Delhi: Oxford University Press.

Kaplan, Marion A. 1985. *The Marriage Bargain: Women and Dowries in European History.* New York: Harrington.

Karlekar, Malavika. 2003. 'Domestic violence', pp. 1127-1157 in Das, Veena (ed.). *The Oxford Indian Companion to Sociology and Social Anthropology.* New Delhi: Oxford University Press.

Madan, T.N. 1975. 'Structural implications of marriage in north India: Wife givers and wife takers among the Pandits of Kashmir'. *Contributions to Indian Sociology* (N.S.): 9: 217-243.

Mandelbaum, David G. 1972. *Society in India.* Bombay: Popular Prakashan.

NFHS-2. 2000. *India* (National Family Health Survey-II, 1988-99). Mumbai: IIPS and ORC Macro.

Nair, P.T. 1978. *Marriage and Dowry in India.* Calcutta: Minerva Associates.

GOI. 1998. *Crime in India 1996.* New Delhi: National Crime Records Bureau, Ministry of Home Affairs, Government of India.

GOI. 1999. *Crime in India 1998.* New Delhi: National Crime Records Bureau, Ministry of Home Affairs, Government of India.

GOI. 2002.*Crime in India 2000.* New Delhi: National Crime Records Bureau, Ministry of Home Affairs, Government of India.

Parry, J.P. 1979. *Caste and Kinship in Kangra.* London: Routledge and Kegan Paul.

Oldenburg, Veena Talwar, 2003. *Dowry Murder* (The imperial origins of a cultural crime). New Delhi: Oxford University Press.

Ramu, G.N. 1977. *Family and Caste in Urban India: A Case Study.* New Delhi: Vikas Publishing House.

Ross, Aileen D. 1961. *The Hindu Family in its Urban Setting*. Toronto: University of Toronto Press.

Sharma, Ursula. 1999. 'Dowry in North India: Its consequences for women', pp. 341-356, in Patricia Uberoi (ed.), *Family, Kinship and Marriage in India*. New Delhi: Oxford University Press.

Singh, J.P. 2002. 'Social and cultural aspects of gender inequality and discrimination in India', *Asian Profile*: 30:2: 163-176.

Singh, J.P. 2003. 'Nuclearization of household and family in urban India', *Sociological Bulletin*: 52:1: 53-70.

Singh, J.P. 2004. The contemporary Indian family', in Bert N. Adams and Jan Trost (Eds.), *Handbook of World Families*, California: Sage Publications Inc.

Singh, K.S. 1997a. *The Scheduled Castes* (People of India, Vol. II). New Delhi: Oxford University Press.

Singh, K.S. 1997b. *The Scheduled Tribes* (People of India, Vol. III). New Delhi: Oxford University Press.

Singh, K.S. 2003. *Introduction* (People of India, National Series, Vol. 1). New Delhi: Oxford University Press.

Srinivas, M.N. 1984. *Some Reflections on Dowry* (J.P. Naik Memorial Lecture, New Delhi). New Delhi: Oxford University Press.

Tambiah, S.J. 1973. 'Dowry and bridewealth, and the property rights of women in South Asia', pp. : 59-169 in Jack Goody and S. J. Tambiah (eds.), *Bridewealth and Dowry*. Cambridge: Cambridge University Press.

TOI. 2002. *The Sunday Times of India* (New Delhi), 8 September, p. 4.

TOI. 2003. *The Sunday Times of India* (Patna, New Delhi) , 18 May, p. 12.

Vatuk, Sylvia. 1972. *Kinship and Urbanization: White-collar Workers in North India*. Berkeley: University of California Press.

This is a revised version of the paper which first appeared under the same title in *The Eastern Anthropologist*: 58:2:2005:199-220. It is included here with the prior permission of the author and the Editor, *Eastern Anthropologist* and the *Ethnographic and Folk Culture Society*, the publishers of EA. J.P. Singh is Professor, Sociology, Patna University, Patna-800005. Address for email correspondence is: jpsingh1950@hotmail.com.

CHAPTER - THREE

Crisis of Masculinity in Haryana: The Unmarried, the Unemployed and the Aged

Prem Chowdhry

The growing numbers of unmarried and/or unemployed men along with the elderly men are experiencing and generating unimaginable levels of tension in Haryana society especially with regard to their masculinities. The construction of masculinity is in itself a historical process, full of tension and contradiction. Implicated in historical change, the status of being unmarried and/or unemployment is linked in a major way with masculinity, which remains a primary way of signifying relationship of power. Its shifting and changing contours have redefined social relations between men and produced their subordinate and marginal masculinities. This article engages with this complexity of masculinities and its relations to power by uncovering those aspects of political economy in contemporary Haryana that structure and restructure them. Although the effect of these shifts are profound upon women and reference to gender equations are unavoidable and even necessary, this paper concentrates on understanding this crisis of masculinity. Operating in the era of new technologies, globalization and rampant consumerism, combination of these complexities, despite their contradictions, is leading to greater aggression and violence, worsening gender equations and also entails greater exploitation of other subordinate categories, the consolidation of repressive social forces and the strengthening of casteism. Such masculinities are affording an unprecedented role to illegal and unconstitutional bodies like the caste *panchayats*. Dominated and dictated by a core group of elderly men drawn from among dominant caste groups, these caste *panchayats* offer the means through which contradictions between men are dissolved and masculine hierarchies (including those based on age) are legitimized and sustained through a public show of masculine collectivity, aggression and solidarity. This all-male public spectacle enables the marginalized categories among the dominant caste male populace to come into their own.

I

Unmarried Males and Demographic Pressure

Statistically, Haryana has inordinately high figures of unmarried men. In the 1991 Census 36.24 per cent of men in the category of 15-44 years of age (the so-called reproductive or marriageable age) were tabulated as being unmarried.[1] In some of the districts like Rohtak the percentage of unmarried males between these ages is as high as 44 per cent.[2] A combination of factors like the adverse sex ratio, the practice of polygamy, widower remarriage and the still persisting custom of bride price among the lower strata, may help explain the phenomenon of the continued existence of a large number of unmarried men in Haryana.[3] Among these, the high adverse female sex ratio plays a major contributory role.

The female sex ratio, as recorded in the decennial census operations, has been declining since the colonial period.[4] In the post-colonial period, introduction of new technologies has wrecked havoc in this ratio. The recent and rampant use of sex determination tests and sex-selective abortions has put the very existence of females at stake. A state with a vast network of motorable roads, availability of electricity, fairly extensive urbanization, has led to the penetration of this modern technology to some of the remotest corners of Haryana. Accessibility to this technology, along with other factors such as economic surplus and small-family (two child) norm has resulted in the materially advanced regions of Haryana showing the most adverse sex ratio. For example, of the top 10 worst districts in India with adverse female sex ratio, Haryana contains three. The provisional figures of 2001 show 865 females to 1,000 males in Haryana. In parts of Haryana it is much less; for example, in Kurukshetra, it is merely 770, in Sonepat, 783 and in Ambala, 784. The activists in Haryana observe that in some villages it is as low as 500-550. The government, according to them, is pressurising the village authorities not to disclose this fact or recognize it officially. Although the Pre-Natal Diagnostic Techniques (Regulation and Prevention of Misuse) Act is more than a decade old, yet there is hardly any news of cases being successfully filed or prosecuted.

Admittedly, a one to one relationship cannot be made between adverse sex ratio and the number of unmarried men or women. Yet, this link is accepted at the local level. It is acknowledged and focused upon by the regional newspapers. *The Dainik Bhaskar,* a popular daily in Hindi, for instance, maintained in its front page "161 men out of 1,000 to remain unmarried in Haryana".[5] This was followed by a news item indicating that between 15 and 24 years of age group there were only 756 girls to a thousand males.[6] An even more sensational heading appeared in its December 18, issue which maintained 'Youth voters in Bhiwani all unmarried". The news item said that "all the 7,500 new male voters in this district were unmarried, but all 5,000 new voters among the girls were married".[7] This unmarried status of men in Haryana is however not something new. Though figures are not available, the common existence of bachelors among agricultural caste groups was noticeable even in the colonial period [Kensington: 1893: 160].

How does this link-up between adverse female sex ratio and the unmarried status of men translate on the ground? The answer to this lies in understanding its effects in relation to different strata of Haryana society. In a situation where status hypergamous marriages are the norm, such an equation leaves a surplus of brides at the top but a pronounced deficit at the bottom. In either case the effects on society are profound. For instance, this has led to a situation in Haryana where on the one hand the employed male is in a commanding position in relation to getting married while on the other hand, the unemployed lower-class male finds it difficult to get married.[8] In the marriage market it is the employed and not the unemployed that is a "suitable boy". The limited number of "suitable boys" gives them leverage in the marriage market as it means a competition to net them in marriage. This competition for "suitable boys" shows a surplus of girls at this stratum that feeds into the dowry economy. The size of the dowry is considered relative to the "worth" of the groom. Consequently, the ranks of "suitable boys" register a different kind of masculinity, at once self-assured, aggressive and more importantly, manipulative of market forces.

Employment of men not only confers social status and position but also translates as an asset in ensuring a good marriage, i.e, a marriage with a large dowry. Ajay Kumar, 26 years old and unemployed, though highly qualified, in village Dobaldhan in district Jhajjar, for example, was waiting (at the time of my fieldwork in 2002) to get employed before getting married.[9] He recognized that "he was well past the age of marriage" (which is ideally preferred to be between 18 and 25 years of age), but wanted to get married only after he secured employment a sentiment shared by many of his other friends. Employment, he hoped would secure him a "good marriage", i.e, marriage with a large dowry and a "better girl" (meaning an earning girl) from "a well-to-do family", just like his older brother, whose wife is a schoolteacher and from a well-connected family.

Employment has arguably come to influence marriage decisions: when to marry and who to marry. It is not as if the unemployed do not get married or do not get "good girls" as brides. They do, but a lot depends on the financial and social status of the family they come from. But generally it can be observed that the unemployed either settle for lesser matches or do not get married at all. Indeed, a substantial number of the unmarried are to be found among those who are unemployed, which is also popularly held responsible for pushing up the age of marriage for males,[10] thereby causing a great deal of anxiety. Anxiety around the unmarried status of men is reflected in a popular observation in Haryana: "If you want to seek help from someone in order to get your work done, then start talking about the possibility of his son's marriage"![11] In fact, there is a prior presumption about the unemployed status of an unmarried man.

II

Unemployment

Unemployment in Haryana is a massive problem. The avenues for new employment are too few and slow to open, and the existing ones have seen a constriction.

Privatization in the wake of new economic policies has meant severe retrenchment in various departments. According to one estimate, in the initial three and a half years of Om Prakash Chautala's government (2000-05) 40,000 employees were laid off.[12] The numbers of the unemployed in Haryana have more than doubled in less than 20 years from 3,59,255 in 1980-81 to 8,11,359 people in the year 1999- a staggering rise of 125 per cent.[13] These include both the educated and the uneducated unemployed. The number of unemployed persons on the employment register, however, in no way reflects the genuine number of unemployed in Haryana. For example, in 1999, there were only 1,173 employers using the employment exchanges. This means that hopes of getting employment through them are very few.[14] Many youths vouched for this and said that they had not felt motivated to register themselves with the employment exchange. Although it is difficult to split the official figures of the unemployed population according to age and sex field observations suggest that the male population form a major chunk of the unemployed. The employment aspirations of females are still extremely low.

Of 7,030 vacancies filled in the year 1999, from a total of 14,687 notified vacancies in the government jobs, there were 49,627 submissions made. This is the situation when the government has raised the fee for application forms from Rs. 100 and Rs. 125 to Rs. 500 and Rs. 600, inhibiting many from even applying for government jobs.[15] It is a notorious and openly acknowledged fact that whatever jobs are created, they are sold off to the highest bidder by those at the helm of affairs. The *Dainik Jagran* reported that in the month of August 2000, there were 91,285 applications for recruitment to 2,000 posts of constables in the police. Many of the aspirants had MA degrees.[16] Reportedly, just to survive some of the educated young men, holding BA and MA degrees, have even taken to petty self-employment like running tea-stalls, selling eatables or plying rickshaws.[17] The situation speaks for a great deal of frustration among the youth. According to a recent survey, by December 2002, among those who were unemployed, there were 74.37 per cent who were educated as against 25.63 uneducated.[18] Higher education is no guarantee for a job, let alone a good one in the organized sector. The standard of rural education remains abysmally low. Generally, most political commentators agree that low educational and training accomplishments of prospective rural job aspirants stand in their way of getting jobs in the private sector.[19]

The educated have also been known to be averse to going into agriculture. The income generation in the green revolution areas has driven away rather than attracted the younger generation to agriculture. Many villagers are of the opinion that even those boys who have studied up to the secondary level and have in fact qualified by "*nakkal*" (copying or cheating) want jobs in the white collared professions.[20] This stand is confirmed by another study which shows that a large chunk of the educated and semi-educated rural population under the age of 25 in Haryana, ranging from the majority category of "10th class failed" to "BA third class" want non-farm jobs only and cannot get them [Bhalla: 1981:1022:30]. In the scale of different work-related masculinities, as understood by sociologists writing on changing masculinities [Morgan: 1992], the white collared professions in Haryana may well be evoking or may be in the process of evoking a higher and much coveted masculinity than the one associated purely with agricultural work. This suggests a subtle shift of preference away from agricultural work associated with an aspect of masculinity such as muscle power or the body, as has been argued by a recent work [Chopra: 2004]. This preference for "*naukri*" (salaried job) is not something new. It has existed historically. In the colonial period it was related to an economy kept deliberately backward which did not allow any economic surplus and made for below subsistence level living [Chowdhry: 1986: 264-88]. Although this rationale is no longer valid in the agriculturally rich states of the post-colonial period, other extraneous considerations may well have worked towards a reiteration of this preference.[21]

Notwithstanding this predilection, in the absence of employment opportunities in the secondary and tertiary sectors, unemployed youth, educated or uneducated, are compelled to fall back on agriculture. Over time agriculture's capacity to absorb labour forces has also come down drastically; therefore unemployment is growing day by day. A recent work shows the relative weakness of the rural employment market in the wake of the economy opening up in the post-reform period. It argues that the proportion of rural persons engaged in agriculture (inclusive of field crop operations, plantations, livestock, forestry and logging and fishing) declined noticeably during the years 1983 to 1999-2000.[22] Indeed, the withdrawal of the state and public sector investment in agriculture in the wake of economic liberalization, and neglect of almost all the essential prerequisites of growth has led to "a crisis in agriculture", especially in terms of declining output and employment.[23]

Industry in Haryana has certainly grown at the rate of 8 per cent between 1981 and 1991,[24] but this growth remains insufficient. In Haryana the rate of industrialization which has shown some upward swing, still lags far behind the rate of urbanisation,[25] which outstrips it massively (industrialization is defined by the percentage of a state's active people employed in industry). Analyzing the number of industrial workers between 1981 and 1991 can provide evidence for this. For example, there has been an increase in the total number of industrial workers in Haryana from 5,68,467 in 1981 to 6,27,654 in 1991 (ibid). But in terms of industrial workers as a percentage of the total working force in Haryana there has been a decline from 15.51 per cent in 1981 to 13.30 per cent in 1991. Clearly, Haryana has undergone rapid urbanization without concomitant economic development. Although a great deal of research needs to be done in this field, part of the reason may well lie in the newly established industries in places like Gurgaon and Faridabad, that prefer and employ migrant labour from Uttar Pradesh and Bihar rather than recruiting locally.[26] A 10 village *panchayat* which met in village Kasan, district Gurgaon, in July 2004 gave vent to its frustration and anger against the industrial houses, who refused to employ "their boys" in industries set up on "their land", procured at throw away prices, and blamed also the government for not putting pressure upon these industries to employ the locals.[27] Even the massive "out-sourcing" occurring in the information and technology sector has benefited "outsiders" rather than the *Haryanavis*, or at best a very small section of them.[28]

Politicians agree that unemployment in Haryana is the "number one problem".[29] Oft-repeated government promises to create jobs for the benefit of the unemployed has been regularly belied. In December 2002 hundreds of youths from the neighbouring villages of Gohana attacked the government sugar mill.[30] Armed with agricultural implements and supported by the local villagers they tried to burn it down. It was alleged that the villagers had given land worth crores of rupees for the establishment of this mill on the promise that the village youth would be absorbed in the jobs that were to be created. This did not materialize. The result was a near riot situation where many were injured.

The unemployed youth of Haryana provide raw material for all the agitations in the state. Although the role of employed males cannot be discounted, the unemployed sections are known to take a lead in whatever violence that occurs. In May-June 2002 confrontation between the government and the farmers regarding payment of water tax, in Kandela village, district Jind, a strong contingent of unemployed youth wielding "*latthis*", openly stated that if they had jobs they would not have been in the agitation.[31] Even the movement for the reservation of seats for *jats,* the dominant land owning caste group in Haryana, is directly connected with the rampant unemployment problem. Seizing upon the enormity of the problem politicians of different hues in their election strategy in the assembly elections of February 2005, promised unemployment "*bhatta*" for the educated unemployed.[32]

As popularly acknowledged there is also a connection between unemployment and crime.[33] Certain villages in Haryana have become so notorious for crime, that people do not wish to marry their daughters into those villages, notwithstanding the "employment status" of individuals.[34] Confirming this, a newspaper report mentioned that in such a village in Bhiwani district, there were 1,000 young unmarried men, for whom no marriage proposals were forthcoming.[35] There appears to be a strong connection, though still unexplored, between unemployment, unmarried status and growing incidents of suicides in Haryana.[36] In Faridabad, for instance, in one month alone there were 60 suicides.[37] There are different reasons for these suicides. However, the men involved were between 15 and 40 years of age and were all unemployed. The newspapers of Haryana frequently comment on the suicide attempts by the young unemployed and still unmarried men in the villages.[38] Although it is difficult to give figures of overlap between unmarried and unemployed status of males, in the opinion of most rural people, there exists an unquestionable association.

III

Masculinity: Marginalization

The extremely tight situation in relation to employment and marriage has put unemployed, unmarried men, in different age groups, under great pressure. This is primarily because masculinity is popularly located in the 'working' men whether involved in agricultural or non-agricultural work. Unemployment has been accepted as one of the major challenges to masculinity [Morgan 1992: 99-119]. Some of the popularly cited proverbs, currently in usage, exemplify the local sentiments adequately. I cite just a few of them:

> *"Mard moocchalaa hi aaccha laage sai"*
> *(Only a man with a moustache is liked)*

Thus, a moustache is popularly associated with masculinity.

> *"Aurat ka khasam mard, mard ka khasam rozgar"*
> (The lord of a woman is a man; a man's lord is his livelihood)

The proverb underlines the overwhelming importance given to work in a man's life and the role of a bread-earner as the primary one in an adult male life.

> *"Mariyo naar kulacchanni, mariyo marad nikatthu"*
> (A characterless woman and an idle/unemployed man are better dead)

Unemployed men are considered a burden on society. Finally, a very telling proverb reveals how the unemployed may thwart all aspirations of the parents by maintaining:

> *"Bette hue sayanne, dilladar hue puranne" (Once the sons grow up, poverty vanishes).*

Unemployed sons, on the other hand, are seen as adding to poverty rather than alleviating it. This proverb reiterates the role of a male as a bread-earner. Being a man is not sufficient in itself to merit a "masculine status". The halo of masculinity rests on his fulfilling the idealized norm of an earner.

Unemployment and its various socio-psychological effects are compounded by the unmarried status of men, which has a significant bearing on other social questions. In a society where marriage is seen as an opportunity for social mobility, unmarried men are not an asset. They are a threat. Culturally, marriage and fertility are highly valued in rural India not only for women, as popularly believed even in academia, but also for men. Men, as much as women, are expected to marry and reproduce for economic, social and lineage purposes. For those engaged in agriculture, the process of becoming male and acquiring "manliness" may certainly be conditioned by their work in agriculture and performing "hard labour", as argued by Radhika Chopra (2004: 36-59), but this process is not complete till a man gets married. This is vital given the importance of female labour to agriculture. Great deals of agricultural and female family members in Haryana, especially by the incoming "*bahus*" or daughters-in-law, perform animal husbandry work.[39] A dilemma seems to exist regarding the utilization of a daughter's labour in view of the temporary nature of her stay in her father's home. This makes a man's marriage an "economic necessity". The same was acknowledged even in the colonial period by officials who did not expect an "*akela adami*" (single man) to perform well agriculturally, and considered his marriage a "valid necessity", and gave all incentives to men to get married.[40] The importance of women in agriculture has not only continued in the post-colonial period especially in the aftermath of the green revolution, it has even been enhanced for certain sections of them [Chowdhry: 1993].

At the same time, even after marriage, a man is still not fully considered a "man" till he has had an offspring, specially a son (same expectation as from a woman). One of the popular sayings is: "*beta hua jub janiye, jeeb pota khele baar*" (you can claim to have a son only when the grandson plays in your doorway). If a man is married but is without a child, it is certainly touted as a woman's fault or her barrenness rather than the man's inability. A barren woman is considered highly inauspicious [Chowdhry: 1986: 130-32, 138-41]. In fact the word "*banjh*" (barren) is used as an abuse, and generally a man is never considered infertile. Yet, there is some amount of ambiguity in fixing cultural responsibility on a man in case of childlessness. Rural males are well known to flock to sex clinics that promise them progeny, especially male progeny. This puts the onus on them, even though publicly it may well be the woman who is held responsible.

On the other hand, if married and with a child, but unemployed, he is still not masculine enough. The wife of one such youth in village Chhara, district Jhajjar, whispered confidentially: "Snide remarks or open taunts are all that my husband and I get. My husband does not say any thing and my in-laws do not allow anyone of us to speak." In the rural cultural milieu, masculinity is linked to the ability of a man to protect and materially support a family. An unemployed man is an emasculated one at best. Unmarried young men as well as those well past their youth are considered immature and likened to boys, who are not fully men, or in other words are "*namard*". It is a sexual insult and an abuse of a man to be considered sexually inadequate and/or immature. This de-sexualisation also challenges a man's bravery and courage [Marsh and Campbell: 1982]. Clearly, it is not only women but also men as well who find it difficult to live up to the stereotypes of a patriarchal setup.[41]

It may be underlined that in peasant societies, where the basic unit of production and consumption is the domestic group, the more you reproduce the more you produce. In such a situation unmarried men are an aberration and against the law of nature. The unmarried status of a man creates a lot of anguish and frustration in the family as well as in the individual. Although the "unmarried male" has existed historically, as referred to earlier, the status is still not considered healthy and marriage is perceived as linked in a major way to masculinity. There is clearly a great deal of unquiet and perturbation about marriage issues, which in turn makes unmarried men potentially inflammable.

Complicity of the Unemployed

As unemployed men, both unmarried and married, tend to be treated as "immature" who have not quite grown up, their voices and opinions are likely to be overlooked, unless they are in consonance with the dominant voice. Such men are likely to seek a masculine identity outside domestic life. The construction of a public masculinity is possible. In the rural areas it is possible through the community collective. The spectacle of an all-male *panchayat* (a public world of men where women are absent) puts the male power on public display. This traditional *panchayat* (I am using the word traditional *panchayat* to distinguish it from the statutory *gram panchayat* established in the early 1950s. Traditional *panchayat* incidentally is not a single *panchayat* but a set of *panchayats*) offers an opportunity to the unemployed unmarried men to demonstrate their masculinity under the surveillance of other men's approval in what may be described as "homosocial enactment" [Kimmel: 2001]. Men prove their manhood in the eyes of other men not necessarily through demonstration of wealth and other accomplishments, as suggested by Michael Kimmel (ibid), but by supporting/participating and implementing the decisions of the dominant caste male leadership who call the shots in the traditional *panchayat.*

Masculinity is established not only in relation to femininity but also in relation to the evaluation of male peers and male authority. Such cases call masculinity into question, as unemployed and unmarried men are more vulnerable to the charge of emasculation/effeminacy. The fear of taking a stand, which might humiliate or shame them in the eyes of other men, helps explain a great deal about the support offered to the dictates of a traditional *panchayat* in social matters. Such men are unlikely to take a confrontationist stand against their elders in social matters.

There are many reasons for this complicity. A large number of the unemployed are dependants. The dependence of the unemployed individuals and therefore vulnerability, both psychological as well as economic, imparts to them a heightened sensitivity to the family/community/public approval and loyalty to its dominant opinions. The unemployed are keen in not wanting to show themselves disloyal or "*namak haram*". An educated youth, for example, maintained that "since the elders control the purse string" it was "prudent" to toe the line rather than stand in opposition. The young in any case are not allowed to voice their opinion, especially in the *panchayat,* when any other older male member of the family is present. They are reprimanded, "Why do you speak when your father/elders are present?" In rural north India, age and experience is still prioritized and change is favouring the youth, but slowly. The decision of such a body, with the older generation monopolizing and directing its course, is projected and implemented as a unanimous decision democratically arrived. It is asserted as "*sab ka mat yo hi sai*" (we all are of the same opinion). The dissenters are dismissed as of "no importance".

Unemployed men opined that in case they venture to voice their opinion, the community, which may be generally sympathetic to them, comes down with a heavy hand. Public taunts are likely to follow to make them aware of their "inferior position". They are likely to be regarded as a "problem" and slotted into the stereo-typical categories of louts, troublemakers, loafers, wasters, drunkards, etc. The unemployed are frequent recipients of open criticism. Such criticism is devastating, as villagers, especially caste fellows, often know one another closely. As a result, the unemployed do not raise their voice against the upholders of tradition and caste-cultural norms, even if they do not approve. An unemployed son is likely to support his elders to earn for himself the epithet of a "good son" or an "obedient son" if not an employed one.

IV

Assertion: Bonding of the Marginalized

The support of unemployed/unmarried men to the working of the caste *panchayat* is conspicuous in matters dealing with the breach of marriage norms, like territorial and clan exogamy or caste endogamy. Such cases are mostly those of elopements and runaway marriages. These are highly sensitive issues and the caste *panchayats* have taken a hard, uncompromising and dictatorial line. As witnessed recently these *panchayats* have inflicted death penalty on "errant females" and/or their partners, have attempted to change conjugal relationship by turning legally wedded couples into brother and sister, compelled couples to divorce, humiliated them in public by blackening their faces, cutting off their hair, making them ride donkeys and beating them with shoes, to name just a few cases of extreme violence. In other cases, entire families and communities as a whole have been boycotted and expelled from the villages. In all these cases the caste *panchayats* have gone against all human rights and acted in violation of the law of the land. Under the law the introduction of modem concepts like adulthood and sanctity given to individual rights has turned the individual settlement of marriage between two consenting adults to be legitimate.[42] In other words, any legal restrictions on marriage of two consenting heterosexual adults are almost non-existent.[43] The legal position means that all decisions made by caste *panchayats* in relation to the alleged breach of marriage norms are illegal and unconstitutional.

The unemployed/unmarried male segment of Haryana society has been the major supporter and implementer of such decisions. Indeed, not being married and deprived of a "family life", with no "future" (no son/s) to issue the extension of name and lineage, socially and economically marginalized, the unemployed/unmarried men, are likely to see the transgression of marriage norms in a more problematic way. It has as much to do with the breach of caste and customary norms as with the patriarchal concern with masculinity. Knowing that they have the popular public opinion with them, they get overly anxious, verging on the belligerent, when traditional norms in marriage are breached or when other caste girls are sought to be brought in to their caste fold or even worse if their caste women marry across caste, class and status lines.

Many such alliances involve the members of the *dalit* community and form a significant category of their own. The split in the ranks of marginalized then becomes obvious. Subaltern men become a casualty of dominant masculinities, with caste emerging as an integral part of the dynamic between masculinities. The *dalits,* though totally marginalized, are not necessarily a part of the other marginalized, i.e, the unmarried/unemployed, drawn from among the dominant caste groups. Class and caste determine any bonding between them. Massive unemployment plays further havoc in their relationship, especially in relation to the institutionalized reserved category in jobs for *dalits* and now the other backward castes (OBCs).[44] Any liaison involving the *dalits* fuels the increasing resentment against them. The end result in such cases is particularly vicious and brutal. Consequently, on many occasions such marriage liaisons or runaway cases are made a pretext to settle wider issues by the dominant community, working through the *panchayat* and aided and abetted by its unemployed/unmarried fellow members [Chowdhry: unpublished].

The resultant violence stands justified. The disturbance of the social structure brought about by a breach of marriage norms provides it with a good enough rationale. Those who disturb it must be punished. This makes for a widespread acceptance of violence. In rural areas aggression and violence is closely related to leadership qualities and masculinity. Inflecting violence gives an opportunity to present "masculinity" before different audience. Marriage matters give the marginalized men an opportunity to prey upon other men who have failed to control their women's behaviour. Such men gain in "honour" by punishing the "dishonoured" men and women. A man is "dishonourable" or feminized as "weak" when his daughter elopes or is "stolen" by another man. The manifestation of violence by the unemployed/unmarried can be read as a desire to express power over others in a context of relative powerlessness. Exercise of power is equated with manhood. Both older men and younger ones want to be seen exercising it as much against women as against other men.

In this violence they have the full support and backing of the traditional caste leaders. There exists a workable bond between the two male segments: the unemployed/unmarried men and the traditional leadership drawn from the elderly male members of the village. The truly old may be inactive in the *panchayat* but they are there by virtue of the seniority of age and genealogical position in the lineage. This bonding between the "youth" and the "aged" defies understanding as the aged and the youth in Haryana do not enjoy an easy relationship. It is very often a conflictual one. The elderly, both men and women, are extremely critical of the youth. The rural young have rapidly adopted the consumerist practices visible in the lifestyle of the urban male population. In any case the rural-urban categories are overlapping categories in Haryana [Chowdhry: 1994]. The role model is set by the rural affluent (who are indistinguishable from their urban counterpart) and others emulate their conspicuous consumption. In the rural areas, consumerism has meant new standards of behaviour and lifestyle, new ways of spending time and money. In this, the consumption of liquor features prominently. Its intake is enormous and growing. Alcoholism is rampant in Haryana especially among its unemployed, school and college students, teachers and army men.[45] Within this the unemployed men indulge in it more than others. With no regular source of income and without any regular job, most, with some exception, have been swept away by a wave of lumpenisation. As one woman put it: "*kaam dham to hai na eeb ladke sab piyen sain aur badmashi karen sain*" (unemployed boys have time to get drunk and be troublemakers). Disagreements over lifestyle and rampant consumerism frequently result in the kind of confrontation between parents and adult male children that generally would not have been expressed in the past. A frequent refrain heard repeatedly is: "*ladke haath se nikal gaye*" (the boys are out of one's control).

These changes are not superficial; they are structural and value changes about people and relationships leading to intergenerational conflict. It has had the effect of exacerbating the existing unease between the older and the younger generation and in fact pitted them against each other not merely within the family but also outside the family. Such anxiety and concern was voiced in January 2003 in the "*sarv khap*" *panchayat* (of 38 *khaps)*, in village Wazirabad, Gurgaon; it was well represented by 2,260 villages. They ascribed it to the modernisation process. The path to development and modernization is erroneously considered as synonymous with westernization.

With the antipathy and generation gap in Haryana noticeably visible even to a causal visitor, what is it that brings the elderly and the youth especially among the unmarried/unemployed together?

The answer lies in marginalisation and diminished masculinity experienced by these male segments. With the gradual decline of the provider's role, ageing and later life has also come to be associated with a subordinate form of masculinity [Varley and Blasco: 2001]. The term "elderly" or the "aged" however is not very precise, as the ageing experience shows gender and class differences.[46] Also a large number among the Indian population may not really know their ages. As an age group, the so-called "the aged" has been defined as persons who have completed 60 years and more.

According to the all-India data available, 85 per cent of the aged rural males (60 and above) are declared to be heads of their households.[47] However, it is more likely that the effective control of the aged on household resources might be less than indicated by the report. However, accurate data on the "real heads of households" in terms of decision-making within the household are difficult to come by. How much power the elderly are able to command in these households remains an open question. All groups of population have elderly people who have little status and power. Any time, by a rough estimate, about half of the aged are fully dependent on others or only partly dependent.

With age, men suffer in prestige, as they are unable to establish a new role for themselves at home or outside. They openly speak of the underlying tension inherent in the family system, ranging from seeking and giving advice in keeping with a sense of self-esteem, and control over family resources, in the face of their declining ability to contribute materially to the family's subsistence. The traditional advisory role of the elderly is also greatly diluted, if not altogether lost in the aftermath of the green revolution. The increase in the level of agricultural technology, control of machines and contact with the outside world, decisions with regard to disposal of grain, its timing, location, price and persons or agencies to whom it has to be sold, taking and re-payment of bank loans, are well beyond the capacity of the elderly. A majority of them are illiterate, as they belong to a period when schools and education was limited.

Importantly, post-colonial India has witnessed a considerable erosion of the traditional power base of the caste leadership due to the introduction of different state structures, such as the elected statutory *panchayat* (since 1950) and election mechanism, based upon equal citizenship and adult franchise. The statutory *panchayat*, which has become the focus of political life of the village, has thrown up much younger, new socially mixed groups, in many cases drawing substantial representation from the lower social strata. A 1985 study of the leadership of the statutory *panchayats* in Haryana shows 77.5 per cent of *panchayat* members are below 50 years [Singh 1985:39]. Only 12.7 per cent are from the age group 51-60 years and 9.8 per cent above 60 years of age. This suggests a perceptible shift of power to the younger men in rural Haryana, belonging to different castes and class categories. They are elected officers of the *gram panchayat*, exercising statutory power, or the local administrators who along with bureaucracy and police constitute the formal structure in post-colonial India. There may be a variety of reasons behind this phenomenon,[48] but the moot point is that age, which was an important factor of dominance in the past, is losing its significance as a criterion for selection of village leadership. This has caused a lot of heart burning among the elderly, created a great deal of insecurity and widened the generation gap. A contemporary review of the decisions taken by the traditional *panchayat* leadership shows that the vocal and self-appointed people among the older generation drawn from among the dominant caste group do not fulfil any role in the authority structure.

It is only when these marginalized aged act in a *panchayat* or in some semi-official capacity that they can be said to have authority. The traditional *panchayat* offers them a way to consolidate and legitimize their positions and control over certain processes. It provides them with an open venue to become prominent personalities and emerge as upholders of what constitutes the village norms, its customary and cultural practices, as well as stand as guardians of public morality. Checkmated in certain spheres, this generation wants to retain its hold over certain matters-marriage and morality is one such domain.

The anxiety to maintain this domain is in its essence connected with the wider male concern with the upkeep of patrilineal inheritance. The Hindu Succession Act, 1956, by enabling daughter, sister, widow and mother to inherit land with full proprietary rights to its disposal, introduced enormous insecurities among the male populace [Chowdhry: 1997, 1993a]. The only ideal and "*izzatwala*" (honourable) pattern of inheritance is acknowledged to be by males from males. This means basically that daughters and sisters who are potential introducers of fresh blood and new descent lines through their husbands are to be kept from exercising their inheritance rights to ensure a patrilineal inheritance on which the "honour" and "unity" of the village is based. Thus tightening controls over marriage is a popular "masculine matter", worthy of support, an issue over which all men, notwithstanding differences of caste, class, creed and age, are united.

Factionalism in the Village

Notably, the village unity, a wholly utopian unity of yore, stands acknowledgely fragmented in post-colonial India. The pressures exercised by unprecedented expansion of participation through adult franchise, competitive elections and state intervention has sharpened the cleavages on caste and status considerations on the one hand and polarized villages into fluid cross-caste factions on the other. Politicization of village India is a fact. Existing factionalism and litigation in the villages feed into unstable political conditions, fragmenting it more. Growing conflict over caste, community and land has become an important aspect of rural politics in India. This fragmentation has meant that no particular group has been or can be in a position to speak for the whole village or for the entire membership of a particular community. Yet the intervention of the traditional *panchayat* in social field on the basis of preserving certain values of village life-its culture, customary practices has the effect of closing ranks. Such an attempt imposes a temporary "*aika*" through a fragile cohesion on what has been and continues to be a highly fragmented village life. The political labels are obliterated to impart a non-partisan a political look to the "*panchas*".

In matters other than those related to village culture and tradition, the traditional *panchayat* may or may not be effective, for example, in matters relating to land use or other material resources which frequently erupt into conflicts. In such cases, the traditional *panchayat's* decisions are often challenged because there is a clear division or factionalism in the village, and the aggrieved party, egged on by others as the economic stakes are high, is quick to move the court. But in cases involving village honour, culture and tradition and its breach by individuals, a united front is maintained. All dissidence is silenced by the show of unity achieved by threatening the isolation of the dissident/s or through use of force, if necessary.

In the changing scenario, the traditional leadership of the village bigwigs derived from the ranks of those born to power and prestige is pushed to the margins of power structure, much the same as the unmarried/unemployed men. These two segments, with doubts around their masculinity and value to society, join hands to empower each other, the former by giving decisive though biased leadership and the latter by supporting and implementing their illegal decisions. It represents a direct attempt at shrugging off their diminished and devalued masculinity and assertion of power by both the segments.

In many such instances of intervention, it is this unemployed single/unmarried segment who constitute an important circle of support to the *panchayat's* decision. Headed by the youth among them they are the first to protest and the elders follow later. In village Jondhi, for example, the caste *panchayat* that attempted to turn in July 2000 a legally wedded couple with a one-and-a-half-year-old child into brother and sister, it was a section of youth male population who first took an openly belligerent stand.[49] They were the ones who physically barred them from entering the village or their houses. They were the ones who kept a vigil on their families to stop any social interaction between them and the villagers. This attempt at forcibly changing a conjugal relationship was repeated more recently in 2004 in village Asanda. In the Jondhi case the victimized woman in question and onlookers described this section of unemployed, unmarried men as "*tamashbeen*" (idlers or curious onlookers). According to her and others, this section was most vocal in supporting the controversial decision of the *panchayat*. The employed, they opined, have no time for such matters.[50] This is not to say that the employed do not share their opinion or do not support the *panchayat*. They do.

V

Solving Single Status-hood

'Marriage' of Sorts

The situation delineated above shows men and masculinities in crisis in Haryana. This picture gets complicated with the surfacing of highly "dubious marriages". For lower class unemployed men, ranked low in the local marriage market the demographic pressure and social shifts have resulted in a dramatic increase in the highly contentious practice of "purchase of woman". Unable to find a wife locally, some of these men have taken recourse to purchasing women from other regions. With this region's emphasis upon observing caste endogamy in marriage, how are such alliances looked at? Are they able to restore or provide some succour to the diminished masculine status experienced by these men? How does the local populace look upon this practice? The answers throw up a highly regressive and exploitative social situation that has further complicated the masculine status of the men involved. This practice is however not something new. The British had recorded such a practice in the colonial period as "purchase of brides".[51] The payment of "bride price" was, however, considered "a low caste practice" both in the colonial and pre-colonial period. In the contemporary period those very caste groups that had condemned and denigrated this practice earlier are reviving it, perhaps in a different form.

There has always been a very thin line between purchase of a woman as a wife or a concubine. In the present context these women are not necessarily "wives" in the strict sense of the term. They occupy an unrecognized and indefinable status in contemporary Haryana. Brought or bought from poor families by "*dalals*" (touts), whose modus operandi remains unknown and unexplored, these women are mostly purchased by the lower class males who have not been able to get married on account of a variety of reasons: health, disability, age, poverty and unemployment. For some of the men it is a secondary marriage and not a primary one. Such a marriage has been traditionally allowed. These young females, with ages ranging from 10 onwards, hail from places like Orissa, Bengal, Mizoram, Assam, Bihar and Nepal.

Most of these purchased women do not even know the language or participate in any of the cultural activities of this region. With severely limited or even non-existing communication, these women are isolated and experience an extreme sense of alienation from the families they are supposed to belong. Many of them even physically live on the periphery, or in the "*khet*" (fields) of their "owner". The other women of the family, who have come through a proper ritual wedding and a dowry, refuse to give them any recognition. Not incorporated fully into the rural household, the "married" status of these women remains highly ambiguous. Although some of them even have their "marriage photo-graph", showing the couple with garlands around their necks, it is clear that no ritual wedding has ever taken place. They are not allowed to visit their families or keep in touch with them in any way. The so-called husband does not keep any relationship or even contact with the "wife-givers" and relationship between "in-laws" is non-existent. Instead, their purchase price is openly flaunted. Not more than bonded labour, they are subjected to extensive exploitation of all kinds. In case they wish to flee or make an attempt to contact their families they are told in no uncertain terms that the money spent on them must be recompensed, before claiming their freedom. Such dubious marriages can hardly afford a 'status' to the men concerned or resolve the contradictions faced by men in relation to their masculinity.

Yet, this social solution to the problem faced by the growing numbers of single status men in Haryana has widespread approval. It is ironic that a society given to inflicting extreme violence upon their own youth who breach customary norms of marriage by bringing in local women of other caste groups "permit" women from different regions and castes.[52] They are in fact given to encouraging such liaisons/ associations as a matter of necessity. Also it may be remembered that it is the men who are breaking the norms not women. Women are not given in marriage to men of other caste groups. However, even for men such an arrangement has limited and uncertain validity. Such men are not held at par with other married men. The legal status of such marriages is suspect. Such men remain with devalued masculinity for seeking an association with a woman of uncertain origins and caste. Such an association, borne of necessity does nothing to enhance the man's marital and social status, or give a boost to his masculinity, although it does fulfill the other physical and labour requirements of the owner. The dominant opinion of both men and women is given to rationalizing this association, which is calculated in terms of money spent on the purchase of such women. This expenditure, they opine, must be honoured. Some women who find it difficult to adjust or manage the extreme hard work involving the household, animals and the fields are even resold to defray the cost they have incurred. Yet others change hands several times. Clearly, the problem is multifaceted.

The state government is not willing to recognize this problem, much less tackle it. For them it is a non-issue. Perhaps taking a cue from the dominant opinion based upon ground situation, the Haryana government's "*Mahila Ayog*" (Women's Commission) has shockingly declared this practice to be "beneficial" for both men and women. "The men get wives and the women get food, clothing and shelter", they opine. "What is then the problem?" they inquire.[53] The problem continues to grow. Although there are no figures available, a rough estimate puts two to three cases of such "marriages" in each village of Haryana.[54]

Meanwhile, the first generation of these unacknowledged and illegal unions has started to surface.[55] It is doubtful if these women or their children would be able to prove that the marriage had taken place. The legal difficulty of proving a marriage is well known.[56] In many instances fatherhood is denied as men in the family have a free access to the purchased woman who may technically be called the property of just one of them or may be "wife" of one of them. Even if some of these children were to be acknowledged, they may still fall short of social recognition and acceptance. For children having a mother of uncertain social and caste background can become a hindrance in more ways than one. This was amply clear in the colonial period that shows the importance given to the caste and status hierarchies even of the male child. In the years to come, the children born of such liaisons are going to be a major source of tension and conflict when the question of their inheritance rights comes up. Also, amidst a rapidly changing social scenario of escalating land prices, fragmentation of landholdings, population growth, severe unemployment and inheritance rights granted to women, the customary practice observed by the community (at best a selective appropriation) of giving recognition to the children born out of wedlock may not come to the aid of such children. Claims to and appropriation of tradition is after all highly selective. The inability of such "marriages" to do anything towards uplifting the status of men is substantiated by the lack of recognition for the offspring of such alliances. The growing cases of such "marriages" are already creating major social and sociological problems for a society undergoing rapid changes. Apart from accentuating dominant and subordinate masculinities in the private and public spheres, it also has singularly negative effect on gender relations.

VI

Conclusion

The unmarried, unemployed and the aged are recognized by the ruling class and the politicians of different hues as politically, highly troublesome categories. Although no solutions are in sight for their problems, these categories have been used for mobilization and their concerns as election strategies. For example, the promise to provide a "solution" to the unmarried status of young men in Haryana was used as an election strategy in 2003-04 *Lok Sabha* elections in the state. The then Chief Minister, Om Prakash Chautala said in a public meeting in village Nanheda of district Panipat, "If there are boys of marriageable age in the village, do not worry. To get these boys married is my responsibility now. You only put your stamp on my election symbol, the spectacle."[58] This was certainly recognition of sorts, of the enormity of the problem. But the fact that it is crucially linked up with the demographic pressure and the wider political economy remains to be officially acknowledged or recognized. The societal attempt at solving this problem by entering into highly dubious marriages by purchasing women is wrecking widespread havoc and unimaginable levels of violence and exploitation in rural areas. Similarly, the issue of unemployment and promises to tackle it has figured in the election manifestos of all political parties for the February 2005 assembly elections in Haryana.[59] The categories of the unmarried/unemployed are both in contradiction and at connivance with the traditional leadership and the ageing population of this region. From 6,19,027 in 1981, the aged, i.e, 60 and above (both men and women), have more than doubled in 10 years. In 1991 they stood at 12,75,731, and formed roughly 15 per cent of the total adult population of the province.[60] A large number of them live in the rural areas, which has far more "aged population" than the urban areas.[61] The importance of their numbers as a possible vote bank can be made out from the fact that Devi Lal government in 1987 started a pension scheme for those above 60 years of age, under which they were to be given Rs. 100 per month. His son and the then Chief Minister, Om Prakash Chautala subsequently raised this to Rs. 200 per month. There were plans to raise it further.[62]

Despite the wooing by different political parties, the basic problems of all these categories of people are not being addressed. Consequently, all of them continue to experience diminished masculinity, powerlessness and marginalisation. Despite their devalued masculinities, such men are in a continuous process of strategizing to shape their relations with others. Their united attempts to assert themselves through the exclusive male preserve of the caste *panchayats*, in crucial social matters relating to village and caste customs, has led to the strengthening of highly regressive and illegal trends in society. Although their actions have challenged and subverted the authority of the state, the latter and its functionaries stand as mute onlookers, unable and unwilling to intervene. In their success and failure these marginalized categories despite the question mark around their masculinities, constitute a highly combustive material in society.

Notes

1 Out of a population of 39,70,390 males, a total of 1,43,897 males in the age group of 15-44 years are unmarried. See Census of Haryana, 1991, Socio-Cultural Tables, series 8, Pt IV-A, Series C, pp. 22-23. Legally, the minimum age of marriage for men is 21 years. However, locally, "marriage age" is highly flexible. For men it is calculated from what is considered to be the "reproductive age", which is put at 15 years.

2. In Rohtak, out of a total male population of 9,77,075 (between the age group of 15-44), 5,47,922 were unmarried. Ibid.

3. For details of these factors see Jonathan P. Parry, *Caste and Kinship in Kangra,* New Delhi: Vikas Publishing House, pp. 237-46.

4. Sex-ratio of females per thousand males in Haryana from 1881-1951 was as follows: 1881-85: 866; 1886-90: 868; 1891-95: 898; 1896-1900: 914; 1901: 867; 1911: 835; 1921: 844; 1931: 844; 1941: 869; 1951: 871. Source: Figures for 1881-1900 are for the undivided Punjab, *Census of India, Punjab,* 1931, Vol. XVII, part I, report, p. 152; figures for 1901-1951 taken from *Census of India,* 1991, India Series India-I. Paper I of 1991, Provisional Population Tables, Registrar-General and Census Commissioner, India, New Delhi, 1991, p. 76.

5. *Dainik Bhaskar* (daily newspaper in Hindi), April 18, 2001, p. I. Also see March 28, 2001, p. 2.

6. *Dainik Bhaskar,* December 7, 2000, p. 3.

7. *Dainik Bhaskar.* December 18, 2000, p. 2.
8. It may also be pointed out here that in the opinion of many ruralites the demand for dowry is not being vocalised so openly as earlier in view of the difficulties currently being faced in procuring a bride. Yet, expectations have not diminished. The high premium placed on a girl's marriage ensures it. These expectations are more so among the employed.
9. Interview, Ajay Kumar, village Dobaldhan, district Jhajjar, December 3, 2000.
10. The male age of marriage is calculated to be in the 25-29 age group as compared to females, majority of whom get married between 10 and 24 years of age. *Census of Haryana, 1981,* Series 6, Part XII, pp. 52-53.
11. Communication from Jagmati Sangwan, Rohtak.
12. *The Hindu* (daily newspaper in English), September 28, 2003, p. 5.
13. Government of Haryana, *Statistical Abstract of Haryana, 1999-2000.*Chandigarh, Economic and Statistical Organisation, Planning Department, 2001, pp. 530-31.
14. A current joke going around speaks of an old man who goes to a government office with an appointment letter. He looks very dejected. When asked as to why he should not be rejoicing he answered: "I got registered in the employment exchange 40 years ago. I have got this letter now. There are only two days left for my retirement".
15. See letter to the editor in *Dainik Jagran* (daily newspaper in Hindi), Sepember 14, 2003, p. 5.
16. *Dainik Bhaskar,* August 23, 2000, p. 2. Commenting upon the reigning corruption in police recruitment drive, Bansi Lal, the former Chief Minister of Haryana, stated in a public meeting that the forms for such recruitment were not available free but had to be purchased after a payment of Rs. 500. See *Dainik Jagran,* December 20, 2002, p. 7.
17. Interview, Ajay Kumar, village Dobaldhan, district Jhajjar, December 3, 2000.
18. Out of the total numbers of educated unemployed, there were 3,90,902 who had passed class 10; 99,796 were above matric but below BA; 92,467 were BA; 13,733 were MA and Ph D. See Economic Survey of Haryana, 2002-03, cited in *Dainik Jagran,* March 18, 2003, p. 4.
19. As Haryana has a lot of private capital being invested in private schools, this is sought to be corrected now. So much so that Haryana is considered to have the fastest growing business in schools, preferably English medium. See Shekhar Gupts's comments, 'Writings on the wall' in *The Indian Express* (daily newspaper in English), June 7, 2003, p. 8.
20. So widespread is the epidemic of "*nakkal*" in Haryana that Brigadier O.P. Chander, Chairman, Haryana School Examination Board, recommended in August 2003 the use of the "Indian army to stop cheating in examination". According to him, this widespread practice had "broken all bounds and refused to be curbed". See editorial in *Dainik Jagran,* August 21, 2003, p. 8.
21. A lot of this has to do with a stable monthly income, power and patronage as well as the scope it provides for illegal gratification. To these may be added the changing lifestyle and consumerist culture available in the cities that are extremely attractive to the youth.

22 In terms of percentage this decline was as follows: 77.1 in 1983 to 77.7 in 1993-94 to 68.4 in 1999-2000. See G.K. Chaddha and P.P. Salve, 'Post-Reform Setbacks in Rural

Employment: Issues That Need Further Scrutiny', *Economic and Political Weekly,* May 25, 2002:38:21:1998-2026. Only trade and commerce has gained from 22.75 per cent in 1981 to 27.98 per cent in 1991.

23. For details see G.S. Bhalla, *Nehru and the Indian Peasantry,* Nehru Memorial Museum and Library, New Delhi, 2003.
24. *Statistical Abstract.* 1999-2000, p. 59.
25. For extensive urbanisation of Haryana, see Sheila Bhalla, 'Islands of Growth', pp. 1022-1030.
26. The industrialists consider the migrant labour docile and hence controllable. The locals are perceived to be reluctant workers given to making a lot of mischief because of their wider linkages with their communities in the villages. The only way the locals can avail of these jobs is by getting false affidavits and certificates from UP or Bihar. Communication from Rakhi Sehgal, currently working on problems of labour and industrilisation of Gurgaon.
27. *Dainik Jagran,* July 5, 2004, p. 17.
28. The increasing number of letters to the editor on the problem of unemployment is significant in this respect. See for example, *Dainik Jagran,* June 13, 2004, p. 18.
29. O.P. Chautala, the then Chief Minister of Haryana in a public speech in Rewari. See *Dainik Jagran,* September 16, 2002, pp. I, 13. In the recent assembly elections in February 2005, Chautala, speaking in a public rally in village Narwana, went to the extent of promising a job even to the "the child in the womb". He said: *'jo tumhari lugai ke pet mein bachcha hai use bhi main naukri doonga'* (I shall give a job even to the child in your wife's womb). Also reported in *The Indian Express,* February 2, 2005, p. 7.

30 *Dainik Jagran,* December 11, 2002, pp. I, 13.

31. *The Indian Express,* June 2, 2002, p. 13.
32. *Dainik Jagran,* April 27, 2003, p. 18.
33. This is especially visible in Haryana's recent past. During the days of prohibition introduced by the then Chief Minister Bansi Lal, a very large number of the youth took to bootlegging and enjoyed enormous prosperity. Within a year this prohibition had to be lifted. Used to a certain standard of living and behaviour,and to make an easy living the vast numbers of earlier bootleggers took to other crimes like stealing, kidnapping, etc.
34. Interview, Umed Singh Shaukeen, village Chhavala, Delhi, August 24, 2002.
35. *Dainik Tribune,* August 25, 2000, pp. I, 9.
36. This emerges from the fieldwork as well as the media reports. In Jind for instance "a middle aged" man committed suicide because he was unmarried. See *Dainik Jagran,* March 26, 2003, p. 5.
37. *Dainik Tribune* (daily newspaper in Hindi), September 5, 2000, p. 4.
38. For instance see *Dainik Tribune,* November 6, 2000, p. 5.
39. For details of work which women, specially married women, performed see Prem Chowdhry, 'Customs in a Peasant Economy: Women in Colonial Haryana' pp.302-36 in Kumkum Sangari and Sudesh Vaid (eds), 1989. *Recasting Women: Essays in Colonial History,* New Delhi: Kali for Women.

40. Recognising the importance of a wife for an agriculturist, they even gave legal sanction to the sale of ancestral immovable property for the purchase of a wife. There are several cases that can be cited. See for instance *Punjab Records,* Lahore, W.E. Ball, 1910, Vol. XLV, Asa Rani vs Sawan Singh, pp. 232-34; *Indian Cases,* Lahore, Law Publishing Press, 1927, Vol 99, Gujjar Singh vs Kehar Singh, pp. 619-20; *All India Reporter,* Lahore Series, Nagpur, V.V. Chitaley, 1929, Piru vs Dila Ram, p. 377, 1931, Bhan Singh vs Ram Singh, pp. 559-600.
41. A 2001 documentary film by Rahul Roy called "Majma" makes a note of the fact that patriarchy oppresses men too.
42. See Hindu Marriage Act in Sunderlal T. Desai, 1966. *Mulla Principles of Hindu Law,* Bombay: N.M. Tripathi Pvt. Ltd., pp. 599-751.
43. Certain persons however could not marry under this act: those related *assapinda* (shared body relationship), unless the custom or usage governing them permitted marriage, those with a living spouse or those of unsound mind, suffering from mental disorder and incapable of giving consent and those subject to recurrent attacks of insanity and epilepsy.
44. Despite the limited growth in education,the enormous increase in the number of educated unemployed in Haryana has meant a great deal of competition for the existing jobs, making even the petty jobs attractive. The intense competition provided by limited jobs offered (especially in the lower class categories) by the local district and state administration, has led to isolation and targeting of the reserved posts for the scheduled castes (SCs) and the other backward castes (OBCs) under the implementation of the Mandal Commission Report in 1994 which are blamed for limiting the jobs for others. It evoked huge protests and violence in Haryana among the upper caste groups, comprising the dominant landowning caste groups like the Jats, Rajputs, and others as also the trading and business castes like the Banias and Brahmins. The agitation was used to demand abolition of reservations altogether. Contradictorily, while condemning reservations, the dominant Jats of Haryana have demanded to be included among the OBCs like in Rajasthan and Delhi.
45. It is an open secret that school-going boys even below the age of 15 readily purchase and consume liquor at their will. The declining age group of alcohol consumers is a constant worry among the Haryana populace. This can be evidenced in the resolutions of the *gram panchayats* demanding prohibition in their territorial limits, as well as in the fact that this menace has provided a basis for periodic bout of anti-alcohol agitation spearheaded by women. The rampant consumption of liquor in Haryana has changed "*des me des Haryana, jit dood dahi ka khanna*" (Hail Haryana, a place of milk and curds) in to "*des me des Haryana, jit jagah jagah ban gaya daaru khaanna*" (Hail Haryana, where flows liquor at every place).
46. For similar reservations regarding the definition of the word "aged" and the overstatement in the number of proportion of the aged, see Pravin Visaria, 'Demogrphies of Ageing in India', (II) *Economic and Political Weekly:* 2001: 36:23: 2081-87.
47. *Dainik Jagran,* July 22, 2001, p. 2.
48. The upper hand of youngsters in rural leadership may be explained by the fact that elections may not suit the temperament of the old traditional leaders. It requires hectic election campaigning and requesting for votes to persons of lower castes and of lower status. Secondly, the traditional leaders may feel it below their prestige to contest

against the youngsters. Thirdly, the apprehension of loss of traditional prestige due to possible defeat in the election may also be an important reason. Ibid.

49. See a full analysis of this case in Prem Chowdhry, 'Caste Panchayats and the Policing of Marriage in Haryana: Enforcing Kinship and Territorial Exogamy', *Contributions to Indian Sociology:* January-August: 2004: 1-42.
50. In such situations, they (the employed) were either out to their respective works or otherwise occupied. Significantly, in village Jondhi, within a span of two weeks, eight meetings of the committee appointed by the panchayat and three meetings of the panchayat were held to come to grips with the problem.
51. See note 46.
52. According to Ravinder Kaur, such women are treated as "foreign" women. And, as their origins, social and economic status is ambiguous, it is measured with a different measuring rod. The non-local status of the woman, according to her, impacts the local standing of the family much less than if the woman had been a local one. See her "Across-region marriages: Poverty, female migration and the sex ratio", *Economic and Political Weekly:* 2004: 39:25: 2595-2603.
53. Communication from Manjeet Rathee, Rohtak.
54. Communication from R.S. Dahiya, an associate professor of surgery and an activist, Rohtak. According to him villages like Baliyana, Bahu Akbarpu in district Rohtak and Bhadtana in district Jind have as many as 10 such women who have come from different regions.
55. Ravinder Kaur in her article discuses certain across-region and across-caste marriage cases that go back 20 years. The woman in question is accepted by the society as a wife and a mother and now a mother-in-law. This full incorporation into the family and society needs to be further investigated before such cases can be clubbed together with lower class alliances that fall in to an altogether different category. Such cases are rapidly coming to surface in Haryana. See her' Across-Region Marriages', pp. 2595-2603.
56. According to Menski, simple marriage rituals may be denied recognition by Indian courts at any time, especially in view of the fact that "*saptapadi*" and "*homa*" (ritual sacrifices into the sacred fire offered at the time of marriage, including seven circumbulations of the fire), are essential ceremonies for all Hindu marriages. See Werner F Menski, *Modem Indian Family* Law, Surrey, UK, Curzon, 2001, pp. 9-46.
57. This is amply argued out in the still to be published work of the author.
58. *Dainik Jagran.* December 8, 2003, p. 5.
59. See for example *Hindu.* January 18, 2005.
60. *Statistical Abstract* of *Haryana,* 1999-2000, p. 64.
61. In district Gurgaon alone there were 57,545 aged who were getting their old age pension. *Dainik Jagran,* July 22, 2001, p. 2.
62. More privileges for the aged, at least for the men among them, have been on the cards. For instance, the Chautala government had plans to build an old age home in every village "to honour the old as they are heads of our families'. Notably, these old homes were conceived essentially for men, where, as officially stated, they could "smoke *hooka*, play cards, sit and chat".

References

Bhalla, Sheila. 198l. 'Islands of Growth: A Note on Haryana Experience and Possible Implications'. *Economic and Political Weekly:* June 6: 16:23: 1022-30.

Chopra, Radhika. 2004. 'Encountering Masculinity: An Ethnographer's Dilemma' pp. 36-59 in Radhika Chopra, Caroline Osella and Filippo Osella (eds), *South Asian Maculinities: Context of Change, Sites of Continuity.* New Delhi: Women Unlimited.

Chowdhry, Prem. 1986.'The Advantage of Backwardness: Colonial Policy and Agriculture in Haryana'.*Indian Economic and Social History Review:* 23: 3: 264-88.

Chowdhry, Prem. 1993. 'High Participation and Low Evaluation: Women and Work in a Green Revolution Province in India (Haryana)', *Economic and Political Weekly:* December 25:28: A35- 48.

Chowdhry, Prem. 1993a. 'Conjugality, Law and State: Inheritance Rights as Pivot of Control in Northern India', *National Law School Journal,* Special issue on Feminism and Law, 1993: 95-116.

Chowdhry, Prem. 1994. *The Veiled Women: Shifting Gender Equations in Rural Haryana-1880-1990.*New Delhi: OUP: 388-90.

Chowdhry, Prem. 1997. 'A Matter of Two Shares: A Daughter's Claim to Patrilineal Property in Rural North India', *The Economic and Social History Review:* July-September: 34: 3:289-20.

Chowdhry, Prem. unpublished. 'First Our Jobs Then Our Girls': The Dominant Caste Perceptions on the 'Rising' Dalits.

Kensington, A. 1893. *Customary Law of the Ambala District,* Vol. X, Civil and Military Gazette, Lahore, p. 160.

Kimmel, Michael S. 2001.'Masculinity as Homophobia: Fear, Shame and Silence in the Construction of Gender Identity' pp. 266-87 in Stephen M. Whitehead and Frank J. Barrett (eds), The *Masculinitie of Reader,* Cambridge: Polity.

Marsh, Peter and Ann Campbell. (eds). 1982. *Aggression and Violence* Oxford: Basil Blackwell: pp. 145-46.

Morgan, David H.J. 1992. *Discovering Men,* London and New York: Routledge: pp. 96-97.

Singh, Hargian.1985. *Panchayati Raj Administration* in *Haryana,* Gurgaon: Indira Publications: p. 39.

Varley, Ann and Maribel Blasco. 2001. 'Exiled to the Home: Masculinity and Aging in Urban Mexico' pp. 15-38 in Cecil Jackson (ed.), *Men at Work:Our Masculinities, Development.* London: Frank Cass.

The paper was first published in the *Economic and Political Weekly*: 40:49: 2005: 5189-99.It is included here with the prior permission of the author and Editor, *Economic and Political Weekly*.Address for email correspondence: premchowdhry@vsnl.net

Chapter - Four

From Violence to Supportive Practice: Family, Gender and Masculinities

Radhika Chopra

I

Introduction

Gender studies, gender theory and gendered interventions have always been arenas inhabited by women. It is lives and the contexts of women's material and social conditions that provide key issues for research and interventions. One of the critical concerns of gender studies is the issue of women's agency and autonomy. While feminist writing and research has established the fact that women are not passive subjects, but are agents and subjects in their own lives, their agency and subjectivities are not fixed or absolute. Neither is women's agency wholly recognized. A great deal of attention has been paid to the unacknowledged nature and 'subterranean' existence of women's subjective agency, as well as to the way that these subjectivities need to 'surface' through a discourse of rights, claims and entitlements. Some feminist theorists have insisted that agency cannot only be understood as an exercise of volition in the abstract. Martha Nussbaum has, for example, argued that the exercise of agency is a human right [Nussbaum: 2000]. Further, it has been asserted that both agency and human rights have a location in material conditions of everyday life such as access to health, adequate nutrition, education, income, safety and other indices of human development. Thus, agency as an issue has to address the horizons within which it is articulated and realized as a political and substantive position.

None of these material conditions of autonomy or agency are produced outside of social relations that give shape to human existence. Social relations create conditions of survival and relations of deprivations or entitlements. The politics of gender and feminist research have outlined the deprivations and unequal entitlements in the lives of women. It is precisely this frame of women's agentic positions located within material conditions of existence that has also produced the view that understanding women's lives is incomplete without looking at their everyday locations within families that must, of necessity, include relations with men.

It is the conceptualization of the material world producing conditions for the exercise of volition that gives us a way of entering the debates around entitlement and deprivation. Entitlement and deprivation can be thought of as absolute concepts. There is no denying the absolute deprivation of nutrition during food scarcity conditions, for example. At the same time, it is important to recognize that entitlement or deprivation are not only about absolute access or loss of some object, like money, medicine or safe streets; they are also entitlements vis-à-vis someone else, in relation to some other person or sets of people. Within households, not every member has equal rights and entitlements to food or health. There is enough evidence to demonstrate the unequal gendered distribution of critical resources, an inequality that is weighed against women. When gender is combined with age, or with caste, then the question of entitlements and deprivation becomes part of a politics of distribution, a relational politics shaped and sustained by cultures of deprivation.

It is clear that entitlement and deprivation are related to each other. The next question therefore is whether all conditions of entitlement and therefore *all entitlements* translate equally and exactly across all cultural and political locations. If we take the social and cultural unit of the household as an object of analysis, it has been adequately demonstrated that men have greater entitlements to household resources, like food. Does this entitlement and access remain true for men across all household contexts? If an individual man works as a domestic labourer in households and with families other than his own, does the fact of his gender and entitlements associated with his gender 'move' with him, from his own home into the homes of others? Are both families and households identical in terms of the way in which he can translate his entitlements, define his power and articulate his subject positions? How does a person negotiate and experience entitlement within different households? How do culture and power become critical sites that define deprivation and animate agency when located within contexts of unequal distributions?

Aspects of class enter to divide a household and family along lines of entitlement and deprivation. The household is an arena of political divisions along fractured lines of deprivation. However, the fact that households are part of different social, cultural and class locations impels us to reopen the issue of how men's entitlements are to be understood and evaluated. The *experience* of being male needs to be placed within these questions and masculinity as an identity has to be understood as a complex negotiation between gender, class and power.

Outlining deprivation has produced another dynamic: the need to redress unequal distribution. This redressal is part of a politics that seeks to 'enter' households and rework inequality and gender imbalances through what has been termed gender intervention and gender sensitization. The interesting point about this politics of entry is that it moves along a terrain of materiality in effect: it seeks to address the issues of power and deprivation by looking at health availability, food access, educational assistance, safe work spaces, equal pay, and so on. Thus for example, the provision of micro-credit has sought to provide women with the means to secure livelihoods for themselves and their families. Micro credit enters the house through a material path-loans and skill formation but its translation into household dynamics and household micro-politics expands the loan beyond the monetary. Micro credit provisions gender relations by expanding the role and attributes of the breadwinner, displacing the role away from the male household head to include women (and sometimes, younger men and children).

In part the politics of entry seeks to change material conditions within households. Simultaneously it seeks to encourage the emergence of a form of domestic democracy. The efforts of this entry, via programmes of intervention, are geared towards persuading the 'entitled' members-mainly the men to play a more supportive role in the lives of their more deprived partners-mainly the women, but also children. Men-as-supportive-partners campaigns undertaken after the 1994 International Conference on Population and Development, Cairo and the 1995 United Nations Fourth World Conference on Women, Beijing, or the Men-in-Maternity programmes of the Population Council [Caleb, et al: 2002] focus primarily on involving men in reproductive healthcare.[1] However, both the Conference agendas and the Population Council programmes focus primarily on a single category of men in households-husbands. The campaigns also focus primarily on one category of women-wives in the reproductive phase of their lives. Within the focused terms of these campaigns husbands are being encouraged to play an active role in the lives of women in specific areas like women's reproductive health. The rationale for this encouragement is to animate the view that babies and their pre-and post-natal care is not the work of women alone, but must include men. Such intervention, in fact, seeks to expand the role of men beyond the sexual and actively demystify the view that the only part men need to play is to make babies, not tend them. The attempt at involving men in the healthcare of their wives and children is to encourage men to think of reproductive health as 'their' work as well. Equally, encouraging men to participate in the reproductive health of women seeks to rework men's *subject* positions within the home-by expanding and elaborating the role of men beyond the sexual, into the intimacies and the 'work' of care. Such interventions shift the 'target' from women to men. Unlike micro-credit schemes that focus on provisioning women with the means to sustain themselves and their families, and in the process expand the number of breadwinners within a family or a household, newer policies of reproductive health strategise ways and means of getting men involved in the work of pre-and post-natal care. The outcome of including men in reproductive health reworks the division of labour within the household, and locates men directly into the domestic work of care and reproduction.

The dimensions of gender violence and violence in the family are another point of entry into households through gender interventions that address issues of gender inequality. Studies like the International Council for Research on Women research on masculinity and domestic violence [ICRW: 2002], or the National Health and Family Survey, rounds I and II [GoI: 1999, 2001; Chopra: 2002] have been important in outlining the range and categories of violence within the household. These studies have analyzed the dimensions and forms of violence against women. Domestic violence is categorized variously as abuse, molestation, battery, rape and so on, or occurring within more than one set of relations and across different contexts. Further, the data in these and other studies [Visaria: 2000, Menon-Sen and Kumar: 2001] demonstrate that violence is also framed and formed by cultures of power and deprivation.

Violence within a household does not remain untouched by political ideologies of violence and valour or cultural dimensions of caste. Histories of Rajput celebrations of violence against the self, for example, enter the household not only through men's violence against women, but women's violence against themselves through their understandings of '*sati*' (self immolation, for example), which is not a historical issue alone, but a contemporary 'real choice' for women [Sangari and Vaid: 1981, Sunder Rajan: 1993]. Equally, caste is critical in the way it generates violence between women and men as well as between men [Anandi and Jeyaranjan: 2002]. Social and cultural contexts make the question of men's role in violence a problematic issue, and one that needs closer attention and explorations. Men need to be located through a series of subjective, agentic positions, as perpetrators, victims, witnesses, and narrators of violence. The question of violence and men demands that we rethink the ways in which men inhabit particular subject positions in relation to violence.

More critically, no analysis that seeks to understand men can confine itself to understanding men only in relation to violence. Any analysis of cultural contexts reveals the multiplicity of subject positions that men inhabit. Investigation that is one-dimensional is incomplete because it mutes a range of aspects that define human relations. Feminist analysis of women's resistance has enabled us to pay attention to everyday speech and 'hear' what lies within and behind a statement. The question this raises is that when men give accounts of themselves, do they always use the language and idioms of violence to talk about themselves and-their subjective perceptions? An analysis of men's everyday speech will allow us to tease out another dimension of gender relations that has remained muted, the support that men extend towards their families.

The concept of supportive partners is a relational question because support can really only be understood in its relational context. If support is relational it is also context-specific. Just as the question of men across different households (as heads of households and as domestic workers) gives a sense of their different locations as subjects of power, equally the idea of supportive relations must open us out towards the question of a multiplicity of support relations and supportive positions. Like violence, support is not homogeneous and can be both material and ideological. In the way that dimensions and forms of violence against women have been analyzed in their various categories as abuse, molestation, battery, rape and so on, or occurring within more than one set of relations, or for more than one reason [Visaria: 2000] it is important to look at the opposite scenario. We need to address ourselves to the forms and dimensions of support as a substantive set of practices. In south Asia, for example, there is a cultural expectation that sons need to extend support to older parents, particularly widowed mothers, an aspect that the men-as-supportive partners programmes overlook. In these campaigns the position and role of men is restricted to a single dimension of their subject positions within households-as husbands, but not as fathers or sons. There is no denying that the conjugal partnership is critical within the family. Young pregnant women are often the most vulnerable in the household, and need vital health and nutritional care. But it is equally important to be self-conscious that 'gendered interventions' that focus only on men as husbands mute whole sets of practices that define the roles and subject positions of men as sons, fathers and brothers. Taking these other roles into account enables an expansion of the idea of men-as-partners and is conducive to working with men in households.

One of the ways to think through the question of the multiplicity of support relations is to think of support as social practice, and therefore part of everyday contexts. Locating support within the frame of the ordinary and the everyday alerts us to the fact that supportive practices need to be culled from existing gender relations and not just from those that come into being through interventions like gender sensitization programmes. Those who seek to enter the household through interventions need to ask whether supportive practices already exist at the level of the everyday. It is presumptuous to assume an absolute absence of male supportive practice within families and households of south Asia. At the very least, existing practices of support may be an *ideology* that might be drawn upon and elaborated when the whole question of domestic democracy and gender equality are sought to be addressed.

Further, the concept of the everyday highlights the fact that everyday practice and patriarchal social structure are not necessarily the same. Structures of power do not necessarily translate wholly or exactly, nor are they identically replicated, in everyday practice. Supportive practices need to be located in relational contexts between men and women, as well as between men and men. In other words, we need to address a dimension of relationships that patriarchal *structure* often hides or mutes and look more closely at the everyday *practices* of men.

There is a need to explore men's perceptions of supportive practices. Perhaps we need to ask whether men already have notions of supportive practice 'for' the family. To reiterate a point made earlier: when men give accounts of themselves, do they always use the language and idioms of violence to talk about themselves and their subjective perceptions? More pertinently, do they use 'talk' of supportive practice as a disguise to veil violent practices? Do supportive practices have no existence per se in the life histories of individual men in their relationship with women or with other men? Is there no substantive material existence to the support that men say they give to their families?

II

Researching Supportive Practice of Men

The research undertaken for the project 'From violence to supportive practice: Family, gender and masculinities in India' (Department of Sociology, University of Delhi and UNIFEM, South Asia Regional Office) sought to raise and address some of these issues. The research offered a view of support in its substantive material manifestations as well as at the level of ideology. However, in the way that women's work remained invisible in its doing until feminist research and analysis uncovered its histories, the doing of support by men may also have remained unaddressed, if not invisible. Through this research, an endeavour was made to make visible the 'doing of support' by men.

It is important to outline the choices that were made before the fieldwork was undertaken. The first was the choice of the family as the single most definite institution within which to explore the lives and everyday relational practices of men. It is more accepted to outline public expressions of masculinity. Nevertheless masculinity is equally expressive within the contexts of domesticity and family. It is important to understand that age, work, space and class differentiate male subjectivities within the home. Understanding masculinities is an exercise that must address itself to key institutional locations like the family and not confine itself to 'public' spaces like streets or factories. In South Asia, family plays a comprehensive role in defining relations of gender, as the arena where the ideologies of difference are expressed and learnt, where everyday forms of power and resistance are articulated. Thus the site of the family was an important starting point for the exploration of masculinity and maleness.

The second choice was to demarcate the kinds of contexts within which to explore masculinities and male supportive practices within families. In the literature on south Asia, one of the missing or muted areas is relations between men and women. Men's relations within the family and their relations with one another was therefore a critical focus. Four field sites were demarcated for this exploration.

Since the father-son relationship is a significant one and defines the parameters of male-male relationships within the family, it was important to select a field site where the father-son relation would be fore fronted and most articulate. Family businesses were chosen to begin an exploration of this relationship. The research enabled a view of the father-son relationship within the domestic domain as well as the expansion of the family ideology beyond the immediate boundaries of the home.

To explore the manner in which the question of hegemony and dependence work in male relations within the domestic and family domain, the second field site was the lives and histories of male domestic workers. Since work has been posited as the crucible of male identity, this field site allowed us to probe further the issue of men and work. However, by choosing to look at *unconventional* work performed by men we were able to analyze both existing paradigms of divisions of labour and how these are contravened in everyday choices that very ordinary men make.

It was important to push the understanding of the relation between men and work. A critical examination of the assumptions in the literature on men-as-breadwinners highlighted the fact that this literature has based itself primarily on an examination of men in conventionally male arenas of work or in the domestic division of labour within their own homes. It became important, therefore, to outline the substantive and material choices that confront men when they enter the world of work. There is no guarantee that 'male work' is always readily available to men. Any analysis of men and work must therefore focus on work that is 'unconventional' in the way it lies outside the accepted division of labour. For example, when men worked as domestic labourers, work that they talked of as 'effeminate' or 'not male' within the division of labour, they said that they did domestic work despite this feminine orientation 'for the sake of the family'. The doing of effeminate work and the doing of support were telescoped in workers' narratives; one was offered as the reason for the other. The primary methodological focus of the research was not to 'change' the way people think. Rather it was to track the way people think differently with the horizons and limits of their cultural and social positions. The fact of doing work that flew in the face of their entitlements made the entire reeach team recognize and acknowledge the extraordinary choices that ordinary men make to support key people in their lives.

Such a frame enabled us to look at the modes and styles of male-male relations within workspaces, as well as examine the way that these relations subvert hegemonic convention. The third field site was therefore also one that looked at men in work situations that were unusual and 'normally' associated with women. Male beauty parlour workers were the focus of the third piece of research. The deliberate choice of a non-family field enabled an exploration of the *ideology* of the family as an institution of care and learning and the way that care is articulated in non-family contexts. Thus, the deliberate choice of a non-family field like the beauty parlour enabled an exploration of the ideology of the family and the ways it is elaborated and given substance. How do the idioms of care, usually associated with the women in the family, translate into 'beauty care'? How does the fact of creating a 'beautiful' body rework concepts of femininity and effeminacy? Most of all does the socialization of men into beauty work replicate or mime socialization and learning practices undertaken by women in families? Does the ideology of protection that contours parent-child relations translate into relations between employers and workers? Does kinship as an idiom transcend its own boundaries and inform practices outside the family?

On the other hand, a site like the boys' club in Kolkata, the fourth field work site, provided an opportunity to explore formations of masculinity in the public, or non-domestic, domain. At the same time, it let us analyze the extent to which boys' clubs were actually 'free' of familial ideologies. For example, boys' clubs made visible the process of 'passing on maleness' from adult men to adolescent boys, through the process of 'learning', replicating modes of inheritance within the family. Structures of familial authority between father and son were imitated in the relations between adults and adolescents. The passing on of vital knowledge between elder club members and new or potential members imitated, in some part, the idea of passing down inherited knowledge that was more overt in the family-businesses. Two field sites therefore directly addressed 'the family' in customary, recognizable and institutional ways. The non-family field sites, on the other hand, enabled the exploration of the ideology of the family and the supportive practices that exist between men who work or forge relationships 'for the sake of the family'. While each research was distinctive in the issues and questions it raised, all four-research sites also crosscut and interlinked with each other in terms of the way in which family, masculinity and gender identity are framed in south Asia.

III

'Doing' Support

In the first research area of the family business, small, urban-based family businesses, with a minimum life span of 40 years, and with at least a three-generational family structure, were chosen for analysis. This delimitation enabled an exploration of the way the family is reproduced, not just as a biological unit but also as a social, cultural and economic entity through inter-gender, and inter-generational, support relations. The analysis of family businesses highlighted the material substance of supportive practices and the affirmation of the ideology and ethos of the family when extended towards the economic institution of the shop or business. The ethos of the family shapes the outlines of the business, and in turn, is forged and changed by the support structures that develop over the life cycle of the business. The father-son relation, the paradigmatic relation between men, explored within this expanded familial domain of the three-generational business enabled us to track the variety of supportive practices across time and through various male-male relationships (for example between fathers and sons, uncles and nephews, employers and '*karigars*' (artisans) employees).

The second location was of male domestic workers, in families other than their own. The exploration of this 'expanded' family location indicated the ways in which male domestic workers form a bridge between two families-their own and the family of their employers. Living between two families in two startlingly contradictory positions as a fully entitled male member in one family context, and as a partial member in the other the subjective position of the man is 'split' between the two contexts in which power dynamics play out very differently. The domestic worker is 'party' to the creation and establishment of both power dynamics as a man of entitlement and as a man deprived of that entitlement. The point at issue is that the family needs to be viewed as an arena within which not just women, but particular categories of men occupy positions of deprivation as subalterns. Domestic workers may exemplify this position, but their situation and experiences draw attention to the aspect of gender and deprivation translated within the micro-politics of the family and in relations between men of the family.

The methodological imperative of doing fieldwork has also raised a number of other questions and highlighted some issues that do not relate directly to support. But they do point our attention toward the subject positions of men, the cultures of male existence, and the formations of masculinity. For example, the question of hierarchies between men is one critical issue. At the same time, this hierarchy is counterpoised with the 'spirit of egalitarianism' that also seems to be crucial in forming relations between men. There is some literature on the peer group that has outlined egalitarian relations between boys belonging to the same age-set. Forms of egalitarianism have been specifically explored in the context of urban street gangs in cities and metropolises in the west [Brake: 1980; Jankowski: 1991; Willis: 1975]. But in such cultural locations egalitarianism as a value or a principle of group dynamics is tied in with adolescent rebellion and a deliberate forging of an anti-hierarchic, anti-structure and anti-adult stance [Osella and Osella: 1998] by the gang members. Much of the analysis of street gangs is in fact placed within a discourse that produces adolescents as social problems needing to be 'solved' through impositions of control and regulation. The gang and the street are one formation within which all-male egalitarian relations are explored. Urban institutions and spaces like pubs or beer halls have also been analyzed as arenas of friendship and equality between men.

The choice of the boys' clubs of Kolkata was made to explore some of the assumptions of this literature. The masculinist spaces of the boys' clubs that are part of every city neighbourhood and small locality give the city of Kolkata a distinctive character. The club as male space, outside of home and work, is a distinctive space like the pub or the street. One of the issues that emerged from the field-based study was the fact that these clubs are not hidden or marginalized spaces. They are part of every urban neighbourhood of the city of Kolkata. The clubs are supported by donations of land and money by the people of the neighbourhood for whom the club is an intrinsic, albeit entirely male, institutional space within the locality. These all-male institutions are accorded an authorized existence; in turn their young members contribute to the collective life of the neighbourhood. The point that this study highlighted was the value placed on friendship by men, who nurtured, enabled, and supported the bonds. Why was friendship given such value at all? What place does friendship have in the lives of men? These questions emerged through the research and were sought to be addressed in the analysis of the field material.

Most interestingly, it was the men who worked in beauty parlours who provide an insight into the value of friendship as social and cultural capital. Many parlour workers were migrants into cities and led precarious, footpath lives. In almost every case it was their friends, or informal networks of friendship, that enabled them to get work in beauty parlours, in jobs that sustained them and their families. It was friends who 'taught' them the skills necessary for beauty work and passed on valuable knowledge and skills in a spirit of friendship. It is this 'spirit' that translates substantively into supportive practices between men, and if extended and elaborated, by men 'for the sake of their friend's, families'. Thus men's supportive practices may not only orient themselves towards their own families, but to other families as well. The doing of support for other families was also clear in the context of family businesses. Help was extended to families other than a man's 'own' or nuclear family. This support could come by way of loans, labour, exchange of goods, sitting at shops to 'help out', or advice. Support towards the extended family had an additional material and substantive existence in inheritance patterns where uncles and nephews rather than fathers and sons, were placed in relations of inheritance and support. Uncles were key players in business families in creating the circumstances for young men who often began their careers in their uncle's shops and businesses. This expansion of the role of fathering undertaken by a variety of men is not unusual in south Asian contexts. The expansion allows us to view the whole context of the authority of the father as both re-enforced and simultaneously dissolving as it expands beyond the single person of the genitor. Further it questions the focus on one person as fulfilling prescribed roles. In fact the dispersal of father in/over many men demonstrated the need to think about supportive partners in a more elaborate and a far more nuanced way.

The two field sites 'outside' the family provided a contrast for the research within the family. In addition, these two sites simultaneously enabled the possibility of understanding how work and non-work were key issues in the formations of masculine identities in the lives of men. The first point to note here is that as researchers we were not attempting to dismiss or nullify the fact of work as a 'crucible' of male identity. Rather, our objective was to take the statement and then begin to explore the issue of the relationship between men and work. Therefore, it was more important for us to explore what the men were saying (and in the process explore the formations of masculine identity) by questioning ourselves as well as the statements that men made. Thus, if men said they work for the sake of the family, and offer themselves and their bodies as 'sacrifices' to ensure the survival of their families, then what kinds of work are they willing to undertake for the sake of their families? How does the need and, necessity to work for the sake of the family translate into substantive choices that men make in the course of their working lives? Male domestic workers always cite this reason ('*mazboori*' need, necessity or compulsion to support their families) when explaining why they made the choice to enter servitude and compromise their autonomy and their maleness in this effeminized position.

As researchers seeking to excavate supportive practices of men, the lives of exemplar men like Gandhi, Nehru or Rammohan Roy are readily available and provide insights into extraordinary, but, clearly upper class lives. We think of these men as extraordinary in many different respects, but most crucially, as models for other men. Unfortunately, biographies of ordinary men often disappear from the pages of histories, even though they are a rich source for understanding changing social contexts within which lives are lived and choices made. In the course of recording the working histories and narratives of ordinary men doing domestic work or beauty palours, all of us were struck by the nature of the choices these men made. They transgressed divisions of labour, made a break with 'masculinist' work ethics and without self-consciously professing a politics of the personal, 'passed on' these transgressive choices to their friends as a form of help and support. We thought of these men as extraordinary because in their own small way their lives are 'models' for others to rework how gender identity is made, fixed and remade, within the limits and horizons of social and economic conditions.

It is their statements that led us to explore the question of effeminacy, work and identity further. It is the link between work and effeminacy that enabled us to question the single stranded way in which effeminacy has been framed solely in relation to sexuality. The research highlighted the way that the concept of effeminacy needs to be expanded to be able to address sexual identity through work and labour. Labouring bodies confront the issue of male identity and effeminacy in extremely complex ways that complicate the relationship between sexual identity and effeminate bodies.

To explore the link between work and effeminacy, it was therefore important to look at a profession that, like domestic work, has been associated primarily with women. The work in beauty parlours yielded important insights and allowed us to explore both the subversions of masculinities and the reassertions of the male self through the performance of work.

There is interesting literature on male 'body work'. But most of this has focused on sports like wrestling, football, polo [Alter:1992; Archetti: 1999; Hargreaves: 1987] and so on through that the physical body is produced as 'powerful' and virile. While the emphasis is on the anatomical, this literature also demonstrates the way the male body becomes a sign for the display of power and virility. The second set of literature that draws attention to the male body is the work on initiation ritual [Bloch: 1986; Herdt: 1981, 1984 among others] through which the male body is adorned and marked as a transformed body. The point that is important for this research is the way that initiation rituals produce masculinity through transactions between men.

An aspect that emerged from the research and analysis in the context of beauty parlours was the nature of care that men extend to other men. Beauty work entails a physical exchange between the bodies of men who 'care' for the appearance of the male self. New formations of masculinity and the male self are produced through cultures of body care. Caring for the body and the production of a beautiful masculinity are a joint endeavour of clients and workers who share a particular view of the male body and the presentation of the masculine self. In a broader sense, caring through hands may be said to be a way in which support is extended between men when one man places himself, literally and metaphorically, in the hands of another.

One of the critical arenas of support between men was through friendship. Friends were responsible for enabling migrants to get jobs as domestic workers or as beauty parlour men. Friends created the context for an entry into the work and also taught men the techniques of how to work. Jobs and skills were key modes through which men 'passed on' something of value to their friends. Like inheritance patterns within family businesses, which moved along kinship and family networks, male friends worked 'like family' to enable their friends to work and earn 'for the sake of the family'.

Friendship networks were critical at significant junctures of men's lives. On the one hand, they enabled entry into working lives and the reproduction of necessary skills. On the other hand, friendship networks were the context for men to re-articulate autonomy, a sense of male self 'lost' through the performance of 'women's work'. Hanging around with their friends ar the milk-booth or playing volleyball with friends in neighbourhood parks made it possible for male domestic workers to capture a part of the sense of autonomy and masculinity away from the family of their employers. Friends, and friendship groups, provided the context for this reassertion. Friendship groups enabled the emergence and the re-articulation of agency and autonomous subjectivities.

If friends are a key group within which male selves are articulated and supported, then clearly this is a significant group for exploration. Here the boys' clubs provided insights. One of the puzzling questions was why young boys are permitted to be away from the direct control of their fathers and families and spend so much time hanging out and seemingly doing nothing at the club. No work happens in the club. Sometimes no games take place either. In fact, nothing of significant 'social' value seems to happen. The real question was why such license was permitted to the boys given the structures of patriarchal obedience and dependence that mark adolescent males' lives vis-à-vis powerful fathers and adult men.

Clearly, there was something else that lay within the 'hanging out' that was not immediately apparent. Our attention was drawn to the hidden social value of hanging out by the substantial contributions made to the club by the entire neighbourhood. Despite the seeming waste of time the club the space and context of this hanging out-adults of the neighbourhood supported it in myriad ways (via donations, money, land and permissions). It seemed clear, therefore, that the entire community recognized the club as a significant institution and were willing to donate valuable resources, like land and money, to establish the club and keep it going.

It is these substantive support practices extended by the neighbourhood to the club that impelled a different understanding of what the hanging out represented in the eyes of the community. It made us recognize that hanging out in the club is a way in which something of value-time-is given or spent freely to create something of value-the all-male friendship group. A second aspect was the way these clubs are spaces and sites for the articulation of formations of masculinities 'outside' the home. The clubs are collective bodies that initiate and introduce boys into worlds outside the family. Unlike schools, however, they are non-formal sites of socialization of boys into the world of power and support. Boys and men of various ages go to these clubs, within which each age-set forms their own group forming friendships through an exchange of ideas, views and feelings.

The non-family location of the club draws attention to the friendship group and its independent logic. The spirit of egalitarianism is a fundamental principle of the friendship group that counters relations of hierarchy in which boys, as adolescent 'incomplete men', are placed within the family. In constituting support and supportive practices, it was interesting to track how support was extended between men along egalitarian lines of friendship and community. The egalitarian mode or the idiom of fraternity was most apparent in the boys' clubs, but emerged in nascent and overt ways in narratives of male domestic workers and beauty parlour workers as well.

The spirit of egalitarianism can be posed against the structures of hierarchy in understanding relations between men. In terms of relations of support this opposition has a particular significance. Within the hierarchic mode (and in relation to the field research) the father-son relation might be said to be the paradigmatic representation of the hierarchies that operate between men. The figure of the father represents the epitome of the authoritarian patriarch. Feminist literature has drawn attention to the figure of the patriarchal father, a figure that has represented and been the focus for articulating a series of oppressions experienced by women within patriarchal structures of power. Given the relative positioning of senior and junior, adult and adolescent, father and son, it is possible to assume that the latter positions (junior/adolescent/son) are the natural place to look for supportive practices. The former positions in the oppositional dyad (senior/adult/father) would be the site of autocratic, repressive practices. One of the issues raised by this research, most importantly in the field of family businesses, but also in the other field sites, is the ways in which practices that constitute fathering might also be placed within the context of supportive relations and support practices.

In fact, what is importantly demonstrated is that fathering is a role centred on more than one single man. As an ideology fathering extends beyond the single man, the father, and is taken on, as it were, by men other than the genitor or the 'biological' father. Business families, for example, adopt strategies of deflecting conflict that might be inherent in the father-son relation. Within the family business (the expectation is that the son step directly into the father's shoes), it is often nephews who inherit businesses from their uncles, resolving, through deflection, the conflict inherent in the direct line between the father and son. By looping inheritance outwards on to tangential lines of affinal and collateral kin, a key relationship within the family, the father-son relation is protected from disruptions. The family business is continued not necessarily in a direct lineal or agnatic line, but along affinal or collateral lines. This looping out has a bearing on the issue of fathering and fathering practice because it brings forward the idea that the doing of fathering as a supportive practice is not done by the genitor alone, but by a whole group of men who stand in place of the father. It draws attention to the fact that just as there might be a proliferation of businesses that make up 'the family business', there is the equal possibility of a proliferation of fathers who play a critical role in the lives of younger men, not necessarily their sons.

Therefore, it cannot, and should not, be assumed that relations of hierarchy are divested of all forms of support. Support was offered along lines of hierarchy like father-son, uncle-nephew in family businesses as well as between higher and lower castes among barbers and their higher caste clients. Adult or older members of clubs offered advice to newer members, passing on skills of organizing locality affairs, account keeping and so on.

Thinking about the substance of support and its locations, the question of fathering as a wider set of practices done by a group of people highlights the material and the ideological existence of support. Support in business is substantive and actualized in loans, labour, space in shops and business networks. It also has a social and cultural existence through advice, business and craft skills, ways of the family, and, most importantly, social networks inherited from elders. The social networks of support are those that are drawn upon during times of need and times when a family affirms and celebrates itself (at ritual moments, or family occasions, for example).

Certain individuals exemplify this aspect of institutionalized support networks. In the life histories of such individual men, support might be extended along lines of hierarchy in the beginning, but may translate into friendship or egalitarian forms of support at subsequent periods of time. Deepchand, a man belonging to the caste of barbers, was supported in the initial stages of his working life by a high caste village fellow, who was also a professor at the University of Delhi, and then later, by the university's vice chancellor. Both men helped him establish his barber's shop on the university campus. Like the young men in the club, Deepchand cultivated his networks of support that constituted his social capital. In his latter years, the caste distances and hierarchies have given way to more egalitarian relations. Now, Deepchand is formally invited to his clients' homes and they send their cars for him in gestures of friendship, acknowledging his 'worth' as a friend not just as a barber of a low caste.

IV

Reflections on Research and Method

Research such as the kind described above engages with the social worlds and the narratives of individual people in their different locations or contexts and begins from a stance that is critically different from the stance adopted by intervention research. For the sake of clarity I will term the two kinds of research practices as 'anthropological' research and 'intervention' research. The two forms of research methodologies differ in their stances, strategies and methodological practices. Anthropological research begins with the assumption that its project is to discover what people say both obviously and subtly. The assumption is that people have their own conceptual capital and this must form part of the research 'findings' as much as the researchers' own conceptual frame. The point, of course, is that by choosing a particular paradigm or a set of questions (like the shift from violence to supportive practice when talking about men in families), anthropological research displays a prior point of view through which an anthropologist frames the issues at hand. Such framing will necessarily enter the process of interpretation as well.

Intervention research is far more self-conscious in performing this exercise. There is a choice already made, for example, involving men in women's health and the agenda is to work out how best this objective may be achieved through strategies that involve rather than alienate the target group. So in some senses we might acknowledge the more up-front nature of intervention research, which anthropological research may not so readily display. The problem with intervention research is that it is not always self-conscious of own power position in relation to target groups. 'Intervention' is a political word in that it expresses a relationship that positions the person who intervenes as 'active' and the people towards whom this intervention is directed as 'passive'. In its action, intervention does in fact seek to penetrate a target audience with a set of agendas and in so doing it comes accompanied by the politics and practices of power. In essence, intervention echoes the same problems that lie in words like penetration. Feminist writings have alerted us to the power of penetration, which blanks out agency and subjectivities of those who are positioned as penetrated. Both penetration and intervention involve notions of active bodies, influential points of view and powerful subject positions directed towards those who need to be altered, changed and transformed, as passive recipients of new knowledges, different roles and good practices.

This is not to claim that transformation is not a valid agenda. But I think it is important to recognize that people confront and engage with change and transformation continuously in their everyday lives. Daily lives are altered through movements of migrants, through doing effeminate work, by expanding the role of fathers towards other adult men. As researchers of all hues, we need to collectively understand the dynamics of these transformations, acknowledge their existence and then draw on them to think through ways of engaging with people's lives and their own conceptual capital as a source for our own supportive practices. It is an exercise in engagement that we need to strive towards, not the politics that underlies intervention.

V

Conclusion

A few issues emerge when thinking about practices of support. First, it is quite clear from the field research and analysis that support has a material and a non-material aspect. Second, support practices are diverse in terms of the cultural contexts within which they are articulated. Thus family businesses and boys' clubs are both contexts in which supportive practices can be configured, but each context has its own set of distinctive practices.

Third, supportive practices are distinguished between those that already exist and those that come into existence or are created when people find themselves in situations of deprivation and a perceived loss of autonomy. In the latter instance, supportive practices have a transformative potential, as, for example, among male domestic workers who reaffirm their 'loss' of maleness by asserting friendship networks. Friendship is a form of capital that 'grows' into social networks of support. Therefore, not just by those, who are engaged in its immediate creation (like the boys of the neighbourhood clubs), but even the adults, who enable the formations of friendship gangs, place great value upon creating friendship bonds. Friendship is an investment in the future and may, in fact, be viewed as if it had a material existence.

Neither is support at least among men-taken for granted. It is cultivated with care and time (a thing of value) is freely spent in the cultivation of support networks. Strategies are developed to enhance support and deflect conflict within the family especially where the reproduction of family fortunes depends on the continuance of the family. Conflict between the father and son standing in a direct lineal relation may be 'diverted' by overemphasizing the support from 'other' fathers (maternal uncles, for example). The future reproduction of the family is assured by the strategic displacement of support and the consequent deflection of conflict.

How do these conclusions engage with the larger issue of gender equality and domestic democracy? This research has tried to bring into focus the way that men's support can be outlined and reflected upon. Men's friendship groups may become an enabling site within which issues of domestic democracy can be parleyed into a discursive context. This potential of the friendship group is already present and was demonstrated by the example of the boys' club group in the role it played in the resolution of a marital dispute within a neighbourhood family. Second, older men in the family play very different roles, and offer different kinds of support to younger men. Apart from uncles in business families, hierarchically placed upper caste men do assist low caste men to get work and support their families, indirectly entering as 'supportive partners' of lower caste men. Often the most direct kin relative may not be the most critical player in the life of a younger man.

Drawing from these instances it may be possible to argue that in the case of women's reproductive health, the husband (the most direct partner) may not necessarily be the most supportive partner. A woman's genitor-her father in her natal home-may, in fact, be a more supportive partner in the context of her reproductive health than her husband or her father-in-law. Such support is already in place within the kinship networks at least of north India and might be drawn upon and expanded. The elaborations of fathering through the practices of group fathering helps us think through the idea of 'deflection of conflict' and the locating the key supportive partner in deflected rather than direct relations.

Asserting support as a frame enables us to engage with a particular language and practice of masculinity. In talking about themselves and their lives, men did not have a very articulate vocabulary to speak about themselves, except when they were narrating the support they received or had given. Supportive practices are therefore more than and 'alternative' frame within which to place men. They enable us to hear an aspect of men's lives and expressions of their subjective positions in ways that have not so far been addressed. Supportive practices are an idiom that explicate agentic subjectivities and provide a language of engagement with the lives and cultural locations of men.

Note

1. As part of the 'Frontiers Programme in Reproductive Health', the Population Council's Men-in-Maternity Study was designed to help men".. .redefine their roles in reproductive health.. .(and) to assess the impact of male partnership in improving pregnancy outcomes and reproductive health...(because) studies suggest that the lack of men's participation in reproductive health actually undermines women's health...[Caleb, et al: 2002: 1-2].

References

Alter, J. 1992. *The Wrestler's Body: Identity and Ideology in North India*, Berkeley: University of California Press.

Anandi, S. and J. Jeyaranjan. 2002. 'Masculinity and Domestic Violence in a Tamil Nadu Village', ICRW.

Archetti, E.P. 1999. *Masculinities: Football, Polo and Tango in Argentina,* Oxford: Berg.

Bloch, M. 1986. *From Blessing to Violence: History and Ideology in the Circumcision Ritual of the Merina of Madagascar,* Cambridge: OUP.

Brake, M. 1980. The Sociology of Youth Culture and Youth Subculture: Sex, Drugs and Rock n' Roll, London: RKP.

Caleb-Varkey, L., A. Das, A. Mishra, E. Ottalenghi and D. Huntington. 2002. 'Frontiers in Reproductive Health', Research Update, (No. 2), Population Council, New Delhi, April.

Chopra, R. (ed). 2002. *From Violence to Supportive Practice: Family, Gender and Masculinity in India,* UNIFEM, South Asia Regional Office.

Dutton, K.R. 1995. *The Perfectible Body: The Western Ideal of Physical Development,* London: Cassell. Gol.1999 and 2001.

National Health and Family Survey, Rounds I and II. 1999, 2001, Mumbai, IIPS.

Hargreaves, J. 1987. 'The Body, Sport and Power Relation' in J. Home et al (eds.), *Sport, Leisure and Social Relations,* London: RKP.

Herdt, G. 1981. *Guardians of the Flutes: Idioms of Masculinity,* New York: McGraw Hill.

Herdt, G. (ed). 1984. *Ritualised Homosexuality in Melanesia,* Berkeley: University of California Press.

Herzfeld, M. 1985. *The Poetics of Manhood: Contest and Identity in a Cretan Mountain Village,* Princeton: Princeton University Press.

ICRW. 2002. *Men, Masculinity and Domestic Violence in India: Summary Report of Four Studies,* New Delhi.

Jankowski, M.S. 1991. *Islands in the Street: Gangs and American Urban Society.* Berkeley: University of California Press.

Menon Sen, K. and A.K. Sliva Kumar. 2001. L. *Women in India: How Free?How Equal?* New Delhi: UNDP.

Nussbaum, Martha, C. 2000. *Women and Human Development: The Capabilities Approach,* New Delhi: Kali for Women.

Osella, C. and F. Osella.1998. 'Friendship and Rirting: Micropolitics in Kerala, South India', *IRAI (incorporating Man)* 4: 189-206.

Sangari, K. and S. Vaid. 1981. *Sati in Modem India, EPW:* August 1.

Sunder Rajan, Rajeshwari. 1993. *Real and Imagined Women: Gender, Culture and Post-Colonaialism,* London: Routledge.

Visaria, L. 2000. 'Violence against Women', *EPW,* May 13.

Willis, P. 1975. 'The Expressive Style of a Motor Bike Culture' in J. Benthall and T. Polemus (eds.), *Body as a Medium of Expression,* London: Allen Lane.

The paper was first published in the *Economic and Political Weekly*: 58:17: 2003: 1650-57. It is included here with the prior permission of the author and the Editor, *Economic and Political Weekly*. Address for email is: radhika.chopra@gmail.com< rchopra@sociology.du.ac.in

Chapter - Five

Human Security and Gender Violence

Radhika Coomarswamy

The Commission on Human Security, a product of the 2000 UN Millennium Summit, defined human security as "protecting fundamental freedoms-freedoms that are the essence of life. It means protecting people from critical (severe) and pervasive (widespread) threats and situations. It means using processes that build on people's strengths and aspirations. It means creating political, social, environmental, economic, military and cultural systems that together give people the building blocks of survival, livelihood and dignity."

How a society confronts the issue of violence against women goes to the heart of how women experience security. Freedom from violence and the threat of violence is the first measurement of women's capacity for survival and empowerment. The United Nations Declaration on the Elimination of Violence Against Women states in its preamble that violence against women is a product of the "unequal power relations" that characterize gender relations in all parts of the world. The declaration recognises that in addition to individual acts of violence, it is this history of unequal relationships that is at the core of widespread and pervasive nature of violence against women. Violence against women is a universal reality but at the same time it is invisible. Yet such violence is underreported if not "normalized" as acceptable social behaviour. South Asia has been classified as the worst region in terms of indicators with the highest rates of different forms of violence against women [UNICEF: 2001].

The historically unequal power relations between men and women have been manifested in a variety of ways. As the first report of the UN Special Rapporteur on Violence Against Women (VAW) states, "the system of male domination has historical roots and its functions and manifestations change over time. The oppression of women is therefore a question of politics, requiring an analysis of the institutions of state and society, the conditioning and socialization of individuals, and the nature of economic and social exploitation" [Report of Special Rapporteur on VAW: 1995]. Recognizing the important role that states can play in transforming legislative, administrative and judicial practices, the report points to the fact that states are nevertheless also perpetrators of violence against women whether in prisons, jails or during armed conflict and when turning a blind eye to violence against women that takes place in their society.

Economic and social exploitation of women and their labour also contributes to violence against women. Women are often employed as bonded labour and as low paid labour in many economic enterprises around the world; as migrant workers they face enormous hardships. The refusal to recognize women's economic independence and empowerment is one of the main reasons for violence against women, accentuating thereby, their vulnerability and abuse.

Violence against women also takes place in the most intimate of places, the family. Though the family is often a site of nurture and care, it can also be a place where male power is brutally expressed and where women are socialized to accept their inferiority and vulnerability. It is the family that often first teaches women to have negative, disempowering self-images and it is in the family that young men first learn about female subordination.

As the special rapporteur writes, in the context of power relations, it is also men who control the knowledge systems of the world. Whether it is science and modern technology or religion and its edicts, women are often excluded from creating symbolic systems or analyzing and transmitting knowledge. In these systems of knowledge, women's experience is devalued and privatized and the public world becomes the site of the struggle for power and the vindication of rights. The public private distinction relegates women to the sphere of domestic activity, immune from scrutiny and activism, while men control and determine public power and the priorities of a society as a whole.

Recommendation 19 of Convention on the Elimination of Violence Against Women (CEDAW) and the United Nations Declaration on Violence Against Women calls on states to take immediate steps with regard to ending gender-based violence in the family, in the community and by the state. They call on the states to enact national plans of action, to train and sensitize their criminal justice system, to provide social support to the victim survivors and to collect data and information of violence against women in their societies. In a survey conducted by the office of the UN Special Rapporteur on Violence Against Women in 2003, except for a handful of countries most countries had taken some measures with regard to eradicating violence against women. Countries had begun to enact or reform laws that related to domestic violence, rape, sexual harassment and trafficking, began training and sensitizing their criminal justice systems and had begun running campaigns to prevent violence against women. Some had also adopted social programmes for the women victims in partnership with NGOs .

These newly emerging international norms and standards are still very aspirational in content. The reality on the ground has not changed dramatically.

The WHO's report on Violence and Health (2002) still points to widespread violence against women in all parts of the globe and many parts of the world where women victims of violence accepted violence as an ordinary part of their lives. In all studies south Asia continues to be a region where violence against women is prevalent, some say even "normalized" as an accepted pattern of behaviour.

Forms of Violence

South Asia has particular cultural and religious practices that also accentuate the problem of VAW in the region. The general low status of women in the region and the entrenched nature of discriminatory structures have led to what is seen as a "Lifecycle of VAW". Even before birth women suffer from sex selective abortion, at infancy they may face female infanticide, as young children they will have to put up with incest and son preference, as adolescents they may be sexually abused or trafficked, as young women they may suffer rape, sexual harassment, acid attacks; as wives they may experience domestic violence, dowry related violence, marital rape or honour killings, and as widows they may be required to self immolate or be deprived of property and dignity. The vulnerability to violence at every stage of the life-cycle makes VAW a terrible south Asian legacy that requires concerted regional, national and local level action.

Armed Conflict

Rani lives in the east coast of Sri Lanka. Rani is a Sri Lankan Tamil. About fifteen years ago the Sri Lankan army took away Rani's husband and she has not heard from him since. The Liberation Tigers of Sri Lanka took her son, who was still a child of 12. She has lost touch with him and does not know whether he is dead or alive. Rani and her daughter eke out a living doing handicrafts with the help of a local NGO. They barely have enough to survive. Her daughter suffers from nightmares and depression since she was attached to both the father and the brother. Rani doesn't like to speak much-speech is dangerous in the east coast with so many young men with guns. Tears swell in her eyes when she speaks. For solace she goes to the nearby oracle to find out about her husband and her son. The oracle tells her that they are alive so she lives in hope (author's notes).

Armed conflict has been an important part of the post-independence legacy of south Asia. Whether on the Afghan border with Pakistan, in Kashmir, in the Chittagong Hill Tracts, among Maoist rebels or in the north and east of Sri Lanka, armed conflict is a terrible reality that many women in south Asia have to face. Women are affected by armed conflict in different ways. First, they are often the victims of direct violence especially sexual violence by armed soldiers or militants. Rape during wartime is one of the oldest war crimes and is now clearly prohibited by the statute of the International Criminal Court (Articles 7,8). However, none of the countries of south Asia have become parties to the ICC. There have been some prosecutions for custodial violence in south Asia. In Sri Lanka in the famous case of Krishanthy Kumaraswamy, the court handed the death penalty to the perpetrators. However, in most of the cases there is no prosecution and the perpetrators remain unpunished [Special Rapporteur VAW: 1994-2003]. Sexual violence during wartime continues in all parts of south Asia and there is a sense of impunity on the part of the perpetrators.

Another way in which women are affected during wartime is as internally displaced persons (IDPs). Eighty per cent of IDPs are women and children. As IDPs they live in terrible circumstances. They are given meagre rations; they live in large communal halls without any privacy, often only separated by a sari. Women are often sexually harassed in these camps by officials and inmates and there are minimal sanitation facilities. They are also subject to restrictions on their freedom of movement. They often dream of returning home but are in these camps for a very long period of time. When the armed conflict is over, resettlement is an even longer process. They often find their lands and homes occupied or destroyed. They usually do not have the communal infrastructure to begin a new life and they are subject to a great deal of bureaucratic regulation. Women and children in these camps continue to have psychosocial problems and long-term adjustment problems. Women are also affected by war in that they become war widows, often losing their husbands. In very patriarchal societies that oppress and discriminate against women, these young widows have special problems and concerns. They become among the poorest and most vulnerable communities in the country [Tiruchandran: 1999]. Research suggests that they survive because of the future they envision for their children.

In some wars women actually become combatants such as in Sri Lanka. Here the ambiguity of the Geneva Convention on the protection of women combatants raises a whole host of issues. Moreover, in the post-conflict situation, other parts of the world such as Columbia point to obstacles in the reintegration of women cadres into civilian life especially in patriarchal societies. Women as warriors, though exciting because of the transgressing of gender roles, raise other issues relating to the realisation of women's rights within the framework of military imperatives and war.

Trafficking

Chamoli was 16 years old and living with her father and stepmother. Her stepmother did not like her very much and used to beat her often. One day a young man from outside came to the village. Chamoli fell in love with him and he promised to marry her. She eloped with him to India. He then took her to a big house and he saw money exchange between her new lover and the madam of the house. After that her lover disappeared and she found she was in a brothel. She was literally tortured into submission. She had to service about ten customers a day and was living in a cubicle the size of a bed. Finally Maiti Nepal, a Nepalese NGO, came to her brothel and "rescued her". She then spent seven months in an Indian "protection home" before she was sent back to Nepal. When she got there doctors as Maiti Nepal discovered that she was suffering from AIDS. Chamoli refuses to return to her family because of the shame and because of her fear of her stepmother (author's notes).

Trafficking of women and girls, especially into the big cities of India, remains a serious problem in the south Asian region. Increasingly young girls between the ages of 10 and 14 are trafficked to different parts of India from within India as well as Nepal and Bangladesh. In other countries there are smaller trafficking enterprises taking place. It is estimated that there are about 2,00,000 young girls from Nepal in India of which 45,000 are in Mumbai alone. Women are often trafficked by close friends and family.

Sometimes trafficking is linked to traditional contexts and practices. In Nepal, the exploitative experience of the *badi caste*, which provided entertainment services to feudal elites and who now must respond to market forces has led to the trafficking of their daughters and wives who leave Nepal in search of a better future. Traditional temple dancers such as *devadasis, jogins, matamma* and *deukis* were once children pledged by their parents to the temple and who become sex workers associated with the temple. These women also become vulnerable to further trafficking once they become older.

Trafficking is also complicated by the legal regimes that are in place for the regulation of prostitution. Some countries in south Asia have "moralistic" legal regime that criminalize everything associated with prostitution, the sex worker, the client, the middlemen, etc. This is true especially in Islamic countries of south Asia. Sri Lanka and India have the "abolitionist model" contained in the 1949 convention, where the women is seen as a victim and is not criminalized whereas those who exploit her prostitution are. Though on the books, the law is rarely implemented. In both these frameworks the criminal justice system is an integral part of the regime and abuse and corruption in the system often ends up victimizing the trafficked women. This has led to many people in south Asia asking for more liberal legal regimes for prostitution to allow the sex worker a certain social legitimacy and more social and economic rights.

However, trafficking is perhaps most complicated by its link to migration. Research clearly shows that most of the women who are trafficked have a strong desire to migrate and are thereby abused in the process. Women desire to migrate often because there is abuse in the home, in the community or because of dire poverty. To counter trafficking by preventing women's migration is to lock them into domestic systems of oppression. Measures taken to prevent women from migrating such as requiring permission of male members of the family or government sanction may actually compound the problem. What is needed is an effective system that prevents women from being abused during the process of migration and this can only take place if the approach to trafficking is designed within a human rights framework.

The human rights framework would also require a different approach to the women survivor once she leaves sex work. Instead of the usual approach of "rescue", "rehabilitation" and "repatriation" which has conditioned the mainstream approach to trafficking, there is now an emphasis on consulting the women on what she really wants to do. Does she want to remain in sex work? Does she wish to return home? Does she wish to stay in her host "country? Does she wish to go back to her parents? These approaches then require a partnership between the police, immigration officials and women's support groups who can counsel the women survivor. These approaches are not present in south Asia where the approach to trafficking is very much oriented towards rescue, rehabilitation (or protection) and repatriation.

Asha Rani was a young bride. Her poor family gave her a small dowry but after marriage her in-laws wanted another Rs 5,000 or an auto-rickshaw. Her father who had seven daughters could not provide the amount. When he refused, the in-laws beat his daughter in front of his eyes. A few weeks later Asha Rani was dead, "burnt while making tea". According to her in-laws, her synthetic sari caught fire on the stove. But the post-mortem revealed otherwise. The Supreme Court finally ruled that she did not die of accident nor did she commit suicide. She was murdered [Umar: 1998].

Domestic Violence

Newspaper pages in south Asia are full of tales of domestic violence. In 2002, 450 honour killings were reported in Pakistan. 15,000 young brides are burnt to death every year in India, and 10 women a week are subject to acid attacks in Bangladesh [OXFAM: 2004]. Violence by intimate family members is one of south Asia's darkest legacies. Forty per cent of all sexual abuse cases in India are about incest. In a survey on violence against women in India, 94 per cent of the cases involved an offender who was a member of the family [Naved: 2004].

The violence against women in south Asia often begins before birth. It is estimated the 50 million women are missing in India either through sex selective abortions, female infanticide or female neglect. So much so that the sex ratio in certain states of India is very disturbing. There are 79.3 girls for every 100 males in the Punjab and 87.8 girls for every 100 males in Gujarat [OXFAM: 2004: 10].

Domestic violence rates in south Asia do vary from com-munity to community and depend on the questions asked. A survey of 1,842 women in Uttar Pradesh and Tamil Nadu in India presented a rate of 40 per cent of women interviewed stating they were victims of wife beating. In Pakistan, a survey of 1,000 women indicated that 55 per cent in the urban areas and 35 per cent in the rural areas stated that they were victims of domestic violence. In Sri Lanka, one survey put the figure at 60 per cent, another at 32 per cent [UNIFEM: 2004:10].

Research on indicators of domestic violence in the region highlights issues such as the fact that children, who themselves are abused or who have witnessed violence in the family, are far more likely to beat their wives than other children. In south Asia alcohol and drug use also accentuates domestic violence. Patriarchal societies where men control all decisions often witness greater violence when women seem to question or go outside the framework of such decisions. If a society seeks to resolve conflict through the use of violence then violence in the home is also on the increase. The lack of economic independence on the part of women and their inability to move out of a violent situation and state inaction against perpetrators of violence helps perpetuate an ideological belief that violence may even be justified and even if it is not, it is not a terrible matter that requires concerted action.

The insensitivity of the criminal justice system has also been highlighted in many studies. Police stations rarely respond though with the new policewomen desks this situation is marginally better. A survey of judges in the region (south Asia) pointed to the fact that 48 per cent of judges agreed that it was justifiable for men to beat their wives and 74 per cent endorsed the view that even in cases of violence the preservation of the family should be the primary concern. The international standard calls on states to draft national plans of action, ensure a trained and sensitive criminal justice system, support systems for victims, ensure sensitive health professionals and to also maintain data collection and analysis about the incidents of domestic violence. Some countries in south Asia, for example, India and Sri Lanka, have begun to respond to these standards in a progressive manner.

Rape and Sexual Harassment

Mathura was a young girl from the *dalit* community. She ran away from home and married her boyfriend. Her family threatened her and her husband. When she went to the police station to make a complaint, she was gang raped by the policemen. Her case so scandalized India that Parliament passed an amendment to the penal code making special provisions to protect the rights of victims who are subject to rape in state custodial institutions.

Rape and sexual harassment continue to be important issues in the south Asian context. In 1998, the Human Rights Commission of Pakistan reported that one person is raped every 354 minutes in Pakistan. In India for the same year, there were over 15,000 reported cases while so many go unreported. Such cases of gang rape of *dalit* women by upper caste men in the rural areas are often compounded as an act of political violence. A CNN survey in New Delhi pointed to the fact that 50 per cent of all workingwomen claimed that they were sexually harassed in the workplace. In Pakistan, the Alliance Against Sexual Harassment in the workplace claimed that 93 per cent of women working in the public and private sectors had experienced some form of harassment in the workplace. Marital rape and sexual violence as a means of initiation are also reported in some of these surveys, a factor that will influence the marriage relationship for years to come [UNIFEM: 2004: 17]. This is the case even though marital rape is not a crime in all the countries of south Asia.

The issue of rape was what first galvanised the women's movement in India and to some extent in the other south Asian countries. The rape of the *dalit* girl Madura in a custodial setting led to a national campaign for the reform of the rape laws. The Law Commission set up to look into this matter decided that in cases of custodial rape the onus of proving consent would shift to the accused. In Sri Lanka penal reforms of 1995 gave more serious punishment for custodial violence but like its Indian counterpart called for mandatory enhanced punishments.

Feminists have been challenging the rape laws of their countries for over a generation now. The need to take away language like "against her will" that requires physical bruises, the need to define rape broadly as sexual assault and not only as penis penetration, the need to make sure that a woman's past history is not introduced into the evidence and the need to get rid of evidentiary procedure that requires corroboration. The National Commission for Women in India drafted amendments to the Indian Penal Code on issues relating to rape is very much along these lines.

In this context, given the terrible nature of the crimes against women many young legal scholars are questioning whether the legal system can be effective in dealing with crimes against women and whether other alternatives to prosecution and punishment should be explored. Statistics for a given period in Mumbai show that of the 504 cases that were registered, only 469 were charge sheeted, of which there were 13 convictions, and 10 acquittals, the vast majority were pending trial or never really got to the trial stage [Agnes: 1990:48]. Furthermore, feminists fear that the rape trial often becomes a "pornographic spectacle" [Menon: 200: 91]. Even when judgments convict, the rape survivor emerges brutalized and sometimes a "scandal figure" in a still very patriarchal society. For this reason most women continue to be silent when they are victims of sexual violence.

The inability of the legal systems to deliver justice in the case of women and the reliance on the prosecution arm of the state has created unease among some women's rights activists. They argue that reliance on the legal strategy alone is not enough and that a more broad based approach aimed at transforming attitudes and social structures is necessary [Kapoor and Cossman: 1996].

Customary Practices

Samia was married to an abusive husband. One day she ran away from home stating that she wanted a divorce. There were rumours that she had found someone else. Finally her family said they were granting her wish. Her mother, her uncle and a stranger came to the lawyer's chambers to discuss the case. Suddenly the stranger pulled a gun out and shot Samia and aimed over the head of the lawyer. The security in the office shot the stranger but the mother and the uncle escaped taking one of the members of the law firm as hostage, who was later released. The police have not prosecuted the case since they felt it was an "honour" killing.

The failure of the law is particularly relevant when it comes to customary practices in a region that is violent toward women. South Asia is perhaps the region with the largest number of customary practices that are violent toward women. The response to the international critique of such practices has been mixed. Some regard these as internal issues and not a concern to the rest of the world; some practices are justified by the internal logic of indigenous cultural systems and any attempt to critique and eradicate such customs is part of the arrogant legacy of colonialism and westernization. However, women's groups within these societies have also taken up these issues and highlighted them as evidence of the low status of women in south Asian societies. These customary practices are in conflict with the international obligations that south Asian states have voluntarily taken upon themselves. The charge of westernization is also disingenuous since many of these societies are rapidly globalizing and the question of culture seems primarily relevant only to the subordinate position of women. The duality between public and private has a special meaning in south Asia where scholars have claimed that the private is also seen as "eastern", "spiritual" and the domain of the women. To change customary practices would entail a necessary transformation of the private and therefore threaten the "eastern" and "spiritual" nature of south Asian societies [Chatterjee: 1989]. As a result, attempts to eradicate customary practices that are violent toward women meet with local level resistance and require both a political as well as a legal approach.

Another customary practice that is associated with south Asia is the practice of bride burning. Bride burning reached its height in the early 1990s. Dowry related murders increased from 437 deaths in 1983 to 4,856 in 1991 and to 5,582 in 1993; these are the reported cases [Umar: 1998:12]. In Delhi, in the early 1980s, the frequency of unnatural deaths of housewives was one every 12 hours. While dowry in certain communities was linked to land and immovable property, giving women some sense of security, it has in the modern world become a morbid symptom of a customary practice. Today a dowry consists of first, gifts to the bride in terms of clothes, jewellery and household gifts. Second dowry consists of luxury items for the husband, clothes, wrist-watch, gold chain, etc; thirdly it may include immovable property written in the husband's name and finally modem electronic items such as televisions, fridges, video cassette players, etc. [Umar: 1998:67]. Material gifts and cash are paid to the bridegroom, who if he is widowed and then marries again receives dowry a second time.

Women are burned as brides either because of dowry, incompatibility between husband and wife, the rigidity of the divorce laws, or a desire to have a son. In recent times the Indian penal code was amended to deal specifically with dowry deaths. Since 1986 the law has provided for punishment not less than seven years and up to life imprisonment for a husband or family member if a woman's death occurs due to bums, injuries or other unnatural circumstances and she was subjected to cruelty or harassment in connection with dowry [Lawyers' Collective: 1992]. The number of dowry deaths has decreased in recent years due to the penal sanctions but they do still occur in many parts of south Asia.

Family members often direct acid attacks at women who, in the protection of honour, reject the advances of men. These attacks have received recent attention in Bangladesh but still continue in certain parts. Linked to the concept of honour it is difficult to eradicate as long as women's emotional and sexual behaviour are seen as reflecting on the honour of the men who are intimately connected to them.

Another south Asian practice that has received international attention is the practice of *sati* or widow burning in certain parts of India. The case of Roop Kanwar, who in the late 1980s committed *sati* on her husband's pyre in a public spectacle created major national and international furore. *Sati* is often always committed under coercive circumstances and a tolerance of *sati* could make many families urge their young widows to commit *sati* to prevent having to take care of them. For this reason women's groups have not only argued against *sati* as a practice but also the ideology of *sati*. Luckily the Indian state responded firmly [Hawley: 1994].

The practice of *sati* reminds us that violence and discrimination against widows is a common cultural practice in south Asia. Besides *sati*, this often manifests itself in witch killings. In Bihar an average of 200 women are killed every year as witches. In many of these cases there is some dispute over land with the victim's husband's family. The lack of economic independence and security for a widow makes her particularly vulnerable. Supposed to be inauspicious, she is socially secluded and discriminated against. If her presence drains the family of its resources, in some cases there is a cultural form of killing or exclusion that allows families to deal with unwanted widows. Again the criminal justice system rarely prosecutes families for killing their widows.

Another customary practice in south Asia that denotes violence toward women is the practice of child marriage. In Nepal 40 per cent of marriages involve girls under the age of 15 [UNIFEM: 2004: 16]. In Pakistan the "*watta satta*" marriage is another form of marriage that violates the rights of women. Women become part of barter between men. A woman is given in marriage to a man in return for another woman. The case of 12-year old Reshma, who was given in a *watta satta* marriage but the marriage took place after a terrible dispute between the two families. On her wedding night her husband shot her dead claiming she had committed adultery [OXFAM: 2004: 8]. These traditional forms of marriage held together by the concept of honour and community deeply oppress women but are so firmly embedded in south Asia that unless there is concerted action with the state taking the lead, such practices will never change.

At the root of much of the violence against women in customary practices is the palpable son preference seen in south Asian societies. Amartya Sen has chronicled how with regard to food, hospitals and schooling there is terrible discrimination against the girl child. Young girls are taken to hospital only if they are very ill, young girls are more malnourished than young boys and in schooling, only 15 per cent of girls in rural primary schools go beyond the fifth grade. The gender gap in school enrolment is 14 per cent in India, 19 per cent in Nepal and 24 per cent in Pakistan [UNIFEM: 2004:14-16]. This son preference and the discrimination against the girl child lasts a lifetime leading to a lifecycle of violence and discrimination.

Violence against Women and Masculinity

Customary practices such as those outlined above require the state to create a normative framework that frowns on such practices and criminalizes those who engage in such activities. However, for the most part, because of political unpopularity, states shy away from insisting on international standards on the protection of women from violence. As a result, there is a sense that the violence is "normal", or "usual" and that severe action should not be taken against the perpetrators. This normalization of violence shows the interlinkage between ideology and violence against women. In Bangladesh in a recent survey the majority of men argued that violence against their wives was all right in certain circumstances as corrective punishment [UNIFEM: 2004]. This normalization prevents men from seeing the violence as wrong prevents women from asserting that the violence is a violation and paralyses the criminal justice system in trying to attain justice.

Another linkage that is often made is that women's lack of economic independence and empowerment has a great deal to do with the levels of violence in south Asian societies. Women's lack of economic security forces them to put up with extreme acts of violence for the sake of survival. Inheritance laws and practices, the lack of access to land, the lack of education and the denial of mobility contribute to keeping women locked into situations from which there is no escape. David Levinson in a 90 country study found that the lack of economic independence is one of the main reasons for violence against women [Levinson: 1989].

In south Asia women's access to economic resources has always been limited. Bina Aggarwal and Govind Kelkar have written extensively about these issues with regard to India and south Asia. Since a large part of south Asia is agricultural, systems of inheritance laws and cultural practices preclude women from having access to important economic resources [Kelkar: 1993: 117]. Some south Asian societies following Islamic laws give differential access to inheritance between sons and daughters. Nevertheless, even in societies and personal law systems where there is equal inheritance, the right of the testator to will his property often results in women being excluded and in being restricted to "dowry" property. Dowry, a negative customary practice then becomes the marker of a woman's inheritance. As Gail Omvedt writes, 'The basic economic dependence of women, their propertylessness and resourcelessness renders them fearfully weak in standing up and challenging the violence and power that is used against them in society" [1993:120].

The right of widows to inherit and to live secure lives free from violence, social ostracism and discrimination still remains an important need in the south Asian context. Poorer women, who have no access to inheritance or land, are economically marginalized, earning 40 per cent of male wages, doing the more labour intensive tasks and often sexually abused and raped by the upper caste landlords on whose fields they work. The rape of *dalit* women by upper caste men in India remains a major area of human rights violations having caste, class and gender implications. In land rights movements women fought for "*izzat*", the right to live in dignity and to be free from the threat of rape along with the right to parity in agricultural wages and access to land. The discrimination with regard to the distribution of land by the state is also manifold. Govind Kelkar in studying land distribution by the *Bihar Kisan Samiti* in 1989 points to how only five women (three of whom were widows) received land compared to 110 men who did and that of the 120 acres distributed women received only 7.85 acres. Discussions urging women to receive land was not well received by the male leaders of the village who saw any such suggestion as a major threat [Kelkar: 1989: 137].

Models of masculinity in the south Asian region also contribute to violence against women. In certain communities, violence is closely linked to honour and the assertion of masculine status. If being a man means controlling and domesticating your wife, then behaviour patterns emerge accordingly. Given the deeply held values and time honoured "masculine" traditions, changing these models and expectations may only take place over generations. For this, there have to be other masculine non-violent traditions that capture the imagination of young men. In modern times, some of these traditions are emerging in south Asia but they are in a nascent phase [Chopra: 2004].

Pradeep Jeganathan in a study on masculinity in Sri Lanka points to two models of masculinity that appear to exist side by side. The first, based on traditional notions of restraint, point to a respectable, responsible adult male who protects traditional virtues. This is perhaps the model inherited from the nationalist phase and Sinhalese preoccupation with shame and fear of ridicule. The other model centres on modern notions of "fearlessness" whether it is the soldier, the politician, the guerrilla, the "criminal thug" and this fearlessness contains elements of criminality and violence. The emergence of this masculine category in post independent south Asia as a dominant paradigm has worrisome implications for violence against women [Jeganathan: 2000].

Thomas Michael Walle's study into Pakistani models of masculinity also point to this dichotomy between what he calls the "moral" model i.e, those men who follow the edicts of the Koran and the "immoral" model of the drinker and the womanizer. Both exist side by side and are deployed accordingly. In both models women are seriously compromised as the "moral" man carries with him a legacy of patriarchy and the "immoral" man a hint of violence, wantonness and eventual abandonment. According to Walle "love-marriages" are discredited in this society and there is an implication of weakness for a man who takes his woman too seriously [Walle: 2004].

In her work Radhika Chopra points to a variety of masculinity models in India- the householder who is the great provider, the Gandhian renouncer. The nationalist depiction of Gandhian "effeminate" males in India has been replaced with notions of a virulent Hindu male confronting "the other", especially "the Muslim". This "restoration" of an aggressive Hindu masculinity also has implications for violence against women. Ashis Nandy's famous article (1998) pointing to the "feminine" vision of Gandhi and the so-called masculine vision of his assassin seems to have played itself out in post-independent India with aggressive, violent manifestations of masculinity taking the upper hand in the 1990s.

Linked to notions of masculinity is also a belief in the proper emotional and sexual behaviour of women. A great part of violence against women has to deal with female sexuality. Rape is about sexual violence, trafficking is often about sex work, sexual harassment is about discrimination in the workplace, domestic violence is often about a woman's refusal to have sex with her husband and many so-called customary practices such as honour killings or female genital mutilation are linked to the control of female sexuality. For this reason it is important that the protection of women from violence must be accompanied by the recognition of the reproductive rights and freedoms of women. This linkage is extremely important if we are to create conditions for women to be free from the fear of violence.

Costs of Violence against Women

Violence against women has costs for the individual victims as well for the society at large. With regard to individual victims, the first cost is that of damage to the health of women. The WHO report (2002) lists the costs of domestic violence/abuse on women in terms of health consequences. These include physical consequences, such as injuries, bruises, welts, disability, chronic pain syndrome, fractures, gastrointestinal disorders, lacerations and abrasions, ocular damage and reduced physical functioning. It has sexual and reproductive consequences such as gynaecological disorders, infertility, pelvic inflammatory disease, miscarriage and pregnancy complications, sexual dysfunction, sexually transmitted disease, unsafe abortion and unwanted pregnancy. It has psychological and behavioural consequences which include alcohol and drug abuse, depression and anxiety, eating and sleeping disorders, feelings of shame and guilt, phobias and panic disorders, physical inactivity, poor self-esteem, post-traumatic stress disorder, psychosomatic disorders, smoking, suicidal behaviour, and unsafe sexual behaviour. The health consequences can also be fatal such as homicide, suicide, maternal mortality and AIDS-related mortality. As a result of all these complications abused women are also long-term users of a country's health services and facilities with the hospital as an important location for women victims of violence.

Violence against women also exacts economic costs for the women concerned and therefore for the society. Research shows that women with a history of partner violence were more likely to be unemployed, to experience job turnover, and a negative impact on job performance [UNIFEM: 2004: 29]. In Canada a study states that violence against women costs Canada 1.6 billion dollars a year in terms of medical care and loss of productivity [UNIFEM: 2004:31].

Violence against women also has a profound effect on the children in the family. There appears to be a correlation between violence against women and child mortality. Children who witness violence are at a higher risk for a whole range of emotional and behavioural problems including anxiety, depression, poor school performance and low self-esteem. The children are also more likely to become abusers when they become adults. A study in Nepal found that in communities where women were beaten often, children aged 6-36 months had a higher risk of stunted and wasted growth than did children in communities where beatings were not reported [UNIFEM: 2004:31].

Perhaps the greatest consequence of violence against women is fear and the chilling effect it has on women's empowerment and mobility. A recent study in Bangladesh points to the fact that only about 18 per cent of women feel comfortable enough to leave their houses alone. Less than 1 per cent of working women said they felt safe in the workplace, citing dark corridors and ill lit places as sites they fear; 81 per cent of women stated that they would not go out unless they covered themselves properly for fear of violence [UNIFEM: 2004: 19-24]. Fear and insecurity then condition women's lives in a profound way because of anticipated violence. There is fear of the violence and fear of the shame if violence was to occur. Living in anticipation of violence curtails their priorities and the choices they make for the future. It makes women search out men for protection rather than companionship and makes women dependent and vulnerable. Fear then socializes women to conform to the very ideological norms that ensure their subordination.

State and Civil Society

Responses in South Asia

International instruments such as CEDAW recommendation 19 and the UN declaration on violence against women spell out the measures that states should take to eradicate violence against women in their societies. The so-called "responsibilities" of due diligence duty as spelled out in international instruments involve:

(i) The duty to pass legislation and other measures that provide a framework for preventing and punishing crimes of violence against women;

(ii) The duty to enact effective procedures and to train and sensitize the criminal justice system to ensure that they are aware of the issues and that they take violence against women to be a serious issue that demands concerted action. Included in the criminal justice process are the police, prosecutors, judiciary and forensic medical professionals;

(iii) The duty to provide support services for victims of violence such as shelters, legal and psychological counselling, training in income generating endeavours, etc, with the assistance of NGOs and other civil society organizations;

(iv) The duty to collect data and conduct research into what is often an invisible phenomenon so as to identify the problems related to violence against women in any given society; and

(v) The duty to comply with international obligations and the duty to report to international treaty bodies.

All the governments of the SAARC region have responded positively to the challenges posed by violence against women in their region. In the last decade, there has been a great deal of advances, especially in the area of standard setting and the enactment of policies and programmes. Though a great deal may not have changed at the local level, the policy framework has been developed in most of the countries of the region.

Bangladesh has responded to the challenges posed by violence against women in the region by declaring openly in its national strategy for economic growth, poverty reduction and social development that it plans to substantially reduce or eliminate violence against women and children by 2015. In 2000, Bangladesh adopted the Prevention of Oppression against Women and Children Act that deals comprehensively with crimes of violence against women. Bangladesh has also set up National Advisory Council for the prevention of violence against women with committees to prevent VAW in every district. There are also four investigative cells in the police station and a multi-sectoral programme which was adopted in 2000 that tries to combine the efforts of the health services, the police, access to justice and public awareness.

India too has taken positive measures with regard to violence against women. With regard to sex selective abortions, in 1994, India adopted the Pre-Conception and Pre-Natal Diagnostic Techniques Act and this has been amended twice as recently as 2003. The recently passed domestic violence legislation is quite comprehensive. The law was drafted in partnership with women's NGOs especially the Lawyers' Collective. In contains many provisions combining civil and criminal remedies and providing support for women survivors of violence. India is also in the process of adopting other legislation with relevance for fighting violence against women.

The Indian government is also considering the possibility of introducing legislation on trafficking. At the moment the main legislation to tackle the problem of trafficking is Immoral Traffic (Prevention) Act. Though the Act does not criminalize sex work, it criminalizes related activities including soliciting, procuring, maintaining a brothel, etc.

In Nepal in the last decade, a great deal has been done in the area of trafficking. The ministry of women, children and social welfare has proposed a new bill to replace the Traffic in Human Beings (Control) Act. The bill broadens the definition of trafficking and has strong provisions with regard to punishment and evidentiary procedure. In the late 1990s, the ministry also adopted a national anti-trafficking policy, and a rehabilitation home for victims of trafficking. The Human Rights Commission of Nepal also created a National Rapporteur on Trafficking.

In Pakistan, though many crimes of violence against women are dealt with under the Offence of Zina (Enforcement of Hudood) Ordinance, which has difficult evidentiary provisions with regard to the women victim, the National Commission on the Status of Women has now been requested to review all laws, rules and regulations affecting the status of women. The Commission also set up a committee of experts to review the Hudood and Zina Ordinances. In 2004, the Parliament in Pakistan adopted legislation criminalizing honour killings with strong punishments for the perpetrators. The law treats honour killings as an aggravated form of murder. The Pakistan Supreme Court has also stated that honour killings are murder and violate a woman's fundamental right. Crisis centres have been established for women in distress in Islamabad, Vehari, Lahore and Sahiwal.

In Sri Lanka, the decade witnessed the drafting of the Penal Code Amendments in 1995 that was a major step forward with regard to meeting the challenge of violence against women. Rape is defined without the limiting words "against her will" and special provisions exist for judicially separated couples and statutory rape. There is enhanced punishment for custodial rape, rape of a pregnant woman, rape of some one under 18, rape of a mentally disabled person and gang rape.

There are also provisions for mandatory sentencing. In Sri Lanka a draft law on domestic violence is also pending. The draft law defines domestic violence broadly and provides for a broad range of remedies including interim and permanent protection orders, emergency monetary relief and compensation.

The countries of south Asia have all ratified CEDAW though some of them have done so with reservations. The countries of south Asia have also signed the SAARC Convention on Preventing and Combating the Trafficking in Women and Children for prostitution. The Trafficking Convention defines trafficking narrowly and it is not in conformity with the international definition. It provides for cooperation among member states, repatriation and rehabilitation of women survivors, and has certain measures to ensure prevention [Report on Violence against Women E/ CN 4/2003/7 5/ Add].

Conclusion

The above survey points to the fact that all the states in the south Asian region have responded to some of the challenges posed by violence against women in the region. Many have passed laws or are entertaining draft laws to deal with some of the important questions. Ten years after Beijing, it is still a concern that except for India none of the countries of the region have adopted domestic violence' legislation or made the necessary changes to anti-trafficking legislation. However programmes and policies are in place. Ministries dealing with women and welfare, national commissions and individual government departments have carried out a great deal of activities. There have been many training programmes also for senior level police officers and other members of the criminal justice system.

The changes in south Asia have also been made possible by the activism of civil society and the foresight of many NGOs. They have conducted research, suggested legal reform and put in place constructive programmes, which actually assist women victims of violence. They have trained policemen, lobbied politicians and judges and also put together shelters and crisis centres. They have taken cases to court, demonstrated for women's rights and in some countries mobilized people at the risk to their own lives. They have counselled and cared for many victims of violence breaking their silence and allowing them to regain their dignity.

Research from around the world points to the fact that violence against women can only be combated if there is a healthy partnership between women's groups and the state apparatus. While women's groups must protect their independence, on certain issues they have to work effectively with the criminal justice system, joining forces to protect the rights of women victims. However, this also poses a major dilemma. The decade ends with the triumph of a certain "law and order feminism" which aims at punishing the perpetrator, using draconian provisions in the law. Whether in trafficking, rape or sexual harassment, there is a punishment rhetoric that belies a complex reality. South Asia is particularly receptive to this excess of law enforcement. Provisions in trafficking legislation, in sexual offences legislation, in preventing women from migrating procedures, are so draconian that they raise questions about the human rights of the perpetrators and an over reliance on the criminal justice system to solve complex social questions. Though they provide an immediate sense of something being done, in the long run they pose serious dilemmas. In the end judges and juries just do not convict if they feel that the law is too harsh or unreasonable. Fighting violence against women will only succeed if it is done through the lens of human rights, protecting the rights and dignity of the woman survivor while ensuring a fair trial for the perpetrator. Any other course of action will not stand the test of time and important legislation will fall into disuse. Fairness must be a central concern for women even when they are dealing with abusers. Moreover, the law is an important tool but it is one of the many strategies available to women.

While fighting for justice through the legal system, there should also be attempts to put in place education policies, health strategies and community level programmes that promote equality between men and women and teach non-violent methods of resolving conflict. A multi-pronged approach to violence against women will result in far-reaching changes, transforming attitudes and practices so that women and men can live in equality and dignity.

References

Agnes, Flavia. 1990. *Journey to Justice,* Mumbai: Majlis.

Chatterjee, Partha.1989. 'The Nationalist Resolution of the Women's Question' in Kumkum Sangari ,et al (eds), *Recasting Women.* New Delhi: Kali for Women.

Chopra, Radhika, et al. 2004. *South Asian Masculinities: Context of Change, Sites of Continuity, Women Unlimited,* New Delhi: Sage Publications.

Chowdhry, Prem.1993. 'Inheritance Rights as Pivot of Control in Northern India', *National Law School Journal,* Bangalore: NLS.

Hawley, J.S. (ed). 1994. *Sati: The Blessing and the Curse.* Oxford: Oxford University Press.

Jeganathan, Pradeep. 2000. 'A Space for Violence-Anthropology, Politics and the Location of a Sinhala Practice of Masculinity' in P. Chatterjee, et al (eds), *Community, Gender and Violence,* New Delhi: Permanent Black.

Kapur, Ratna and Cossman, Brenda. 1996. *Subversive Sites: Feminist Engagement with the Law in India,* New Delhi: Sage.

Kelkar, Govind. 1990. 'The Bodh Gaya Land Struggle' in Ilina Sen (ed.) *A Space within the Struggle: Women's Participation in People's Movements,* New Delhi: Kali for Women.

Kelkar, Govind 1993. 'Women, Land and Agrarian Reform: Issues of Gender and Class in Improving Women's Effective Access to Land', *National Law School Journal,* Bangalore: NLS.

Lawyers' Collective. 1992. *Domestic Violence,* New Delhi: Kali for Women.

Levinson, David.1989. *Family Violence in Cross Cultural Perspective, Frontiers, of Anthropology Series,* Vol. I, Delhi and London: Sage Publications.

Menon, Nivedita 2000. 'Embodying the Self: Feminism, Sexual Violence and the Law', New Delhi: Permanent Black.

Nandy, Ashis. 1998. 'Final Encounter: The Politics of the Assassination of Gandhi', in A Nandy *(ed.), At the Edge of Psychology,* New Delhi: OUP.

Naved, Ruchira Tabassum. 2004. A *Situational Analysis of Violence against Women in South Asia,* UNIFEM.

OXFAM. 2004. 'Towards Ending Violence against Women in South Asia', OXFAM International, UK.

Perera, Susana. 1999. *Stories of Survivors: Socio-Political Contexts of Female Headed Household in Post-Terror Southern Sri Lanka,* New Delhi: Vikas.

Special Rapporteur on Violence. 1994-2003. Special Rapporteur on Violence against Women, its Causes and Consequences, International, Regional, and National Developments in the Area of Violence against Women 1994-2003, Addendum I. EICNAI2003175/Add.1.

Violence against Women.1995. (Preliminary Report) submitted by the Special Rapporteur on Violence against Women, its Causes and Consequences, *EICN.4I1995/42.*

Tiruchandran, Selvy. 1999. *The Other Victims of War: Emergence of Female Headed Households in Eastern Sri Lanka,* New Delhi: Voices.

Umar, Mohammed. 1998. *Bride Burning in India,* A *Socio-Legal Study,* New Delhi: APH Publishing Corporation.

UNICEF. 2001. A *Reference Kit on Violence against Women and Girls in South Asia,* ROSA, Katmandu.UNICEF.

UNIFEM. 2004. Say No to Gender-Based Violence: Responses from South Asia, New Delhi.

Walle, Thomas Michael. 2004. 'Virginity vs Decency: Continuity and Change in Pakistani Men's Perception of Sexuality and Women' in Radhika Chopra, et al (eds.), *South Asian Masculinities: Context of Change, Sites of Continuity,* New Delhi: Kali for Women.

WHO. 2002. *World Report on Violence and Health,* Geneva: WHO.

This paper was first published in the *Economic and Political Weekly*: 40:44-45: 2005: 4729-4736. It is included here with the prior permission of the author and the Editor, *Economic and Political Weekly*. Address for email correspondence is: rcoomaraswamy @yahoo.com

CHAPTER - SIX

Broken Lives, Desperate Choices: The Political Economy of Global Sex Trafficking

Susan Runkle

In recent years, the Indian media has done several exposes on how global sex trafficking mafias have set up shop in India and how the women they bring from the former Soviet bloc countries and the collapsed regimes of Eastern Europe as sex workers are hot favourites with the nouveau riche Indian men because of their fair skin and western appearance. This article provides a glimpse into the factors and conditions that force women from these countries to be sucked into sex trade. This article is based on the author's field and archival research under very dangerous conditions in Armenia.

Millions of women throughout the world are trafficked each year, brought from their homes to perform sex work in conditions which often provide them with little to no pay, as well as inadequate food and housing. Often, they have initially been promised jobs that do not involve sex work. These women are victimized because they are poor, because they have little or no other prospects for employment, and, above all, because they are women. Definitions aside, the reality of the situation is essentially this: comparatively privileged men buy the bodies of poor women, because they can. Politico-economic analyses (e.g. Bishop: 1998) have been particularly enlightening, as they allow for an analysis of the root causes of sex trafficking in specific historical and cultural locations.

Louise Brown succinctly describes the reasons for the existence of trafficking as transcending poverty, noting that it represents a macro-level view of the distorted power relations between men and women, the wealthy and the poor and those who have access to resources and those who do not. "The sex industry makes money because it buys cheap raw materials and packages them well" she notes, "It turns vulnerability into a commodity and that commodity into a profit"(2000:60).

This commoditization of vulnerability makes it all the more essential to draw a very sharp defining line between what constitutes labour migration and what it means to be trafficked for sex work.

The Interpol Working Group on Trafficking in Women and Children, ratified by its 181 member countries in 2000, distinguishes migration from trafficking because in the case of trafficking "the intention is to exploit the victim after the illegal entry has been accomplished, whereas the smugglers' relationship with the victims normally ends once the illegal entry has been achieved" (2000). As such, it is clear that women who are *victims of sex trafficking face a special set of issues that migrants do not, not least of which is the lack of option to return to their place of origin of their own free will.*

A Crime Against No One

In the case of Armenia, as in most areas where it is an issue of concern, sex trafficking is a problem with both multiple facets and limited scope for solutions. It is a product of a historical period in which criminal elements are able to capitalize on the economic and socio-political instability of the countries of the collapsed socialist bloc through the relatively simple acquisition of forged passports as well as a pool of women who have few, if any, other resources with which to support themselves and their children.

It is far too easy to condemn the actions of the traffickers, or, more insidiously, the women who choose to migrate to perform sex work, without understanding the context in which the problem itself has arisen. In Moldova, for example, 30 per cent of women who are returned to their place of origin after being victims of trafficking "disappear" within months of their return, as they find themselves in the same unstable economic situation that they initially sought to escape.

Factors that Facilitate

In 1920, the Red Army forced Armenia to accept a communist- dominated government in which Armenian autonomy was subjugated to Soviet rule. Since then, political and economic instability have combined with natural calamities, like the earthquake of 1998, to make a large proportion of the population internally displaced persons (IDPs) or migrants to neighbouring states like Russia. This added to the trend of seasonal migration of labour that has prevailed since the 1960s.

In September 1989, Azerbaijan and Turkey began a blockage of Armenian fuel and supply lines over the disputed territory of Nagorno-Karabakh. The war over Nagorno-Karabakh produced 218,950 refugees on the Armenian side and 185,000 on the Azeri, with the creation of an additional 72,000 internally displaced persons. In the winter of 1991-1992, 80 per cent of industry and transport could not function due to a complete lack of electricity leading to more than 250,000 people leaving the country. The Armenian diaspora numbers 5.5 million people, approximately one and a half times the population of Armenia, and since 1991, between 800,000 and 1 million people have emigrated out of a total population of four million.

Socio-political crises have resulted in the creation of a situation in which it has become relatively easy for traffickers to exploit existing weaknesses in a destabilized social structure. The dissolution of the Soviet Union meant that its population registration system was also destroyed, which makes it extremely difficult to ascertain the numbers of women trafficked each year from Armenia. Social structures which would have formerly served to support women have been fundamentally destabilized following the breakup of the Soviet bloc, and the privatization initiatives of the Government of Armenia between 1998 and 2000 only further served to marginalize women, who cross culturally form the bulk of the poor.

Indeed, women have been most affected by socio-economic crises in Armenia. As an increasing number of men migrate for work, one-third of Armenian households are currently female-headed. Although women constitute 45 per cent of the workforce, they also constitute 66 per cent of the unemployed, and women's wages are just over half that of men's. 70 per cent of the officially registered unemployed are women, and women form the majority of workers in the informal sector. Such statistics are complicated by the existence of what are often termed "traditional" gender roles, which position men as the main economic unit in the household and further marginalizes women who are single parents.

These inequalities make young, divorced or abandoned women particularly vulnerable to being trafficked. An unstable economic situation, limited opportunities for employment, coupled with gender norms which consider divorced women and single mothers abnormal and even "anti-family", positions such women as social outcasts who have to negotiate a larger social structure which effectively works against them at every turn. Migration is often seen as the only source of income with which to support themselves and their families.

A Desperate Choice

Women constitute the majority of illegal migrants from Armenia. It is impossible to ascertain the percentages of these women who are performing sex work, or how many undocumented workers exist. At some level, however, the numbers are irrelevant, as the existence of the problem itself warrants concern.

It is crucial to remember that women who choose to migrate to perform sex work, as well as those who are deceived by traffickers with offers of legitimate employment abroad only to be forced into sex work are not making irrational decisions. *While their choice to leave their place of origin is definitely risky, it is also the result of a life situation in which there are often no other choices to be considered.* As such, it is imperative that analyses of trafficking be sensitive to the fact that *women who migrate are not making unintelligent decisions, but rather desperate ones.*

Who are the Traffickers?

Sex trafficking is a high profit, low risk criminal activity in that it generates an enormous amount of profit for those in control of it while presenting very little possibility of prosecution. Because traffickers prey on the most marginalized members of society, poor women, their activities are often ignored. This is, of course, compounded by the fact that reliable documentation on the extent of trafficking is nearly impossible to ascertain due to its clandestine nature. Unlike drug trafficking, which presents a relatively high risk of being caught along with a high profit margin, *sex trafficking can often be masked via the construction of false fronts such as employment agencies and marriage bureaus, enabling traffickers to justify the movement of women across borders without much interference at the state level.*

Yet, traffickers are as often a part of informal networks as they are of the large-scale organized criminal networks that operate mainly in Ukraine, Belarus, Russia and Bulgaria. Such networks exist simultaneously, which allows for the loose organization of trafficking networks, a characteristic that enables them to fragment and reform quickly even when disrupted by police intervention. Above all, *traffickers are criminal elements that thrive in situations of instability, war and economic hardship, exploiting human suffering to their own advantage.*

Far beyond Armenia, sex trafficking is part of a global phenomenon which moves women from areas as diverse as Myanmar to Cambodia, rural to urban Thailand, Nepal to India, Ukraine and the Commonwealth of Independent States (CIS) to Dubai and Turkey, the Philippines to Japan, China to Malaysia and Singapore. *Ethnicity also plays a role in the demographics of trafficking, with the movement of women* from Southeastern Europe to Southeast Asia, Eastern Europe to Central America and the CIS to the Gulf countries.

In Armenia, an estimated 45 per cent of women have experienced domestic violence, a crime that can seriously compromise one's sense of self-worth. As such, it is essential to consider that *many women who are trafficked are victims before they even leave the country.*

Means of Control

Traffickers derive their power from a variety of sources, all of which combine to create a situation from which escape is often impossible. The primary source of their power lies in the *system of debt bondage*, in which women are forced to perform sex work without pay, sometimes for years, in order to "repay" the cost of being trafficked, including their plane fare and dubious fees which are more often than not fabrications. Traffickers also maintain *control over women through physical and linguistic isolation.*

Women's documents, especially their passports, are often taken from them once they reach their destination, which robs them not only of their proof of identity, but also of their sense of self. Without documentation, women are powerless to escape, even if they have the opportunity to do so. In addition to this, traffickers use *violence and fear, as well as threats of reprisals against the victim's family, in order to guarantee their acquiescence. Psychological torture, the systematic deprivation of contact with others who are not clients, is another, particularly destabilizing, technique by which traffickers gradually assert complete control over their victims.*

Despite these circumstances, however, women do survive the dehumanizing experience of being trafficked. This rhetoric of victimhood serves both to infantilize women and to obscure the realities of sex trafficking. *Trafficking is not primarily about sex: it is about the systematic exploitation of those who have no other choices in life.* However, prevailing cultural assumptions about the nature of sex work often serve to complicate not only the lives of women who perform sex work, but also the efforts at combating the problem.

Fighting an Unseen Foe

On October 14, 2002, Resolution No. 591-A established the Interdepartmental Committee on Trafficking in Armenia, which created protocols for the investigation and prosecution of traffickers as well as a pan governmental board of individuals who will ideally work together to combat trafficking. This legislation defines trafficking as "the recruitment, transportation, transfer, harbouring or receipt of a person by means of coercion, or by abduction, fraud or deception, abuse of power or position of vulnerability" and proposes a punishment of three hundred to five hundred times the minimum national salary (which is currently at 13,000 drams, or approximately $23 per month), one year of public service, or imprisonment from one to four years. Sentences increase to prison terms of four to seven years if the trafficking case has involved a minor or use of force or threats against life, and to a period of five to eight years if an organized criminal group has been involved in the case, or if the death of the victim has been caused.

Yet, the main question remains: how can formal legislation combat what is essentially a clandestine phenomenon? It is perhaps in recognition of this fact that the International Organization for Migration (IOM) concluded that the solutions to the problem of trafficking are five-fold. The first is creation and raising awareness, which includes public information campaigns, the sensitization of public officials (particularly those who work with travel documents which are necessary for the trafficking of women), media and NGOs and the training of staff working in Armenian embassies and consulates.

Throughout the CIS, increasing of awareness has taken the form of post-card size leaflets, designed for quick distribution in public places, which are extremely evocative in nature. The images on them are extremely graphic, as well as effective; from a picture of a doll-like woman trapped in a plastic box, the label of which reads "Lorena" to one of a woman covered by a bar code such as one would find on an item for sale in the grocery store, holding the bars and crying, these images convey the reality of trafficking. One of the most powerful images, however, is the least graphic: it shows a Georgian woman looking disturbed, yet resolute, as a male hand extends money toward her while another male hand tries to take her passport. The caption reads, in emphatic red Georgian and English letters, "You are not for sale!"

The second IOM recommendation to combat trafficking is, of course, *the prosecution of traffickers.* This is easier said than done due to the ability of the criminal elements that form trafficking networks to fragment and regroup much more quickly than law enforcement is able to respond. IOM advocates longer prison terms for those convicted of trafficking, as well as the development of legal mechanisms for the confiscation of the assets gained by traffickers in order to make them available as compensation for their victims. In addition to this, IOM suggests that the Government of Armenia regulate and monitor all companies that arrange for young women to travel abroad, as well as undertake greater measures to combat corruption at all levels of the government in regard to trafficking.

The third IOM recommends the *adoption of protection and assistance measures to victims via the establishment of links between various organizations, from NGOs to women's groups, in order to better serve women who have been victims of trafficking.* This would further involve the creation of shelters, improved access to psychological and health care as well as assistance in finding employment. IOM also advocates the implementation of measures that would provide what they term "a safe and dignified return" of women to Armenia.

Additional IOM recommendations in order to improve the situation in regard to trafficking in Armenia are *further research into the subject, as well as economic development in the region.* Certainly, such wide ranging, albeit important, recommendations underscore the *extremely problematic nature of trafficking as a social phenomenon*, and raises the question as to how to improve life for the most marginalized members of society when there is so very much else to be done.

Politico-Economic Roots

It would be ludicrous to assert that men have not also been victimized by the vast economic changes that have swept the countries of the former Soviet Union since 1991. The difference between the experience of men and women, however, is a profound one, and lies in the deeply embedded gender norms that are endemic throughout the world. When economic systems are in a state of flux, women's bodies, whether via their *commoditization of the female form in institutions like the Miss India pageant* (Runkle: 2004) or the international sex industry (Chapkis: 2002), are all too often viewed as objects for sale.

The problem of sex trafficking is not just about changes in an economic system, but something much more profound: *a view of women that perceives them as items available for male consumption.* Were it not for the existence of pre-existing gendered social structures such as sex work itself, sex trafficking could not exist. *In looking for solutions it follows that broader understandings of what it means for women to survive in a gendered world need to be incorporated into the formulation of recommendations to ameliorate what is clearly a mere symptom of the greater disease of gender inequality.*

References

Acharya, Usha D. 1997. *Country Report on Trafficking in Children and Their Exploitation in Prostitution and Other Intolerable Forms of Labour in Nepal*, Kathmandu: International Labour Organization.

Bangladesh National Women Lawyers' Association. 1997. *Survey in the Area of Child and Woman Trafficking*, Dhaka.

Butler, Judith, 1993. *Bodies That Matter,* New York: Routledge, Caouette.

Therese, M. 1998. *Needs Assessment on Cross-border Trafficking in Women and Children: The Mekong Sub-region. Bangkok,* Bangkok: UN Working Group on Trafficking in the Mekong Sub-region.

Government of Pakistan. 1997. "Combating Child Sex Trafficking, Sexual Exploitation and Involvement of Children in Intolerable Forms of Child Labor", *Country Report on Pakistan.* Islambad.

Hart, Angie. 1998. *Buying and Selling Power: Anthropological Reflections on Prostitution in Spain,* Boulder: University of Colorado Press.

Held, David, Anthony McGrew, David Goldblatt and Jonathan Perraton, I.(eds.).1999.

Global Transformations, Stanford: Stanford University Press.

International Organization for Migration. 2001. *Trafficking in Women and Children from the Republic of Armenia: A Study,* Yerevan.

Interpol Working Group on Trafficking in Women for Sexual Exploitation. 2002. *Manual For Investigators.*

Kempadoo, Kamala and Jo Doezema. 1998. *Global Sex Workers: Rights. Resistance and Redefinition.* London: Routledge.

Lim, Lin Lean. (ed.). 1998. *The Sex Sector: The Economic and Social Bases of Prostitution in Southeast Asia,* Geneva: International Labor Organization.

Minna, Hiltunen and Seppa Teija. 1999. *The Beach Boys: Child Sex Tourism Phenomenon in Sri Lanka,* Unpublished Master's Thesis: University of Kuopio.

Muecke, Marjorie. 1992. "Mother Sold Food, Daughter Sells Her Body: The Cultural Continuity of Prostitution", *Social Science and Medicine:* 35:891-6.

Mukherjee, KK. 1997. *Child Prostitution in Rajasthan,* Delhi: National Commission for Women. Government of India.

National Commission for Women. 1997. *The Velvet Blouse,* Delhi: Government of India.

Niesner, Elvira and Jones-Pauly, Christina. 2001.*Trafficking in Women in Europe.*

Prosecution and Victim Protection in a European Context, Bielefeld.

Rozario, Rita. 1986. *Trafficking in Women and Children in India,* Delhi: Uppal Publishing House.

Runkle, Susan. 2004. "The Making of 'Miss India': Constructing Gender, Power and the Nation" *Journal of South Asian Popular Culture:* 2: 2: 16-26.

Shelly, L. 2003. "Crime and Corruption: Enduring Problems of Post Soviet Development", *Demokratizatsiya:* 2:1:110-114.

Sinha, Indrani and Carolyn Sieightholme. 1996. *Guilty Without Trial: Women in the Sex Trade in Calcutta,* New Brunswick: New Jersey: Rutgers University Press.

The paper was first published in *Manushi:* 146: 2005:16-21. It is included here with the permission of the author and Editor, *Manushi.* The author has done her Ph.D in Cultural Anthropology at Syracuse University.

PART - II

SURVIVAL, REPRODUCTION AND PROTECTION FROM LETHAL THREATS

CHAPTER - SEVEN

Survival of the Girl Child: Tunneling out of the *Chakravyuha*[1]

Satish B. Agnihotri

Abhimanyu, the legendary prince of Mahabharata, died during the epic war, trapped inside *Chakravyuha*, the wheel shaped formation of the enemy columns. His death was destined while he was in his mother's womb. Many an Indian girl children seem destined to die likewise today and in their case the *Chakravyuha* has invaded the womb itself resulting in their death even before they are born! Provisional results of 2001 census give rise to both alarm and despair on this score.

How can we begin to rescue the girl children out of the *Chakravyuha* of sex selective abortions? Do we wait for a 'revolution', or for that illusive entity called 'political will' to be forged or for the miracle of total enforcement of the PNDT Act to happen or expect a change of heart among the foeticide service providers who worship profit at all costs?

We first need to map the contours of the problem by locating the 'epicentres' of female child deficit. We need next to move to a mix of possible, even if partial solutions, to mitigate the situation rather than seeking a blueprint for a perfect solution. That will be like 'Waiting for Godot'.

In short term, we need to support and strive for universal coverage in survival inputs like immunization, supplementary nutrition or even birth registration to minimize the gender gap. As girl children usually face discrimination in accessing these inputs, universalisation benefits them more. But in the longer term, we need to create objective conditions so as to minimize the 'unwantedness' of a girl child. This necessitates a modicum of economic and physical security being guaranteed to women.

At the same time, civil society must also debate the ethical dimension of sex-based elimination of a segment of the population. This could well be the thin end of the wedge that provides in its wake currency to eliminate other segments of population based on other criterion. We must also question the current model of development, where discrimination necessarily appears to accompany development. Success stories of alternative 'development' must be provided visibility and highlighted as role models for society to follow.

Sex ratios in the Indian population are becoming rapidly masculine. A marginal increase of 6 points in the female to male ratios of the overall population; 933 in 2001 from 927 in 1991, has not given rise to much euphoria as it did in 1981 (Chhabra: 1981; Padmanabha: 1981) and rightly so. This is because there has been a sharp decline of 18 points in the f/m ratios among children (0-6 years) during the same period. This pattern, the Registrar General of India warns us, will continue to haunt the society for decades to come (Paper–1 of 2001), unless of course, corrective measures are taken.

Results of the first population census of the millennium reveal a number of significant changes in the sex ratio patterns in the country. Firstly, the sex ratio decline among children in the 0-6 age group turns out to be sharper in the urban areas (32 points) than in the rural. Table 1 provides state level data on the changes in sex ratio between 1991 and 2001 in the rural and the urban population. It can also be noticed that the decline in urban f/m ratios among children in most of the states is significantly larger compared to that in the rural areas.

Above pattern is seen more sharply in the distribution of the decadal decrease in sex ratios in the rural and the urban areas in different districts of the country. Figure 1a and 1b give this distribution. While the mean decline in rural areas of the districts is 16, it is as high as 28 in the urban segment. Further, the number of districts where the f/m ratios have declined by 60 to 100 points it is much higher in the urban areas.

The second important change is of the breach in the much written about north-south divide in the sex ratio patterns[2] across the Narmada-Sone or the Bharuch–Chhotanagpur axis. This can be seen from figure 2 which maps the urban f/m ratios among children in 0-6 years age group. Four broad categories of districts can be identified by f/m ratio; below 865, between 856 and 910, between 910 and 960 and above 960. Districts in the first two categories are the ones where the female deficit is strong. These are no longer confined to the north of Narmada but have moved considerably southward, making ingress into nearly entire Gujarat, a number of districts of Maharashtra, and surprisingly, certain pockets of Orissa. The traditional north-south divide stands significantly modified and the 'northernisation' of sex ratios (a term used by the Caldwells: 1990) is rapidly taking the urban route. Even the north–east is not unaffected from this malaise, urban Kamrup that is essentially Guáwahati shows a f/m ratio of 888 for children in the 0-6 years age group.

Sharp decline in the f/m ratios among children in urban areas can not be explained away by any of the three popular escape hatches of yesteryears i.e. migration, undercount or biologically ordained high sex ratios at birth. Unlike adults, children below 6 years do not migrate sex selectively; urban areas should suffer much less from undercount than adjoining rural areas and biologically, sex ratios at birth cannot become masculine so rapidly.

Table 1
Decline in FMRs (Females per 1000 males) in the 0-6 Year Population: 1991-2001

State	FMR 06U01	FMR 06R01	FMR 06U91	FMR 06R91	Decline U	Decline R
INDIA	903	934	935	948	32	14
Punjab	789	795	936	952	147	157
Dadra & Nagar Haveli*	885	995	977	1015	92	20
Gujarat	827	905	909	937	81	32
Haryana	809	824	884	877	76	53
Daman & Diu*	935	920	996	933	62	13
Delhi*	866	853	917	900	51	48
Uttar Pradesh	880	922	928	927	48	4
Himachal Pradesh	858	900	904	955	46	55
Uttrakhand	874	914	913	898	39	-16
Chandigarh*	844	852	879	891	35	39
Goa	919	948	953	972	35	24
Andaman & Nicobar Islands*	940	976	970	973	31	-3
Maharashtra	908	923	934	953	27	30
Bihar	924	940	950	953	26	14
Madhya Pradesh	906	941	931	944	25	4
Nagaland	935	983	959	1001	24	17
Assam	931	967	955	977	24	10
Orissa	927	954	949	969	23	15
Rajasthan	886	914	909	919	22	4
Chhatisgarh	941	982	960	988	19	6
Jharkhand	931	973	950	985	19	13
Sikkim	925	991	936	967	12	-24
Karnataka	939	954	951	963	12	9
Lakshadweep*	920	1010	932	951	11	-59
Pondicherry*	951	971	962	963	11	-7
Tripura	948	978	959	968	11	-10
West Bengal	948	967	955	969	7	3
Tamil Nadu	951	931	955	945	4	14
Meghalaya	964	977	968	989	4	12
Mizoram	961	978	965	973	4	-6
Andhra Pradesh	958	965	962	979	3	14
Kerala	958	964	958	958	-1	-6
Manipur	980	956	972	975	-8	19
Arunachal Pradesh	981	957	946	986	-35	29

* Female to Male Ratios (Urban) among children (0-6 years) Census 2001.
Source: Census of India, 2001

The rapid decline in the urban f/m ratios among children clearly points out to one factor; sex selective abortion or female foeticide that has gained currency

Figure 1: Urban and Rural Decline in the FMR 0-6 between 1991 and 2001, Districtwise

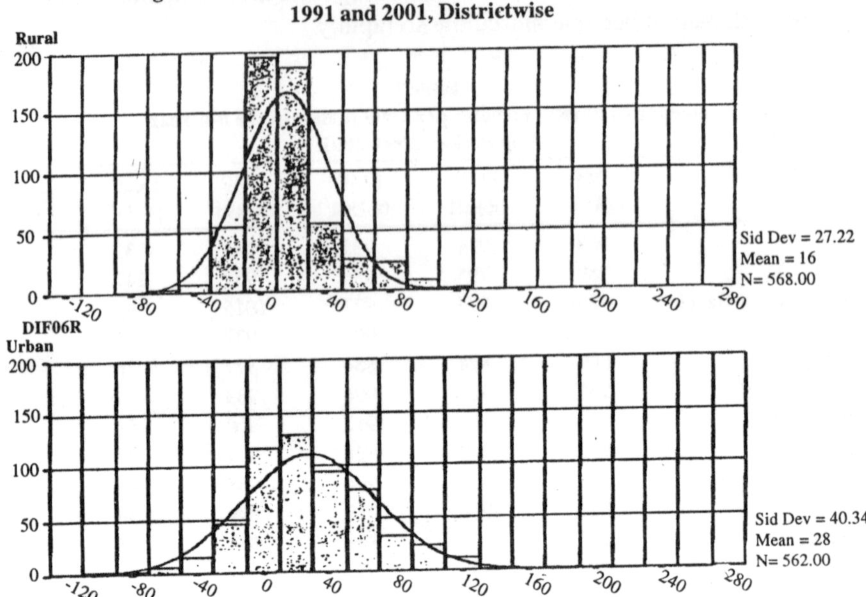

Figure 2: Female to Male Ratios (Urban) among Children (0-6 Years), Census 2001

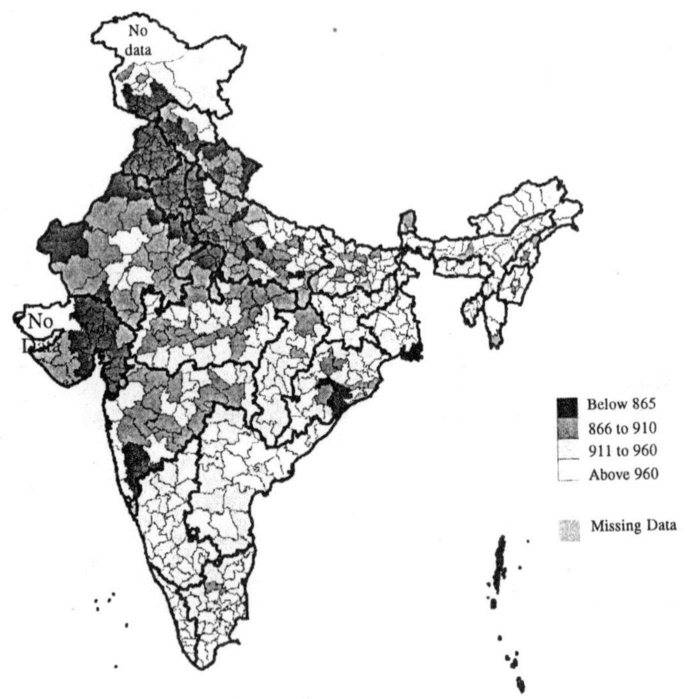

Source: Census of India.

during the 80s and more sharply in the 90s. The sex of the foetus is identified through techniques of amneocentesis or use of ultrasonography. Abortions are carried out either as an 'attached' service' or independently. Compared to female infanticide, this became a more acceptable mode of disposing of the 'unwanted' girl child. Infanticide is an overtly 'barbaric' practice, carried by non–professional and less powerful persons e.g. traditional '*dais*' or an old lady in the household. It does not allow parents to distance themselves from the event i.e. killing of the child, and be free of any guilt (McKee: 1984). 'Professionals', superior in the power hierarchy, on the other hand, carry out sex selective abortion. They use scientific techniques, hardware and skills; sanitize the process of eliminating the foetus and reduce the burden of guilt on parents.

Concentration of medical facilities and professionals in urban areas, and, more important, their absence from the rural areas is well known in our society. Naturally, the facilities for sex selective abortions and other sex selection techniques will be available in the urban areas first and that is precisely what we are seeing in the results of 2001 census.

It is important to highlight here the importance of state specific analyses of the problem. Many a nuance of the state level decline is not revealed in the national perspective. This can be elaborated with the example of Orissa, a state where it was hard to imagine such widespread decline in sex ratios even if the decline is confined to urban areas. The spatial pattern of the decline is shown in figure 3a and 3b. In 1991, only two districts, Kendrapada and Jagatsingpur, had low f/m ratios, 942 and 941 respectively. But in 2001 as many as 12 districts had f/m ratios

Figure 3a: FMR among Children 0-6 years (Girls per 1000 Boys): Orissa 1991

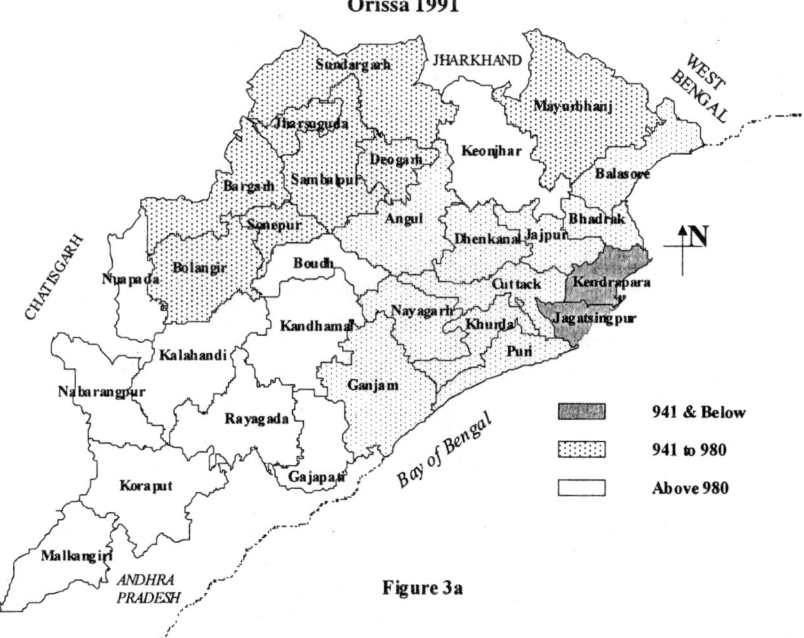

Figure 3b: FMR among Children 0-6 years (Girls per 1000 Boys): Orissa 2001

Figure 3b

Figure 4: Urbam FMR among Children 0-6 years (Girls per 1000 Boys): Orissa 2001

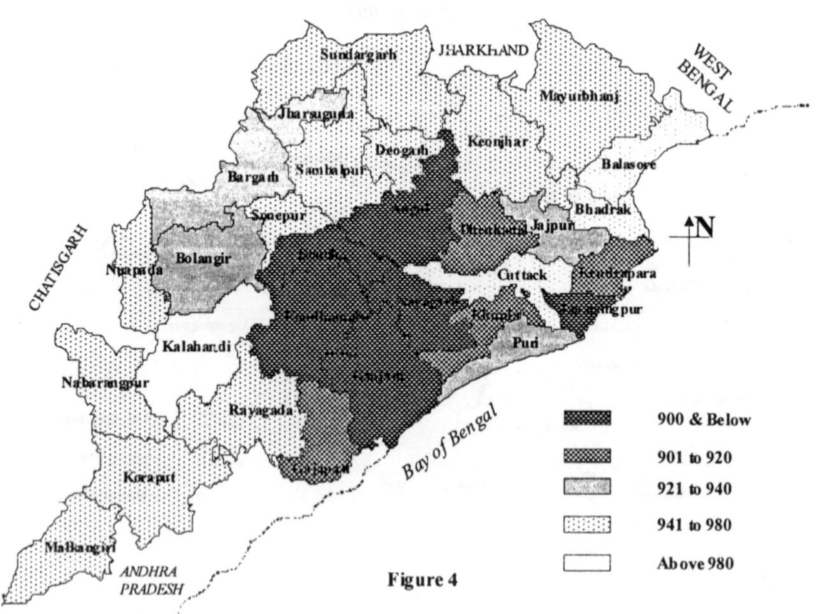

Figure 4

below this level, lowest being in Nayagarh (901). The contiguity of these 12 districts is striking; low f/m ratios show a remarkable cluster and not a scatter.

But the contiguity of districts with very low f/m ratios in urban population is more disturbing (Figure 4). Three adjoining districts, Ganjam, Nayagarh and Boudh have f/m ratios (urban) below 860; a figure comparable to some of the districts of Haryana and western UP. These are flanked by Kandhamal (896), Angul (898) and Dhenkanal (902), Khordha (908) and Gajpati (920). Two districts, Kendrapada (916) and Jagatsingpur (889) are not contiguous but separated by a strip of Jajpur (926), Cuttack (948) and Puri (930); even these ratios are not quite high. The belt of low f/m ratio also stretches along the Bolangir (921), Bargarh (938) and Jharsuguda (931).

It is plausible to argue that the low urban f/m ratios for the 0-6 age group could also be attributed to statistical fluctuations due to the small population size. This is especially so for urban child population of Nayagarh, Boudh and Kandhmal. It is intriguing, however, as to why the 'fluctuations' should point out in the same direction. Further, even if we add the urban population of these contiguous districts, f/m ratios in the 0-6 age group will remain low. The 'fluctuation' argument does not therefore help.

It is possible to take this kind of analysis to sub-district level and quite fruitfully. This part of the research is currently underway and is progressing as per the availability of the census 2001 sub-district data.

II

How does the lowering of f/m ratios in urban areas affect the rural segment of the population? It is necessary to study this pattern and anticipate the changes that are likely to occur. We have talked of the 'foeticide service providers' operating from the urban centres in the previous section. As their practice and the profit[3] 'roars' in the urban area, the doctor–entrepreneur starts attracting clients from the rural catchments. At the same time, the number of such 'service providers' increases and in many instances, they start providing mobile service. Gradually a larger segment of the rural population starts availing of these 'services'. As the use becomes widespread the sex ratios in the child population become more and more masculine in the concerned area and tell tale signs appear through the sex ratio figures.

High-school physics textbooks describe a phenomenon called 'sympathetic resonance'. Imagine two cloth-strings on which clothes are kept for drying. If one string is shaken, up and down vertically, the other string does not respond initially. If the oscillations persist, the second string slowly begins to respond. Gradually its oscillations become comparable to those of the first string. In the extreme case of 'coupled oscillations', it is possible for a bridge to collapse as soldiers march in unison and the rhythm of their march coincides with the 'natural' frequency of the bridge!

The response of the rural sex ratios to growing masculinity of the urban sex ratios follows a similar pattern (for details, see Agnihotri: 2002). Initially these remain indifferent to the changes taking place in the urban f/m ratios. If we draw a graph showing the urban f/m ratios on x-axis and the rural sex ratios on the y-axis, we can expect a horizontal line. This is indeed the case in most of the eastern and the southern states (with exception of Tamil Nadu and Orissa), Chhattisgarh and Jharkhand as shown in figures 5a to 5i. This pattern has remained the same in these states for both 1991 and 2001.

Figure 5a Child Sex Ratios: Andhra: Urban - Rural

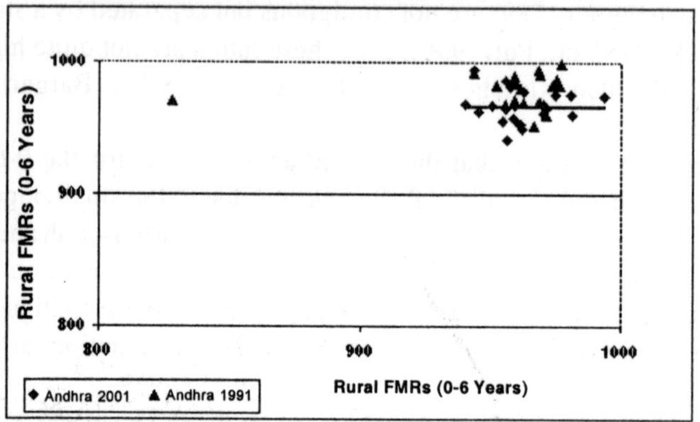

Figure 5b: Child Sex Ratios: Kerala: Urban - Rural

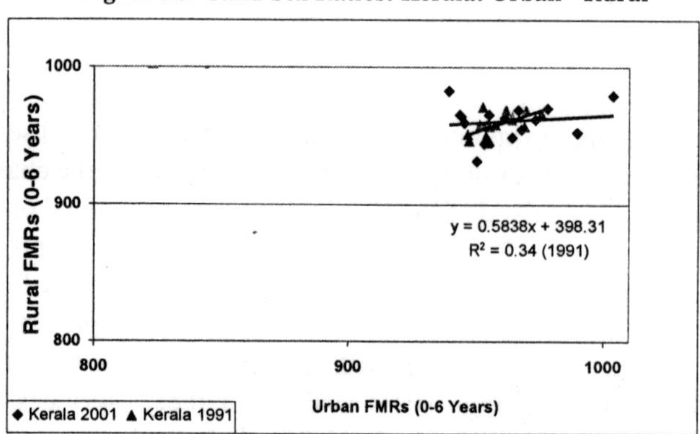

Figure 5c: Child Sex Ratios: Karnataka: Urban - Rural

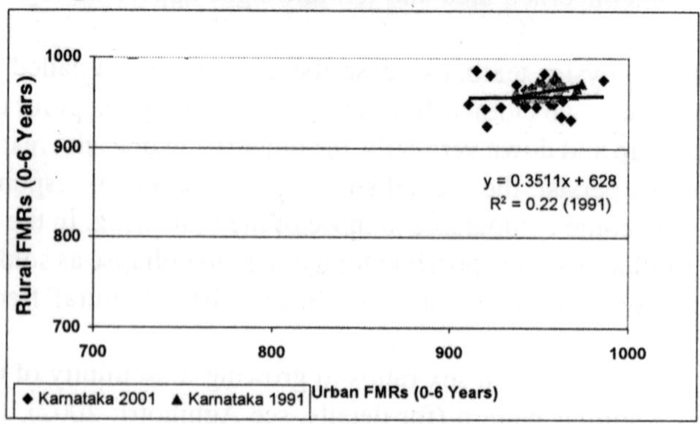

Figure 5d: Child Sex Ratios: Chhattisgarh: Urban - Rural

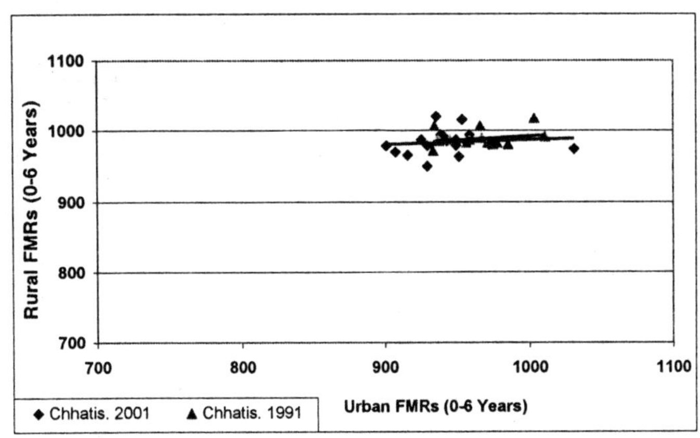

Figure 5e: Child Sex Ratios: NE: Urban - Rural

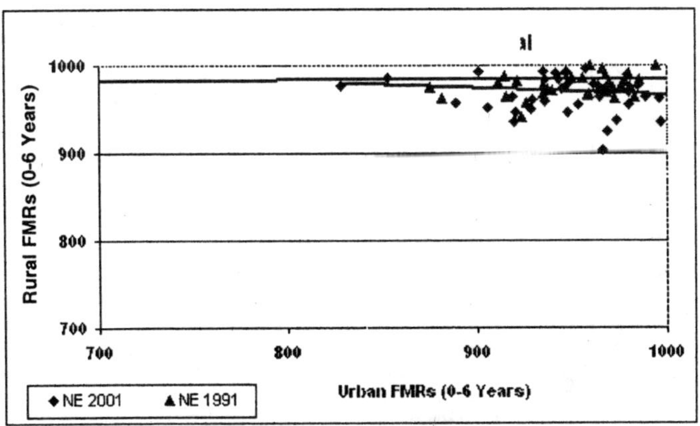

Figure 5f: Child Sex Ratios: Assam: Urban - Rural

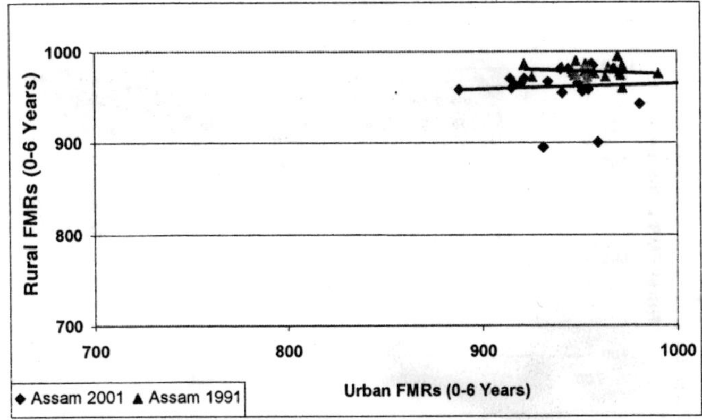

Figure 5g: Child Sex Ratios: WB: Urban - Rural

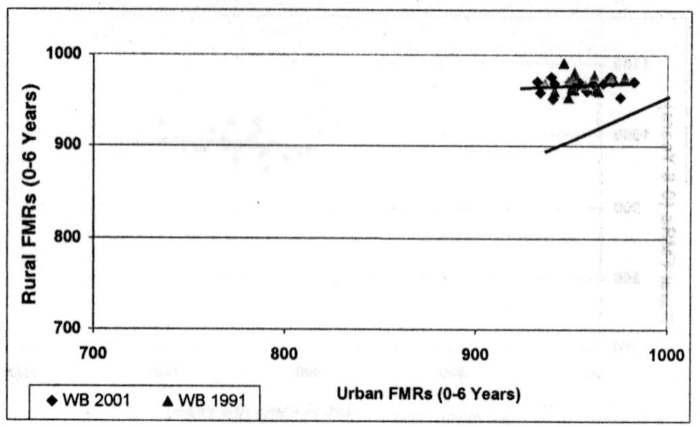

Figure 5h: Child Sex Ratios: Jharkhand: Urban - Rural

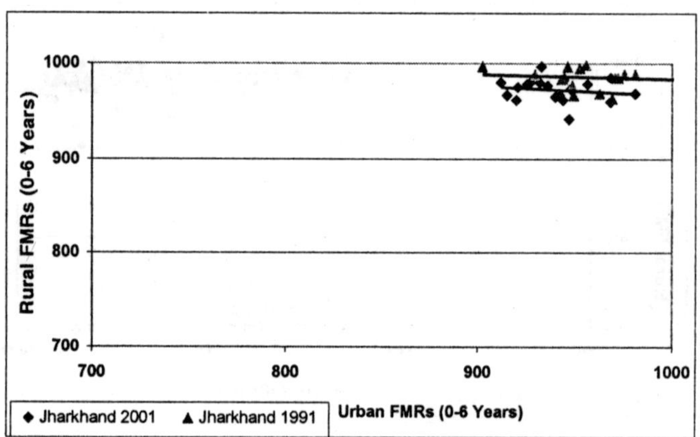

Figure 5i: Child Sex Ratios: Orissa: Urban - Rural

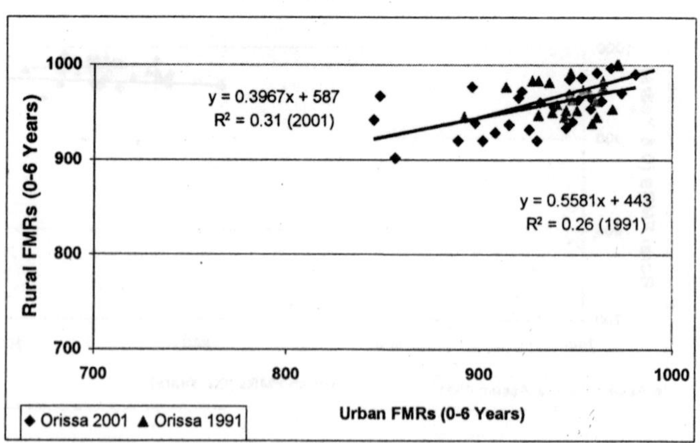

Figure 5j: Child Sex Ratios: Bihar: Urban - Rural

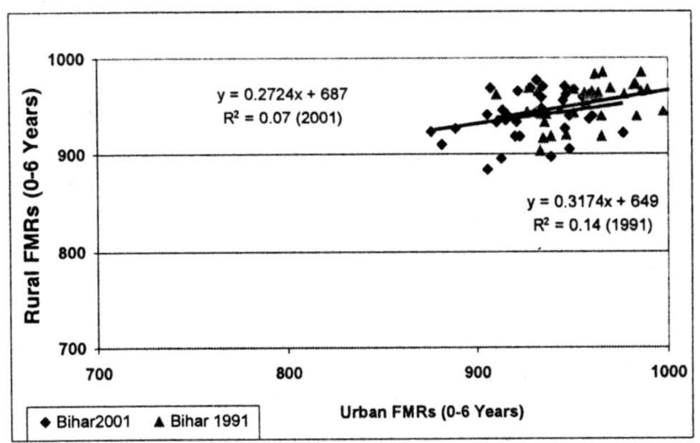

In the states where the rural sex ratios have 'begun responding slowly', the line starts sloping downwards. As the urban f/m ratios decline, rural ratios decline but not very strongly. Bihar, Orissa and Uttaranchal are examples of such states (Figures 5k to 5m).

Figure 5k: Child Sex Ratios: Uttaranchal: Urban - Rural

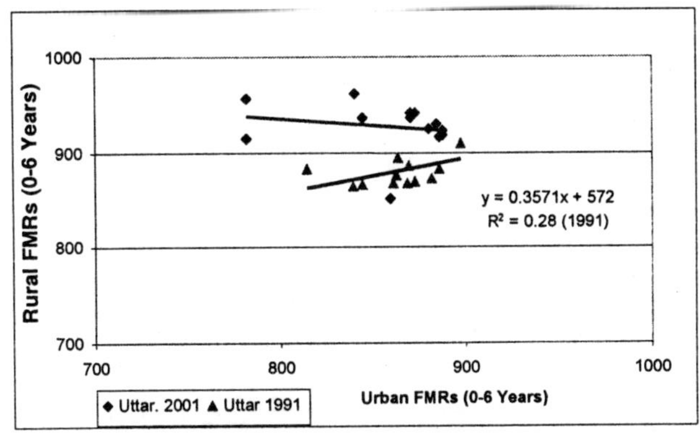

Figure 5l: Child Sex Ratios: Punjab: Urban - Rural

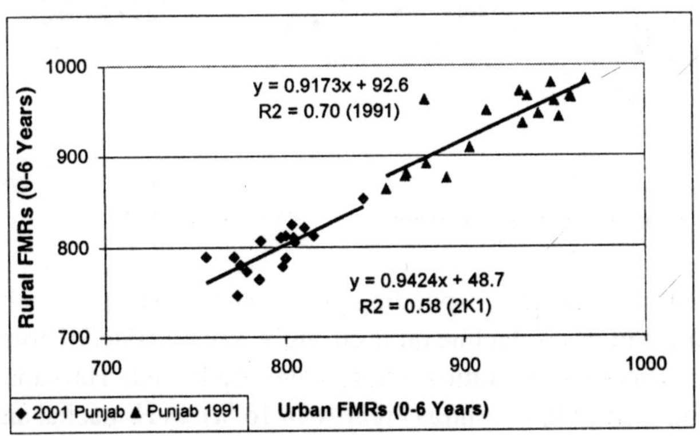

Figure 5m: Child Sex Ratios: Haryana: Urban - Rural

Figure 5n: Child Sex Ratios: UP: Urban - Rural

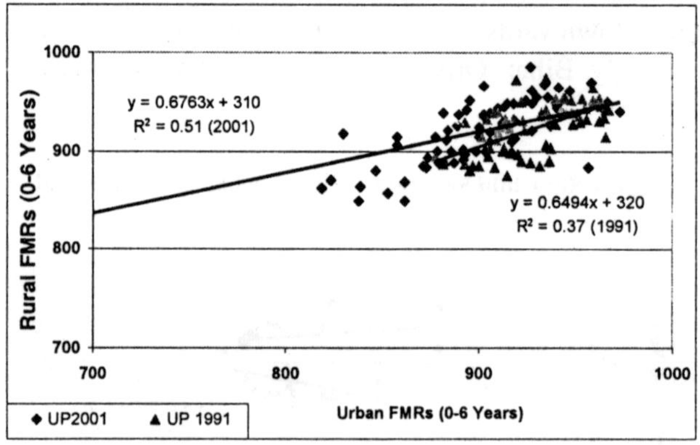

Figure 5o: Child Sex Ratios: Himachal: Urban - Rural

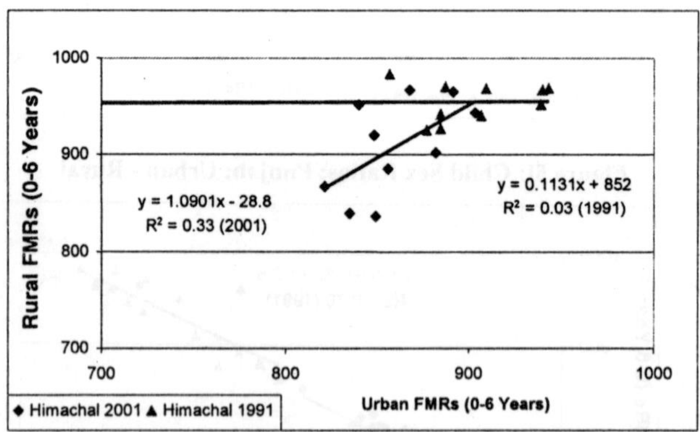

In the list of 'strongly responding' states, the line slopes further downwards. Here the rural f/m ratios decline quite strongly, say by 50 to 90 points for a decline by 100 points in urban f/m ratios. These states are Punjab, Haryana, UP, Himachal Pradesh, Gujrat and Maharashtra (Figures 5n To 5t). In Himachal and Maharashtra, the deterioration between 1991 and 2001 is sharp, while in Gujarat it has been bad in 1991 itself. Rajsthan presents an interesting case where the situation appears to have improved. But this needs further and a more detailed look.

Figure 5p: Child Sex Ratios: Rajsthan: Urban - Rural

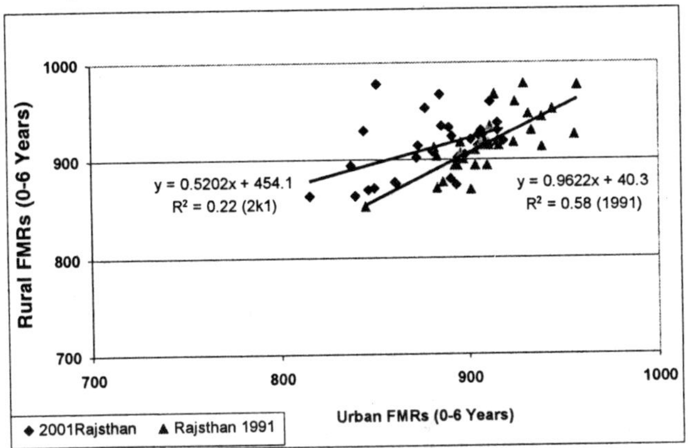

Figure 5q: Child Sex Ratios: MP: Urban - Rural

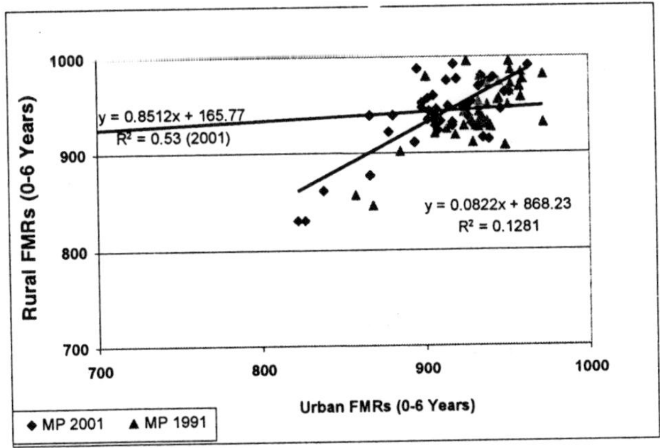

Figure 5r: Child Sex Ratios: Maharashtra: Urban - Rural

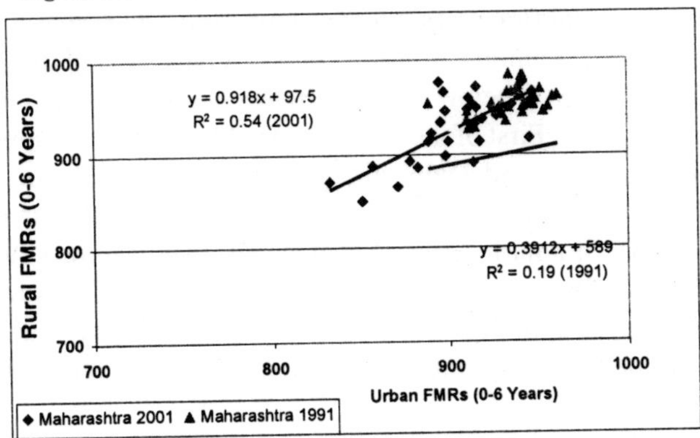

Figure 5s: Child Sex Ratios: Gujarat: Urban - Rural

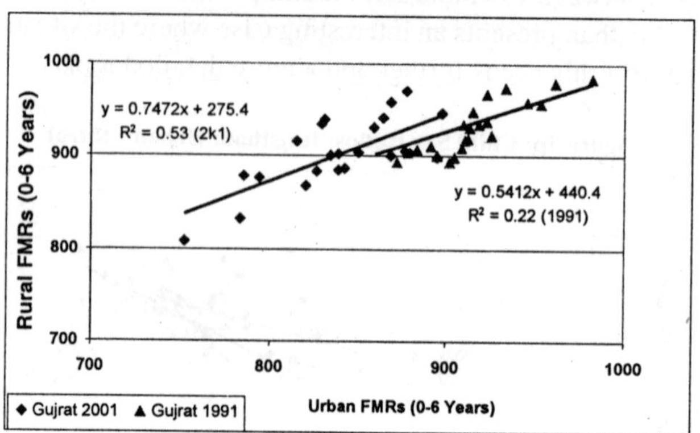

Figure 5t: Child Sex Ratios: TN: Urban - Rural

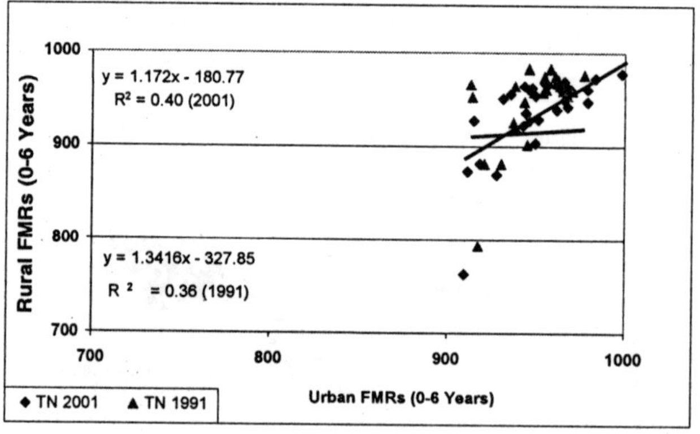

Among southern states, Tamil Nadu presents alarming trends for both 1991 and 2001. Unlike most other states, the rural f/m ratios among children in a number of districts have been lower than the urban ratios and have declined faster than the urban ones too.

This analysis will remain incomplete without mentioning the 'terminal cases' or districts where rural f/m ratios 0-6 are significantly more masculine compared to the urban f/m ratios among children. Table 2 gives a list of districts where the rural f/m ratios 0-6 are (a) below 920 and (b) less than 10 points or more compared to urban f/m ratios 0-6. First of the three discernible clusters comprises of districts from Punjab, Haryana and Delhi along with Kangra (836) in Himachal and Hardwar (850) in Uttrakhand. The second cluster is in Bihar comprising of Darbhanga (884), Sitamarhi (896), Saharsa (897) and Munger (905). The third cluster is in Tamilnadu with Salem (763), Theni (873), Namakkal (882), Dharmapuri (869) and Madurai (903). These districts may have an earlier history and prevailing pattern of infanticide co-existing with or replaced by provision of foeticide.

Table 2
India/State/Union Territory/District

	F/M Ratios in the 0-6 Population				
	FMRO6R 0-6 Rural	*FMRO6 U 0-6 Urban*	*FMRO6T 0-6 (R+U)*	*Urban 0-6 per cent*	*Diff 06 R-U*
India	934	903	927	22	31
Leh (Ladakh)	911	966	929	34	-55
Kangra	836	849	836	4	-14
Fatehgarh Sahib	747	774	754	28	-27
Patiala	764	786	770	31	-22
Sangrur	779	798	784	29	-20
Rupnagar	787	800	791	30	-13
Ambala	772	812	784	31	-41
Rewari	811	830	814	16	-19
South West	798	852	845	86	-54
Delhi.	853	866	865	92	-14
South	870	888	886	90	-18
Sikar	880	891	882	19	-11
Karauli	873	894	876	13	-20
Meerut	849	861	854	43	-12
Bijitor	898	917	902	22	-19
Mau	883	956	897	19	-73
Darbhanga	884	906	885	6	-22
Sitamarhi	896	913	896	5	-17
Saharsa	897	939	900	7	-42
Munger	905	948	915	24	-43
Bishnupur	903	966	925	35	-62
Jorhat	895	932	901	15	-36
Hailakandi	900	959	903	5	-60
Puri	920	930	921	12	-10
Bhopal	916	936	931	75	-20
Tikamgarh	915	939	919	15	-25
Sola pur	890	914	897	29	-24
Washim	917	945	921	17	-28
Salem	763	910	826	45	-147
Theni	873	911	893	54	-39
Namakkal	882	919	896	38	-37
Dharmapuri	869	928	878	15	-59
Madurai	903	950	927	53	-47

III

The patterns above are linked to a question agitated for some time now in the received literature. Bardhan (1974) had pointed out how the relatively poorer regions in the country e.g. Kerala, appear to treat their daughters better than the more prosperous states in the northwestern India. Within a given region too, Miller (1981) has discussed the differences in sex ratios among the 'propertied classes' and others. Most recently, Premi (2001) has stressed the need to examine as to why the largest decline in the child sex ratio (0-6 years age group) has occurred in the well-developed districts.

At a different level, sociological and anthropological literature provides many instances of increased female subordination among the more prosperous groups (e.g. Goody: 1990; Papaneck: 1990; Berreman: 1993). This leads to unequal access to life sustaining resources e.g. food, nutrition, health care, for the female members (Dasgupta: 1987; Miller: 1981). In a harsher manifestation of this inequality, direct denial of life chances through infanticide or sex selective foeticide can take place among these groups.

A concern over the masculinity of sex ratios in the wake of prosperity at district level is one matter; corroborating this with quantitative data is quite another. As the mainstream population census data did not provide sex ratio data by prosperity level, this important issue has remained un-addressed in the demographic literature.

One exception to this trend was Krishnaji (1987) who analyzed the NSSO (National Sample Survey Organisation) data on composition of the family and the prosperity level represented by the MPCE (Monthly per capita expenditure) class. The household consumer expenditure surveys of NSSO do provide data on the composition of the household in terms of the adult and the child (0-14 years) population by 12 different AMPCE classes. As the AMPCE reflects per capita expenditure, the family size does not affect the measure and it can be taken as a good surrogate for prosperity[4].

Very recently, while all eyes had been fixed on the results of the 2001 population census for data on sex ratios, NSSO report on the 55th round reported an important and disturbing observation. The report (No. 457: 17) blandly provides the following information based on a survey of over 1.20 lakh households in the country (rural 75% and urban 25%):

Table A
Demographic differences between lowest and highest MPCE classes

Population characteristic	*Rural*			*Urban*		
	Bottom 5%	*Top 5%*	*All*	*Bottom 5%*	*Top 5%*	*All*
Sex Ratio	1005	858	941	949	837	900
Sex Ratio (Adults)	1067	873	966	993	840	908
Sex Ratio (Children)	946	804	900	903	819	883

Source: Report of the National Sample Survey Organisation, NSSO No. 457 "Level and pattern of consumer expenditure in India: 1999-2000.

This information is significant. It shows how masculine the sex ratios are among the prosperous groups both in rural and in urban areas. It also points out towards the trend of more masculine sex ratios in urban households compared to the rural households.

Before invoking the escape hatch of migration explain away these findings, it will be useful to remember that the sex ratio among children does not suffer from sex selective migration. Further, the difference of 142 points in rural and 84 points in urban households between the bottom 5% and the top 5% of the households is too large to be explained away by migration. The observed distortion in the sex ratios is clearly man–made.

Before proceeding further, it is pertinent to look at the sex ratio figures by the 12 different AMPCE (Average Monthly Per Capita Expenditure) classes. Table 3a gives the details of the AMPCE classes, number of households surveyed, mean AMPCE in each class and the sex ratios among these for the total as well as the child (0-14 years) population in rural areas. Table 3b gives corresponding information among the urban households.

Table 3a
Sex Ratio by MPCE Class, India (Rural) NSSO Survey
Round 55, July 1999-June 2000

PCE Class	*AM PCE*	*No 01 Hhs*	*Log AMPCE*	*f/m Ratio (0-14)*	*f/m Ratios (All)*
0-225	191	2547	2.28	948	1004
225-255	242	2451	2.38	951	990
255-300	279	5147	2.45	950	988
300-340	321	5588	2.51	925	971
340-380	361	5892	2.56	914	946
380-420	400	5895	2.60	948	955
420-470	445	6783	2.65	895	940
470-525	497	6635	2.70	832	904
525-615	567	8253	2.75	853	921
615-775	686	9383	2.84	820	904
775-950	853	5337	2.93	854	908
<950	1345	7474	3.13	804	858

Table 3b
Sex Ratio by MPCE Class, India (Urban) NSSO Survey
Round 55, July 1999-June 2000

PCE Class	*AM PCE*	*No of Hhs*	*Log AMPCE*	*11m Ratio (0-14)*	*11m Ratios (All)*
00-300	256	1585	2.41	903	949
300-350	326	1586	2.51	977	988
350-425	389	3290	2.59	948	961
425-500	464	3886	2.67	894	941
500-575	537	3926	2.73	915	958
575-665	619	4374	2.79	885	913
665-775	719	4785	2.86	875	898
775-915	841	5150	2.92	840	871
915-1120	1010	5677	3.00	795	848
1120-1500	1286	6651	3.11	798	815
1500-1925	1692	3901	3.23	810	847
> 1925	3074	4113	3.49	819	836

A consistent decline in the f/m ratios (females per 1000 male population) as one moves up the AMPCE range is clearly discernible. This is so for both rural and the urban households and for the 0-14 years as well as total population.

For urban areas the relationship can be linearly described as:

f/m ratios(All - age) = 1368 – 163.1 x LogAMPCE (Urban) Adj. R. Sq = 0.76
f/m ratios(0-14 yrs.) = 2188 – 728.5 x LogAMPCE (Urban) Adj. R. Sq = 0.65

Once again, the constant term and the slopes are significant at 1% level and so is the f–value in both the equations. However, as figure 6b indicates, the relation can more correctly be described as a quadratic one (the adj. R. Sq. values marginally improve):

f/m ratios(All - age) = 1368 – 728.5 x LogAMPCE + 96.4 x $(\text{LogAMPCE})^2$
f/m ratios(0-14 yrs.) = 2367 – 877.5 x LogAMPCE + 122.7 x $(\text{LogAMPCE})^2$

Figure 6a: Sex Ratios by Prosperity: Rural India 1999-2000: NSSO 55th Round

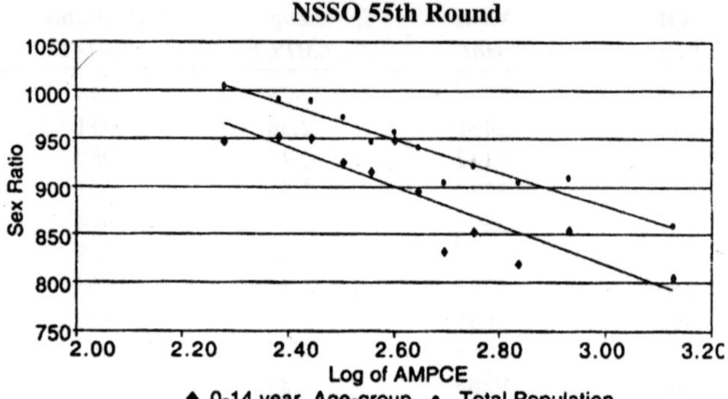

Figure 6b : Sex Ratios by Prosperity: Urban India 1999-2000: NSSO 55th Round

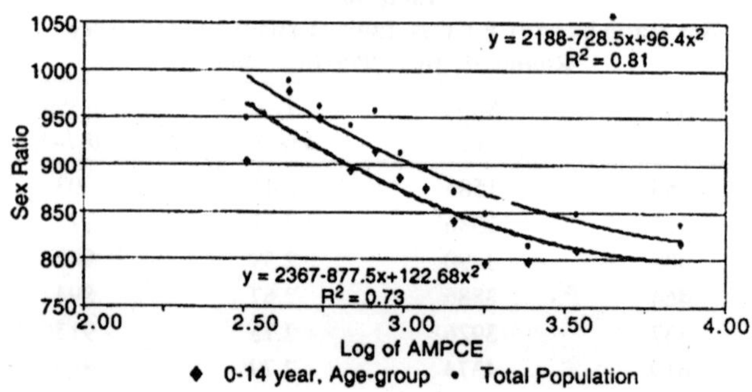

Above pattern is not 'one off'. A similar trend is seen in the 43rd and the 50th round. It is observed not just at all–India level but in different states as well (Agnihotri, et al: 2003: Forthcoming). What is disturbing is that the lowering of the f/m ratios has intensified in most regions across the three rounds.

This analysis is important for another reason. As against the observed reality of increased female subordination in the wake of prosperity, certain economic literature expresses 'prosperity optimism'. Briefly speaking, it is similar to the 'trickle down' hypothesis based on an inverse U shaped relationship (Kuznets curve) between inequality and prosperity. It tells us that inequalities initially increase as nations become prosperous. Beyond a 'turning point', however, these decline as fruits of prosperity trickle down to the lower strata as well. Similar relationship holds, some economists argue (Haddad and Kanbur: 1992), in the household domain. Inequalities rise with prosperity initially reaching a maximum at the 'turning point' of prosperity level. Beyond it these reduce and everybody lives happily ever after!

I have elsewhere (Agnihotri: 2002: Chapter-8) argued against this 'prosperity optimism' on three counts. First, the existence of a U-shaped relationship begs three important questions; at what level of prosperity does this turning point come? how attainable is it? and most important, how severe is the inequality at this turning point? Second, at this turning point the inequality is at its peak. As such one has to prosper a lot more before it comes down to some 'acceptable' level. Third, it is naïve to assume that the inequality in terms of different life sustaining inputs behaves identically. A prosperity level, at which inequality in consumption of rice may have disappeared, can co-exist with strong inequality in access to protein or more crucially in the access to medical care. The net result will still be that the survival of the girl child may get more adversely affected. The NSSO data so far indicates this to be the case. Finally, it can be shown from analytical considerations that it is not the prosperity per se, but the female contribution to prosperity that is relevant in deciding her lot; a result intuitively obvious to sociologists and anthropologists, but not necessarily so in economics!

IV

Against this backdrop of despair, how do we rescue the girl child out of the '*Chakravyuha*'? Her situation is, to use an analogy from physics, like that of a particle in a well. Imagine a ball in a bowl-shaped pit. The walls of the pit provide the barrier that the ball must overcome in order to get out of the pit. The higher the barrier, more difficult it is for the ball to overcome it. The extreme example of this is the black hole where the barrier is so high that even light is unable to escape out of it!

Traditional solutions offered by classical physics essentially require enough energy to be imparted to the ball so that it overcomes the barrier. Either the kick imparted to it has to be sufficiently strong or one could just pick it up and place it outside the pit or, radically, break the barrier to allow the ball to roll out. In short, single drastic solutions are on the offer. But in reality particles do emerge out of these barriers even without such solutions. Alpha particles breaking from the stranglehold of the nucleus and even black holes emitting matter! How does it happen? Quantum physics tells that they 'tunnel' through the barrier; a non–radical solution indeed but does help them break free.

We can likewise wait for radical solutions to happen i.e. for a revolution[5], for the perfect enforcement of the PNDT act, for emergence of that elusive entity called the political will or await a change of heart among foeticide service providers who worship profit at all costs. While each of these solutions must be explored, it is useful in the meantime, to look at some seemingly non-radical solutions as well.

One such set of solutions is to consolidate the position of the girl child in areas where barriers to her survival have not yet become formidable. Even in these areas, gender inequalities in respect of basic entitlements do operate e.g in birth registration, in immunisation, in nutrition or in schooling. It stands to reason that any effort towards complete coverage will reduce the gender gap in the coverage. Attempt should therefore be made for *complete coverage as an anti-dote to the gender gap*. Three specific examples from the field will amplify this.

Data on nutritional status of children in the 0-3 age group in the ICDS do show a gender gap in the incidence of moderate and severe malnutrition[6]. I have experienced this in respect of at least three different states: Orissa, West Bengal and Maharashtra. Data show that girls in this category often outnumber boys and the differences in the incidence of moderate and severe malnourishment between them are statistically significant. Further, the gender gap appears to aggravate during lean seasons when malnutrition peaks; an observation supported in literature (Behrman: 1988).

The implications of these patterns were brought home dramatically before me during a zonal ICDS review meeting conducted by me as the Secretary to Government of Orissa in the Women and Child Development Department at Sambalpur, in 1999. I did on purpose ask a couple of ICDS Project Officers to read out the gender break up of moderately and severely malnourished children in different sectors in their project. As they started reading out the statistics, it was clear that girls were invariably outnumbering boys. This explicit revelation created a sudden if uncomfortable silence in the meeting hall with many of Project Officers murmuring that they too had experienced similar pattern. It did dawn on most of them that a campaign to eliminate severe and moderate malnutrition benefited the girl child more. Interestingly all the *Anganwadi* workers, sector supervisors and Project Officers in Orissa are women and yet, the point had to be explicitly made with supporting data!

A similar and explicit recognition came up recently during a review meeting of a UNICEF supported intervention in certain blocks of West Bengal. This project "Positive Deviance' aims at improving nutritional status of children on a sustainable basis through mobilisation of mothers and the community. Initial results indicate that the nutritional status of girl children improves more for the simple reason that they are the more deprived to begin with!

Gender gaps also mark child immunisation especially for drop out between, say, the first and the third dose of the DPT. Once again, an NGO, SPCO (Shibpur Peoples' Care Organisation) that has taken up a campaign for complete immunisation of *all* children in seven Gram Panchayats 'realized' that girls benefit more on this account. The reason again is simple; they were the more deprived to begin with.

It is necessary therefore, to remove the 'veil' of aggregation from the data, look at the critical gender gaps and press for a universal coverage in order to give the girl child her due. The reality, however, is that the gender-wise break up of data are often not provided, and when provided often not analyzed by gender. In one unusual case, the gender break up has been dropped from routine reporting in the name of efficiency in a Department entrusted with responsibility of women's development [7].

Three unintended outcomes of this 'universal' coverage can be anticipated. In less regressive regions, it consolidates the 'female friendly' milieu while in others it improves her 'entitlements perspectives', even if non-radically. Second, a ripple effect across entitlements takes place. Complete coverage in immunisation can, for example, pave way for complete birth registration of girl children. Finally, as we move closer to complete coverage, the service delivery infrastructure and social attitude towards girls may both improve.

It is necessary, therefore, to follow this strategy for basic entitlements like registration, nutrition, immunisation and more important literacy/schooling. As universalisation is the stated goal of the state for these entitlements, this strategy needs serious consideration by both civil society and the state. But the next climb is steeper still. How to stem the alarming increase in sex selective elimination of the girl children?

V

One front on which the activist groups are fighting hard is implementation of the PNDT Act 1994. I have myself provided modest methodological inputs in this regard. These help highlight the emerging 'epicentres' of female child deficit at the district and sub-district level and may perhaps help take more effective implementation. It is useful to remember, however, that f/m ratios have been low well prior to the 90s due to excess female child mortality in the 1-4 age group, and in many a states in the post neo-natal period itself.

Roots of sex selective elimination need to be traced to the perceptions about 'unwantedness' of the girl child and tackled at that level. These perceptions are shaped primarily through viewing a daughter as a liability in economic and physical security sense. A substantial part of this perception is shaped by the prevailing status of women.

Received literature is nearly unanimous that high work-force participation by women goes together with higher sex ratios (Murthi, et al: 1995). It is not however, a necessary condition for high sex ratios, if culture takes care of survival (Agnihotri: 2000). However, a distinction needs to be made between wage-work where women have control over their earnings and work not explicitly linked to wages e.g dairy activity, where the blessing may be mixed depending on the control women have over the earnings (Sharma and Vanjani: 1993).

Among non-poor households, the dynamics of withdrawing women from work force for purposes of 'status production' (Papanek: 1989) in the wake of prosperity needs to be noted. But this creates a conflicting situation for the concerned woman; her status within the society goes up while her bargaining power within the household declines. She therefore hopes for the best but is not 'prepared for the worst'. Once withdrawn from the labour market, her ability to re-engage with it erodes steadily, often sharply, giving rise to an increasing sense of insecurity. Basu (1992: 222) has summed this up very aptly when she observes "probably the best placed mother is one who does not work herself but knows that there are no restrictions on her finding work … should the need arise".

Creation of employment avenues for women from the non-poor households has to take into account above observations. Our policy preoccupation today is mostly with work force participation of women from poorer households. That is useful in the poverty context. But if we wish to create a dent in the epicentre, flexible employment avenues must be created for women from non-poor households. Once women are able to access these '… should the need arise', their status within the household will perceptibly go up. This is important since the social dynamics within this class creates role models for the upwardly mobile groups.

However, a parallel campaign has to be mounted about the deteriorating crime situation in the public sphere as it affects women more adversely than men. The tendency to withdraw women from external employment is also influenced by the safety perceptions about the workplace and the road leading to it! This is one area where activism, civil society groups, media and judiciary has to play a proactive role to merely expedite judicial processes. I am quite convinced that it is the swiftness and certainty of punishment and not the harshness of a punishment that acts as a deterrent. The proactive role should identify to begin with, the weak links in the criminal justice processes because a chain snaps not at its strongest link but at its weakest one. The devil truly lies here in these weak links.

Two specific interventions need to be mentioned here which may contribute to reduce the 'unwantedness' of daughters. The first relates to mobility in the non-metro urban towns. Girls do not enjoy the same mobility as boys do because their access to two-wheelers, especially bicycles, is limited. I seriously think this must go. It is anecdotal, but not uncommon, to find parents mentioning that daughters cannot run errands as the sons do as they lack mobility. Riding bicycles should become part of a movement for girls.

The second issue is of married adolescent girls. Notwithstanding the legal age of marriage being 18 years, a large percentage of number of girls get married below this age (RCH 1998-99), the percentage in some districts going as high as 70. These girls find their social communication avenues sharply curtailed after marriage (Judith Bruce: personal communication). Further, they cannot become part of any SHG as they are below 18 years of age. They thus get initiated into an unequal position, burdened with the task of social and biological reproduction at low information base. It is necessary to bring this group into the fold of SHG activity as trainees or affiliates so as to improve their social communication avenues if not economic power.

There is a view that the role of SHGs is exaggerated and these are mostly insensitive to social issues once they pursue economic goals. The solution to this, in my opinion, is not to write these off, but to sensitize them to social issues. In any case the importance of gaining economic security for oneself through participation in SHG cannot get negated merely because the person does not become sensitive to an activist's level of satisfaction.

Finally, a specific intervention to highlight the supporting role of daughters to parents in old age is called for. There is a growing realization in metros and rural areas alike that sons do not necessarily look after parents in old age these days. In both these areas, son-drain due to long distance migration is significant and there is a considerable, anecdotal again, evidence to show that it is the daughter who comes to help in the time of need or crisis. There is a strong need to highlight this role through visual media.

VI

It is important to debate here the ethical dimension of sex-based elimination of a segment of the population. Once this is sanctified, it could well be the thin end of the wedge that provides in its wake, currency to eliminate other segments of population based on other criterion whether religion or caste or the colour of the skin or the shape of the nose!

Development, frankly, cannot be viewed in isolation; it is important to know how it combines with discrimination, gender based one in particular. If we remain underdeveloped and yet aggravate discrimination, that is the worst-case scenario. If underdevelopment co-exists with lack of discrimination, life gets tolerated but not enjoyed. But highly developed society with high discrimination levels as in our 'epicentres' is not a great goal for women either. We must therefore strive to become a society where development goes hand in hand with absence of discrimination against its women.

We must therefore question the current model of development where discrimination necessarily appears to accompany development. It is not that success stories of alternative 'development' do not exist; Kerala, Goa or Manipur provide examples where social indicators have developed, but not at the cost of gender equity. This is the role model that the society has to follow and not the model of the Punjab, Haryana and western UP where discrimination appears as 'inevitable'.

But that necessitates that the fight against gender–based discrimination has to become part of the larger fight against all other discriminations. In fact, gender based discrimination gets aggravated when combined with other inequalities. It becomes necessary therefore to identify the most unreached and the most unserved, within the gender domain and advocate strongly for improving their lot. Just as different inequalities multiply the misery of the affected, reducing these together also gives multiple benefits. Willy-nilly we are talking here of eliminating the *Chakravyuha* of discrimination altogether rather than its specific manifestation we began with, so that no child dies an avoidable death, let alone a girl child.

Notes

1. This is a revised version of the 2nd annual lecture on Girl Child delivered under the auspices of the IACR (Indian Alliance for Child Rights). The views presented here are author's own and not of UNICEF.

2. More appropriately a northwest and southeast divide with more masculine sex ratios in the former and less adverse f/m ratios in the latter (See e.g. Sopher: 1980; Miller 1981 & 1989 and Agnihotri: 2000. Miller: 1989) talks in particular of the growing masculinisation of the f/m ratios between 1971 and 1981.
3. None of these foeticide service providers, who often claim to be rendering 'national service', provide the service free; even for some of their poor clients!
4. Question regarding different saving levels or disposable and non–disposable income for the same MPCE level can be raised here. But by and large, higher per capita expenditure will indicate higher prosperity.
5. While one may agree or disagree with the governance in North Korea, son preference there is next to nil in stark contrast to the strong son preference in South Korea traced to religio- cultural context of a Confucian society (Goodkind: 1999).
6. I am quite puzzled by the persistent divergence on this issue between the ICDS data and the survey data from, say NNMB and NFHS that seem to indicate a much lower or insignificant gender gap.
7. The ICDS reporting format had reportedly been 'modified' with an aim to reduce drudgery at the field level and what gets dropped is the gender-wise break up of nutritional status. I strongly hope my information is either incorrect or outdated!

References

Agnihotri, S.B. 2000. *Sex ratio patterns in the Indian population-A fresh exploration*, N. Delhi: Sage.

Agnihotri, S.B. 2002. 'Setting daughters' of Urban India: Locating the epi-centres of female deficit' *Proceedings of the International symposium on Girl Child*–January 2002, IIPS, Mumbai.

Bardhan, P.K. 1974. "On life and death questions". *Economic and Political Weekly*, Special Issue No. 9: 1293-1304.

Basu, A.M. 1992. *Culture, the status of women, and demographic behaviour*, Oxford: Clarendon Press.

Behrman, J. 1988. "Nutrition, health, birth order and seasonality: Intra-household allocation among children in rural India" *Journal of Development Economics*. 28.

Berreman, G.D. 1993. "Sanskritization as Female Oppression in India" pp. 366-392 in Miller, B.D. (Ed.), *Sex and Gender Hierarchies*. Cambridge: Cambridge University Press.

Caldwell, J.C. and Caldwell, P. 1990. *Gender implications for survival in South Asia*, Health Transition Working Paper No. 7, Canberra: NCEPH, Australian National University.

Chhabra, R. 1981. "India's sobering Census" *People*, 8:3.

Dasgupta, M. 1987. "Selective discrimination against female children in rural Punjab, India" *Population and Development Revie:* 13: 77-100.

Goody, J. 1990. *The oriental, the ancient and the primitive*. Cambridge: Cambridge University Press.

Haddad, L. and Kanbur, R. 1992. "Is there an intra-household Kuznets curve? Some evidence from the Philippines" *Public Finances:* 47.

Krishnaji, N. 1987. "Poverty and sex ratio-some data and some speculations ?" *Economic and Political Weekly*: 22:23: 892-897.

McKee, L. 1984. "Sex differentials in survivorship and the customary treatment of the infants and children", *Medical Anthropology*: 8:2: 91-108.

Miller, B.D. 1981. *The Endangered Sex*. Ithaca, N.Y.: Cornell University Press.

Murthi, M., Guio, A. and Dreze, J. 1995. *Mortality, fertility and gender bias in India: A district level analysis*, DERC Discussion Paper No. 61, London :London School of Economics.

Padmanabha. P. 1981. "The decisive decade: A note on the provisional results of the 1981 Census of India", *Yojana*: 25:9.

Papanek, H. 1989. "Family status production work: Women's contribution to social mobility and class differentiation" pp. 96-116 in Krishnaraj, M. and Chanana, K. (Eds) *Gender and the Household Domain*, New Delhi: Sage.

Premi, M.K. 2001. "The missing girl child" EPW: 36:21: 1875-80.

RGI: 2001, *Provisional population totals; Paper–1 of 2001*, N. Delhi: Office of the Registrar General and Census Commissioner, India.

Sharma, M. and Vanjani, U. 1993. "When more means less - Assessing the impact of Dairy development in the lives and health of women in Rural Rajasthan (India)" *Social Science and Medicine*: 37:11:1377-89.

The paper was first published in *Economic and Political Weekly*: It is included here with the prior permission of the author and the Editor, *Economic and Political Weekly*.Address for email communication is: sbagnihotri@yahoo.com

CHAPTER - EIGHT

Food Security: How and For Whom?

Maithreyi Krishnaraj

The following set of papers[1] deal with the influence of gender on food security. Before we go into the issues raised in these papers, it may be useful to recall some of the ongoing discussions pertaining to this problem. How is food security conceptualized? what steps have been taken? and how appropriate are the questions that arise in this context? Food security (hence-forth FS), is contingent on three basic parameters-availability, accessibility and affordability. Availability comes from production and related aspects of productivity that sustain a desired level of production. Accessibility is about distribution. Spatial constraints are not the major ones as much as social-political ones. People can afford food if they can buy it and have the means to do so. It is also possible to get FS through self-provisioning. Both these are linked to what Amartya Sen calls endowment and exchange entitlements. One can buy food if one has the resources to do so and such resources have to come from assets such as land and other productive means or wage labour. How adequate these are, determine one's capacity to buy food affordability.

These papers deal precisely with this problem of endowment and exchange entitlement as regards women. Self-provisioning either through subsistence farming or commercial farming of food crops that yield a marketable surplus hinge on a host of enabling conditions-land, credit, technology, infrastructure, availability of water, and other necessary inputs that enhance soil fertility but more than any other, the major impediment can arise from institutional arrangements that exist for negotiating such access to these means of production. These are pretty simple truths. Falling very much within the political economy sphere, they are also most difficult to confront.

Assuming that there are those who can produce a surplus and this can be distributed to others, the terms and conditions under which this is done are additional hurdles on the way. There is a good deal of controversy on whether farmers benefit more from commercial farming with modern technology or traditional subsistence farming. Given the fact that in India the average size of holdings that was around two hectares in the 1970s has come down to 0.2 hectares, and that the majority of the hundred million holdings are small and marginal, solutions to enhance productivity on these are not easy. Some would argue forget agriculture-let people do non-farm work or increase urbanization. While there is merit in this option, given the size of the rural population, such drastic measures are likely to further intensify the problem of rural poverty and lead to decreasing returns from agriculture-which is what in fact has been happening. Intensive farming, which took place under the green revolution, has run its course. No doubt it boosted production of wheat and rice, but confined as it was only to three states, there was neglect of other areas. Besides, the intensive farming through high inputs of water, fertilizers and pesticides have brought in devastating environmental outcomes that have made continued pursuit of such methods difficult if not impossible. Agricultural policy pursued so far has not benefited the small and marginal farmers. Subsidies in the form of free power and irrigation have only benefited the richer sections. With declining public investment in agriculture, the prospect of a reprieve is ever more distant. Well, to put the matter succinctly, production and productivity then have been deeply affected by macro policies.

Secondly, they have affected most the vulnerable farmers. Another rescue line mooted is contract farming. But as Sharma in his passionately argued article (2004) says where it has been tried, as in Punjab and other places, it has favoured agribusiness.[2] Potato, tomato or other produce may give the farmer an assured price, but the cost and risks are borne by the farmer. Contract farming which was ushered in with great fanfare in Latin America has been a mixed blessing. Market-oriented production can pose risks to household food security. An IFAD study in Andhra Pradesh found that conversion of paddy land to growing export crops like cotton, flowers and aqua culture had the following short-term results: (i) less land was available for growing food crops; (ii) the lack of land reduced the amount of food produced for the family, and decreased women's control over income and therefore food supply since women do not market cash crops; (iii) cash income led to greater alcoholism, which reduced the amount of income available for family food and used up also a proportion of grains for brewing liquor; (iv) because of the decreased family food supply, women in many households had to decrease their own food intake, but at the same time work harder to get cash income; and (v) many more had to rely heavily on wage income and PDS for survival [IFAD: 2005].

Recent farmer suicides show how relying on fickle export markets can bring disaster. The risks are too heavy for farmers who rely on debt to take advantage of commercial opportunities. Development projects that promote market-oriented production should ensure some buffer for poor households with a minimum basic level of food, as those facing the greatest risk are those with limited land and labour and insufficient financial resources to carry them through the transition.

Other undesirable outcomes have been the concentration on monoculture to the detriment of biodiversity, critical for environmental health and long-term sustainability [Hawtin: 2005]. To quote a telling passage from Hawtin:

> *"Poor farmers are aware of the relationship between the stability and sustainability of their production systems and the diversity of crops and crop varieties on their lands. Their management and use of a diverse range of plants have soften helped them to survive under difficult conditions. Crops mature at different times and can be easily stored.. .they also provide a nutritionally balanced diet."*

The singular neglect of dry land farming and cereals other than wheat and rice in policy has led to deterioration in the nutritional level of the poor. Well so much for the production angle.

What about distribution? The government of India set up the Food Corporation of India (FCI) under a special Act in 1964. It had three goals: (i) effective price support for farmers; (ii) distribution of food grains through ration shop outlets to consumers at prices they could afford the Public Distribution System (PDS); and (iii) maintain a satisfactory level of buffer stocks. Catering to a population of over one billion and covering 582 districts in the country, FCI has a turn over of rupees 650 billion. It procures from the states more than rupees 76 billion worth of grain [FCI statistics on the web]. An incredibly massive enterprise! Behind these wonderful figures lies a sad story, a story so paradoxical and tragic. According to a report of the standing committee of Parliament, the cost to the nation that FCI imposes is a staggering Rs. 62,000 million! The tragedy of how FCI has forfeited its authentic goals through PDS has been discussed many times in the pages of Economic and Political Weekly. The distortions are: uneven distribution and the failure of PDS to reach the needy, its patently urban bias and poor quality and unreliable supply in the ration shops. This implies that the poor for whom it was meant were forced to rely on the open market. But after liberalization, the introduction of targeting needy families by making a distinction of below poverty (BPL) and above poverty (APL) categories has exacerbated problems, as BPL and APL are notoriously subject to manipulation by interested parties. At best of times, the BPL families meet barely 25 per cent of their needs through the PDS. What really went wrong with the FCI's system is that the minimum support price assured to surplus farmers through procurement kept rising under pressure from the farm lobby and the issue price of the grain began to be closer to the market price. In effect the supposed 'subsidy' to the consumers really went to the rich farmers in three states who supply the bulk of the FCI procurement. Even in the food for work programmes the central government meets only 50 per cent through grain while the states are expected to supply the cash component. Given the cash strapped condition of the states, this was not of much help.

Prashant Goyal, secretary to the chief minister, Pondicherry, with a candour rare among the bureaucracy admitted (he says, it is his personal opinion): "There is need to shift from the existing expensive, corruption ridden institutional arrangements to those that will ensure cheap delivery of requisite quality grains in a transparent manner, that are also self-targeting" [Goyal: 2002]. But who is to bell the cat?

Alternatives suggested have been to go for village level grain banks. These have so far been tried in isolated pockets through NGOs but nowhere have these been accepted as feasible at all India level. Other initiatives attempted by NGOs are for seed collection to improve biodiversity. These are all private endeavours here and there.

Defining Food Security

We have been talking of food grain supply and its distribution but FS is a broader concept. There are many definitions [Ayalew: 2005]. To the World Food Programme, it is 'the assurance of balanced supply and demand of staple foods in the international market'. Considering the international market is not all that friendly to poor nations, this definition seems to imply that if the rich nations have enough that takes care of all of us. Decades ago, in 1948, the UN Declaration of Human Rights included the right to an adequate standard of living including food. In 1966, the International Covenant on Economic and Social Rights sought to ensure 'an adequate supply of staple food in relation to need'. Then in 1974, the Universal Declaration on Eradication of Hunger and Malnutrition enunciated that 'every man, woman and child has an inalienable right to be free from hunger'. All these pious, global declarations have done little to alter the reality that 433 million in India survive on less than 1.00 $ per day and that India has the largest number of the world's poor. The World Bank's definition is more acceptable: 'access by all people at all times to enough food for an active and healthy life'. FS is not a one off matter. FS has to be sustainable over time. Suicides by farmers in India prove that temporary cash flow does not guarantee FS over time. Nor did the green revolution.

Under liberalisation, agricultural exports are emphasised. Our government sounds pro-poor in international meets. In the agricultural committee of WTO, India advocated a "market plus approach'. In the agreement on agriculture (AOA) at the Uruguay round there was ostensibly a concern to bring discipline to one of the most distorted areas of trade. Europe and North America coddle their agricultural sector with massive subsidies and protectionist policies and trade is tilted in their favour while they talk of non-trade barriers for other countries. The preamble in AOA recognised the importance of non-trade concerns like food security and environmental protection. This applies especially to countries like India with a significant population dependent on agriculture for which maintenance of livelihood is critical. India argued for a flexible approach within AOA. To what extent this will be honoured is anybody's guess?

FS is not just a matter of food-quality of food that ensures nutrition, and healthcare that protects people from debilitating diseases or intestinal parasites that leak nutrition are all part of it [Radhakrishna: 2005]. Hence, solutions cannot be a single one but an integrated approach. Investment in rural and urban development that ensures the livelihood of people in a measure that enables them to get exchange entitlements and build up their endowments like assets, skill, and appropriate technology are critical, but above all social and political power matter most. Public expenditure on safe water, sanitation, health care, and public assistance for affordable food are all part of ensuring FS. "One cannot invest in one aspect of poverty. There is need for a balanced approach, with large projects in education, health, nutrition, and rural infrastructure. At present the government spends 4 per cent on education and less than 1 per cent on health" [Sachs: 2005].

The Planning Commission will be setting up a Food and Nutrition Security Watch to function as a think tank on food and nutrition security issues and review programmes. Acknowledging that his party had ridden to power on a wave of agrarian distress, Prime Minister Manmohan Singh committed his government to a new deal for rural India. We hope it will be translated into a concrete reality [ToI: 2005]. A Food Insecurity and Vulnerability Information and Mapping System (FIVIMS) at the International level has been set up and the government of India will undertake food and nutrition surveillance in three states of India [FAO: 1999].

M.S. Swaminathan Research Foundation (MSSRF) has produced a Food Insecurity Atlas for India (2002). It follows the FAO definition of FS: 'FS is a situation which exists when all people at all times have physical and economic access to sufficient, safe and nutritious food to meet their dietary needs and food preferences for an active and healthy life' .The Atlas uses 17 indicators that include food affordability, availability, absorption, access, access to housing, discrimination in livelihood access, access to sanitation, health and nutritional outcome. Problems of urban poverty are as severe and multifaceted as that of rural distress.

The health and growth outcomes due to poor food security have been documented both by family health surveys and the Nutrition Foundation of India. There is a high proportion of stunting and wastage among children, prevalence of anaemia among women, high incidence of diseases like tuberculosis, and blindness due to vitamin A deficiency. Poor nutrition is also the cause of maternal deaths.

Gender and Food Security

> *Women are active at every point in the food chain and are often responsible for protecting the integrity of food and ensuring its wholesomeness and safety [FAO: 2005].*

Coming to the set of papers referred to here, they do not address FS directly. They do not go into issues of intra-household distribution of food but draw attention to the resources available to women for procuring food mainly through employment. They focus on exchange entitlements and narrate trends that they find disquieting. Apart from inadequate opportunities for wage labour, lack of command over productive resources act as a major constraint for those women who do undertake farming for the household. Participation in the production of food does not guarantee commensurate returns. Independent land rights may not be a panacea. Household prosperity may lead to loss of autonomy. As long as marriage is the basis of security and social prestige, women may prefer to bank on compliance with social norms. One of the things that the feminist discourse, concerned with domestic violence and subordination of women in the family, forgets is that households undertake many cooperative tasks and women as members of households have high stakes in its stability and social esteem. They derive their basic identity from the family-household. Nitya Rao and Praveena Kodoth address the issue of land rights but from different angles. Rao questions the premise underlying policy and discourse that independent land rights for women will reduce poverty. Kodoth examines the effect of progressive land reforms in West Bengal and Kerala and concludes that they resulted in regressive effects on women.

To Rao, the shift in policy regarding agricultural production and land management, nationally and internationally, is based on the premise that since agriculture is increasingly becoming the domain of women, enhancement of women's endowment through land will increase production, reduce poverty and ensure food security. This is inspired more by an instrumental approach rather than out of a commitment to equal rights and social justice. She sees no evidence that land ownership reduces poverty given that land sizes are so small and agriculture has become a sinking ship for the majority of poor farmers who constitute the bulk of our rural population.

Experiments in wasteland development through women's collective have been successful only where there is considerable support from NGOs. It is true women have fought for land rights in Bodhgaya but here again it is through the intervention of social activists and support by local men. Even here once women did get rights, they preferred not to transfer it to daughters as daughters move away to their marital home. Let us remember that there is not much public land for distribution. Arable land is transferred only through inheritance. Land is a marker of social status, prestige and identity. Women see land as related to the family. The male role is perceived to be that of the provider (even if males repudiate it often and abandon women if thing get rough). With the drastic reduction of the role of agriculture in supplementing household income, work burden on women and girls has increased greatly. "In a situation of restricted mobility and restricted choices, women prefer the security of marriage" as Rao says. It is the socially embedded nature of kinship and marriage systems, its strong association with cultural identity and symbolism that makes it different from other aspects of gender relations such as sexual harassment, violence, etc.

Rao advocates diversification of employment for women. This was also the conclusion arrived at by Krishnaraj and Shah (2004). However, as diversification is not going to be easy in the short run, Rao would have us emphasize public works and food subsidy. Rao implies in her reference to Santhal Parganas that men everywhere provide the basics for the household while women provide the 'extras' through working as migrant labour as if it is a general phenomenon. On the contrary, it is the other way- in most parts, women provide the basics while men provide the extras. In my own fieldwork in Maharashtra in agriculture as well as crafts, subsistence was the predominant role of women. Accounts in this section from eastern Uttar Pradesh and the north-east indicate how women ensure subsistence.

Kodoth with data about the impact of progressive land reforms in West Bengal and Kerala, chosen for their dominant Left presence has somewhat controversial conclusions. She notices increase in dowry practice even among the poorer sections. Alienation of land on account of dowry is pronounced among agricultural labour and small peasant households as well as among working classes and lower castes in Kerala who previously did not own land but received some in Kerala. This is accompanied by withdrawal from paid labour for women. She sees this as the aspiration for a higher social status. There are contrasts between West Bengal and Kerala with respect to underlying conditions. Kerala had gone through social reform that resulted in consolidation of castes and therefore has strengthened caste identities. In the background of politicized caste and religion, radical reforms got watered down, strengthened former tenants and middle sections while inherited social norms were retained. Women had already lost property with the withering of matriliny. Marriage became important in redefining property relations. The emergence of dowry after the 1960s and increase in expensive marriages and expenditure on life cycle ceremonies are expressions of new found prosperity, fuelled also by remittances from gulf migration among sections of the population. Kodoth marshals data from many field studies to establish these trends.

In West Bengal, agricultural production increased in the 1980s and small peasants carried on rice cultivation. There was no aggregation of caste interests, caste divisions were fragmented and the Left was unable to rise above the interests of the middle and upper sections. There has been a progressive shift from bride price to dowry and girls are married young to escape dowry. Social group interests always determine inheritance. The government of India's stipulation regarding joint *pattas* was ignored. While in both states, the proportion of women in non-farm activities increased, in Kerala it was more in household industry. This diversification of women's employment was intertwined with gender conservatism. The net result has been women's livelihood security has been anchored in marriage. In this scenario, widows, divorced or single women are at a disadvantage.

Kodoth's observation regarding the pull of social mobility is valid and well taken. However, one also has to understand that if women agree to dispense with independent income earning work, it is not entirely due to conservative social norms that grants higher status to 'female seclusion', but also the sheer burden of hard physical labour with low returns, the double burden of family work plus outside work, the long hours, the terms and conditions of that work. These are equally influencing factors. Many of us, who are in white-collar professions, fail to grasp the enervating, soul killing aspects of the drudgery involved in manual work. All through human history, people have tried to escape manual labour and social privilege meant that they get some thing else (those who are vulnerable, without resources) to do their job India perfected this system by a superbly articulated caste system.

Thelma Paris, Abha Singh, Joyce Luis and Mahbub Hossain in their paper on impact of male labour migration on women in rice farms in eastern Uttar Pradesh document the high responsibility for keeping the family farm imposed on women left behind. They take over all farming responsibilities including management and decision-making. However lacking the resources for enhancing productivity, the yields are not satisfactory either among the households with migrants or without migrants. The remittances by migrants go to meet social and religious obligations and for gaining assets like *pucca* houses. These findings drive home the point that responsibility on women does not make for more equitable gender relations. While family farm management does provide for a measure of food security, it is laid unilaterally on the shoulders of women.

'Feminization' of Agriculture

By looking at census data, Swarna Vepa arrives at similar conclusions regarding 'feminization' of agriculture. However census data or macro data is not helpful to establish trends as definitions and coverage leave much to be desired. Despite efforts made over the years to improve coverage of women's work in rural areas by proper inclusion of unpaid productive work, there has been only marginal improvement. The definition of cultivators in the census relies on ownership of land so that even though women actually cultivate they are seen as family labour. Hence this fact is not reflected in the proportion of men and women cultivators that make some people dispute that there is feminization of agriculture in India. Leaving aside these technicalities, no one can deny the fact that women continue to be immersed in agriculture and bear a heavy burden of farming tasks with less access to non-farm work than men. Sumi Krishna captures this reality that the price of rice is gendered-in other words the cost of food security is borne by women. She examines in detail the farming system in the northeast. Women here have preserved biodiversity; have extensive knowledge of seeds and their characteristics. In terms of total amount of work, women's share far exceeds that of men. The majority of the societies are patrilineal with the exception of a few, like the Garos and Khasis. Generally because women have more freedom to move about, undertake marketing, have less strict sexual codes, are not bound by oppressive marriages, the reality that women's lives are subject to underlying social norms and practices is obscured. Women are excluded from community decisions. Poor economic conditions that necessitate greater cooperation in joint activities hide unequal power in gender relations.

Barbara Harris deals with post-harvest work of women and delving through history traces the marginalisation of women from an earlier pre-eminent position in these activities due to commercialization and commodification. It is a very complicated paper where she tries to apply two theories-that of Esther Boserup and Ursula Huws to the post-harvest rice operations in order to demonstrate that both are off the mark and are only partially right. Boserup's thesis is that plough agriculture reduced opportunities for women in productive work in south Asia. Huws talked of 'commodification' namely, how products or services that had use value became objects for sale and purchase. Harris shows that women did not lose productive work but became wage labour within rice farming systems in addition to engaging in petty production and trade. Instead, a remarkably stable structure of demand for basic wage goods and services under petty production survived and expanded in India. In Bengal, women husked paddy through the traditional '*dheki*' for cash-hiring themselves out or hiring others. With the introduction of rice hullers this task was taken over by men. In the second phase, with the introduction of modern rice mills this trend was further accentuated. In the Punjab, there was more of casual male labour with mechanization and women in family farms subsidized the activity by cooking food for labour.

The introduction of modern mills increased the scale of commercialization, it also led to a lot of by products-husk as fuel for the mills, rice bran as cattle feed, bran as industrial solvent extractors, broken rice powdered as organic fertilizer and as base for cosmetics. Family concerns as well as companies run these mills. Huws theory of commodification applies only to women in the households where mills are commercial enterprises. Here women perform no productive work in post-harvest activities but buy and sell what they used to do for themselves earlier. The theory does not apply to the majority of rural women.

The introduction of rice mills increased the number of live-lihoods - sub-agents, paddy brokers, petty mill producers, new puffing units, itinerant traders, new rental markets, markets for second-hand machines, drying fields for rice, parboiling units, parboiling machinery units and a host of related activities. Rice enters the food chain as rice, cooking oil and meat (produced by cattle feed of bran). The Harris saga ends on a sadder note-while women's employment expanded, real wages increased, actualization and insecurity were attendant features. Self provisioning which gave women direct control over food supply is now replaced by the need to look for non-farm work with poor returns relative to labour.

The papers deal with rice farming, as this was the subject of the seminar for which it was intended. They do not deal with quality of food or other developmental needs like health, sanitation or safe water. They are however illustrative of the general situation regarding food insecurity among poor women and point to the urgency of public measures for protection of this vulnerable section.

Notes

1. The six papers referred to here were drawn from a series of seminars conducted by M.S. Swaminathan Research Foundation in 2004, the International Year of Rice, on the general theme of Gender, Rice, and Food Security. Five of the six papers were presented at the seminar on 'Gender Concerns and Food Security Issues in Rice Livelihood Systems in India' held at Chennai on September 2 and 3,2004 while the sixth paper, by Sumi Krishna, is drawn from her keynote address at the seminar on 'Gender Concerns and Food Security in Rice Farming systems', Workshop on 'Rice Heritage of Northeast-Challenges and Opportunities', ICAR, Umiyam, Meghalaya: November 5-6,2004. These papers, as they appeared in the *Economic and Political Weekly*: 40:25: 2005:2508-63, were: Nitya Rao: Gender Equality, Land Rights, and Household Food Security: Discussion of Rice Farming Systems: pp. 2513-21; Thelma Paris,Abha Singh, Joyce Louis and Mahbub Hossain: Labour Outmigration,Livelihood of Rice Farming Households and Woman Left Behind: 2522-29; Barbara Harriss-White: Commercialization, Commodification ana Gender Relations in Post-Harvest

Systems for Rice: 2530-42; Praveena Kodoth:Fostering Insecure Livelihoods: Dowry and Female Seclusion in Left Development Contexts in West Bengal and Kerala: 2543-54; Sumi Krishna: Gendered Price of Rice in North-Eastern India: 2555-62; and Swarna S. Vepa: Feminization of Agriculture and Marginalisation of Their Economic Stake: 2563-68.

2. Quoted by Sharma: he does not give the date.

References

Ayalew, Mdaku. 2005. 'What is Food Security? *Famine and Hunger'*. http://Iwww.brad.ac.uk.

FAO. 1999. 'Development of Food Insecurity and Vulnerability Mappingj Systems in India: A Report', FAO, Rome.

FAO. 2005. 'Gender and Food Security'. http://www.FAO.org/gender/17687.

Goyal, Prashant. 2002. 'Food Insecurity in India', *The Hindu,* January l0.

Hawtin, Geoffery. 2005. 'Genetic Diversity and Food Security.International Plant Genetic Resources Institute, UNESCO Courier, May.

IFAD. 2005. 'India: Impact of Market Oriented Production', International Foundation for Agricultural Development. http://www. FAO.org.

Krishnaraj, Maithreyi and Amita Shah. 2004. 'Women Farmers in India: Declining Options and Future Posibilities', Draft Report. Ahmedabad: Gujarat lnstitute of Development Research.

M.S. Swaminathan Research Foundation. 2002. 'Food Insecurity Atlas. Chennai: MSSRF.

Radhakrishna. R. 2005. 'Food and Nutrition Security for the Poor in India'; *Economic and Political Weekly.* April 30.

Sharma, Devinder. 2004. 'Alternative Strategies for India's Development.http:// www.manfully.org. foodlndia.

The Hindu: India. 2002. 'Together Organization Report on Malenadu Sen Collection', January 10.

The Times of India. 2005. 'Plan panel to set up Food Security Watch/ March 8.

The paper was first published in the *Economic and Political Weekly*: 40:25: 2005: 2508-12. It is included here with the prior permission of the author and the Editor, *Economic and Political Weekly*. The address for email correspondence is: maithreyi_ krishnaraj@yahoo.com

CHAPTER - NINE

Perceptions on Safe Motherhood: An Analysis

G. Rama Padma

Safe motherhood means ensuring that all women receive the care that they need to be safe and healthy through pregnancy and childbirth. It is estimated that at least 1,600 women die every day from complications related to pregnancy and childbirth. Complications of pregnancy and childbirth are the leading cause of death and disability for women (aged 15 to 49 years) in developing countries [World Development Report: 1993]. Over one-fourth of deaths of women in reproductive age in many developing countries are related to pregnancy. Of all the health statistics monitored by the World Health Organization, maternal mortality has the largest discrepancy between developing and developed countries.

Maternal mortality is just the tip of the iceberg of the health problems women face. Many women do not die of causes related to pregnancy but suffer severe morbidities. Due to miscarriage, induced abortion, and other factors, about 40 per cent of the pregnancies in developing countries result in complications, illness, or permanent disability for the mother or child [WHO: 1992a]. Another study indicates that, for each maternal death, a further 10-15 woman suffer from serious impairments in developing countries [Measham and Rochat: 1987 as cited in Bhatia: 1993]. A study in India reported that 78 per cent of the maternal deaths that were reported in the study could have been prevented by specific timely actions [Bhatia: 1993].

The tragedy of maternal mortality and ill health has largely remained neglected for years. It has been neglected because those who suffer from it are neglected people, with the least power and influence over how national resources be spent; they are the poor, the rural peasants, and above all women. Only recently has serious attention been paid to the full complexity of this problem. The safe motherhood conference, that took place in Nairobi, Kenya in February 1987, had as its goal "not only to draw attention to maternal mortality, but more importantly, to mobilize immediate and concerted action at the national and international levels to prevent the continued tragedy" [World Bank: 1987]. Thus with a changed attitude to belief that 'Pregnancy is Special' safe motherhood initiative was launched at the conference. Safe motherhood initiatives have clearly defined these in its four pillars. These are family planning practice, antenatal care, clean/safe delivery, and essential obstetric care. Subsequently at the international conference on population and development at Cairo in 1994 safe pregnancy was reiterated in terms of not only survival but also complete well being of a woman. i.e., free of morbidity, during her reproductive ages.

Literature Review

The purpose of including family planning as one of the pillars of safe motherhood is with an assumption that it helps women from being exposed to 'maternal risk' by ensuring planned and wanted pregnancies. Experience shows a positive correlation between family planning and maternal health. In a rural sub district of Bangladesh, maternal mortality has declined substantially because of new approaches to family planning and maternity care. An effective community based family planning project has raised contraceptive prevalence to above 50 per cent in the study area as compared with 23 per cent in the control area, and reduced the maternal mortality rate by about one-third. Family planning succeeded in decreasing total pregnancies, and thus the number of pregnancy related deaths, but did not change the risk of death faced by pregnant women. However, a combination of basic family planning and maternal care has reduced the maternal mortality rate by more than one-half [World Bank: 1993].

A number of studies have stressed the role of socio-economic and demographic factors in influencing demand for and, utilization of family planning and mother and child health services [Ray, et al: 1984, Kanitkar and Sinha: 1989, Elo: 1992, Swenson, et al: 1993, Barlow and Diop: 1995, Ahmed and Mosley: 1997]. Many of these studies have also shown that women's education strongly affects the utilization of maternal and child health services. Chatterjee (1990) has argued that when permission and ability interact with need, a demand for health services is generated. Actual utilization of health services occurs when this generated demand connects with availability. In the Indian context, the situation is further complicated by women's perceptions of illness, which are affected by women's cultural conditioning to tolerate suffering. Because of this tolerance, which varies considerably across regions of India, even when the actual need is great the perceived need for health services can be small. It is argued that women's health seeking behaviour, especially related to pregnancy and childbirth, is considered a natural state of being for a woman rather than a condition requiring medical attention and care.

Every time a woman is pregnant, she risks a sudden and unpredictable complication that could result in her death or injury. At least 40 per cent of all pregnant women will experience some type of complication during their pregnancies. According to Rodhe (1995) the main purpose of antenatal care is for early detection of some complications or risk factors. Antenatal care refers to the pregnancy related care provided by a health worker in a medical facility or at home. In theory, antenatal care should address both psychological and medical needs of women, within the health care delivery system and the culture in which she lives [WHO: 1996]. The purpose behind periodic check-ups during the pregnancy is to establish confidence between a woman and her health care provider, to individualize health promotional messages and to identify and manage any maternal complications or risk factors. In this regard, a WHO technical working group recommended a minimum of four antenatal visits for a woman with a normal pregnancy. However some women will require more than four visits especially those who develop complications. It was further emphasized that this recommendation is to focus on the content of care and to set a basic essential standard for quality. Content of coverage is important especially in resource poor settings, and in this regard some have suggested that unnecessary antenatal visits should be reduced in favour of fewer and effective visits [Khan-Neelofur, et al: 1998].

Government of India has proposed a minimum of three antenatal visits during a pregnancy. This includes at least three antenatal care visits, iron prophylaxis supplementation, and two doses of tetanus toxoid vaccination, detection and treatment of anaemia in mothers, high blood pressure check-ups and management of high-risk pregnancies. Commonly used factors to identify risk are height, weight, age, parity and previous history. Other factors such as antenatal bleeding, sexually transmitted diseases, and transverse presentation are also identified as risk factors. In rural areas, an auxiliary midwife posted at sub-centre level is responsible for registering pregnant women, motivating them to obtain antenatal and post-natal care, assessing their health throughout pregnancy and postpartum period, and referral of high-risk pregnant women to a hospital.

The objectives of this paper are, first to analyze the levels of safe motherhood in the rural areas of Andhra Pradesh vis-à-vis other southern states, viz, Karnataka, Tamil Nadu and Kerala. Secondly, the paper tries to understand limiting causes, based on perceptions, which come in the way to achieve safe motherhood.

For examining the present levels of safe motherhood data were taken from the second National Family Health Survey (NFHS-2) conducted during 1998-99. The NFHS provides information on the first three components of safe motherhood, viz, family planning, antenatal care, and clean/safe delivery and thus, to this extent the analysis of levels of safe motherhood in rural areas is limited. To examine the second objective, data were drawn from an ongoing study on maternal morbidity. As part of the study Mahbubnagar and Guntur, a less developed and a better-developed district, were selected. In both the districts one PHC and a RCWHC (round the clock women health centre) were selected purposively. In each of the health centres 10 per cent of the villages were selected for the study at random. To understand the causes that come in the way to achieve safe motherhood, analysis was based on the perceptions collected from various groups of people who were directly related to it. As mentioned earlier women's health seeking behaviour depends not only on the availability of facilities but also on one's own perceptions on the need. Thus focus group discussions (FGDs) were organized with married women in the reproductive age groups. Women were further grouped as young and old based on their fertility status. Old women were defined for the present study as those who had at least one child and had not conceived since past five or more years. The remaining married women were considered as young. Studies have shown that often men play an important role in making decisions related to fertility and the ability to utilize health services by women depends upon the permission granted to them by men.

Hence the perceptions of the men with respect to maternal health and related issues were collected through FGDs. Also availability of the health care providers becomes vital in terms of utilization of health services. So, discussions and in-depth interviews were also held with auxiliary nurse midwives (ANMs) and informal health care providers such as traditional birth attendants and registered medical practitioners (RMPs), who play a vital role in promoting maternal health at rural areas. Therefore, the present paper is based on 30 focus group discussions and a few in-depth interviews conducted during the major part of the study.

This paper is organized into six sections. A brief review of literature on the concept and components of safe motherhood is presented in first section. In the second section, a comparative analysis of safe motherhood in rural Andhra Pradesh vis-à-vis other southern states of India is carried out based on the NFHS- 2 data. The third section deals with perceptions of women on various aspects related to safe motherhood. The fourth section narrates the understanding of rural men about maternal health. Fifth section discusses the perceptions of health care providers in promoting and implementing safe motherhood in rural areas. Conclusions and policy implications are given in the last section.

Results from NFHS

Family Planning

Estimates of the family planning indicators of safe motherhood in rural areas of the states of Andhra Pradesh, Karnataka, Tamil Nadu and Kerala are given in Table 1. According to the second National Family Health Survey [NFHS 1998-99] the awareness levels of any one of the contraceptive methods is almost universal in all these states. Although nearly all the currently married women know at least one method of contraception, only 58 per cent of rural women in Andhra Pradesh are using a method. Proportion of rural women currently using any method of contraception is higher in Kerala (63.2). A majority of these women are users of permanent methods of contraception. In other words, these users are protected permanently from being exposed to pregnancy or saved permanently from maternal risk. The median age at sterilization is the lowest in Andhra Pradesh (23.6 years). This in turn might imply that 58 per cent of the rural women in Andhra Pradesh are free of maternal risk for 21 years, i e, more than half of their reproductive span of life. This seems to be an encouraging phenomenon for policy-makers from the point of view of controlling population and permanently saving more years of reproductive span of life from risks of dying due to complications of pregnancy. At the same time consequences due to sterilization cannot be ignored. Some of the studies have shown that there is an evidence of morbidity associated with sterilization. While a few of the studies emphasized on the immediate post operative complications as a consequence of the procedure and timing of sterilization but others have focused on the physiological and psychological morbidity experienced over a period of time [Khairullah, et al: 1992, DeStefano, et al: 1985, Neil, et al: 1975, Wilcox, et a1: 1992, Miller, et al: 1991]. The government's policy to promote sterilization to lower number of children per woman in the larger interest of controlling population growth needs to be reassessed from the overall reproductive health perspective.

Table 1
Family Planning Related Indicators of Safe Motherhood in Southern States

Indicators	*India*	*Kerala*	*Andhra Pradesh*	*Karna-taka*	*Tamil Nadu*
Knowledge of any modern contraceptive method (per ceot) Current use of contraceptive method (per cent)	98.7	99.7	98.7	97.8	.99.9
–Any method	44.7	63.2	58.3	57.0	48.8
–Permanent method	35.4	51.0	56.9	49.4	45.6
–Temporary method	9.3	12.2	1.4	7.5	3.2
Median age al sterllisation	25.7	26.5	23.5	26.5	25.3
No method used before sterilisation (per cent)	81.9	57.9	94.4	90.0	87.5
Unmet need (per cent) for					
–Permanent method	7.8	4.9	2.4	3.3	6.6
–Temporary method	8.9	7.1	5.3	5.5	7.1
Reasons (per cent) for not using					
–Fertility related	66.4	52.2	80.2	77.1	62.9
–Opposition to use	7.3	10.4	2.5	6.8	5.3
–Lack of knowledge	4.5	1.3	1.1	3.6	0.4
–Method related reasons	14.4	12.9	11.3	7.2	28.7
Total fertility rate	3.07	2.07	2.32	3.03	2.23
Per cent of births by birth order					
–Birth order 3	18.2	15.9	17.5	16.1	15.6
–Birth order 4+	29.9	7.7	16.6	11.5	11.4
Per cent of births by Interval since previous birth					
–Less than 18 months	12.3	10.2	10.5	11.1	13.1
–18-23 months	15.6	12.4	14.6	19.6	17.0
Median age al lirst					
–Marriage	16.0	20.0	14.9	16.8	18.5
–Cohabitation	16.8	19.9	15.1	17.6	18.6
–Pregnancy	19.1	21.4	17.9	19.6	20.0

Note: Both rural and urban.
Source: NFHS-2, 1998-99.

Over decades, the number of children per woman has been brought down since the launch of family planning programme in 1951. The total fertility rate has come down from 6.1 in 1951 to 2.32 in 1998 for rural Andhra Pradesh. At the same time more than one-third of births in Andhra Pradesh are at birth order of three and above (NFHS-2). This also suggests that women with high birth orders are yet to be covered with contraceptives. Safe motherhood also addresses spacing between pregnancies. Percentage of rural women using any of the spacing methods of contraception is lowest in the state when compared to the other southern states. Also percentage of women who used no method before undergoing sterilization is highest in Andhra Pradesh (94.4). It is surmised that the programme is not satisfying the needs of large group of women who wish to space their births [Measham and Heaver: 1996]. Space between two successive pregnancies is a matter of concern. In Andhra Pradesh 10 per cent of births occur within 18 months of previous birth and 25 per cent within 24 months in rural areas. Within the unmet need, there has always been a higher need for temporary methods of contraception than for the permanent ones. The data from two consecutive NFHSs reveal that the unmet need for spacing methods still continues at the same levels, whereas there is an overall decrease in the total unmet need. Further, an analysis of the non-users of any contraceptive method reveals that a substantial percentage of women are not using because of either some method-related problems or they are opposed to using any method.

In terms of safe motherhood, adolescent fertility is an area of serious concern. An ICMR study has documented that the existing poor nutritional levels in Indian girls have shifted their physical maturity to later ages of 18 or 19 years [Behrman, et al: 1996]. The poor nutritional status in the adolescent girls results in incomplete development of pelvis. The incidence of other complications of pregnancy like obstructed labour; fistulae and pregnancy-induced hypertension are more common among adolescent girls [Saramma: 1996]. According to NFHS-2 median age at marriage in Andhra Pradesh (14.9) is close to the BIMARU states (14.9, 14.7, 15.1 and 15 years respectively). Median age at first cohabitation and age at first pregnancy in Andhra Pradesh (15 years and 17.9 years respectively) are lowest in the country indicating a majority of women in rural parts of the state are at maternal risk.

Antenatal Care

In all the southern states proportion of mothers receiving antenatal check-up is far better than the country as a whole [NFHS-2: 1998-99]. In rural areas of the country, still four out of ten women had no antenatal check-up (Table 2). Despite the uniformity in the programme design throughout the country, there is a considerable regional diversity in antenatal care received by women. In Kerala and Tamil Nadu, almost every woman had an ANC. In Andhra Pradesh nine out of 10 women, and in Karnataka eight out of 10 women in rural areas had an antenatal check-up. Though the number of women covered by an antenatal check-up is encouraging in the rural Andhra Pradesh, the percentage of women who had the recommended

Table 2
Antenatal Care in Southern States

Indicators	*India*	*Kerala*	*Andhra Pradesh*	*Karna-taka*	*Tamil Nadu*
No antenatal care (per yent)	39.8	0.4	9.5	17.3	1.3
Three or more anlenatal check-ups (per cent)	36.6	98.1	76.0	64.9	89.1
Median number of cheek-ups	2.5	8.5	4.0	3.8	4.4
Median months pregnant at first check-up	3.9	2.2	3.5	3.4	3.4
Antenalal measurements (per cent)					
–Weight measuled	48.3	78.9	72.1	58.4	85.0
–Height measuled	22.2	26.9	33.8	44.9	57.5
–Blood pressure checked	55.5	96.5	84.9	69.0	80.4
–Blood tested	51.4	94.8	74.1	64.5	70.0
–Urine tesled	46.9	96.3	71.8	55.5	71.5
–Abdomen examined	70.2	94.2	85.2	85.9	87.9
–Internal examination	31.4	60.4	57.8	25.7	63.8
–X-ray	3.5	3.7	4.4	2.9	5.4
–Sonography or Ultra sound	11.8	40.6	16.0	13.2	25.7
–Amniocentesis	1.9	2.4	0.7	1.4	7.5
Antenatal advice (per cent)					
–Diet	63.9	71.4	71.2	74.2	92.6
–Danger signs 01 plegnancy	31.7	41.2	41.4	44.9	38.9
–Delivery care	37.4	36.9	41.2	42.2	77.5
–New born care	34.0	32.7	35.6	36.1	79.8
–Family planning	26.1	29.9	36.5	34.6	53.6
IFA tablels given (per cent)					
–Who received supply for 3 + months	80.5	93.2	86.1	94.5	91.0
–Who consumed all the suppfy	79.4	92.6	77.3	85.8	79.4
Had 2 or more TT injections (per cent)	62.5	86.5	78.9	70.3	95.9
Pregnant women with anaemia (rural and urban) (per cent)	49.7	20.3	41.8	48.6	57.1

Source: NFHS-2, 1998-99.

number of antenatal check-ups is far less (76). Median number of checkups by mothers is slightly encouraging in Andhra Pradesh (4.7). Apart from the number of check-ups, timing of the first checkup is important for initiating adequate care. Barring in Kerala, women in the remaining states preferred to have their first antenatal check-up at the end of the first trimester (median month is 3.5). Contents of antenatal check-up are important, as it would guard woman from being exposed to maternal risk. In Andhra Pradesh every three out of four women had undergone the necessary tests for identifying a risk in pregnancy. Antenatal check-up also includes health promotion. Most commonly given advice during a check-up is an advice on diet. Provision of antenatal care such as coverage of women by IFA tablets/syrup and TT injections is relatively higher, that is more than the number of women who received three or more ANCs. Indeed these are the most commonly provided aspects in antenatal care in the rural areas. Yet compared to the other southern states, per cent of women who received three or more months of IFA tablets/syrup and those who consumed the given supply is lowest in Andhra Pradesh. About 42 per cent women in the state are found to be anaemic during pregnancy.

Delivery Care

Sixty per cent of rural mothers in the state are having non-institutional deliveries. Though number of deliveries attended by traditional birth attendants or untrained members in the state are less than that of the country as a whole yet it is a substantial percentage (42). Though the percentage of mothers who had a post-partum check-up in the state (45) seems to be far higher than the national figure, yet it is not even one out of two women had a post-partum check-up within two months of a delivery. Of those whose deliveries were attended by medical or paramedical personnel, only half of them had a post-partum check-up. Percentage of women reporting with post-partum complications is highest in the state compared to other southern states.

Perceptions of Women on Safe Motherhood

During focus group discussions care was taken to see that women belonging to all castes were represented. To encourage better involvement, discussions were organized separately for women from forward castes and scheduled castes or backward castes. In each of the groups six to eight women were included. In Mahbubnagar district, more women were from socio-economically weaker sections than those from Guntur district. Nine out of 10 women in Mahbubnagar district were illiterates whereas in Guntur district every second woman was a literate and a majority of them had studied up to primary level. Nearly three out of four women in Mahbubnagar district, and one out of two persons in Guntur district were working outside home. Most of the women worked as agriculture labour. Women were also engaged as daily wagers in non-agricultural work such as in stone-cutting, building construction activities, tobacco and cotton processing units, etc.

All the participants believed that attainment of puberty makes a girl eligible for marriage. Though everyone from both the districts agreed that 18 to 21 years is an ideal age for marriage, most of the women in Mahbubnagar district and a few in Guntur district stated that for personal reasons they get their girls married within two or three years after attaining puberty. Among scheduled castes, most of the girls were married even before they attained menarche. Every one expects a woman to bear a child within a year or two after marriage in most communities. Culturally, pregnancy is highly valued. First pregnancy is revered in families. Women perceive that there is an elevation in their 'status' within the family once they are pregnant. Being pregnant is a moment of joy and pride for husband and parents. Also a few women, especially from scheduled castes and backward castes, mentioned that if one is not pregnant till two years after her marriage, she is subject to criticism. Therefore after the marriage many preferred to conceive at the earliest.

All women in the Guntur district and most of them in Mahbubnagar district (75 per cent) have a favourable attitude towards family planning methods. They feel that but for the availability of these methods, a woman would continue to bear children all through the reproductive age. Though women were in favour of limiting the size of the family, yet many were not in favour of using a method before first conception or between pregnancies due to the fears of not conceiving when desired. Women are also worried about the health problems associated with usage of temporary methods. Some young women belonging to upper castes and backward castes from both the districts, however, wished to postpone first pregnancy. Though they had no adequate knowledge about health consequences related to teenage pregnancy, their main concern was not to get involved into the responsibilities of motherhood soon after marriage. In such cases women felt that husbands' cooperation was very much needed. Otherwise, they felt that it was embarrassing for them to go to a shop to buy or get a contraceptive from the health centre. However in the villages where ANMs regularly visit, some women requested them for supply of contraceptive pills.

Health Care Seeking Behaviour of Women

Women were asked on the need and type of care to be taken by them during pregnancy. The first response by most of the women irrespective of their caste in the backward region was a query on the need for additional care. When they were sick during pregnancy the only care they took was to rest for a while or abstain from wage work. However the inability to work for wages left them with a sense of guilt. This was mainly because of the financial compulsions. On the contrary in the developed region, though some women from scheduled castes and tribes also felt that pregnancy and childbirth as a natural process, many of them strongly agreed that an extra care in terms of medical care, nutritious food, and rest was essential. Depending on the family's financial position, they either went to a private nursing home or to a public health facility for an antenatal check-up. Some women visited a private doctor for a check-up and also they went to a public health facility especially for receiving TT injection and IFA tablets. All of them believed in following a doctor's advice. Most of them consumed the given IFA tablets/syrup. Though many of them did not have a specific knowledge about desired health care during pregnancy or after childbirth, but the attitude to follow doctor's advice made them utilize the health facilities.

On the other hand most of the women from Mahbubnagar met mainly informal health care providers, viz, registered medical practitioner (RMP) or *dai* or traditional healer. When women received IFA tablets, most of them from backward castes, scheduled castes, and scheduled tribes did not like to consume them. They felt that by taking the tablets a woman would give birth to a 'large' baby and delivery at home will be unmanageable. They also opined that every hospital delivery will lead to a caesarean section and finally became expensive. Similarly some women were reluctant to take a tetanus toxide injection as well. At the same time a few women from forward castes realized the importance of following a medical advice during pregnancy. It is reflected from following annotations:

- It is good to follow a doctor's advice. I was advised to take complete rest, but all the time it is not possible. My earlier pregnancy ended in an abortion.
- This is my fourth pregnancy in last three years. First I had a daughter and she is a healthy baby. Next two pregnancies resulted in abortion. Doctor advised me not to conceive immediately. She said it would be better to give a gap of one year at least. My parents in-law and my husband want me to bear a son. I have no choice. Now I am pregnant again. I am praying god to bless me with a son. Otherwise again I may be forced to become pregnant soon.

The above comments also suggest that even though women in this district had realized the need for medical care, they were not in a position to follow medical advice due to the inability to exercise their will in the house.

Most commonly received advice from health personnel by most of the women in both the regions was the prescription of iron capsules or syrup, multi-vitamin tablets, and about nutritious diet. Most of the women from Guntur district took interest to have nutritious diet during pregnancy, whereas women in Mahbubnagar district did not take additional care mainly because of financial problems and also due to the ignorance. They normally took *roti* made of *jowar* with chilly-powder, called as *'vellulikaram'* on normal days and as well as during pregnancy. In two of the focus group discussions a few women belonging to scheduled tribes and castes said that they took liquor during pregnancy, as they believed that it helped the foetus to move actively in the womb. They also took it after the childbirth to regain their 'lost strength'.

The kind of care required during and after childbirth is not seriously perceived by many women. As it is believed to help in easy delivery, consumption of homemade concoction is given to women during delivery. There is hardly any planning made for a safe delivery. Usage of a new blade and a thread to cut and tie the umbilical cord is the only care perceived to be the most important by women during home deliveries. In Mahbubnagar district, many preferred home deliveries. Women opined that home delivery was equally safe and costed less. Some of their expressions were:

- If one goes to a private hospital, doctors unnecessarily insist on a caesarean to make money.
- "An ordinary delivery at hospital will cost not less than Rs. 1,500-whereas if it is done at home we pay Rs. 50 to the dai. If an ANM assists we pay her Rs. 100. Don't you think it is much cheaper than a hospital delivery?
- Once we go to a PHC, staff insists us to go for an operation (tubectomy). In Guntur district most of them preferred to have childbirth at an institution either a private hospital or a public health centre. Women from lower socio-economic status still preferred to have a delivery at home with the help of a dai in Guntur. The type of care given to woman during post-partum period is generally related to food intake, that too in the form of restrictions on diet. After childbirth, attention is largely shifted towards the newborn child. If it is a male child, celebrations are performed with joy. Though specifically girl child is not ill-

treated, rarely a celebration is followed. In some families, the mother and girl child are looked down and subsequent care is not volunteered or at times denied.

Table 3
Delivery Characteristics in Southern States

Indicators	*India*	*Kerala*	*Andhra Pradesh*	*Karna-taka*	*Tamil Nadu*
Non-institutional births (per cent)	75.3	8.4	59.9	61.5	27.5
Births attended by TBA and others (per cent)	66.2	6.3	41.5	53.2	22.1
Delivered by caesareen section (per cent)	4.9	27.4	11.9	7.1	12.2
Birth weight (per cent)					
–< 2.5 kg.	4.2	15.3	6.5	6.1	12.2
–Not weighted	78.6	9.7	64.3	66.2	30.5
Post-partum check-up within 2 months of birth (per cent)	16.1	–	45.2	34.3	51.4
–Of those attended by Doctor/Nurse/ Midwife/LHV (rural and urban) (per cent)	29.3	–	53.0	55.7	60.8
Post-partum complications (per cent)					
–Massive vaginal bleeding	11.4	9.6	19.0	6.1	7.8
–Very high fever	13.4	11.5	14.9	6.5	5.1

Note: Not Available.
Source: NFHS-2, 1998-99.

Women's awareness about health problems was mainly related to their experiences rather than about the seriousness of a problem. Findings suggest that lesser the experience of problems, lesser was the awareness about it. By and large a few women had mentioned problems during pregnancy in Guntur district than those from backward district (Table 4). When asked to mention about various problems they may face during pregnancy, the women spontaneously stated that 'vomiting' was the most commonly experienced problem. Women in Mahbubnagar mentioned that 'headache'; 'giddiness'; 'do not feel like eating'; and 'indigestion' were the next commonly experienced problems. In Guntur district 'weakness during pregnancy', and 'not feeling like eating' was reported as the common problems next to 'vomiting'. Women's knowledge was very poor about the problems, which might lead to risks in pregnancy. Only a few of them felt that 'high blood pressure', 'convulsions', 'vaginal bleeding' could be serious. Knowledge about problems during delivery was very poor. Most of the women in the Mahbubnagar villages believed that it was better for a woman to have menstrual bleeding for a month after delivery. They thought that bleeding helped in throwing off the unnecessary particles from a woman's uterus. Similarly, after delivery, 'less bleeding' or 'bleeding for few days only' was perceived as detrimental to health. On the contrary, a few women in Guntur district perceived excessive bleeding as unhealthy.

Table 4
Perceptions of Rural Women about Maternal Health Problems in Andhra Pradesh

Local name	*Problems*	*District*	
	Closest English Translation	*Mahabubnagar (N = 86)*	*Guntur (N = 91)*
During Pregnancy	*During Pregnancy*		
Vantulua	Vomiting	100.0	98.9
Tala noppi/tala tiragatam	Headache/giddiness	73.3	19.8
Tina Buddi veyadu	Do not feel like eating	59.3	40.7
Aragadu	Indigestion	43.0	–
Vollu noppi	Body ache	37.2	32.9
Tella batta	White discharge	31.4	–
Rechikati	NIght blindness	29.1	–
Nirasam	Weakness	22.1	64.8
Potti Kadupu noppi	Abdominal pain	20.9	1.1
Pindam tiragaka povatam/ jaripovatam/tirugutunte badha	Problems related to movement of fetus	19.8	–
Ayasam	Breathlessness	16.3	5.5
Podukovalanipastundi	Feeling sleepy	13.9	24.2
'Akkada' raktam povatundi	Vaginal bleeding	11.6	3.3
Kalisinappudu noppi/raktam	Pain/bleeding during coitus	7.0	6.6
Gundello noppi	Chest pain	4.7	–
Nirupadutundi	Edema	4.6	8.8
Ekkuva raktapotu	High blood pressure	1.2	7.7
Gurrapuvatam	Convulsions	–	7.7
Visugu/Kopam	Irritation/angry	–	7.7
During Delivery	*During Delivery*		
Takkuva raktam potundi	Less bleeding	60.0	–
Ekkuva raktam potundi	Excessive bleeding	–	12.1
Kallu/Nadumu gunjutayi	Pain in legs/abdomen	3.5	8.8
Maya tondaraga padadu	Delayed placenta	3.5	5.5
Bidda addangatirigindi	Baby in transverse position	2.3	4.4
Gurrapuvatam	Convulsions	–	2.2
Nadumu-noppi	Bakache	–	2.2
Bhayam	Fear	–	3.3
After Delivery	*After Delivery*		
Tkkuva raktam	Less bleeding	62.8	5.5
Rommu noppi	Breast pain	12.8	–
Vollu noppi	Body ache	11.6	8.8
Danurvatam	Tetanus	–	3.3
Raktam ekkuva pote neerasam	Weakness due to bleeding	7.0	–
Garbesanchi jarutundi	Uterus prolapsed	7.0	–
Nadumu noppi	Back ache	4.7	2.2
Jalubu and talanoppi	Cold and headache	4.7	–
'Akkada' noppi	Pain at birth canal	1.2	3.3
Kadupulo gadda	Cyst in abdomen	5.8	–
Navva/durada	Itching sensation	4.7	–

Source: Based on Fieldwork.

Perceptions of Men and Women

Many women felt that men did not accompany women to a doctor or health centre during pregnancy, delivery or after delivery. Most of the elderly participants said that it was not nice to expect men to leave their work and go with wife to a doctor. These women opined that it was not an area for men to get involved in. At the same time all women felt that men never understood what a woman underwent during pregnancy and after childbirth. Some of the grievances of women against men were:

> *Men never understand what a woman undergoes during pregnancy. They want us to serve them with care like on normal days. If we tell them about the discomfort, they think that we are making excuses. Men demand for 'it' (sex) and if we feel uncomfortable during pregnancy, they beat us or go to another woman. So we accept their demand. They never try to understand a wife.*

After childbirth the women think men are less cooperative. Women feel that they need to attend to the newborn child, whereas husband does not understand their additional responsibility.

Not everyone agreed, however, that encouraging men's participation in reproductive health activities was a good way to improve women's reproductive health. By and large men being the main decision-makers of a household, therefore in this particular context an attempt was made to understand men's knowledge levels and their perceived role towards safe motherhood.

All the men, young and old, alike were aware about menarche. All men felt that attaining menarche reminded everyone at home that the girl had reached marriageable age. Older men felt that a girl should be 'given' in a marriage as soon as she attains puberty. Especially among low castes and poorer families, they felt that delay in marriage after reaching menarche was a social stigma. Some of their comments about it were:

- The earliest we perform her marriage after puberty, better will be our respect in the community. If delayed more, we will be subject to criticism by society.
- I know I should not delay my daughter's marriage. Last year they were asking Rs. 10,000. Then I did not have enough money so I was forced to wait. This year they are asking for Rs. 15,000 and a bicycle. From where can I get that much? I wish I had married her off before she became 'big' (attained menarche).
- Nowadays we should not delay girl's marriage after puberty. From TVs they are learning every thing. It is better for us to be careful. Otherwise one day they will not allow us to raise our head in the community.

On the contrary, some of the young men feel that a woman should go for a marriage after she attains the legal age at marriage because by then she would be grown completely both physically and mentally. Some of their comments about it were:

- If married at a young age she would not know how to respect parents-in-law nor be able to understand how to behave in our family. Before 18 years of age she will not know completely sexual needs and will not be able to cooperate with husband properly in 'it' (sex).

- A majority of the young men want to postpone first pregnancy. They feel that one needs to enjoy life for a few years. They complained that wives did not understand this. On the contrary older men felt that it was better to have a first child at the earliest.

Majority of the older men related conception to the mercy of god whereas younger husbands associated it to the physiology of the body. Relatively older men as compared to younger men, and among younger men, those from Mahbubnagar were less aware about the type of health care needed during pregnancy. The older men said that a doctor would prescribe some tonics and medicines, which a woman was required to follow. The younger men were aware about the need to take 'iron' tablets, tetanus toxide injections, and the necessity for clinical tests and scanning during pregnancy. Awareness about the problems a woman may face during pregnancy was poor among most of the men. All they know was that a pregnant woman would vomit till fifth or seventh month of pregnancy and got tired faster than on normal days.

Most of the husbands felt that they had no specific role to play towards a pregnant wife. Some of their remarks in this regard clarify this:

> *What are we supposed to do if one is pregnant? It is the duty of her mother or other women to take care of a pregnant woman. We give them money to go to a doctor. What more should a man do? We help her in having an easy delivery by participating in 'it' (sex) till seventh month of pregnancy.*

On their behaviour towards a pregnant wife, many said there would be not much of a specific change. A few husbands, however, said they brought food of wife's choice like sour tasting fruits or eatables during pregnancy. Some were generous to say that they would not beat their wives during pregnancy while others continued to beat them, if they thought she had been disobedient. A few men said that they did take care of pregnant wife by not letting her to lift heavy objects. They took their wives to a doctor and if they were busy they made alternate arrangements.

Usually wives went to parents place for first two pregnancies and in most of the cases husbands were not present at the time of delivery. Even if they were present, mainly the female members of the family or dai or health worker played a vital role. Only in case of an emergency, that is, if baby was in a transverse position, other elderly male members and husband were involved in making necessary arrangements for transportation. The older men from Guntur district said that it was usually their wives who planned for daughter's delivery. They gather information about hospitals, doctors and cost particulars through the experiences of other women in the village. Based on the cost, reputation of a place or doctor the male head of the family decided the institution for a delivery. In Guntur district most of the men were in favour of institutional delivery. However, a few men preferred home delivery for cost reasons. Similarly a large number of men in Mahbubnagar district decided that their women deliver at home. Husbands also perceived that they had no role to play after their wives' delivery. Rather many thought that their wives neglected them as their main concern shifted towards the newborn child. Most of the husbands, especially from Mahbubnagar, felt that their wives forbid them to have coitus for nearly six months after delivery. Thus they felt that when women did not cooperate with them, it was not necessary for them to think of needs of the wives. A few men, however, realized the importance of immunization. So they took the child and wife to a doctor/health centre.

In Mahbubnagar district, two men said that initially they planned a home delivery for their wives. However, after six to 12 hours of trial, the local *dai* and other elderly women expressed their inability to handle the cases. In one case labour pain started on an early evening. Initially the family members did not anticipate it to be serious. Otherwise the last bus from the village to town was available at 6 p m. After waiting for six hours they hired a jeep and took the woman to the nearby private hospital in the nearest town, Dharur, which was around five km from the village. The doctor helped in having a safe delivery. In another case, the woman started having labour pains by late evening. After five hours of efforts, then dai said that the woman needed to be shifted to a hospital. The husband of the lady requested one of the villagers, who owned a jeep, to carry his wife to a hospital. However the head of the family, father-in-law of the woman, decided to wait till morning. In the early hours they took the woman to a hospital. Before the doctor could attend to her, the woman died.

In Guntur district, two of the fathers had planned for their daughters to have deliveries at home. After two to three hours of effort by dais and RMPs, they took the women to nearby health facilities. One woman was brought to a RCWHC. Another woman was taken to a private hospital at Ponnur. Both the women had safe deliveries.

Older men thought that it was better to have a desired number of children and then to limit further pregnancies by a terminal method. On the contrary, younger men felt that it was better to postpone first birth for a year or two after the marriage. They felt wives should take interest and use the contraceptive pills. At times a few of the husbands got the pills. The younger men felt that elders disapproved their decision and thus they needed to maintain secrecy. Whether young or old, everyone agreed that a smaller family of two children was an ideal family size. While some in Guntur district thought that even a single child was acceptable, some men in Mahbubnagar thought that there should be three children for a desired family size.

ANMs, Dais and RMPs

Most of the ANMs from both the districts had basic knowledge about obstetric care and each one of them agreed that antenatal check-ups include not only physical aspects but also an advice on health promotion. Compared to the ANMs in Mahbubnagar district, ANMs from Guntur district could tell more specifically about the timing of check-ups and indications of risk pregnancy. However, in reality there was a wide gap in the knowledge and actual role played by ANMs. Some of the ANMs have not visited all the villages that are allocated to them since past a month especially in the villages of Mahbubnagar district. They were not aware about the number of pregnant women in the SC/ PHC village, if not in other villages. A few of the ANMs from Mahbubnagar district justified this situation to the lack transportation, distances and more population. ANMs perceived that local RMPs and traditional healers acted as an obstacle for their work by misguiding women. Another major difficulty ANMs thought was the attitude of villagers towards them as family planning workers rather than as health care providers. As a result, women did not inform them about pregnancy nor cooperated with them. Many a times they found difficulty in convincing pregnant women about their genuine desire to help them. Women from tribes, backward and scheduled castes did not consume the given IFA tablets and often ANMs had to physically monitor whether they are consuming the tablets or not. ANMs in Guntur district were instructed not to handle a home delivery but to refer the pregnant women to the health centre under *Sukhibhava scheme.* In case of emergency staff nurse at health centre refer the woman to a nearby private hospital because of closer proximity. If a family cannot afford the cost, then at an earlier stage she advises the woman to be taken to a first referral unit.

A *dai* is generally an aged woman from a lower caste. Usually women from scheduled and backward castes and among tribal groups often seek health advice from *dais*. In Mahbubnagar district women from other castes too consulted *dai* for specific women's health problems. Women go to dais to seek advice on menstrual problems, during pregnancy and mainly for assistance during childbirth. *Dais* normally suggested homemade remedies for any health problem. In the villages of Guntur district too, women sought advice from *dais*. *Dais* felt that their role and income had been largely taken over by RMPs and qualified medical staff. *Dais* themselves sensed that their role was going to disappear in these villages.

The trained *dais* recalled that they were informed during training about the importance of IFA tablets, TT injections and need for nutritious diet during pregnancy. However, in practice both trained and untrained *dais* in Mahbubnagar district advice women not to take more quantity of food and IFA tablets. They believed that by taking more food a woman might have to experience difficulty during childbirth. In Guntur district the emphasis was on type of food. *Dais* felt that specific planning was not required for childbirth. *Dais* washed their hands before assisting in childbirth. In addition *dais* from Guntur district also used surgical gloves. All of them opined that a new blade and a thread were essential items required for a safe delivery. *Dais* in Guntur district advised hot tea to be served to the woman before childbirth whereas in Mahbubnagar district in some villages women were advised to take country liquor apart from homemade concoctions. *Dais* opined that for a majority of cases there was no need for a referral and they could handle it by themselves. Only if baby was in transverse position or if the woman developed convulsions, it was risky. Thus she suggested a family member to take woman to a hospital but did not refer a particular place. The RMP actually referred the cases to the hospital. *Dais* thought that a post-partum care was largely related to massaging of the body with herbs and oils, care of birth canal, kind of bathing, avoiding certain types of food, and care related to nursing and handling of the baby. Some of their advices about postpartum care could be gauged from the following comments.

On fifth or eleventh day after delivery, the woman needs to have a proper massage with neem leaves, turmeric powder, 'vajapodi' (local herb) and oil. This strengthens the muscles. This should be followed for three months after delivery Cotton soaked in country liquor or neem leaves and black pepper soaked in oil has to be placed at mouth of the birth canal We advice women to drink only boiled water for a month or two after delivery.

Registered medical practitioners (RMPs) referred to as 'doctors' by the villagers play an active role in health delivery system. Only a few of them were the registered medical practitioners, whereas rest are quacks. In Guntur district, each RMP went for a yearly contract with some of the families in a few villages. He either treated them or referred the case to a doctor, usually a private practitioner. In addition, he also dispensed outpatient services at fixed timings where women usually from lower castes went. Unlike in Guntur, in few cases RMPs in Mahbubnagar also assisted in a delivery.

Most of the RMPs believe that intake of nutritious food and supplementary tonics/tablets would keep a pregnant woman in good health. They prescribed IFA tablets, vitamins, and administered TT injections. All the RMPs did not have adequate knowledge about the risks involved in a pregnancy. Though villagers preferred a woman, i.e, a *dai* or an ANM to assist the pregnant woman during childbirth, RMPs were definitely called upon at the time of childbirth. This was because people opined that in case of an emergency he would be of help in guiding them to go to a hospital as most of them maintain an association with the private hospitals. Most of the RMPs opined that *dais* delay in referring a risk case for want of fee; otherwise they could save more women from suffering. Only a few of them were knowledgeable about risks involved in a pregnancy and the type of care to be taken during and after delivery. However they judged themselves as more knowledgeable than the *dais*.

Conclusion

At a glance, the NFHS-2 data suggest that the rural women in rural Andhra Pradesh are experiencing safe motherhood. However, social and group perspectives reveal that many women are exposed to unsafe motherhood and often non-biomedical causes influence the medical determinants of safe motherhood. The paper brings out the differences in perceptions in a backward district (Mahabubnagar), and a developed district (Guntur).

Age at marriage and age at first pregnancy in Andhra Pradesh are the lowest in the country. Early age at marriage is mainly related to social problems like dowry and fear of fathers about social disgrace attached to their inability to make daughters married. Thus it requires to be handled at a broader level, not merely by enacting laws. If early marriages cannot be discouraged, all efforts must be made to delay the occurrence of an early pregnancy. Information should be given on the benefits of delaying pregnancy by providing adequate knowledge on temporary methods. Low usage of temporary methods and the un-met need for them is a reflection of gaps in implementing the need-based approach. The desire of the younger couples to postpone first pregnancy vis-à-vis fears related to infertility and health problems caused by using some temporary methods has to be talked off by spreading correct reproductive health knowledge and persuasion. Availability and accessibility of contraceptives has also to be reviewed periodically. Apart from targeting younger couples, educating older members of the family, both men and women, to develop a favourable attitude towards temporary methods has to be considered for effective implementation of safe motherhood practices.

Women perceive that motherhood confers on them a relatively a higher 'status' within the family. Across all socio-economic classes, the stages of pregnancy are still celebrated in traditional ways. However, the real care and protection in ensuring safe motherhood has not reached desired levels. The main problem in these rural areas is the lack of awareness about the need for maternal health care. Especially in the backward district, women perceive pregnancy and the problems associated with it as a natural process. Even when women realize the need for health care, their inability to convince family members leave them to unsafe motherhood practices. In addition unfriendly attitude of the governmental health staff does not encourage women to utilize antenatal care facilities at public health centres. A few ANMs in backward district also find it difficult to cover all the assigned villages because of a large geographical area and poor transportation facilities. Because of their poor financial status, most of the rural women in Mahabubnagar district, unlike those in Guntur district, do not go to private health facilities for antenatal care. In the backward district, the women frequently go to untrained health care providers, viz, RMPs, dais, and traditional healers. The most commonly received antenatal care in both the districts is the supply of IFA tablets and TT injections. Among the women who receive the IFA tablets, all do not consume them in backward areas due to misconceptions.

Depending on one's own financial position, the male elderly members of a family decide the place for a delivery. The role played by local non-institutional health care providers is detrimental to the health of the women. Most of these providers are inadequate in their own knowledge levels on maternal risk factors. Comparatively *dais* are better aware than RMPs. Fearful of missing their fee *dais* do not refer a serious case at an early stage. RMPs on the other hand would want to refer to a private hospital for their own benefit. At the same time villagers trust them. It is, therefore, necessary to acknowledge their role and derive methods to co-opt their services in providing better maternal health care. Unfriendly behaviour of some of the governmental health staff and the uncontrolled levels of fee charged by private health centres, and fears of unnecessary caesarean sections imposed by private hospitals are forcing the lower economic sections to opt for home deliveries. People in the backward district are experiencing more of such problems. Even in places where governmental health staff is willing to extend sincere services, the already existing notions against them make people to take decisions against utilisation of services from public health centres. Concerted efforts are urgently needed to remove such notions in these areas.

Maternal care includes not only care during pregnancy and delivery but also during post-partum period. Care after delivery is highly neglected by both women as well as health care providers. The health workers in rural areas appear to be burdened with multiple tasks. Thus, they divert their efforts more towards immunization programmes and meeting the sterilization targets rather than on post-partum care. Women's knowledge levels are also very poor with respect to delivery and postpartum care. They wrongly perceive that many a problem could occur only during pregnancy rather than during delivery or post-partum period.

References

Ahmed and Mosley. 1997. 'Simultaneity in Maternal-Child Health Care Utilisation and Contraceptive Use: Evidence from Developing Countries', Hopkins Population Centre Papers on Population, WP 97-03: Baltimore.

Barlow, R. and Diop. 1995. 'Increasing the Cost-Effective Health Services through Changes in Demand', *Health Policy and Planning:* 10:3: 284-95.

Bhatia, J.C. 1993. 'Levels and Causes of Maternal Mortality in Southern India', *Studies in Family Planning:* 24:5:310-18.

Behrman, R.E. and Kliegman A. Raymond Nelson. 1996. *Textbook of Paediatrics,* Bangalore: Saunders and Prism Books.

Chattterjee, M. 1990. 'Indian Women: Their Health and Economic Productivity', Report No 109, Washington, DC: World Bank Discussion Papers.

DeStefano, F., et al. 1985. 'Long-Term Risk of Menstrual Disturbances After Tubal Sterilisation', *American Journal of Obstetrics and Gynaecology:* 152: 488-98.

Elo, Irma T. 1992. 'Utilization of Maternal Health Care Services in Peru: The Role of Women's Education', *Health Transition Review,* 2:1: 49-69.

IIPS. 1993. *National Family Health Survey (NFHS- 1),* Mumbai: International Institute of Population Sciences.

IIPS. 2000. *National Family Health Survey (NFHS-2),* Mumbai: International Institute of Population Sciences.

Kanitkar, T. and R.K. Sinha. 1989. 'Antenatal Care Services in Five States of India' in S.N. Singh, M.K. Premi, P.S. Bhatia, and Ashish Bose (eds), *Population Transition in India,* Vol. 2, Delhi: B.R. Publishing.

Khairullah, Z., et al.1992. 'Declining Mortality in International Sterilization Services', *International Journal of Gynaecology and Obstetrics:* 39: 41-50.

Khan, Neelofur, M.R., M. Gulmezoglu and J. Villar. 1998. 'Who Should Provide Routine Antenatal Care for Low-Risk Women, and How Often? A Systematic Review of Randomised Controlled Trials', *Paediatric and Perinatal Epidemiology:* 12: Supplement 2: 7-26.

Mathai, Saramma T. 1996. *Women and Health System in improving Women's Health in India,* Washington, DC: The World Bank, and IDRB.

Measham, Anthony R. and Richard A. Heaver. 1996. *Supplement to India's Family Welfare Programme: Moving to a Reproductive and Child Health Approach.* Washington, DC: The World Bank.

Miller, W.B., et al. 1991. 'The Predictors of Post-Sterilization Regret in Married Women', *Journal of Applied Social Psychology:* 21:1083-1110.

Neil, J.R. et al.1975. 'Late Complication of Sterilization by Laproscopy and Tubal Ligation', Lancet: 2: 699-700.

Ray, S.K., B.B. Mukhopadhoyay, R. Das, M.M. Ganguly, A. Maidal, and S.C. Roy. 1984, 'Extent of Utilization of Maternal Health Care Services of PHC by Families of a Rural Area', *Indian Journal of Public Health:* 28:3: 122-27.

Rodhe, J.E. 1995. 'Removing Risk from Safe Motherhood', *International Journal of Gynaecology and Obstetrics,* 50: Supplement 2: S3-S 10.

Wilcox, L.S. et al. 1992. 'Menstrual Function after Tubal Sterilisation', *American Journal of Epidemiology:* 135:1368-81.

WHO. 1992. *Antenatal Care and Maternal Health: How Effective is it?* Geneva: World Health Organization.

WHO. 1996. *Care in Normal Birth: A Practical Guide,* Geneva: World Health Organisation.

WHO.1996. *Antenatal Care, Report of a Technical Working Group,* Geneva: World Health Organisation.

World Bank. 1987. *Preventing the Tragedy of Maternal Deaths,* A report on the International Safe Motherhood Conference. Washington, DC:

World Development Report. 1993. Investing in Health, Washington, DC: The World Bank.

This work is based on a prospective study on Maternal Morbidity in Andhra Pradesh sponsored by Rockefeller Foundation. This paper was first published in the *Economic and Political Weekly:* 38:39: 2003:4173-81. It is included here with the prior permission of the author and the Editor, *Economic and Political Weekly.* Address for email correspondence is: ramapadma@cess.ac.in

CHAPTER - TEN

Abortion Services and Providers' Perceptions: Gender Dimensions[1]

Sunita Bandewar

Introduction

Gender constitutes an important dimension of the socio-cultural and political context within which interactions between health service providers and users take place. Users as well as providers of health care services are part of a social system governed by patriarchal norms. By patriarchal norms we mean a worldview that considers males as inherently superior to females, and values and privileges men. Medical training institutions, medical curricula and the organization and management of health services are not without the impact of patriarchal and gender biased value system. Thus, even though they may not be aware of it, service providers are more likely than not to reflect gender biases. In addition, their knowledge allows them to have an authority and upper hand while interacting with service users, which means that service users may find themselves at the receiving end of discriminatory attitudes and practices on the basis of gender.

This paper explores the gender dimensions of abortion-service providers' perceptions of users. Gender norms and values related to femininity and what is appropriate for women to do govern a whole range of issues related to women's abortion needs. Gender power relations between women and men place women in a situation where they are often without power and authority in negotiating sexual relations with men. They may also have limited access to contraceptives and power to use these even when available. Ironically, however, it is women who bear the brunt of non-use of contraception, while men seldom take responsibility for preventing pregnancies either through abstinence or through uses of contraception themselves. When faced with an unplanned or unwanted pregnancy, women may once again find themselves facing barriers to termination of the pregnancy from their male partners and from others, including service providers.

Providers' responses to a particular abortion situation are shaped largely by their attitude towards women, to women's health care needs in general and to abortion care needs in particular. Their understanding of woman's status in the family and society, of the power dynamics between women and their partners and family members, all these have implications-desirable or un-desirable-for women's access to abortion care and quality of care that they receive.

The significance of providers' perceptions and attitudes is evident when viewed against the fact that according to the Medical Termination of Pregnancy (MTP) Act, it is the medical doctor who decided whether or not an abortion seeker fulfils the criteria spelled out in the Act. It is for the medical professionals to decide as to how liberally or restrictively to interpret the Act in a given socio-political context. In addition to other factors, providers' attitude towards and understanding of women and their abortion needs influence the interpretations of the Act and is an important variable influencing women's access to abortion services.

In this paper, we examine providers' perceptions on women's abortion needs in terms of whether these perceptions reinforce the gender based value system victimizing women or facilitate a gender sensitive (and not a gender neutral) value system empowering women. The information discussed in this paper was collected as part of a larger initiative entitled 'Research and advocacy programme for improving access to abortion' taken up by CERAT, a non-governmental research and advocacy organization. Research under this larger initiative was conducted primarily to assess the quality of institution–based abortion care services. Providers' perception about women's abortion needs was studied because we believed that this would have an important influence on the quality of services provided.

II

Study Area and Methodology

The study area consisted of seven sub-districts in two districts of Maharashtra, India. The study units were health care facilities. We undertook enumeration of health care service centres in the selected study area using the snowballing technique to define the universe, viz, abortion care facilities, as there was no information available on these facilities. One hundred and thirty (130) providers from 115 facilities participated in responding to questions regarding perceptions of providers about women's abortion needs. More than one third (36.2 per cent) of the respondents were women, and about half of the respondents were not qualified to perform abortions as per the MTP Act.

Providers were requested to express their views about: abortion as a spacing method, abortion in case of failure of contraception, abortion after sex determination, second trimester abortion situations, and abortion as a woman's right. In addition, they were also asked to articulate as to who are responsible for women to face abortion situations in general. Women researchers conducted interviews of head of the institutions and abortion service providers at health care facilities, which together lasted for about 90-120 minutes.

III

Providers' Perceptions

Providers held either individuals and/or individuals' circumstances responsible for women's abortion situations. Some providers articulated the dynamics among various factors and often-shared information on specific situations.

The spectrum of individuals held responsible for abortion was wide and included those closest to the woman seeking abortion. Husbands alone were held responsible by about 35 per cent of the providers, the woman herself by 41 per cent and both the woman and her husband were held jointly responsible by 44 per cent of the providers. In addition, about 8 per cent of the providers held family members and relatives responsible and about the same number explained situations of abortions among single women specifically.

It is worth taking note of the fact that the woman seeking abortion was held responsible for being in that situation by more women providers than men (more than half as compared to only about one third), more urban than rural providers (45 per cent vs 32 per cent) and more private practitioners than public providers (44 per cent vs 20 per cent). One reason why public providers and rural providers tend not to blame the women may be that they interact with women from comparatively poorer communities and are better able to understand the situation of the abortion seeker. It is difficult to understand why women abortion providers are unable to empathize with women seeking abortions. Could it be that their privileged position alienates them from the experiences of average women?

Providers who held husbands responsible offered many, different explanations. According to them, husbands did not accept available male contraceptives and forced their wives to undergo abortion in case of unplanned pregnancies. Husbands/men not having education was thought to be the reason why they did not understand the significance of planning pregnancies and using contraceptives to achieve the same. Providers felt that husbands dominated decision-making in this regard. Some providers talked about the power dynamics between married couples in terms of sexual negotiations. In case a woman did not fulfill her husband's sexual demands or meet the family's expectations regarding sex composition of their family, another wife replaced her. It was the fear that they were utterly dispensable which forced women into situations of unwanted pregnancies.

As mentioned earlier, a larger number of providers held women responsible for facing the situations of abortion. Men were not to be expected to know about how women's bodies worked and what the risks of pregnancy in specific situations were: ...Wife must know about it (conception during post-delivery amenorrohea). Males do not know about such things. Women alone should know about that. Others said that women needed to be more firm and decisive in implementing their decisions regarding the number and spacing of their children. It was women's responsibility to communicate with their husbands on matters related to regulating fertility, and make their husbands understand the difficulties involved in adding one more mouth to feed.

Many providers felt that women were not the helpless victims they were made out to be, and that they were perhaps not genuinely interested in planning and avoiding pregnancy. Contradictions, according to them, are too obvious to be ignored. For example, how was it possible that a woman be coerced and forced into unwanted or unprotected sex on the one hand, but be independent enough to terminate the resulting pregnancy? Why was it that educated women were not aware of reversible contraceptives when even uneducated women and women from the older generation knew about it? Why were women unwilling to use reversible methods of contraception even when these were available?

Providers often categorized the abortion needs of unmarried and other single women differently from those of married women. Opinions as to who was responsible for abortion situations of these women were divided. Widows, separated and even unmarried women facing situations of abortions were held responsible because they were the 'sexually indulging type'. In cases of abortion situations arising of rape, men were squarely held responsible.

There was a strong disapproval of premarital sex. Families were held responsible for not keeping watch on young unmarried girls who had a natural tendendency to seek sexual pleasure and also denied that such a thing existed earlier in the past.

> *"Pregnancies among unmarried women (indicative of extra-marital sex) are increasing. People's attitudes are changing. One's character (moralities) is not valued now. People are after momentary pleasures in life. I think society is responsible as a whole."*

Only a few providers felt that women's lack of decision-making power was responsible for their unwanted or unplanned pregnancies. Parents and parents-in-law played a decisive role in whether or not a woman could use contraceptives, on the number and sex composition of her children, among others. They said that women in joint families had no rights or autonomy to make reproductive decisions. While highlighting specific situations such as men migrating to cities for work, providers spoke of men's tendency to have complete control over women's sexuality by not allowing their wives to use reversible contraceptives. At the same time, neither did they use any contraceptive when they visited their families, and often caused unwanted pregnancies.

There were also a number of social factors mentioned by providers as responsible for women having to undergo abortions, including son preference, lack of sex education, ignorance about contraceptives and misconceptions about side-effects of available contraceptives.

Abortion as a Spacing Method

India's MTP Act allows abortions for the indication 'failure of contraceptive' and is silent about use of abortion as a spacing method. Of the total MTPs recorded in

India in 1990-91, about 42.2 per cent were done for failure of contraception [Chhabra and Nuna: 1994].

A community-based study conducted in Maharashtra recorded a whooping 74.1 per cent of abortions either because desired family size was achieved or because pregnancy was mistimed [Ganatra, et al: 1997]. In another community based qualitative study, contraceptive failure did not get overwhelming support by women as a reason for abortion [Gupte, et al: 1997]. But the same study indicated that women do resort to abortion as a spacing method and/or failure of contraceptives, reflecting its inevitability in absence of guaranteed access to safe and sure contraceptives. These data suggest that (a) there is an increase in resorting to abortion for the reasons of spacing and (b) abortions are not denied when sought for as a spacing method.

In the present study, opinions about use of abortion as a spacing method varied between two extremes-concern for women's health and using women's vulnerability to make business.

A large majority of the abortion providers (96/130) held the view that use of abortion as a spacing method was 'inappropriate', 'not good', 'not advisable' when there are a wide range of reversible contraceptives available. A substantial number of them explicitly articulated the consequences of abortion to women in terms of ill-health-bleeding, irregular menses, aches and pains, secondary infertility and life-threatening risks arising of anaesthesia. The procedure being invasive many emphasized the risks involved in abortions. According to some, use of abortion as spacing method also implied women's exposure to repeat abortions and thus, increased risks. A substantial number of providers (41/130) said that women should prevent unwanted pregnancies rather than going through the ordeal of an abortion.

Other providers said that they did not think it was their job to prevent unwanted pregnancies. They did not counsel for post-abortion contraception because it was of no use. Women's repeat abortions because of non-use of contraception for spacing had earned abortion providers their business. They argued that by charging a higher fee from women of rich rural households who did not care for family planning, they would be able to provide abortions at subsidized costs to poorer women.

Forty-three providers (43/130) were of the opinion that use of abortion as a spacing method cannot be completely eliminated. It was thought that despite contraceptive use or intention to do so, accidental conceptions do take place and change in reproductive intentions after conceiving will make abortions necessary in any society.

From a medical point of view, compared to the first trimester abortion second trimester abortions involve more risks of complications because of physiological reasons. However, India ranks among countries with the largest number of second trimester abortions. Of the total MTPs recorded in 1990-91 for India, the share of the second trimester MTPs was 15.69 per cent [Chhabra and Nuna: 1994: 42]. According to a community based study conducted in Maharashtra, about 29.1 per cent of the abortions were recorded in the second trimester [Ganatra, et al: 1997:8]. Community based qualitative research studies have shown that women are faced with second trimester abortions owing to the complex decision-making processes related to abortion seeking [CEHAT: unpublished data, ICMR: 1989].

Providers interviewed by us indicated multiple reasons for women facing second trimester abortion situations. 'Abortions followed by sex detection' was the single most important reason mentioned by the majority of abortion providers. Some went as far as saying that sex selection was the only reason for second trimester abortion. Ignorance about indications of a pregnancy, negligence during lactational amenorrohea, missed periods mistaken as amenorrohea were the reasons mentioned by a significant proportion of providers. Some providers attributed ignorance to women being 'illiterate'.

The stigma attached to an act of abortion, the societal pressures that women have to face and their efforts to maintain confidentiality were some of the other frequently stated reasons for second trimester situations. According to some, the social stigma attached to an act of abortion also caused time lapse because women tried to terminate pregnancies using various other methods, and also because of delays in decision-making about terminating pregnancies.

It was said that in the case of unmarried women, delays in disclosing 'illegitimate' conceptions led to second trimester abortions. They added that in such situations, disclosure was feared because of its devastating social consequences given the severe social sanctions against such sexual 'indulgence'. Further, according to them, because of social sanctions, which caused delays in getting an abortion done, many providers denied unmarried women abortion.

The above-mentioned reasons stated by a large number of providers did not find significant variation across various analytical categories. Unmarried women can't approach. If they do, it may create problems. Doctors refuse to provide services. As a result they face second trimester abortion situation. In case of unmarried, they tell us that they had not come in contact with anyone. Women refuse to accept interaction with anyone about sexual issues. Those asleep could be awakened but not the ones who pretend to be asleep!

A few (14/130) also stated that women's domestic constraints such as work load, financial inability, lack of time which obstruct them to approach service providers in time. Most of the providers who said so (12/14) were males. A few providers acknowledged malpractices that their fellow practitioners were engaged in, which caused women to face second trimester abortion. This included their lack of expertise and use of irrational drugs such as EP Forte, and involvement in providing abortion services by unqualified health personnel and general practitioners without a license to provide medical termination of pregnancy.

Thus, according to the providers, sex selection, social sanctions against seeking abortions by certain groups of women, women's own gender-related constraints and lack of access to safe abortion services contribute to second trimester abortion situations. In addition, malpractices by the medical community also contributed to second trimester abortions.

Sex Selective Abortion

A community based study documented 16.8 per cent of the abortions were after detecting the female foetus [Ganatra, et al: 1997]. It is difficult to come across any community-based study that would tell us sex selective abortion rates. A woman underwent nine sex selective abortions consecutively after having three daughters [CEHAT: unpublished data]. The decreasing sex ratio has also been considered as one of the indicators suggesting increased sex selective abortions. For India, the sex ratio exhibits a downward trend over the decades. Providers' perceptions on the issue need to be viewed against this backdrop.

There were three major trends reflected in providers' position on the issue at hand. The majority (64 per cent) said that they are against sex selective abortions; another 10 per cent said that they too were against it but they had to do it; and the rest (about 24 per cent) approved the practice of sex selective abortions. Most of the providers tended to explain their position on the issue of sex selective abortion.

There was not much variation across providers working in public/private health care facilities or rural/urban location of their practice. However, the pattern was different across men and women providers. Of the total men providers, about 28 per cent approved of sex selective abortion practice whereas it was much less in case of women providers (17 per cent). Correspondingly, higher percentage of women providers (68 per cent) compared to men (61 per cent) were against such a practice and this trend continued in case of the position taken 'disapprove but have to do it'.

Of those-the majority-who opposed the practice, some said that they would not ever compromise on ethical principle and therefore had never indulged into abortion service provision at the cost of negative implications for their medical practice. Some of them expressed their opposition sharply by saying, 'it should be banned', 'it is criminal', 'it is inhuman', 'it is matter of principles (ethics and human rights)', 'discrimination based on sex is objectionable', 'I feel agitated to realize such practices prevail'. However, the majority who clearly stood against the practice did not always speak in terms of 'opposition to discriminatory practices'. The various other explanations offered included, 'it causes ill-health to women', 'balance between men and women will be disturbed', 'tests are not reliable and thus it is futile', 'for women to become mother is important and adequate'.

Those who disapproved of the practice of sex selective abortions but engaged in it against their principles expressed their helplessness. On the other hand some spoke of compulsions at their ends for two reasons. One, pressures arising out of unhealthy competition in the health care service sector were an important motivating factor. It was stated that if they had not provided abortion care services, some others would have provided them anyway. Two, the pressures those arise out of implications that women may have to face back home in case they did not get abortion done. Many talked of compulsions that women have at their ends to go for sex selective abortions arising either out of social norms fostering son preference or because their lives are put at stake in case they do not produce son. Some also said that unwanted girls run the risk of severe ill treatment at their natal homes causing them emotional and mental trauma. Either way, providers' empathy for women's social needs for sex selective abortions seems to have been a major factor.

Among those who responded in favour of sex selective abortion, there prevailed convictions about the legitimacy of sex selective abortion practice in the "interest of society" and "nation's larger objectives for everybody's good" without any regrets about violation of medical ethics or human rights issues involved in discriminatory practices. The explanations offered were 'people should be allowed to choose sex composition of their families', 'it contributes to population control goals of the nation', 'ill treatment that the unwanted girls would receive'. A large majority of them appeared to be concerned about the number of girls (unwanted) born while waiting for an arrival of a son that adds to the burden on the family and/or to the state by increasing the population.

Some responses by one or two providers are quite revealing. One of them perceived the technique of ultra-sonography as having the sole utility of sex identification. And they felt that it should be made use of to control population and advised that government should allow use of such techniques for the purpose of sex detection. When there are techniques available for sex determination, why one should not do it? Otherwise what is the use of these (sonography) machines? ... The government should open (allow) up sex determination.

Thus, the views oscillated between 'opposition to' and 'in support of sex selective abortions, between those who were willing to forgo their practice by not engaging themselves in unethical medical care and those who were capitalizing on demand for sex selective abortions by indulging in unethical practices. Once again social compulsions and population control concerns featured prominently.

As discussed earlier, the MTP Act is restrictive in nature as it allows abortion only for certain reasons. Though it has decriminalized abortion, it does not recognize abortion as women's right despite its revolutionary characteristics, such as allowing abortion for failure of contraception and not requiring husband's consent for undergoing abortion. Women perceived abortion rights more as an answer to their pragmatic needs without really being able to find answers to moral dilemma they face in various abortion situations [Gupte, et al: 1997]. They tended to be conditional while recognizing abortion as woman's right. However, they have been able to overcome the various obstacles while striving to access abortion care facility when required. In that sense, women have been able to exercise their right to abortion and had their own ways to translate the abstract concepts in to reality. Their articulation was different than the feminists' understanding of abortion as woman's right. The latter looked at abortion as one of the important means to have control over the matters related to one's own body and articulate this in the context of women's human and political rights.

The majority of providers interviewed (70 per cent) said that women should have right to abortion, 17 per cent qualified their approval by specifying situations in which women should have right to abortion and mentioned that women should exercise this right responsibly. Ten (8 per cent) providers felt that it should be couple's right. Five (4 per cent) of the providers (Male-4, female-1) were against women having right to abortion. The variation across public/private and rural/urban was not noticeable. However, it does show a different pattern across males and females in that about 76 per cent of males supported the idea of women's right to abortion unconditionally and about 10 per cent qualified their support; about 10 per cent said it should be couple's right and about 5 per cent were against it. The same percentages in case of female were 60 per cent, 30 per cent, 4 per cent and 2 per cent respectively.

Those who approved of abortion as woman's right explained their position further. Among these the principal argument was that the women who shoulder the responsibility of child bearing and rearing should have right to decide about number of children. Besides, new trends as regards woman's career aspirations, their entry in the workforce and the responsibilities arising there from were also seen as a reason for women having right to abortion. Some articulated factors relating to her secondary status in family, which has implications for her reproductive life. Coercive sex within marriage, lack of decision-making power in most of the family matters including child bearing, poor economic status and the trouble mothers face in bringing up children without adequate support from the family members, husband's irresponsibility vis-à-vis contraception, poor health status of women, negative health consequences of frequent deliveries, ill-effects on the foetus in case it is not wanted, were the various explanations offered in support of their approval for women's right to abortion. Some other reasons less frequently mentioned were that it would help unmarried women and rape victims, women engaged in farm labour during peak seasons, women who have lost their husbands when carrying. In couple of instances, it was said that it is not women's duty to beget children and they should have scope and space to develop themselves. A few felt that such a right would contribute to population control.

Those who qualified their approval/conditional support to women's right to abortion explained the situation specifically. They specified that a woman should have right to abortion in case of woman's ill health, contraceptive failures and foetus anomaly and probable teratogenic effects. Some very explicitly mentioned that it should not be abused, for example, for sex selective abortions. Some others stated that in situations of primies, and failure of contraception women should have such right. Some squarely denied commercial sex workers right to abortion. Similarly, some also said that unmarried and singles should not have such right to abortion. Women should not use such a right to damage Indian culture; women should not set trends of not giving birth to children using this right. She should not evade her responsibility as wife were some of the critical concerns expressed by providers while specifying what responsibility it implies that women have to bear in mind. Providers often emphasized that women should use their right to abortion responsibly.

Thus, single women's right to abortion was both approved and disapproved. It was approved because it was perceived that women get cheated and deceived. Those who opined against it feared that such a right to women would encourage promiscuity among women to a large extent.

The range of responses were along these lines:

"I do not think they should have! If it happens, life would be with no reins. The child is also of the husband. If all rights are entrusted to her, husband will have no value. Women may start telling lies. If it is for the reasons of one's career, then it is fine. But it may encourage illegitimate relationships and therefore women should not have such a right. It should be a couple's right! Tomorrow if women get commercial (about sex), poor husband will have to suffer. (Women's) licentiousness will increase. ... It would not be too far that we have to open the (abortion) centres at colleges. Should be... But those engaged in sex business (commercial sex workers) should not have such a right...They may entrap a man. Unmarried (women) should not be given such a right! Our culture hasn't yet become that matured. They should have the maturity to use contraceptives. But married women should have right to abortion as otherwise they have to keep producing children. Sometimes pregnancies are forced on them because of a want of son."

IV

Providers' Perceptions: Gaps and Contradictions

Some common issues emerge from the data presented and summarized till now. For convenience the discussion that follows is organized around these emerging issues with the central focus on implications of providers' gender biased perspective for quality of abortion care services.

In general, how people's ignorance and apathy towards contraceptives contributes to women's abortion needs corroborates earlier research findings and also falls in line with the reality.

However, providers' perspective about reasons for non-utilization of contraception is devoid of analysis of larger health care system and lacks understanding of gender biased policies/programmes. People's ignorance about and apathy towards contraception cannot be seen in isolation without looking at the way the 60 year old family welfare programme is being implemented; its underlying anti-people philosophy-population control obsessions, and gender biased approach, over emphasis on female contraceptives and sterilsation; commercialized and unregulated private sector; dynamics between public and private health care sector; and the larger development paradigm, which is not able to create equitable access to resources. Besides, providers seem to have sidetracked the critical fact that in addition to having knowledge about contraceptives, they should be available and accessible for people to use them.

Providers have a significant role to play in this sphere. This is because they have the necessary knowledge and potential opportunities to interact with the people on this. Also, most importantly people's trust with the medical community could be utilized for the benefit of people. However, the providers have said not much about their role in addressing the issue of people's ignorance about and apathy towards contraceptives.

Women were blamed and held responsible for abortion situations in two diametrically opposite contexts-one, various situations within marriage, and two, various situations outside marriage, including single women's pregnancies.

Married women are held responsible for being ignorant about the basics of sexual life, for being illiterate, for not being able to negotiate with their husbands on the issue of sexual relationship, not being able to convince and make husbands understand about circumstantial constraints, for being dependent on husbands and families, all of which lead them to face abortion situations some time or the other. These situations do occur in women's lives, which providers have captured quite aptly. However, holding women alone responsible for all these seems to be naive and fragmented analysis. Providers expected women to be firm and determined to exercise their rights in these matters.

Contradictions are more than obvious. Firstly, in the male dominated society where even men are not aware of these matters, expecting women to be knowledgeable is a misplaced expectation. Secondly, in situations where men know about these matters, their responsibility to educate their women has not been mentioned. Thirdly, assuming that women become aware of these matters, expecting them to be in a position to initiate dialogue or negotiate with their men is quite an utopian fantasy being imagined by the medical community.

Internal contradictions in positions of providers about women's responsibility for their abortion situations/needs are revealed by aggregate response. On the one hand, women's secondary status and absence of any voice in any familial matter is said to be responsible for her to face an abortion situation. On the other hand, women are expected to convince their partners about significance of using contraceptives. These are the misplaced contemplation of providers about women's knowledge about contraceptive methods and her power to negotiate-be it sexual or otherwise-with their partners/husbands.

Contradictions also arise when providers hold women entirely responsible by saying that it depends upon women to avail of opportunities for education and to be able to have a voice in family matters. It appears that somewhere providers have missed out on the fact that women are part of the larger social system, which is patriarchal and gender biased.

In case of unmarried women, some saw their indulgence in undesirable sexual relationships being responsible for getting pregnant and facing abortion situations. While women's sexuality was questioned all the time, men went scot-free. It reflects on prevailing tendencies among providers to think of women in isolation and not as an integral part of the social system.

Pre-marital or outside marriage sex has strong connotations of 'illegitimacy' in our culture. Consequently, such 'illegitimate' connotations also obstruct those involved from taking adequate measures to have safe sex. These (mis) conceptions and (biased) opinions of providers about singles' abortion needs would affect quality of abortion care she receives, if any.

These one-sided views, disjoined from social realities will have mostly negative implications for quality of care. That patriarchal compulsions in the form of son preference, which translate in reality in sex selective abortions, are at work at both ends-women and providers, have also figured in the observations made by the providers. Providers articulated the fact that women are easily dispensable in their own homes in case they do not meet reproductive expectations of their in-laws. Either they are not able to give progeny or are not able to provide male heir to the family line.

One can easily understand and empathize with patriarchal compulsions at the women's end given her subordinate status in the family and within society. However, it is difficult to do so in case of the medical community, which justifies their indulgence in sex selective abortions. The medical community has mostly argued that it finds itself in a helpless situation. In this context, two points need to be taken note of. One, it was the medical community, which opened the door to prenatal diagnostic for sex detection. Medical ethics were compromised then and it continues to be so. Two, the fees charged to the same technique of ultra-sonography are much higher when used for sex detection. Sex selective abortions are also costlier compared to non-sex selective second trimester abortions. The views about the compulsions emerging of patriarchal value system, which force providers to conduct sex selective abortions, therefore, seem to be out of place and naive.

It is baffling to see the contradictions in this context. On the one hand sex selective abortions were justified on grounds of socio-cultural and patriarchal compulsions at both ends-medical community and women. On the other hand, in the process of 'salvaging' women's married life, they justified the role the medical community is playing in eliminating female foetuses without realizing the damage they are causing to the society, both in long- and short-terms.

Participation of a powerful and respected community like medical professionals in such anti-women practices has potential to legitimize them. In fact over the last decade, it has been shown to be true. It contributes to the consolidation of unhealthy patriarchal norms. In fact, as reality indicates the impact on people's attitude of medical community's participation in these practices is massive. As of today people assume that they too are contributing to 'nation's good' by eliminating female foetuses.

Providers have justified their engagement in abortion service provision in different situations of women's abortion needs including sex selective abortion needs on the grounds that it helps contributing to population control. The contradictions in these arguments and justifications put forward by the medical community is too glaring to be ignored. On the one hand, people's capacity to make informed choices about contraceptives is underestimated attributing it to their ignorance and lack of education. On the other hand, they are engaged in providing abortions care services without complementing it by quality contraceptive counselling.

This not only leads women to face repeat abortion situations, but also contributes to promoting and legitimizing abortion as a spacing method. Concerns expressed by some about ill-health that abortion causes to women do not seem to reflect in the abortion practice of medical community in general. Assuming that medical community is genuinely concerned about the 'population explosion' and possesses the scientific knowledge of ill consequences of abortion, it will not be erroneous to expect that it played a significant role-needless to mention, along with others in averting unwanted pregnancies and in reducing women's abortion needs.

V

Providers' Perceptions on Quality of Care

Perceptions of providers about women' abortion needs are divided. Although some providers have been insightful and had a sensitive understanding of certain aspects of women's abortion needs, not all providers share this understanding about the full spectrum of women's abortion needs and their socio-cultural context. The gaps in their understanding are glaring. Contradictions in their views are also obvious as regards range of abortion care situations.

In the presentation below, we have tried to briefly articulate the possible implications of providers' perceptions for quality of abortion care.

Ignorance, Apathy and Negligence

Provide s' concern for women's health and well-being has the potential to reflect in the abortion service provision by way of counselling on contraceptive methods and making them and other concerned persons understand the negative consequences of abortions and the need to avoid repeat abortions. Similarly, providers and/or others from health care facilities can also play the role of educators given the fact that women and men are ignorant about various physiological aspects.

Providers understand the inevitability of women using abortion as spacing method are expected to bring empathetic texture to their communication with women during abortion care service provision. However, provider's attitude that women and others concerned were not bothered about using contraceptives, may lead to victimizing women seeking abortion care. Besides, their articulation that abortion care service provision fetches them business has a tremendous potential to exploit women's abortion needs. It may lead to pushing women to face repeat abortion by keeping them away from knowledge about contraceptives and also physiological aspects.

Those who believed that women's "illegitimate sexual indulgence" has been responsible for their abortion needs are likely to formulate their own punitive measures, for example, by charging them exorbitantly. It may also lead to ill treatment to such women and exploiting their vulnerable situations. Women's desperation to get an abortion in such situations naturally tends to be high and thus leads to having a reduced bargaining power with the medical community. As a result it is more likely that the quality of abortion care services they receive will be much poorer.

One anticipates that pressure of compulsions on providers for being in favour of sex selective abortions, among others, would make providers more sensitive to women seeking abortions in these situations, and will not charge exorbitantly, and will also make efforts to dissuade women and others concerned from doing so.

Those who believe that the sex selective abortions contribute to the 'noble objective' of population control will engage themselves in providing contraceptive counselling services to women in other situations. However, one can anticipate that they themselves may be engaged in sex selective abortion care service provision, which in turn may help promote such sex discriminatory practices. As the majority was in favour of women's right to abortion, one anticipates that women would have easy access to humane abortion care services.

Abortion Practices

In the same study, we explored circumstances under which providers allow women to have access to abortion care at their health care facilities. Additionally, we also studied provider women interactions for 40 women who sought abortion care services at 23 abortion care facilities to understand softer facets of quality of abortion care.

Of these 130 providers, 113 said they did not provide services of abortion care to women coming alone. 'Pregnancies outside marriage', 'lack of resources-human power, finances', 'need for confidentiality' were reasons mentioned by providers for women seeking abortion care on their own. This reflects on the absence of a good fit between providers' empathy for women's abortion care needs at the level of perceptions and their abortion care service practices.

Of 130 providers, 51 (public-4 of 20; private-47 of 110) said that they insist on the husband's signature before they conduct abortion. Of 130 providers, 36 (public-9 of 20; private-27 of 110) said that it was mandatory for women to adopt some method of contraception post abortion at their health care facilities.

Of the 40 women who sought abortion care at the sub-sampled abortion care facilities, 30 (75 per cent) had sought it for the purpose of family planning. Providers did not seek any information from 27 of 40 women about their contraceptive history.

This pattern of practice once again indicates that perceptions and concerns for women's health in the context of their abortion needs do not go with their abortion care service pattern. This is because a large number of providers have mentioned that it was not advisable for women to use abortion as a spacing method. One expects that they would provide contraceptive counselling to women seeking abortion care to avoid repeat abortions. It needs to be noted that there was no contraceptive counselling offered to these women or their partners. Instead, contraceptives were forced without leaving much space for making informed choices and denying opportunities to educate themselves vis-à-vis contraceptives. Demanding husband's signature not only is a non-legal practice, but it also contradicts providers' favourable opinions about women's right to abortion care.

Sex selective abortions were generally charged more than other abortions. Similarly, abortions in case of unconventional or 'illegitimate' pregnancies were charged exorbitantly and women had to bear the humiliation and the ill treatment by the medical providers and other paramedical staff. Once again the gendered understanding of women's abortion needs seem to be more a face to show and exhibit, as their abortion care practices often did not match their perceptions.

Against this pattern of abortion care service provision, the overwhelming response of the medical community in favour of 'abortion as women' right' would carry little meaning for women. In general, their commercial interest in abortion care service provision seems to overpower their understanding of women's abortion needs, which is swamped with gaps and contradictions.

This anecdotal information is suggestive perhaps of medical community attempting to be 'politically correct' while articulating their perceptions of women's abortion needs. These gaps between perceptions and practices could be better explained with the help of forces at work that are pushing medical care service sector towards its commodification. Commercial interests of the medical community in abortion service provision in particular can further explain these gaps. Combating the irrational and unethical abortion care practices in isolation without understanding the dynamics of the larger health care system will be a difficult and perhaps even futile task. However, the gap between the perceptions and abortion care practices perhaps forms a solid case to look into the health care delivery system, which is paralyzed with the obsession of commercial interests of the medical community. This is complemented by the convenient patriarchal attitudes towards women specific health care needs, such as, abortion care needs.

One concrete strategy to repair the damage and bring back the humanitarian and ethical spirit in health care service provision is to revamp the entire health/medical education system in which ethics and gender are integrated and an organic link is established between health care practices and users of health care services. A number of interim strategies-organizing gender sensitization workshops for members of the medical community, improving regulatory mechanisms, motivating bodies like IMA to play a proactive role-could be designed for actually making the services gender sensitive and ethically sound.

Note

1. The research study has an elaborate component built in to delve into patterns of abortion care practices. Presentation of the data on that dimension does not fall under the scope of the present paper. Only the anecdotal information to highlight the gaps between perceptions and practices is provided.

References

Chhabra, R. and S.C. Nuna. 1994. *Abortion in India: An Overview.* New Delhi: Veerendra Printers.

Ganatra. B.R, S.S. Hirve, S. Walawalkar, et al. 1997. 'Induced Abortion in a Rural Community in Western Maharashtra: Prevalence and Patterns' unpublished manuscript.

Gupte, M., S. Bandewar, H. Pisal. 1997. 'Abortion Needs of Women in India: A Case Study of Rural Maharashtra', *Reprodutive Health Mailers:* 9: May: 77-86.

Indian Council for Medical Research. 1989. *Illegal Abortion* in *Rural Areas:* A *Task Force Study,* New Delhi.

Acknowledgements are due to the research team members Madhuri Sumant. Hemlata Pisal, Mugdha Lele. This paper was first published in the *Economic and Political Weekly*: 38:21: 2003:2075-81. It is included here with the prior permission of the author and the Editor, *Economic and Political Weekly*. Address for email correspondence is: sunitavb@vsn1.com>

CHAPTER - ELEVEN

Women's Reproductive Health Security and HIV/AIDS in India

Saseendran Pallikadavath and
R. William Stones

There is overwhelming evidence that HIV/AIDS infection is increasing among women than among men, although men had a higher infection rate when the epidemic began more than a decade ago [Amaro: 1993:24; Gorna: 1996:2; Lepri, et al: 1994; Sherr: 1993:42]. However, in absolute terms, in all parts of the world except South Africa, there are more men infected with HIV [UNAID b: 2000: 4; see Table 1]. According to the UNAIDS (December 2000) report, there were 36.1 million HIV/AIDS infected people living in the world by the end of 2000. Of these, 16.4 million were women. The pace at which HIV/AIDS epidemic is spreading to women is alarming. A UNICEF [UNICEF: 2001 a] document reports that in 1998,43 per cent of all people over 15 years of age living with HIV/AIDS were women: this is 2 per cent higher than the per cent reported in the previous year. In the UK, Gorna (1996:2) estimated the rate of HIV increase among women to be at least 15 per cent faster than among men. In the US, Sherr (1993:42) showed that in the early 1990s the number of AIDS cases increased by 29 per cent for women as compared to 18 per cent for men. In Africa, the infection rates in young women are reported to be far higher than in young men-the average rates for teenage girls were over five times higher than in teenage boys [UNAIDS: 2000a: 11]. The Indian National AIDS Control Organization [NACO: 2001a] reports that the HIV epidemic in India continues to shift towards women and young people with an accompanying increase in vertical transmission and paediatric HIV [NACO: 2001 a]. Thus, globally there is an increasing trend of HIV infection among women.

Although the overall sex ratio of the HIV/AIDS infected population impacts more men than women, the death statistics show that so far more women have died of HIV/AIDS than men. In 1999 alone, 2.3 million women were infected with HIV compared to 2.5 million males in the same year. However, the number of women dying of AIDS in the same year was 1.3 million compared to 1.2 million male deaths due to AIDS [USAIDS: 2000 b]. Furthermore, up to the end of 2000, the AIDS disease killed 9 million women compared to 8.5 million men [UN AIDS: 2000b]. Clearly, globally the epidemic has taken more women's lives than men's with far reaching implications for families and communities. Thus, globally not only the proportion of women infected with HIV is increasing, but also there are more women dying of HIV/AIDS.

Table 1
HIV/AIDS Infection among Women, Regionwise, End of 2000

Region	*Adults and Children Living with HIV/AIDS*	*Adul Prevalence Rate (per cent)*	*HIV Positive Adults Whoare women (per cent)*
Sub-Saharan Africa	25.3 million	8.80	55
North Africa and west Asia	4.00,000	0.20	40
South and south.east Asia	5.8 million	0.56	35
East Asia and Pacific	6,40,000	0.07	13
Latin America	1.4 million	0.50	25
Caribbean	3,90,000	2.30	35
Eastern Europe and central Asia 7,00,000	0.35	25	
Western Europe	5,40,000	0.24	25
North America	9,20,000	0.60	20
Australia and New Zealand	15,000	0.13	10
Total	36.1 million	1.1	47

Source: UNAIDSb: 2000:5.

The UNAIDS reports 3.7 million HIV infected cases in India by the end of 1999-more than any country in the world except South Africa which had 4.2[1] million HIV/AIDS-infected people in 1999 [UNAIDS: 2000a: 12]. As per the USAID/INDIA-HIV/AIDS (2000) document 21[2] per cent of the total HIV/AIDS infected cases, by the end of 1999, in India were women. This proportion compared to some of the countries is very low, particularly those in the African region in sub-Saharan Africa, 55 per cent of the HIV positive cases among adults were women. However, given the large population base in India a small proportion would not negate the HIV/AIDS issues of women in India. For example, approximately 0.78 million women were estimated to have been infected with HIV in India by the end of 1999. This number would approximately equal to the total number of HIV/AIDS infected people living in North Africa and west Asia, Caribbean, and Australia and New Zealand (0.8 million). Clearly, the number of women living with HIV/AIDS in India is enormous. Actions are urgently required to protect women from the epidemic without waiting for a higher proportion of them to be infected.

Given the trend in the HIV epidemic in India and elsewhere it is most probable that HIV cases of women would increase further before it stabilizes or declines. Evidence revealed by the National AIDS Control Organization (NACO) also suggests that the HIV epidemic is spreading from the high-risk groups to the general population indicating that more women would be infected in the future (NACO: 2001 a). Age wise data of HIV infected people in India further shows that the age group 15-49 accounts for nearly nine-tenths of the HIV infected cases. Clearly, this is more alarming because they are in the reproductive age group with tremendous potential to transmit the virus to their spouses or partners and even to their children (UDAIDS/INDIA-HIV/AIDS: 2000). Thus, women having HIV has a multiplier effect in terms of both vertical and horizontal transmission of the virus.

The increasing proportion of HIV and the higher HIV/AIDS death rate in women is a serious cause for concern. We consider focusing on women in this paper because women's reproductive health is linked with HIV infection. Furthermore, focusing on women's reproductive health is vital because of its connections with the well being of family, community and the nation, and of course women's own well-being. We focus on India in this paper for the following reasons. Firstly, in India the number of women with HIV infection is already high and is most likely to increase in the future. Secondly, there is a higher mortality of HIV/AIDS infected women than men. Furthermore, death of an infant is often associated with the death of her/his mother-infants are more likely to die if their mother has already died. The number of orphans due to HIV/AIDS related death of parents is on the rise for the reason that if the wife is HIV infected, it is more likely that the husband too is HIV infected. Thirdly, women in India possess relatively low status, economic and social, in the family leading to discrimination in access to food and nutrition, health care, and education. This dimension of discrimination could further increase if they have HIV/AIDS resulting in poor health, becoming destitute, and possibly an early demise. Fourthly, Indian women traditionally take care of the children and family, hence their survival is essential for the welfare of the traditional Indian family. This is more important in the context of demographic transition leading to nuclear as well as to small families. Fifthly, since India is currently undergoing economic reforms, public spending on health is unlikely to be enhanced further. This implies that there will be no additional funding from the government to meet the needs of the generally weak public health system in India, or to meet the new challenges posed by the HIV/AIDS. Thus, if women, particularly some of the vulnerable groups among the population, are not targeted for protection from HIV infection it is most likely that they would become victims of the HIV epidemic in India.

Given the above background the objectives of the paper are:

(a) To examine HIV/AIDS features in India

(b) To discuss the concept of reproductive health security of women

(c) To discuss important reproductive health security issues of women in the context of HIV/AIDS epidemic

(d) To discuss strategies to achieve reproductive health security in the wake of HIV/AIDS epidemic

HIV/AIDS Management System

The NACO is the national level government body managing the HIV/AIDS programmes in India. Since it was essential to have a fairly good idea of the number of HIV infected cases in the country for the control and prevention of HIV, a surveillance system was set up in 1994 with 55 surveillance sites in various parts of the country (NACO: 2001 a). Later, the surveillance system was expanded, and in the year 2000 there were 232 sentinel sites in India-109 sites in STD clinics, 110 antenatal clinics, 11 sites among intravenous drug users and two sites from areas frequented by men having sex with men. These sites and population groups were chosen based on information of risk behaviour for HIV infection.

In India, most of the information on HIV infection comes from the sentinel surveillance system. The national AIDS control organization (NACO: 2001 a), based on the 2000 sentinel surveillance data collected from the 232 sites, classified Indian states and union territories into three major groups based on the HIV prevalence in adult population. The various groups of states are given below:[3]

Group 1: Maharashtra, Tamil Nadu, Karnataka, Andhra Pradesh,Manipur, and Nagaland where the HIV infection has crossed one per cent or more in antenatal women.

Group 2: Gujarat, Goa, and Pondicherry where infection is below one per cent in antenatal women.

Group 3: Includes remaining states where HIV infection in any of the high-risk groups is less than five per cent and is less than one per cent among antenatal women.

The above details indicate that the HIV/AIDS infection has so far made its way mainly into the southern and in the northeastern states. Some claim that better data collection in the southern states is the reason for the higher HIV/AIDS prevalence [Mehendale: 2000].

In India the first AIDS case was detected in 1986 from Chennai.[4] Latest data suggests that HIV infection has reached into almost all Indian states and union territories. However, as evident from the classification of states given above, India's HIV epidemic is highly diverse. While some states have almost no HIV infection, others have reached adult HIV prevalence rates of 2 per cent and above. Table 2 gives state wise distribution of AIDS cases reported during 1986 to 2001 period. The states that show the highest AIDS cases are Tamil Nadu, Maharashtra, Karnataka, Andhra Pradesh, Gujarat, Delhi and Manipur. Each of these states so far has reported more than 500 AIDS cases. This figure is most likely to be an underestimate and the actual number could be much higher.[5]

Data from the sentinel surveillance system further suggests that there is an urban-rural dimension to the HIV infection in India. The HIV infection among women attending antenatal clinics in the seven metro cities in India showed that HIV infection has crossed two per cent in Mumbai, more than one per cent in Hyderabad, Bangalore, Chennai and is below one per cent in Calcutta, Ahmedabad, and Delhi (NACO: 2001a). Comparison of HIV infection rates of the metros with rural population clearly indicates that HIV infection in India is more in the urban areas compared to the rural population. However, this could reflect limited surveillance in rural areas. Time series data are needed to conclude whether or not there has been a narrowing or widening trend in rural-urban HIV infection incidence rates.

In India the major mode of HIV transmission is through heterosexual contact: over four-fifths of the infections were by this route. HIV infection through blood transfusion, perinatal transmission, and homosexual contact is very low in India (Table 5). The most common HIV virus found in India is HIV-I type,[6] responsible for over nine-tenths of the cases (NACO: 2001 b). Nearly 87 per cent of the AIDS cases in India are in the 15-44 age group. The HIV prevalence in India is reported to be highest among sex workers, intra-venous drug users and STD patients.

Table 2
AIDS Cases in India, 1986-2001

State	AIDS Cases	Per cent
Andhra Pradesh	661	3.12
Assam	110	0.52
Arunachal Pradesh	0	-
Andaman and Nicobar Islands	13	0.06
Bihar	44	0.20
Chandigarh	306	1.44
Delhi	520	2.45
Daman and Diu	1	-
Goa	40	0.19
Gujarat	756	3.56
Haryana	48	0.23
Himachal Pradesh	87	0.41
Jammu and Kashmir	2	-
Karnataka	918	4.33
Kerala	267	1.26
Lakshadweep	0	-
Madhya Pradesh	664	3.13
Maharashtra	4715	22.22
Orissa	55	0.26
Nagaland	110	0.52
Manipur	808	3.8
Mizoram	18	0.08
Megahalaya	8	-
Pondicherry	141	0.66
Punjab	131	0.61
Rajasthan	272	1.28
Sikkim	2	-
Tamil Nadu	10164	47.90
Tripura	0	-
Uttar Pradesh	297	1.40
West Bengal	57	0.27
Total	21215	100.00

Note: Indicates nil or very low.
Source: NACOb: 2001.

Although the HIV/AIDS infection has reached close to four million people in India, no HIV testing or treatment is offered under the government public health system. Therefore, in most of the cases, those who are infected with HIV do not know their HIV status. In general, a lot more needs to be understood about HIV/AIDS in India. In sum, very little is known about the HIV infection dynamics in India.

Women's Reproductive Health Security

The 1994 international conference on population and development (ICPD) defines reproductive health as 'state of complete physical, mental and social well-being in all matters related to the reproductive system and to its functions and processes'. We recognise that the HIV/AIDS epidemic, particularly the way in which it is spreading to women and children, poses challenges to the reproductive health of women as defined in the ICPD. Since HIV has no cure and there is no vaccine available, the issue of HIV among women in India needs to be considered not only with an objective of preventing its infection, but also from the point of providing medical, social, and economic support to those already infected. It is in this context that reproductive health security is emerging as an imperative in financing health services. We define reproductive health security as the financial, social, and health care support that is required to maintain the reproductive health of women. Although reproductive health security captures a spectrum of issues, in this paper we discuss two aspects. First, preventing HIV infection to women. Secondly, providing social, financial and health care support for those women infected with HIV/AIDS. We examine four key areas of women's domain in this regard-family planning; access to health care; marriage, sexuality and childbearing; and breastfeeding and maternal and infant mortality to examine how far the two reproductive issues related to HIV infection are met in the Indian context.

Family Planning Services

Family planning has been a long-standing policy objective since 1951. The National Population Policy 2000 encapsulates a commitment to the ICPD reproductive health agenda and this is now starting to translate into service provision [NPP: 2000]. However, the full impact of HIV epidemic is yet to be assimilated into policy and service provision. There is a serious risk that the reproductive health agenda will be negated once the HIV epidemic takes hold. Specific issues requiring action are as follows:

> *One of the important reproductive health security issues of women is to guard them from HIV infection. How far is the current family planning programme equipped to protect women from HIV infection? With regard to the family planning acceptors, a worrying issue crucial to HIV transmission is the very high proportion of sterilization acceptors among the total family planning adopters-about 75 per cent [NFHS: 2000: 136]. Moreover, female sterilization alone accounts for 71 per cent of the current contraceptive users. That means these women would not be using condom for preventing pregnancy in their sexual relations, marital or*

non-marital. If HIV infection is a potential threat to couples that have already accepted sterilization, it is important that they use condoms to prevent HIV infection. This is going to be a major task for the family planning or HIV control programme in India.

Sexual behaviour of sterilized men and women is an important determinant of the potential risk for HIV infection. For example, studies have shown that truck drivers have sexual relations with multiple partners while on their long distance trips. A study conducted among long distance truck drivers in the Orissa-Andhra Pradesh border showed that a significantly higher proportion of men over 40 years were promiscuous compared to those men under 21 years [Rao, et al: 1999]. While men in their 40s or their wives may have sterilized to limit their family size, the chances of the male partners transmitting HIV virus to their wives does not stop with sterilization. Studies have also shown that older women, mostly sterilized, have promiscuous relations with adolescent boys of their neighbourhood [Jejeebhoy: 2000: 46]. This raises the issue of motivation for condom use among the sterilized men, both in their marital and non-marital sexual relations. And to sterilized women needs to insist on condom use in their sexual relations. There is a cultural dimension to this issue. For example, man insisting on condom use in marital relations would mean that he is promiscuous, which is unacceptable to a wife; similarly the woman insisting for the man to use condom could mean she is promiscuous.

Thus, if condom use is central to the HIV infection control strategy in India, its implication in terms of the supply required to meet the demand will be huge. The NFHS-2 reports condom use among the currently married women at 3.1 per cent. If the family planning or the HIV control programme intends to increase condom use from the current level of about 3 per cent to whatever level is considered adequate to curb HIV infection, the implications in terms of finance and management are critical to the programme.

Financial aspects include meeting the growing demand for condoms, particularly when the services are to be given to at least some of the already sterilized people and those who are yet to join the family planning club. UNFPA estimates that globally funding required for contraceptive commodities for family planning and condoms for preventing sexually transmitted infections, including HIV/AIDS, will rise from $ 940 million in 2002 to $ 1.8 billion per year by 2015 [UNFPA: 2001]. While such estimates for India are not readily available, it is almost certain that the financial burden of family planning programme planning services needs to evolve altogether a fresh strategy as the existing supply-networks will not be able to cope with the increase as well as diverse demand for condom and other contraceptives. There is already a high deficit of trained manpower and inadequate health infrastructure in the Indian public health system. The National Population Policy 2000 (NPP 2000) estimated that Indian primary health care system is short of 23, 190 sub-primary centres, 1,513 primary health centres and 2,899 community health centres. In the case of trained manpower the shortage is estimated at 27,501 auxiliary nurse midwives (ANMs), 64,860 male multipurpose workers, and 4,224 lady health visitors (LHVs), 5,126 health assistants (male), 2,475 medical officers in PHCs, 1,429 surgeons, 1,446 gynaecologists, 1,525 physicians, 1,774 paediatricians, and an overall shortage of 6,635 specialists (NPP: 2000).

Thus, the crucial issue, much to do with policy, is the shift required in the family planning programme of India. As is well known the family planning programme in India is predominantly a sterilization programme, although it does not officially favour any particular method explicitly. If condom use is to be popularized/increased as a part of the family planning programme, there is definitely a need for a sincere departure from the implicit emphasis on the sterilization programme. This needs to happen at all levels, from top management to the grass roots level workers at the sub-primary health centre (sub-PHC) level of the public health system in India. Under the current contraceptive target free system that became operational in 1997 it may be easier to make such a shift in emphasis to condom use from sterilization in the family planning programme. But a great deal of political will is required.

One of the issues that came up for discussion in the meeting of international union for the scientific study of population (IUSSP) in 1996 was: do family planning programmes need to change to fight against AIDS? In the IUSSP meeting most of the discussions were reported to have taken place on the assumption that changing the nature of family planning services will help the fight against AIDS. The key change needed was re-focusing family planning efforts around condom promotion and STD diagnosis and treatment [Zaba: et al:1998: 15]. This stand is further supported by the fact that about nine-tenths of HIV positive individuals worldwide do not know they are infected: the only safe options are sex without penetration or sexual intercourse protected by condom use [UNAIDS: 2000 b: 11]. In India too majority of the HIV infected population does not know their HIV status. Thus, the sooner the Indian family planning programme re-focuses around condom promotion the better it would be for HIV prevention and control.

In sum, we argue that sexual behaviour, emphasis on sterilization in the family planning programme, and the enormous funding required to make condom available in the public health system together make women vulnerable to HIV infection. Alternative strategies are to be identified in order to guard women from HIV infections.

Access to Health Care

Ensuring access to health care to women in order to protect them from HIV infection and to provide health care services to those women infected with HIV are important reproductive health security measures. Issues that have direct links to women's access to health care discussed in this section are: (i) issues related to low status of women; (ii) lack of preparedness of the health system to provide health services to HIV infected women; (iii) non-availability of HIV testing and treatment at government facilities; (iv) influence of opportunistic infections on HIV; (v) impact of economic reforms; (vi) options for delivery.

Issues related to low status of women: Access to health care is an important issue for those infected with HIV as well as those not infected with HIV. However, access to health care is more important for women infected with HIV because of their specific health needs. However, in general women have limited access to health care because of their low status deriving from their illiteracy and economic dependence on men. Studies have shown that women are less likely to be taken to a hospital or given medical care for any given health need as compared to men. This is particularly a serious issue in the rural areas where women depend on men for economic and social security. Given the lesser numbers of women with STIs consulting a health professional because of social and other reasons, such women are at greater risk of HIV infection because STIs facilitate HIV infection. Thus, the status of women is an important variable influencing the risk of HIV infection [Rankin and Wilson: 2000].

Preparedness of the health system to provide health care to HIV infected women: Another issue related to health care is preparedness of the health system-whether government or private-to provide health care services to HIV infected women. This is particularly relevant to women because some of the reproductive health care services to women require physical examination of the reproductive system. Reports indicate that private hospitals in India seldom admit HIV patients fearing boycott from the other potential clients. It further shows that although the actual risk is very low, doctors and nurses fear HIV transmission to them if they attend HIV positive patients [Dongaonkar: 2000; Ramasubban: 2000: 176]. This could be a more serious issue in the case of women requiring caesarean section where the medical staff would come in direct contact with patient's body fluids containing the HIV virus. Thus, there is great resistance in providing health care to HIV infected women. This could be even more serious in rural areas where correct information about HIV/AIDS is limited.

Non-availability of HIV testing and treatment at government facilities: Knowing HIV status is a vital item of information for providing care to the infected person and preventing the virus from spreading to other people. There is no public facility under the government for HIV testing in India. Consequently, there is no treatment or care available for HIV/AIDS under the government system.[8] Thus, the lack of public facilities to test the HIV status of women, or for that matter anyone, presents a serious obstacle to providing services.

Impact of economic reforms: Presently the public health care system provides only some of the needed medicines and prescribed tests to their clients free of cost. Since there is a constraint in government spending especially following the economic reforms, health services using government funds are unlikely to receive increased resources in the future. Indeed, there is a great fear of funding cuts in the health sector. Under the circumstances it is more likely that the already ailing health care system would find it difficult to provide any assistance to HIV infected women requiring free or subsidized medicines. Thus, if adequate steps are not taken, reproductive health security of women may be negated under the wave of economic reforms in India.

Table 3
HIV Prevalence in India, Various Groups and Years

State/City	*Year*	*Group*	*HIV Prevalence (per cent)*
Bombay	1987-88	Sex workers	1.1
	1992	Sex workers	41.2
	1986-92	ANC	1
	1994	ANC	2.5
	1998	Pregnant women in a study	3.7
Rajasthan	1994	ANC	0.8
Pune	1994	ANC	0.7
Gujarat	1992	Blood donors	0.1
Madras (Chennai)	1991-92	Blood donors	0.35
New Delhi	1992	Blood donors	
Manipur	1991-92	ANC	0.2
India	Up to 1991	Blood donors/recipient of blood products	0.22
		Intravenous drug users	39.04

Source: Dongaonkar: 2000; Low-Beer, et al: 1998.

Threat from opportunistic infection: This is one of the key areas of concern for health care to HIV positive patients. Tuberculosis is one of the major infectious diseases found in India. Epidemiological analysis of reported AIDS cases in India has revealed that the major opportunistic infection in the AIDS patient is tuberculosis[9] indicating a possibility of a dual epidemic of TB and HIV in the future. In 1997, the estimated incidence of smear positive tuberculosis in India was 8,04,855 [Nicoll, et al: 1999]. A review paper suggests that although Commonwealth countries (including India) represent only 29.5 per cent of the global population, they account for 60.5 per cent of cases of HIV and 42.3 per cent of those of tuberculosis [Nicoll, et al: 1999]. Since HIV infected persons die in most cases because of opportunistic infections of various kinds in which TB is important, effective ways to curb TB must be in place to tackle the issue of AIDS. On the other hand, if HIV infection is not curbed an epidemic of TB is to be anticipated. A WHO report indicates that HIV, TB, and malaria cause over 300 million illnesses and more than five million deaths each year [WHO: 2001].

Caesarean section: Delivery by caesarean section can reduce the possibility of maternal to child transmission of HIV as it avoids exposure to the virus during the process of delivery [Duong, et al: 1999]. However, in developing country settings widespread increase of caesarean section would have potentially disastrous effects on women's health exposing them to the risk of surgery in unsafe conditions. In India, rates of caesarean section have risen steadily in urban areas among economically secure classes and this has been the subject of controversy. A major driver is remuneration to obstetricians that is significantly greater compared to vaginal delivery. Caesarean section may be a viable option for an HIV positive mother who is economically secure, but widespread adoption of this practice in rural areas would be disastrous because of the attendant complications, especially haemorrhage and infection.

In sum, health care support needed for preventing HIV infection and treating HIV infection in India is far from adequate. Under the current scenario, it is highly likely that HIV epidemic in India would further aggravate the already poor reproductive health status of women.

Marriage, Sexuality and Childbearing

Marriage is a vital element of reproductive health of women because of its links to childbearing. In India marriage is almost universal. Marriage is particularly of interest in India because it paves the way for childbearing, as reproduction is, by and large, confined to wedlock. To be able to marry or not determines both the social and physiological aspects of women's reproductive health. HIV epidemic poses very crucial questions in this regard. For example, will a girl with HIV be accepted for marriage? Or, can HIV positive women conceive and have a normal baby? Since both marriage and childbearing are gratifying to women and their parents, it is very important from a social perspective to get married and to have children. Although there are no Indian studies published on this aspect, available evidence indicates that HIV/AIDS infection could debar a girl from being eligible for marrying. Scholars report stigmatization of HIV/AIDS in India. The social status of an HIV/AIDS infected person could very well compare with that of a leper in India. Thus, HIV infection of an unmarried woman is very likely to influence the social and psychological aspects of her reproductive health.

Other aspects of the institution of marriage have implications for reproductive health in the light of current social changes taking place in India. They are: (i) increasing age at marriage and (ii) early debut to sex. The NFHS surveys revealed that the age at marriage of girls is on the rise in India.[10] This suggests that the period between puberty and age at first marriage will increase.[11] Studies also support that that age at first sex is relatively low in India, whether in rural or urban areas [Jejeebhoy: 2000]. As these social changes are likely to increase the occurrence of premarital sexual relations in India adolescent girls will be a higher risk of HIV or other STIs in the absence of adequate health education.

Since most of the people in India do not have easy access to HIV testing it is not possible to know who is HIV infected and who is not. Thus, while knowing the HIV status of an unmarried girl can push her to remain unmarried, not knowing about it can spread the virus to her husband (if not already infected) and possibly to her children. These issues have not yet become the subject of wide public discussion, but a lack of reliable information may lead to a significant social impact. We speculate that in the near future urban brides and grooms would demand an HIV status certificate of their prospective spouse.

Childbearing becomes an important reproductive issue in the light of the reports that younger persons with HIV will take longer to develop full-blown AIDS than do older persons with HIV. For example, a study of 1,199 subjects with a known date of seroconversion to HIV in Italy showed that older subjects progressed to AIDS more rapidly in all exposure groups considered, for both men and women, and for different definitions of AIDS [Pezzotti, et al:1996]. A similar finding is also reported in a study conducted in London [Phillips, et al: 1994]. In the context of increasing the period between HIV infection and AIDS, issues relating to treatment to infertility [Gilling-Smith, et al: 2001], and maternal and childcare are likely to be of concern in the longer run.

In the shorter run, a crucial reproductive health issue for HIV infected women is their capacity to bear children, particularly children not infected with HIV. This is particularly important when only one of the partners is HIV positive. In India this problem would become serious when the HIV epidemic spreads to young women. UNICEF (2001) estimates that young people, aged 15-24 years, constitute more than half of the HIV infected population worldwide. In India the latest NACO report suggests that nearly 45 per cent of AIDS cases were less than 30 years of age [NACO: 2001b]. Since reproduction does not end at 30 years of age among women in India as indicated by the NFHS-2 survey, fertility aspirations of HIV infected women would be a key reproductive health issue. However, this is going to happen on a large scale only when HIV testing becomes available in the public health system in India.

Table 4
AIDS Cases in India up to April 2001

Sex	*Number up to 2001*
Male	16,204
Female	5,011
Total	21,215

Source: NACO: 2001b.

Table 5
Mode of HIV Transmission among the AIDS Cases up to April, 2001

Sexual	17,552	82.73
Perinatal	397	1.67
Blood and Blood Products	816	3.85
Injectable drug users	858	4.04
History not available	1,592	7.50
	21,215	100.00

How could HIV infected women's sexual life be qualitatively different from that of HIV free women? Review of the literature suggests that there is hardly any research available on this aspect of HIV. Research studies from both medical and social perspectives are needed in this area to develop counselling and educational programmes to enable as normal as possible a sex life for HIV infected women. Some of the questions to which answers are required are how HIV infected women's sexual life differs from the rest of the population in terms of frequency of sexual relations, satisfaction levels, willingness of a non-HIV infected partner to have sex with an HIV infected woman, and disturbance of menstrual function.

For non-HIV infected women, an important issue that could influence her sexuality is about the fear of HIV infection through sexual relations. This could happen in a typical commercial setting, in casual friendships, marital and non-marital relations. Some of the pertinent issues in this regard, associated with status of women, are a woman's control over sexual relations and her ability to refuse sex without a condom. Condom use in sexual relations in commercial settings could be very difficult to propagate as reported by Kerkwijk (1995) from fieldwork among Thai sex workers. It was shown that money and the promise of a profitable relationship often limited condom use among sex workers. Studies from India show the powerlessness among women to enforce condom use in commercial settings for fear of assault or the customer being lost on this account.

In a review of studies on mapping of locations of sexual contacts, Pelto (2000: 105-106) indicated that sex workers are not confined to cities only. The review indicated that women sex workers were found in most villages. Among others who provide sex in the villages include widows, poor, and low caste women. Pelto's (2000) review suggests that non-marital sexual activities, including visits to sex workers are common in rural areas as they are among urban populations. This is highly relevant information for targeting reproductive health services to such populations in the rural areas.

Breastfeeding and Maternal and Infant Mortality

Breastfeeding is common in India. According to the NFHS-2 survey, 72 per cent of mothers exclusively breastfed their under one-month-old children. Research shows that breastfeeding could increase the chance of a child getting HIV from the mother. A UNICEF (2001) report indicates that women who are HIV positive and breastfeed face about 15 per cent chance of transmitting the virus to their infants through breast milk if no intervention takes place. It further states that since the beginning of the HIV/AIDS crisis, between 1.1 million and 1.7 million children are believed to have contracted HIV through breastfeeding [UNICEF: 2001].

There is awesome support from African countries that breastfeeding does increase the risk of perinatal transmission. Although Indian data on this aspect are not readily available to provide any estimate of children infected with HIV as a result of transmission from mother, globally it is estimated that nearly all HIV infected children less than 10 years of age acquired HIV from their mothers and are in developing countries. A study conducted in Mumbai showed that the highest rate of perinatal transmission of HIV was found among the breastfeeding population [Dongaonkar: 2000] suggesting the risk involved in breastfeeding mothers infected with HIV.

Breastfeeding may also put HIV positive women at a higher risk of mortality [Chaudhry: 2001: 1324]. A recent study from Nairobi in Kenya revealed that mortality among the HIV-I mother was higher in the breastfeeding group than in the formula group. The attributable risk of maternal death due to breastfeeding was 69 per cent. The study also revealed an association between maternal death and subsequent infant death, suggesting the need for ensuring maternal survival for infant survival [Nduati, et al: 2001]. It is argued that lactation involves high metabolic activities and HIV positive women engaging in breastfeeding face more problems due to HIV infection and other opportunistic diseases. Therefore, nutrition interventions to breastfeeding HIV positive women in poor households need to be evaluated.

Although avoiding breastfeeding by HIV positive women may be a good strategy for maternal survival and controlling mother to child transmission, serious doubts have been posed on various issues surrounding formula feeding. While formula feeding could be a good alternative to breast milk, studies have pointed out financial constraints, little access to drinking water and sanitation, fear of stigmatization, cultural practices, or inadequate health infrastructure as obstacles in formula feeding [UNICEF: 2001; Nduati: 2001:1651; Latham and Preble: 2000:1656]. A research study done in Durban, South Africa, showed that exclusive breastfeeding in the first few months reduced vertical transmission compared to that associated with mixed feeding.[12] It is believed that breastfed infants probably maintain a health gut epithelium that acts as a viral barrier, and that breast milk contains immune factors that have been shown in vitro to have antiviral and anti-HIV effects. Lathman and Preble (2000) revealed that mixed breast and formula feeding is the most dangerous feeding option for the young infant as it increases the risk of HIV and other infections. They further argue that, quoting an urban Kenayan trial, it is difficult to ensure exclusive formula feeding even among mothers who had been carefully counselled and had agreed to give formula milk provided free of cost. Lathman and Preble (2000) recommend that because the morbidity and mortality resulting from not breastfeeding are higher in the first six months of life than at older ages, consideration must be given to reducing the duration of breastfeeding by infected mothers.

Early weaning is linked to fecundability. There is a concern that early weaning or total dependence on formula food would decrease the duration of postpartum amenorrhoea (PPA) which in turn would result in the early resumption of ovulation and hence increase the chance of pregnancy while the last child is still an infant. The worst fear is not only that the child may acquire HIV infection from the HIV positive mother, but also that subsequent children become orphans.

Table 6
Age-Sex Category of AIDS Cases up to April 2001

Age Group	*Male*	*Female*		*Total*
0-14	486	299	785	3.7
15.29	6,198	2,456	8,654	40.79
30-44	8,064	1,793	9,857	46.46
45+	1,491	428	1,919	9.0
Total	16,239	4,976	21,215	100

Note: Figures in parenthesis indicate percentages.
Source: NACO: 2001 b.

Considering the wide range of issues around avoiding breastfeeding, Zwi and Soderlund (2000: 1659) suggest that studies of antiretroviral treatment for the prevention of vertical transmission are a priority. They believe that the best feeding method for infants whose mothers are HIV positive is unclear.[13]

Since breastfeeding in India is near universal, its implications for maternal and child health is crucial. Furthermore, in populations where maternal and infant mortality is high, like many northern states in India with over 400 maternal deaths to 10,000 live births, HIV infections among mothers who are feeding both breast milk and non-breast milk could fuel the already high maternal and infant death rates to further heights. Research is required on these issues in the Indian context.

Breastfeeding in the above context is a highly complex policy issue for any government. There are several aspects involved in this issue. Should India discourage HIV positive women from breastfeeding? It may be noted here that the Indian government has been promoting breastfeeding with a view to improving child survival. Reversing such a long-standing policy would require serious consultation and probing as to the consequences on child survival. Furthermore, issues such as the cost of formula food, clean water and social pressure to breastfeed need research in the Indian context. Taking the above facts in to account, in 1997 WHO, UNICEF, and UNAIDS established a basic policy on appropriate approaches to the prevention of mother-to-child transmission of HIV. The policy affirms that breastfeeding remains the best and safest choice for women who are HIV-free or who do not know their HIV status. The policy also states that in order to stop effectively the spread of HIV from mother to child while at the same time protecting the health of infants the following steps are necessary. First, that voluntary and confidential HIV testing be made available to all people; second, that HIV positive women be provided with sound antenatal care and that they be offered anti-retroviral drugs that lessen the risk of HIV transmission to their infants; third, that they be counselled on the benefits and risks of all available feeding options, based on the best available information; fourth, that the choice of feeding option is that woman's by right; fifth, once a woman makes a choice, she be fully supported in that choice; and sixth, that when an HIV positive woman chooses to breastfeed, she be counselled on the means of doing it most safely [UNIEFE: 2001].

For India, one thing that is clear from the above review is that research on the issue of mother to child transmission and its relation with breastfeeding is almost non-existent in published work. Since HIV testing is not done in India for every pregnant woman to find out her HIV status, it is impossible to know pregnant women's HIV status. In developed countries it is shown that increased antenatal HIV testing is contributing to a decrease in vertical transmission of HIV [Ferriman: 2000: 1430]. Absence of HIV testing in India would limit any intervention strategy based on policies on breastfeeding among HIV infected women in order to control mother to child transmission and control maternal mortality. A lot of research is needed in India in this vital area.

Women's Specific Reproductive Health Issues in the Context of HIV Epidemic

The precursor to provide reproductive health security to women in India, in the context of HIV, is to introduce voluntary counselling and testing for HIV infection.

Only though this and by knowing HIV status can an effective reproductive health security strategy for women with HIV be implemented. Such information is also vital for guarding women from HIV infection. The following specific reproductive health security issues need to be addressed in order to protect women from HIV infection and to provide services that can help them to maintain reproductive health.

Heath Care/Family Planning Services

- Access to basic health care (including admissions in private health care facilities)
- Access to HIV/STI treatment, in particular anti-retroviral treatment during pregnancy
- Access to family planning services particularly condoms

Social/Family/Community Aspect

- Right to have freedom (non-discrimination) in social life (at home, community, work place, etc)
- Protection from exploitation and coercion through caste and economic pressures

Women's Status/Empowerment

- Control over sexual relations in commercial settings
- Refuse sex without condom use in commercial settings
- Refuse sex without condom use in non-marital relations
- Ability to use contraception in any kind of relationship
- To know husband's/partner's HIV status
- To have married life and to know prospective husband's HIV status

Information

- Right to have latest information about HIV/AIDS
- Right to information and right to choose infant feeding methods

Reproduction/Delivery

- Right to decide whether or not to have children and when to have children
- Right to terminate pregnancy
- Right to decide the option for delivery in the light of best available information

Economic Security

- Access to economic security to outcaste and destitute women from brothels and such commercial outfits

Strategies to Guard Women

Benefit linked voluntary confidential counselling and testing for HIV (BVCCT): Benefit linked voluntary confidential counselling and testing (BVCCT) for HIV should be made available to adolescents and sexually active women both in the rural and urban areas. This does not mean that the entire adolescents and women should be tested for HIV, but rather than those who suspect their HIV status-for example those who have received blood transfusion, wives of truck drivers and other high risk groups sex workers, those who have had unprotected sex with multiple partners-may come forward for this facility at an appropriate health facility. The most crucial part of this is ensuring some benefit through providing treatment and support to those identified as positive.

Women workers in organized/government sector: While for BVCCT to become operational at the national level may take some time, it is important to begin interventions in organizationally easier areas. Organized sectors may be a good starting point to begin BVCCT. Women working in organized sectors may be given BVCCT at their request, with testing undertaken at any medical facility decided by her. An assurance that the results will not be disclosed to her employer or any other person would be essential. Towards this, organized sectors must evolve insurance schemes that could cover HIV testing, treatment and support in the event of a woman testing positive. The public sector insurance companies are well placed to consider such schemes and initial discussions have been reported in the national media.

Targeting and prioritizing government services to women home-makers: As of today most of the HIV-infected people in India would not know their HIV status. However, once HIV testing becomes acceptable to people, it is possible that people belonging to some specific groups may come forward in order to know their HIV status. One way of helping these HIV positive women and also encouraging others to come forward for HIV testing is by ensuring medical care. We suggest that in both rural and urban areas HIV infected women must get priority in consultation, getting relevant tests done, receiving medicines and care at all public funded health facilities. Furthermore, such facilities in the rural areas must be within the easy reach of women.

HIV/AIDS information, education and communication: Unlike traditional medical disciplines, HIV/AIDS is a key domain of medical and social research, currently being investigated on a war footing internationally. Hence, there is a flow of new information almost every day. It is important that the general public but especially HIV infected people, health providers and those responsible for health service management know about the developments taking place in medical and social research on HIV/AIDS. Governments and media must undertake careful scrutiny of information before making interpretations and policy statements. HIV education packages must be a part of the health training for undergraduates at medical colleges and as an element of continuing professional development.

Insurance for brothels and sex workers: The huge costs involved in HIV/AIDS treatment as well as the economic and social impact of HIV/AIDS require that women sex workers have access to at least minimum health security which could take care of their health needs. We recommend that steps should be taken to enable brothels to organize group insurance. Research studies are needed in this area to find out the feasibility of such insurance programmes and possible contributions from the government. We also recommend that individual sex workers in non-organized settings are enabled to access insurance using their earnings. All these efforts need the willingness of insurance companies. Studies that could recommend possible strategies to the government on these issues are needed.

Targeting condoms to high-risk populations: The Indian family planning programme is predominantly a sterilization programme. While sterilization may effectively provide a means to limit population growth, it has a very limited role in curbing the spread of HIV infection. Considering the benefits of condom use for both population limitation and HIV control, it may be important for the Indian family planning programme to give an extra focus on condom use in the family planning service. We recommend that government efforts could be targeted to the HIV/STI high-risk population groups. This would possibly lessen the burden compared to services given to untargeted population.

Private involvement in providing condom: Inability of governments to meet public services is now evident from the spending cuts in various service sectors of the government. Marketing research could help identify the extent of people's willingness to pay for condoms in both rural and urban areas. Innovative sales strategies need to be developed to change people's mindset about condoms from a family planning device to a 'tastemaker' or a 'security-device'. This would possibly increase condom use among adolescents who reportedly have less condom use in India. TV and other communication channels could be explored for this purpose.

Introduction of female condoms: While medically it is not yet proved that female condoms can be effectively used to control HIV and other STD infections, it is recommended for use when the male partner is not willing to use a condom. The most important advantage of female condom is that it is in the control of women. Female condoms are of particular importance in commercial setting where men refuse to use condoms. In India, where HIV infection is mainly through heterosexual contact, female condoms can be very effective in preventing the spread of the virus. As a first step female condoms could be made available to women who are less powerful in demanding male condom use, in particular sex workers from both formal and informal settings. Unfortunately experience with female condom dissemination from African programmes is not encouraging.

Targeting schools and colleges: Given the early debut in sexual life among adolescents in urban and rural areas [Ramasubbhan: 2000] that often accompany unsafe sex practice [Jejeebhoy: 2000], an effective safe-sex education is needed to address those in the schools and colleges. We recommend that schools and colleges must be targeted for education about safe sex and HIV. It should not be confined to the curriculum, and frequent sex education activities must be organized in colleges and high schools. NGOs could play a vital role in this programme in collaboration with students groups who could engage in fund-raising and publicity to create participation and ownership in the programme. Schools could identify the agencies to conduct such programmes. The government must facilitate this type of activity by giving constructive guidance for schools.

Screening of blood: Blood transfusion is the second highest mode of HIV infection in India; the NACO (2001) estimates it at 5.52 per cent. Although blood transfusion accounts for only a small proportion of HIV infection in India the number of people infected through this is large. A report indicates that about 30 per cent of blood in India comes from commercial sources and only a portion of it is tested for HIV. Furthermore, although the Supreme Court of India banned the use of blood from professional blood sellers because they are considered high-risk group for HIV, according to the blood transfusion safety division of the WHO, these professional blood sellers now claim to be family members of patients needing blood [Sharma: 2000: 1026]. This makes the safety of blood transfusion more complicated. In this context it is inevitable that blood tests for HIV be made mandatory irrespective of the source, before it is transfused. Blood banks in India must be expanded with proper HIV testing facilities.

Conclusions

In this paper an attempt was made to examine reproductive health security issues of women in the wake of the developing HIV/AIDS epidemic in India. Women's health is central to this paper, recognizing that globally the proportion of women infected with HIV is on the rise, and so far more women have died of HIV/AIDS than men. While the definition of reproductive health used in this paper is that of the 1994 ICPD the concept of reproductive health security is the financial, social and health care support needed to maintain the reproductive health of women. Thus, while reproductive health security encompasses a much larger number of issues the two central issues that we discussed in the paper are (i) protecting women from HIV infection and (ii) providing services to already HIV/AIDS infected women. We noted that lack of HIV testing and treatment facilities in the public system poses a great challenge to providing and targeting services. Since condom use is central to the HIV infection control strategies the present family planning programme must take a major chunk of such responsibility for condom supply. However, it seems that the government family planning programme is not fully equipped to take up such responsibilities, as it would require significant financial and management interventions. Involvement of the private sector is therefore a possible alternative that must be explored seriously. Access to health care for HIV -infected women appears to be far less than satisfactory-both provider and client issues account for this state of affairs. The transmission of HIV to younger unmarried girls would mean an attack on the institution of marriage and childbearing. Social changes leading to the increase of age at marriage and pre-marital sexual relations could make adolescents vulnerable to HIV and other STI diseases. Existing sexual networking in rural areas would facilitate HIV transmission to low risk populations. As no treatment is offered to prevent mother to child transmission of HIV, interventions through breastfeeding in Indian context need research and documentation. Moreover, linkages between HIV-infected mothers' breastfeeding and maternal mortality need to be researched in the Indian context as part of the evolution of appropriate prevention strategies.

Notes

1. Latest report shows that about 4.7 million South Africans have HIV virus compared to 4.2 reported in 1999.
2. However, the per cent of AIDS cases that are women is about 24 per cent of the total, AIDS cases until 2001 (NACOb: 2001).
3. The methodology of estimating HIV infection among the adult population is $\Sigma V = (P/T)(R)$. Where V is the total estimate, P is the number of HIV positive, T is the number of samples tested and R is the estimated size of population. For more details see NACO: Estimation of HIV infection among adult population. *http:// naco.nin.in.Type* the formula.
4. The first cases of unusual immune deficiency were identified among gay men in the US in 1981. See '20 years of HIV/AIDS', UNAIDS, 2001.
5. See for example, Mudur 2000, Indian agency admits publishing "wrong" HIV figures, *British Medical Journal,* Volume 321.
6. There are two major HIV viruses known, HIV-I and HIV-2.
7. Ramasubban (1990:175-76) reports that an advertisement by a premier teaching hospital for applications from medical and paramedical personnel wishing to work in a "leading medical field" received enthusiastic response. However, when appointments were issued and it became known that the positions were in the proposed AIDS department, all selected candidates declined the appointment.
8. It may be noted that Brazil is the only developing country that provides HIV treatment through their public medical system.
9. Such results are also revealed in studies conducted overseas. See for example Poznansky, MC, et al (1995).
10. In rural areas, the median age at first marriage is more than one and one-half years higher for women aged 20-24 than for women aged 45-49, and in urban areas it is also more than one and one-half years higher for women aged 25-29 than for women aged 45-49 years (NFHS: 2000:55).
11. Studies also show that age at menarche in India is declining because of improved nutritional status among girls, which also contributes for a longer interval between puberty and age at first sex.
12. See also news coverage by Wise, J, 'Breastfeeding Safer than Mixed Feeding for Babies of HIV Mothers', *British Medical Journal,* 2001: 322 (3 March).
13. For a detailed debate on this issue see, 'Education and Debate', *British Medical Journal:* 320: 1656-1660.

References

Amaro, H. 1993. 'Reproductive Choice in the Age of AIDS: Policy and Counseling Issues' in S Wilkinson (ed), *Women and AIDS: Psychological Perspectives,* (First ed *Gender and Psychology).* London: Sage Publications.

Chaudhry, S. 2001. 'HIV Positive Mothers Who Breast Feed May Die Sooner', *British Medical Journal:* 322, June 2.

Dongaonkar, D. 2000. 'Perinatal Transmission of HIV' in *Modelling to Evaluate Options for Diagnosis and Treatment of STIs in Women,* Pune.

Ferriman, A. 2000. 'Antenatal Testing Reduces Vertical Transmission of HIV', *British Medical Journal*: 321, December 9.

Gilling-Smith, C., J.R. Smith, and A.E. Semprini. 2001. 'HIV and Infertility: Time to Treat', *British Medical Journal*: 322, March LO.

Goma, R. 1996. 'Vamps, Virgins and Victims: How Can Women Fight AIDS', London.

Cassel Jejeebhoy, S. 2000. 'Adolescent Sexual and Reproductive Behaviour: A Review of Evidence from India' in R. Ramasubban and S.J. Jejeebhoy (eds), *Women's Reproductive Health in India,* Jaipur: Rawat Publications.

Kerkwijk, C.V. 1995. 'The Dynamics of Condom Use in Thai Sex Work with Farang Clients' in H.T. Brummelhuis (ed), *Culture and Sexual Risk: Anthropological Perspectives on AIDS,* Luxembourg: Gordon and Breach Publishers.

Latham, M.C. and E.A. Preble. 2000. 'Appropriate Feeding Methods for Infants of HIV Infected Mothers in Sub-Saharan Africa', *British Medical Journal,* 320, June 17.

Lepri, A.C., et al. 1994. 'HIV Disease Progression in 854 Women and Men Infected through Injecting Drug Use and Heterosexual Sex and Followed for up to Nine Years from Seroconversion', *British Medical Journal,* 309.

Low-Beer, D, et al. 1998. 'HIV and AIDS' in C.J.L. Murray and A.D. Lopez (eds), *Health Dimensions of Sex and Reproduction,* Harvard:The Harvard School of Public Health.

Lundgren, J.D., et al .1994. 'Survival Differences in European Patients with AIDS, 1979-89', *British Medical Journal,* 308: 6936: pp. LO68-1191.

Mehendale, S. 2000. 'Epidemilogy of HIV and AIDS' in *Modelling to Evaluate Options for Diagnosis and Treatment of STIs in Women,* Pune.

National Family Health Survey (NFHS) 1998-99. 2000. International Institute for Population Sciences (IIPS) and ORC Macro: Mumbai.

NACO (National AIDS Control Organization) 200la. *Status and Trend of HlV/AIDS Epidemic in India up to* 1999.

NACO. 2001b. *HIV/AIDS India Scenario.*

Nduati, R. et al. 2001. 'Effect of Breastfeeding on Mortality among HIV-I Infected Women: A Randomized Trial', *The Lancet:* 357, May 26.

Nicoll, A. and P. Godfrey-Faussett. 1999. 'HIV and Tuberculosis in the Commonwealth, Heads of Governments Can Learn from One Another's Success', *British Medical Journal,* 319, October 23.

Pelto, P.J. 2000. 'Research on Sexuality and Sexual Behaviour in India:The 1990s', in R. Ramasubban and S.J. Jejeebhoy (eds), *Women's Reproductive Health in India,* Jaipur: Rawat Publications.

Pezzotti, P. et al. 1996. 'Category of Exposure to HIV and Age in the Progression to AIDS: Longitudinal Study of 1199 People with Known Sates of Seroconversion', *British Medical Journal,* 313.

Phillips, A.N. et al. 1994. 'Use of CD4 Lymphocyte Count to Predict Long-term Survival Free of AIDS after HIV Infection', *British Medical Journal,* 309.

Poznansky, M.C. et al. 1995. 'HIV Positive Patients First Presenting with an AIDS Defining Illness: Characteristics and Survival', *British Medical Journal,* 311 (6998): 156-286.

Ramasubban, R. 1990. 'Sexual Behaviour and Conditions of Health Care: Potential Risks for HIV Transition in India' in T. Dyson (ed.), *Sexual Behaviour and Networking: Anthropological and Socio-Cultural* Sill *dies on the Transmission of HIV*, International Union for the Scientific Study of Population: Belgium.

Ramasubban, R. 2000. 'Women's Vulnerability: The Recent Evidence on Sexually Transmitted Infections' in R. Ramasubban and S.J. Jejeehoy (eds.), *Women's Reproductive Health* in *India.* Jaipur: Rawat Publications.

Rankin, Wand C. Wilson. 2000. 'African Women with HIV'. *British Medical Journal,* 321.

Rao, K.S. et al. 1999. 'Sexual Lifestyle of Long Distance Lorry Drivers in India: Questionnaire Survey', *British Medical Journal:* 318: 162-63.

Sharma, R. 2000. 'South East Asia Faces Severe Shortage of Safe Blood', *British Medical Journal,* 320, April 15.

UNAIDS. 2000a. *Report on the Global HIV/AIDS Epidemic,* June 2000,

UNAIDS: Geneva. 2000b. *Global Summary of the HIV/AIDS Epidemic,* December 2000.

UNFPA. 2001. 'Nearly $1 Billion Needed for Family Planning Supplies and Condoms for HIV/AIDS Prevention, Says UNFPA Executive Director.

UNICEF. 2001. 'Preventing the Spread of HIV through Breastfeeding'.

UNICEF. 2001a. 'Adolescents and HIV/AIDS.

UNICEF. USAID/INDIA, USAID/INDIA-HIV/AIDS Programmes, 2000.

World Health Organization (WHO). 2000. HIV, TB and Malaria–Three Major Infectious Diseases Threats', Background for the G8 discussions, Backgrounder No. 1, July, WHO Information fact sheet.

Zwi, K. and N. Soderlund, Commentary. 2000. 'The Feeding Debate is Still Unresolved and of Secondary Importance', *British Medical Journal,* 320, June 17.

This paper was presented at the National Consultation on Health Security organized by United Nations Development Programme (UNDP) and Institute for Human Development at India International Centre. New Delhi, during July 26-27, 2001. It was first published in *the Economic and Political Weekly*: 38:39:2003: 4173-81: It is included here with the prior permission of the authors and the Editor, *Economic and Political Weekly. Address for email correspondence is:* sasee61@hotmail.com

PART - III

EDUCATION: ISSUES IN ACCESS, CHOICE AND SUBSTANCE

CHAPTER - TWELVE

Reaching Global Goals in Primary Education: Some Gender Concerns for Tamil Nadu

R. Akila

I

Introduction

That each child should have the chance to complete primary education in every country is one of the most serious goals currently supported across the world. Despite rapid educational improvement during the 1990s even in poor countries, thanks to the widespread education-for-all (EFA) efforts, India alone still holds about one-quarter of south Asia's out-of school children, who are more often girls than boys.

Consequent to acknowledging the limitations in meeting this challenge, India has joined 189 countries to assert its commitment to a set of eight millennium development goals (MDGs) in September 2000 of which two goals are pertinent to note: goal 2 of the MDG is to achieve the completion of a full course of primary education for all girls and boys by the year 2015, and goal 3 is to promote gender equality and empower women by addressing elimination of gender disparity in primary and secondary education by 2005, and at all levels by 2015. An incentive to achieve these goals is that by crossing the minimum threshold level of five to six years of learning, countries may be able to trigger off more benefits of development through education.[1]

But, so far, estimates of India's progress suggest that while it may possibly meet the goal of achieving primary school completion by 2015, it is unlikely that it will achieve the goal of gender equality by 2005, because both access and completion have been difficult to achieve for girls in some sections. Data for 1995 on a commonly used indicator of universal primary completion, namely, literacy status of the 15+ population, shows wide gender disparities, with 64 per cent of urban males and not even 15 per cent of rural females as those completing primary education [World Bank: 2001].

Despite the reported gross enrolments of 100 per cent at the class one level in some of the major states, estimates still show that children who do not attend a school may be about 33 per cent of all children in the 6-14 age group, two-thirds of these being girls. Even among those who enrol, completion rates have been very low, especially among girls.

Currently, both domestic (such as the SSA) and international efforts (such as the DPEP) are promoting primary education in a big way, and the centre, state and civil society[2] have assumed greater responsibilities for meeting needs of the disadvantaged sections. In the context of India's commitment to reach the global goals in primary education, namely, to achieve universal access and completion by 2015 with elimination of gender disparities by 2005, this paper highlights some gender concerns in the primary education scenario in Tamil Nadu. It discusses the current status in Tamil Nadu, and highlights certain issues for attention regarding access to and completion of primary education among girls. The paper is divided into four sections. Section II sketches the education scenario in Tamil Nadu by providing current details on literacy, and particularly enrolment, retention and achievement at the primary education level. Section III discusses interventions that have produced results for the state, and issues that need further consideration. Section IV points out the state's financial commitment towards primary education, and the role of private schooling in terms of its implications for including girl children. Finally, some concerns are highlighted for policy attention.

II

Tamil Nadu's Education Scenario

The 'education balance sheet' of India [Haq and Haq: 1998] shows that it is still the world's most illiterate country, holding about 30 per cent of the world's illiterates. About 35 million children continue to be out of school. Even among those who enrol, about 37 per cent drop out before reaching class five. Girls lag behind even in states like Tamil Nadu that have had a tradition of successful formal schooling. Hence, in the context of the global goals in primary education, it may be useful to assess Tamil Nadu's literacy status[3] and focus on issues in girls' primary education.

Literacy rates: The inter-censal period between 1991 and 2001 has been remarkable across the country for various breakthroughs. Importantly, but for the 'BIMARU' states, all others have managed to achieve a literacy rate of above 50 per cent for women. Twenty-three of the 35 states and Union Territories, including Tamil Nadu have shown more than a 10 percentage-point difference in their literacy rates between 1991 and 2001.

Age-specific and gender-specific literacy: Although Tamil Nadu's overall literacy rate is ahead of many other states, there are problems in terms of age-specific and gender-specific literacy. Comparative age-specific literacy data for

2001 has not yet been published, but such data for 1981 and 1991 already showed that Tamil Nadu's growth rates in literacy between 1981 and 1991 for certain age categories were lower than the national average [Radhakrishnan and Akila: 2002]. Particularly, the lower rates among 7-14 age females, but not males, indicated that progress in primary education among girls was poorer than that among boys. Thus, if girls remained disadvantaged even at the primary level, their relative access to higher levels may be even poorer.

Gender gaps in *literacy:* While Tamil Nadu's inter-district data for 2001 may indicate good news about female literacy in general, gender gaps in literacy would show that the female literacy rate (65 per cent) is much lower than male literacy (82 per cent). As Table 1 shows, although the male-female gaps have narrowed between 1991 and 2001, with higher increase in literacy among females than males, the improvement in female literacy has not been significant in many districts. Examples include both educationally advanced and backward districts. In fact, but for Chennai and Kanyakumari, all districts have a male-female gap of more than 15 percentage points. The gap is wider in Dharmapuri, Tiruvannamalai and Nilgiris, which have a high concentration of SCs and STs. Cuddalore, Namakkal, Salem and Villupuram also lag behind both in terms of overall and female literacy. Further, the female literacy rate has not gone above 80 per cent in any district except Kanyakumari, while 21 districts have reached this level for males.

Caste-based disparities in *literacy:* Despite the overall improvement in literacy and a relative decline in regional variations in Tamil Nadu, disparities in male-female, and SC/ST-others tend to be considerable.[4] Gender gaps in rural areas and among disadvantaged communities still owe basically to the interlinkage between caste and gender and its repercussions on the schooling of girls.

Enrolment, retention and achievement: As literacy rates are only indicative of overall progress or decline, specific indicators of enrolment, retention and achievement are sought to address primary education. While gross enrolment ratio (GER) and age-specific enrolment ratio, were conventional indicators to gauge enrolment, recently more specific indicators such as net enrolment ratio (NER), non-attendance or discontinuation ratio, and dropout rate at each class or level are also being used widely.[6]

It is believed that 95 per cent of India's population now has access to primary schools within 1 km of their habitat [Govinda: 2002]. Tamil Nadu achieved this even earlier. Tamil Nadu's enrolment trend is unique because its enrolments have actually decreased due to the successful reduction in the size of its younger population. Although its gross enrolment has at times been above 100 per cent due to the enrolment of under-aged and over-aged children, and possibly an offshoot of the push for enrolment during the beginning of the 1990s, Table 2 shows that there is positive adjustment in recent times.

Nevertheless, as Table 3 shows, district wise data on GERs are a matter of some concern. Tamil Nadu's primary level GER is 97 per cent, with 98 per cent among boys and 96 per cent among girls. It is important to recognize that in many districts there is a direct correlation between low enrolment of girls and low overall

Table 1
District-wise Gender Disparities in Tamil Nadu's Literacy, 1991-2001

District	*Literacy Rate*					
	1991			*2001*		
	Male	*Female*	*Male-female Per cent Point Difference*	*Male*	*Female*	*Male-female Per cent Point Difference*
Ariyalur	63.19	34.47	28	77.92	52.03	28
Chennai	87.86	74.87	13	84.71	75.32	9
Coimbatore	76.45	55.73	21	83.82	69.80	14
Cuddalore	71.53	45.21	26	82.76	60.86	22
Dharmapuri	57.21	34.23	23	68.82	49.10	20
Dindigul	69.19	43.94	25	80.29	59.30	21
Erode	65.54	41.58	24	75.49	55.26	20
Kancheepuram	77.11	55.51	22	84.82	70.21	15
Kanyakumari	85.70	78.39	7	90.88	85.38	5
Karur	69.62	42.59	27	80.42	57.30	23
Madurai	79.93	57.90	23	87.24	69.93	17
Nagapattinam	77.03	54.43	23	85.61	68.35	17
Namakkal	66.65	41.71	25	78.02	57.04	21
Perambalur	64.74	38.57	26	77.68	54.26	23
Pudukkottai	71.78	43.62	28	83.22	60.94	22
Ramanathapuram	74.73	48.84	26	82.96	63.55	19
Salem	63.51	41.31	22	75.25	55.61	19
Sivaganga	76.90	49.59	27	83.70	62.12	22
Thanjavur	77.26	55.01	22	85.45	66.95	19
The Nilgiris	81.79	61.47	20	89.63	73.39	16
Theni	72.70	47.51	25	82.50	61.41	21
Thiruvallur	77.03	54.90	22	84.62	68.23	17
Thiruvarur		54.73	23	85.59	68.36	17
Toothukudi	82.02	64.57	17	88.66	75.64	13
Tiruchirappalli	79.50	57.69	22	87.19	71.19	16
Tirunelveli		54.23	23	85.89	68.50	17
Tiruvannamalai	66.71	39.25	28	80.14	56.31	24
Vellore		48.58	24	82.67	63.53	19
Villupuram	60.92	35.38	26	76.02	53.16	23
Virudhunagar	75.67	50.17	25	84.56	64.09	20
Tamil Nadu	73.75	51.33	22	82.33	64.55	18

Table 2
Proportion of Enrolment to School-Age Population

Level	*School Age Popn*			*Enrolment(in lakh)*			*Per Cent of Enrolment*		
	1993	*1998*	*2001*	*1993*	*1998*	*2001*	*1993*	*1998*	*2001*
Primary	79.8	68.8	57.5	80.2	66.7	56.7	100	96.9	98.6
Middle	36.8	37.5	37.6	35.4	33.8	35.2	96.2	90.1	93.6

Source: Policy notes of respective years, Government of Tamil Nadu.

Table 3
Districtwise Distribution of Primary and Middle Schools, and GERs by Age Category, 1998-99

District	*Per Cent Distribution of Schools*		*Enrolment Ratio (6-11)*			*Enrolment ratio (11-14)*		
	Primary	*Middle*	*Boys*	*Girls*	*Total*	*Boys*	*Girls*	*Total*
Chennai	0.9	4.0	108.2	75.4	89.7	96.0	91.9	94.0
Coimbatore	4.8	4.0	120.7	112.1	116.4	115.8	98.7	107.1
Cuddalore	3.9	3.9	97.2	92.3	94.8	94.8	90.0	92.5
Dharmapuri	6.4	3.4	82.1	78.6	80.4	81.9	76.1	79.0
Dindigul	3.9	3.5	117.34	117.4	117.7	107.0	101.6	104.4
Erode	4.9	3.4	122.2	119.1	120.7	126.1	91.0	106.8
Kancheepuram	3.5	4.4	86.3	106.2	94.8	76.4	79.9	78.1
Kanyakumari	1.1	2.7	103.7	106.9	105.3	94.6	86.5	90.6
Karur	2.2	1.5	116.8	115.2	116.0	113.8	106.1	110.0
Madurai	3.3	3.7	86.9	85.7	86.3	83.1	80.2	81.7
Nagapattinam	2.7	3.2	111.0	107.6	109.3	103.6	106.5	105.0
Namakkal	2.6	102	127.4	161.4	141.8	120.9	112.3	006.7
Perambalur	2.3	2.1	108.0	107.1	108.0	102.6	98.6	100.7
Pudukkottai	3.7	3.2	95.1	71.0	81.5	87.4	76.7	81.9
Ramanathapuram	3.2	2.8	87.9	89.8	88.8	88.4	83.6	86.0
Salem	4.1	2.9	96.3	124.3	107.9	90.1	86.3	88.3
Sivaganga	3.2	2.8	95.0	98.9	96.9	87.1	88.8	87.9
Thanjavur	3.6	4.0	92.0	89.1	90.6	86.0	88.0	86.9
Theni	1.4	2.8	87.9	87.7	87.8	86.4	81.5	84.0
Tirunelveli	5.0	6.8	91.4	96.0	93.6	88.4	103.5	95.2
Tiruvallur	3.6	3.5	88.6	116.0	100.3	77.4	82.3	82.7
Tiruvannamalai	4.8	3.4	87.3	85.9	86.6	83.0	82.3	82.7
Thiruvarur	2.2	2.2	118.0	115.0	116.5	110.6	113.5	111.7
Toothukudi	3.5	5.1	96.4	103.2	99.7	89.0	91.6	90.3
Tiruchirappalli	3.3	4.7	90.7	90.9	90.8	87.0	83.9	85.5
Udhagamandalam	1.3	1.1	106.9	98.5	102.7	99.0	86.4	92.8
Vellore	5.4	5.6	95.4	85.2	90.1	84.6	74.1	79.0
Villupuram	5.6	5.1	81.9	77.5	79.7	79.6	75.5	77.6
Virudhunagar	3.5	2.9	89.8	92.5	91.1	107.5	75.3	89.3
Tamil Nadu	100.0	100.0	97.9	96.0	96.7	92.7	87.5	90.1

enrolment. Examples are Dharmapuri, Tiruvannamalai and Villupuram, which, on that account, received special attention from the DPEP's gender-specific strategies. On the other hand, Salem, Kancheepuram, Namakkal, Tiruvallur and Toothukudi have higher GERs for girls than boys. If this may be due to better reach of schemes targeting girls' primary enrolment, relevant field-based evidence would be useful as lessons for other districts.

While establishing more schools to ensure greater enrolments is in practice, it should be borne in mind that the number of schools in a locality and its GER are not always directly correlated. For instance, while Kanyakumari, with the highest GER in the state, has only 1 per cent of the primary schools, Tiruvannamalai, one of the poor achievers, has almost 5 per cent of the primary schools in the state. However, this is not to argue against establishing the essential number of easily reachable schools in every needy location. In 2001, Tamil Nadu had 31,488 primary schools, and more may be established in suitable locations. But some caution against mushrooming of inefficient schools and against reproduction of the myth about the availability of schools as the sole factor for improving enrolments will nevertheless help. Evidence shows that caste and class equations also continue to play a major role, due to which *dalit* children remain relatively disadvantaged [Nambissan: 1996].

While more schools and higher enrolments may mark a beginning, it is important to ensure that all the enrolled children are retained in the system by due promotions. In this regard, retention data from the 43rd NSS round for 1987-88 and the 52nd round for 1995-96 is quite disturbing, as close to 60 per cent of the out-of-school children in the ages of 6-11 in Tamil Nadu are girls [Ramachandran et al: 1997]. The average discontinuation rate[7] in Tamil Nadu has also been considerable and in fact higher than the corresponding national average. While at all-India levels, discontinuation is only 6 per cent among children enrolled in a primary class in a rural area, the same is 11 per cent for Tamil Nadu. Further, Tamil Nadu also displays a high incidence of discontinuation among children in the 12-14 age categories, often girls, probably owing to the demands of domestic and remunerative labour on them. Factors causing poor retention or high discontinuation are either supply related (such as school-based difficulties), demand based (need to work) or customary, such as the need for girl children for sibling care at home. In Tamil Nadu, customary factors are more prevalent [Parikh: 1999].

Table 4 compares the rates of discontinuation among the 6-14 age group children for India and Tamil Nadu with data for 1992 and 1994. It shows that discontinuation is increasing rather than decreasing in Tamil Nadu, and is especially high among girls. This suggests the need to focus more attention on the regular attendance of girls, especially in backward districts.

Table 4
Discontinuation Rate Among 6-14 Age Children

	Ever Enrolment Rate for 1992 (Per cent)			*Discontinuation Rate (Per cent)*					
				1992			*1994*		
	Boys	*Girls*	*Total*	*Boys*	*Girls*	*Total*	*Boys*	*Girls*	*Total*
Tamil Nadu	90.9	84.3	87.7	6.2	7.9	7.1	7.5	14.8	10.9
All-India	77.1	64.8	71.4	6.0	7.8	8.0	4.8	7.6	6.0

Source: Quoted from Parikh: 1999.

Another key indicator that deals with the nature of retention among primary school children is their repetition rates. It is a sign of wastage, as repeating children do not move from one class to the next higher, but stagnate in the same class.

While the government's current practice of compulsory pass until class five may have its own repercussions, for want of more recent data, the one available for the year 1993 is presented in Table 5. Tamil Nadu's repetition rates, both for boys and girls, are considerably higher than the corresponding national average. Further, its repetition rates are slightly higher for boys than girls, not only in class one but also in classes four and five. This indicates that girls get lesser chance to repeat, and that in cases of failure to study, migration, demands for child labour and the like, girls may greatly lose their access to schooling rather than win chances to repeat. That girls suffer more denial of schooling than boys do probably reflects in their differential dropout status, as Table 6 shows.

Table 5
Repitition Rate among Girls and Boys in Primary Classes, 1993

	Class 1		*Class 2*		*Class 3*		*Class 4*		*Class 5*	
	G	*B*	*G*	*B*	*G*	*B*	*G*	*B*	*G*	*B*
Tamil Nadu	15.3	15.9	13.1	13.1	14.1	14.1	16.1	16.6	11.2	11.4
All-India	9.2	9.0	7.2	7.0	10.3	9.9	7.8	7.6	7.1	7.2

Source: Sixth All India Education Survey.

Table 6

Year	*in Classes 1-5*		*in Classes 1-8*		*in Classes 1-10*		*in Classes 1-12*	
	Boys	*Girls*	*Boys*	*Girls*	*Boys*	*Girls*	*Boys*	*Girls*
1986-87		25.06		57.83		78.59		89.64
1991-92	17.71	21.16	37.48	46.50	64.45	71.93	83.92	86.07
1996-97	14.05	16.20	26.38	34.78	58.63	67.05	78.21	83.09
2001-2002	12.73	15.95	35.46	34.53	57.34	57.79	79.69	79.32

Source: Policy notes on respective years, Government of Tamil Nadu.

Table 6 shows that there has been some drop in Tamil Nadu's dropout rates across time, and this has been quite considerable for girls across all levels. But there are still gender gaps to be addressed even in the primary stage, and this would be more urgent in some districts than others. Dropout data disaggregated at the district level is presented in Table 7.

As has already been indicated, districts such as Dindigul, Dharmapuri, Tiruvannamalai, Theni, Villupuram and Virudhunagar need sharper focus in terms of curtailing their dropout rates. Further, in most of these districts, the dropout rate among boys is not very high (not higher than the corresponding state average), but those among girls is quite high (higher than the state average). If primary education and completion for all has to be a reality, effective tackling of dropout among girls should be immediately prioritized.

While it is true that children who drop out of the system fail to gain from it, not all those who continue in the system actually do gain either. This is evident from the very low attainment levels of children. The government does not publish data on these lines. But, data available for the phase I DPEP districts on the achievement levels of class one and class four children showed that although the average levels of learning among children in all the concerned districts had risen from 1994 to 1997, the attainment level reached was quite low. Children's poor achievement, probable elsewhere in the state too, raises concerns related to the burden of non-comprehension in schools, which was highlighted in the government of India report titled, 'Learning without Burden'. In sum, primary-level enrolment, retention and attainment need greater attention in Tamil Nadu. They are currently suffering due to several reasons, some of them home-related, and some school related. While home-related factors may either be generational and indicative of cumulative backwardness (such as a tradition of illiteracy), or may be contemporary (such as the economic demands on children in poor families), they are nevertheless more complex to solve than school-related factors. But it is increasingly recognized that many of the home-related difficulties could be effectively tackled by appropriate school-related developments. In this context, it may be useful to assess the role of the state in terms of its supply provisions for universal primary education in Tamil Nadu.

Table 7
Districtwise Dropout Rate by Class and Sex, 1998-99
(Per cent)

District	*Class I-V*			*Class I-VIII*		
	Boys	*Girls*	*Total*	*Boys*	*Girls*	*Total*
Chennai	12.7	14.8	13.7	35.6	41.2	39.7
Coimbatore	12.7	14.8	14.1	39.3	33.1	36.0
Cuddalore	13.3	17.2	15.1	36.3	42.7	40.4
Dharmapuri	13.5	16.0	15.1	41.6	35.0	38.1
Dindigul	12.9	16.7	14.5	38.2	32.1	35.1
Erode	13.4	14.4	14.2	41.1	34.6	37.7
Kancheepuram	13.0	16.7	14.8	34.6	39.9	42.7
Kanyakumari	12.4	14.8	13.5	32.4	27.3	30.1
Karur	12.8	15.5	14.4	35.0	29.4	32.1
Madurai	12.8	16.0	14.3	38.4	32.3	35.3
Nagapattinam	13.2	16.3	14.4	35.0	29.5	32.2
Namakkal	13.4	14.6	14.3	25.8	21.7	23.7
Perambalur	12.8	15.4	14.4	35.0	29.4	32.1
Pudukkottai	13.1	15.8	14.7	40.8	34.4	37.4
Ramanathapuram	13.6	16.6	14.7	37.2	31.3	35.1
Salem	13.4	14.6	14.3	25.8	21.7	23.7
Sivaganga	12.8	16.0	14.4	39.9	33.6	36.6
Thanjavur	12.6	15.8	14.1	35.0	29.5	32.2
Theni	12.8	16.3	14.3	38.4	32.3	35.3
Tirunelveli	12.5	15.8	14.1	36.1	30.4	33.3
Thiruvallur	13.0	16.5	14.8	34.6	39.9	38.0
Tiruvannamalai	13.4	16.8	15.0	42.0	35.3	38.7
Thiruvarur	13.2	16.2	15.0	35.0	29.5	32.2
Toothukudi	12.6	15.8	14.1	38.5	32.4	35.6
Tiruchirappalli	12.8	15.4	14.4	35.0	29.4	32.1
Udhagamandalam	13.6	13.9	14.1	39.6	33.3	36.5
Vellore	13.3	16.6	14.9	39.0	32.8	35.9
Villupuram	12.7	17.3	14.8	36.3	42.7	40.4
Virudhunagar	13.6	16.9	15.2	41.1	34.6	37.8
Tamil Nadu	13.0	16.2	14.5	36.9	33.4	35.2

Source: Government of Tamil Nadu, Statistics Department.

III

Government Primary Schooling

That primary education is largely a state responsibility is now well established. The political commitment to educating all children through government schools under state responsibility was recognized quite early in Tamil Nadu. It has been a pioneer in not only implementing innovative schemes like the nutritious noon meal scheme, but also passing legislation for compulsory elementary education. Regarding its compulsory elementary education, however, there has been a long delay in implementation since passing the bill in 1994, the bill becoming an Act in 1995, to actually notifying it for implementation in 1998. Meanwhile, a number of concerns have been raised, some focusing on whether the phrase 'free and quality primary education' should be suffixed with 'compulsory', some others arguing that the penalty clause of the act victimizes poor parents rather than ensuring more state responsibility. There have also been claims for amendment because the act does not cover children up to 14 years of age (while elementary education conventionally extends up to this age), but stops with inclusion up to 11 years only, when incidence of dropping out (especially for child labour) has been proven to be considerable.

Currently, awareness for primary education is being created across all districts and there is hope that parental motivation for enrolment is likely to improve further in the light of education becoming a fundamental right of all citizens. In this context, the state needs to be equipped better for both sufficient and qualitative supply.

The role of the state is even more conspicuous in Tamil Nadu than in other states because of the spread and popularity of its schemes like the noon meal scheme, introduced in 1982 for children from class one to five, and extended since 1984 to cover all children of classes six to 10 also. Allied benefits like free textbooks are also given to beneficiaries of the noon meal scheme. In fact, each year, the Tamil Nadu Textbook Corporation distributes about 400 lakh textbooks to children through the Departments of Education, Adi Dravidar and Tribal Welfare, BCs and MBCs, and the Directorate of Rehabilitation. The government's welfare schemes also include free supply of slates to class one children, uniforms, bus passes and even bags and slippers to many children. Besides the state implemented the Tamil Nadu integrated nutrition project from 199I to 1997, and provides a package of services through the integrated child development services since 1975. However, while the probable impact of these measures on enrolment has been shown by some studies [Radhakrishnan and Akila: 2002], field-based evidence on its role in reducing gender gaps in primary education is wanting.

Schooling Availability and Quality

In the current scenario of time targeting the goals of universal primary completion, it should be recognized that the quality of schooling offered with currently available funds should become a central concern. The first step, namely, schooling availability and access, is not problematic as far as lower primary schooling is considered.

But in terms of upper primary schooling, data for 1993-94 has shown that only 81 per cent of Tamil Nadu's habitations have an upper primary school within one km. The need to bridge lower and upper primary schooling in Tamil Nadu is vital, given the high discontinuation rates in classes four and five, and that especially among girls.

Despite the fact that the budget allocation for classroom construction has been increasing in every annual state budget, many schools are also in need of classrooms. This apart, *panchayat* union schools construct their own buildings, and recently the DPEP has also constructed buildings and classrooms using locally available resources. Play-walls and swings and special care for disabled children have marked a difference in some such schools. The state also gets maintenance grants from the central government's EFA scheme. Yet, the improvement in meeting the need for classrooms does not seem significant. The sixth all-India survey had noted that 50 per cent of the state's schools suffered from inadequate number of classrooms in 1993. This may have improved. There is still no category wise compiled data on overcrowded classrooms, those used for non-teaching purposes, and those in dire need of repairs. However, an indirect development in this regard is the government order of 1994-95 that all primary schools should establish a parent-teacher association (PTA) to ensure not only enrolment and quality but also to facilitate legitimate collection of funds for construction of classrooms and compound walls or expenditure for infrastructure. PTAs, village education councils (VECs), and community participation in general are expanding in rural Tamil Nadu, and have the scope to ensure local monitoring as an effective strategy, although resources in poor and illiterate areas may need greater attention. In any case, unless the parents of girls are satisfied with the quality of schools that their children may attend, targeting all girls will remain a distant dream.

Schooling infrastructure is an important criterion in this regard. The sixth all-India survey in 1993 found that there was no drinking water in one-third of Tamil Nadu' s government schools, no blackboards in one-fifth, and no basic furniture for teachers and students in about 70 per cent of the cases; 91 per cent had no toilets, and the provision of sanitation, especially in girls' schools, was very poor. About 80 per cent had no electricity. Playgrounds were not available in about half of the schools. This has been despite the fact that the state has completed all four phases of the Operation Blackboard scheme.[8] Random field visits do show that the problem continues in many villages across districts.

Apart from the points discussed so far in the vein of correction for proper expansion of primary education benefiting especially girls who have remained excluded from EFA, two major issues regarding teachers are even more crucial. One is their availability, which can be gauged in terms of the teacher-school ratio,[9] and teacher-pupil ratio. The other is their efficiency in terms of creating and sustaining interest in learning and thus producing greater attainment levels among children.

The Tamil Nadu government has been facing a crisis regarding the teacher-pupil ratio. In fact, while it held 1:20 as a healthy ratio in the early 1990s, it soon readjusted it to I: 40 by a government order (GO No. 525, December 29, 1999). It is important to reckon that reducing the class size will help teachers use their time with students more effectively.[10]

Regarding the efficiency of teachers and teaching, the directorate of teacher education and training gives a number of programmes across the state [DTERT: 1993]. 'Joyful learning', supported by UNICEF has been chief among these. The government has also given grants for teaching-learning material. However, despite the generally high educational level of teachers and their attaining qualifications, it is true that many teachers have greater responsibilities than they can handle. The low motivation levels among teachers translate into indifferent classroom practices, teacher absenteeism, and low turnout of students in terms of both numbers and attainment levels. The state's strategy to have more male teachers and to encourage monitoring by the parent community and *panchayats* offers some promise for targeting more girls. In a number of cases, sensitized and motivated community participation seems to hold the key to ensuring that all children are in school.

IV

Funds for Primary Education

Allocating sufficient resources by prioritizing needs is central to improving educational performance across the country. But despite increases in budgets for education, public spending on education is still low, at just about 3 per cent of GDP. Although it is increasingly being said that allocating 6 per cent of GDP on education is essential to achieve UPE at least by 2007, the share of GDP spent on education has paradoxically fallen from 3.65 per cent at the beginning of the 1990s to 3.48 per cent in 1996-97 [Sipahimalani: 2000]. Further, as mobilization of additional resources becomes difficult, restructuring of the available educational budget is becoming the solution. In this regard, it is important to note the features of intra-sectoral allocation.

As Table 8 shows, in Tamil Nadu's Eighth Five-Year Plan for 1992-97, plan outlay of Rs. 25.25 lakh was allocated for elementary education (nearly 50 per cent of the total outlay), while secondary and higher education received about half, namely, Rs. 12.59 lakh. But as there is greater upgradation of primary schools to middle, with more children completing primary education, increasing resources for them may be needed at these levels as well.

Similarly, the inter-functional allocation of resources is also vital. Many components are in dire need of funds, as 90 per cent of the funds for primary education are being used for teachers' salaries, and building construction takes away a major portion of the rest of the share. It is difficult to curtail funds for Tamil Nadu's noon-meal and related welfare schemes, as already a number of children seem to suffer due to the resource crunch that has led to prioritizing the most disadvantaged and needy among them to avail of such benefits. In this context, shifting the priorities for resource allocation would also be difficult.

Table 8
Intra-Sectoral Allocation of Resources in Education, 1992-98

Sector	*8th Plan Outlay (in as lakh)*	*Per cent per sector*
Elementary education	25,247	57.4
Secondary and higher secondary	12,585	28.6
University	2,150	4.9
Adult and non-formal	4,000	9.1
Language development	18	0.1
Total outlay for education	44,000	100

Source: 8th Five-Year Plan, Government of Tamil Nadu.

It is in this regard that the government has been encouraging private contributions to primary education. As 80 per cent of its elementary schools are managed directly by the state, at the household level, current expenditure on primary education per student in Tamil Nadu is only Rs. 470, while the all-India figure is Rs. 539. In this context, as Chennai, Tirunelveli and Toothukudi have a major share of established private aided schools, there are suggestions that other districts may also be encouraged to establish private schools so as to reduce the state's burden. But this needs careful consideration in terms of not only quality but also certain gender concerns. For instance, the India Development Report [Parikh: 1999] has shown that in terms of girls' education, government schools are a safer bet than the private fee-collecting schools, since among the 6-14 age children, the female-to-male ratio was close to I in government schools, while it was only 0.73 in private schools. This indicates parental preference for educating boys rather than girls when educational expenditure becomes higher. Hence the state must shoulder more responsibility both for quantity and quality rather than depend on private schooling that may adversely affect female education. Fortunately, private unaided schools, where the financial burden may be even higher on parents, form a very small percentage in Tamil Nadu, suggesting the effective control it wields against mushrooming of market-oriented and inefficient schools.

V

Conclusion

Some critical issues and priorities for action have emerged in the course of discussion in this paper. As far as Tamil Nadu is concerned, a closer look with regard to the following concerns for policy and implementation may help to effectively achieve primary education for all girls.

- Elusive EFA goals are to be urgently met. Regarding literacy attainment, male-female disparities, considering both rural-urban and OBC-SC/ST factors, should be reduced. Social and gender equity can be achieved only by creating better awareness of primary education among the disprivileged and minority groups in every district.

- There is a need to bridge the gap between availability and access at lower and upper primary schooling. Bridging the gap between primary and middle levels with special focus on the needs of girls will also be essential as more children complete primary education.
- The trend of increasing wastage needs to be curtailed, and repetition in primary classes needs proper attention. Timely tackling of discontinuation can help to curtail dropouts at all levels. Effectively implementing the Compulsory Elementary Education Act with due recognition of the special disadvantages of girls and their parents is urgent.
- Integrating gender perspectives in all functional areas is a must. The currently used gender focus for increasing female enrolment should get sharper to ensure their retention and attainment. Some important areas can be sensitizing all teachers, and encouraging mothers' participation in PTAs and VECs. Tamil Nadu's local escort system for ST girls is commendable, and more of such innovations are welcome.
- Inadequate spending, at the present 3 per cent share of GDP, has to be rectified. In fact, the Kothari Commission had recommended this even as early as the 1960s.

Notes

1. Azariades and Drazen (1990) are considered to be the first to conclusively state this critical threshold for reaping tangible benefits from education. Sen (1999) and Sen and Dreze (1999) noted that education provides people with 'human capabilities', the power to reflect, make choices and seek a voice in society. Hanushek and Kunko (2000) proved that low levels of human capital go with poverty, and inefficient diffusion of knowledge hinders increasing productivity. A number of others have also presented compelling justification for investing in girls' education [King: 1990, Lockheed and Verspoor: 1990]. Research in India has corroborated most of these findings [Bhatty: 1998, Govinda: 2002].
2. Some recent developments in this context are the 73rd and 74th Constitutional Amendments in the early 1990s that paved the way for decentralized management in many fields including primary education through *panchayati raj* institutions. Further, the 83rd Constitutional Amendment in 1997 argued for education as a fundamental right, and the 93rd Constitutional Amendment in 2001, with Presidential assent in 2002, has made education a fundamental right of all children between the ages of 6 and 14. A nationwide campaign is calling for the fulfillment of it through formal schools under state responsibility.
3. See Radhakrishnan and Akila (1993) for an analysis of Tamil Nadu's literacy in the all-India context during the 1980s, and Radhakrishnan and Akila (2002) for a similar account in the 1990s.
4. Athreya and Chunkath (1996) have already shown that Tamil Nadu has a contiguous low literacy belt consisting of Dharmapuri, Periyar, Salem, South Arcot, and Tiruvannamalai. Its other major illiteracy belt is the contiguous area of Dindigul, Madurai, Thanjavur and Tiruchchirappalli.

5. Akila (2000) documents the socio-historical role of the interplay of caste and gender in determining the low educational status of women in Madras Presidency and later in Tamil Nadu.
6. As the NER is a proportion of the population of a particular age group enrolled at a specific level of schooling to the total population in that age group, it is more reliable than the GER, which does not consider age, and the age-specific enrolment ratio, which does not consider the level or class of enrolment. Secondly, while non-attendance and discontinuation rates caution about the absence of students in schools, they are indicative of dropout at a later date.
7. This indicator refers to the percentage of ever-enrolled children who discontinued their studies at any time during the age of 6 to 14 years. It is therefore an average for an 8-year period, and only a rough estimate, which provides context to non-attendance, later often leading to dropout.
8. Operation Blackboard is one of the largest projects for improving school infrastructure. It basically has three main components, namely, the building component, teacher component and equipment component. Although the majority of funds under this scheme have gone into building construction and teacher appointments, it is still popularly known for its equipment component including provision of blackboards.
9. Data from the policy notes of the government during the 1990s show that on average there are four teachers for primary schools, which generally have five classes. The government has been taking account of surplus posts in some schools and is using a transparent method of transferring teachers to needy schools. Even by the policy note of 2001-02, there are 7,987 surplus posts in *panchayat* union schools, and the number is higher in other types of schools.
10. Some interesting studies have focused on the ideal class size for students to benefit from schooling. Haq and Haq (1998) noted that students in a class of five will spend an estimated 90 per cent of their time on learning activity; in a class of 20 they will spend only 60 per cent of their time on learning; and in a class of 100 the learning time will further drop to just 12 per cent.

References

Akila, R. 2000. 'Caste and Gender in Women's Education: A Study of Tamil Nadu, 1854-1996', unpublished PhD. thesis, University of Madras.

Athreya, V. and S. Chunkath. 1996. *Literacy and Empowerment.* New Delhi: Sage Publications.

Azariades, C. and A. Drazen. 1990. 'Threshold Externalities in Economic Development', *Quarterly Journal of Economics:* 105: 2.

Bhatty, K. 1998. 'Educational Deprivation in India: A Survey of Field Investigations', *Economic and Political Weekly:* 33:27: July 4.

Dreze, J. and A. Sen. 1995. *India: Economic Development and Social Opportunity.* New Delhi: Oxford University Press.

DTERT. 1993. *Strategic Plan of Action to Achieve Universal Primary Education in Tamil Nadu by 2000 AD,* Chennai: Government of Tamil Nadu.

Govinda, R. 2002. *India Education Report: A Profile of Basic Education,* New Delhi:Oxford University Press and NIEPA.

Hanushek, E. and Kunko. 2000. 'Schooling, Labour Force Quality and the Growth of Nations', *American Ecollomic Review:* 90:5.

Haq, M. and K. Haq. 1998. *Human Development in South Asia.* Oxford: Oxford University Press.

King, E. 1990. *Educating Girls and Women: Investing* in *Development.* Washington, DC: The World Bank.

Lockheed, M., A. Verspoor and Others. 1990. *Improving Primary Education* in *Developing Countries: A Review of Policy Options.* Washington, DC: The World Bank.

Nambissan, G. 1996. 'Equity in Education? Schooling of Dalit Children in India', *Economic and Political Weekly: 31:16* and 17: April 20-27.

Parikh, K. (ed). 1999. *India Development Report.* New Delhi: Oxford University Press.

PROBE. 1998. *Public Report 011 Basic Education in India.* New Delhi: Oxford University Press.

Radhakrishnan, P. and R. Akila. 2002. 'Progress Towards Education For All: The Case of Tamil Nadu' in R. Govinda.(ed). *India Education Report:* A *Profile of Basic Education.* New Delhi: Oxford University Press and NIEPA.

Radhakrishnan, P. and R. Akila.1993. 'India's Educational Efforts: Rhetoric and Reality', *Economic and Political Weekly: 28:48*: November 27.

Ramachandran, V.K., V. Rawal and M. Swaminathan. 1997. 'Investment Gaps in Primary Education', *Economic alld Political Weekly:* 32:I and 2: January: 4-11.

Sen, A. 1999. *Development and Freedom.* New York: Alfred Knopf.

Sen, A. and J. Dreze. 1999. *The Amartya Sen and Jean Dreze Omnibus: Comprising Poverty and Famines, Hunger and Public Action. India: Economic Development and Social Opportunity.* New Delhi: Oxford Unversity Press.

Sipahimalani, V. 2000. 'Financing of Elementary Education in India in the 1990s'.Washington, DC. The World Bank, Report No. 2, http://www.worldbank.org

World Bank. 2001. 'Expanding and Improving Upper Primary Education in India', Report No. 20347-IN. http://www.woridbank.org

The paper was first published in the *Economic and Political Weekly*: 39:25: 2004: 2617-22. It is included here with the prior permission of the author and the Editor, *Economic and Political Weekly*: Address for email correspondence: akilar2000@ yahoo.com

Chapter - Thirteen

Battling for Education: The Challenges of Educating Girls in Rural Maharashtra

Chetna Gala Sinha and Michelle Rosenthal

The salary 16-year-old Savitra Mane receives for a week of backbreaking field labour is less than the cost of the 10th standard examination fee. As a member of the Kaykadi nomadic caste, she is the first in her family to have reached this far in her education, yet she faces no choice now but to drop out of school in order to support her aging and ill family. Born to uneducated and illiterate parents, Savitra was always a bright and eager student, whose parents nurtured her desire to learn and insisted that she never miss school for fieldwork. Also a dedicated daughter, Savitra soon took it upon herself to assume more and more of the housework, in order to relieve her mother's burden as a basket-weaver and homemaker.

When Savitra was in the 10th standard, her father fell ill, and she found herself sharing his burden making it increasingly difficult to remain awake long enough to study, after rising early and working late in her home. As a result, she failed her 10th standard state examinations this March and has become a full-time field labourer, in addition to taking on all of the housework. She still nurtures the hope of returning to school, but fears that even if she is able to carve out precious study time from her packed schedule, she will not be able to afford the 150 rupees monthly fee for vocational school training. Remarkably, her parents have offered to make do without her meagre, but necessary, field salary so that Savitra could return to school. But she is determined to balance her studies with field and housework so that she can continue supporting her family. For Savitra, education has enabled her to gain more confidence, and while she insists she is not proud of herself, she is clearly a source of pride for her parents.

Savitra is not alone in her dilemma. Thousands of rural girls across the country are forced to drop out of school due to financial constraints and educational fees. While Savitra's specific circumstances may be unique, her desire to be educated and the simultaneous self-imposed guilt she feels for the additional sacrifices her family must make on her behalf, are shared by thousands of other rural girls. *Contrary to the opinion of many, school drop out does not result from a lack of desire on the part of the girls or a lack of support from their families. Rather, girls drop out of school due to a lack of resources, and the financial constraints, in actual and opportunity costs, of education.*

Making Schools Complete

This difficulty is common knowledge to rural families, but that does not mean it need remain an immutable fact. The *Mann Vikas Samajik Sanstha*, a NGO, in coordination with the *Mann Deshi Mahila Sahakari Bank*, has successfully executed an innovative model to find a solution to this problem. The main objective of the Bank and its partner *Sanstha* is to empower poor rural women, and they have coordinated many programmes designed to improve the lives of women by promoting education and economic independence. The Savitribai Phule Gram Puraskar or "Education for All Girls: Rural Girls Education Campaign" is one such programme intended to encourage 100 per cent school attendance for the girls in rural Maharashtra by offering villages a large cash reward, courtesy the Bank of India, if they achieve the goal.

The idea for the competition came from the women of the Bank's Self Help Group Federation, during the Bank and Sanstha's 2002 annual meeting. These women articulated the need to make education for rural children, particularly girls, a priority, and so the competition was designed with the involvement of Self Help Groups, *gram panchayat* members, teachers, and village citizens in the block.

Ten villages immediately expressed interest in supporting girls' education through the competition, and two villages committed to achieving 100 per cent enrollment this year. Over the next few years, the *Sanstha* will steadily expand the scale of the competition until all of Mann Taluka is included. Part of the inspiration for this type of competition is the government's *Sant Gadgemaharaj Swachhata Abhiyan* (Sant Gadgemaharaj Cleanliness Competition), which has so effectively cleaned up rural villages by providing the incentive and the infrastructure to achieve cleaner and healthier communities. The government has expressed strong interest in implementing the Girls' Education Competition at the state level, because it has already had the remarkable effect of uniting citizens to cooperate and take responsibility for supporting girls' education in their villages, as well as strengthening village pride, unity, and excitement.

A Committed School

The village of Waghmodewadi, in rural Maharashtra, is a case in point. This village, comprised of 175 families and 1,500 people, has been an exemplary model for girls' education, and will receive the Rs. 50,000 reward for winning this year's competition. Virtually 100 per cent of the girls in the village attend school, and their parents have shown strong support for their daughters. In a comprehensive survey of the village, we found that with very few exceptions, girls do not miss school to do fieldwork or to attend to the family's animals. While most girls assist with cooking, cleaning, and fetching water (a time consuming and arduous task in a village with a single water tank that is often empty as a result of ongoing drought) they still find time to study. Younger children are fortunate enough to have an easily accessible primary school within the village, but all children wishing to continue past the 4th standard must travel to school. Thus, each day begins with a ritual of morning chores for the older girls, before they embark on the long and dusty walk into the neighbouring village of Gondavle for school. Children are forced to carry their own food and water to school, as the school's supply of water is unfit for drinking.

Since none are rich, families make significant sacrifices to keep their girls in school. For virtually everyone, paying for education is a constant difficulty, and parents frequently share fields and finances with their siblings to help support the extended family's collective children. Those who can buy bikes to ease the commute to school are a privileged few, and most feel fortunate when they can afford the notebooks and uniforms their children need. Although the government has just started supplying books, it still costs an average of Rs. 2000 per child each year, a staggering sum for families who live hand to mouth on the fruits of their drought ridden fields. Given these circumstances, the commitment to education of the village of Waghmodewadi and those like it is truly remarkable. Families say they believe education will help their daughters "stand on her own two feet" and "have a bright future" and for these reasons they have made innumerable sacrifices.

Insufficient Education

Sadly, many of these sacrifices are in vain. Girls are rarely able to continue their education beyond the 10th standard, even if they are able to reach that far. In the rare cases when a girl is able to continue to the 12th standard, her career prospects are barely enhanced by the additional years of schooling, so she will most likely still be consigned to a life of marriage and housework. The lack of opportunity results in part because of the low quality of education provided by government schools, and in part because most rural girls will not be able to afford to continue their education through the university level. Thus, while a junior college degree has the positive affect of postponing marriage, it rarely provides the professional training necessary to earn an income outside of the fields. Those girls who are fortunate enough to receive vocational training are far more likely to attain self-sufficiency than those who only complete the 12th standard but ironically, vocational training is primarily made available only to those girls and women who dropped out of school before the 10th standard. *Wider access to vocational training for women is an important intermediate step on the road to improving girls' education.* Vocational skills, such as tailoring or salon skills, allow women to become financially independent. Research has shown that these women are more likely to support their own daughters' education in the future because as income increases, opportunity and commitment to education do as well.

Ingredients for Success

Despite the dim prospects that often face girls after their schooling, the quality of the education they receive and the support given to them by their schools can have a profound affect on a girl's future. The Navachaitanya High School and Junior College in Gondavle BK has made great strides in working with parents and students to improve the quality of their education, and the girls of Waghmodewadi and neighbouring villages have benefited as a result, but there is only so much a single school can do without sufficient resources from the government.

Drawing primarily from four villages in the Satara district of rural Maharashtra, the female enrollment of the Gondavle High School almost equals the male enrollment. The percentage of girls who pass the 12th standard examinations exceeds that of boys, although fewer girls reach this level. For example, there are only 26 girls compared to the 47 boys enrolled in the 12th standard, but 76 per cent of those girls passed the state examinations, compared to 69 per cent of the whole class that passed. Interestingly, this year there are 56 girls in the 10th standard and only 35 boys, a prominent contrast from last year, when there were 49 male and 49 female students. Whether this is indicative of an increased commitment to girls' education in the region or is merely a statistical anomaly remains debatable, but *evidence suggests that families are truly beginning to understand the importance of educating all their children.*

The Gondavle School in particular boasts a strong working relationship with parents, and a dedicated administration that works hard to implement their suggestions. For example, at their most recent teacher parent assembly, parents suggested increased teacher accountability and homework regularity, while teachers recommended parents take a more active role in ensuring that their children complete assignments thoroughly and on time. Both sides agreed to begin implementing the others' suggestions, making the school a true model for the type of cooperation that is necessary for students and schools to succeed.

According to Gondavle's teachers, there are two primary difficulties they face when trying to educate rural children. The first is *parental illiteracy*. Despite supporting their children's education, rural parents who have not been educated themselves cannot adequately assist their children with homework or ensure that they spend sufficient time studying. Because the education of parents directly impacts the ability of their children to succeed in school, it is an urgent necessity that this generation of Indian youth is properly educated. The second pressing issue is the need *to make education more employment oriented. Students and their families are loath to sacrifice for the sake of an education that cannot supply them with a job and additional income in the future. These issues must be addressed on a broad scale if education in India is to improve.*

The Obligation of the Government

Thus, the burden no longer rests with the rural families of India, or even with individual village schools. They have shown a commitment to educating their girls and have sacrificed immensely on their behalf. It is now time for the educational system to reform its half of the deal. Girls deserve an education that will benefit them in the future and a government that is committed to supporting their future with viable and honest policies and officials. The current government scheme to encourage education is called "Education for All" and it has been all but useless. The crux of the programme revolves around village education committees, comprised of *gram panchayat* members, the school principal and parents. Ideally, these are the people best equipped to evaluate their local schools and teachers and make recommendations for their improvement. In reality, however, these committees have little power to make changes in their village schools and even less opportunity to sway policy. For example, these committees are responsible for evaluating teachers and requesting transfers of those teachers who are continually absent, abusive, illiterate, or simply lazy. These requests are not made lightly and the situation is often quite serious before an impassioned plea is issued to the government. However, transfers are almost never issued, despite glaring abuse and incompetence. This is because teachers receive virtually the largest salary in any village community and are, thus, able to bribe politicians to cancel their transfer. This not only secures their jobs against the will of the local community, but also allows them to remain in their home villages and exert more energy on their fields than on their students.

Tuning to Local Conditions

Work in the fields plays a central role in the lives of teachers, parents, and students in this area, and educational reform cannot be effective unless it takes this reality into account. Maharashtra is primarily a rural state and children often help their families in the fields from an early age. For the last three years, the state has suffered from severe droughts, stymieing an already stagnant agricultural economy. This scenario negatively affects both education and literacy rates, making rural Maharashtra's literacy rate of 58 per cent fairly impressive, when compared to the 54 per cent national average. In the district of Satara, home to the village of Waghmodewadi, total literacy rates are at 66.67 per cent. For rural males the level is at 79.27 per cent, substantially higher compared to the 50.75 per cent rate for rural females. Literacy has a clear correlation with education, and the drop out rate among girls remains high, averaging 54.59 per cent to the 44.87 per cent for the boys. Despite increasing familial support for girls' education, the fact remains that more help in the house and fields is demanded of girls, who also face greater challenges finding time and resources to attend schools outside of their villages.

The presence of a nearby school substantially increases the likelihood that girls will continue with their education. While most villages boast a primary school with high enrollment, dropout increases dramatically as girls in rural areas are forced to travel long distances, often by foot, to attend their secondary schools. If the school is not reachable on foot (or by bicycle in the rare instances where families can afford to buy them for their girls), there is little likelihood that families will allow their daughters to travel alone to school, leaving girls with no choice but to drop out altogether.

Bikes for Boys, Guilt for Girls

Although families in Waghmodewadi provide educational resources to their male and female children with more equity than in many villages, the fact remains that boys' education is considered an undisputed right, while for girls it is a hard earned privilege. In addition to the fact that girls are expected to help with house and fieldwork far more than their brothers, they also frequently feel guilty for imposing a burden on their families for the sake of their education. As a result, they either drop out earlier or study harder and appreciate their education more than their brothers. In contrast, most boys take their education for granted, and unlike girls, they don't consider familial burden a reason to drop out, but rather cite academic failure or boredom as the reason for not attending the school. In addition, boys who attend school through the 12th standard are unwilling to return to the fields, yet possess no greater vocational skills than their female counterparts, who are more likely to swallow their pride and bow to the necessity of earning an agricultural income despite their school degree.

Practical Reforms

Rural families must make immense sacrifices in order to educate both their sons and their daughters, and it is unfair to reward their efforts with futile government programmes that provide low quality teachers, minimal resources, and few vocational skills. What families and villages need in support of their efforts are the assets necessary to provide a viable education for their girls, and the government has the power to rethink its policies, priorities, and resource allocation in that pursuit. Rather than issuing bus passes to girls in villages whose roads have never touched the wheels of a bus, the government should roll out programmes similar to the *Mann Vikas Samajik Sanstha's Saraswati Yojana Freedom Ride Bicycle Programme o*n a much wider scale. This programme lends families the money to buy bicycles interest free. It has allowed scores of young girls to attend schools who otherwise would have been stymied by the distance.

- The government should provide uniforms to families, rather than wasting money preparing inedible rice for primary school students.
- The government should also make sure that the educational facilities are equipped to actually educate students. Schools should have clean water for their students. They should also own computers and provide classes that teach students how to use them with proficiency.
- Schools should also offer professional and vocational training for students, especially those girls who will otherwise drop out to work in the fields.
- Teachers should be held accountable to parents and students, and censured or removed if they prove inadequate.

These are not the ideas of an outsider, critiquing a system only briefly examined. These are the words of the parents and girls themselves, eager to avail themselves of an education they can use. The passion for education exists in abundance in rural India. It is now a matter of harnessing that energy with an effective system, designed to maximize the benefit of educating girls.

Hope for the Future

A system of this sort would benefit an eager and enthusiastic young girl like Savitra immensely. Savitra is from Waghmodewadi, and despite all the obstacles in her path, when she and her family heard about the Girls'Education Competition, it served as the final catalyst necessary to encourage her to go back to school. With a loan from the Mann Deshi Mahila Sahakari Bank, she has now enrolled in a vocational school in Gondavle and will earn her tailoring degree in a few months. Eager to support their daughter's education, but also intent on helping their village improve its school by winning the award, her family serves as an example of how this programme can truly have an impact on individual girls, village pride and the rural educational system. *As Savitra has demonstrated, educating girls in rural India is not a hopeless task; rather it requires a commitment from the government to follow the lead of its citizens and provides the requisite resources for good quality schooling to village children.*

This paper was first published in *Manushi*: 143: 2004:34-39.It is included here with the permission of the authors and the Editor, *Manushi.Chetna* Gala Sinha is President of *Mann Deshi Mahila Bank, Mann Vikas Samajik Sansatha and Director of Mann Deshi Udyogini*. She was a 2002 Yale World Fellow, as well as an Ashoka Fellow. Michelle Rosenthal was a senior at the Yale University in the US and spent the summer researching and implementing the Girls' Education Competition, while interning at the *Mann Deshi Mahila Bank* in Mhaswad, Maharashtra.

Chapter - Fourteen

Simultaneous Analysis of Child Labour and Child Schooling: Comparative Evidence from Nepal and Pakistan

Ranjan Ray

I

Introduction

There has been, in recent years, growing interest in the subject of child labour[1] among academics, public officials and the media. There are few topics in the core of the development literature today that enjoy as much importance and evoke as much passion as that of child labour. The subject has moved from the national to the international arena. The prominence accorded to the subject of child labour at the WTO meeting in Seattle a couple of years ago is a reflection of its pivotal importance in the international policy arena. Basu (1999b) provides a lucid exposition of the policy implications of child labour for the setting of international labour standards in an era of rapid globalisation. Fallon and Tzannatos (1998) discuss ways in which the World Bank can assist member-nations in reducing child labour.

Notwithstanding almost universal agreement that child labour is undesirable, there is wide disagreement on how to tackle this problem. The formulation of policies that are effective in curbing child labour requires an analysis of its key determinants, namely, identification of variables that have a significant effect on child employment. In view of the close interaction between child labour and child schooling, such an analysis needs to be extended to the latter. Moreover, evidence on the nature of interaction between child labour and child schooling is needed in formulating effective policies designed to improve the welfare of the child. The present study provides south Asian evidence on these issues. There has been, in recent years, a rapidly expanding literature on child labour that provides empirical evidence on its nature and determinants (see Grootaert and Kanbur: 1995,

Basu: 1999a and Jafarey and Lahiri: 2000b for surveys). While some of these studies [for example, Knight: 1980, Horn: 1995] discussed mainly the qualitative features of child labour, the recent literature has focused attention on the quantitative aspects taking advantage of the increasing availability of good quality data on child employment. Within the empirical literature on child labour, there has been a shift in emphasis from mere quantification (that is, exclusive reliance on descriptive statistics) to an econometric analysis of its determinants. The present study is in this latter tradition.

Table 1
Child Labour-Aggregate and Distribution

	No. of Children (below 15 years) working (in thousands)		
	1980	*1985*	*1990*
World	87,867	80,611	78,516
	(19.91)	(na)	(11.32)
Africa	14,950	14,536	16,763
	(30.97)	(na)	(24.92)
Latin America and the Caribbean	4,122	4,536	4,723
	(12.64)	(na)	(8.21)
Asia	68,324	61,210	56,784
	(23.42)	(na)	(10.18)
East Asia	39,725	33,463	22,448
	(na)	(na)	(na)
South-east Asia	6,518	6,079	5,587
	(na)	(na)	(na)
South Asia	20,192	19,834	27,639
	(na)	(na)	(na)

Note: Figures in brackets denote child labour participation rate
Source: Basu (1999a, Table 1)

While the majority of the econometric studies on child labour have used Latin American data [see, for example, the volume edited by Grootaert and Patrinos: 1998], the corresponding literature on south Asian child labour is relatively limited. And, yet, as Table 1, reproduced from Basu (1999a) shows, south Asia contains the largest concentration of child labour in the world. Nearly one in three child labourers is from south Asia. However, the child labour participation rate in south Asia lags behind that in Africa. The chief motivation of the present exercise is to extend the literature on estimating the determinants of child labour and child schooling to the south Asian context. The previous literature on south Asian child labour includes the classic monograph by Weiner (1991) Chaudhuri and Wilson (2000), Ray (2000c), Cigno and Rosati (2000) on India, Ravallion and Wodon (2000) on Bangladesh, and Addison, et al (1997), Ray (2000a, b) on Pakistan. However, there exists no comparative study of child labour or child schooling between the south Asian countries. That is one of the features of this exercise. The countries chosen for the present exercise are Nepal and Pakistan. The corresponding data sets are fairly comparable. These country surveys provide comparable information not only on the nature and magnitude of child labour and child schooling, but also on the individual, household and community-level attributes that provide their potential determinants.

This study provides empirical evidence on the impact of poverty and inequality on child labour and child schooling. There is no consensus in the literature on the role of poverty in forcing households to put their children into employment. Bhatty (1998), Ahmed (1999) and Lieten (2000), among others, argue that poverty has only a limited role in explaining child labour. Bhatty (1998: 1734) cites a variety of studies on Indian child labour in support of the view that "income and related variables do not seem to have any direct significant effect on children's work input......children are often put to work as a deterrent to idling rather than as an economic necessity". As a referee pointed out, significant schooling costs (such as, costs of textbooks and, tuition) prevent school attendance from being viewed as an alternative to 'idling'. Lieten (2000: 2038) observes that "the correlation between regional poverty and child labour indeed is inconclusive" and explains the lack of a strong correlation by the fact that poor regions are characterised by high fertility rates and low labour opportunities. Lieten's view is supported by the Pakistani evidence of Addison, et al (1997), who observe, "low incomes do not increase child labour". Ray (2000a) also provides evidence that shows that household poverty has an insignificant impact on the child's labour market participation in Peru and Pakistan. Swaminathan (1998: 1514) explains the observed weak relation between incidence of child labour and incidence of poverty by suggesting that at "the micro-level, poverty ensures a supply of child labour... it is the structure of demand, however, that determines the use of child labour". In contrast to these empirical findings, income and poverty variables play a crucial role in the analytical results on child labour derived in Basu and Van (1998).[2] Also, Ray (2000b) provides evidence from Pakistan that suggests that there is a strong positive association between child labour hours (unlike labour force participation rates) and poverty, though this result does not extend to the Peruvian data. Ray (2000c) provides Indian evidence that shows that while household poverty is a significant determinant of wage-based child employment, this is not so for more generally defined 'economic activities'. Against this background of a lack of consensus on the link between poverty and child labour, the new evidence on this on data from Nepal, presented here, acquires some significance.

In examining the impact of poverty on child labour and child schooling, we depart from previous studies in distinguishing between 'household poverty' and 'cluster poverty'. While the former is a household attribute and is based on the household's income shortfall from the poverty line,[3] used in the Foster, Greer and Thorbecke (1984) measure of poverty, the latter, which is a community level variable, uses the headcount poverty rate to measure economic affluence, or the lack of it, of the cluster of residences of the household. The income shortfall is measured by $P = \frac{(z-x)^{\alpha}}{z}$ where z is the cluster-specific poverty line, x is the per capita expenditure of the household, and a*** is the 'poverty aversion' parameter. The parameter a*** was set at 2.0 in the present exercise. Note that this extends the treatment of the poverty variable in Ray (2000a, b) which set a***= O and, consequently, ignored the income variation between the poor households. The distinction between household poverty and cluster poverty that we draw here is quite significant for it allows the possibility that the household is not 'poor' but resides in an economically depressed cluster with considerable poverty, or vice versa. The transmission mechanism from household poverty to child labour, if present, can be classified as a 'supply side' phenomenon; namely, economic necessities pushing a child from a poor household into employment. In contrast, cluster-level poverty would control poverty-related variables from the 'demand side' since, as suggested by Addison, et al (1997) and Lieten (2000), among others, households living in poor clusters have only limited opportunities for employment. As our results show, the estimated coefficients do not always agree, thus underlining the need to make this distinction. Following conventional practice, the cluster-specific poverty line was set at half the sample median of per capita expenditures in the cluster. The large sample ensured that the number of observations in each cluster was never too small to rule out meaningful statistical inference. The idea of 'relative poverty', implicit in setting the poverty line at a fraction of the sample median, was favoured over 'absolute poverty'since the latter requires accurate estimates of subsistence expenditures in the two countries, which were not readily available. Note, incidentally, that the use of cluster dummies, instead of cluster poverty, did not yield significant or sensible estimates since such dummies were controlling for a lot of other heterogeneous factors between clusters, besides poverty. Moreover, while it is easy to interpret the estimated coefficient of the cluster poverty variable, this is not so for the cluster dummy variable.

This study also provides evidence from Nepal and Pakistan on the impact of inequality[4] and credit constraints on child labour and child schooling. There has been much discussion recently on these variables in the context of child labour [Jafarey and Lahiri: 2000a, Ranjan: 2001], but relatively, little empirical evidence exists on their impact on child employment. Inequality could have an impact on child labour principally in three ways. First, high inequality provides demand for child labour from the more affluent households. Second, such inequality offers a pool of child labour supply from among children in the less affluent households. Third, high inequality implies that credit is siphoned off to the more affluent leaving the less affluent households to rely on child labour to smooth their income fluctuations. Ray (2000c) reports on Indian NSS data a V-shaped relationship between child labour force participation rate and inequality. Swinnerton and Rogers (1999) demonstrate analytically the importance of inequality in explaining child labour and provide support to the view of Grootaert and Kanbur (1995:198) that "general economic development, equally distributed, is the best and most sustainable way of reducing child labour". Ranjan (2001) derives analytically a positive relationship between inequality in the distribution of income and the incidence of child labour. Inequality of income leads to severe credit constraints.

Ranjan (2001), and Jafarey and Lahiri (2000a) highlight the pivotal role that increased credit availability can play in switching children from labour market to schooling. If, as some argue, households look to income from child labour to compensate for income shocks and lift them out of poverty, then improved credit provision can play a significant role in keeping children in schooling and out of employment. As Ranjan (2001) and Jafarey and Lahiri (2000a) both argue, the link between credit markets and child labour may result in trade sanctions, currently touted as a way of reducing child labour, making matters worse by driving the children from credit-starved households on to the labour market. This calls for much needed empirical evidence that this study provides, on the impact of credit availability on child labour, and child schooling. Similar to the distinction made earlier in the context of poverty, we distinguish between cluster level credit, measured by credit received per household in the cluster, and household level credit recorded by the amount of net credit inflow into the household. Analogous to the poverty case, we allow for a credit-starved household to live in a credit rich cluster and vice versa.

Another key distinguishing feature of this study is that the child labour, child schooling and poverty variables are jointly estimated using a 3SLS estimation procedure that takes note of the simultaneity of these variables. This exercise, therefore, extends Ray (2001) that assumed that the poverty variable is exogenously determined in the estimation. In this study, we pay particular attention to the interaction between a child's labour hours,' her/his schooling experience and the economic circumstances of the child, as measured by the poverty status of the household that the child resides in. As the results reported later show, the endogeneity of poverty and its joint estimation with child labour and child schooling provides some interesting empirical insights into the nature of interaction between these three crucial ingredients of child welfare. Moreover, there are some significant differences between the 3SLS estimates for boys and girls. As the present results confirm, there is a strong gender dimension in the results on child labour and child schooling that should be recognised in policy analysis.

The joint estimation of the child labour hours, child schooling years and the household's poverty status variables, that we report later needs to be justified. We wish to make the following comments in this context.

First, both the annual labour hours of a child and the years of schooling received by that child are long-run decision variables. Child labour hours, especially the annual hours used here, reflect long-term parental considerations, socio-economic factors and institutional features, just as in the case of child schooling. For example, there is now unpublished evidence that suggests that the children of parents who themselves worked long hours in their youth tend to work longer hours than other children. The situation is analogous to the case of child schooling since children of better-educated parents tend to stay in schooling longer and drop out much later than other children. Moreover, given the cross-sectional nature of the data sets used here, the household's poverty variable reflects the longer-term economic status of the household.

Second, while the endogeneity of child labour and child schooling is quite obvious, this may not be true of the household poverty variable, especially vis-a-vis child schooling. We provide three principal reasons for this treatment.

1. Child labour earnings, especially if the child is working longer hours can, in theory, alter the household's economics. Since child labour and child schooling are jointly determined, the potential dependence of household poverty on the former automatically translates into a dependence on the latter. The latter link appears more clearly from the tradeoff between child labour and child schooling that we report later. If a household has to depend on more child labour hours and earnings to move out of poverty, it must depend on less child schooling as well.
2. As Ray (2000b) has shown, there is evidence of a close nexus between the adult female and child labour markets in Pakistan. Consequently, changes in-child schooling will have an impact on adult female labour hours through the child labour hours and this, in turn, will alter the household's economic status.
3. Besides child labour and child schooling, there are a host of demographic and socio-economic factors that can and do affect the household's economic status, thus, justifying the present treatment of household poverty as an endogenous regressor.

The above discussion raises the issue of robustness of the qualitative results to a departure from the 3 SLS, simultaneous equations estimation methodology proposed above. The paper provides evidence on this by reporting the results of multinomial logit estimation that analyses child labour and child schooling participation rather than the annual labour hours and schooling years respectively. We allow four possibilities: (1) the child attends school but does not work, (2) combines schooling with employment, (3) does neither, and (4) works but does not attend school. The paper provides comparative evidence between Nepal and Pakistan on the impact of some key child and household level variables on the probability of the child being in one of these four states.

The rest of this paper is organised as follows. Section II discusses the methodology, describes the data sets and focuses on some of its summary features. The empirical results are presented and discussed in Section III.We end on the concluding note of Section IV which spells out the policy implications of the results of our study.

II

Methodology and Data

The empirical exercise is based on the simultaneous equations estimation, using three stage least squares (3SLS), of a set of three equations, namely, the annual labour hours of the child, the years of Child Schooling and Child Poverty Status schooling experience of that child and the poverty status (l = poor, 0 = non-poor) of the household that the child belongs to. The 3SLS estimation procedure not only takes note of the joint endogeneity of these three variables but also recognises the mutual interaction between the equations through allowing a non-diagonal covariance matrix of the errors of the estimated system. A key feature of this exercise is that we examine the impact of a child's current school attendance on her/his labour hours. This last aspect of our empirical exercise is of considerable policy significance since many have argued that compulsory schooling or, alternatively, encouraging schooling via an enrolment subsidy is a useful vehicle for reducing child labour.[5]

The Nepalese data on child labour comes from the Nepal Living Standards Survey (NLSS) conducted in June 1995 by the Household Survey Unit of the Central Bureau of Statistics (CBS). The main objective of the NLSS is to collect data from Nepalese households and provide information to the government to monitor progress in national living standards and to evaluate the impact of various policies and programmes on the living conditions of the population. The sample size for the NLSS is 2,288 households. The Pakistani child labour data came from the Pakistan Integrated Household Survey (PIHS), carried out in 1991 when PIHS teams visited 4,800 households residing in 300 urban and rural communities.

The data on child labour force participation and on the child's labour hours were obtained by combining information from a number of sources. The information on wages, especially child wages, was often not readily available or simply not available at all. In the latter case, we used imputed wages based on the mean wage rates of the cluster of residence of the household. This introduced a high degree of arbitrariness in the constructed wage data, which suggests that the wage coefficients should be interpreted with considerable care.

Tables 2 and 3 present respectively the age-specific participation rates of children in the two countries in the labour market and in schooling. The following remarks apply. In both countries, the child participation rate in the labour market increases with child age. The sharp gender disparity in the child's labour market participation rate in Pakistan contrasts sharply with a more even gender balance in case of Nepal. It is possible to compare other key characteristics of the two data sets by looking at sample means (Table 4). A typical Pakistani household contains more children than a typical Nepalese household. A much larger percentage of children live below the poverty line in Pakistan than in Nepal. On average, a child works similar hours in the two countries, with the figure (372.12 annual hours) being somewhat higher in Nepal than in Pakistan (305.46 hours). While the ratio of the child's to the man's labour hours is quite similar between Nepal and Pakistan, the corresponding ratio of the child's to the woman's labour hours is sharply lower in Nepal than in Pakistan. The latter result is due to the relative lack of labour market activity by Pakistani women. It is also worth noting that in both countries a high proportion of children has never received any schooling (31.92 per cent in Pakistan, 31.12 per cent in Nepal). The evidence on India provided in Ray (2000c) suggests that this picture is true of the entire south Asian region. These percentages provide cause for considerable alarm, especially if one recalls that the comparable figure is only 2.00 in case of Peru [Ray 2000b: Table 3].

Table 2
Participation Rates (in percentages) of Children in Employment

Age	*Nepal*		*Pakistan*	
	Boys	*Girls*	*Boys*	*Girls*
10	17.60	27.80	14.90	18.70
11	22.33	28.40	16.10	19.60
12	33.30	42.20	25.40	22.80
13	36.40	42.70	30.30	21.30
14	41.30	45.40	36.30	28.30
15	48.70	55.60	36.30	28.30
16	53.50	55.40	51.20	26.70
17	52.60	53.30	48.40	25.80

Table 3
Participation Rates (in percentages) of Children in Current School Attendance

Age	*Nepal*		*Pakistan*	
	Boys	*Girls*	*Boys*	*Girls*
10	78.16	57.37	77.30	51.10
11	79.46	65.16	82.20	54.80
12	75.18	50.60	73.50	49.00
13	77.30	57.71	72.10	45.30
14	67.69	48.09	66.80	39.00
15	61.10	43.03	56.90	33.40
16	44.60	40.50	50.70	28.10
17	46.90	38.00	48.80	28.20

Table 4
Household Characteristics of Nepal and Pakistan (Sample Means)

Characteristic	*Nepal*	*Pakistan*
Number of children in the household	3.69	5.61
Ratio of girls to boys	0.47	0.48
Percentage of children living in households below the poverty linea Boys Girls		
Boys	18.23	27.11
Girls	18.15	25.57
Ratio of the most educated woman's educational experience to that of the most educated man in the household	0.54	0.39
Ratio of the child's to the man's educational experience	0.59	0.68
Ratio of child's to the woman's educational experience	0.85	1.75
Average age of child	12.43	13.16
Percentage of households that are female headed	11.24	1.87
Percentage of children living in households with electricity	24.58	76.45
Percentage of children living in urban areas	80.41	53.67
Ratio of child's labour hours to man's labour hours	0.16	0.13
Ratio of child's Jabour hours to woman's labour hours	0.23	0.60
Percentage of children involved in child labour	36.49	27.92

Characteristic	*Nepal*	*Pakistan*
Percentage of children who have never received any schooling	31.12	31.92
Atkinson Index (E = 2.0) of Cluster Inequality	0.281	0.277
Percentage of households where at least one adult works	97.94	88.00
Percent of children who are currently attending school	62.74	55.25
Annual labour hours worked by a child	372.12	305.46
Years of schooling received by a child	3.28	3.97

Notes: (a) The poverty line is set at 50 per cent of the median non-child household income per adult equivalent in the sample.
(b) Measured in years of schooling.

Source: *Nepal Living Standards Survey* (NLSS) 1995 *and Pakistan Integrated Household Survey* 1991.

III

Results

The 3SLS estimates of child labour hours, schooling experience and the child's poverty status equations are presented in Table 5 (Nepal) and Table 6 (Pakistan). These Tables report, for each country, the estimates obtained by pooling the observations for all children with the child gender-dummy capturing the heterogeneity between boys and girls. The gender-disaggregated estimates are presented later. While the numbers in these Tables are worth examining individually and provide considerable empirical insights into child labour and child schooling in each country, a comparison between them helps to keep these results in perspective by establishing the robustness or otherwise between countries of the principal qualitative results.

Table 5
3SLS Estimates of Child Labour Hours, Child Schooling Years and Child Poverty Status!' in Nepal!

Labour Hours		*Schooling Years*		*Povertv Statusb*	
Variable	*Coefficient Estimate*	*Variable*	*Coefficient Estimate*	*Variable*	*Coefficient Estimate*
Child Characteristics		**Child Characteristics**		**Child Characteristics**	
Currently Attending	-389.66d	Annual Child Labour	-0.01d	Annual Child Labour	0.00
School (0=no, 1=yes)	(25.75)	Hours	(0.00)	Hours	(0.00)
Age of Child	5.31	Age of Child	0.52	Years of Schooling	-0.02c
	(94.41)		(0.81)	Experience	(0.01)
(Age of Child) 2	0.63	(Age of Child) 2	0.01	Child Gender	-0.04d
	(3.78)		(0.03)	(0 = boy, 1 = girl)	(0.01)
Child Gender	-60.84d	Child Gender	-0.93d	Child Wage	-0.00
(0 = boy, 1 = girl)	(21.21)	(0 = boy, 1 = girl)	(0.18)		
Child Wage	13.43d	Child Wage	0.11d		
	(.46)		(0.01)		(0.00)
Family Characteristics		**Family Characteristics**		**Family Characteristics**	
Household Poverty	705.60d	Household Poverty	4.09c		
	(207.46)		(1.78)		

Contd....

Labour Hours		*Schooling Years*		*Povertv Statusb*	
Variable	*Coefficient Estimate*	*Variable*	*Coefficient Estimate*	*Variable*	*Coefficient Estimate*
1Region of Residence (1 = urban, 2 = rural)	21.77	Region of Residence (1 = urban, 2 = rural)	-0.15	Region of Residence (1 = urban, 2 = rural)	-0.13d
	(64.32)		(0.55)		. (0.04)
No. of Children	-15.75d	No of Children	-0.16d	No of Children	0.03d
	(5.49)		(0.05)		(0.00)
No. of Adults	9.34	No of Adults	-0.01	No of Adults	0.00
	(6.04)		(0.05)		(0.00)
Gender of Household Head (0 = male, 1 = female)	-54.49	Gender of Household Head (0 = male, 1 = female)	-0.30	Gender of Household Head (0 = male, 1 = female)	0.03
	(36.84)		(0.32)		(0.02)
Age of Household Head	-1.33	Age of Household Head	-0.01	Age of Household Head	-0.00
	(0.87)		(0.01)		(0.00)
Years of Education of Most Educated Male Member	-3.38	Years of Education.of Most Educated Male Member	0.12d	Years of Education of Most Educated Male Member	-0.Q1d
	(3.20)		(0.03)		(0.00)
Years of Education of Most Educated Female Member	-5.28	Years of Education of Most Educated Female Member	0.11d	Years of Education of Most Educated Female Member	-0.00
	(3.50)		(0.03)		(0.00)
At least one adult works (0 = no, 1 = yes)	154.60	At least one adult works (0 = no, 1 = yes)	2.01d	At least one adult works (0-= no, 1 = yes)	0.14c
	(85.14)		(0.74)		(0.06)
Maximum wage earned by the Male Members	-0.24	Maximum wage earned by the Male Members	-0.00	Maximum wage earned by the Male Members	-O.OOd
	(0.46)		(0.00)		(0.00)
(Maximum wage earned by the Male Members) 2	0.00	(Maximum wage earned by the Male Members) 2	0.00	(Maximum wage earned by the Male Members) 2	O.OOd
	- (0.00)		(0.00)		(0.00)
Maximum Wage earned by the Female Members	-0.68c	Maximum Wage earned by the Female Members	-0.00	Maximum Wage earned by the Female Members	0.00
	(0.31)		(0.00)		(0.00)
Credit Received by the Household	-0.00	Credit Received by the Household	-0.00	Credit Received by the Household	0.00
	(0.00)		(0.00)		(0.00)
Cluster/Community Cha racteristies		**Cluster/Community Characteristics**		**Cluster/Community Characteristics**	
Atkinson Inequality	-602.52	Atkinson Inequality	1.90	Atkinson Inequality	3.04d
	(1061.24)		(9.13)		(0.69)
Atkinson Inequality 2	946.75	Atkinson Inequality 2	-4.18	Atkinson Inequality 2	-4.66d
	(1730.57)		(14.88)		(1.13)
Cluster Poverty	34.70	Cluster Poverty	0.78	Cluster Poverty	1.18
	(129.35)		(1.11)		(0.08)
Cluster Credit Availability	0.00	Cluster Credit Availability	0.00	Cluster Credit Availability	0.00
	(0.00)		(0.00)		(0.00)
Water Supply (1 = yes, 0 = no)	6.01	*Water* Supply (1 = yes, 0 = no)	0.04	Water Supply (1 = yes, 0 = no)	0.04c
	(24.91)		(0.21)		(0.02)
Electricity Supply (1 = yes, 0 = no)	-48.74	Electricity Supply (1 = yes, 0 = no)	-0.39	Electricity Supply (1 = yes, 0 = no)	-0.03
	(34.59)		(.030)		(0.02)

Notes: a Standard errors in brackets. b Poverty status = 1 if the child comes from a 'poor' household, 0 otherwise. c Significant at 5 per cent level; d Significant at 1 per cent level.

Table 6
3SLS Estimates of Child Labour Hours, Child Schooling years and Child Poverty Status in Pakistan

Labour Hours Variable	*Coefficient Estimate*	*Schooling Years Variable*	*Coefficient Estimate*	*Poverty Status Variable*	*Coefficient Estimate*
Child Characteristics		**Child Characteristics**		**Child Characteristics**	
Currently Attending School (0= no. 1 yea	-506.53^{d}	Annual child labours hours	-.01^{d}	Annual child labours hours	-0.00
	(26.50)		(0.00)		(.00)
Age of Child	-89.91	Age of Child	.02	Years of schooling experience	-.01^{d}
	(108.54)		(.96)		(.00)
(Age of Child)^2	5.05	(Age of Child)^2	.04		
	(4.36)		(.04)		
Child gender	-225.73^{d}	Child gender	-2.26	Child gender	-0.02
(0=boy,1=girl)	(23.51)	(0=boy,1=girl)	(.20)	(0=boy,1=girl)	(.01)
Child wage	22.39^{d}	Child wage	0.18^{d}	Child wage	.00
	2.33		(.02)		(.00)
Family characterstics		**Family characterstics**		**Family characteristics**	
Household poverty	-444.11^{c}	Household poverty	5.92^{d}		
	206.56		(1.82)	Region of residence	.04^{d}
Region of residence	52.50	Region of residence	.59^{c}	(1=urban,2=rural)	(.01)
(1=urban,2=rural)	(27.06)	(1=urban,2=rural)	(.24)	No of children	.02^{d}
No of children	-0.55	No of children	-.00		(.00)
	(4.41)		(.04)	No of adults	-.01^{d}
No of adults	-19.65^{d}	No of adults	-.25^{d}		(.00)
	(6.23)		(.06)		
Gender of household head	86.22	Gender of household head	.90	Gender of household head	.06
(0=male, 1=female)	(84.06)	(0=male, 1=female)	(.74)	(0=male, 1=female)	(.03)
Age of hosehold head	2.19^{c}	Age of hosehold head	.02	Age of hosehold head	.00
	(1.01)		(.01)		(.00)
Years of education of most	-1.04	Years of education of most	.07d	Years of education of most	-.00^{c}
Educated male member	2.67	Educated male member	(.02)	Educated male member	(.00)
Years of education of most	8.71c	Years of education of most	.16d	Years of education of most	.00
Educated female member	(3.44)	Educated female member	(.03)	Educated female member	(.00)
At least one adult works	170.68^{d}	At least one adult works	1.44^{d}	At least one adult works	.07d
(0=no,1=yes)	(39.30)	(0=no,1=yes)	(.36)	(0=no,1=yes)	(.02)
Maximum wage earned by the	-3.88	Maximum wage earned by the	-.03	Maximum wage earned by the	-.00
Male members	(2.24)	Male members	(.02)	Male members	(-.00)
Maximum wage earned by the	.03	Maximum wage earned by the	.00	Maximum wage earned by the	-.00
Male members^2	(0.03)	Male members^2	(.00)	Male members^2	(.00)
Maximum wage earned by the	-5.78^{d}	Maximum wage earned by the	-.05^{d}	Maximum wage earned by the	-.00

Labour Hours		*Schooling Years*		*Poverty Status*	
Variable	*Coefficient Estimate*	*Variable*	*Coefficient Estimate*	*Variable*	*Coefficient Estimate*
Female members	(1.59)	Female members	(.01)	Female members	(.00)
Credit received by the household	-.001 (.001)	Credit received by the household	.00 (.00)	Credit received by the household	0.00[c] (.00)
Cluster/community characteristics		**Cluster/community characteristics**		**Cluster/community characteristics**	
Atkinson inequality	-786.91[d] (258.11)	Atkinson inequality	-6.48[d] (2.31)	Atkinson inequality	.17 (.10)
(Atkinson inequality)^2	1027.71[d]	(Atkinson inequality)^2	8.63[d]	(Atkinson inequality)^2	-.19
Cluster poverty	(319.87) 145.11	Cluster poverty	(2.86) 1.56	Cluster poverty	(.13) (.03)
Cluster credit availability	0.00 (0.00)	Cluster credit availability	(.80) (.00)	Cluster credit availability	-.00
Water supply (1=yes,0=no)	-5.55 (6.52)	Water supply (1=yes,0=no)	-.07 (.06)	Water supply (1=yes,0=no)	.00 (.00)
Electricity supply (1=yes, 0=no)	15.77 (54.58)	Electricity supply (1=yes, 0=no)	.55 (.48)	Electricity supply (1=yes, 0=no)	-.00 (.02)

Notes: a. Standard errors in brackets.
b. Poverty status = 1 if the child comes from a 'poor' household, 0 otherwise.
c. Significant at 5 per cent level.
d. Significant at 1 per cent level.

The following features are worth noting from these tables.

1. In both countries, the current school attendance by a child significantly and sharply reduces her/his labour hours-by 390 labour hours annually in Nepal, 506 in Pakistan. Again, in both countries, a ceteris paribus increase in the child's labour market activity has a significantly adverse impact on her schooling experience. The trade off between child employment and child schooling is clearly established from these Tables. The policy implication is clear-compulsory schooling or measures such as free school meals that encourage enrolment provide effective means of reducing child labour hours.
2. In both countries, boys work significantly longer hours in market activities than girls, though the gender disparity is much more in Pakistan (225 annual labour hours) than in Nepal (60 hours). Similarly, girls experience significantly less schooling than the boys in both countries. However, the impact of household size and composition of child labour and child schooling varies considerably between two countries. For example, a ceteris paribus increase in the number of children in the household significantly reduces both the labour hours and the schooling experience of the child in Nepal but has little impact in Pakistan. Household credit variables have little impact in either country, contrary to the claims made in the analytical literature. This suggests that households do not necessarily use the credit to smooth their income fluctuations as a substitute to their income from child labour.

3. An interesting result with considerable policy significance that seems to hold for both countries is that while rising levels of adult education significantly and positively influence child schooling, its anticipated negative impact on child labour is considerably weaker in absolute magnitude to the point of statistical in significance in several cases. This result, which was observed in Ray (2001), stems from the joint endogeneity of child employment and child schooling. It suggests that the previously observed negative impact of rising adult education on child labour (Ray 2000a,b) worked through the positive impact of adult education on child schooling and the subsequent trade off between child schooling and child labour. Once the latter has been incorporated in the estimation, as in this study, the residual impact of adult education on child's labour market activity is quite limited. This points, once again, to enhancement of child schooling as the core strategy for making a dent on the problem of child labour. Such an enhancement can be made by increasing the benefits and relevance of schooling in the eyes of the poor, through more non-formal education, and by increased public awareness, as discussed below.
4. Household poverty, though significant determinant of child labour and child schooling, does not always have an impact on these dependent variables in the manner expected. However, it does explain longer child hours in case of Nepal and less child schooling in case of Pakistan. In contrast cluster poverty, that is, economic environment that the child lives in, does not have any impact on her/his employment or schooling. In both the countries, presence of one or more employed adults in the household adds to the schooling experience in children.
5. Of particular interest in these estimates is the impact of cluster inequality on the labour hours and schooling of children residing in the cluster. Inequality has strong U–shaped impact on child labour hours and child schooling in Pakistan, but the effect is considerably weakened to the point of statistical insignificance in case of Nepal. In other words, Ahmed (1999) observation that high inequality is a cause of child labour is confirmed by the evidence for Pakistan, but the supporting evidence is not so strong in case of Nepal. However, as we report below, the gender disaggregated estimates for Nepal show much stronger support for the V-shaped impact of inequality on labour hours in case of Nepalese girls.
6. A distinctive feature of this study is the endogenising of the poverty variable and its joint estimation with the child labour, child-schooling equations. The coefficient estimates of the poverty equation are, therefore, of special interest. In both countries, a child who has, ceteris paribus, more schooling experience comes from a more affluent household than one with less schooling. In contrast, neither a change in the annual child labour hours nor the child wage rate significantly alters the economic background of the child. Both countries also show that a child Iiving in a household containing a large number of children is more likely to be living in poverty than a child residing in a household with

fewer children. Ceteris paribus, while the rural child in Pakistan is poorer than the urban child the reverse is the case in Nepal. In both countries, especially in Nepal, cluster inequality has an inverted V-shaped impact on the child's poverty status. In other words, as cluster inequality increases, the child's poverty status initially worsens but improves sharply thereafter as the negative quadratic coefficient dominates the positive linear coefficient. The strong significance of the positive cluster poverty co-efficient estimate confirms that, in both countries, a child from a poorer cluster is much more likely to be living in poverty than a child from a more affluent cluster. In both countries, especially in Nepal, rising levels of adult male education play a strong role in ameliorating the poverty of the child.

The above discussion overlooks possible child gender differences in the estimates. To examine such differences, Tables 7 and 8 present the gender disaggregated 3SLS estimates of child labour hours and child schooling years in Nepal and Pakistan respectively. We have, for space reasons, omitted the corresponding gender disaggregated estimates of the child's poverty status equation, though these are available on request.

Table 7
Gender Disaggregated 3SLS Estimates' of Child Labour Hours and Child Schooling Years in Nepal

Variable	*Labour Hours*		*Schooling Years*	
	Boys	*Girls*	*Boys*	*Girls*
Child Characteristics				
Currently Attending School	-455.68[d]	-302.77[d]		
(0 = no, 1 = yes)	(32.45)	(44.92)	-	-
Annual Child Labour Hours	-	-	-.01[d]	-.01[d]
			(.00)	(.00)
Age of Child	-46.47	93.45	.43	1.23
	(117.70)	(138.71)	(.89)	(1.02)
(Age of Child)2	2.49	-3.10	.01	-.03
	(4.71)	(5.56)	(.04)	(.04)
Child Wage	15.15[d]	13.15[d]	0.11[d]	0.10[d]
	(.65)	(.69)	(.01)	(0.02)
Family Characteristics				
Household Poverty	-198.10	2661.16[d]	-2.82	18.90[d]
	(264.71)	(297.53)	(1.99)	(2.21)
Region of Residence				
(1 = urban, 2 = rural)	-72.04	136.12	-.93	1.13,
	(78.22)	(105.25)	(.59)	(.78)
No of Children	-9.57	-24.50d	-.09	-.23d
	(7.18)	(8.26)	(.05)	(.06)
No of Adults	4.75	10.34	-.08	.01
	(7.89)	(9.07)	(.06)	(.07)
Gender of Household Head	-129.65[d]	7.48	-.76c	.04
(0 = male, 1 = female)	(45.27)	(60.11)	(.35)	(.44)

Variable	*Labour Hours*		*Schooling Years*	
	Boys	*Girls*	*Boys*	*Girls*
Age of Household Head	-1.46	-1.31	-0.01	-0.02
	(1.09)	(1.37)	(:01)	(.01)
Years of Education of Most Educated	2.81	-3.32	0.31[d]	-0.01
Male Member	(4.56)	(4.59)	(.03)	(.03)
Years of Education of Most Educated	-5.34	-9.74	-.00	.33[d]
Female Member	(4.01)	(6.88)	(.03)	(.06)
At least one adult works	198.48c	86.04	1.69[c]	2.11
(0 = no, 1 = yes)	(98.21)	(149.10)	(.76)	(1.10)
Maximum Wage Earned by the	-1.55d		.94	-.01[d]
Male Members	(.60)	(.69)	(.00)	(.00)
(Maximum Wage Earned by the	.00[c]	-.00	.00[c]	.00
Male Members)2	(.00)	(.00)	(.00)	(.00)
Maximum Wage Earned by the	-.43	-.59	.00	-.01
Female Members	(.38)	(.50)	(.00)	(.00)
Credit Received by the Household	-0.00	-0.00	.00	.00
	(.00)	(.00)	(.00)	(.00)
Cluster/Community Characteristics				
Atkinson Inequality	1706.16	-3314.50[c]	21.32[c]	-24.74[c]
	(1343.98)	(1664.36)	(10.11)	(12.54)
(Atkinson Inequality)2	-2497.94	5150.88	-32.88[c]	37.97
	(2210.83)	(2695.11)	(16.63)	(20.26)
Cluster Poverty	537.22d	-630.81[d]	3.77[d]	-4.14[d]
	(160.17)	(207.79)	(1.25)	(1.56)
Cluster Credit Availability	.00	.00	.00	.00
	(.00)	(.00)	(.00)	(.00)
Water Supply				
(1 = yes, 0 = no)	-64.99[c]	65.04	-.44	.49
	(30.66)	(37.40)	(.24)	(.28)
Electricity Supply	-51.56	-42.26	-.42	-.33
(1 = yes, 0 = no)	(43.76)	(54.08)	(.33)	(.40)

Table 8
Gender Disaggregated 3SLS Estimates of Child Labour Hours and Child Schooling Years in Pakistan

Variable	*Labour Hours*		*Schooling Years*	
	Boys	*Girls*	*Boys*	*Girls*
Child Characteristics				
Currently Attending School	-833.56d	-21 0.34d	-	-
(0 = no, 1 = yes)	(31.26)	(43.12)		
Annual Child labour Hours	-	-	-.OOd	-.02d
			(.00)	(.00)
Age of Child	-35.34	-110.09	1.03	-1.82
	(125.71)	(174.35)	(.74)	(3.51)
(Age of Child)2	3.41	5.26	-0.00	.11
	(5.04)	(7.00)	(.03)	(.14)
Child Wage	22.53d	16.21d	O.11d	.32d
	(2.34)	(4.97)	(.02)	(.12)

Contd...

Variable	*Labour Hours*		*Schooling Years*	
	Boys	*Girls*	*Boys*	*Girls*
Family Characteristics				
Household Poverty	-47.53	-310.61	-1.10	-7.31
	(223.75)	(362.79)	(1.32)	(7.25)
Region of Residence	-19.74	82.31	-.12	1.93e
(1 = urban. 2 = rural)	(31.24)	(43.75)	(.18)	(.90)
No of Children	4.90	-7.9.5	.03	-.16
	(5.13)	(7.07)	(.03)	(.14)
No of Adults	-23.60d	-14.16	-.20d	-.37
	(7.42)	(9.73)	(.04)	(.20)
Gender of Household Head	44.84	118.38	.41	2.56
(0 = male, 1 = female)	(92.34)	(143.79)	(.55)	(2.88)
Age of Household Head	-.55	5.49d	.00	.11d
	(1.17)	(1.63)	(.00)	(.04)
Years of Education of Most Educated	5.90	-5.60	.12d	-.04
Male Member	(3.09)	(4.27)	(.02)	(.09)
Years of Education of Most Educated	5.66	3.99	.10d	.19.
Female Member	(3.97)	(5.59)	(.02)	(.11)
At least one adult works	182.10d	147.24[e]	1.07d	2.78[c]
(0 = no, 1 = yes)	(46.53)	(61.79)	(.28)	(1.41)
Maximum Wage Earned by the	-6.11e	-3.12	-.03	-.05
Male Members	(2.62)	(3.57)	(.02)	(.07)
(Maximum Wage Earned by the	.03	.05	.00	.00
Male Members)2	(.03)	(.05)	(.00)	(.00)
Maximum Wage Earned by the	-7.38d	-.71	-.03d	-.03
Female Members	(1.72)	(2.96)	(.01)	(.06)
Credit Received by the Household	-.00	-.00	.00	.00
	(.00)	(.00)	(.00)	(.00)
Cluster/Community Characteristics				
Atkinson Inequality	-194.74	-1400.89d	-.23	-27.92[d]
	(297.30)	(416.21)	(1.76)	(10.01)
(Atkinson Ineejuality)2	339.64	1652.54d	.72	33.32d
	(369.05)	(515.18)	(2.18)	(12.13)
Cluster Poverty	-151.77	429.91d	-.41	8.48[e]
	(102.40)	(147.23)	(.60)	(3.52)
Cluster Credit Availability	-.00	.00	.00	.00
	(.00)	(.00)	(.00)	(.00)
Water Supply	1.68	-7.44	-.01	-.18
(1 = yes, 0 = no)	(7.53)	(10.48)	(.04)	(.21)
Electricity Supply	-66.89	106.04	.32	2.24
(1 = yes, 0 = no)	(62.59)	(88.30)	(.37)	(1.80)

Notes: a Standard errors in brackets.
b The estimates of the poverty status equation are available on request.
c Significant at 5 per cent level.
d Significant at 1 per cent level.

The trade-off between child labour hours and the child's school attendance, reported and discussed earlier, holds strongly for both boys and girls in each country. It is interesting to observe, however, that in both countries the current school attendance of a child reduces that child's labour hours by a much smaller amount for girls than for boys. This is particularly striking in Pakistan, where the reduction in annual labour hours on account of school attendance is 834 hours for boys but only 210 hours for girls. This gender disparity is explained by the fact that school attendance comes at the expense of mainly non-market (mostly domestic) hours for girls, but market hours for boys. Household poverty has a significantly positive impact on labour hours of girls in Nepal but not for boys in that country. Cluster poverty has a strong impact on the labour hours of boys and girls in Nepal but in exactly opposite directions. The V-shaped impact of cluster inequality on child labour hours holds more for girls than for boys in both countries. The result, noted earlier, that rising adult education levels have a much weaker impact on the child's labour hours than on her schooling experience holds for both boys and girls in each country. The credit variables, at both household and cluster levels, register very little impact on child labour hours and schooling experience, irrespective of the gender of the child.

Before concluding this section, we report the results of the multinomial logit estimation. Table 9 presents the marginal probabilities implied by the multinomial logit estimates of the four choice outcomes (1)-(4) for a selection of comparable variables between the two countries. The multinomial logit estimates will be made available to interested readers. The marginal probabilities show the marginal changes in the probabilities of the four outcomes when the corresponding child, family or community characteristic changes by one unit. In both countries, older children are more likely to combine schooling with employment. However, the impact of child age on the probabilities of the other outcomes varies between the two countries. Again, in both countries, girls are more likely than boys to be neither in schooling nor in employment, and less likely to combine schooling with employment. In both Nepal and Pakistan, girls are much less likely than boys to be exclusively in schooling with no outside work involvement. The effect of child gender is generally stronger in Pakistan than in Nepal. The effect of urbanisation on child labour is also quite similar between the two countries. The urban child is more likely than the rural child to be in the 'school only' category and less likely to be in the 'work only' category in both countries. A significant point of departure is the 'neither school nor work category', namely, those that have been described as 'no-where children' in the south Asian context [Chaudhuri and Wilson: 2000]. In Pakistan, such children are less likely to be found in urban areas, more likely in the rural. The reverse is indicated for Nepal. Household poverty tends to have a detrimental impact on child schooling in both countries by discouraging a child from attending school with or without simultaneous child employment. Household poverty encourages a child to be in the 'work only category' in both countries. The marginal probabilities show, however, that the poverty effect on the four outcomes is much stronger in Nepal than in Pakistan. This is consistent with the 3 SLS estimates of the child labour hours equation, presented in Tables 5 and 6, which show that household poverty impacts on child labour hours in Nepal much more strongly than in Pakistan, and in the expected direction, unlike in Pakistan. The positive role that adult education can play in encouraging schooling at the expense of child labour is seen from the fact that children from households with better educated female adults are more likely to be in the 'school only' category and less likely to be in the 'work only' category than other children. A comparison of the female education marginal probabilities shows that the impact of increasing female education on child behaviour is much stronger in Nepal than in Pakistan, similar to the impact of household poverty.

Table 9
Multinomial Logit Marginal Probabilities for a Selection of Variables

Variable	*Nepal*				*Pakistan*			
	School Only	*Both School and Work*	*Neither School Nor Work*	*Work Only*	*School Only*	*Both School and Work*	*Neither School Nor Work*	*Work Only*
Age	Q.0827	0.0330	0.0125	Q.0372	0.0275	0.0412	Q.1173	0.048
Gin	Q.2233	Q.0948	0.1426	0.1755	. Q.2363	Q.0754	0.2858	0.0251
Urban	0.1854	Q.1712	0.0741	-.0883	0.2029	Q.0412	-0.1055	Q.056
Nchild	Q.0168	0.0132	0.0016	0.0020	- 0.0061	0.0002	0.0035	0.002,
Nadult	Q.0017	Q.0033	0.0074	Q.0024	0.0246	Q.0019	Q.0036	Q.01
FHH	Q.0619	0.0142	0.0658	Q.0181	Q.0468	0.0207	0.0154	0.010
Headage	-0.0012	-0.0002	0.0015	-0.0001	Q.0012	-0.0001	0.0007	0.000
Maxfemed	0.0679	0.0122	Q.0285	Q.0516	0.0283	-0.0009	Q.01O4	-Q.016
Pov	-0.8625	-2223	0.6801	0.4047	Q.1144	-0.0225	0.0890	0.047

Notes: Age = Age 01 Child; Girl", 1, jlgirl, 0 ilboy; Urban = 1, if child resides in urban area, 0 ilchildresid in rural area; Nchild = no 01 children in the household; Nadult = no 01 adults in the househo FHH = 1 if child belongs to a female headed household, 0 otherwise; Headage = Age of househl head; MAXFEMED = years 01 education 01 the most educated female in the household of the child Pov = 1 if the child resides in a poor household, 0 otherwise.

IV

Conclusions

While there is universal agreement about the harmful effects of child labour, there is not much consensus on effective ways of dealing this phenomenon. Proposed action plans range from legislative measures that ban child labour to concerted international trade sanctions by developed countries against the import of products made by underage children in developing countries. The linkage of child labour, under the guise of 'labour standards', with trade has led to the hijacking of this issue by the WTO from child welfare agencies such as the UNICEF and the ILO. The recent international outcry over child labour has provoked talk of measures designed to satisfy several lobby groups, not all of whom are directly interested in the welfare of the working children in third world countries. There has not been much attempt, until recently, to examine systematically the causes of child labour with a view to identifying factors that could lead to its reduction and eventual elimination. That is now changing with a proliferation of empirical studies on child labour. These have either taken the form of case studies of a particular region inside a country with high incidence of child labour or they involve econometric investigations based on sample survey data containing information on child labour and child schooling. The present study, which belongs to the latter tradition, compares the results of two countries (Nepal and Pakistan) from one of the poorest regions (south Asia), which accounts for a significant proportion of child labour in the world.

This study has some special features that distinguish it from previous investigations. First, we distinguish between household level and cluster-level poverty in examining the importance of poverty as a determinant of child labour. The significance of this distinction is evident from the fact that the two poverty variables do not always agree on the nature of their impact on child labour or child schooling. Second, this study provides evidence on the impact of inequality on child labour and child schooling, and examines the relative importance of inequality vis-à-vis poverty as a determinant. Third, the study examines the impact of borrowings, both at household and cluster levels, on child labour and child schooling. While there has been much analytical work and related discussion of the inequality and credit variables in the context of child labour, there has not been much empirical evidence to guide policy action in this regard. Finally, and quite crucially, we report the results of simultaneous estimation of child labour hours, years of child schooling and the child's poverty status using a framework that recognises their joint endogeneity. The endogeneity of child poverty marks a significant point of departure from previous studies.

An important finding of this paper, arising out of the joint estimation of child labour hours and child schooling experience equations, is the significant role that a child's current school attendance plays in sharply diminishing her labour hours. Alternatively, long hours spent in work by the child have a detrimental effect on her schooling. Notwithstanding the rhetoric in public statements, the record on primary schooling in south Asian countries is quite disappointing, leaving the children prone to long labour hours. Rising education levels of the adult members in the household and increased public awareness have a highly significant, positive impact on child schooling and, consequently, can play an important part in reducing the child's long labour hours. Improvements in the schooling infrastructure, by making them more relevant to the child's needs as viewed by the parent, and locating them near places of child employment will be conducive to shorter working hours and encourage combination of child labour with child schooling to a greater extent than has happened in countries such as Pakistan in relation to Latin American countries such as Peru [Ray: 2000a]. A common feature of the Nepalese and Pakistani results is the sharp gender bias in favour of boys' schooling in both countries. However, the extent of the bias is much larger in Pakistan. Government-assisted programmes such as the district primary education projects and the integrated children development schemes (ICDS) in India [Fallon and Tzannatos: 1998: 15] can play a useful role in promoting schooling. The role of household credit that is tied to its use in keeping the child in school and to compensate the household from its consequent loss of child earnings can also be very useful in this regard. The results obtained in this study warn that untied lending to the household may be misused and can make matters worse by increasing child labour.

Since tying is administratively costly and loan is fungible, a more effective strategy could be the use of mid-day school meals and enrolment subsidy that will encourage parents to keep their children in school and out of employment.

Notes

1. According to the World Bank [WDR 1995:72] "perhaps 100 million or more children in the world below the age of 15 participate in substantial economic activity at some point during the year".
2. The World Bank lists poverty as one of the main causes of child labour [WDR: 1995:72].
3. Following conventional practice based on the 'relative' view of poverty, the poverty line was defined as half the sample median of the per capita household expenditure distribution in the cluster.
4. The inequality variable used in the regressions is based on the Atkinson inequality measure with the 'inequality aversion' parameter set at 2.0.
5. See Ravallion and WOO (2000) for evidence on Bangladesh. The results of their study show, however, that an increase in school enrolment does not lead to a large reduction in child labour.

References

Addison, T., S. Bhalotra, F. Coulter and C. Heady. 1997. *Child Labour in Pakistan and Ghana: A Comparative Study,* Centre for Development Studies, University of Bath, UK.

Ahmed, I. 1999. 'Getting Rid of Child Labour', *Economic and Political Weekly:34:* 27: 1815-22.

Basu, K. 1999a. 'Child Labour: Cause, Consequence and Cure with Remarks on International Labour Standards', *Journal of Economic Literature:* 37: 3:1083-1119.

Basu, K.1999b. 'International Labour Standards, Globalisation and Marginalisation, with Special Reference to Child Labour', Mimeo, Cornell University, background paper prepared for the WDR, 2000.

Basu, K. and P.H. Van. 1998. 'The Economics of Child Labour', *American Economic Review:* 88:3: 412-27.

Bhatty, K. 1998. 'Educational Deprivation in India: A Survey of Field Investigations', *Economic and Political Weekly:* 33:27: 1731-40 and 28: 1858-69.

Chaudhuri, D.P. and E.J. Wilson. 2000. 'The Challenge of Child Labour in Rural India: A Multi-Dimensional Problem in Need of an Orchestrated Response', University of Woolongong Working Paper, No. 2000-2: Australia.

Cigno, A. and F.C. Rosati. 2000. 'Why Do Indian Children Work, and is it Bad for them'? IZA discussion paper, No. 115: Bonn.

Fallon, P. and Z. Tzannatos. 1998. *Child Labour: Issues and Directions for the World Bank.* Human Development Network, Washington DC. The World Bank.

Foster, J., J. Greerand E. Thorbecke. 1984. 'A Class of Decomposable Poverty Measures', *Econometrica:* 52: 761-66.

Grootaert, C. and R. Kanbur. 1995. 'Child Labour: An Economic Perspective', *International Labour Review:* 134: 2: 187-203.

Grootaert, C. and H. Patrinos. (eds.). 1998. *The Policy Analysis of Child Labour:* A *Comparative Study,* New York: St. Martin's Press.

Horn, P. 1995. *Children's Work and Welfare:* 1780-1890. Cambridge: OUP.

Jafarey, S. and S. Lahiri. 2000a. 'Will Trade Sanctions Reduce Child Labour? The Role of Credit Markets', discussion paper No. 500, Department of Economics, University of Essex.

Jafarey, S. and S. Lahiri. 2000b. 'Child Labour: Theory, Policy and Evidence', discussion paper no. 2000-09, University of Wales, Swansea.

Knight, W.J. 1980. *The World's Exploited Children: Growing Up Sadly,* Monograph 4, Bureau of International Labour Affairs, Washington DC:US Department of Labour.

Lieten, G.K. 2000. 'Children, Work and Education-I', *Economic and Political Weekly: 35:* 25: 2037-43.

Ranjan, P. 2001. 'Credit Constraints and the Phenomenon of Child Labour', *Journal of Development Economics:* 64: 81-102.

Ravallion, M. and Q. Wodon. 2000. 'Does Child Labour Displace Schooling? Evidence on Behavioural Responses to an Enrolment Subsidy', *The Economic Journal:* 110: C158-C175.

Ray, R. 2000a. 'Analysis of Child Labour in Peru and Pakistan: A Comparative Study', *Journal of Population Economics:* 13: 3-19.

Ray, R. 2000b. 'Child Labour, Child Schooling, and Their Interaction with Adult Labour: Empirical Evidence from Peru and Pakistan', *The World Bank Economic Revie:* 14: 2: 347-67.

Ray, R. 2000c. 'Poverty, Household Size and Child Welfare in India', *Economic and Political Weekly:* September: 3511-20.

Ray, R. 2001. 'Child Labour and Child Schooling in South Asia: A Cross Country Study of Their Determinants', mimeographed, School of Economics, University of Tasmania, September.

Swaminathan, M. 1998. 'Economic Growth and the Persistence of Child Labour: Evidence from an Indian City', *World Development:* 26: 8: 1513-28.

Swinnerton, K. and C.A. Rogers. 1999. 'The Economics of Child Labour: Comment', *American Economic Review:* 89: 1382-85.

WDR. 1995. *Workers in an Integrating World,* New York: Oxford University Press.

Weiner, M. 1991. *The Child and the State* in *India,* Princeton: Princeton University Press, N.J., USA.

The author is grateful to Geoffrey Lancaster for his research assistance for this paper. This research was supported by a grant from the Australian Research Council. The paper was first published in the *Economic and Political Weekly*: 37: 52: 2003: 5215-24. It is included here with the prior permission of the author and the Editor, *Economic and political Weekly*. Address for email correspondence: ranjan.ray@utas.edu.au

CHAPTER - FIFTEEN

Gendered Inequality in Educational Transitions

Divya Vaid

I

Introduction

Schooling has innumerable benefits, and yet a vast majority of Indian children, especially girls are deprived of these. Despite various measures undertaken by the government and local bodies to reduce the inequality in education between genders, castes, classes and religions, this inequality still persists. The aim of this paper is twofold. Firstly to highlight the factors responsible for this inequality for both boys and girls from socially deprived origins, and secondly, to highlight in particular the inequality faced by girls at each educational transition stage.

In order to tackle the issues at hand, I begin this paper with a brief overview of the persisting inequality in education in India and a summary of past research. A section follows this on the aims of the present paper and a discussion of the major hypothesis. I then lay down the methods employed to study this inequality and the data and variables used in this research. This is followed by an explanation of the models used and the results obtained. I end the paper with a discussion of these results and a summary conclusion.

> *The state shall endeavour to provide, within a period of ten years from the commencement of this Constitution, for free and compulsory education for all children until they complete the age of fourteen years.*
>
> *(Art 45, Part IV, Directive Principles of State Policy, The Constitution of India, 1951)*

A far cry from the provisions of the Constitution, India, a land of more than a billion people has slightly less than one-third of the world's non-literate population aged 15 years and above.[1] The goal of universal education, as set out in the Constitution, seems elusive even after five decades. The original period of 10 years to achieve this goal was extended to 16 years after the government failed to meet its target. The Education Commission in its report in 1966 regretted this failure on the part of the government and pushed the date further. The new target date was 1985. In 1986, the National Policy on Education extended the date by another 10 years. In 1993, the department of education, in its report 'Education For All', set the date at 2001.[2] Despite the government's apparent failure in meeting its goals,[3] a preliminary review of the 2001 Census data reveals that the last decade has seen a phenomenal rise in literacy rates in India, especially for women [see Ramachandran and Saihjee: 2002 for a discussion].

Table 1 depicts the literacy rate in India by gender. A cursory glance of these official figures seems to show that the literacy rates have risen for both men and women, but this is not enough to study how the disparity in educational attainment or the 'inequality of opportunity' between men and women has changed over the years. This is because marginal changes such as the expansion of the education system or other structural changes in the education system could confound the picture.

Table 1
Literacy Percentage 1901 to 2001[4]

*Year**	*Males Per Cent of Total Male Population*	*Females Per Cent of Total Female Population*	*Odds Ratio***
1901	9.83	0.60	11:1
1911	10.56	1.05	12:1
1921	12.21	1.81	7:1
1931	15.59	2.93	6:1
1941	24.90	7.30	4.1:1
1951	24.95	7.93	3.7:1
1961	34.44	12.95	3.5:1
1971	39.45	18.69	2.8:1
1981	56.50	29.85	3:1
1991	64.13	39.29	3:1
2001	75.85	54.16	2.7:1

Notes: * 1901-1941 figures are for undivided India, 1991 figures exclude the state of Jammu and Kashmir, where the census was not conducted due to disturbed conditions.
** Odds Ratios calculated from the official government figures.

Source: Data on Literacy from 1901-1991 is from Education Statistics; sub Table IX, Department of Education, Government of India web site. Figures for 2001 are from the provisional population totals from the Census of India, 2001, Government of India web site.

Looking at Table 1, the gender gap would appear to have increased in absolute terms. But, in order to see the real change minus these marginal changes, ie, to study the relative chances of women and men one needs to look at the odds ratios. Odds ratios are the ratios of the odds of a woman being literate as compared to a man. A comparison of the odds ratios would help to see if and how the relative chances of literacy have decreased between the two sexes, after allowing for the marginal changes.

Figure 1 is a graphical description of the odds ratios presented in Table 1. The odds of a man having greater access to education as compared to a woman have clearly declined, indicating a decline in inequality between the two genders, though in 2001, the odds still stand at 2.7: 1.The relative gender inequality in rural/urban literacy too has declined over the decades as can be seen in Figure 2 (see Appendix 1 for the table). The odds ratio for the rural gender gap has fallen from 4.6 in 1951 to 2.82 in 1997. But interestingly the gap seems to have fallen and then increased in the urban areas, it has reverted back to its 1951 level of 2.85. This has left the gap in the rural and the urban areas at approximately the same level, thus going against the widely held belief that the gender gap is higher in the rural areas.

Figure 1 then reveals that since the beginning of the century, gender inequality in literacy has declined, but more importantly what it also reveals is that the relative chances of women and men have remained fairly stable in the last few decades. What this means then is that despite the rapid expansion of the educational system and other government policies, the gender inequality seems to be persisting.

Figure 1: Odds Ratios for Male and Female Literacy 1901-2001

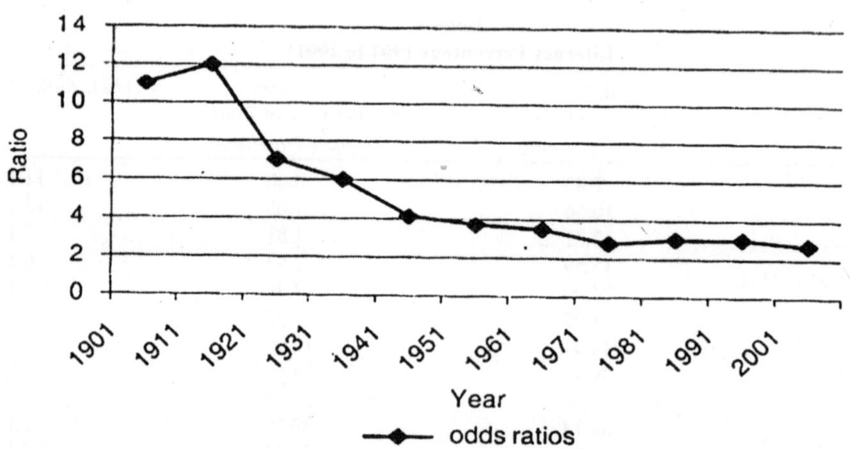

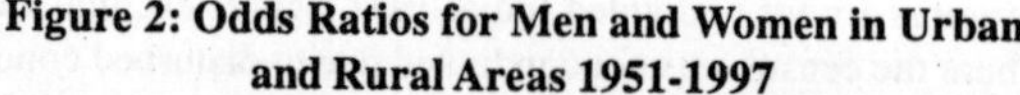

Figure 2: Odds Ratios for Men and Women in Urban and Rural Areas 1951-1997

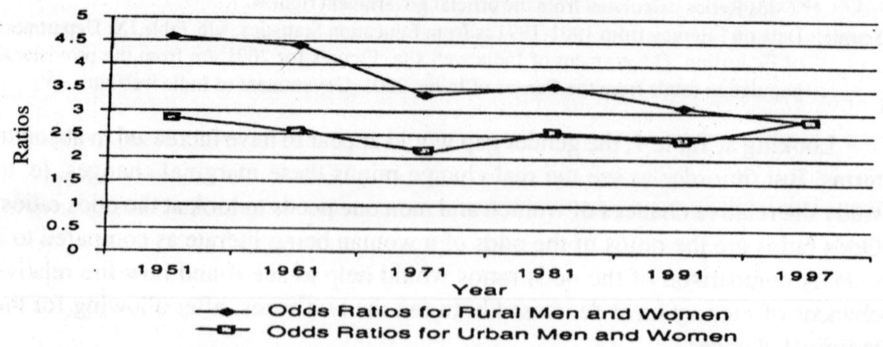

Inequality in educational opportunities is not only a 'gender' problem in India. The presence of the schedule caste (SC) and schedule tribe (ST) groups[5] who are historically deprived both socially and economically makes the situation quite complex. Official figures for the backward castes in India, especially the scheduled caste and the scheduled tribe community reveal that they consistently lag behind the higher 'twice born' castes. The literacy rates for SC's and ST's (combined) were 56 per cent in 1991 as compared to 76 per cent for the other castes,[6] ie, an odds ratio of 2.5: 1.

Why This 'Persistent Inequality' in Education?[7]

The benefits of schooling are unquestionable. According to the human capital theory, labour productivity is a direct function of the amount of schooling received. Higher schooling is expected to increase cognitive development and leads to economic modernisation [Colclough: 1982]. The individual and social returns from women's education are believed to be exceptionally high especially where the lowering of fertility and infant and child mortality rates are concerned [Kingdon: 1999; World Bank: 1997]. In addition, rising levels of education of women lead to improvements in nutrition and health care facilities and the improvement of children's educational achievements [Sengupta and Guha: 2002; Colclough: 1982].

Despite the fact that the non-monetary returns to schooling appear to be quite high [Colclough: 1982], many parents still don't send their children especially their daughters to school. Several reasons have been put forth for this. Using Indian household data, Rosenzweig and Schultz (1982) find that children who are expected to be more economically productive as adults receive a larger share of family resources. Sathar and Lloyd (1994) seem to agree and conclude that parents decide the amount of education a child receives on the basis of present and future anticipated costs and returns. 'Returns to educational investments in girls are likely to be seen by parents as lower than in boys because of their more limited opportunities in the labour market and the near certainty that they will marry out of the family and devote their future time and earnings to their husband's family' [Sathar and Lloyd: 1994:113-14].[8]

In India, a predominantly agrarian country,[9] a substantial number of girls are expected to contribute to the family income by their own labour or to look after their younger siblings [Aggarwal: 1987]. The opportunity cost of educating girls is thus especially large in rural and low-income families [Sengupta and Guha: 2002].

The National Committee on the Status of Women in India (1975) accepted that poverty plays a major role in the attitude to girls' education especially for people below subsistence level.[10] Prejudice against the education of girls has a strong detrimental effect on the amount of schooling they receive. According to Sopher (1980) this prejudice exists because an exclusively domestic role is seen as an ideal for a woman. Men, in his opinion, believe that education 'un-suits' women for that role, because an educated female and he quotes Krishnan and Shyam (1973), ... may become a doubtful character, or may not be capable of adjusting in the joint family system, or may not participate in obligatory agricultural operations, or may not remain under the control of her husband' [Sopher: 1980: 138].

Certain other background factors are believed to affect enrolment and dropout rates in school, and are believed to be magnified in the case of girls. Ramachandran and Saihjee (2002), in a study of District Primary Education Programmes (DPEP), have found that 'general household characteristics like income, caste, occupation and educational level of parents continue to determine access, attendance, completion and learning achievements' [Ramachandran and Saihjee: 2002: 1611]. According to Sengupta and Guha (2002) in a study of girl children in West Bengal, the strongest factors with regard to school participation, enrolment and dropout were household factors such as parental, especially maternal schooling, household income and the father's occupation. They also found that caste and religion were important determinants of schooling. They found that the Muslim girls, irrespective of whether they lived in a rural or urban area, received less schooling than other religious communities. According to their results residing in an urban area had strong positive effects on the education of girls.[11]

The National Committee on the Status of Women in India (1975) also accepted the postulation that apart from slow growth of women's literacy, there were 'several imbalances in educational development between advanced and backward classes and between regions'.[12]

II

Present Study

The persisting inequality in opportunity where education is concerned thus becomes apparent through an analysis of official figures as well as through a study of past research. Several factors such as caste, class, religion, and parental characteristics emerge as important determinants of educational inequality.

But what most past research seems to be lacking is a holistic view of the interplay of all these social and economic forces together. For example, not many researchers seems to have looked at how gender could magnify the other social inequalities leading to an even worse position of the women from those deprived communities. One researcher who does mention this issue albeit theoretically and with little empirical analysis is Raju (1991). Through her analysis of literacy data Raju (1991) shows that non-scheduled caste urban females emerge as a better-off group as compared to the rural males of all categories including non-scheduled caste males. What she suggests then is that a distinction needs to be made between women as well, and research on women cannot ignore social class relations in various spheres in which males are as integral a part as women.

In light of the above, the purpose of the present paper is twofold. Firstly I aim to empirically test the factors that are responsible for the inequality of educational opportunities for both boys and girls from socially deprived origins. Secondly, I would emphasise in particular the inequality faced by girls as compared to boys from the same origins, at each stage of the educational process.

III

Hypotheses

This section lays down some of the hypmheses that I will test in order to identify the factors that could affect the inequality in educational transitions.

I begin by testing what I call the *poverty* hypothesis. For this hypothesis to hold, two results should emerge. Firstly, the effect of father's class on educational transitions should be significant, and the results should show that both boys and girls from higher classes are more likely to make a transition to the next educational stage as compared to those who come from lower classes. But in addition, girls from lower classes should not only do worse than the boys and girls from the higher classes, but should do worse than the boys from these same lower class itself. This is because parents are expected to invest in their sons more than their daughters, especially when resources are low [Sengupta and Guha: 2002]. In other words there should emerge an interaction effect between gender and class, which would show that the gender gap is the least at higher levels of the class schema, as parents have more resources to invest in their daughters. The opposite should hold for girls from the lower classes.

Secondly, community characteristics such as caste and religion are expected to adversely affect the relative chances of children from deprived backgrounds in achieving the same levels of education as the children from more advantaged communities. Some social scientists [Sengupta and Guha: 2002; Raju: 1991] believe that both religion and caste should interact with gender and lead to a greater inequality for women from the depressed communities. Higher caste as well as Hindu girls should be in a better position than lower caste and Muslim girls, where transitions to the next stage of the educational process are concerned. I call this the *community* hypothesis.

Thirdly, I will test the *household resources* hypothesis or the *family background* hypothesis. This hypothesis posits that other family characteristics such as mothers and father's literacy should prove to be important determinants of the educational decisions made by their children [Sengupta and Guha: 2002; Burney and Irfan 1991; Sathar and Lloyd: 1994]. Thus parental literacy must emerge as a strong determinant of the likelihood of a child making the next educational transition. In addition there should also emerge a strong relationship between gender and mother's education. According to Sathar and Lloyd (1994) mother's literacy has a larger effect on enrolment of children, and this effect is larger especially for girls. In order to test this, the interaction of mother's literacy and gender should emerge stronger than that for father's literacy and gender.

Fourthly, under the *regional variation* hypothesis two aspects will be studied. These are the rural/urban aspect and the state aspect. There should be lower levels of gender discrimination in urban areas [Raju: 1991], as well as in the states that have traditionally had an above average level of literacy. This is because the traditional investment in education for girls as well as the social acceptance of girls' education should be higher in these regions (for example Kerala, the state with the highest level of literacy especially for women).[13] The opposite should hold for states like Bihar and Rajasthan, which have historically lagged behind the national average rate of literacy for girls. The transitions to later stages of education should be lower in these states for all children and the position of women should be even worse.

And finally the expansion of the education system as well as recent government initiatives to educate girls should be evident in the *Cohort Effect.* Younger cohorts of both boys and girls are expected to do better than the older ones and girls in these younger cohorts should have a relatively better chance, due to more opportunities available to them [Sengupta and Guha: 2002].

In sum, for each hypothesis I will test for the presence of a main and an interaction effect for gender, to study inequalities in educational attainment not only between communities and classes, but within the same communities and classes where gender is concerned.

IV

Brief Overview of the Indian Education System

India has two distinct streams of education, the formal education stream and the non-formal one. The formal stream begins at the age of six with primary school (Figure 3), which continues from grades I-V. Middle school is from grades VI-VIII.[14] Together primary and middle schools comprise elementary school. High school includes grades IX-XII. In this paper, I will club all colleges (with and without degrees) together.[15]

The non-formal stream is expected to provide education to students between the ages of nine and 14. For the government the non-formal stream is an alternative path to education for children employed in the labour market and deprived of education in the formal stream [Acharya: 1994; Aggarwal: 1989]. But serious doubts remain among theorists [Acharya: 1994] about the quality of this kind of education and its relevance in the lives of these children. As there is no information on the nonformal educational stream in the National Election Study Data set that I use, I am unable to deal with these issues.[16] For the purpose of this paper I concentrate wholly on the formal stream of education.

V

Methods

Ordinary Least Squares regression (or linear regression) and logistic regression are two methods most often used by the sociologists to study the effects of socio-economic background variables on educational attainment.[17] The linear regression method treats the highest qualification obtained (measured in the number of school years completed) as the dependent variable and regresses that on the independent background variables like parental education and father's class. The logistic regression method on the other hand treats the outcome as a dichotomous variable,

Figure 3: A Simplified version of the Indian Education System

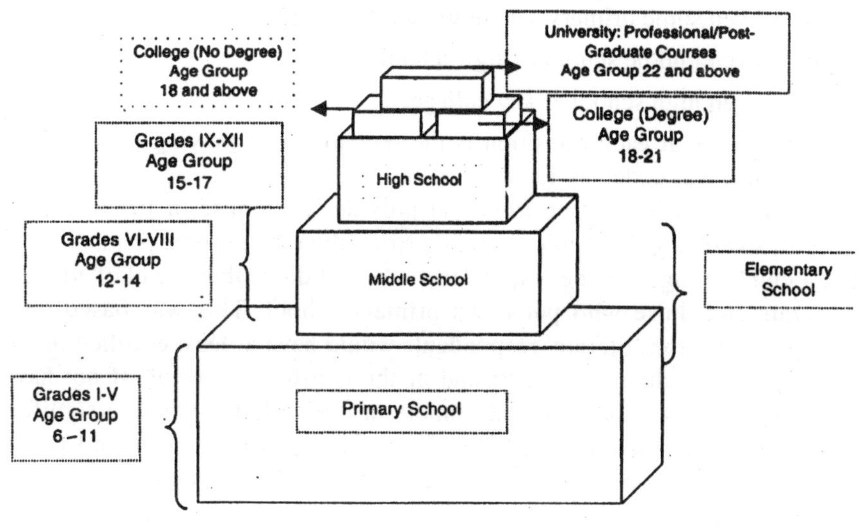

and studies whether the background variables have an effect on the likelihood that the subject makes a transition to the next stage of the educational process, given that she has completed the previous stage.

Keeping in mind my initial research questions, for the purpose qf the present paper I weighed the merits and drawbacks of both these methods. According to Mare (1981) linear models could conceal important social changes by summarising two offsetting trends; 'the univariate dispersion of formal schooling and the multivariate association between school attainment and socio-economic background characteristics' [Mare: 1981:83]. He goes on to add that 'the parameters of the logistic response model measure-in a sense-'pure' inequality of opportunity because they separate the distribution and allocation of schooling, and measure the latter explicitly' [Mare: 1981: 86].

In light of the possible drawbacks of the OLS regression and the advantage of logistic regression, especially with reference to studying inequality at different transition points, in the present analysis I decided to use a series of logistic regressions similar to those expressed by Mare (1980, 1981). In these models (henceforth called the Mare Model), I treat 'survival' at different transition points as the dependent variable [Jonsson: 1993].

The advantage of this model is that it helps to throw light on the inequality in educational opportunity for boys and girls without being affected by the degree of educational expansion or contraction [Shavit and Blossfeld: 1993]. The Mare Model views the educational process as a series of transitions, where at each level the subject's decision to continue till the next stage or dropout from the educational process is adjusted for in the model.

In order to use the Mare Model, I specified a series of transitions at significant points in the Indian education system. These transitions were:

(a) From illiterate to some primary school
(b) Given some primary school to middle school
(c) Given middle school to high school
(d) Given high school to any college.

The success at each transition is the probability of moving on to a higher transition and was coded as 1.

The first is a broad transition and provides a glimpse of the factors that affect the likelihood of a subject moving from illiteracy to some primary school. Here I clubbed together the respondents who put down their level of education as literate and those who put down primary school. This was based on the assumption that the 'literate' respondents would have at least enrolled in some sort of primary school (in the formal or the non-formal sector) if not having completed it. This transition is an important one in India, where a significant proportion of the children might not have the opportunity to attend primary school. This transition could thus help identify reasons why some children never make it to school.

The second and the third stages look at the transition from one level of school to another, and the last transition could help identify the factors that affect the likelihood of a subject making it to college. In the final transition, I clubbed the three categories of 'college no degree, college degree, and professional/postgraduate courses' under 'any' college.

VI

Data and Variables

The data for the present paper comes from the National Election Study (NES), 1996, conducted by the Centre for the Study of Developing Societies (CSDS), Delhi. The data, collected by a nationally representative, stratified random sample of 9,614 respondents from the electoral rolls contains roughly the same 'number of men and women.[18] As the electoral registration rates in India are high, and the onus of registration rests with the state, any selection bias in this data set should thus be minimal.[19]

This NES is a unique data set, and the 1996 data is especially useful for the present study. What sets this data apart from others is the inclusion of detailed background information not only on the respondent but also has detailed information on the respondent's parent's caste, class, education, religion and other background variables.

Success at each of the four educational transitions, mentioned above, was treated as the dependent variable.

Keeping in mind the expected determinants of the likelihood of educational transitions previously laid out in this paper, the independent variables in this study are gender, father's class, caste, father's education, mother's education, locality (rural/urban), and religion. What has not been looked at in much detail in previous studies is the variation of gender inequality by states. India is a vast country; rural areas steeped in poverty flank highly developed cities. In such a diverse country, the level of education too varies from one region to another. Kottayam in Kerala has one of the highest rates of literacy in the south Asian region, with 95.72 per cent of its population educated. On the other hand district Jhabua of Madhya Pradesh has the lowest rate of total literacy of 19.0 I per cent according to 1991 Census.[20]

The gap in literacy between women and men too varies widely by region.[21] Kerala[22] again has the highest level of literate women, while Rajasthan has the dubious distinction of having some districts with only 8 per cent educated women.[23] In the light of these variations, it becomes essentiai to study the gender differential in education and its variation by region or state.

I now turn to a brief discussion of the explanatory variables used in this study.

Class

A country with more than 60 per cent of its population in the farming and subsistence sector, but with one of the fastest growing IT industries, India is unlike any country in the west. For this reason, to simply apply the class categorisation used in studies in the west to the Indian scenario could provide a skewed and unclear picture. For this purpose I will be using the class schema developed by Heath, et al (2002) especially for the Indian case.[24] I use a modified version of their 8-class schema.

Original Classes [Heath, et al: 2002]:[25]

1. Higher salariat = executives, professional, white-collar workers.
2. Lower salariat = Class IV employees.
3. Business = small-scale and large-scale businessmen.
4. Petty business = Small storeowners and road side businesses
5. Skilled and semi-skilled manual labourer = mechanics, electricians, tailors, weavers, carpenters and craftsmen, and rickshaw pullers.
6. Unskilled manual labourer = manual labourers, excluding those in the agricultural sector (e g, construction workers, sweepers)
7. Farmers = owner and tenant cultivators with more than five acres of land
8. Lower agriculturists = less than five acres of land, sharecropper, agricultural labourer, landless labourer, tea plantation worker, dairy farmer, fishermen, shepherds, hunters.

Modified Categories

1. Class I = higher salariat + business
2. Class II = lower salariat

3. Class III = skilled and semi-skilled manual + petty business + farmers
4. Class IV = unskilled manual labourer + lower agriculturists

Caste

A unique feature of the data set is its enumeration of caste. The last Indian census to collect data on caste was in 1931. Since then, the census only collects data on the scheduled castes (SCs) and the scheduled tribes (STs).[26] This procedure has left a conspicuous gap in the data on other backward castes (OBCs) in India, who like the SCs and the STs also suffer from numerous inequalities, an important one being access to education. The present data set thus overcomes this lacuna as it includes variables on the OBCs, SCs, STs, as well as on the higher twice born castes.

It must be kept in mind at this point that the caste categories that I use for the purpose of this paper are by necessity a generalised picture of caste per se in India. Castes are not homogeneous categories, and there appears to be stratification within the same caste itself.[27] But the broad caste categories were considered sufficient for the purpose of this paper.

Figure 4[28] shows the break up of the castes in this data with regard to the different educational stages. Due to the small sample size of the STs that made any analysis difficult, I clubbed the SCs and STs together.

Figure 4: Castes and their Educational Attainment

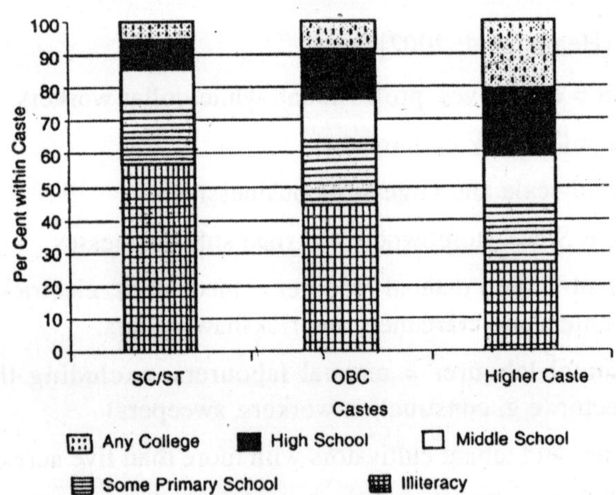

Region

In order to study regional disparity I look at two indicators, the state one belongs to and whether one comes from a rural or from an urban area. Dummy variables were created for each state in the sample (there were originally 21 states, but states with a small N were merged with their nearest large state, leaving me with 15 states).[29] I treated Assam as a 'middling state' (an average state where education and size is concerned) and made that the base category, in order to observe the distribution around it. For rural/urban differences I coded rural as 0 and urban as 1. Together these two indicators of state and locality make up the variable of region, which would highlight any impact of regional variation on the educational transitions made.

Parental Characteristics

The data on the respondents' parent's (both the mother and fathers) educational attainment is an important aspect of this data. For both parents, being literate was coded as 1 and being illiterate as 0.

Religion

For the purpose of this paper I divided religion into three categories; Hindu, Muslim and 'other'. The 'other' category is quite heterogeneous and includes Christians, Sikhs, Jains, Buddhists and Parsis. Despite this simplification these religious categories do help in a broad comparison between these communities. I treat Hindu as the base category in the regression, in order to see how these religious minorities fare educationally with regard to the majority Hindu population.

Cohorts

Age groups were converted into five cohorts, and the base category was taken to be the oldest cohort of respondents born prior to 1940. The youngest cohort was born between 1971 and 1978.

VII

Models and Results

Table 2 depicts the models that were constructed using logistic regression at the first transition point. Similar analyses were conducted at each educational transition, but in order to simplify the analysis these tables for the last three transitions are excluded from the present paper. Instead of presenting tables for all the four transitions, Table 4 brings together the significant models at each of the four transitions.

Models 1-8 within Table 2 are successive models controlling for additional main-effect background variables. In model 8 only the significant states have been shown (to make the tables easier to interpret), though all the states were a part of the analysis.[30]

Model 8 emerged as the most parsimonious main-effect model, and was treated as the baseline model for the addition of interaction effects.

The last column in Table 2 depicts the model with interaction terms. This model (Model 9) was derived by adding various interactions as shown in Table 3 (all interactions are with gender). The changes in chi-square and the changes in degrees of freedom were used to judge the fit of the model. The model with the best fit was deemed the most parsimonious one and was included in Table 2 as Model 9.

Table 2
Mare Model–Logistic Regression Parameters for the, Transition to 'Some Primary School from Illiterate'

Independent Variables	*Model 1*	*Model 2*	*Model 3*	*Model 4*	*Model 5*	*Model 6*	*Model 7*	*Model 8*	*Model 9*
Gender	-1.214	-1.325	-1.387	-1.397	-1.646	-1.709	-1.725	-1.847	-1.947
(Male=O)	(0.048)	(0.051)	(0.053)	(0.053)	(0.061)	(0.062)	(0.063)	(0.066)	(0.081)
Class 1		2.909	2.641	2.643	1.583	1.585	1.276	1.362	1.399
		(0.129)	(0.131)	(0.131)	(0.147)	(0.148)	(0.151)	(0.153)	(0.155)
Class 2		1.668	1.69	1.704	1.056	1.051	0.763	0.875	0.886
		(0.192)	(0.195)	(0.195)	(0.212)	(0.213)	(0.215)	(0.220)	(0.220)
Class 3		0.511	0.479	0.476	0.269	0.262	0.169	0.178	0.185
		(0.053)	(0.054)	(0.054)	(0.061)	(0.062)	(0.063)	(0.068)	(0.068)
Caste (OBC)			0.508	0.547	0.329	0.397	0.408	0.432	0.423
			(0.063)	(0.063)	(0.070)	(0.071)	(0.072)	(0.077)	(0.077)
Caste (Higher)			1,169	1.212	0.776	0.906	0.898	1.075	1.061
			(0.069)	(0.071)	(0.080)	(0.082)	(0.083)	(0.090)	(0.091)
'Other' Religion				0.535	0.442	0.491	0.495	0.308	-0.446
				(0.125)	(0.142)	(0.144)	(0.145)	(0..154)	(0.216)
Muslim				-0.211	-0.186'	-0.276	-0.357	-0.430	-0.430
				(0.089)	(0.099)	(0.101)	(0.103)	(0.108)	(0.109)
Moth. Lit. (liliterate=O)					1.912	1.875	1.845	1.62	1.596
					(0.138)	(0.139)	(0.140)	(0.144)	(0.144)
Father Lit.					1.668	1.576	1.557	1.458	1.295
(1Illiterate=O)					(0.069)	(0.070)	(0.070)	(0.073)	(0.105)
Cohort 1						1.155	1.200	1.356	1.356
('71-'78)						(0.100)	(0.102)	(0.106)	(0.106)
Cohort 2						0.848	0.874	0.959	0.954
('61-'70)						(0.097)	(0.098)	(0.102)	(0.102)
Cohort 3						0.555	0.568	0.641	0.630
('51-'60)						(0.103)	(0.104)	(0.107)	(0.107)
Cohort 4						0.198"	0.185'	0.224'	0.219'
('41-'50)						(0.114)	(0.115)	(0.118)	(0.118)
Locality							0.802	0.738	0.757
(Rural=O)							(0.084)	(0.095)	(0.096)
Bihar								-0.611	-0.636
								(0.176)	(0.175)
Gujarat								1.965	1.949
								(0.274)	(0.275)
Tamil Nadu								0.703	0.664
								(0.189)	(0.189)
Rajasthan								-0.917	-0.579
								(0.201)	(0.225)
Kerala								1.857	1.787
								(0.337)	(0.338)
G' Other Religion									1.357
									(0.287)
G ' Father's Lit.									0.317
									(0.139)
G'Rajasthan									-1.111
									(0.294)
Constant	0.957	0.507	o.oor	-0.020'	-0.302	-0.957	-1.034	-1.005	-0.934
	(0.035)	(0.043)	(0.058)	(0.058)	(0.064)	(0.099)	(0.100)	(0.176)	(0.177)

Contd...

Independent Variables	*Model 1*	*Model 2*	*Model 3*	*Model 4*	*Model 5*	*Model 6*	*Model 7*	*Model 8*	*Model 9*

N=7808

Chi Sq 668.19 1608.37 1907.86 1934.25 3392.17 3575.26

3668.79 3966.43 4010.62

(1 d.f.) (4d.f.) (6 d.f.) (8d.f.) (10d.f.) (14 d.f.)

(15d.f.) (29d.f.) *(32d.f.)*

Notes: Standard Errors in parenthesis.

Parameter is less than twice its standard error. Omitted Variables: Class 4, Caste (SC/ST), Religion (Hindu), Cohort 5 (those born before 1940), State (Assam). See text for more details. Interactions are with Gender and are shown as 'Goo.'20'2"'1

Table 3
Deriving the Most Parsimonious Model for the Transition 'Some Primary School from Iliterate'[31]

Model 1	*Model Chi Sq*	*Model d.f.*	*ΔChi Sq*	*Δd.f*
Baseline model	3966.425	29	-	-
Model2a				
Class1	3966.846	30	0.421	1
Model2b				
Class2	3966.911	30	0.486	1
Model2c				
Class3	3966.519	30	0.094	1
Model2d				
Caste (OBC)	3966.970	30	0.545	1
Model2e				
Caste (Higher)	3966.550	30	0.125	1
Model2f				
Religion (Other)	3989.376	30	22.951	1
Model3a				
'Other, 'Muslim	3991.547	31	2.171	1
Model3b				
Other, 'Mother Lit.	3991.923	31	2.547	1
Model 3c				
Other, 'Father Lit.	3995.316	31	5.940	1
Model4a				
Other, 'Father Lit., Cohort 1	3998.069	32	2.753	1
Model 4b				
Other, 'Father Lit, Cohort 2	3997.900	32	2.584	1
Model4c				
Other, 'Father Lit, Cohort 3	3996.687	32	1.371	1
Model4d				
Other, 'Father Lit, Cohort 4	3996.326	32	1.010	1
Model4e				
Other, 'Father Lit, Locality	3996.078	32	0.762	1
Model4f				

Contd....

Model 1	*Model Chi Sq*	*Model d.f.*	*ΔChi Sq*	*Δd.f*
Other, 'Father Lit, 'Bihar	3996.299	32	0.983	1
Model4g Other, 'Father Lit, Gujarat	3996.424	32	1.108	1
Model4h Other, 'Father Lit, Rajasthan	4010.618	32	15.302	1
Model 5a Other, 'Father Lit, Rajasthan, 'TamilN	4011.648	33	1.030	1
Model5b Other, 'Father Lit, Rajasthan, 'Kerala	4010.618	33	0.000	1

Notes: N=7808.
Standard Errors in parenthesis
Parameter is less than twice its standard error
The Base Line Model is Model 8 in Table 2. This includes all the main effects, but no interaction terms.
Interactions are with Gender and are shown as 'Goo.
Gender and state interaction is only shown for the states that had a significant main effect parameter.

I will begin by explaining the results of the first transition, from illiteracy to some primary school, and in the next section of the paper will supplement these results with information from the other transitions. In the final discussion, results will be culled from all four transitions to provide an overall picture of educational transition decisions and the changing effect of gender and other background variables on these decisions.

The next section provides a detailed explanation of Tables 2, 3 (see footnote 31) and 4. Readers interested solely in the results can turn to the 'discussion' section of this paper, which puts these results into perspective.

Main Effects

Table 2 shows the parameter for gender and the other independent variables at the stage of transition to some primary school.[32] The parameter for gender remains negative and highly significant and increases after controlling for additional independent variables. The parameter for father's class is positive and significant, and the parameter for class I is consistently larger than for the other classes. The addition of caste in the model does not change the parameter for class by much. Though belonging to the twice born higher castes has a stronger parameter than belonging to the other backward castes (OBC) in contrast to the base category of the scheduled castes and tribes. The coefficient for religion is seen to be highly significant. For Muslims this parameter is negative, while for 'other' religions it's positive as compared to the base category of Hindus.

The addition of variables for mother's and father's literacy leads to a large increase in the parameter for gender but decreases the parameter for father's class.

The parameter for mother's literacy is higher than that for father's literacy even after adding all the other main effects. A clear cohort effect is visible; the youngest cohort (born between 1971 and 1978) has a strong positive parameter as compared to the base category of the oldest cohort (respondents born before the 1940's). Similarly regional parameters of locality and state were added to the model. Belonging to an urban area has a positive parameter even after controlling for the state of the respondent.

Interaction Effects

The above model with the main effects assumes that class, caste, parental education, region, and religion have the same effects at all levels for both men and women. Interaction terms help us to see how the effect actually varies across groups. The interactions that were added were for gender and father's class, gender and caste, gender and religion, gender and parent's education, gender and cohort, gender and locality and gender and state. Each interaction in turn was broken up into its sub-parts, for example, gender *caste (OBC), gender *caste (higher).

At the first transition to some primary school, one can see that the only significant interactions were for gender and 'other' of Rajasthan. The interaction of gender with Rajasthan too is significant at the first three transitions. The implications of these findings will now be discussed.

Comparison with Other Transitions

The above was a description of the main and interaction effects for the first transitional stage. As mentioned earlier, similar analyses were conducted at all four transitions. I will now highlight the patterns that emerge through a comparison of the most parsimonious models at each transition level. Table 4 puts together all parsimonious models from each transition, and helps to interpret how inequality in opportunity varies at each transition stage.

Controlling for all the background variables, Table 4 shows that the impact of gender is negative at all stages. Though it declines at later stages particularly at the stage of moving from high school to college, where the parameter becomes insignificant.

The impact of the father's class on the other hand is relatively stable at all transitions. Belonging to class 1 (professional, managerial or big business) as compared to class 4 which is the base category (unskilled manual labour, lower agriculturists) seems to have a positively significant effect on the relative chance of making the next transition. The interaction of gender and class is not significant at any transition.

Belonging to the higher castes has a positive and stronger parameter than OBc. But these caste parameters become insignificant at the last stages. The parameter for caste is weaker than for class 1 at each transition stage. The interaction of caste with gender was barely significant at the second stage, but became insignificant after the other interaction terms were added.

Table 4
Logistic Regression Parameters for All Main and Interaction Effects at Each Transition

Independent Variables	*Some Primary School from Illiterate*	*MiddleSchool Given Some PrimarySchool*	*HighSchool Given Middle School*	*College (any) Given High School*
Gender (Male=O)	-1.947	-1.174	-0.781	-0.198′
	(0.081)	(0.122)	(0.163)	(0.155)
Class 1	1.399	1.069	0.893	0.762
	(0.155)	(0.138)	(0.137)	(0.147)
Class 2	0.886	0.256'	-0.588	-0.128′
	(0.220)	(0.206)	(0.214)	(0.311)
Class 3	0.185	0.254	-0.079′	0.030′
	(0.068)	(0.086)	(0.100)	(0.132)
Caste (OBC)	0.423	0.303	0.018′	0.040′
	(0.077)	(0.102)	(0.124)	(0.163)
Caste (Higher)	1.061	0.866	0.287	0.103′
	(0.091)	(0.127)	(0.125)	(0.157)
Other religion	-0.446	0.380	-0.059′	0.460
	(0.216)	(0.180)	(0.247)	(0.194)
Muslim	-0.430	-0.786	-0.598	-0.520
	(0.109)	(0.123)	(0.138)	(0.180)
Moth Lit (1Illiterate=O)	1.596	0.928	0.605	0.714
	(0.144)	(0.108)	(0.105)	(0.118)
Father Lit (1iIliterate=O)	1.295	0.921	0.551	0.874
	(0.105)	(0.085)	(0.102)	(0.147)
Cohort 1 ('71-'78)	1.356	1.725	0.649	0.668
	(0.106)	(0.151)	(0.183)	(0.224)
Cohort 2 ('61-'70)	0.954	1.549	0.628	0.527
	(0.102)	(0.136)	(0.175)	(0.222)
Cohort 3 ('51-'60)	0.630	1.176	0.348′	0.353′
	(0.107)	(0.142)	(0.184)	(0.234)
Cohort 4 ('41-'50)	0.219′	0.762	0.392′	0.262′
	(0.118)	(O.160)	(0.213)	(0.268)
Locality (Rural=O)	0.757	0.530	0.168′	0.111′
	(0.096)	(0.102)	(0.123)	(0.133)
Andhra Pradesh	-	-	-	-
Bihar	-0.636	-	-0.672	-
	(0.175)		(0.275)	-
Delhi		-	-1.032	-
		-	(0.280)	-
Gujarat	1.949	-	-0.790	-0.819
	(0.275)	-	(0.299)	(0.311)
Karnataka		-		-
Haryana, Himachal and Punjab	-	-0.825	-	
		-	(0.333)	-
Orissa		-0.914		-
		(0.257)		-
Maharashtra		-		-0.555
		-		(0.270)

Independent Variables	*Some Primary School from Illiterate*	*MiddleSchool Given Some PrimarySchool*	*HighSchool Given Middle School*	*College (any) Given High School*
Madhya Pradesh		-0.624	-1.049	-
		(0.233)	(0.293)	-
Tamil Nadu	0.664	-	-0.718	-1.401
	(0.189)	-	(0.270)	(0.296)
Rajasthan	-0.579	-0.791	-1.064	-1.597
	(0.225)	(0.280)	(0.339)	(0.418)
Uttar Pradesh		-0.286′	-0.788	-
		(0.217)	(0.253)	-
Kerala	1.787	-	-0.570′	-1.390
	(0.338)	-	(0.291)	(0.306)
West Bengal		-0.680	-1.422	-1.022
		(0.220)	(0.267)	(0.293)
G'Higher (Caste)		-0.195'		-
		(0.163)		-
G'Other (religion)	1.357	-	0.743	-
	(0.287)	-	(0.356)	-
G'Father's Lit.	0.317	-		-
	(0.139)	-		-
G'Cohort 1		0.464	0.448	-
		(0.170)	(0.185)	-
G'Rajasthan	-1.111	-1.301	-1.822	-
	(0.294)	(0.463)	(0.701)	-
G'UP		-0.628		-
		(0.216)		-
G'Locality		-	-0.446	-0.688
		-	(0.186)	(0.217)
Constant	-0.934	-1.346	0.332′	-1.503
	(0.177)	(0.231)	(0.291)	(0.334)
Chi Square	4010.618	1238.240	465.288	406.239
	(32d.f.)	(33d.f.)	(33d.f.)	(30d.f.)
N	7808	4554	3132	2112

Notes: Standard Errors in parenthesis; Parameter is less than twice its standard error; '-' The insignificant parameters for states and theinsignificant interactions with gender are not shown. States that had a significant main effect parameter but became insignificant with the introduction of interaction effects are shown in the table. Omitted Variables: Class 4, Caste (SC/ST), Religion (Hindu), Cohort 5 (those born before 1940), State (Assam). See text for more details.Interactions are with Gender and are shown as G'.

With Hindu as the omitted category, one can see the impact of belonging to a Muslim background or belonging to the 'other' religious community. Being a Muslim has a strong negative effect at each stage of educational transition, though the effect is smallest at the first stage. It rises sharply for the transition from some primary to middle school, and then falls for the subsequent transitions. But what is interesting is the interaction of 'other' religion with gender, which is positive at the first and third transitions, its main effect on the other hand was negative at these transitions.

Mother and father's education too has the expected positive effect on the probability of going to the next level of school. At each level mother's literacy seems to have a stronger effect on the educational transition of a child than the father's literacy, except at the level of transition to college given high school completion. Gender and parental literacy interaction is only significant for father's literacy at the first stage. There is a strong cohort effect as expected, and the cohort gender interaction is significant at two transitions.

The effect of locality seems to decline, and becomes insignificant at the last two transitions. The one state that has a consistently significant parameter at all transitions is the state of Rajasthan. The interaction of gender with Rajasthan too is significant at the first transitions.

The implications of these findings will now be discussed.

VIII

Discussion

The statistical analysis makes it clear that controlling for a host of background variables, the gender inequality in educational transitions still remains, though it does decrease by the last transition, where its parameter becomes insignificant. As already mentioned, the model with the main effects assumes that all background characteristics have the same effects at all levels for both men and women. Interaction terms help us to see how the effect actually varies across groups. The inclusion of interaction effects thus highlights some interesting results. These interactions highlight in particular the additional inequality faced by girls while making educational transitions. Figure 5 depicts some of the prominent results that have emerged as a part of the analysis.

In support of the poverty hypothesis (as laid out in an earlier section of this paper) one finds that father's class, as was expected, plays a decisive role in the

Figure 5: Graphical Description of Selected Parameters

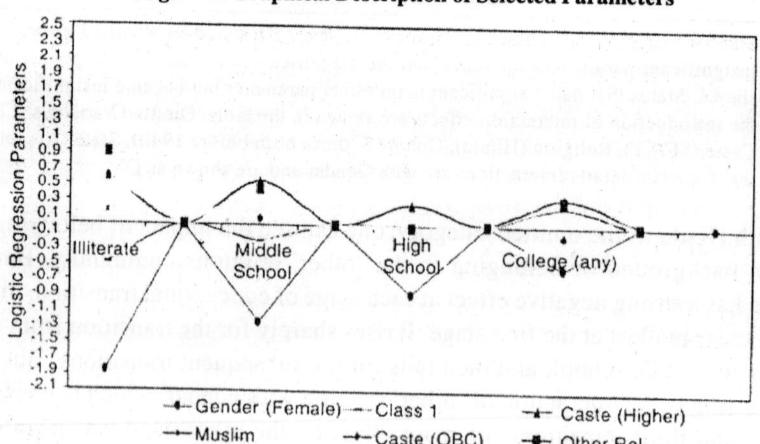

transition likelihood of the subject. Father's class has a consistently high parameter at all stages of the educational process. According to the second part of the poverty hypothesis the effect of gender should vary by class at different transition points. But interestingly this hypothesis finds no support in my analysis, as the interaction between gender and class was insignificant at each transition stage. Put another way what emerges is that the gender odds ratio is the same for all four classes, which refutes the notion of a more egalitarian Indian middle class.

It is observed that higher castes fare better than the backward castes where education for both boys and girls is concerned, but surprisingly caste does not appear to play as decisive a role in the decision to make a successive transition, as does father's class. The parameter for caste becomes insignificant in the last transition stages, whereas that for class I remains positive and significant at all levels. What this means really is that caste no longer distinguishes among the 'survivors' at later stages. In other words there has already been a kind of natural selection at each stage, in which only the most determined women or men from the backward castes have made it.[33] It is important to note that the interactions that were tried between caste and class were not significant, similarly the interaction between gender and caste was insignificant.

The second part of the community hypothesis posits that caste and religion should interact with gender; in other words, girls from lower castes, or from religious communities that do not encourage long-term investment in the education of girls should fare worse than boys sharing the same background. Particularly for Musiims it is believed that girls do much worse than the boys [Sengupta and Guha: 2002]. But contrary to these studies, my analysis refutes this claim, as there emerges no interaction between gender and belonging to the Muslim community. What does emerge though is that girls from 'other' religious communities do stand a better relative chance, as the gender and religion interaction parameter is strongly positive for this community. This could be because the 'other' religion category is quite heterogeneous and includes communities like the Christians, Parsis and Jains who are known to encourage the education of girls.[34]

Next I turn to the household resources hypothesis. I find that mother and father's education both play an important part in the transition likelihood of the subject. A mother being literate has the strongest impact on the child's transition to some primary school from illiteracy, but by the last stage (transition to college) it is the father's education that has a stronger effect. This would seem to support the view that a literate mother would encourage all her children irrespective of gender to stay on in school [Sathar and Lloyd: 1994] as suggested through the parameter of the main effect. But here again I find that there emerges no interaction between mother's literacy and gender. Thus implying that the belief that a more educated mother would lead to a higher education for the daughter [Sathar and Lloyd: 1994; Sengupta and Guha: 2002] does not hold. On the other hand father's literacy and gender interact and have a significant parameter at the first stage from illiteracy to some primary school.

Under the regional variation hypothesis support was found for the state aspect, but only partial support was found for the rural/ urban aspect. Coming from an urban area has a strongly positive parameter in the first two transitions, which would support the view that an urban background could lead to a higher likelihood of making successive educational transitions at least till the level of entry into middle school for both boys and girls. But interestingly the interaction of gender and locality does not have a significant parameter at the first two transitions, and reveals a negative parameter at the last two transition stages, which could possibly be due to the selection processes at the later educational stages discussed above.

But what really stands out with regard to the regional variation hypothesis are the parameters for states as well as the interaction of gender and states. The state of Kerala has a strong positive parameter, and that of Rajasthan has a high negative parameter, which seems to empirically support the view that coming from a state with historically high or low levels of literacy could reduce or add to the gender inequality in educational transitions. But what needs special attention is the interaction between gender and Rajasthan. The negative and highly significant interaction parameter at the first three stages of the educational transition process throws light on the extreme gender inequality in this state. In addition to the rural/ urban effect then one also observes a strong regional or state effect. In sum, it emerges that in India girls have a relatively poorer chance than boys to make successive educational transitions, but in Rajasthan their chances are even poorer than elsewhere.

Conclusion

Historically the education of girls in India has lagged behind that of boys [Aggarwal: 1987; Agrawal and Aggarwal: 1994]. In addition studies have shown that certain communities and classes fare much worse than the others. Recently, some researchers have attempted to lay down the determinants of the inequality in educational attainment for boys and girls. Only a handful of these [Sengupta and Guha: 2002; Raju: 1991; Burney and Irfan: 1991; Sathar and Lloyd: 1994][35] have explicitly looked at the factors responsible for the relative gender inequality in educational attainment. But none of these [except Sathar and Lloyd: 1994][36] deal with the relative chances that girls have vis-a-vis boys keeping background characteristics constant.

The aim of this paper has then been twofold. Firstly to highlight the factors responsible for the inequality in educational opportunities for both boys and girls from socially deprived origins, and secondly to highlight in particular the inequality faced by girls at each transition stage. In other words the aim was not only to see how social background variables affect children's schooling, but keeping all else equal to study how girls from a particular community or class fared as compared to boys from the same community. This was achieved through interaction effects between gender and all the background variables.

Logistic regression was considered the most appropriate method to conduct the present analysis. The major results of this study seemed to be only partly consistent with previous research. Using the 1996, National Election Study (NES) data, I found that class emerged as a strong determinant of the relative chance of a child continuing in school. But no support was found for an additional class effect where the education of girls is concerned, thus refuting the notion of a more egalitarian middle class. I found only partial and weak support for the effect of caste. Adding caste to the analysis did not appreciably lead to a decline in the parameters of class, and it then emerges that given caste and class together, class seems to have a greater impact on the education that a child receives. This is not to deny the fact that caste has an important part to play in social interaction, especially in blocking certain avenues of education to the minority backward community. But what it does really is to highlight the fact that for better or for worse class appears to be an important determinant of who gets ahead and who lags behind.

The effects of other background characteristics like parental education, religion and region were found to be important determinants of the likelihood of an educational transition for a child. Parental literacy (especially father's literacy), state (especially the state of Rajasthan), and religion (belonging to the 'other' religion category) had strong interactions with gender.

The decrease of gender inequality as seen in the west [Shavit and Blossfeld: 1993] has not yet come into play in India, where the education of girls is still not considered a necessity (see Table 1 and Figure 1 in this paper, which depict the odds ratios calculated using census figures. These ratios reveal a relatively stable pattern of gender inequality in the past few decades). This could well be due to the dynamics of an agricultural society, where children are an asset on the farms and the opportunity cost of educating them (and doing without their labour) is quite high.

While interpreting the results of the present analysis one must bear in mind that the method of logistic regression is not without its drawbacks. According to Mare (1993: 352) 'the more that unobservable factors affect school continuation and the greater the degree of selectivity, the more difficult it is to estimate social background effects, and the more important to compare background effects across social contexts.' This problem of unmeasured heterogeneity could be overcome in subsequent studies by the introduction of additional control variables, which are conceptually believed to affect the schooling of girls. These could be the availability of schools, the availability of female teachers, the quality of schools available, the distance of the schools from the village and girls labour force participation. Even though the present data does not include information on these variables, nevertheless, in my opinion, the data does help to shed light on gender inequality where education is concerned and is a step in the right direction to understand this inequality. A future qualitative field study could also complement the current research and would provide a clearer picture of factors that affect the schooling of girls and boys.

Keeping in mind the results of this study, many avenues for further research emerge. It would be interesting to study if and how caste and class mediate with education to affect the job opportunities for women and men. This could be a good test of the human capital approach [Colclough and Tembon: 1999; Kingdon

1999] which posits that the job opportunity structure could be biased against women, and parents knowing well that their daughters will not get good enough jobs in the labour market, prefer to invest in the education of their sons instead.

The present paper is a first step, albeit a small one, to analyse some of the determinants of inequality in educational transitions in India with particular emphasis on gender inequality.

Appendix 1
Odds Ratios for Rural Men and Women as well as for Urban Men and Women

Year	*Rural Men Per cent of Total Rural Male Sample*	*Rural Women Per cent of Total Rural Female Sample*	*Odds Ratios for Rural Men and Women*
1951	19.02	4.87	4.59
1961	29.10	8.55	4.41
1971	33.76	13.17	3.36
1981	49.69	21.77	3.55
1991	57.87	30.62	3.12
1997	68.00	43.00	2.82
Year	*Urban Men Per cent of Total Urban Male Sample*	*Urban Women Per cent of Total Urban Female Sample*	*Odds Ratios for Urban Men and Women*
1951	45.06	22.33	2.85
1961	57.49	34.51	2.57
1971	61.27	42.14	2.17
1981	76.83	56.37	2.57
1991	81.09	64.05	2.41
1997	88.00	72.00	2.85

Source: Data on Literacy is from Education Statistics, sub-Table X, Department of Education, Government of India web site.

Appendix 2
Number of Respondents by Caste and Education

	Illiteracy	*Some Primary School*	*Middle School*	*High School*	*Any College*	*Total*
SC/ST	1215	400	212	204	109	2140
Per cent within caste	56.78	18.69	9.91	9.53	5.09	100
OBC	1337	558	392	448	261	2996
Per cent within caste	44,63	18.62	13.08	14.95	8.71	100
Higher	702	464	416	537	553	2672
Per cent within caste	26.27	17.37	15.57	20.1	20.7	100
Total	3254	1422	1020	1189	923	7808
	41.68	18.21	13.06	15.23	11.82	100

Source: NES, 1996, CSDS Data Unit.

Appendix 3
Respondents by Final Grouped States
(this table is for the section on 'Region' in the text)

State	*Respondents*	*Per cent of Total*
Andhra Pradesh	685	7.1
Assam	337	3.5
Bihar	880	9.2
Delhi	563	5.9
Karnataka	494	5.1
Gujarat	483	5.0
Himachal, Haryana, Punjab	425	4.4
Kerala	343	3.6
Madhya Pradesh	707	7.4
Maharashtra	861	9.0
Orissa	373	3.9
Tamil Nadu	723	7.5
Rajasthan	539	5.6
Uttar Pradesh	1432	14.9
West Bengal	769	8.0
Total	9614	100.0

Note: This table includes the total number of respondents including the ones that were later dropped due to missing cases.
Source: NES, 1996, CSDS Data Unit.

Appendix 4
Mare Model: Logistic Regression Parameters for all Main Effects

Independent Variables	*Some Primary School from Illiterate*	*Middle School Given Some Primary School*	*High School Given Middle School*	*College (any) GivenHigh School*
Gender (Male = O)	-1.847	-1.238	-0.875	-0.536
	(0.066)	(0.084)	(0.093)	(0.113)
Class 1	1.362	1.028	0.867	0.770
	(0.153)	(0.135)	(0.135)	(0.146)
Class 2	0.875	0.255′	-0.608	-0.134′
	(0.220)	(0.205)	(0.214)	(0.311)
Class 3	0.178	0.260	-0.089′	0.024′
	(0.068)	(0.085)	(0.100)	(0.131)
Caste (OBC)	0.432	0.306	0.007′	0.043′
	(0.077)	(0.102)	(0.124)	(0.162)
Caste (Higher)	1.075	0.762	0.269	0.112′
	(0.090)	(0.108)	(0.125)	(0.157)
Other Rei	0.308	0.374	0.298′	0.452
	(0.154)	(0.179)	(0.185)	(0.193)
Muslim	-0.430	-0.779	-0.583	-0.522
	(0.108)	(0.121)	(0.137)	(0.179)
Mother Lit (1Illiterate:O)	1.620	0.934	0.611	0.712
	(0.144)	(0.108)	(0.104)	(0.117)
Father Lit (1iliterate=O)	1.458	0.909	0.530	0.865
	(0.073)	(0.084)	(0.101)	(0.147)

Contd...

Independent Variables	*Some Primary School from Illiterate*	*Middle School Given Some Primary School*	*High School Given Middle School*	*College (any) GivenHigh School*
Cohort 1 ('71-'78)	1.356	1.885	0.778	0.679
	(0.106)	(0.138)	(0.175)	(0.225)
Cohort 2 ('61-'70)	0.959	1.506	0.604	0.554
	(0.102)	(0.134)	(0.174)	(0.223)
Cohort 3 ('51-'60)	0.641	1.138	0.340	0.389′
	(0.107)	(0.141)	(0.183)	(0.235)
Cohort 4 ('41-'50)	0.224′	0.730	0.376′	0.284′
	(0.118)	(0.159)	(0.212)	(0.269)
Locality (Rural:O)	0.738	0.507	0.322	0.317
	(0.095)	(0.101)	(0.104)	(0.116)
Andhra Pradesh	-0.289′	-0.111′	-0.266′	-0.155′
	(0.189)	(0.243)	(0.291)	(0.289)
Bihar	-0.611	0.000′	-0.687	-0.425′
	(0.176)	(0.233)	(0.274)	(0.299)
Delhi		-0.039′	-1.038	-0.400′
	(0.224)	(0.258)	(0.279)	(0.282)
Gujarat	1.965	-0.366′	-0.818	-0.797
	(0.274)	(0.251)	(0.298)	(0.310)
Karnataka	-0.277*	0.230′	-0.307*	-0.329′
	(0.200)	(0.264)	(0.306)	(0.323)
Haryana, Himachal and	0.171′	-0.330′	-0.828	-0.305′
Punjab	(0.242)	(0.288)	(0.333)	(0.379)
Orissa	0.097′	-0.912	-0.346′	-0.545′
	(0.217)	(0.257)	(0.338)	(0.337)
Maharashtra	0.248′	-0.142′	-0.459′	-0.568
	(0.183)	(0.223)	(0.265)	(0.269)
Madhya Pradesh	-0.291′	-0.660	-1.049	-0.553′
	(0.179)	(0.233)	(0.292)	(0.344)
Tamil Nadu	0.703	0.050′	-0.747	-1.403
	(0.189)	(0.228)	(0.270)	(0.295)
Rajasthan	-0.917	-1.079	-1.310	-1.615
	(0.201)	(0.263)	(0.326)	(0.419)
Uttar Pradesh	-0.109′	-0.503	-0.789	0.126′
	(0.165)	(0.206)	(0.253)	(0.259)
Kerala	1.857	0.243′	-0.590	-1.409
	(0.337)	(0.268)	(0.290)	(0.305)
West Bengal	-0.122′	-0.677	-1.437	-1.044
	(0.181)	(0.220)	(0.267)	(0.292)
Constant	-1.005	-1.260	0.292′	-1.602
	(0.176)	(0.229)	(0.290)	(0.333)
Chi Square	3966.425	1212.385	444.412	396.082
(29d.f.)	(29d.f.)	(29d.f.)	(29d.f.)	
N	7808	4554	3132	2112

Notes: Standard Errors in parenthesis. ¢Parameter is less than twice its standard error. Omitted Variables: Class 4, Caste (SC/ST), Religion(Hindu), Cohort 5 (those born before 1940), State (Assam). See text for more details.

Notes

1. Source: World Education Report (1998), and the section on Education Statistics at the Department of Education, Government of India website (henceforth called the DOE website) at http://www.education.nic.in/ htmlweb/edusta.htm.
2. For a detailed study on the receding goal of universal elementary education, see Acharya (1994). See Agrawal and Aggarwal (1994) for a historical look at policies on education. For a review of the National Policy on Education 1986, see Aggarwal (1989).
3. According to the 1991 Census, only 45 per cent of the total female population aged 6-10 years was in school In addition only 57 per cent of the male population in the same age group was enrolled in school. Source: Census Data Online, Table 15; The Census of India, 1991, Government of India web site at http://www.censusindia. netlcendatl datatablel5.html (henceforth called census data online).
4. 'The decadal census collects information on literacy. For the purpose of census, a person is considered literate if he or she can read and write with understanding in any language. However, a person who can merely read but cannot write is not literate'. (Education Statistics, DOE web site).
5. Scheduled castes and tribes are the former untouchables who at the time of the drafting of the Constitution were included in a constitutional list or 'schedule' and preferential policies for their upliftment were laid out (for details on preferential policies see Weiner, et al (1981).
6. Source: Education Statistics, Sub-Table XVIII, DOE web site.
7. Shavit and Blossfeld (1993) in their cross national comparison of 13 western countries reveal persisting class inequalities. According to their study the gender inequality seems to have been reversed in the west. This has not happened in India, as this paper will show.
8. For a discussion on this aspect of girls' schooling especially with regard to the labour market see Kingdon (1999), Colclough (1999), Sengupta and Guha (2002).
9. According to the 1991 Census, about 67.7 per cent of the Indian population were engaged in agriculture (Source: census data online).
10. For a discussion on the status of women's education in India, see Aggarwal (1987).
11. Similar studies in the neighbouring country of Pakistan show that household income, parental education and the size of the landholding has a positive impact on a household's decision to send a child to school [Burney and Irfan: 1991]. Sathar and Lloyd (1994) too, in their study of primary schooling in Pakistan conclude that the basic decisions of children's entry into school and completion of the primary level are largely determined by parent's education, particularly that of mother's and household income [Sathar and Lloyd: 1991:103]. They believe that an important determinant of girls' education seems to be the accessibility of 'appropriate' girls' schools. They conclude that mother's education far outweighs father's education especially where the education of girls was concerned.
12. For a detailed look at basic education in India see the PROBE team report (1999) and also the World Bank paper on primary education in India (1997). See also Dreze and Kingdon (1999) for a look at factors affecting school participation in rural India.
13. The high rate of literacy of women in Kerala has been attributed to the large Christian missionary community in this state and also to the unique matrilineal structure of society here (see Sopher: 1980 for a discussion, especially p. 140).

14. There might be some discrepancy here about the grades, as some schools have their middle school from grades VI-VIII, while others have it till grade IX. For the purpose of this paper, I follow the grades as set out by the National Policy on Education, 1986. See Aggarwal (1989) for a discussion. For detailed information on the grade system in different states see the Department of Education website.
15. There are various kinds of colleges and vocational education options available to students after completing their high school. But as 1 will be looking at the determinants of education at different levels and not within a level, for the purpose of this study it was considered enough to know whether a respondent went to college or not, and not what kind of college he went to.
16. See Acharya (1994) for a discussion on the non-formal stream and its weaknesses.
17. Shavit and Blossfeld (1993) present the study of educational inequality in 13 countries using a combination of both these methods.
18. After deleting from the data all the respondents that had missing information on any of the variables used in the study, I was left with a final sample of 7,808 men and women.
19. Though this does not exclude the possibility of official bias while including people on the electoral register, the bias should still be minimal.
20. Source: Department of Education website, Education Statistics, Sub Table XI.
21. For an interesting discussion on the geographical picture of sex disparity in Indian literacy, see Sopher (1980), in which he studies reasons why certain regions in India have consistently lagged behind others where equality of educational opportunity is concerned.
22. For a study on what sets Kerala apart from the rest of the country see Jeffrey (1992).
23. The districts of Barmer and Jalor of Rajasthan have the lowest literacy of 7.68 per cent and 7.76 per cent respectively. Source: Census of India 1991, Department of education website.
24. See Heath, et al (2002) for a discussion of these categories.
25. Father's class is computed from the data on the occupation of the father.
26. For a discussion on the enumeration of caste in the census see a commentary by Kumar (2000). See also Sundar (2000).
27. For an example of the divisions between the category of *'dalits'* or scheduled castes, see Shah (2002).
28. See Appendix 2 for the Table corresponding to Figure 4.
29. See Appendix 3 for a table with the final 15 states.
30. For a comparative picture of all four transitions see Appendix 4, which puts together the most parsimonious models with the main effects but no interaction terms at each transition point (including the parameters for each state, whether significant or not).
31. Similar procedures were used to derive the most parsimonious model at each transition. The tables for each transition are not included here due to space constraints.
32 The logistic regression coefficients or parameter estimates are the fitted log odds. According to Mare (1981: 83) they 'denote the change in the log odds of grade progression per unit change in an independent variable.' These coefficients are the

parameter estimates for each successive transition given the completion of the previous one.

33. One observes a decline in the background effects on each successive transition as would be expected under the life course hypothesis [Shavit and Blossfeld: 1993], which posits that background effects should be particularly strong at the lower levels of the education system, and should diminish as one moves higher up the education ladder. This could either be because towards the end of the educational career, the subject has become independent enough not to depend on parental resources, or what is more likely is that there could have been a kind of a natural selection.
34. See Sopher (1980).
35. Sathar and Lloyd (1994) and Burney and Irfan's (1991) study is based on education in Pakistan.
36. Raju (1991) only mentions the need to deal with this issue, but does not empirically tackle it herself.

References

Acharya, P. 1994. 'Universal Elementary Education: Receding Goal', *Economic and Political Weekly:* 29:1 and 2: 27-30.

Aggarwal. J.C. 1987. *Indian Women: Education and Status.* New Delhi: Arya Book Depot.

Aggarwal. J.C. 1989. *National Policy on Education, 1986: An Appraisal.* Delhi: Doaba House.

Agrawal, S.P. and J.C. Aggarwal. 1994. *Third Historical Survey of Educational Development in India: Select Documents.* 1990-1992. New Delhi: Concept Publishing Company.

Burney, N.A. and M. Irfan. 1991. 'Parental Characteristics, Supply of Schools, and Child School Enrolment in Pakistan', *The Pakistan Development Review:* 30:1: 21-62.

Colclough, C. 1982. 'The Impact of Primary Schooling on Economic Development: A Review of the Evidence', *World Development:* 10:3: 167-185.

Colclough, C., P. Rose and M. Tembon. 'Does Poverty Cause Gender Inequality in Schooling?' *Id21 Insights,* Issue 29. Also available on the World Wide Web at http://www.id21.orglinsights/insights29/insights-iss29art05.html.

Dreze. J. and G.G. Kingdon.1999. 'School Participation in Rural India', *Development Economics Discussion Paper Series.* No. 18, Suntory and Toyota International centre for economics and related disciplines.

Heath, A.O. and S. Kumar. 2002. 'The Determinants of Social Mobility in India', *Economic and Political Weekly:* 37: 29: 2983-87.

India. Education Commission. 1966. *Report of the Education Commission, 1964-66: Education and National Development,* New Delhi: Ministry of Education, Government of India.

India. Government of. 1986. *National Policy on Education.* 1986. New Delhi: Ministry of Human Resource Development.

Jeffrey, R. 1992. *Politics, Women and Well-being: How Kerala Became a 'Model',* Basingstoke: Macmillan.

Jonsson, J.O. 1993. 'Persisting Inequalities in Sweden' pp. 101-32 in Y. Shavit and H.P. Blossfeld (eds), *Persistent Inequality: Changing Educational Attainment in Thirteen Countries*, Boulder, CO. Westview Press.

Kingdon, G.G. 1999. 'Gender Gap in India's Schools: Is the Labour Market a Factor?' *Id21 Insights*. Issue 29. Also available on the worldwide web at http://www. Id21.org/ insights/insights29/insights-iss29-art06.html.

Krishnan, G. and M. Shyam. 1973. 'Spatial Perspective on Progress of Female Literacy in India: 1901-1971', *Pacific Viewpoint:*14: 203-06.

Kumar, R. 2000. 'Caste Enumeration in Census: Constitutional Imperative', *Economic and Political Weekly:* 35:35 and 36: 3100-02.

Mare, R.D. 1980. 'Social Background and School Continuation Decisions', *Journal of the American Statistical Association:* 75: 295-305.

Mare, R.D. 1981. 'Change and Stability in Educational Stratification', *American Sociological Review:* 46: 72-87.

Mare, R.D. 1993. 'Educational Stratification on Observed and Unobserved Components of Family Background' pp. 351-76 in Y. Shavit and H.P. Blossfeld (eds.), *Persistent Inequality: Changing Educational Attainment in Thirteen Countries,* Boulder: Westview Press.

National Committee on the Status of Women (India). 1975. *Status of Women in India: A Synopsis of the Report of the National Committee on the Status of Women, 1971-1974. New Delhi:* Indian Council of Social Science Research.

PROBE. 1999. *Public Report on Basic Education in India,* New Delhi: Oxford University Press.

Raju, S. 1991. 'Gender and Deprivation. A Theme Revisited with a Geographical Perspective', *Economic and Political Weekly:* 26:49: 2827-39.

Ramachandran, V. and A. Saihjee. 2002. 'The New Segregation: Reflections on Gender and Equity in Primary Education', *Economic and Political Weekly:* 37:17: 1600-13.

Rosenzweig, M.R. and T.P. Schultz. 1982. 'Market Opportunities, Genetic Endowments and the Intra-Family Distribution of Resources: Child Survival in Rural India', *The American Economic Review:* 72: 4:803-15.

Sathar, Z.A. and C.B. Lloyd. 1994. 'Who Gets Primary Schooling in Pakistan? Inequalities among and within Families', *The Pakistan Development Review:* 33:2:103-34.

Sengupta, P. and J. Guha. 2002. 'Enrolment, Dropout and Grade Completion of Girl Children in West Bengal', *Economic and Politic Weekly:* 37: 17:1621-37.

Shah, A.M. 2002. 'The 'Dalit' Category and Its Differentiation', *Economic and Political Weekly:* 37: 14:317-18.

Shavit, Y. and H.P. Blossfeld (eds.). 1993. *Persistent Inequality: Changing Educational Attainment in Thirteen Countries,* Boulder, CO: Westview Press.

Sopher, D.E. 1980. 'Sex Disparity in Indian Literacy' pp. 130-88 in D.E. Sopher (ed.), *An Exploration of India: Geographical Perspectives on Society and Culture,* London: Longman.

Sundar, N. 2000. 'Caste as Census Category: Implications for Sociology', *Current Sociology:* 48:3: 111-26.

UNESCO. 1998. *World Education Report.* Paris: United Nations Educational, Scientific and Cultural Organisation.

Weiner, M., M.F. Katzenstein and K.V.N. Rao. 1981. *India's Preferential Policies: Migrants, the Middle Classes, and Ethnic Equality.* Chicago: University of Chicago Press.

World Bank. 1997. *Primary Education in India.* Washington, DC: World Bank.

The author thanks Anthony Heath for his encouragement. She would also like to thank the Data Unit of the Centre for the Study of Developing Societies, Delhi for permission to use their 1996, National Election Study data set. The paper was first published in the *Economic and Political Weekly:* 39:28: 2004: 3927-38. It is included here with the prior permission of the author and the Editor, *Economic and Political Weekly.* Address for correspondence: divya.vaid@nuffield.ox.ac.uk

Chapter - Sixteen

Contemporary Challenges to Women's Education: Towards an Elusive Goal?

Nandini Manjrekar

In the 1970s, struggles by women around issues of domestic violence, women's employment and livelihoods, communalism, representations in the media, etc, provided the impulse to women's studies, which has been referred to as the 'academic arm' of the women's movement. Critical inquiry into the structural and cultural bases that characterize the maintenance and reproduction of patriarchy in India at the familial, community and state levels have been carried out by women's studies scholars. Women's studies gained well-earned legitimacy within academia firstly through state support for its institutionalization in the 1980s, and more significantly, through the substantial contributions of feminist scholarship to the so-called mainstream disciplines. By questioning the value-neutrality of disciplinary perspectives, pointing to exclusions and invisibility, recovering women's voices and concerns from the margins, and often from outside the pages of mainstream academic discourse, and constantly unveiling and exploring the complex relationship between power and knowledge, women's studies have engaged directly with the politics of knowledge.

It is somewhat surprising, then, and worthy of critical attention, why feminist engagements with the politics of knowledge, both in the academic arena and through activism, have bypassed the field of education in a larger sense and school education in particular. The effects of formal education on Indian women over the so-called silent years between independence and the early 1970s was captured in the *Towards Equality* report [GoI: 1974] which indicated its role in sharpening class inequalities between women. The findings of the Committee on the Status of Women in India should have alerted the women's movement to the need to interrogate the social character of formal education in India, which has acted to divide women by class, caste and ethnicity. Larger feminist critiques of development policies and paradigms have unfortunately overlooked the ways in which formal education, in its organization and processes, offers a narrow range of subject positions for girls and women, locating and even objectifying them as mere instruments in the narrative of national progress.

The absence of critical thinking on formal education indicates the low status educational studies hold in the hierarchy of knowledge, even feminist knowledge, in India. Feminist scholars of education in the west have contributed to understanding the relationship between schooling and the reproduction of gender relations in capitalist society. They have examined how race, class and gender intersect in the making of policy, school knowledge, the formation of gendered and raced identities, and modes of resistance from a feminist perspective. Given the paucity of theoretical work in our own contexts this literature is largely what many of those interested in educational issues in India have to refer and draw from. In India, we still do not seem to share a discourse within which to discuss how educational visions have been highly gendered, both within nationalism as well as in the post-independence era; or to examine girls' education in relation to issues of their labour and sexuality.

There is, however, a large body of literature from which to construct frameworks to understand these issues in our own context. Feminist perspectives within the different disciplines, as well as the availability of a wide range of sources (women's writings, histories of women's organisations, women's journals, policy documents, NGO reports, etc) provide a base for theoretical understanding of gender and education. However, this important work of analysis remains to be done. Meanwhile, those of us who work on education within women's studies and the women's movement will have to continue to nudge and push: for inclusion of gender perspectives in educational fora, and the inclusion of educational concerns within the women's movement.

The above discussion is not intended to underplay the significant interventions made by the women's studies movement. Largely due to the persistence of women's studies scholars, in 1986 the National Policy on Education (NPE) specifically emphasized the necessity of reorienting education to promote women' sexuality, and envisioned education playing a positive interventionist role in the empowerment of women. The policy recommended revision of textbooks to eliminate gender bias and stereotyping and the training of teachers towards greater gender sensitivity. The NPE 1986 was a radical policy intervention in that it placed gender equality through education as a social and political commitment of the state; and it has continued to guide advocacy efforts for women's education. However, even this major intervention at policy level was limited by the fact that education, and school education in particular, had remained marginal to knowledge building within the women's movement and women's studies. Thus the NPE Review Committee (NPERC) in its critique of the 1986 policy noted that gender was markedly absent in the chapter on 'Content and Process of School Education' except for a mention that 'equality of the sexes' is to be one of the 10 core areas (para 6). It also pointed out that the task of addressing gender is fraught with complexity:

> *...A gender perspective in the content of education means more than the elimination of sexist bias and stereotypes from text-books... The task of bringing a gender perspective into the curriculum is a complex one and requires research inputs, discussion and debate...[NPERC: 1990: 44].*

Gendered access to educational facilities, sexism in school textbooks and stereotyping of curricular choices are issues that have been extensively examined by women's studies scholars. These are extremely important issues in themselves, but are not independent of other processes of schooling. Forms and representation of knowledge in school curricula reflect the discourses of formal education and the pattern of social relations in society-framing, normalizing and legitimizing social inequalities, processes in which the state plays a critical regulatory role.

We need to critically analyze why education has been peripheral to the concerns of the contemporary women's movement in India, given the legacy of struggle by women to establish their right to education. It is worth considering whether the assumed instrumentalist nature of formal education, particularly in the post–independence era, has not inhibited more radical interpretations of what formal education means for girls, both in terms of self perceptions as well as materially. The very premise of girls' education, especially education of poor girls-and here it is difficult to disentangle policy rhetoric from popular perceptions is based on an understanding that education is critical to social development-lower fertility, better child-rearing practices and so on. On one hand, these normative positions on the 'benefits' of women's education are persuasive and compelling; on the other, the struggle for the right of girls and women to education gets reduced to issues of access alone. The absence and avoidance of issues of conflict and contestation in mainstream education and curriculum discourse adds to this uni-dimensional understanding.

It has been easier for women's groups and NGOs to work with girls outside the system of formal education, especially the government system of education, which is notoriously inflexible. At the risk of repeating familiar statistics it is instructive to draw a picture of what it means to be schooled in India. There are data to show that the large majority of children, especially poor children, are in government schools. Conditions in most of these schools are hardly conducive to meaningful learning. A minuscule percentage of government schools possesses the very basic set of facilities such as adequate classrooms, toilets and drinking water, teaching-learning materials and libraries. There is evidence to show that physical inaccessibility, irrelevance of curricula, repeated 'failure' and even harsh treatment in schools contribute to children dropping out or never enrolling in school; it has been seen that in the case of girls, the influence of these factors is even more acute [Anandalakshmy: 1994:118, Jalaluddin: 1991:33, PROBE: 1999]. According to a NSSO survey (1995-96), about 26 per cent of those who had dropped out cited reasons other than poverty-unfriendly school environment, doubts about usefulness of schooling and inability to cope with studies. These factors accounted for over 75 per cent of dropouts among girls in rural areas [NSSO: 1998]. Dropout percentages among girls are extremely high in schools: figures for 1997-98 indicate that 41 per cent dropout at the primary level, 58 per cent at the middle school level and 72 per cent at the secondary level [GoI: 2000]. Discontinuation rates of rural girls have been found to be twice as high as those of boys [Sudarshan: 1998: 19]. Literacy and numeracy skills are abysmal among children who attend govern-ment schools, and are further devalued for poor girls who leave school, most often into environments that do not promote or sustain literacy.

New Challenges

Part of the challenge in thinking through our concerns about gender and education lies in uncovering the dialectical linkages between the formal education system and larger social and economic processes, and their influence on girls' and women's lives. In the present context, we are now seeing how an education system, already fragile and alienated from its objectives, is increasingly facing the combined onslaught of rightwing reaction and the market. Both portend the deepening of social divisions and inequalities.

A serious issue affecting girls' education is the appropriation of curriculum discourse by the Hindu Right. The National Curriculum Framework 2000 has a clear-cut position on gender issues, which embodies a break from the rhetoric and approach of earlier policy documents. It seeks to posit women as recipients of a benevolent if not empowering culture, promotes the idea that gender equality is an organic part of our cultural legacy and that the education of girls has a place to play in social cohesion, rather than social transformation. The glorification of women as mothers and the pronouncement that gender equality will be promoted through 'non-adversarial' positions signifies the considerable shift from the NPE 1986 [GoI: 1986], which spoke of education as an interventionist agency to promote gender equality in Indian society.

Studies show that privatisation of school education, hitherto restricted to urban centres, has been on the increase in rural areas since the early 1990s. The withdrawal of the state from formal education has been legitimized and endorsed by neo—liberal discourse, most prominently by the Ambani-Birla report (2000), which classifies education as a non-merit good.

Several micro-level studies indicate that families are investing scarce resources in sending their sons to private rather than government schools. There is a perception that English, widely taught in private schools across a wide spectrum from elite to substandard, holds the key to competing for scarce jobs in a shrinking labour market. It is necessary to study the implications of these trends on exacerbating gender divisions and the long-term effects on girls' participation in education. These trends are serious reminders to us that the women's movement must intensify its engagement with issues concerning women's education.

National Curriculum Framework

The National Curriculum Framework (NCF), officially released in 2000, reflects the efforts of the Hindu Right to seize the opportunity of commandeering the ideological state apparatus of education to push through its regressive agenda at the national level. The NCF marks a significant departure from earlier frameworks (1975, following the 1968 Education Policy; and 1988, following the 1986 Education Policy), which stressed the inculcation of values of democracy and social justice, and national integration through appreciation and understanding of the commonalities of different sub-cultures. The debate on the NCF 2000, and the strong criticism against it (articulated in a petition to the Supreme Court and discussed to some extent in the media), highlight the deeply ideological character of education. Spectacular in its shoddiness and banality, the text of the NCF is an ominous narrative of the Right's educational agenda. It is significant that the framework nowhere addresses the huge deficits in education at all levels.

History holds a key position in the reformulation of social knowledge in the NCF. Apprehensions expressed by historians, who have been protesting against the framework since 2000, have been vindicated, with textbooks now published (after the vacation of the stay by the Supreme Court) revealing gross distortions of history with a fetishist preoccupation with a glorious Hindu past. Religious education, thinly disguised as education for values, permeates all sections of the NCF. Value education is the main plank for launching the 'spiritual and moral renewal' of India through education.

> *"Schools can and must strive to restore and sustain the universal and eternal values oriented towards the unity and integration of the people, their moral and spiritual growth enabling them to realize the treasure within. People must realize who they are and what is the ultimate purpose of human life. Self-recognition would come to them through proper value education that would facilitate their spiritual march from the level of sub-consciousness to that of super consciousness through the different intermediary stages. Value based education would help the nation fight against all kinds of fanaticism, ill will, violence, fatalism, dishonesty, avarice, corruption, exploitation and drug abuse" [NCF: 2000: 17].*

According to the NCF, it is through learning of the 'lives of prophets, saints and the sacred texts' (p. 35) that children can achieve higher SQs (Spiritual Quotients) and EQs (Emotional Quotients) (p. 13). Value education is envisaged to form an integral part of the child's school experience. The child, in the vision of the NCF, is to be immersed in an environment where values, not derived from rules of citizenship in a democratic polity, but from religion, will predominate.

Value education and education about religions would not form a separate subject of study or examination at any stage. These would be so judiciously integrated with all the subjects of study in the scholastic areas and all the activities and programmes in the co-scholastic areas that the objectives thereof would be directly and indirectly achieved in the classrooms, at the school assembly places, play-grounds, cultural centres and such other places [NCERT: 2000: 33].

Quite apart from the dreary drivel it contains, the framework is an enormous setback to the women's movement. It portends a future for women's education that is deeply disempowering. The lack of seriousness with which the NCF approaches social disadvantage can be seen in the manner in which a range of citizens is subsumed within a single disadvantaged category: women, *dalits, adivasis*, along with children with impairments. Valorisation of religious tradition, the leitmotif of the document, negates the essentially oppressive role tradition plays in women's lives to curb and control their sexuality, labour and individuality.

It is not surprising that the NCF, displaying its ideological position on women, includes education of girls in a section titled 'Education for a Cohesive Society'. Here, we get a glimpse of how girls can be educated the 'Right' way. Patriarchal oppression and the struggle for equality and justice are non-issues in a social order in which caste and gender hierarchies are non-conflictual, harmonious elements in the seamless fabric of the great Indian tradition:

[Besides,] making education accessible to more and more girls, especially rural girls, removing all gender discrimination and gender bias in school curriculum, textbooks and the process of transaction is absolutely necessary. *Moreover, it will be the most appropriate thing to recognize and nurture the best features of each gender* in *the best Indian tradition. After all, India gave her women the right to vote without any prolonged battle for it unlike* in *the west. There* is *a need to develop and implement gender inclusive and gender sensitive curricular strategies to nurture a generation of girls and boys who are equally competent and are sensitive to one another, and grow up in a caring and sharing mode as equals, and not as adversaries* [NCERT: 2000: 9, emphasis added].

The 'vision' of the NCF neatly accommodates the pervasive instrumentalist view of education for girls and women, in which women are seen primarily as reproducers. Equality of the opportunity [sic] of access to education is necessary if more women are to become the agents of change. Therefore, education of women is an important key to improving health, nutrition and education in the family, and also empowering them to participate in decision-making. Investment, both in formal and non-formal education of young children in general, and of the girl child in particular is expected to yield exceptionally high social and developmental returns [NCERT: 2000: 19].

It may be tempting to dismiss the NCF as the usual hocus-pocus regularly churned out by the cultural nationalists who command so much media space these days. However, it is important to remember that the framework will influence the ways in which millions of children understand their social worlds and identities through textbooks. Ironically, moreover, the anti-modernity of the NCF's vision of education is entirely compatible with the processes of globalization. 'Indianising' and 'spiritualizing' the curriculum is not antithetical in the least to orienting education to the market. Vocationalisation, a recommendation of the NCF, was originally envisaged as an alternative to college education, which students could opt for after Class XII. It has been a non-starter in Indian education, with less than 5 per cent of students opting for vocational courses [Visaria: 1998]. Vocational courses for girls are highly gendered-typing, tailoring, etc, which only allow them entry, if at all, into low-paying jobs in the unorganized sector. The NCF now recommends vocational streaming after Class X. This will only serve to heighten inequalities by caste, class and gender, by further restricting the access of poor girls, *dalits* and other marginal groups to higher education, and decreasing their representation at this level.

In Gujarat, the crucible of *Hindutva,* one can see from where documents like the NCF derive their force and purpose. Education has been a key focus of mobilization by *Hindutva* organizations over at least the past five years in Gujarat. In Panchmahals, where we happened to do some fieldwork in schools in 2000, government-appointed *vidya sahayaks* were holding *satsangs* in schools and participating in VHP programmes [Manjrekar and Surti: 2000]. In 1998, a fact-finding team investigating the communal violence which visited Sanjeli-Randhikpur in Gujarat following the marriage of a Muslim youth with an *adivasi* girl, met school teachers who justified the violence against Muslims and supported the actions of the VHP-Bajrang Dal in the area (PUCL report). With the ascendance of the BJP in elected governance, conflict has been emerging in Gujarat over the running of educational institutions in tribal areas between Christians and RSS organizations.

By March 2002, the curriculum was already being revised in Gujarat according to the NCF guidelines, paying little heed to the then ongoing Supreme Court case. It is no surprise that RSS-affiliated organizations have been involved in the curriculum revision. Quite in keeping with the NCF guidelines, post-BJP government textbooks are replete with stories of 'the wisdom of our ancient sages'; according to the guidelines, Sanskrit will be taught from Class 6 in all 'schools. The Gujarat education minister stated that a state-level 'campaign' is necessary for implementing the 'National Curriculum' by June 2003, through seminars with principals and teachers (PUCL-*Vadodara Shanti Abhiyan* 2002 submission to the National Human Rights Commission]. It is now slated to be operational from the next academic session.

In this planned saffronisation of education, emphasis on 'value education' derived from religion and 'tradition' replaces that on social justice, tolerance and plurality. The idea of 'unity in diversity', an educational slogan of the post-independence era, which had some pedagogic value despite its problems, has been given a quiet burial. This new thrust is of a piece with efforts in other spheres to manufacture a majoritarian view of society in which the cultural and political space for all marginalized sections, especially minorities, will progressively shrink. What better place to begin than in school? Experience of the present carnage against Muslims in Gujarat begs the question whether a saffronised school curriculum will not provide a good setting in which intolerance and further injustices against minorities can be justified. The complex ways in which these distortions will affect the identities of girls of different classes, castes, religions and ethnicities, providing an illusion of empowerment for some and drastically disempowering others, is a cause for concern for the Indian women's movement.

Education and Market

Since the introduction of market reforms in India, there has been a steady attempt to devalue the role of the government in the social sector. Undoubtedly, the Indian state must bear the responsibility for its lack of commitment to constitutional directives that mandate that all children must be healthy and educated in independent India. However, we need to consider whether privatization in the education sector is an adequate answer to the government's lack of performance. There is increasing evidence that privatization is likely to exacerbate existing gender inequalities in education.

In April 2000, the prime minister's Council for Trade and Industry submitted a report on a policy framework for reforms in education. The convener and principal member of this 'special subject group' were two leading industrialists. The report outlines in a succinct manner the conditions of education in India, and talks of the different worlds coexisting side by side: the privileged few, the resistance to change from various quarters, the situation of poor children in indefensibly adverse learning conditions. It speaks of raising standards and working to 'create a competitive yet cooperative knowledge-based society'. This report explicitly argues the necessity of opening up the secondary sector to private initiatives, while maintaining that the primary sector needs the full support of the government in order to meet the requirement of Article 45 of the Constitution.

The report unequivocally calls for government support to private investment in secondary education in every *taluka*, and a 'user pays' principle, as well as direct foreign investment, at the higher education level. The report is profoundly lacking in any reflection on what constitutes learning, what and how children should be learning. It talks of creating 'smart schools', which must be competitive and innovative. Our endeavour, it suggests, should not be the creation of an environment that produces industrial workers and labourers but one that fosters 'cutting edge' knowledge resources that can place India in the 'vanguard in the information age' (p. 3).

Several contentious issues in the report need to be debated. Firstly, we must ask ourselves how it is that industry is dictating what national educational priorities must be. Obviously, there is a huge educational market at stake here. A close look at other social sector policies tells us the same story. The National Population Policy 2000, for instance, talks of private investment in basic education for girls and the creation of markets at the village level that will motivate girls to take up vocational training. It is clear that the logic of market intervention in education is related to so-called 'efficiency' and the generation of profit, in the context of education supposedly emerging as a new sector of the global economy. What is frightening, however, is that any educational vision or perspective will be surrendered to this logic. Hence in the Ambani-Birla report, 'knowledge' and information' are viewed as the same, since this justifies entry into the global IT market. But should we not pause to reflect' how this approach, in one imperious sweep, negates the years of struggle and debate on making education relevant and contextual for children as the best way to sustain their interest in school-based learning? Have we not learned from the available evidence that it is because of an information-loaded curriculum that children find school boring and in the face of other difficulties, leave early? But the market will demand information, not local knowledge that children are familiar with and can acquire genuine skills from. We need to contest the report's neo-liberal approach to education on both political and pedagogical grounds.

Privatization: Intensifying Gender Inequalities

Given that up to the 1990s privatization did not find mention in policy documents, it is quite amazing how fast it has gained ground and seized the imagination of our educational decision makers. The government's withdrawal from the education sector and the entry of private enterprise is by design, not by default. The failure of the state to provide basic education to all children takes on a different dimension in the context of structural reform of economies. The experiences of other countries attempting such reforms in the name of efficiency tell us that they serve to further marginalize communities who already find themselves on the periphery of formal education.

Although overall most children are in government schools, the share of enrolments in private schools out of total enrolment has been steadily increasing, as more and more parents feel that the poor quality of learning offered by state-run schools add to further disadvantage their children's life chances [Khan and Manjrekar: 2002, Sudarshan: 1998: 20]. There is no regulation or monitoring of most of these private schools, many of which remain unrecognized. Evidence points to the fact that the standards are poor, teachers are underpaid and facilities are lacking. Then why are they still in demand? Most of them have one selling point: the teaching of English. Hence the demand for private schools is largely related to popular perception that knowledge of English is necessary to survive in the new labour market. It is instructive to see what this means in terms of actual money spent. The average annual expenditure by families per child in government schools is Rs. 317, in government-aided schools it is Rs. 391 and in private schools it is Rs 742 [Sudarshan: 1998: 20]. Private expenditure has increased as a percentage of consumption expenditure from 2.5 per cent in the early 1980s to 3.5 per cent in the late 1990s (p 60) [NSSO: 1995-96, cited in National Human Development Report: 2001: 55-56].

Justified on the basis of returns through employment, increased household expenditure on education will inevitably be discriminatory: boys' education will be favoured over that of girls. There is growing evidence that beyond a certain income level, girls are being sent, if at all, to government schools, whereas their brothers are sent to private schools. For girls, marriageability remains the more critical criterion. Thus, while there is some evidence of increasing demand for girls' education, even in rural areas, the motivation of parents is to seek upwardly mobile marriage to educated salary earners.[1]

Privatization is unlikely to embody the social understanding and vision that can address the real issues behind lower participation of girls in education. Recent developments indicate that policies are becoming increasingly gender-blind. One may even venture to say that they are erasing whatever gains have been made towards girls' well being. We are already witness to drastic reductions in the outlays on the mid-day meal programme, which, with all its problems, has served to ensure some nutrition for poor children, especially girls, and has been shown to have a positive effect on retention in schools [Tilak: 1999]. The 93rd Amendment Bill, declaring education as a fundamental right, does not include the under-6 population from its purview. This effectively means that the entire ICDS programme of early childhood education has been put into jeopardy. It also means that older girls will have to participate for even longer hours in sibling care. The emphasis on income generating activities as a priority for educated women bespeaks this myopia. Education for five years, basic literacy and numeracy skills that can just about sustain these activities, are deemed sufficient for girls. Although economic independence is an important aspect of women's empowerment, it cannot be reduced to income generating activities, which more often than not mean low-paying, insecure jobs, often within the parameters of the traditional domestic roles of women.

It is a telling commentary on our caste, gender and occupational hierarchies that the Kothari Commission's recommendation of neighbourhood schools could never be put into practice. Neighbourhood schools would perhaps have altered the very texture of our society, and generated questions missing from the educational agenda today, such as the social contexts of learning and content of curriculum. Despite the claims of privatization to being a great social leveller based on merit alone, for girls, and particularly poor girls, it is likely to be yet another mode of discrimination within the family and economy. As Mary Warnock (1977: 26) puts it: 'There is a world of difference between the equal right to education and the right to equal education'. Class, caste and gender inequalities in education are only going to increase without strong state commitment to equality. That the Indian state has failed to stem these inequalities is not in doubt. However, we should recognize that entrenched privileges of the elites functioning within Indian patriarchal society have contributed to this failure. These interests will continue to influence privatization as well. We may recall that 25 years ago, J.P. Naik (1979: 177) said that equal opportunity in education cannot be seen in isolation from enhancing opportunity on the political and economic fronts to 'destroy privilege itself'.

What is to be done?

Where democratic spaces are increasingly shrinking under the weight of a majoritarian state and the forces of the market, how can the women's movement re-engage with questions of education? In this paper, I have tried to raise a few issues that could be addressed as a tentative beginning to this re-engagement. To my mind, there is need for intensive monitoring of new developments that are likely to impact girls' education. Women are central to the contemporary politics of culture embodied in the NCF. The struggle for an egalitarian and democratic culture should be extended to a struggle for an education that is critical of received ideologies and can promote such a culture. For this we may have to work to mainstream gender concerns into alternative educational discourse. Unfortunately, as I have attempted to point out here, there is a gap between those who are part of the more radical debates on education, most of whom are sensitive but hesitant to address gender issues, and women's studies scholars and activists who do not direct their analysis of gender and society towards questions of educational theory, pedagogy and curriculum.

Many women's activists and organizations participate in sessions with teachers where gender issues are discussed. Teacher training is an important area of intervention, but we should be a little wary of training in isolation from the experience of teachers in schools. At a recent seminar on school education, a participant lamented that a standard response of school administrators to problems of girls' education is to suggest a training course. She said that the idea of training as a solution has become so commonplace that schoolteachers and even NGOs have unquestioningly accepted it. This brings to mind an interesting experience we had two years ago while studying social contexts of schooling in Panchmahals district in Gujarat [Manjrekar and Surti: 2000]. A single teacher managing five classes in a single room (a new room constructed under the District Primary Education Programme (DPEP) lay unused because it was close to collapse) told us that she had learned a great deal from the gender training course she had received under the DPEP. How do you use some of the ideas in your classroom, we asked. She told us that she made the girls and boys sit together, because in the course she had learned that gender segregation was not a good practice. She added that the arrangement prevented social interaction in the classroom making it easier for her to teach in that difficult situation. Now, in many co-educational schools, seating girls and boys next to each other rather than in the more usual segregated manner is employed as a 'shaming' technique, used by teachers to prevent 'indiscipline' in the classroom. The above example highlights the absurdity of reducing concerns about gender in school education to 'gender training', from which teachers take away what is most practical to their pressing needs in undoubtedly adverse situations.

Privatization is another area we must keep monitoring. The devaluation of government schooling over the past twenty years or so has been speeded up by market reforms since the early 1990s. Data from urban areas shows that corporation and government schools now mainly have poor girls and very poor children from other marginal communities; in many cities, municipal schools with good infrastructure are lying vacant. It is important to engage with government bodies to see what can be done to improve the quality of schooling so that more girls can attend these schools and attain an acceptable level of education.

Finally, in the face of multiple pressures, can we debate our feminist-understanding of what it means to be educated as a girl/woman in contemporary India? Can we put forward an alternate perception of girls' education? Young girls today are facing newer, more complex, forms of regulation. For instance, our experience in an urban context suggests that young school going girls, under the influence of the market and the media, are experiencing new consumption-related desires, such as the desire to look good. We have also found that poorer girls engage in piece-rate work after school hours to earn enough to fulfill these new needs.

After the violence against Muslims in Gujarat, there have been apprehensions that Muslim girls may be withdrawn from schools. Indeed, this is an issue that came up repeatedly in interactions with victims of the violence, in particular, women and young girls [PUCL-Shanti Abhiyan: 2002, Panjabi, et al: 2002]. A few of us have been meeting young Muslim girls in a school to discuss issues of education. Questions of physical insecurity loom large in these discussions, as can be expected after the trauma that Muslim women and the community as a whole have been through, and the insecurity that continues to loom large over their lives. What has struck us, however, is the determination of many of these girls to continue with education. Many of them said they wanted to be lawyers and teachers. Why, we asked. To fight for our rights, and teach girls well so they can fight too, they said. Can education engender such resistance? Is this the alternate, critical consciousness we have been hoping to articulate as an aim for girls' education? And does it necessarily have to come at so heavy a price? As Brecht said, too many questions.

Note

1. The dichotomy that has been set up between boys-superior, private-and girls-inferior, government-has its own tragic consequences for the self-esteem and identity of girls. In my own work I have spoken to girls who, with considerable anguish, question but also resign themselves to this divide that casts them as educationally less deserving than their brothers. This is an important aspect of the social consequences of privatization and one that needs further study.

References

Ambani, M. and Birla K. 2000. 'Report on a Policy Framework for Reforms in Education', New Delhi: Prime Minister's Council on Trade and Industry, Government of India.

Anandalakshmy, S. (ed). 1994. *The Girl Child and the Family*, Department of Women and Child Development, New Delhi: MHRD, Government of India.

Government of India. 1974. *Towards Equality: Report of the Committee for the Status of Women* in *India,* New Delhi: Ministry of Women and Child Development.

Government of India. 1986. *National Policy on Education,* New Delhi:Department of Education, Ministry of Human Resource Development.

Government of India. 2000. *Annual Report 1999-2000,* New Delhi: Ministry of Human Resource Development, Department of Education.

Government of India. 2001. National Human Development Report, New Delhi: Government of India,Planning Commission.

Jalaluddin, A.K. 1991. 'Development Imperatives for Universalisation of Basic Education' in School Education in the 1990s; Problems and Perspectives, New Delhi: NCERT.

Khan, F. and N. Manjrekar. 2002. Contexts and Constraints of Schooling: Operation Blackboard Ethnographic Studies: A Summary Paper, unpublished.

Manjrekar, N. and T. Surti. 2000. 'Schooling on the Margins of Development: A Study in Shivrajpur, Panchmahals District, Gujarat', New Delhi: National Institute of Educational Planning and Administration (unpublished).

Naik, J.P. 1979. 'Equality, Quality and Quantity in Indian Education', *International Review of Education,* Jubilee Number.

National Council of Educational Research and Training. 2000. 'National Curriculum Framework', New Delhi:NCERT.

National Sample Survey Organisation.1998. *Attending an Educational Institution* in *India: Its Level, Nature and Cost—*1995-96. *NSS 52nd Round (1996-97),* Report No. 439, New Delhi: Department of Statistics, Government of India.

Panjabi, K., K. Bandopadhyay and B. Gangopadhyay. 2002. *The Next Generation: In the Wake of the Genocide* (A Report by Independent Citizens on the Impact of the Gujarat Pogrom on Children and the Young), supported by Citizen's Initiative, Ahmedabad.

PROBE. 1999. *Public Report on Basic Education,* New Delhi: Oxford University Press.

PUCL- Shanti Abhiyan. 2002. At *the Receiving End: Women's Experiences of Violence* in *Vadodara,* Vadodara.

Ramachandran, V. 1998. 'Promises, Promises', *Seminar* (Right to Education):April: 54-63.

NPERC (1986). 1990. *Towards an Enlightened and Humane Society,* Acharya Ramamurthi Report, New Delhi: NCERT.

Sahiyar Stree Sanghathan, Gujarat Forum for Women's Studies and Action, NAWO, Movement for Secular Democracy and PUCL, Fact-finding Reports into Sanjeli-Randhikpur Incidents, August-September 1998.

Sudarshan, R. 1998. Where Are We? *Seminar* (Right to Education): April: 18-21.

Tilak, J.B.G. 1999. 'National Human Development Initiative: Education in the Union Budget', *Economic and Political Weekly:* March 6-13: 614-20.

Visaria, P. 1998. *Unemployment among Youth in India,* Employment and Training papers 36, Geneva:International Labour Organisation.

Warnock, M. 1977. *Schools of Thought,* London: Faber and Faber.

The paper was first published in the *Economic and Political Weekly*: 38:43: 2003: 4577-82. It is included here with the prior permission of the author and the Editor, *Economic and Political Weekly*. Address for email correspondence is: manjsam@ d2visp.com.

PART - IV

WOMEN IN TRADITIONAL ECONOMIC ACTIVITIES: PRESENCE, AGENCY AND CONTROL

CHAPTER - SEVENTEEN

Portrayal of Working Women in Indian Popular Literature-Changing Scenario

Aruna Sitesh

With the spread of education and the changing social ethos, there has been a marked change and departure from tradition in our society creating new pressures, new situations and new attitudes. The new crossing to a technological-metropolitan society has altered the spectrum of choices available to the Indian woman. Workingwomen are no longer seen as a stigma on the family as the inability of the patriarchal head to provide for the family. The power structures of the nuclear families have also changed creating new roles and responsibilities. It has become an accepted pattern to expect the daughter, especially the eldest daughter, to take up a job and help settle her younger brothers and sisters. The trend is very explicit in our literature also which is regarded as major tool of true image of the society. This article reviews literature to examine the portrayal of working women by eminent women writers. The analyses of the characters in the Indian popular literature are actually representing the society as such hence their analyses clearly reflect the attitudinal changes in the society in context of working women. This article tries to capture *the change in the trend as* reflected in the novels during the last few decades written by various women writers.

Sushma in Usha Priyamvada's *Pachpan Khambhe Lal Deevaren* (1966), Ranjana in Rajani Paniker's *Pahali Ladaki* (1973) and Malti in Shashi Prabha Shastri's *Naven* (1974) take up jobs as soon as they have completed their studies because of economic pressures faced by the family. The fallacy of the belief that economic independence would help them control their destinies soon becomes apparent. Even though these girls have jobs, they are not really economically independent. Their parents hold or want to hold their purse strings. Parents' self-indulgence can be heartless at times. When Sushma gives up her first teaching assignment because the secretary of that private college tries to take liberties with her, her mother doesn't support Sushma's decision. Parents' indifference to the emotional needs of their working daughters turns callous when they begin to discuss the marriage prospects of their younger daughter. These women represent the paradox of progress that women's education and consequent economic independence has not really meant their liberation in the real sense of the term. *These free women are not really free-they still cannot lead their lives the way they want to.*They internalize the self-sacrificing values and decide that they *live only for their parents and siblings. Exploited thus by their families both economically and emotionally, these women remain on tenterhooks constantly balancing their home needs and career*. The disturbing difference is that while men are allowed to lead their independent personal lives, young women are not. One important reason for that is that sons remain members of the natal family even after marriage while girls, once married, leave their parental homes. After marriage, their earnings, if they continue to work, become the rightful possession of their husbands and in-laws of course exceptions are there.

Not all women however, work to support their parents or siblings. These days most urban middle class girls go for a Bachelor's or Master's degree. Parents find it easier to find a match for their educated daughters. But instead of fooling away their time while the parents are looking for a suitable boy, isn't it better and wiser to take up a job? In Mridula Garg's *Uske Hisse Ki Dhoop* (1976) Vidhu begins to teach in a college because her fiancée plans to marry only after returning from the USA year later with a degree in Management. While waiting to get married, many girls take up jobs, if available. After all, no one can stop you from resigning anytime. Of course, the choice to opt out of employment is not left to them. It is left to the parents-in-laws to let them continue or ask them to give up their jobs.

Some girls get married precisely because they are working. Ajit in Rajani Paniker's *Mahanagar Ki Mita* (1972) might not have married Mita had she not been the college librarian and thus in a position to support him in his studies. In Shashi Deshpande's *The Dark Holds No Terrors* (1980), Sarita might not have been married to Manohar had she not been a medical student. In Neelima Singh's *Satya Ka Sheshansh* (1987) Ranjan Chatterjee marries Ruma not because he finds her better in looks or *smartness* than many other young girls eager to marry him, nor because he cares for the simplicity of her loving heart, but because she gets a handsome salary every month. Shahala's father in Shubha Verma's *Mohtarma* (1984) educates all his four daughters so that he wouldn't have a problem marrying them off. They would earn and pay their dowry lifelong. His arithmetic is however, proved wrong when he is asked to give sufficient dowry by the groom's father commensurate with his son's education. Rohin, the groom also sees nothing wrong in his father's expectations.

It is often argued, and not without reason, that dowry and arranged marriages go together. Give the girls the freedom to choose their life partners and the evil of dowry would automatically disappear. Shahala's experience with Rohin presents an entirely different picture. Shahala's parents allegedly encourage their friendship in the fond hope of getting Shahala married without dowry. Rohin, however, would care to wed the girl of his choice only if a decent dowry accompanies her, thus making the best of both the worlds. Within three months of losing Shahala, he gets married to another girl and is reported to be doing well in life.

Kuni in Chandrakanta's *Apne-Apne Konark* (1995), well settled in life with job and handsome pay, declares that she does not want to marry as lot of money and jewellery was demanded. Her father gets relieved on hearing this and gives his best wishes. But the story that gets into circulation thereafter is that his father doesn't want to marry off his earning daughter. Who would want to lose the goose that lays the golden eggs?

An unmarried girl doing a job and living all by herself in another town is blasphemy. What will people say? Working in the same town or working after she had got married would have been different. *Yet another paradox of our times is that young women can work if their parents or parents-in-law permit them to. Where they should work, how they should work, when they should resign-these crucial questions which would determine the quality and direction of their lives would also be decided by parents or parents-in-laws without paying the slightest heed to the likes or dislikes of the girls concerned.* The majority of women themselves don't think that after marriage, personal fulfillment for a woman in her career or having her own life is justified if the husband does not approve of it. *It is for the woman to make the major adjustment in a marriage even if it means giving up her career.*

Usually husbands don't like/allow their wives to work. They perhaps fear that she would lose her meekness, if not purity, if she competes with men outside the home. *Perhaps a workingwoman clashes with the bourgeois conventional image of a dutifully passive wife.* They perhaps see it as a reflection on their role as a provider of the family. *Also fear that if she becomes economically independent, their sole authority would be eroded.*

Even as Indian women are leaping ahead breaking every male bastion that comes their way, a large number of Indian men, fortunately not all, have not been able to internalize it. Especially if financially comfortable, they expect an extra pat for being so condescending! so liberal, so accommodating as to let their wives work. They feel that their responsibility ends there. The idea of sharing some of the domestic chores with her is quite alien to them. *She, therefore, finds herself in the demanding dual role of a housewife and a workingwoman.*

When a husband begins to harbour the impression that his wife is perhaps more capable than he is, it can develop a backlash in the marriage. And this can take a lot of forms; criticism of her household work, sabotaging her professional aspirations, pushing childbirth on her when she is not ready for it, refusing to help in household chores, physical and emotional abuse, etc. *Successful women very often find themselves dealing with the remnants of a broken marriage. The apparent reversal of traditional gender roles and subsequent power equations constantly threatens the tenuous fragility of their marriage.*

Most of our enlightened, independent women do not want their marriages head towards divorce and a broken home. It is not cowardice that makes many of our workingwomen shun divorce or separation, it is not the fear of social stigma either, *it is an acceptance of their innate need to love and be loved.* Only when the situation turns intolerable, do they decide to walk out of marriage. It is choosing between the devil and the deep sea. As far as possible, *these women would try to reconcile.* While looking for new possibilities of choice, personal control, personal growth, these women don't want to sacrifice the vital human satisfaction of warm loving relationships some of which exist only in a family context. This dualism, best explained in terms of individualism and conformity the desire to want to belong and to being dependent, explains *why these women suffer indignities and tyranny of the family.*

Is the status of a married woman enhanced in the family circles if she earns an income? Is she accorded more respect and treated as an equal by her husband and other family members for bringing a second pay packet to the household? The answer found in the majority of the novels is 'no'. *Their economic status doesn't alter the basic domestic order or power structure. Working within the traditional social and cultural contexts these women take on multiple roles of wives, mothers, daughters-in-law and co-providers.*

In Shashi Deshpande's *The Dark Holds No Terrors* Sarita can no longer tolerate her husband's brutality (marital rape as a sexual weapon) night after night. But Sarita's job gives her the confidence and courage to leave him and home. 'Enough is enough'. In *Satya Ka Sheshansh* Ruma can get away from the chilling brutality of her husband and mother-in-law because she has a job. What fulfillment does/can this life give her is, of course, a moot question? Despite going through hell, her only obsession in life is her husband and her marriage. This emotional bondage dictates the decisions of many of our workingwomen. In a sense it augurs well because it will stop our society from turning chaotic or going the western way. On the other hand, women continue to be exploited for this weakness of theirs.

Broadly speaking however, an economically independent woman doesn't necessarily have to leave her in-law's house only as a corpse as decreed by tradition, she can just walk out. In Raji Narasimhan's *The Sky Changes* (1991) Krishna takes up a job once she is convinced that the man she is married to cannot bring her any fulfillment and to be able to live life in her own way. Perhaps the need for self-assertion and self esteem makes Radha and Rukmani in *Do Sakhiyan* take up jobs even though their husbands are literally rolling in money. We are not told what kind of job satisfaction, if at all, these two sisters get but when Radha's only son Kartikeya turns a drug addict at 18 and is expelled from college, her husband blames her for it.He argues that if she had not been obsessed with her job and had been available to the son instead of insisting on keeping him in the hostel, Kartikeya could/would have been saved. Radha's husband, *most husbands and housewives blame the working mother for her child's delinquency. This is another striking anomaly of our times.* On the one hand, housekeeping and childcare are considered inferior activities demanding little intelligence or enterprise or strain; on the other hand, the sociologists invariably cite absence of mother from home for long hours leading to an emotional void in the tender hearts as a major cause for the rising incidence of juvenile delinquency.

Not only husbands, even children don't like their mothers going out to work. In Shashi Deshpande's *The Binding Vine* (1993) Mandira hurts Vanaa by saying all sorts of nasty things because she feels her mother neglects them her and Pallavi. She keeps saying Vanaa should not be working. No one blames the father for not being around. Vanaa tells her Urmi aunt that she would leave the job and stay at home to look after the children. Urmi aunt wants to know what she would do when her children grew up and go away and they don't need her any more.

Kunni of *Apne Apne Konark* faces an unusual situation. She remains unmarried and helps her brother to settle down and set-up homes. Her brother Divakar's wife Kaveri is not happy about the presence of this unmarried sister-in-law at home. Her presence makes them feel guilty and affects their freedom. Once the parents die, Kuni will become the liability; they will have to look after her. Kuni is stunned to overhear this. She hadn't thought that far ahead! She hadn't thought of herself at all when she had put her foot down to declare that she would not marry and push her family to the verge of desolation and destitution. She hasn't yet started thinking of her age. She decides to try for a transfer, as she does know how else to move out without hurting her parents.

When Sushma *(Pachpan Khambhe)* turned away from Neel to gratify her parents, she obviously had inkling of how her siblings were going to treat her a few years after. This is the home front. What's about the work place? Shahana Choudhury in Shubha Verma's *Freelancer* (1981) gives a distressing account of the sexual harassment women journalists have to undergo. Shubha Verma is the only writer who has written at length about the problems of women journalists not their personal, domestic problems but problems they confront trying to discharge their professional duties. Shubha Verma's long experience as a journalist has obviously stood her in good stead. Shubha Verma's novels delve deep into the day-to-day life of professional women journalists. The situation is far more complex and problematic than that meets the eye. If there are men ever ready to exploit their female colleagues and subordinates, there are women eager to take advantage of their boss's carnal weakness and clinch an out of turn promotion or assignment or extension. In *Hartal* (1987) Shubha Verma introduces us to Ketaki who, even after her retirement, has been soliciting and seducing the General Manager Mehta hoping to get a few year's extension or a few more permanent columns.

The appalling situation of the majority of these women characters is not a remnant of the archaic systems of patriarchy. *They are a product of modern development. In modern society money and social esteem go together. Those without money are also denied esteem.* For this very reason housewives occupy a low social status. They earn nothing and, therefore, deserve no recognition. Domestic chores and childcare are not measured in monetary terms and hence considered inferior. Women left at home are troubled by a sense of futility and worthlessness. *With the passage of time women themselves become aware in ever increasing numbers, in the cities at least, that all their energy was taken up by making food and love and that there was perhaps more to life than this. It is this craving for recognition that compels Vismita of Manjul Bhagat's Tirchhi Bauchhar (1984) to take up a job. By all accounts she is a well-adjusted wife and mother. Yet she must work to prove to herself that life exists beyond the four walls of her home and that she can find/make a place for herself there.*

How do these women perceive their new roles outside the home? What is the quality of their output? Suryabala's *Oeekshanta* (1992) deals with the decline in the moral standards of our academics. Among latter there are *women of leisured class who work because they want the added charm of the intellectual label attached to them.* Suryabala focuses on the endless search for independent status of these very rich women who are only interested in flaunting their chiffons and sandals and perfumes. On the other extreme is the ambition of the lower middle class women to go up the socio-economic scale. These middle class women would also like to have all the privileges of the leisured class. With no commitment to their jobs both are equally insincere and shallow. Without any qualms both these groups of teachers would not take classes, would not teach beyond 15 minutes, if at all. Students are not interested in studies anyway. So why waste their breath on them? *What does one do about such self-opinionated shirkers?*

Usha Puri's *Mukhauton Ke Beech* (1986) also exposes this total lack of commitment to work in a number of women. They turn the staff room into the arena of politics the way the earlier women used the inner courtyard for gossip and petty jealousies. Pramila Rajdan in Shubha Verma's *Katmangur* (1989) has absolutely no scruples about getting along with anyone at any time, if it boosts her ego or interest. Job is only a cover for her. Anju tells Neeta that "women like Pramila Rajdan who allow themselves to be used by their bosses and in turn use everyone they can lay their hands on for their own vested interest have vitiated the lives of working women. Anyone who knows about Pramila would conclude that all those who go out to work are like her".

It should be noted that in all these novels focusing on the campus life, women teachers have not been favorably portrayed. It becomes still more significant in the light of these writers being themselves teachers. May be they are trying to caution us against this *rapidly rising decline in work ethic so that these can be set right before irreparable damage is done to the image of women as a conscientious, industrious and responsible work turf.* Whereas the works of the 60s and 70s dealt with the working girls mainly in their familial and emotional contexts, the last decade has shifted its focus to the workingwomen's performance and professional hazards. Quite a few of these women have been portrayed as victims of circumstances, ambition, callous indifference or casual, non-serious attitude to work.

However, not all have fallen into the rut. Shahana Chaudhury of *Freelancer* has decided to be *a freelancer so that she can retain her freedom and dignity to that extent. She can take the job of her choice without having to slave for anyone against her will.* She gives up the security of her job with the publishing company because a permanent job means many strings. She is a freelancer by choice, "Hard work in the initial stages gives you a standing and then you can be on your own". Shahana is the executive member of the Delhi Journalists' Association and also the National Union of Journalists. She has won three consecutive elections. She enjoys the respect of her fellow workers because of her integrity and dedication to work. When employees strike at work, she provides the required support and leadership by actively participating in all the sit–ins, marches and demonstrations. Beenu Natarajan also sits with the striking workers outside the office braving the scorching sun. Hitherto women were supposed to opt for softer options-keep off strikes and stay home in troubled times.

In Mridula Garg's *Anitya,* Kajal Banerjee, herself a freedom fighter, works because she cannot live with falsehoods and hypocrisy. Had she wanted money or power, she would have stayed on with her minister husband. She divorces him, unsuccessfully fights for the custody of her son but does not compromise with her ideology. Unlike her husband she cannot encash her contribution to the freedom struggle. As a teacher of history she says she cannot mislead and misinform the young minds, cannot tell them that the history of the nationalist movement is really the history of the Congress, cannot teach the history written for us by the British. *She has to resign for teaching. But she is prepared to pay the price for doing what she considers right. We may not always subscribe to her way of thinking but we do respect her for her courage to stand by her convictions.*

Principal Prema Diwan in Shashiprabha Shastri's *Meenarein* (1992) tries her best to discharge her responsibilities with dignity, poise and understanding. She refuses to play a puppet in the hands of the secretary of the college, governing body or the Vice-Chancellor. In Nasira Sharma's *Theekare Ki Mangani* (1989), Mahrukh takes to teaching when she learns that her fiancée Rafat has been living with another foreigner woman in the US and she decides to teach in a village school. Women like Shahana Choudhury, Kajal Banerjee, Shalmali, Prema Diwan and Mahrukh, *work not because of family compulsions but because of their own inner compulsions to carve a niche for themselves as individuals and simultaneously forge a new consciousness in their society.* While the majority of the novels of the 60s and 70s had portrayed working young women as victims-turned-martyrs, the novels of the last decade, in particular, have *depicted women attempting, often successfully, to get out of the social shackles and familial fetters to take their own decisions and even pave the way for a dignified life.*

Summing up, what we considered in the above 'fictional' situations *certain 'factual' situations of workingwomen are outlined:*

- Women who have to work to support themselves and their families,
- Women who work while waiting to get married,
- Women who work to supplement husband's income and raise the economic status of the family,
- Women who work for a label,
- Women who work because they want to feel they are more than breeders and caretakers,

- Women who work because they have a vision, an idea of what they want or don't want in life. They can work towards it only if economically independent.

Teaching occupation is believed to be feminine and compatible with the demands of their primary gender roles of housewife and mother. Hence in most of our novels we have women as teachers. For the sake of family status consistency, a wife should enter an occupation that is almost equal in prestige to that of her husband's or slightly inferior to it. Teaching meets that requirement too. It is taken for granted that when occupational sacrifices have to be made, the wife will make them. She is, in fact, happy to be the one to make them, subordinating her career to that of her husband. These occupations stress the aspect of service. As embodiments of sacrifice, therefore, women are best suited for these jobs. It is significant that most of these writers have themselves been teachers. They, therefore feel at home, writing about the academia. Namita Singh, Neelima Singh, Prem Nandkumar, Suryabala, Usha Priyanvada and Usha Puri have for long been associated with the academia. Mridula Garg taught for a few years before deciding to be a full time writer. Nasira Sharma does teaching stints whenever opportunity and time permit her to do so. Shashiprabha Shastri retired only a few years ago as Principal of a College.

Earlier, women lacked role models in the scientific and technical occupations, in management and public administration. With more and more women taking to unconventional careers, with women engineers, managers, vice-chancellors, airline pilots, IAS officers, etc., we have now many women coming out of their seclusion. Shubha Verma is herself a journalist. It is but natural, therefore, for her to write about the world of women journalists, the world she knows inside out. Shobha De is a journalist too. Even though her forte is soft porn, her experience has enabled her to expose the cine world or socialite lifestyle. It is noteworthy that even though we have had several outstanding women actively associated with the freedom movement, we don't have much literature dealing with women politicians. Kajal Banerjee is perhaps the only exception.

Married women are never treated as primary breadwinners even if they are the sole supporters of the family. The husband would want to put up the facade of having a job, a good job. The wife herself would want it. Only in case of a widow would the people accept her as the sole supporter but here she becomes either a victim of fate or martyr-having been forced to take on this responsibility and hence looking forward to her son (?) growing up and taking the yoke off her shoulders. Instances of a wife choosing to work and support the family all by herself while the husband looked after the home or pursued his own hobbies or accepted the supplementary status are extremely rare. Only in Zai Whitaker's *Up the Ghat* (1992), we are told of a German fellow who looks after his three small children while his wife goes off to Orissa or somewhere to study tribal dance. But he is a German. Significantly none of the Indian couples in this novel have this kind of arrangement or understanding. In fact, few Indian women would themselves agree that they are working because they need the money, while their husband is at home looking after the kids. Ordinarily women would claim to be working to utilize their talent or time. *It is still not considered a respectable thing for a woman to work for money. She works because it would be a pity to let her qualifications go waste.*

Whatever be the motive, workingwomen have no proper support system that can help them cope simultaneously with their professional and personal responsibilities without losing their reason. In the final analysis, *economic independence does give you the freedom to make your own choices-though the price you pay for making a particular choice may at times be very high. Let us hope the women of the 21st century are not called upon to pay such a heavy price, are not called upon to make these hard choices in life.*

References

Bhagat, Manjul. 1984. *Tirchhi Bauchhar,* New Delhi: Rajkamal Prakashan.

Chandrakanta. 1995. *Apne-Apne Konark,* New Delhi: Rajkamal Prakshan.

De, Shobha. 1991. *Starry Nights.* New Delhi: Penguin Books India.

Deshpande, Shashi. 1980. *The Dark Holds No Terrors.* New Delhi: Penguin Books India.

Deshpande, Shahsi. 1993. *The Binding Vine.* New Delhi: Penguin Books India.

Friedan, Betty. 1963. *The Feminine Mystique.* London.

Garg, Mridula. 1976. *Uske Hisse Ki Dhoop.* New Delhi: Akshar Prakshan.

Garg, Mridula. *Anitya.* New Delhi: National Publishing House.

Nandakumar, Prema. 1982. *Atom and the Serpent.* Madras: Affiliated East-West Press.

Narasimhan, Raii. 1991. *The Sky Changes.* Delhi: B.R. Publishing Corporation.

Paniker, Rajani. 1969. *Mahanagar ki Mita.* Jhansi: Setu Prakshan.

Panilter, Rajni. 1973. *Pahali Ladaki,* New Delhi: Pitambar Book Depot.

Priyamvada, Usha. 1966. *Pachpan Khambhe Lal Deevaren.* New Delhi: Rajkamal Prakshan.

Puri, Usha. 1986. *Mukhauton Ke Beech.* Delhi: Sanmarg Prakashan.

Sharma, Nasira. 1987. *Shalmali.* New Delhi: Kitabghar.

Sharma, Nasira. 1989. *Theekare ki Mangani.* Delhi: Saraswati Vihar.

Shastri, Shashiprabha. 1974. *Naven.* New Delhi: Rajkamal Prakshan.

Shastri, Shashiprabha. 1992. *Meenarein.* New Delhi: Kitabghar.

Shivani. 1988. *Do Sakhiyan.* Delhi: Saraswati Vihar.

Singh, Namita. 1995. *Apnee Salibein.* New Delhi: Radha Krishna Prakshan.

Singh, Nilima. 1987. *Satya Ka Sheshansh.* Delhi: Vivek Prakshan.

Suryabala. I980. *Subah ke Intzar Tak.* Delhi: Parag Prakshan.

Suryabala. 1992. *Deekshanta.* New Delhi: National Publishing House.

Verma, Shubha. 1981. *Freelancer.* Delhi: Saraswati Vihar.

Verma, Shubha. 1984. *Mohtarma.* Delhi: Indraprastha Prakshan.

Verma, Shukla. 1987. *Hartal.* Delhi: Vivek Prakshan.

Verma, Shukla. 1989. *Katmangur.* Delhi: Vivek Prakshan.

Whitaker, Zai. 1992. *Up the Ghat.* Madras: Affiliated East-West Press.

The paper was first published in *Women's Link*: 5:4: 1999: 40-45. It is included here with the permission of the author and the Editor, *Women's Link*.Aruna Sitesh is Professor and Head of the Department (English), Indra Prastha College, Delhi University, Delhi.

CHAPTER - EIGHTEEN

Implications of Globalization of Culture at Workplace and Violence on Women

Somen Chakraborty and Shalu Nigam

Parul Sharma, a student of Journalism, *Bharatiya Vidya Bhawan,* New Delhi, confessed in *The Hindustan Times*, November 4, 1998:

> *"Yes, the Generation X is career conscious, appearance conscious, enthusiastic, informed, knowledgeable, desirous of not merely a new lifestyle, but a global style...and so very short-tempered and testy. That is the new generation for you. Ready to bump you off at the drop of a hat. Freedom is what they want at any cost and assert".*

She continues,

> *"One good thing is, they are not slaves of orthodox and conservative viewpoints. They are mature (at least they always think they are) enough to take their own decisions and they dream of a complete, independent life with all its spices and colours. They are not satisfied with the bare necessities of life, but strive religiously for luxuries, which soon dissolve into necessity. A luxury of tomorrow may soon become the necessity of today. They want good things fast and cheap. They equate success in terms of dollars, and hang on to the tame trappings of fame, fortune and flamboyant lifestyles. They are clear only about one thing most: money and status. If the road ahead is full of potholes of compromises, they do not mind the big jolts"(emphasis contributed).*

A new culture is at our doorstep, a new fashion wave-discovery of a new individual self. While discussing the theory of hierarchy, Maslow opined that the most sought-out thing for the majority of human beings was the need of recognition. This is a truism for the Indian society as well. Recognition-financial, educational, social, positional and so on, has been the yardstick of success for a large section of the urban elite. Being a party to the rat race of prosperity and acquiring it through the best of investments is their way of living. The means, by which they achieve it, is not their concern. For them, the globe, and not an individual nation state, is the limit. The entire human world is being gravitated into this new economic orbit-globalization. Globalization evolves not only new symbols for status but also new means or ways of perpetuating the culture of domination over the majority of society. At the economic level it empowers corporatism through MNCs and TNCs, at the political level it propagates for hegemony and in social context it denotes reinforcement of patriarchy. It introduces new work culture, hostile and competitive work environment. It brings forth new forms of sexual violence against women. This paper makes an assessment of the changing character of work place as a result of globalization, and emergence of a new masculine behaviour against women workers. The impacts of globalization are not so vivid in our society. Nevertheless, after the Indian State resolved to liberalize country's economy in many ways the majority of people are victims of this new world economic order.

Globalization: A new phenomenon

Globalization is an advanced form of capitalism. It denotes undeterred capacity of the transnational companies to determine the production process and consumption patterns of a nation and its people. It enables MNCs and TNCs to overstep into the domain of nation states to dictate the values and culture of the human collectives of those places. This is colonialism no doubt, but different from those which we have experienced earlier. Capturing a nation state physically, perhaps, is not the agenda of globalization. 'Free' economic and cultural systems of a nation, however, are made to be regulated by the global marketing framework of TNCs, MNCs and various international financial institutions. This regulation, in the process, takes away the capacity of independent and indigenous way of growing from a nation and from its people. Independent nations become incrementally vulnerable to the global power dictate. Globalization is thus not an administrative invasion. Rather, it is economic penetration and cultural subjugation. It tends to locate itself in the psycho-social settings of a nation. India is one of those countries that are becoming increasingly victims of the stratagem of change and modernization fabricated by the global economic powers.

Under the disguise of development and modernity globalization negates plurality of culture, their origin and destroys the life systems that sustain around different cultural milieu. Plurality is replaced by a monolithic and homogenized culture of the Western design. Many of our value-based, people centered cultural heritages are fast becoming oblivious under the pressure of a global economy.

An unreal world of fantasy

Globalization is transboundary in nature. It is omnipresent but invisible. It is often immune of any particular local identity. Through satellite channels and other modern media mechanisms it further penetrates into the remotest areas. It aims at bringing all human communities, societies and nations under one singular global village. The changes take place quickly, in that it provides no chances to decide what is good and what is bad. It pollutes the native cultures. It vitiates morality, ethics and value system of native societies. Before rationalizing the merits or demerits of media-based simulations, psyche of the recipients gets entrapped by new cultures, values and reasoning. This 'new' then decides what to think and what not, what to value and what not; what to consume and what not; what to do and what not; what to adopt and what not. Everything traditional, easily consumable, and is acquired without hardship, is projected as primitive, anachronic, bad or obsolete. Everything with a western flavour, though untenable, is welcomed. A new world of fantasy opens up before the masses. Fantasy eventually settles in the core of a conscious mind. It eventually destroys the very structure of ideology of individuals. A process of degeneration and demotivation of morals and ethics is intensified.

The expectations thus generated remain unattainable to the majority of a society. Meaning of essential needs in life changes rapidly. On the one hand, new consumer items flood markets, new luxury becomes the way of living. On the other, people's purchasing power continuously declines. People's consumption desires supersedes their economic capacity. Generation gap is quickened. Gap between generations gets widened too. Gap increases between the needs and the capacities of the social majority. A few elites acquire the new luxuries and continue to be the elites. A section of the middle class takes himself or herself to the 'high society' by acquiring them. They feel closer to the West than before. They get continuously alienated from the rest of society. They are the first to absorb the values and cultures emerging from the expansion of globalization. These small Indo-Western group of people are the most coveted manpower in new work places. Through intellectual, academic and cultural exercises these minority group of people then tend to transmit their newly acquired values to the rest of society. This class, in true sense, is not protected by any pro-people ideology. Largely being free from social obligations, this 'new' middle class sells out the academic and intellectual agenda of the West.

A large number of people of the lower income groups follow the footsteps of the emerging middle class and the elite. They dream of having taken themselves to the world of the so-called 'modernity'. A culture of competition among the members of the lower middle class gets sharpened. They aim at transforming their ordinary capacity to a surplus capacity. Members of this class try, fail and try again. They are caught in an indefinite 'merry go round' within the orbit of a vicious cycle. Their strong community bonds reduce to individual self. As globalization penetrates into a nation the intensity of competition goes up. Once an individual acquires any of these dreams, desires or aspirations, he/she denies sharing such precious items with others. The culture of sharing resources with others is replaced by the culture of denial. The consideration of monetary value, howsoever insignificant it may be, conditions social relationships and elevates individual status within those relationships. Individual self gets priority.

People slowly abandon their traditional social life, community ethos, food habits, language, clothing, behaviour, dreams, relationships and so on. Culture becomes the culture of greed, competition, adjustment, compromise and submission. A value-free, morality-free and ethics free life germinates. A new life system pervades majority of the people, society and nation. The growing amnesia of the enriched cultural heritage creates a state of passivity, disabling people to protect, promote and strengthen their own identity. Hegemony of an alien culture, which is, at this moment of history, the Western, becomes widespread. An ambition perpetuates within the individual self-a kind of hypnotism-with all probability, not to become materialized.

Globalization does not provide chances to the poor to become economically stable community to become self-reliant and developing nations to become developed. Frustration and despair do not allow citizens to be creative. Criminalization, sexism, aggression, violence, intolerance, social discrimination and injustice tend to predominate the community ethos. Gap between 'haves' and 'have-nots' is enhanced. The concept of human rights and dignity remain a misnomer.

Every human being, especially women, becomes continuously commodified under the globally operated economic laws. Human mind, body, behaviour, desire, relationship and even psyche becomes available in the market in exchange of a few rupees. People, so far, were selling their labour power, but their mind was free, capable of thinking independently and creatively. By the media driven campaigns for commodities, globalization moulds the mind itself. Trade and commerce comes out of the 'assembly line'. Modem media takes the masses to a new world of consumer worship. Visual reality no way complies with the factual reality. A well-designed psycho-behavioural pattern is slowly injected into people's life system. The Indian society, especially the urban population, of late, has started indicating towards this psycho-social development.

Privatization takes a boom

In the context of globalization state's control over natural and human resources declines. Privatization of business and enterprises is prioritized in the economic policies of the states. Privatization continuously goes away from the control of the state because of deregulation and of society because they are individual profit oriented (Bernard: 1993). Laissez Faire economy, in practice, is regulated by the global economic designs. The unorganized sectors grow at an alarming rate. It does not allow the work force to emerge as a collective and to consolidate itself to resist its marginalization.

The Indian State no more promotes and protects the public enterprises. It refuses to become a welfare state and to fulfill its commitments of bringing about a just social order. It is a pity that the Indian State has largely surrendered to 'the business classes. The private sectors, comprising of national and international corporations, are dictating the terms of trade and commerce. Business has grown global. Economy has become private by virtue of being liberal. A growth model, depending on alien technologies and know how, is surging ahead with all its might.

In globalization, business and enterprise operate under the global market conditions. The principles governing these conditions are that the international standards must be uniform, universal and non-discriminatory. Competition, comparison, perspectives and challenges in trade and commerce are global. It does not tolerate anything outside its domain. That is why globalization is different from internationalism.

New business climate demands new manpower with qualities helpful for business to grow global. Global economy demands free and unprejudiced human interactions. Global market demands global mobility. Open economy needs an open mind. Global competitions require skills, knowledge, education and training of globally applicable standards. Education *per* se distributes the Western technical know how. New technical skills offer new attitudes, values and ideologies. Strong desire for profit making becomes a value in itself. When profit becomes the end in itself, means do not matter. A disguise of progress enables globalization to strip people off their self-dignity and self-respect.

Urbanization

Accordingly a new urban system develops. Urban centres are the hubs of trade and commerce, of the 'best' education, of the latest technical trainings, of the fastest communications, of the costliest living and of course, of modem arts, culture and fashion.

Unfortunately, majority of the urban communities remain deprived of all these advancements. A sizeable number among the city dwellers are in crisis of minimum survival. They desperately look for a place in the new economic system. Most of them are frantic to secure a place in a new work place. They get ready to sacrifice everything to acquire a job in that they intend to obtain the capacity of transforming their dreams into reality. The languages to learn, the dresses to wear and the people to associate with are meticulously decided keeping their future benefits in mind. They do it because they have fascination for a modem life style. Everything traditional, except being a believer of God, becomes outdated. Traditions, howsoever rich and scientific they may be, are reduced to antiques. Eventually, an introvert individual turns extrovert; a defensive goes offensive; a submissive emerges as aggressive, an incompetent becomes competent and everybody aspires for a glamorous appeal. Men and women of the new generation acquire it first. The rest of society follows it later. Prosperity and status are earned through a cut-throat competition. They learn manipulation and acquire the art of corruption. They learn living in the world of fantasies, falsehoods and double standards. An ideology thus acquired, does not attribute value to human concerns and collective good.

This new generation is the most preferred group in the modern work place. They are empowered with apt knowledge, skills and desires. They want to achieve a power-wielding career. They dream of reaching the peak. They desire to have stability in life. They aim at transforming the days of crisis to the days of affluence. New workplace, whatever demand it may impose on them, is a need for them. They are committed to take the business global. They compromise, adjust and survive. Career and status rank the highest in their priorities in life. To be frank, nothing sounds unusual in this dream and aspiration. A stable economic relation is, in fact, the pre-condition for any progress. This looks harmless. Hence, globalization enjoys acceptance from society at large.

Globalization of economy is, of course, a step towards dehumanization. It undermines human dignity and respect for human life. Meaning of ethics gets constantly changed. Relationships between persons, whether it is in a family, in a society or in a nation, get reduced to mere consumer relationships. Money becomes instrumental to materialize people's dreams and desires. Recognition as well as status in society is measured by the size of one's wealth. The warmth of beautiful human relationships fades away. Biological inhibitions in human interactions are commonly viewed as anachronic. The traditional concept of morality is rejected for being a taboo. The institution of marriage starts losing its relevance in societal formations. For many of them free-sex is a symbol of modernity. Sex, too, becomes a market item and often a means to success.

Violence old, methods new

In the era of globalization the work place spreads across national boundaries. The globe becomes the virtual work place for the hefty-paid busy managers in new corporatism. They have very little time for their families, friends and society. Many a good traditional bonds are abandoned for they are considered unproductive. Occupational commitments do not even provide them opportunities to come closer and share emotional feelings with their life partners. Relationships between husband and wife reduce themselves to a time specific sexual encounter. Such relations are largely devoid of emotional bonds of passion and, love. While pleasure is being chased, it continues to remain unavailed. Normal sexual desires are compensated by violent sexual impulses. Individual expressions, in fact, indicate collective perils of a society.

The nuclear family bonds get weakened over time. Many among the urban denizens seek satisfaction outside family. Extra-marital relations or pre-marital sex become common occurrences. Its impact on women is disastrous. Earlier they were instrumental in promoting and preserving social institutions. Under the auspices of feminist perceptions, society since long accumulated knowledge and enhanced the volume of production to meet the needs of the people and in that regeneration of resources was never obstructed. Advent of human civilization had taken place under the strong feminist political will through centuries. Later, with the growth of a patriarchal economy a culture of patriarchy has begun to predominate societal relations. It has started reversing the role of women from construction to deconstruction of civil society. New societal norms victimize women with perpetual violence and indignity. In the era of globalization, the processes of victimization surface with new *forms*. India has not come across the worst of it because fortunately, globalization is yet to fully overshadow our society.

Globalization has potentials to transform the place of work into the potential centre for sexual harassment. Satisfaction in work place has long been associated with some important elements of mental health along with stability of income. An increasing feeling of alienation and pessimism in these new work places reduce the control of a person over the future course of his/her life. Under such circumstances an invisible, omnipresent and all pervasive violence breaks out and yet they remain immune of legal battles. Both males and females fall prey to this sexual aberration and violence.

A report in The Hindustan Times on 10.1.97 goes like this. A young girl, who worked in a computer company, was assigned a challenging task with a lucrative salary package. Her job involved contacting different people to promote the market for her company's product. She was often helped by her friend working in another business organization to venture out for new contacts. One day both of them went out to meet some potential clients. On the way two persons known to them earlier offered them lift. All of them took soft drinks for a break and that young girl became drowsy. The car took another direction. Later, the girl discovered that she was raped. Nobody got to know who the persons were behind this whole ghastly incident and what was their real motive.

Majority of the victims of such sexual violence are the young women entrants in the job market. For they are still under the world of fantasy and have not experienced the harsh realities of life. The sorry tales of Monica Lewnisky, perhaps, do not have any comparison. In popular view it may be perceived as an act of volition. It can also be termed as the power rape in that political and economic hegemony takes the expression of sexual assault against a woman. The sordid incident exposes to the world that a male superior in a modern work place, whatsoever high may be his position, is potential to impose patriarchal domination on the subordinates. Globalization provides space for this new genre of bosses to emerge all over the world. They earn satisfaction by blending monetary gains with fulfillment of certain basic instincts. They gift society with new values, cultures and challenges free from social audit. Their media and institutions make all-out attempts to establish this as people's own desire through stories, news and features. Media apart, various other forces of society, which have already become corrupt, cruel and inhuman, further compel a woman to translate these newly acquired values and cultures into practice. It robs woman of her dignity. A sense of emotional insecurity overshadows her rational mind. The bosses and managers in new work places exploit the world of fantasy of young women employees, take advantage of their state of insecurity and inflict violence on them.

The next potential victims are those women, who witness rapid modernization in their work place at a later stage. Due to over-age, lack of tenacity and competence women workers of this group fail to acquire the new skills and approaches that their work places demand from them. "The quick profit tendency tends to look upon labour as cost component bereft of anything else. There is a lack of human angle in this respect. For any cost adjustment, the first consequence is retrenchment of work force and be more competitive and profit making" (Prayag Mehta: 1994). Women employees of this genre become the primary target of retrenchment. There is hardly any demand for them in the job markets. At the same time a stable and regular earning is a dire need for them and their families. A section of this decaying workforce compensates its deficiency by keeping up their physical glamour to the expectation of their masters. They compromise under absolute compulsions. A new patriarchy thus takes over as a culture, and pervades men as well as women. Patriarchy lies in an attitude of aggression that finds means and ways to subjugate women through anxiety, fear, intimidation and temptation and sexual assaults. The new corporates adopt this strategy mainly to reinforce and reorganize their internal mechanism of power and profit.

Six "NOs" of National Commission for Women

In order to protect women from increasing incidents of sexual violence the National Commission for Women has enlisted the following acts as the indications of sexual violence on women:

- Unsavory and sexist remarks
- Innuendoes
- Forcible physical touching and brushing against any part of the body
- Physical confinement against woman's will
- Display of pornographic or offensive picture, cartoons or pamphlets
- Treat women employees as sex objects.

This is one of the many appreciable steps of the Commission to ensure a violence-free working conditions to women. These six commandments have potentials, indeed, to restrain sexual advances. Whether they will also be effective in liberating women from the mechanisms that colonize, utilize, commodify, transform, displace and destroy women, need serious reflections.

Globalization works more at the psychological level of a person. It creates necessary conditions in a work place in which a female psyche accepts sexual subjugation as a natural development of relationship. It promotes a situation, where a woman volunteers to compromise on sex. A women may not be physically forced but she is compelled by the working conditions to allow her body to be caressed and mind to be 'softened'. A 'free and modern' woman remains confined in her work place for it ensures shelter, food, clothing and ultimately an urban living to herself and her family. It provides her access to new techno-scientific gadgets. It gives her a 'different' she feeling. In a society of individualism and patriarchy, she finds herself alone. She is desperate to survive. She copes with. She commodifies herself. She redefines her values and morality. She becomes modern and smart. She submits to sexual violence-slowly and continuously not necessarily biological but more than that psychologically, mentally and ethically. This has happened to her through the entire realm of advancement of capitalism and now it is intensified in the era of globalization.

Women have their alternatives

Women in India, however, are slowly realizing the danger of globalization. Like the downtrodden of other developing countries, they are strengthening the struggles against globalization. The protest movements by women have virtually created a furore in our society. In a large contingent they are now present in *panchayati raj* institutions. Many of them have proved their potentials in spearheading people's protest movements. They have raised their collective voice for reservation in legislative bodies at all levels. Many of the women groups are struggling for the cause of equal wages and rights for women. A process of revising the state theory is taking place at the grassroots level. The feminist protests are widening their membership base. They are developing distinct gender concepts based on new political ideology. Women collectives at different levels are in search of a new development model that brings about socio-economic changes through continuing exercise of public power. Structuring of a political economy of power based on feminist approaches is in the making (Baxi: 1994). They are refusing to accept globalization as the last answer to the history of civilization. They are denying accepting the present model of modernization and growth, which exposes them to a gender discriminative work climate. They are refusing to become prey of violent sexual impulse of their superiors. They have demanded a new education system which enables people to be gender sensitive. They have demanded abolition of patriarchal values from social institutions. They have voiced for social relationships that ensure justice and equality to human beings through enlarged participation of women.

A much wider network of these movements and protests is now visible in the country. These networks are based on renewed understanding of freedom and liberation. Perhaps, history would demand men and women to share the common platform to fight against globalization. Because globalization, in ultimate analysis, is the economic fundamentalism. It not only targets destruction of women's dignity but human civilization as a whole. Besides protest movements against the male dominated society, solidarity among people, including men and women, is necessary to combat the aggression of globalization. Consolidation of the collective strength of the democratic elements of the masses is necessary to expedite the process of uprooting the genesis of globalization. This seems to be the only feasible alternative to liberate women from new varieties of sexual violence in the changing work places.

References

Baumohl, Bernerd.1993. When Downsizing becomes Dumbsizing, *The Times Magazine*, March 15.

Baxi, Upendra. 1994. *Inhuman Wrongs and Human Rights: Unconventional Essays*, Har-Anand Publications, New Delhi, pp. 60-63.

Mehta, Prayag. 1994. (New Economic Policy, Work Place and Human Development, *Econom-ic and Political Weekly*: 29: 22: M75-M81.

Walse, James.1993. Isle of Despair, *The Times Magazine*, March 15.

The paper was first published in *Women's Link*: 5: 4: 1999: 25-30. It is included here with the prior permission of the authors and Editor, *Women's Link*. Somen Chakraborty and Shalu Nigam are respectively Researcher and Programme Officer at the Indian Social Institute, New Delhi.

CHAPTER - NINETEEN

Life Histories and Long-Term Change: Rural Livelihoods and Gender Relations in a West Bengal Village

Molly Chattopadhyay and David Seddon

Not only do life histories provide insights into the complexity and variety of individual lives and social relationships, they enable us to identify patterns and issues of greater generality. Analyzing the 'life histories' collected in course of fieldwork in a West Bengal village, this paper seeks in turn to understand rural livelihoods, while also exploring the methodological issues involved in using such information to complement other qualitative and quantitative data.

I

Using 'Life Histories'

The recording of 'oral testimony' [Van Onselen: 1993, Aunger: 1995], including 'social biographies' [Angrosino: 1989, Burke: 1993] and 'life histories', and their analysis has been an important component of the research methodology of social anthropologists and social historians for several decades. This paper attempts to study changes through time and change processes itself by using 'life histories' and changes that have occurred in the lives and livelihoods of the people, men and women of Mohula in West Bengal over the last 20 years.

In social anthropology, the interest in modes of investigation and analysis which reveal the lives and experiences of people (what Audrey Richards called "the individual characters, with all their temperamental and physical peculiarities and the dramatic incidents of everyday life" (1939: 160) began during the 1940s and 1950s in part as a reaction against the dominant structural-functional approach which emphasized the structures and principles of social life rather than the ways in which people lived their lives. It was also part of a response to the recognized need (towards the end of the colonial period) to study and analyze processes of social change and the increasing social heterogeneity, if not complexity–for which the structural-functional approach was ill suited. This approach called not only for the investigation of what Malinowski called 'the imponderabilia of actual life' [Malinowski: 1922: 18], but also for coordinated accounts of the actions of specified individuals. By the 1960s many younger social anthropologists agreed with J Van Velsen's views that "the statics of the structure ... should be supplemented and enlivened by an account of the actions–both 'normal' and 'exceptional'–of the individuals who operate the structure, i.e, the processes going on within the structure...". It was also agreed "this new emphasis not only demands a different type of field material, but also raises the question whether and in what form this material should be presented to the reader" [Van Velsen: 1967: 141; Dabbs: 1982: 33].

During the 1970s, social historians influenced by the work of E.P. Thompson (1991) and others concerned with writing the 'history from below' began to make increasing use of sources which enabled the lives of 'ordinary people' to be seen as the real basis for social life and social change. Particularly for those working on 'contemporary history' within the 'Thompson' tradition, oral history became a crucial part of their research methodology. This included African and Asian historians and increasingly, students of development [Terence Ranger, et al: 1993].

More recently, other students of contemporary social change have paid closer and more direct attention to life histories and accounts by people of their own lives as primary sources for the understanding of social change [Shaw: 1980]. Bernstein, et al (1982), for example, in their Third World Lives of Struggle, focus on "the diverse conditions of everyday life of people in the third world ... as much as possible through the 'voices' of those who live these daily experiences" (xi). Importantly, these experiences are seen not as 'typical' or 'accurate' in any sense, but as 'authentic' and 'revealing'.

In his recent collection of biographies of men and women in the Middle East, Burke suggests that a selection of biographies cannot be 'typical', but can serve both "to assert our common humanity" (1993:3) and to indicate "the sheer variety"of lives and circumstances; he emphasizes the fact that while "Middle Eastern men and women responded to often difficult circumstances in different ways...struggle was one dimension of their individual stories" (1993:3) and celebrates the tenacious and often courageous effort of common folk to hang in there, to survive against all odds" (1993:4).

Burke suggests "because it is a primary site for exploring the connections of social and cultural processes, biography has grown in importance if anything in recent times" (1993:5). He argues, "the biographical approach holds out the promise of reinvigorating the relation between social theory and empirical research. The credibility of biographies comes from the concrete details they convey about a particular life and how it was lived. The more accounts of lives we have, the better we will be able to assess their typicality and to understand individual survival strategies" (1993:6).

The 'life histories' collected by the project on Rural Livelihoods and Long-Term Changes in South Asia constitute one source of 'qualitative' information collected during the course of fieldwork to provide the basis for understanding and analyzing rural livelihoods. They complement other sources of 'qualitative' information (derived from various forms of participatory rural appraisal (PRA), including individual and focus group discussions, social mapping and wealth ranking of households, etc) as well as the major source of 'quantitative' information (data collected by means of a household survey using a schedule/questionnaire).

The material contained in 'life histories' enables us, we suggest, to achieve an insight into the complexity and variety of individual lives and social relationships; at the same time, consideration of a number of 'life histories' enables us to identify patterns and issues of greater generality. The 'life histories' allow us to understand socio-economic changes in a more qualitative and in-depth manner through an appreciation of the relationships whereby men and women gain their livelihoods and live their lives [Becker and Harris: 1978, Brewer and Hunter: 1989].

Sampling 'Life Histories'

The research methodology whereby these 'life histories' were collected involved selecting a sample of 30 households, stratified by wealth (on the basis of wealth ranking exercise) into three groups of 10 from each of the 'rich', 'medium' and 'poor' households in the village. This sample cannot be regarded as statistically representative, but it does nevertheless, 'represent' the authentic experiences of particular categories of individuals and households and suggest more general patterns, trends and tendencies. The ideas and hypotheses generated by these insights can be tested by reference to the 'quantitative' data collected for a sample of 50 households by the household survey. In this sense, the two methodologies are complementary.

The life histories were collected, after the household survey had been undertaken, from the members of households included in that survey. Some respondents were reluctant to spare the time necessary for their 'life history' as this involved long hours sitting with members of the research team; some households were therefore replaced by others from within the same 'wealth rank'. The interview itself was semi-structured. Guided by a checklist, it allowed respondents to talk freely while ensuring that they covered: (a) the structure and 'history' of the family (including births, marriages, deaths, etc); (b) history of occupations of family members; (c) current place of work and migration history; and (d) *changing gender relations.*

Initially, the head of the household was interviewed; but wherever possible, other family members were also interviewed. Households headed by the females were selected deliberately as part of the focus on gender relations. The histories were thus 'directed' but structured so as to allow individuals the opportunity to express in their own words and in their own ways their experiences and perceptions of social change, within the family and in the wider social context.

Our interest is in the extent to which and ways in which individual life histories can generate insights into processes of social change, reveal both patterns and regularities. But there are important differences between what might be termed 'full life histories' (in which an attempt is made to explore in-depth, in detail and from many angles the lives and times of particular individuals) and 'brief life histories'. We adopt the term 'brief life histories' to distinguish these from the far more detailed 'life history' methodology adopted by some social historians. Charles van Onselen's recent discussion of the methodology employed to study the life and times of a black South African sharecropper, for example, reveals that "more than 60 interviews with Kas Maine, conducted over a period of six years, as well as another 20 with members of his peer group drawn from the families of similarly placed black farmers" (1993:503) were required. These interviews were supplemented by dozens of other recorded discussions with landlords, lawyers and traders who had been active in the region; while "fifty or more further interviews with Kas Maine's brothers, sisters, two wives, a former lover, his children and many grandchildren gave added insight ..." (ibid 503). This clearly differs from our own 'brief life histories', collected generally in a single interview (or in at most two or three) over a period totaling no more than a few hours at most. Nevertheless, we believe that even 'brief lives' are revealing and allow us to understand better ways in which the lives of individuals both affect and are conditioned by the wider social context and processes of social change.

Table 1
Primary Occupation by Caste 1996

Caste	*Unemp/ hhwife*	*Ag. lab*	*Culttv*	*S crpr*	*Potter*	*Fisher*	*Busi-ness*	*Tea-cher*	*Ser-vice*	*Unskld/ Grazer*	*total*	*Per cent*
GC		1	5		1		2	3	2	1	15	30.0
SC		9		7					1		17	34.0
ST	4	11		3							18	36.0
Total	4	21	5	10		0	2	0	3	1	50	100.0
Per cent	8.0	42.0	10.0	20.0	2.0	0.0	4.0	6.0	6.0	2.0		100.0

Note: See Table 3.

The household survey of the village shows that over the last 20 years there are changes in the primary occupation of the sample households (N = 50). Table 1 shows that service and business as primary modes of livelihood has increased whereas number of owner-cultivators has decreased in the case of caste Hindu households (GC). Access to services by caste Hindu people has increased as they have access to primary education also. In case of business, the ability to provide collateral has also increased their access to business. Land reform implemented in 1981 loosened the control over cultivable land by GCs. That's why the number of owner-cultivators has decreased. This general picture is shown by the information collected from quantitative techniques. It is rather weak in presenting how the caste Hindus are able to enjoy access to education and service.

Within our sample scheduled caste households, a sharp increase in the number of sharecroppers from 1976 to 1996 (Table 2) was noticed. But it failed to project those households who under existing land reform laws are eligible to be sharecroppers, but were reduced to the status of agricultural wage labourer or off-farm daily wage earner. Arun Bagdi, who sells '*chanachur*' and ice cream, narrated later, how land reform laws backtracked in the face of powerful landowners.

Table 2
Primary Occupation by Caste 1976

Caste	*Unemp/ hhwife*	*Ag. lab*	*Culttv*	*S crpr*	*Potter*	*Fisher*	*Busi-ness*	*Tea-cher*	*Ser-vice*	*Unskld/ Grazer*	*total*	*Per cent*
GC	1		8		3		1	1	1		15	30.0
SC	1	9		4		1				2	17	34.0
ST	4	13		1							18	36.0
Total	6	22	8	5	3	1	1	1	1	2	50	100.0
Per cent	12.0	44.0	16.0	10.0	6.0	2.0	2.0	2.0	2.0	4.0		100.0

Note: See Table 3.

The findings from quantitative techniques are limited to the pattern of changes in earning a livelihood. But they fail to show 'how' these changes occurred.

For example, Kalyani Das, a widow, aged 38 years earns her livelihood by preparing puffed rice. She has one son (17 years) and one daughter (15 years). Her husband was a '*pheriwalla*' (who head loads stationary materials and sells on foot). His early death compelled Kalyani to earn her livelihood by preparing puffed rice, which was the only means available to her. Widowed young, she had to face discrimination from her male neighbours. Widows are entitled to a pension that the state government has initiated a few years back, even for those who are not in government service. After she lost her husband, her neighbour Pankaj Sarkar tried to take advantage when she was asleep in her courtyard. Fortunately, she raised an alarm. Next day Pankaj Sarkar went to meet Baidayanath Pal, then elected CPIM member of *gram panchayat* and complained that Kalyani Das was spreading disaffection against him. Outraged, Baidyanath Pal cancelled her application. This was not the only case of victimization. She was unable to apply for IRDP loan because she did not have collateral. Her inability to secure access to institutional resources compelled her to take up the occupation of preparing puffed rice as the only mode available for livelihood.

In case of caste Hindu households it is seen that with changing occupation there are changes in access to educational resources, irrespective of gender. But households headed by the women are deprived of that resource. Kalyani Das's daily life begins at 4.30 am. If she prepares puffed rice within the village then she comes back at 12.30 pm. At 4.30 pm she starts for other households and comes back after four hours. Whenever (and mostly it is so) she gets calls from outside villages she sets out in the evening to reach that place. Next day from 6 am to 12 pm she prepares puffed rice and returns by 2 to 2.30 pm. Her work schedule has an adverse effect upon her daughter's study. Her daughter had to be withdrawn from school after class V and she has been assigned daily household chores.

For the last two decades there have been tremendous changes in respect of per capita income, primary education, family planning due to introduction of HYV seeds, Mass Literacy Campaign (MLC), and land reform initiated by government. But access to these resources did not reach all the households. Households headed by women are worst sufferers and their stories unfold only through life histories.

Arun Bagdi made the decision to break away from the family tradition of agricultural labouring which was their primary occupation to sell 'chanter' and ice cream on foot. In general, Bagdis benefited much from the fruits of land reform all over Birbhum. And with the rise of daily wage rate the lot of agricultural labourers also improved. But his decision to break away from agriculture was forced by the memory of physical abuse meted out to his father by the then landlord BN Pal. His father, Madan Bagdi, was *Kisani* of BN Pal. Just before the government initiated the registration of tenants in 1981, BN Pal terminated his tenancy. When asked why he did not move court, his wife said that '*mukh takiye nieni*' (means considering the cordial relationship with landlord for a long time) such a move was seen as undesirable. Next day we probed further and it was revealed that to avoid conflict with landlord they did not move further. His past experience deterred him from doing so. BN Pal once sent Arun's father to Burdwan to cultivate his father-in-law's land. On the pretext that Madan's son Arun was sick, BN Pal called him back to the village. As he entered the village he was tied with a rope and severely beaten up by BN Pal's men alleging that he had stolen money from the place of BN Pal's in-laws. All these were done to disprove his claim as *Kisani.* Arun Pal witnessed the torture of his father as a child and it had a lasting impact on him. Arun no longer participates in any agricultural activity in the village. His wife and mother still participate as agricultural labourers. Only in *Kharif* season does Arun plough their own land (0.33 acres) for three days that yields 2.4 quintals of rice. This change from agriculture as primary occupation followed by the father to petty business by son has been unfolded only by a narration of their life history.

Individual histories are not always exceptional. Each life history represents a story in the context of general changes taking place.

The story of Balika Hansda, a widow, aged 65 shows how the absence of any male member reduced her to the status of agricultural labourer. Her husband was a sharecropper. After her husband's death his son inherited the right of sharecropping. As her son rarely stayed in the village, the landlord terminated the *barga* arrangement. Now her livelihood comprises of crops from her *patta* (vested) land, daughter's earning from wage labouring and the selling of bamboo (bamboo bush was noticed in her courtyard by the study team). Her grandson (who stays in the same village but belongs to a separate household) ploughs her *patta* land, as any woman cannot do it. Her daughter (who was separated from her husband and stays with her mother in this village) carries out other cropping operations. Her daughter gets 70 labour days per year. They complained that even if she works for more than 8 hours, the landlords would insist that it was less. In lean season she

Table 3
Occupational Changes Collected from Life Histories of Three Caste Groups Over Time

(a) General Castes

	Nature of Primary Occupation							
Years	*Teacher*	*Service*	*Cult.*	*Business*	*Pottery*	*Remit-tance*	*Making Puffed Rice*	*Tution + Cult.*
1976	2	1	4	2	2	0	0	0
1996	1	1	2	3	1	1	1	1

(b) Scheduled Castes

	Nature of Primary Occupation								
Years	*Fishing*	*Ag lab*	*Kisani*	*Chhoto Mahin-dar*	*Bodo Mahin-dar*	*Ag Lab+ Vested Land*	*Cult+ Kisani*	*Share-cropper*	*Culti-vator*
1976	1	3	5	1					
1996		4			1	2	1	1	1

(c) Scheduled Tribe

Years	*Ag Lab*	*Kisani*	*S Cropper*	*Ag Lab+ Vested Land*	*Bandha*
1976	6	1	3		
1996	6		2	1	1

Note: Unemp/hhwfe = Unemployed/Housewife
cullY = Cultivator
Ag lab = Agricultural Labourer
Potr = Potter
S crppr = Share Cropper
Unskld/grazer = Unskilled manual worker/grazer
Bodo Mahinder = Worker (aged> 16) who does both farm and household chores for his landlord and gets yearly Rs. 3,000/- + clothes+daily food + 3 kg of paddy per day. The condition is renewed every year in January with increased annual remuneration.
Chhoto Mahinder = Same as above. Only exception is here the worker is below 16 years of age and gets annually Rs. 1,700/-.
Kisani = Before land reform in 1981, Kisani system was one of the major systems that persisted in Birbhum. Here the tenants used to get 1/3rd of the crop after cultivation. Kisanis were later registered as sharecroppers in 1981.

worked in a brick-kiln. If she does not get it then landlords lends her one-quintal of rice, which is to be repaid by labour days.

Reductions from the status of sharecropping to agricultural labour selling households are documented only by life histories, which would otherwise have been unnoticed by a quantitative survey.

Changing Status of Women

This section is about how women take advantage of their increasing access to education to increase their own autonomy. The notion of autonomy is extremely complex and we will be addressing it partially. It has been defined by Leacock as the extent to which women hold 'decision-making power over their own lives and activities' comparable to the power men hold over theirs (1978: 247). In the present context, the focus is on women's participation in the economic life of the household. In discussing autonomy, we must at all times take into account the powerful economic constraints which affect both males and females because of social class inequities, which in effect set limits on their possible autonomy–the most obvious among them being perhaps the limited amount of disposable income. However, when we are talking about women who are totally dependent on their husbands or on those who provide income for their households, it must also be recognized that there is an overriding social constraint on women's autonomy, resulting from the fact that the wider society and wider social norms tend to favour patriarchy. Thus, our present discussion of autonomy is set within the context of a class and caste-ridden society with a strong emphasis on patriarchal cultural norms [1989:118].

A major change in case of education of women of caste Hindu households was noticeable. The change took place just within one generation. The present generation around up to 22-23 years attends schools and colleges but their mothers were illiterate. Girls from SC households also attend schools regularly, though except one, none had passed school-leaving examination from that village. This is worth investigating because most of the Bagdis are labour-selling households. Tribals still lag behind in terms of primary education. We want to relate access to education by women with their changing autonomy over the last two decades from life histories of both mother and daughter. Autonomy is indicated by women's right to (a) keep the cash that she earns or her dowry money, jewellery in case of caste Hindu households; (b) to reject the prospective groom arranged by her father; (c) whether she can buy things for herself without getting permission from her husband and (d) the extent to which a woman participates in decisions about household matters (such as whether to continue a child's education).

Any discussion of autonomy here must distinguish among three different types of households: general caste (GC), scheduled caste (SC) and scheduled tribe (ST), disaggregated by three wealth ranks.

If we first look at GC households we find that educational resources have reached almost all the households irrespective of their wealth rank. Now the question is whether it has enhanced the autonomy of women. Table 4 shows that the majority of women (who are mainly housewives except one) do not keep cash/dowry money in their hand. Cash is always kept with the husband. Fathers-in-law always handle dowry money. In his absence, husbands control it. Mostly, it is used for husband's sister's marriage, or otherwise spent for the wedding ceremony itself. Only one woman keeps some cash, which is earned by making small earthen pots and then selling it. In two cases, women handle cash. A widow heads one household. In another household the head of the household was a bit indifferent to worldly matters. He was a mendicant, forced into marriage by his parents, and now regrets marrying. He does not want to control the finances of his family.

Table 4
Number of GC Households Where Women Participate in Decision-Making (N=11)

Areas of participation	*Whether GC Women can participate*		
	Yes	*No*	*Both*
Keeping cash/dowry		8	3
saying no to prospective groom		11	
Purchase of own clothes		8	3
Continuation of child's education	3	5	3

Note: Three households belong to high wealth rank, six belong to medium wealth rank and two belong to that of low wealth rank.

In case of rejecting prospective groom, it is seen that there has been no change in this matter. All the 11 households agreed that there is no scope of participation in selection choice of a groom by the bride. It was entirely decided by fathers in consultation with mothers though the age at marriage did increase–for males by eight years and in case of females by four years.

As it is a patriarchal society women going out to purchase clothes is rare. Even households headed by the women do not go out without the company of their sons to the market. In eight cases, male members purchase their clothes. Daughters accompanied by their fathers purchase clothes from market in three cases. But we did not find a single household where a couple can go and make necessary purchases.

Mostly male members share education of child, but young housewives who are slightly educated are taking care of their wards at the primary stage in three cases. In another three cases both husband and wife take care of the education of their children. This is one area where women are coming forward both in terms of accessing educational resources and spending resources for their children irrespective of gender.

At the time of our field work when BN Pal who was the richest person, a teacher in the village was about to get her daughter (20 years) married. She had passed her school-leaving examination and was about to enroll for graduation degree course. We discussed with all the members of the household about the marriage. It was revealed that he would be paying Rs. 50,000 cash, jewellery and other furniture as dowry. When we asked why he was paying so much when he himself had accepted meagre amount of dowry at the time of his marriage, he said that it is worth paying because the groom was educated, held enough land being only one son and was working as part time lecturer in a college. He and his wife both agreed to the marriage proposal and his wife too wanted a groom from Burdwan as it was agriculturally developed and had access to facilities available in towns. But the education of the groom compelled them to take the decision. Did they ask their daughter? His wife had asked her and she said yes. We asked her daughter about her opinion to which she said that parents always do well by their daughters and it was not respectable to negate a parent's choice.

This story is not peculiar. Patriarchy is strong among high caste households and with increasing education, dowry demand too is getting higher.

In case of SC households it is seen from Table 5 that like GC women they also do not control cash. A single woman heads one household, which shows cash being handled by women. There is another household where both husband and wife handle cash; by occupation they are agricultural labourers. Here the husband controls the finance, but whenever the wife needs cash and if her husband does not give her the requisite amount, she forcibly takes it away. That's why we placed this case in the cell 'both'. Otherwise other nine households follow the path of GC women. Husbands or fathers-in-law control dowry. The mother hands over utensils, which are given as dowry to the bride to the in-laws.

Table 5
Number of SC Households Where Women Participate in Decision-Making (N=10)

Areas of participation	*Whether GC Women can participate*		
	Yes	*No*	*Both*
Keeping cash/dowry	1	8	1
saying no to prospective groom		10	
Purchase of own clothes	2	7	1
Continuation of child's education		10	

Note: One household belongs to high wealth rank, two belong to medium wealth rank and two belong to that of low wealth rank.

Like GCs, SC women are also not permitted to say no to the prospective groom arranged by their father. Age at marriage increased by two in case of males and by one year in case of females. Yet parents still want to get their wards married early. They are afraid that increase in age of marriage may lead to allegations of '*kalanka*' (loss of reputation), in case of girls. Though the age at marriage has not increased substantially, like GCs dowry has increased. SCs who hold cultivable land, demand more dowry than sharecroppers.

Only two women stated that they purchased their own clothes, a widow-headed household being one among them. Only one couple went out to purchase cloth. Other seven households are dependent upon their husbands for purchases. During the course of our conversation one SC man commented that 'man is not a man, but a coward if he accompanies his wife to the market'.

Education of children is completely dependent upon the male members of the household. Women are illiterate so they are regarded as incapable of handling education of children.

Rita Bagdi and her husband Nikhil Bagdi are agricultural labourers and own 90 bighas of land. Nikhil earns slightly more than his wife does because in lean seasons he works as soil-cutter whereas at that time Rita works as maidservant. When we asked who kept the cash, Rita replied that "I am the owner of my labour, the owner of my earnings is my husband". They also think that if they get a groom who holds 10 bighas of land or less but is an only son, then they would pay dowry as demanded. Her father-in-law had demanded only Rs. 1,000 as dowry that was spent on the wedding feast. This was 10 years back. To ask their daughters' consent about their choice of groom was beyond their imagination.

There is only one household (Table 6) among STs where a woman kept cash; it is a single (a woman separated from her husband) headed household. In another household, both husband and wife handle cash. Other eight households are same as GCs and SCs. But tribals do not have the system of dowry; they have '*Pon*' (brideprice). '*Pon*' has not increased, but it is heard that at some places grooms are expecting dowry, if they are a sharecroppers. But that is yet to happen here. The '*Pradhan*' (head of the Santal community within the village) handles '*Pon*' and it is very meagre amount of Rs. 12. Other gifts include one wedding sari, which is handed over to the bride.

Table 6
Number of ST Households Where Women Participate in Decision Making (N=10)

Areas of participation	*Whether ST Women can participate*		
	Yes	*No*	*Both*
Keeping cash/dowry	3	6	1
saying no to prospective groom	10		
Purchase of own clothes	3	5	2
Continuation of child's education	1	3	1

• Children from five households do not attend schools.

Note: Two Households belong to medium wealth rank, and eight belong to low wealth rank.

Tribal women are free to choose their spouses, can take decision for separation/ divorce and can marry for a second time. It is reflected in the Table 6, where all the 10 households responded that they could say no to prospective groom. One woman who is single remarked, "When both of us are earning why should I remain committed to a womanizing husband?"

ST women are also free to purchase their clothes. Sometimes women in a group without the escort of any male member go out for purchases. Three women reported that they purchase their own clothes. Two women make all their purchases along with their husbands. The rest are dependent upon their husbands for possible purchases.

Regarding education, ST children lag behind GCs and SCs. Children from five households do not attend school. Out of five households in only one case does the mother take care of her children's education in another case, both of them are equally careful. Otherwise it is felt that fathers are more competent to look after their children's education.

Ganga Kisku, a widow aged 40 years, is a matchmaker among Santals. She is '*bandha*' labourer, which means she is tied to a particular household where she does both farm and non-farm work. She appreciates '*bandha*' system because she does not have to bother every season for agricultural labouring. We asked her of changes in the system of marriage. She remarked that age at marriage has increased slightly, but changes are more in the attitude of wives today. Now that boro labour days have increased, so has the income. That is why wives are separating from joint households over minor conflicts. Dispute between wives and mothers-in-law have increased. Husbands are also indulgent towards their wives. She herself complained that whenever she returns from work her son's wife never offered food to her. When she complained about it to her son, they separated from the joint household. Women, these days are also interested to keep their earnings with them.

Conclusion

In SC and ST households where women retain their earnings, their husbands actually hand over their own earnings, besides what they keep for personal expenses, to their wives for managing their household. But does that constitute autonomy? Given that there are households living always at the edge of poverty even if they are not actually suffering from starvation, it is clear that there is very little that the women can do with their earnings apart from buying food and other essentials. It can be confidently said about ST households that they enjoy autonomy to a greater extent than the other groups. ST women can take decisions of marriage, separation, divorce and remarriage.

All of this leads to a general discussion of women as earners and the extent to which this affects their status in the household. In spite of being an essential economic contributor, there are social constraints, which work against the woman to improve her status and position within the household. Though we lack any concrete data, it is our strong impression that when a woman is more or well educated than her husband she tends to be better positioned than otherwise.

Women's control of the product of their labour depends on many factors. Females who work as agricultural labourers do not automatically enjoy same rights. It is again dependent upon caste hierarchy and the probability of her having a better education than their husbands. A variety of cultural and socio-psychological factors also play a part in how much autonomy a woman has. Some women early in life are able to earn a reputation for being able to handle people and being able to manage things well. Such women are often able to gain considerable autonomy in their households, and even in the community at large. A man who is very family-oriented and understanding can see to it that even a woman who is not exceptionally efficient or good at human relations has more autonomy. Thus, within the social, economic and cultural parameters mentioned above there is still room for significant individual variation among households.

References

Angrosino, Michael V. 1989. *Documents of Interaction: Biography, Autobiography and Life History in Social Science Perspective.* Gainsville: University of Florida Press.

Aunger, Robert. 1995. 'On Ethnography: Storytelling or Science?' *Current Anthropology*: 36 (1): 97-130.

Becker, G.W. and T.O. Harris. 1978. *Social Origins of Depression: A Study of Psychiatric Disorder in Women.* New York: Free Press.

Bernstein, Henry, Hazel Johnson, Raul Hernan and Ben Crow (eds.) 1982. *Third World Lives of Struggle.* London: Heinmann Educational in Association with the Open University.

Brewer, John and Albert Hunter. 1989. *Multimethod Research: A Synthesis of Styles.* Newbury Park, CA: Sage.

Burke. 1993. *A Stained White Radiance.* London: Arrow.

Dabbs, J.M.J. 1982. 'Making Things Visible' pp. 31-63 in J. Van Maanen, J.M.J. Dabbs, and R.R. Faulkner (eds.), *Varieties of Qualitative Research.* Thousand Oaks, CA: Sage.

Leacock. 1978. 'Women's Status in Egalitarian Society: Implications for Social Evolution'. *Current Anthropology*: 19: 2:247-76.

Malinowsky, B. 1922. *Argonauts of the Western Pacific.* New York: Macmillan.

Mencher, Joan P. 1989. 'Women Agricultural Labourers and Landowners in Kerala and Tamil Nadu: Some Questions about Gender and Autonomy' in Maithreyi Krishnaraj and Karuna Chanana (eds), *The Household in Gender and the Household Domain: Social and Cultural Dimension.* New Delhi: Sage Publications.

Onselen, Charles Van. 1993. 'The Reconstruction of Rural Life from Oral Testimony: Critical Notes on the Methodology Employed in the Study of a Black South African Sharecropper', *Journal of Peasant Studies*, South Africa, 20:3: 494-514.

Ranger, Terence and Olufumi Vaughan (eds). 1993. *Legitimacy and the State in Twentieth-Century Africa: Essays in honour of A.H.M. Kirk-Greene,* Basingstoke. Oxford: Macmillan in association with St Antony's College.

Richards, Audrey I. 1939. *Land, Labour and Diet in Northern Rhodesia: An Economic Study of Bemba Tribe.* London: International African Institute.

Shaw, B. 1980. 'Life History Writing in Anthropology: A Methodological Review', *Mankind:* 12:226-233.

Thomson P. 1991. *Customs in Common.*Londom: Merlin.

Velson, Van J. 1967. 'The Extended Case Method and Situational Analysis' pp. 139-62 in A.L. Epstein (ed.). The Craft of Social Anthropology. London: Tavistock.

The authors are grateful to D.K. Bagchi and P.M. Blaikie for their unstinted intellectual support during the authors' collaborative research project on "Long-term Changes in Livelihood Trajectory" funded by ESCOR. The contribution made by Ajoy Ghosh and Arpita Chatterjee is acknowledged. The paper was first published in the *Economic and Political Weekly*: 37:49: 2002:4935-4940. It is included here with the permission of the authors and the Editor, *Economic and Political Weekly*. Address for email correspondence: cmolly4011958@yahoo.com

Chapter - Twenty

Women's Participation in Forestry: Some Theoretical Issues

Debnarayan Sarkar and Nimai Das

Policy makers and advocates of Joint Forest Management (JFM) agree that women should be full participants and their involvement is especially important because of the nature of women's work (Tinker: 1994:367; Hobley: 1996: 19; Locke: 1999: 235). This commitment is increasingly reflected in some of the provisions of JFM legislation and in the debate and documentation of the National JFM Support Group and could provide a genuine basis from which stakeholders within donor organizations, Non-Governmental Organizations (NGOs) and Forest Departments could encourage JFM to address women's concern (Lichbach: 1996). Thus, the gender policy has been informed by instrumentalist positions in the debate over women's relationship to the environment. This paper attempts to examine the extent of women's involvement in Forestry in Non-Timber Forest Products (NTFPs) and their role in JFM in West Bengal where the successful experience of JFM emerges as an exceptionally good example for Government of India to turn this concept as a National Forest Policy in 1990.

This paper is divided into four sections. Section I presents the theoretical framework of the study. Section II deals with the review of studies concerning the formal provision of women's participation in JFM in India along with some research studies in this context. Section-III provides the data set and empirical results. Conclusions in the light of the results obtained in our study are presented in section IV.

I

Theoretical Framework

Mainstream development agencies are not centrally concerned with development theory, but they draw on an instrumentalist line of argument concerning the relationship between women and the environment (Leach and Green: 1995). Mainly two arguments are put forward behind the theoretical explanation of WED (Women, Environment and Development). First, improving the status of women will assist the solution of environmental problems (Jackson: 1993 c). Second, within environmental projects, women's sole participation will lead to improve project efficiency. " Women's productive role", as Tinker puts in, "not their needs, provide the justification for including them in forestry programmes" (Tinker: 1994:370).

The argument of WED in favour of their theoretical explanation is: women are more dependent on nature by virtue of the sexual division of labour. It is said that women are primarily responsible for the gathering of fuel, fodder and wild foods and the growing of subsistence crops for survival, whereas men are seen as mainly responsible for the growing of cash crops for profit (Leach and Green: 1995:7). Women are seen as being the 'most' appropriate participant in environmental conservation as the main victims of environmental degradation (Shah and Shah: 1995). Thus, it is implied that women have a special connection with environment, which are somehow close to nature and men (ibid, 1995; Leach and Green: 1995). The WED's understanding of women's relationship to the environment implies that the central issues for community forestry are formal provisions for women's representatives plus recognition of women's resource-use roles and their special knowledge and values about the environment.

The fact that women have a 'special' connection with the environment derives much weight for its explicit articulation in Eco-feminism. Eco-feminism presupposes a direct connection between women's biology and women's relationship with the environment. In proposing a natural affinity between women and environment, Eco-feminism has been seen as retrogressive by the women's movement, because it proposes a direct connection between women's biology and women's relationship with the environment (Locke: 1999). Whenever women reacted against ecological destruction and chances of annihilation of life, they became concerned about the violence against them. Aggressionism against environment was perceived almost physical aggression against female body (Mies and Shiva: 1997).

Though WED and Eco-ferminism both claim women have a special and close connection with the nature and in that the two approaches have strong similarities, WED does not explicitly subscribe to eco-feminism and has important differences from it. First, Eco-feminism emphasizes the natural and spiritual content of women's 'closeness' with nature (Locke: 1999: p. 237). Second, in proposing a natural affinity between women and the environment, eco-feminism has been seen as retrogressive by the women's movement for it proposes a direct connection between women's biology and women's relationship with the environment. In contrast, the WED's position accepts the socially-constructed nature of women's role in resource-use, but assumes that women in their current roles are more informed and interested in environmental issues (Rocheleau, et al: 1996) and are therefore a 'natural' constituency for conservation interventions (Jackson: 1993 b: 649; Leach and Green: 1995:2). Thus, WED provides ideological support for environmental policies that uphold the given division of labour. Third, while WED is essentially an interventionist position, albeit one that advocates participation, eco-feminism is much more radical political stance that argues for respect for women's indigenous environmental activities (Joekes, et al: 1994:137-38). Eco-feminism also points to women's activism in indigenous environmental movements as evidence of their altruism vis-à-vis the environment (Agarwal: 1992:147; Leach and Green: 1995:10).

The gender and development (GAD) perspective observes women's (and men's) relation to environmental resources merely as a part of general entitlements and capabilities ascribed to individuals by social relations or gender, class and so on (Joekes, et al: 1994:139). In this exposition GAD poses some important differences from WED and Eco-feminism. First, GAD denied any special relationship between women and the environment to both WED and eco-feminism on the basis of the nature of women's work or on the basis of female biology. Second, rejecting the notion of women as an undifferentiated category with particular interests, GAD regards current social roles as established and maintained though power and authority. Third, although eco-feminism glorifies women's altruism, GAD draws attention to debates over intra-household relationships where a women's bargaining power is diminished by the perception that her well-being is of secondary importance to that of other household members (Jackson: 1993a:1958; Sen: 1987:17-30). Considerable evidence suggests that traditional community argument has in practice usually been premised on inequality within and between households (Jackson: 1993b: 651; Quiggin: 1993:1124; Watson: 1989:67).

Therefore, gender analysts have argued for a revolution of women's involvement in environmental movements and women's community managing work. They argue that such involvement in essentially conservative processes actually constitutes the extension of unpaid work for women rather than evidencing women's radical environmental activism (Leach and Green: 1995;19; Jackson: 1993a:1950-52). Moreover, there is increasing recognition of the gendered nature of inter-community environmental issues (Agarwal: 1994, Jackson: 1993a, Shah and Shah: 1995). Although gender analysis can not distil any general relationship between women and the environment that could inform perspective policy (Razavi and Miller: 1995), it suggests that environmental interventions will be a new arena in which gendered bargaining processes will be enacted and contested (Locke: 1999).

Thus, the theoretical viewpoint of WED and eco-feminism recognize special relationship between women and environment or women's 'closeness' to nature on the basis of material role of women, and of natural and spiritual content of women's 'closeness' with nature. But, more importantly, increasing women's participation without attention to addressing gender inequality represents little more than increasing the unpaid contribution of women (Mayoux: 1995:236). Understanding of women's relationship with the environment needs to recognize the relationships of power and authority, negotiations and bargaining and the wider social relations in which decisions about land and trees are embedded (Leach: 1991:19).

The WED approach understands the gender division of labour to be about identifying who uses which forest products–the nature of work; but GAD's approach is directed by social relation of gender, class and so on and is maintained through power and authority of patriarchy. It could be argued that WED is a useful strategic discourse arguing for the involvement of women in environmental projects in a way that is persuasive to policy makers (Li: 1996). But important dimensions of gender concerns regarding forest use are currently hidden in the WED approach and in the kinds of understandings promoted as significant in JFM. Adopting a GAD approach will involve changing policy framework that are grounded in WED, redefining the kinds of understandings needed for gender-sensitive planning, and establishing how to monitor changing gender relations in the context of JFM. The aim of gender sensitive planning for JFM should be to find ways in which women can institutionalize the few bargaining strength they have and in working out leverages and incentives that would insure a voice and space for the most marginalized groups within decision-making processes (Shah and Shah: 1995:81-82). Within gender planning for JFM, this trend has translated into a preoccupation with formal provisions for women's participation in local forest management institutions, and with the necessity of identifying women's preference for forest resources and their knowledge and values about forest resources.

II

Review of Studies

As to the formal provisions for women's participation in JFM, within the various policy statements of the Indian Government, rhetoric about women's role in JFM is minimally present (Locke: 1999: 239). The watershed 1988 National Forest Policy asserted that one of the basic objectives was 'creating a massive people's involvement with the involvement of women (The Ministry of Environment and Forests, MOEF: 1988). This is the only non-bracketed mention of women. The 1990 circular makes no mention of women specifically and refers only to beneficiaries (MOEF: 1990). At the national level in official statements of policy, women are seen as undifferentiated and marginalized category whose inclusion in JFM merits a clause. The token reference to women in these documents largely reflects the accommodation of the Indian State to multiple political pressures, including those from national and international activists and donors, and has justifiably been labeled as 'gender-biased' (Arora: 1994: 695).

Marking a sharp departure for the past, JFM is a direct outcome of 1988 National Forest Policy, which acknowledges the dependence of the rural poor on forest resources for survival. This policy extolled the virtues of people's participation in development and conservation of forestland. In forestry, this process is also found elsewhere in Asia (Hobley: 1996, Lynch and Talbot: 1995). But, India's Joint Forest Programme furnishes as an exceptionally good example of an attempt to turn their concept into reality (Sundar and Jeffery: 1999). Orissa was the first state that passed the first resolution on the subject in 1988, followed by West Bengal in 1989.

In India, JFM programme, implemented through a June 1990 Ministry of Environment and Forests (MOEF), Government of India circular, is to a large extent based upon the successful experience of joint management in Arabari hills in Midnapore district of West Bengal, which have demonstrated beyond doubt that local communities can protect forest patches near their villages and that the forest department too can work with the people if it wants (Mitra: 1997). The key precursor to JFM, from a managerial perspective, was a local-level initiative, dating from the early 1970s, in the Arabari hills in West Bengal. In Arabari, a forest officer worked outside the official rules in an attempt to protect experimental plantation. He discovered that by offering to share the benefits of the regrowth of trees, his own interests in protection could be met (Sivaramkrishnan: 1996a; Sundar and Jeffery: 1999).

But the small amount of information that is available regarding the outcome of JFM for women is disheartening. Women are commonly excluded or unable to participate in community institutions for JFM (Jewitt: 1995, Hobley: 1996). The Overseas Development Administrations (ODA) review of their participatory forest management projects confirm that in India trends in quality, accountability and scope of local decision-making are negative with poor involvement of women and marginalisation of forest dependent groups (Bird: 1996: Annex 2, Table 2). Debates over formal provisions of membership are removed from the realities of effective political representation where male foresters and male villagers have a common interest in perpetuating women's visibility (Arora: 1994:695). In the central Himalayas women are 'effectively conscripted' to forest committees in order to fulfill the formal requirement of JFM resolutions (Britt-Kapoor: 1994: 11).

Individual state resolutions and project policies in JFM 'lack clarity regarding the role of women' in JFM. The resolution of some states stipulates that one adult representative per household may be a member of the general body of the local forest management institutions. Although some resolutions add the qualification that this may be either a man or a woman, in practice it is usually a man (Locke: 1999: 240). Some resolutions stipulate the inclusion of one male and one female member from each household in the general body and a compulsion to include at least two women members in the executive body (Kameswari: 2002).

There are five major constraints to women's formal participation in JFM initiatives which result in their exclusion from the decision-making process–traditional rule, social and cultural barrier, limited experience of women in public speaking (e.g. illiteracy), logistic constraints like time and double work burden and preference of male members by the male forest department staff involved in JFM (Agarwal: 1997). In the context of Karnataka's JFPM programme, Correa (1996) observes how formal provisions are distorted due to lack of gender sensitivity on the part of forest department staff. Despite formal provision of involving women in JFM activities, the actual functioning of Village Forest Committees (VFCs)/

FPCs restricts them to the role of passive receivers of information related to JFM (Kameswari: 2002: 800).

Correa's field survey (Correa: 1999) in Uttar Kannada suggests that at every stage of Joint Forest Progamme Management (JFPM) process participation of women was practically non-existent due to three main points. First, although there was official report on participation of women, the active participation of women was limited to cooking the meals of official staff. Second, the minutes of meeting systematically excluded the views of any women who might have attended the meeting (Kameswari: 2002: 98-99). Third, women who were the members of the managing committee did not know anything about JFPM: they did not know anything of their being members of the managing committee; nor were they practically concerned about the fact that they have to carry out the conclusions of its deliberations. Furthermore, it was also observed that women resigned from executive body of Village Forest Committee (VFC) as their husbands did not approve of their taking part in public activities and beat them up whenever they came to attend the meetings of the executive committee (Kameswari: 2002: 799). Such incidents not only undermine the confidence of the women to express their views in JFM committee meetings but also set precedents for sidelining them during future decision making. This paper thus attempts to examine the extent of women's involvement in forestry and their role in JFM in West Bengal where the successful experience of JFM acted as the key precursor to turn the concept of JFM for India.

III

The Data Set and Findings

This paper is based on secondary data on State Forest Report published from the Directorate of Forests, Government of West Bengal and the official records of the Directorate for the years 1989 to 2000. It also uses a Report of a case study executed by the Directorate of Forest in 1994 relating to extent of women's involvement in forestry on Non-Timber Forest Products (NTFPs) in West Bengal. The major constraints, among others, of these secondary data are that some indices of the contents that are published in one year remain unpublished for some other subsequent years. For the researchers, these constitute limits to represent time-series data of any index in standard econometric analysis. Despite these limitations, we have attempted to examine the extent of women's involvement in forestry in NTFPs and their role in JFM in West Bengal. The procedures like absolute numerical value, simple proportions, compound growth rate, and averages are employed to achieve the stated objectives of this study.

The joint forest management (JFM) in West Bengal has its origin in the success achieved in rejuvenating a patch of 17 hectares of degraded forests under a pilot project implemented during 1972 near Arabari in Midnapore district. About 618 families living in 11 villages lying in the fringe voluntarily protected these forests when in return they were assured provision of fuel wood and fodder from the regenerated forest and employment in forestry activities. In 1987, these villagers were also declared as beneficiaries for these rejuvenated forests and granted 25 per cent share from the revenue earned from the final harvest (State Forest Report: 2000).

Despite its early success, the JFM in West Bengal gathered momentum in 1989 (dated the 12th July, 1989) when Government Orders were issued to formalize the Forest Protection Committee (FPC) wherein the duties and responsibilities of the FPC members, usufructuary and other benefits to which they would be entitled had been laid down. But the amended State Resolution on JFM did not make explicit mention of women as independent entities; the membership was either joint or male/female. Moreover, according to the State Resolution, the executive committee of FPC did not mention a minimum number of representatives from women category; rather it was stated that the number of members under elected representatives of the beneficiaries would not exceed six in the executive committee. Beyond this, the resolution was silent on women's separate role and involvement in committee formation, micro planning, site selection, protection, benefit sharing, etc. Consequently, women, who by their nature of work (WED) and on the basis of their spiritual content (Eco-feminism) are very 'close to nature, lose an important opportunity to participate actively under formal institutional framework in JFM movement in West Bengal. This seems to support the argument of Locke (1998), which remarks that as to formal provisions for women's participation in JFM within various policy statements of the Indian Government rhetoric about women's role in JFM is minimally present.

Table 1
Men's and Women's Involvement in Forestry: Non-Timber Forest Products (NTFPs)

(in percentage)

Activities Related to NTFPs	*Male*	*Female*
Gathering	25.00	75.00
Processing	-	100.00
Marketing	33.33	67.67
Consumption	50.00	50.00

Source: Directorate of Forest, Government of West Bengal.

That women's involvement in forestry is more significant than men seems to be obvious from the report of survey executed by the Forest Department, Govt. of West Bengal in 1994. As may be seen in Table 1, activities related to NTFP like gathering, marketing, female's involvement is dominant or even cent per cent (activities related to processing), but in consumption of NTFP both men and women consume in same proportion. Turning to Table 2, regarding the gathering of NTFP, women's involvement is more pronounced than men. Men's involvement is higher than women's in such an item (like medicinal item of NTFPs), which requires minimal physical labour. These finding might suggest the theoretical explanation of WED, suggesting that women are very 'close to nature' for the nature of their work on the one hand and supports the explanation of GAD, based on unequal division labour and gender relations supporting current social roles as established and maintained through power and authority of men and the women's well-being is of secondary importance to that of men on the other.

Table 2
Men's and Women's Involvement in Gathering of NTFPs

Classified Items to NTFPs	*Number of female Gatherer*	*Number of Male Gatherer*
Food	37(84.10)	7(15.90)
Fodder for Goats	3 (50.00)	3 (50.00)
Fuel	38 (90.48)	4 (9.52)
Structural	2 (50.00)	2 (50.00)
Religious	4 (80.00)	1 (20.00)
Ornamental.	2 (100.00)	-
Medicinal	5 (26.32)	14(73.68)
MinorHouseholdarticles for mats, sal plates	3 (100.00)	-
Total	94 (75.20)	31 (24.80)

Note: Figures in brackets represent percentages.*Source:* Directorate of Forest, Government of WestBengal.

Table 3
Status of FPC 1993 and Its Compound Growth Rate between March 1993 to December 2000

Districts'	*No. 01 FPC*	*Area under Protection (Hectares)*	*No 01 FPC Members*	*Area Protected byFPC/EPC Members*
Bankura	868 (5.287)	81979 (4.238)	77716 (6.309)	1.05 (-1.870)
Midnapore	780 (5.317)	83488 (3.350)	112166 (6.210)	1.32 (-2.698)
PuruJia	432 (6.079)	56774 (1.819)	43483 (5.238)	1.31 (-3.243)
Birbhum	72 (9.163)	7070 (3.619)	5129 (7.352)	1.38 (-3.441)
Burdwan	32 (13.573)	11584 (7.670)	6408 (16.662)	1.81 (-7.738)
24-parganas	10 (18.596)	240 (118.317)	118 (96.874)	2.03 (10.907)
Jalpaiguri	29 (25.849)	7472 (32.067)	4401 (28.756)	1.70 (2.566)
Cooch bihar	29 (23.167)	1237 (33.392)	244 (50.814)	5.07 (-11.534)
Darjeeling	2 (73.328)	599 (71.278)	547 (36.280)	1.09 (25.750)
Total	2235 (6.812)	27912 (8.311)	223076 (8.178)	16.76 (1.769)

To crystallize the idea of JFM in West Bengal that started in 1989 after the issuance of government JFM resolution, the FPCs were set up first in the degraded forest areas of South West Bengal in the districts of Bankura, Midnapore, Purulia, Birbhum and Burdwan and gradually it was extended to other parts of West Bengal with the participation and involvement of the local people living in the fringe of the forests Table 3 supports these facts. It shows that although the compound growth rate relating to the number of FPC, Area under Protection (in hectares), Number of FPC members and Forest Land-man ratio was much lower for the areas of North West Bengal in the districts of Jalpaiguri, Cooch Behar and Darjeeling and one district of South West Bengal–24 Parganas than the areas of South West Bengal between 1993 and 2000, the initial status of FPC in 1993 was much higher for former districts (i.e. the areas other than South West Bengal).

Table 4
Distribution of Men's and Women's Involvement in FP Committee in West Bengal, December, 2001

Districts	*Forest Division*	*Total Number of FPC*	*Members*		
			Male	*Female*	*Total*
Midnapur	Karagpur S F	82	18002 (92.82)	1293 (7.18)	19295 (100)
	Rupnarayan 8 C	182	21358 (96.05)	843 (3.95)	22201 (100)
	East Midnapore	315	41387 (95.17)	1998 (4.83)	43385 (100)
	West Midnaproe	542	45103 (95.72)	1932 (4.28)	47035 (100)
Bankura	Bankura (S)	538	48372 (93.67)	3064 (6.33)	51436 (100)
	Panchet	221	24088 (92.66)	1767 (7.34)	25855 (100)
Purulia	Purulia	174	17912 (97.71)	410 (2.29)	18322 (100)
Birbhum	Birbhum	133	8756 (98.60)	123 (1.40)	8879 (100)
Burdwan	Burdwan	57	13937 (83.41)	2312 (16.59)	16249 (100)
24-Pgs	(S) STR	10	3776 (97.38)	99 (2.62)	3875 (100)
Jalpaiguri	Baikuntnath	55	6082 (96.02)	241 (3.98)	6223 (100)
Darjeeling	Darjeeling	41	2481 (91.21)	218 (8.79)	2699 (100)
	Kalimpong	35	2795 (94.17)	163 (5.83)	2958 (100)
Total		2385	254049 (94.30)	14463 (5.70)	268512 (100)

Note: Figures in brackets represent percentages.

Dealing with women's involvement in JFM committee, Table 4 shows that women's involvement in the JFM committee is insignificant as compared with men in almost all the districts of West Bengal. This is, mainly, due to the fact that as the amended State Resolution on JFM does not explicitly mention women either in the FPC or in the Executive committee of FPC, the Forest Department personnel are not usually interested in motivating women to participate in JFM. Their prime importance seems to relate to the formation of committee, irrespective of gender. It should be mentioned that despite formal provision for involving women in JFM committee in Madhya Pradesh State (undivided) in India, the actual functioning of Village Forest Committees (VFCs)/FPCs restricts them to the role of passive receivers of information whereas men are active senders of information related to JFM (Kameswari: 2001). This dichotomy of an active male sender and passive female receiver derives strength from the existing social norms and cultural values and in turn strengthens the existing gender disparity (Moitra: 1996).

As to the payment of usufracts to FPCs, usufructs from these forests began to flow after protection of these forests by FPC members for a continuous period of 5 years, from the year 1996 when the distribution of usufracts from harvest was made in the month of October and 25 per cent share of the final yield from the harvest were paid as usufracts to a small proportion of FPC members, taking household, *and not women*, as a unit of beneficiaries. Since then such usufracts are being paid to the FPC members from the revenue earned from regular and final harvest of these rejuvenated and matured forests. Table 5 shows that the payment of usufructs is almost confirmed to the beneficiaries of some FPCs in Midnapore and Bankura districts but the significant majority of FPC and their members are out of the scope of the payment of usufracts.

Table 5
Payment of Usufracts to FPCs aHnitial Year (1995-96) and Its Compound Growth Rate, 1995-96 to 1998-99

Districts	*Number of FPC Benefited*	*Percentage of Total FPC*	*Number of Beneficiaries*	*Percentage of Total FPC Member*	*Amount (as in lakhs) Benefited*
Midnapore.	91	11.67	10771	12.90	73.99
	(31.09)		(2.01)		(28.64)
Bankura	56	6.45	48.69	5.94	37.59
	(28.92)		(29.58)		(37.14)
Burdwan	14	43.35	3964	34.22	6.88
	(-12.79)		(-11.60)		(-10.82)
Birbhum	1	1.39	128	1.81	0.68
	(191.29)		(54.93)		(76.99)
Total	162	9.25	19732	10.72	119.14
	(27.65)		(24.19)		(30.23)

Note: Figures in brackets represent compound growth rate.

Table 6
Comparative Characteristics of FPC and Femi;lle FPC in Bankura District, West Bengal, December 2000

Forest Division	*Total Number*		*Average*	*Total Number of Female*		*Average*
	FPC	*FPC Member*	*FPC Member*	*FPC*	*FPC Member*	*Female FPC Member*
Bankura (North)	486	44210	90.97	4 (0.82)	119 (0:27)	29.75
Bankura (South)	538	50192	9.29	9 (1.54)	485 (0.97)	53.89
Panchet	221	24865	112.51	4 (1.81)	401 (1.61)	100.25
Total	1245	119267	95.80	17 (1.37)	1005 (0.84)	59.12

Note: Figures in brackets represent pertentage.

Thus, understanding that women are being deprived of their equal constitutional rights to benefits accruing from the forest, efforts have been made very recently by the Forest Department, Govt. of West Bengal to establish new management system of female FPC in West Bengal. To this end 17 Female FPCs have been established, primarily only in Bankura district in West Bengal. It has been extended to all the three Forest Divisions of the district, though the payment of usufracts to the members of female FPC has not started up to the present time. Table 6 shows that although compared with FPC, the number of female FPC as well as the other members of FPC is insignificant in Bankura district, the movement that has been started by the Government effort seems to motivate women who can function as an important control group in their own FPCs in a large scale forest management in all areas of West Bengal in future.

IV

Conclusion

The experience of West Bengal relating to the extent of women's involvement in forestry and their role in JFM suggests that despite women's greater involvement in forestry in NTFPs, they are commonly excluded from participating in community institutions for JFM. State JFM Resolution does not make explicit mention of women as an independent entity; nor does it mention a minimum representation from the women's category. Beyond this, the resolution is silent on women's separate role and involvement in committee formation, micro planning, site selection, protection, benefit sharing, etc. Women's insignificant role is also reflected in JFM Committee. These findings might suggest the theoretical explanation of WED and Eco-feminism which accept women's 'closeness' with nature on the basis of female biology or the nature of women's work (Jockes, et al: 1994) on the one hand, and the explanation of GAD, which is based on unequal division of labour and gender relations suggesting current social roles as established and maintained through power and authority of men in which women's well-being is of secondary importance to that of man (Locke: 1999), on the other.

But the theoretical line of argument thrown up by the WED, Eco-feminism and GAD approaches respectively argue for GAD approach in which gendered bargaining processes will be enacted and contested (Sundar and Jeffery: 1999, Locke: 1999). GAD's approach is firmly based on the analysis of actual gender relations in which gender-sensitive planning for JFM should be able to find ways so that women can institutionalize the bargaining strength they have. The setting up of female FPC in some areas of West Bengal very recently is an attempt, which supports these theoretical explanations. This new attempt seems to motivate women who can function as important control group in their own FPCs along with their own management system that would ensure a voice and space for these most marginalized groups within decision-making process. Added to this, as the main victims of environmental degradation, women would be the most appropriate participants in environmental conservation under their own management system of micro planning.

Notes

1. Due to various reasons, the old custodial Forest Management systems developed were rendered ineffective in the Fifties and Sixties of the Twentieth century, the major reason being traditional emphasis on production of commercial wood and disregard for local need.

References

Agarwal, B. 1992. 'The Gender and Environment Debate: Lessons from India'. *Feminist Studies:* 18: 1: 119-58.

Agarwal, B. 1994. 'Gender, Resistance and Land: Interlinked Struggles over Resources and Meanings in South Asia'. *Journal of Peasant Studies:* 22: 1: 81-125.

Agarwal, B. 1997. 'Environmental Action, Gender Equity and Women's Participation'. Development and Change: 28:1: 1-44.

Arora, D. 1994. 'From State Regulation to People' Participation: Case of Joint Forest Management in India', *Economic and Political Weekly*: 29:12: 691-98.

Bird, P. 1996. *ODA's Review of Participatory Forest Management: Synthesis of Findings.* London: ODA Review Working Paper 6.

Britt-Kapoor, C. 1994. *A Tale of Two Committees: Villager Perspectives on Local Institutions, Forest Management and Resource Use in Two Central Himalayan Indian Villages.* London: Overseas Development Institution Rural Development Forestry Network Paper 17a.

Correa, M. 1999. 'He need for Emancipatory Research: Experiences from JFPM in Uttar Kannada' in the Jeffery, R. and Sundar N. (eds), *A New Moral Economy For India's Forests? Discourses of Community and Participation.* New Delhi: Sage Publications.

Hobley, M. 1996. *Participatory Forestry: The Process of Change in India and Nepal.* ODI Rural Development Forestry Study Guide 3.

Jackson, C. 1993a. 'Doing What Comes Naturally? Women and Environment in Development', *World Development:* 21: 12: 1947-963.

Jackson, C. 1993b. Environmentalisms and Gender Interests in the Third World', *Development and Change*: 24:4: 649-77.

Jackson, C. 1993c. 'Questioning Synergism: Win-Win with Women in Population and Environmental Policies?' *Journal of International Development: 5:6: 651-68*

Jeffery, R. and Sundar, N. 1999. *A new Moral Economy For India's Forests? Discourses of Community and Participation.* New Delhi: Sage Publications.

Joekes, S., N. Heyzer, R. Oniango and V. Salles. 1994. 'Gender, Environment and Population', *Development and Change*: 25:1.

Kameswari, V.L.V. 2001. 'Gendered Communication and Access to Social Space: Issues in Forest Management, *Economic and Political Weekly*, Feb.23.

Leach, M. and C. Green. 1995. 'Gender and Environmental History: Moving Beyond the Narratives of the Past'. *Contemporary Women-Environment Policy Debates*, Sussex.

Lichbach, M.I. 1996. *West Bengal Joint Forestry Management Project.* London: Overseas Development Administration Report on an Orientation Visit to the Indian Forestry Field Management Office.

Locke, C. 1999. 'Gender Policy in Joint Forest Management' in Jeffery, R. and Sundar, N. (eds) *A New Moral Economy For India's Forests? Discourses of Community and Participation,* New Delhi: Sage Publications.

Lynch, O.J. and K. Talbott. 1995. *Balancing Acts: Community-Based Forest Management and National Law in Asia and the Pacific.* Washington, DC: World Resources Institute.

Mayoux, L. 1995. 'Beyond Naivety: Women, Gender Inequality and Participatory Development', *Development and Change: 26: 2: 235-58.*

Mies, M. and Shiva, V. 1997. 'Eco-feminism in Feminism' in Kemp, S. and Squires, J.P. (ed.). Oxford Readers.

Mitra, A. 1997. 'Joint forest Management: Case studies' *Yojana*, August.

Moitra, S. 1996. 'Wemen, Communication and Science: Identity Question' *Economic and Political Weekly*: 20: 8.

Quiggin, J. 1993. 'Common Property, Equality and Development', *World Development: 21: 7: 1123-138.*

Razavi, S. and C. Miller. 1995. *From WID to GAD: Conceptual Shifts in the Women and Development Discourse.* UNRISD Occasional Paper-1.

Rocheleau, D., B. Thomas-Slayter and E. Wangari. 1996. Gender and Environment: Feminist Political Ecology Perspective', in D. Rocheleau, B. Thomas Slayter and E. Wangari (eds), *Feminist Political Ecology: Global Issues and Local Experiences.* New York: Rutledge.

Sen, A. 1987. *Gender and Cooperative conflicts.* World Institute for Development Economics Research Working Paper 18.

Shah, M.K. and P. Shah. 1995. 'Gender, Environment and Livelihood Security: An Alternative Viewpoint from India': *Economic and Political Weekly:* 26:75-78.

Tinker, I. 1994. 'Women and Community Forestry in Nepal: Expectations and Realities', *Society and Natural Resources: 7: 4:* 367-81

Watson, J.J. 1989. 'The Evolution of Appropriate Resource Management Systems', in F.Berkes (ed.), *Common Property Resources: Ecology and Community-Based Sustainable Development.* London: Belhaven Press.

The paper was first published in the *Economic and Political Weekly*: 37:43:4407-4412. It is included here with the permission of the authors and the Editor, *Economic and Political Weekly.* Debnarayan Sarkar, is a Professor and Nimai Das, a Senior Research Fellow at the Centre for Economic Studies, Presidency College, Kolkata-73. Address for email correspondence is: sarkar_d_n@rediffmail.com.

CHAPTER - TWENTY ONE

Women, Water, Irrigation: Respecting Women's Priorities

Anil C. Shah

I

Women's Needs and Perception

We were visiting the command area of an irrigation project. From the car window I could see some women washing clothes in the canal. I requested the accompanying engineer to stop the car. The engineer told me that quite often they tried to dissuade women from using the canal water for such purpose. But they managed to reach the canal and use it for their purposes. When I asked the women why they were using canal water for washing clothes, they said, there was no other convenient arrangement in their village, so they preferred to walk the 2 kms distance to wash their clothes in the running canal water. The engineer was feeling more uncomfortable. I asked the women: "Is it convenient to wash clothes in the canal?" And they replied: "It is better than what we have in the village. Of course it is difficult to wash clothes on the slope of a slanting canal side." I asked: "If government is ready to help, what kind of arrangement would you like?" The women said: "Some kind of platform made of flat stones on which we can sit and wash clothes, using the canal water".

Back in the car we proceeded further. Now it was engineer's turn to stop the car to show me a group of women washing clothes in another canal. When we reached the women, we found that there was indeed a platform on which women were washing their clothes. To my surprise, I turned to the engineer, how come? He said, "We learnt about the problems of women in a nearby village and therefore constructed this facility." "Is it, permissible? What about the funds?"

The engineer was now in full form. "No problem. After all it is a small expenditure. It can be accommodated in the canal maintenance grant".

Sankarpura (Anand District, Gujarat)

I joined the group of women sitting on the ground. Some of the women had covered their faces with their saree following the *pardha* system. The menfolk were requested to move back so that the women did not have to cover their faces. This created a relaxed atmosphere. After some 'ice breaking' dialogue, I asked women about the various uses of water. As the group was mentioning the uses they were noted in a chart paper: (1) drinking; (2) cooking; (3) bathing; (4) washing clothes; (5) water for animals to drink and, wash; and (6) agriculture.

The discussion turned to how much water was required by each family. They described the requirement in terms of '*beda*' (a *beda* means two pots, one over the other) that women carry on their heads. The number varied from 5 to 15 depending upon the number of people and animals in a family. Then we discussed sources of water. There are two dug wells in the village from which water could be drawn lowering the pot tied to a rope. The women however preferred to carry water from the tube well of a farmer. The extent of trouble would depend upon the distance of the houses from the tube well. This took us to drawing the social map of the village, showing location of houses and their distance from the tube well. Initially hesitant, the women were now drawing the map. Each one tried to mark her house; the wells and the tube well were also shown.

Besides the dug wells and the tube well, was there any other source of water? The women looked at each other. I asked: "I understand there is a canal serving your village?" "Yes, of course, that is for agriculture." I drew their attention to the list they had prepared about the uses of water, which included agriculture. They explained they had in mind buying water from the tube well owner, an expensive proposition. The flow of canal water was not very regular and therefore if the crops required they hade to turn to the private tube well owner. But when the canal water was available, would they use the water for the purposes listed? They liked it but were not allowed by the canal officers and even farmers. They stated that the canal water was for agriculture. If allowed, would they like to use canal water for the listed uses? "Yes, of course, it is, much better than carrying loads of water on the head. We are losing hair, becoming bald!" "At present we carry the clothes as also a wooden plank so that we have some kind of platform to wet, soap and rinse our clothes. If allowed we would like to have a flat platform made of stones where we can sit and wash clothes. We will also use the facility for animals to drink and we can wash them. Women showed readiness to collect contribution if required by the *panchayat* (village council)."

Yadbar (Mehsana District)

We had a meeting with villagers, mostly women, of a backward community. All the women were illiterate. There was a water trough very close to the meeting place. Animals were drinking water and women were bathing and washing clothes. Starting discussion with the villagers at the water trough, I asked various uses and sources of water in the village. There were a number of wells in the village area but except four all had saline water, not fit for drinking and cooking. The water trough and four wells were shown in a map on a chart paper. Also shown were the lanes and houses in the village to find out the distance from the sources of water. Women had to bring 5 to 15 *bedas* to meet the water requirements of the family. I asked: "Since you wash clothes and bathe with the water in the trough, at least you are not required to carry water for bathing". Women said, "Only we (women) come to the trough. We have to carry water home for men's bathing". I exclaimed, women bathe in open and men in the comfort of home! Is it not strange? Women laughed and said that is how our life is organised. What are the other sources of water? I thought they would now mention the canal that was passing by the village. The women mentioned the village pond, which collected rainwater that was sweet. If it filled up dúring rains it could provide water to the village for two years. But that is not happening for last five years. "What could be done?" I wondered loudly. The women suggested that if canal water could be diverted to the pond it could be filled up. "Yes, good idea. Why don't you approach the canal officers?"

I was informed that there was an open channel dug by the village community to divert some canal water to the pond. Later on they laid underground pipe connecting the canal to the pond. They raised funds by contributing Rs. 300 to Rs. 500 per family. "Very good, so your problem is solved?". Sullen and dejected, the women informed: "Yes until the canal authorities plugged with cement concrete the outlet from which the pipeline carried water to the pond. They could not tolerate such unauthorised use!" I discussed with the villagers, mostly addressing women, some options that can be considered for dealing with the problem of water such as roof-top rain water harvesting, approaching the canal authorities for giving permission for taking canal water to the village pond, etc. Women remained sceptical. I did not discuss the question of women's participation in the management of canal for agriculture.

Ravalapura (Anand District)

The meeting with women was arranged in the office of the village milk cooperative. It was a floor above the centre where the society collected milk twice a day for sending to the district milk union for processing and distribution. Late in the evening it was not very convenient time for women to meet and yet, there were more women than we expected. Some carried their children also. It is difficult to conduct a Participatory Rural Appraisal (PRA) on 'Women and Water' in this context. However I started with information on milk cooperative-number of members-4,500, daily collection 1,000, annual sale Rs. 2 million. Both women and men 'poured' milk in the society. Out of 450 members, 70 were women; once there were three women in the executive committee of the society; now there is none. Even though questions were directed to women some men sitting around all the time volunteered to provide information. I requested them to move to an adjoining room. Women felt relaxed and spread out. PRA exercise started with a few women with whom it was possible to communicate.

Uses and sources of water: Uses of water-drinking, cooking, bathing, drinking and washing animals, washing clothes, washing utensils, agriculture. The most important source was piped water supply scheme of the village. The most difficult problem was erratic power supply that kept women waiting for hours. Those who do not have pipe connection at home collected water from the neighbour. There were localities at higher level, where piped water could not reach. There was a washing *ghat* (enclosed water stand with facility for washing and bathing) for women, but inadequate. Without drainage, the surroundings were slushy, dirty. Though all these are very vital for women, there was no time to get into these issues. We were interested in women's perception about the irrigation canal as a source of water to meet their requirements. They did not even mention it. When we referred to the PRA map of the village women pointed out those living close to the canal and who use it for washing clothes. There was a platform for washing clothes constructed by the canal authorities. There was need for extending the platform but most of the women preferred to have facility for washing close to the village.

The village was prosperous. Women were more involved in their household duties and their involvement in agriculture was restricted only to weeding and harvesting operations. To carry out all other operations, as and when required, farmers engaged labourers. Yet these women were expressing their grievances before a stranger how they were suffering because the village leaders do not care for their needs of water for domestic purpose. We left the village without discussing the possibility of women participating in canal management. Programme officers of the development support centre carried out a similar exercise in three more villages, given in Annexure A.

II

Emerging Scenario

The canal served villages that were studied through participatory rural appraisal (PRA) technique for establishing rapport and interaction with village women brought out that the following uses of water are common in all the seven villages: (I) drinking; (2) cooking; (3) washing; and (4) bathing. Five villages mentioned water for animals whereas groups in one village each mentioned water for agriculture, making cow-dung cakes and for construction. Thus primarily women are concerned about the use of water for domestic purposes. Traditionally providing water for these uses has been the responsibility of women.

Water requirement: Except in a village where women have easy access to a stream for washing the utensils and clothes, women have to carry on their head pots of water for all domestic purposes. In terms of '*bedas*' the average number is about 15 per day per family. The pleasure of meeting other women at the water collecting site is far outweighed by the labour and hustle of collecting and carrying water some times from long distances. Water requirement is low during rainy season, increases in winter and reaches the peak in the summer, when carrying water becomes oppressive.

Sources of water: Women from only one village could get water from the home piped supply scheme. Even here, not all houses have water connections.

Those women having no home water supply connections collect water from private wells carrying the load on their heads for long distances and sometimes suffer acute humiliation from the owners of private water sources. They would like to have village pipe water supply made more reliable. Some villages are suffering the problem of saline groundwater. Although all the villages studied were served by canal, only in one village women mentioned it as a source of water. We had to remind the village women of canal water as a source and their response was yes, but it is only for agriculture. Only in one village irrigation authority has provided some facility for washing clothes in the canal. Women of other villages would also like to have a similar facility. The development agencies working for improving water supply and those that have women in the centre of their programme objectives would be well advised to give priority to easing women's problems of obtaining water for domestic purpose. Problems and suggestions relating to different sources of water are given in Annexure B.

III

Women and Canal Irrigation

We may now consider in detail how irrigation sector can contribute to improving supply of water for domestic uses that have the highest priority for women.

Design: In order that canals can serve women's needs of water for domestic use, women should be involved in designing canal systems when it is close to villages. If it is not close, a channel loop may be constructed taking it closer to the village. It should have a facility for women to use canal for washing clothes and for animals to drink and wash. Alternative design for this purpose should be developed that provides convenient facility to women without damaging canal structure and quality of water.

While rehabilitating a defunct irrigation project of Pingot, Bharuch district, Gujarat in 1990, before transferring it to the water users' associations (WUAs), Aga Khan Rural Support Programme, India [AKRSP (I)], an NGO that sponsored the irrigation management transfer, found that the canal was flowing very close to home-stead lands where women tried to raise vegetables. A special order of the government had to be secured to permit canal officers to allow the use of canal water for the homestead lands. This could be made an obligatory part of canal designing. Drawing conclusions in the paper 'Gender and Irrigation Management' Margreet Zwarteveen has rightly mentioned, "explicit consultations should be held with women users and women's ideas and concerns should be included" in designing and managing canal systems. If this is not to be left to chance and on the will of the irrigation engineers there should be explicit government order on how the process of planning and irrigation system should incorporate formal and organized consultation with representatives of women's groups in the villages to be served by the proposed irrigation project.

Redesigning: For the existing canal systems there would be need for redesigning of canals when they pass near village habitations so that they take care of the priority needs of water for domestic uses. After gaining some experience how this can be done, government orders should be issued. That will ensure that women's needs for domestic uses of water is no longer neglected. It sould not leave the village women at the sufferance of canal officers.

Water supply scheduling: Which crops to raise on the farm is an intra family decision. However when there is shortage of water in the irrigation system, canal authorities have to decide when to first release water in a season and how many waterings to provide, with what frequency. This depends upon farmers' views about main crops to be raised. It has been reported in several studies that men prefer cash crops and women prefer food crops for consumption. In Sri Lanka paddy is a 'male' crop, and millet a 'female' crop. When canal authorities consult farmers about planning for irrigation season it should be imperative that they also consult women groups and consider their preferences.

Management: A special requirement that has been brought out in all studies and in fact which is obvious is that women farmers, when they do not have male members in the family, should not be required to attend to night irrigation. While planning rotation/roster, canal officials take care of this probability. Women heads of households manage this problem through mutual understanding. However, as reported by Shilpa Vasavada in Gardi project, experience has shown this requirement was completely neglected even when the management was with WUA. There is need for government order that canal officials should have a list of female-headed farm families and in planning the rotation/roster, they must see to it that women are not required to go to their farm land during the night for irrigation purposes.

IV

Problems of Irrigation Management

L.K. Joshi who was joint secretary in the Ministry of Water Resources, Government of India, in his comprehensive review of irrigation sector in India (1997) presented as 'Paradigm Shift', has listed the followng ailments of public irrgation management in India: (a) Water delivery is unreliable; (b) wafer distribution is inequitable and tail end deprivation is almost universal; (c) small farmers suffer more deprivation of water; (d) water use is very inefficient, leading to over irrigation in part of the command that leads to wastage of water; (e) there is no group/individual incentive for farmers to conserve water and economise its use; (f) service to farmers is poor and marked by insensitivity; (g) levy of water rates and the recovery has no relation to the actual cost of water; and (h) there is widespread deterioration of infrastructure. From the analysis of the performance of 24 irrigation projects carried out by the Central Groundwater Board, India, it is possible to add a few more deficiencies to the list provided by Joshi: (i) excessive canal seepage; (j) inefficient drainage and water logging; (k) main system's deficiencies; and (I) mismatched cropping pattern and water supply calendar. Joshi summarises the weaknesses of the present system in these words: "The approach is top-down. The prescriptions are handed from the top and irrigation is managed more according to standard administrative procedures than by local variable needs."

Left to itself the irrigation establishments will only tinker with these problems. It has a built-in incapacity to undertake bold reforms that are necessary for improving the performance of the vital irrigation sector. There is therefore need for influencing and supporting irrigation reforms by those who have wider understanding of development, particularly rural development and who can look at the issues from variety of perspectives required for serving the cause of improving performance of irrigation sector. Since the irrigation engineers would not take initiative for reforming the system they are managing, pressure has to be brought from outside by those who value the significance of irrigation in economy, particularly rural economy of the country and ensure its benefits for the people including the poor.

Participatory irrigation management: All this indicates need for reforms and the direction of reforms. The management has to be transformed by creating much higher scope for the farmers to participate in planning, construction and management of irrigation systems. This is participatory irrigation management (PIM) that was initiated by NGOs and is being increasingly accepted in policy at least in principle. So far in India, except in Andhra Pradesh, where it is introdoced by law, PIM is making slow progress despite enabling orders issued by state government. Irrigation engineers would implement such orders more as a formality to reach targets given to them. Few NGOs that have taken to PIM are facing resistance from irrigation establishment and hurdles in implementing ehanges in irrigation management. Even the farmers, the highest stakeholders to benefit from PIM, do not show keenness and initiative in availing of the enabling orders. Farmers have settled down in their apathy and passively use the irrigation waters as and when available. In any case water from public irrigation system is almost free. They have not contributed towards investment and water fees do not cover even operations and maintenance cost. They can get away as free riders even when they do not pay such meagre fees. Making a success of PIM is indeed a difficult task, involving motivating and organising farmers into WUAs, guide them to get their organisation registered and contribute share capital; take responsibility for planning of water supply in every season for which applications have to be collected from individual members; managing water distribution to the satisfaction of farmers particularly tail enders against unreliable release of water by the irrigation authorities and out of turn drawl of water by the head reach and other head strong farmers; fixing and collection of fees and paying government charges; maintenance of the system; maintaining accounts, resolving inevitable conflicts and so on. This requires a shake up of the system, which, as I described elsewhere, is in the state of equilibrium, a malignant equilibrium.

Women and participatory irrigation management: Let us now see what women can contribute to the success of PIM, remembering that mainly government irrigation engineers and a few committed NGOs promote PIM. Margereet Zwuarteven, et al, also have mentioned that in Philippines women control the cash flow and therefore their involvement in pricing policy may help in water fees collection. Shilpa Vasavada also narrates experience of her organisation [(AKRSP (I)] that women manage to save money and therefore are in a better position to pay irrigation fees. Margeret also mentions that when PIM requires labour contribution for construction and maintenance of field channels it was found in Gambia that women were expected to contribute labour and they demanded compensation. Sara Ahmed and Shilpa have given examples of women members of the executive committee providing leadership for collecting fees in advance so that the problem of collections is avoided. She also gives example of the women groups managing 2 out of 7 sub-minors in an irrigation project enforcing better discipline in taking water by turn and other regulations.

Shilpa mentions the case of an irrigation project where women have important responsibility of cleaning up channels. She also claims that women handle conflicts more competently in irrigation management, adding that her example pertains to tribal area where men get drunk and are unable to deal with issues in calm and fair manner.

All the authors, advocating the need to bring women in the 'mainstream of PIM' and in strategic position of decision-making in WUAs, recognise the problem of traditional division of gender roles-men dealing with the world outside the home and with the assumed 'hard' tasks in agriculture. Women's world is supposed to be her home and the farm where she provides substantial labour, sometimes exceeding men's contribution. The distinction is more biased, attaching more value to 'men's tasks'" says Margereet Zwuarteven, who recognises "participation may be less attractive for women, partially because the cost spent on travelling and attending meetings may be relatively higher for them; also because norms and values are not always supportive of women engaging in public meeting. Social transaction costs are higher for women, than for men". A woman had told Elena "I have a lot of work around the house. There is no reason for both of us to attend meetings". Studies have shown that women carry more workload than men not only in the household affairs but sometimes in farming also. Though they dislike it and I prefer household duties when the family can afford paid labour to substitute family labour, as found in the Patel community in Ravalapura village.

It is not important to controvert S. Ahmed's assertion based on rather flimsy evidence. Based on the study of cooperative lift irrigation societies, they state, "there is little doubt that women's participation in community irrigation management organisations is critical to both effective functioning of the organisation as well as the sustainability of irrigation system". Ahmed and Shilpa desire and claim 'self-confidence and self-esteem' as well as more respectable status in the society as the other larger benefits flowing from women's participation in irrigation management. Such outcomes are very welcome, but few development agencies, governmental and otherwise, would be keen to incorporate them in their plan of irrigation sector reforms.

Keeping all this in view what may be the right approach for the development agencies promoting PIM moving from the ideal of desirable to the reality of possible? Even Margereet Zwuaarteven, et al have drawn attention to "too much emphasis on what is desirable (empowerment) and too little on what is possible. Irrigation management institutions have the main task of ensuring that right amount of water is delivered at the right time, at right place, cannot be expected to be interested in the empowerment of women, neither they have the capacity to change gender inequities".

Sara Ahmed had reminded us that for irrigation bureaucracy the concept of farmers' participation itself, let alone women's participation, is alien. Amongst the primary duties of irrigation officers is to attend to those 'deprived' farmers who have right to their share of water but are denied because they are tailenders or because of system failure. A study conducted by the writer, "The Deprived" concludes that if the irrigation officers attend to the needs of the 'deprived', it will contribute significantly to reforming the entire system.

Tasks for irrigation agencies: So far as government irrigation agencies promoting PIM are concerned it will be useful to (a) develop in them gender awareness programmes and (b) PR techniques to understand and appreciate women's perception, needs, priorities with respect to water. It should be therefore considered an achievement if they (c) formulate systems and accept as their responsibility to incorporate in irrigation planning and, management the special requirements of women as listed earlier in designing canal system, in redesigning, water supply scheduling, and management of water delivery.

Tasks for NGOs: NGOs, which are committed to efficiency and equity, should ensure that (a) the agenda for reforms should include securing government orders to give importance to meeting the 'domestic' need of water as listed earlier in designing and redesigning canals, in scheduling, in planning water supply rotation; and (b) securing orders will be only the first step. Operating them satisfactorily will be the major task requiring NGOs to orient the irrigation bureaucracy and induce implementation; (c) they should also strive for creating enough space and scope for women to present their special requirements and contribute their strengths to successful working of WUAs. Besides reservation of some position for women in the executive committee, it is important (d) to help the WUA members to elect such women who can conveniently attend meetings and other duties. Elena P. Bastidas has found in her studies that participation of women depends upon their household composition and life stage. She classifies households into four types (i) young couples with small children; (ii) couples with grown-up children (Hi) women headed house households, (iv) old couples. She found that old couples participate more fully. For those women who can conveniently spare time may be encouraged to participate if they exhibit potential for leadership qualities such as education, "urge to do something for the community" as Sara Ahmed quotes Kanshiben. For women to contribute to better working of WUA, it is not necessary to prove that women are farmers and women are irrigators. Even a non-farming educated woman can help WUA in better record keeping. In fact similar criteria are applicable when electing male members: leadership quality and availability of other adult males in the family to look after family business; (e) They may also organise women's group separately so that the women can collectively present their requirements through the women members of the executive committee. Such members in turn can keep the women informed about the discussions and decisions in the executive committee meetings; (f) The NGOs can also provide encouragement to the women through training and exposure visit to WUAs where women are more actively participating and contributing to that success of PIM. Elena has found/out that appointing women staff members helps and trains women to gain confidence and overcome the initial resistance.

Tasks for gender-centred/gender priority NGOs: The NGOs that are gender equity com-mitted, working for women's empowerment, can contribute by (a) demonstrating through examples in diverse cultural situations how women could shoulder responsibility and through leadership qualities ensure better performance of WUAs tribal and non-tribal, good rainfall and low rainfall areas, etc. AKRSP has promoted a unique project of Kevdi in Bharuch district, Gujarat where 50 per cent of WUA, members are women as also in its executive committee. Experience of irrigation management on the basis of equality between men and women would yield valuable lessons. Though 'island of excellence' has its own value, it is considerably enhanced when its feasibility is demonstrated in good number of cases. (b) Detailed documentation of the process, positive gains and problems resolved and unresolved will further add to the value of such examples. (c) For creating an impact on the 'mainstream' PIM, such gender priority organisations should also get the experience of promoting gender-equity approach in new as well as existing WUAs. They can then develop suggestive approaches of introducing gender equity in different stages of WUAs. It may be useful to keep in view Christine Van Wijk's, counsel "Kwaule points out that shifting the balance from men to women is no solution either because it caused men to oppose women's role or even withdraw from the project". To avoid such a backlash, reforms towards desirable have to be pushed with circumspection. (d) Such organisation could also take up the change and get changed that only men are considered as heads of family and therefore entitled to represent family in the WUAs. (e) They would require to work for removing administrative and legal hurdles in women's full membership of WUA. (f) While 'mainstreaming women', they would be well advised not to neglect the mainstream issues of canal irrigation reforms. Unlike other women centred activities like micro-finance, PIM cannot be conducted in isolation at micro level. It is not possible to ignore other requirements of irrigation reforms, many of which are gender neutral, but impact the gender sensitive micro management. (g) Again securing administrative and legal entitlement for women to participate fully in WUA FS would not be enough. Such organisations will have to work for translating such orders into reality on the ground. This has been found necessary, for example, in the case of legal rights conferred on daughters to equal share of ancestral property. This has yet to be translated into reality. Traditional mindset has to be changed to translate legal provisions into reality as has been done by Bina Agarwal in her book, *A Field of One's Own.* A strong case has to be made out not only about the desirability but also about feasibility. These subsequent steps of creating awareness and demonstrating feasibility can be accomplished by promoting actual cases.

Meanwhile the development agencies may better respect women's priorities in water for domestic purpose and see what irrigation can do to meet this requirement. Simultaneously, they should be creating scope and space for their contribution to irrigation sector reform, particularly through PIM. They should hold on to the faith and reality that society is changing towards more gender equity. As is happening in the developed countries, including in the Indian households, the gender roles would change, giving women much more freedom to contribute their strength to the 'mainstream' activities in economic, social and political spheres. This approach demands combination of innovative work and patience, all the time respecting women's 'reproductive' and domestic responsibilities as well as their present perceptions and priorities.

Annexure A

PRA Exercises with Village Women to Understand Their Needs and Priorities about Water

Rajpur taluka Himatnagar, district Sabarkantha: The piped water supply provided water that was used for cooking and drinking for people and animals. Other important water source was a stream passing by the village. When the water is flowing in the stream the women use it for washing utensils, clothes and also washing animals. If such washing were done at home the wastewater would create puddles of nuisance. There is a canal where the women could wash their clothes. Using canal water is difficult; there is no stone platfonn. Women's main concerns were piped water not reaching the elevated parts of the village and irregulat power supply.

Kanzara, taluka Vagdod, district Patan: A meeting was held with village women, which brought out relevant information and issues about the water in the life of women. The uses of water included apart from the usual list-house construction, house repair, make cowdung cakes and mopping of the floor if not tiled. The quantity required 6 '*bedas*' for a typical family of 5 people and 4 animals. Six *bedas* (120 ltr) in winter, 16 *bedas* (240 ltrs) in summer. The main source is the village tube well, from which water is taken by pipes to four stand posts located in different parts of the village. However, the pumping equipment is not properly maintained. Half of the time it is not functioning. Women then have to collect water from the irrigation wells located away from the village site. They might spend 4/5 hours a day. Sometime girls leave their school for bringing water. Sometimes women have to search for water from one well to another because the pumping system may be out of order or because of the insulting behaviour of the farmer. A woman broke down while narrating her experience "when I was in my parent's place I was never sent out for fetching water. Married for five years there are many problems in bringing water for the family. Only yesterday in the hot afternoon I spent 4/5 hours hunting for water leaving behind at home my one year old daughter..." An elderly woman added, "Carrying water on the head women develop pain in the head and in the ears". Some backward communities have problem in approaching 'private' well owners. During days' of shortage of water, mostly women and children may forgo daily bath, develop skin disease. While fixing marriages with the boys in the village the brides' parents are discouraged when they learn about the water problem in the village. Women's main requirement was improving the village water supply system, and drainage facility so that the surroundings of their home may be clean.

Women were willing to take over the management of the village water supply. In fact twice they collected fund and repaired the system. There should be reserve fund built up for repair purpose so that no time is wasted in raising fund. They need a water trough for the animals.

What about the canal water? During years of low rainfall there is no water in the canal. When there is water, it is used by women for bathing and washing. There are some stones in the canal but the women preferred to use their own wooden plank. Women looked upon canal water as if it was meant for domestic use and additionally for irrigation. The election of the village council was only one month away. The women attending the meeting on 'women and water' declared: "We will vote for only those candidates who would assure us that they will solve our water problems". They meant water for domestic use.

Khadalpur, taluka Visnagar, district Mehsana: In meeting with the women of the village they mentioned some uses of water-drinking for family members and animals, cooking, cleaning utensils, washing clothes, etc. Main source of water is supposed to be village water supply system, which is hardly of any use as the ground water is saline. New sites were tried, again the same problem of saline water. In the PRA map exercises the women showed four private wells from which they collected water, on an average of 10-15 *beda* per family. Apart from hours spoilt in fetching water from different private wells women also narrated experiences of abusive treatment of well owners they have to put up with, as there are no other options. Once they collected Rs. 50 per household as contribution for repair of a private tube well.

What about canal water? In good rainfall year when the water flows in canal, it recharges the groundwater. It is also used for animals to drink and also for agriculture. They were also planning to use one of the sub-minors for bringing drinking water to the village from a new tube well, which looked promising. But how to raise funds? The village is backward and had to face 2-3 years of very low rainfall. They cannot raise Rs. 1,000 per household required for installing a new tube well. What can be done? What about roof top water harvesting and storage of rainwater? Women had not heard about it. But if there is assistance available and if they can make contribution by way of labour they were interested.

Khadalpur is in the process of setting up a water users' association (WUA) as required in participatory irrigation management (PIM). The visiting DSC officers were overwhelmed by the problems the women were facing about water for domestic use. The visiting team left the village wondering what can they do to help the women about the problems and priorities of water as perceived by women.

PRA Map Village Ravalapura

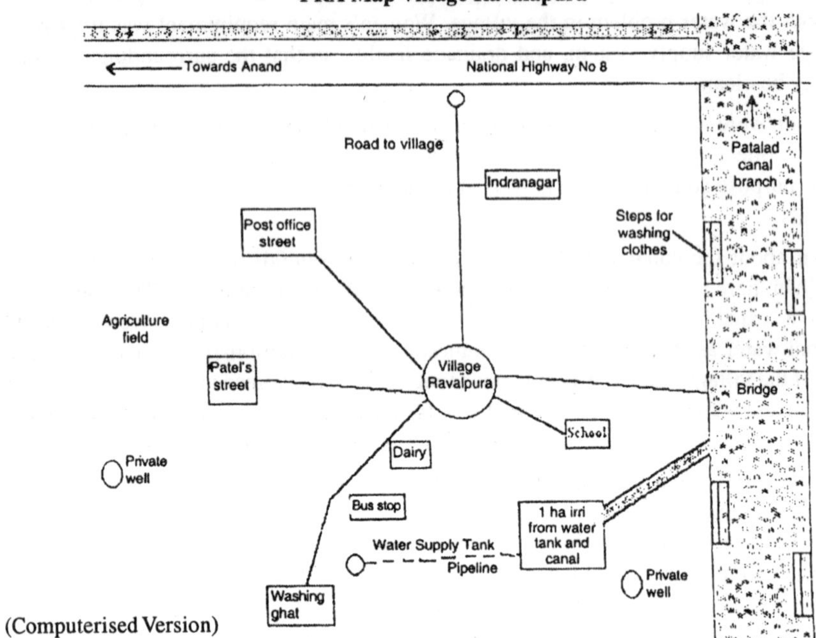

(Computerised Version)

Annexure B

Problems and Solutions of Different Sources of Water

(i) Common Wells

Problems: This most common and ancient form of domestic water supply still remains neglected by the village panchayat that has the responsibility for maintaining it. Village population may be rising and new localities sprung up, but there has been no increase in number of wells. Lifting devices like simple pullies may be damaged or missing. No arrangement for protecting the water supply from wastewater entering the well directly or through seepage from the surrounding area. Band-pumps are supplementing, sometimes replacing the village wells. They are easier to install but they need constant repairs that is usually neglected.

Suggested action: Number of wells/hand-pumps depending upon size and spread of the village should be provided. Also required easier lifting devices, better maintenance, clean surroundings, maintaining water supply in the wells/pumps through recharging.

(ii) Village Pipe Water Supply

Problems: Even in the single village of our survey where the village water supply provided sweet water, it was for a very short duration and not reliable on account of frequent interruptions in power supply. Some localities at higher levels never received water. In another village (and we know this is common in many villages) the maintenance of machinery was unsatisfactory, causing interruptions for days.

Solutions: Maintenance of water lifting machinery and distribution of pipes is very important. The height of the water tank should be enough to supply water to all localities that may beat higher level. To take care of usual power shortage, facility of alternative diesel engine is important.

(iii) Ponds

Problems: Ponds collect rainwater, which is sweet, but it dries up. More so because some farmers divert it or lift it for some agriculture purpose. Women would like to use part of the canal water for replenishing water in the tank.

Suggested actions: Desilting of ponds, protecting its inlet channels and the bunds, restricting water from being diverted for agriculture, replenishing the pond water by canal water, installing hand-pumps and even constructing wells close to the ponds would make it easier for women to collect water and protect the pond from unsanitary instrusions of people and animals.

PRA Map Village: Rajpur

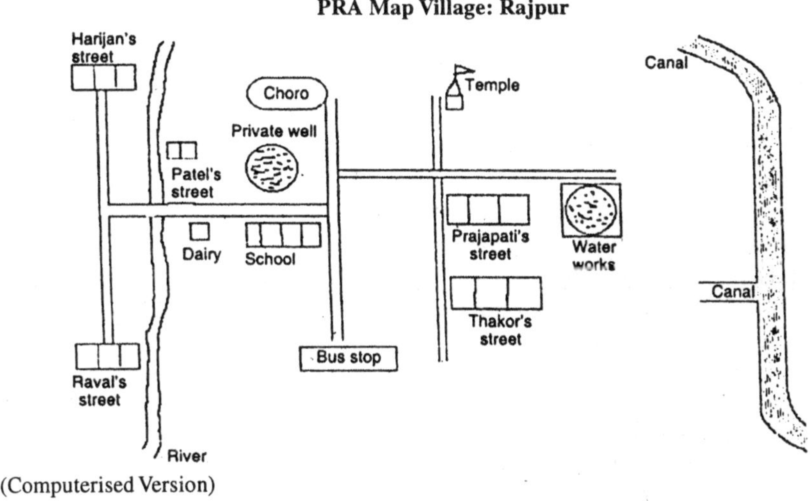

(Computerised Version)

PRA Map Prepared by Women, Village Khadalpur

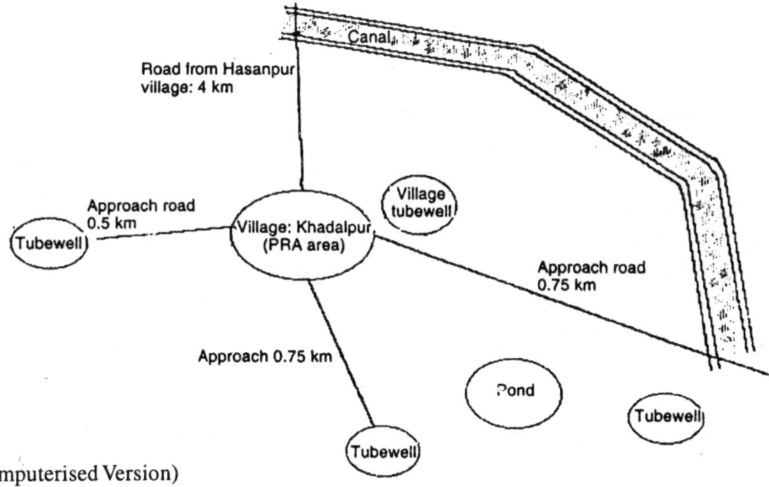

(Computerised Version)

(iv) Private Wells

Problems: This is the least preferred source of water for drinking and cooking. Wells are at long distance and water is collected depending upon the sweet will of the private well owners. Women belonging to backward communities suffer more humiliation. This source therefore is resorted to only when the situation is desperate.

Suggested actions: Though least preferred, fetching water from private agriculture wells may be the only option in some villages more so in a drought year. Fetching water manually pushed/machine operated wheel carts can be arranged by *panchayats* or women's association. When assistance is provided towards the cost of mechanical wheel cart or for propelling it, there are examples of the carts entrusted to contractors who supply water at reasonable charge. Some small entrepreneurs using manually pushed/machine operated wheel carts for supplying water at a reasonable price have been tried successfully. This is a promising option even for taking water from common wells, when they are few and for some houses at long distance.

(v) Canal

Problems: Women know about canal and what its water can do for their agriculture. However while considering their own responsibility for water, canal is thought of only for washing clothes and animals. Only in one village of our study has the irrigation agency provided facility of flat stone platform for washing clothes. Women would like to have such facility in ample measure in all villages.

Suggested actions: In the designing of the canal provision should be made for use of its water for washing clothes and for drinking and washing animals. Need to explore the most convenient arrangement for such use of canal water. This should not be at the sufferance of the canal engineers but as part of the design and system. If the canal is away from where people live, a channel loop can be constructed specially for the purpose of bringing water closer to village for domestic use. Replenishing water in the village ponds should be considered a legitimate use of canal water. The village community or its representative body should be willing to pay for the water supplied for this purpose. Canal water when recharging the village wells would also improve the water quality, particularly through reduction in salinity.

(vi) Salinity

Problems: Salinity in the water supply is a very acute problem in some villages.

Suggested solutions: Salinity in water is an acute and spreading problem in the rural areas, adding to the problem for women who are responsible for cooking and washing clothes that is difficult with saline water. Though canal water can improve the quality of groundwater it may not be available throughout the year and some times for years together when there is continuous drought condition. There is also the option of collecting fresh rain water on the roofs of private houses and store it for use throughout the year. There was a rich tradition of roof rainwater harvesting which has to be revived with the financial and technical support. Participation of women in dealing with these issues is extremely important.

Women's associations can be promoted and where existing can be encouraged to form women's water groups (*mahila pani panchayat*) which can take responsibility for planning and managing the water sources for domestic use. The local village council (*panchayat*) should transfer the responsibility for supplying water for domestic purpose to women's water groups *(mahila pani panchayat)*, which should also be responsible for raising and managing funds for upkeep and management. Development agencies working for improving domestic water supply and those which are gender-centred can develop appropriate PRA techniques for understanding water supply situation in the villages they serve, the perception of women about their needs, priorities, problems and preferred solutions. The development agencies should offer the options from the menu that they should go on developing from their own and others' experiences.

All agencies working in water area should place the water requirement for domestic use as the highest priority in their programme strategies. Strangely some authors including some feminist activists refer to domestic use of water as 'reproductive' as distinguished from 'productive' use for agriculture. Even protagonists like Sara Ahmed have defended 'reproductive' use by pointing out that part of water at home is devoted to 'productive' use as for tending milk animals, backyard vegetables garden, brick making, etc. However 'reproductive' use, like reproductive function itself, needs no defence. It is the basic requirement for existence, survival and, good living.

References

Ahmed, S. 1999. 'Changing Gender Roles in Irrigation Management-Sadguru's Lift Irrigation Cooperatives', *Economic and Political Weekly:* December 18,

Ahmed, Sara, IRMA, 'Empowering Rural Women, Policies, Institutions and Gendered Outcomes in Natural Resources Management', *NEWORD:* 6:3.

Christine, van Wijk, Esther de Lange and David Saunders: 'Gender Aspects in the Management of Water Reseurces'.

Elena, P. Bastidas, 'Gender Issues and Women's Participation in Irrigated Agriculture: The Case of Two Private Irrigation Canals in Carchi, Ecuador' Research *Report: 31:IWMI*: Sri Lanka.

Margreet Z.Zwarteveen .1995. 'Linking Women to the Main Canal: Gender and Irrigation Management', *Gatekeeper Series: SA* 54. London: IIED.

Margreet Z. Zwarteveen. 1997. 'Water: From Basic Need to Commodity: A Discussion on Gender and Water Rights in the Context of Irrigation', *World Development: 25:8:1335-*1349.

Margreet Z. Zwarteveen. 1997. 'Identifying Gender Aspects of New Irrigation Management Policies', paper presented at Sri Lanka at a workshop held by IIMI, 'Women and Water'; September 15-19.

Margreet, Z. Zwarteveen and Nita Neupane. 1995. 'Gender Aspects of Irrigation Management: The Chhattig, Mauja Irrigation System in Nepal', *Asia-Pacific Journal of Rural Development:*5:1: July.

Nagar, R.K. 'Participatory Irrigation Management: Gender and Irrigation Kakdiamba'.

Pinakin, Vyas. 2000. 'Water and Women' in Anil C. Shah (ed.), *Documentation of an Exploratory PRA.* September.

Shvamala, C. Vijava and C.S. Sithapathi Rao. 1999. 'Role of Women in Participatory Irrigation Management: A Study in Andhra Pradesh', paper for the Researcher's Conference, 12-13 December.

Shah, Anil. 2000. 'The Deprived in the Command Area of Irrigation System', Ahmedabad: Development Support Centre. August.

Shah, Anil. undated. 'Supporting Irrigation Sector Reform from Outside', Ahmedabad: Development Support Centre,

Shilpa, Vasavada. 2000. 'Women Irrigators and Participatory Irrigation Management: Policy and Approaches to Mainstream Gender Concerns: Lessons from Aga Khan Rural Support Programme, October.

William, M. Adam, Elizabeth E. Watson and Samuel K. Mutiso. 1997. "Water Rules and Gender: Water Rights in an Indigenous Irrigation Systems, Marakwet, Kenya', *Development and Change:* 28:107-30.

This paper was first published in the *Economic and Political Weekly*: It is included here with the prior permission of the author, and the Editor, *Economic and Political Weekly. Address* for email correspondence is: dsc@satyam, net.in

CHAPTER - TWENTY TWO

Expansion of Markets and Women Workers: A Case Study of Indian Garment-Manufacturing

Deepita Chakravarty

I

Introduction

This study aims at understanding women's relative position inside a firm in the context of expanding market opportunities in India, concentrating on the garment manufacturing industry. Changes in the economic regime in India have led to an expansion of markets and technological modernization with implications for employment in general and women in particular. The literature on the implications of the macro-economic changes to the industrial sector is not gender specific (Chakravarty: 1999; 2002). However, there is a women-focused literature on women as victims of the changes in the policy regime (Jhabvala: 2002; Neetha: 2002).[1]

Expansion of markets leads to shift of resources including labour from non-tradables to tradables especially to the exportable sector. This can create unemployment in the non-exportable sectors because labour mobility is relatively lower than the mobility of other resources of production. Again, due to different socio-economic constraints within the labour force women usually have systematically lower capabilities than men and need different requirements to be mobile. These constraints on mobility restrict women to a certain distinct sectors. Usually, in developing countries, unskilled female labourers dominate the consumption goods branch of the non-tradable sector and the unprotected manufacturing of import substitutables[2] (Collier: 1994). Unemployment generated in those sectors as a result of expansion of markets in a broader sense[3] will consequently affect female labourers disproportionately. Again, from other developing country experiences it may be expected that the retrenched female labourers may get employment in the newly emerging sectors of exportables but only at a lower wage rate than the on-going one in that sector. Garment manufacturing for exports is a case in point (Standing: 1989).

The question to be specifically asked here is: what happens as export oriented industrialization grows over time? Theoretically one would expect either male labour to shift into this activity, or female labour supply to increase, or the productivity of female labour to increase via fresh investments. Unfortunately, no significant research has been done in this direction. The scanty evidence from the traditional exporting countries does not help us to state anything conclusive about the problem.

The paper begins by briefly outlining the experiences of East and South–East Asian countries regarding export orientation and women workers. This is followed by a discussion of the sample firms of our study. The rest of the paper deals mainly with the applicability of the received ideas in the Indian context focusing on the selected firms.

II

The Stylized Facts

It has been found that there are certain universal regularities in the composition of exports of manufactures and related patterns of labour use by gender. Performance of developing countries in their exports of some labour intensive manufactured products such as clothing, footwear and processed foods followed by (when diversification takes place) production of electronic products for consumer and business use was typically good (United Nations: 1995). That successful industrialization, or, for that matter, presence of export-led industrialization largely depended on a considerable expansion of female labour is already on record. Taking cue from these findings, we look at the scenario from the Indian context. Does this tendency of higher female labour take place as export-led industrialization gets emphasis after a long period of the import substitution regime?

The reasons for the increased absorption of female workers in export manufacturing are well known. The labour intensive products exported by the third world countries are by nature low technology-intensive ones. This is especially true for the clothing industry.[4] Consequently, the increasing cost competition in the export markets leads entrepreneurs to search for newer sources of cheap labour. It has been argued that 'young women, particularly in the newly industrialising countries of Asia, have been oppressed, both socially and economically for so long that they are forced to develop low "aspiration" wages as well as low "efficiency" wages' (Standing: 1989: 1080). These women are ready to work for very low wages and for longer hours under exceedingly inhospitable conditions of work. Their 'oriental docility' normally does not let them join unions and agitate against the management (Standing: 1989). Joekes (1995) maintains that the most important, though not the sole reason behind the differential distribution of male and female workers of different branches of industry, is the gender gap in wages in manufacturing.

An additional reason, as Joekes noted in 1995, behind women's increasing absorption in the export oriented manufacturing, as pointed out by many researchers, (for example, Barbezat: 1993), is their alleged high turn-over rates which help make a flexible work force (Lim: 1984); that is, women workers are less likely to protest layoffs. This in fact is a corollary of the docility argument. We shall bring the reasons for gender preference (if any) into special focus later in our study.

Finally, in export manufacturing, the production process of electronic goods is highly technology-intensive and is going through continuous modernization. Though clothing is comparatively less technology-intensive, studies have pointed out a substantial amount of technological modernization taking place in the larger garment-manufacturing firms, mainly involved in exports. These changes in the production process have led to some significant changes in certain job categories. However, in the case of clothing industry, the main production line machinery, methods and tasks of production remain almost untouched by the technological modernization. It has been claimed that the new, highly skilled posts (resulting from technological change) tend to be filled by male workers. As a result, the labour force in exporting industries is not entirely female. Moreover, Joekes (1982) claims:

> *"Some men continue to be taken in production line positions (paid a higher wage) to act as agents of social control: they break up female solidarity."*

With these stylized facts in mind we now turn to India.

III

The Study Firms

Secondary data show some indications of differences between the experiences of the early exporting countries and that of India (Goldar: 2002). However, macro information often hides substantial sector-specific differences. Therefore, we decide to narrow our field of inquiry down to garment manufacturing of India. The reason behind the choice of this sector is its increasing export intensiveness combined with technological improvement propelled by the policies for expansion of markets from the early 1980s. Moreover, garment manufacturing has been one of the most women intensive sectors in India from the beginning. For the detailed study we have chosen Hyderabad and the surrounding areas, where a large number of manufacturing units have come up in recent years. More importantly, the government of Andhra Pradesh has established an apparel export promotion park in the year 1998-1999 near Hyderabad. The firms in this park generally have high export shares in their net sales and are technologically quite sophisticated.

According to the Handloom and Textile Department of the Government of Andhra Pradesh there are altogether 31 garment-manufacturing firms in and around Hyderabad. In order to get sufficient contrasts we divide the firms primarily on the basis of export shares, categorizing those with 60 per cent or more as export-oriented units. Firms under the two categories of market orientation then have been classified by their female labour intensity and level of technological modernization. Since female labour intensity is generally much higher in the domestic-market-oriented firms compared to export-oriented ones, we employ a slightly different definition to decide the relative women intensity in the two groups of firms. For the domestic-market-oriented firms, relatively high female intensity relates to percentage of women being 80 or above and in the case of export-oriented firms it is 70 or more. Information collected from the Community Development Centre of the Apparel Export Park helped us to categorize firms in terms of modernization.

For selecting the sample, the present study has adopted a purposive sampling procedure since we are not trying to make any quantitativè generalization. Table 1 describes the procedure followed. While M1 represents the domestic market oriented firms, M2 represents the firms that mainly cater to the export market; H1 and H2 stand for relatively low and high women intensity respectively and finally T1 and T2 represent technologically advanced and non-advanced units respectively. Table 1 gives the eight-fold classification of units.

Table 1
The Categorization of Firms[5]

Type of Market	*Domestic (M1)*		*Export (M2)*	
Percentage of Women Workers	Relatively High (H1)	Relatively Low (H2)	(H1)	(H2)
Technologically Advanced (T1)	H1T1 (A)	H2T1 (C)	H1T1 (E)	H2T1 (G)
Technologically not[1] Advanced (T2)	HIT2 (B)	H2T2 (D)	H1T2 (F)	H2T2 (H)

Note: A, B, C and D in parenthesis thus emerge as specific types. For example, firm A is a technologically advanced, relatively more women intensive unit which caters to the domestic market.

Table 2
Basic Information About the Sample Firms

Firms	*Year of Inception*	*Number of Workers*	*Percentage of Women Workers*	*Percentage of Exports in Total Sales*	*Level of Technological Modernization*	*Performance*
A	1999	900	80	40	Modernized	Profit Making
B	1996	25	85	Nil	Non-Modernized	Do
C	1995	140	69	Nil	Modernized	Break even
D	2000	30	70	Nil	Non-Modernized	Loss Making
E	2000	75	70	100	Modernized	Profit Making
F	1998	100	80	60	Modernized	Break even
G	1998	100	50	75	Modernized	Break even
H	2001	20	10	75	Modernized	Profit Making.

Considering the detailed and minute nature of information to be collected we have decided to consider only one firm under each of the 8 categories described in the Table 1.

Table 2 summarizes the important information about the sample firms of our study.

The main sources for secondary information for the study were the documents collected from the Handloom and Textile Department of Andhra Pradesh and the Community Development Centre in the Apparel Export Park. These secondary sources apart, we have collected data through long interviews with the management and at least one worker from each category of every single firm. We have also laid our hands on different firm level accounts kept by the management.

IV

Issues of Discrimination

The issues of employment and wages of the women workers in the sample firms constitute the themes of this section. According to Table 3 total employment has increased over the years almost in every firm except in the case of firm D within the group of domestic-market-oriented firms. The decline in the total number of workers in the case of firm D is considerable. However, this is the only firm in our sample that is making losses consistently since its inception. The percentage of female employment, however, has not increased in any of these firms catering mainly to the domestic market. While employment percentage of women has, in fact, declined in the cases of firms A, C and D, firm B shows a constant female percentage share at two points of time. The decline in the case of firm A is as sharp as 8 per cent points. But the total number of women working in the three firms A, B and C has not declined.

Table 3
Percentage of Women Workers in Sample Firms in the Year of Inception and in 2002-03

Firms	*Percentage of women in the year of inception*	*Total number of workers in the year of inception*	*Percentage of women in 2002-03*	*Total number of workers in 2002-03*
A	80 (720)	900	72 (720)	1000
B	85 (21)	25	85 (23)	27
C	69 (97)	140	68 (99)	146
D	70 (21)	30	69 (9)	13
E	70 (53)	75	70 (84)	120
F	80 (80)	100	71 (107)	150
G	50 (50)	100	44 (45)	102
H	10 (2)	20	Nil	18

Note: Total number of women workers is given in the parenthesis.
Inception years are given in Table 2.

Turning to the export-market-oriented firms, we find that the total employment has improved generally except in the case of firm H in the year 2002-03 when compared with the years of inception. However, even in the case of firm H the decline is marginal. Percentage share of women workers on the contrary has declined, except in firm E, in the year 2002-03 in this group as well. In the case of

Firm E the percentage, however, has not increased, but remained constant at the two points of time. While the employment of women workers has increased significantly in firms E and F, the total number of women workers has declined in firms G and H. In fact, in the year 2002-03, there is no woman worker in firm H. Therefore, according to Table 3, percentage share of women's employment has declined irrespective of market orientation as well as degree of female intensity in the sample firms.

According to the stylized facts stated above technological modernization in the clothing industry changed certain job categories where new skills are essential, requiring more formal training and experience. Moreover, Joekes, in her 1982 study claims that such positions tend to be filled by male workers. This is part of the reason, she claims, why the labour force in exporting industries is not completely female.

Since the late 1980s some of the well-established exporters in the garment sector in India have started modernizing their units (Koshy: 1997). The liberal import policies for the exporters played a major role in these initiatives. Is it then the level of technological modernization that leads to the general decline of the percentage of women workers in the sample firms? In order to get an answer let us have a quick look at the level of technological modernization in the sample firms in comparison with the available standard technical advancement.

Table 4
Level of Technological Modernization of Different Firms

Description of technological advancement	*Name of the firms where the specific technological advancement is available*
1. Light box checking machine	A, E, F and G
2. Computer aided designing	A, E and F
3. Mechanized cutting	A, C, E, F, G and H
4. Computer aided manufacturing	A, C, E, F and G
5. Micro-processor controlled checking	A, E, F and G

Notes: Firm E does not perform computer-aided designing in the Apparel Export Park. However, the designs come from their parent firm generated by computer-aided designing. Since firm H produces garment accessories and not garments, the technological processes for this firm are not comparable with those of other units in the sample. However, the management of firm H considers their unit as technologically semi-modernized in terms of available technological advancement.

Table 4 demonstrates that the level of technological modernization in firm A among the domestic market oriented firms, along with all the export market oriented firms except H, is internationally comparable. Firms C and H can be considered semi-modernized and finally firms B and D are technologically non-advanced ones.[6] Thus, it can be concluded that export-oriented firms are generally technologically more advanced when compared with the domestic market-oriented firms except firm A. However, it is worth mentioning here that firm A is continuously increasing its share of exports in its net sales and in the year 2002-03,the share has reached 55 per cent.

Combining the facts revealed from Tables 3 and 4 it becomes evident that the percentage decline in women's employment is much sharper in the case of technologically advanced firms than in the technologically backward ones irrespective of their market orientation except in the case of firm E. However, firm E cannot be held wholly as an exception here because much of its activities that relate to higher technology, such as computer aided designing, are carried out in its parent firm in Coimbatore. Moreover, production diversification of this unit is extremely limited here; in fact, men's shirts are the only product of this firm. These evidences hint at the confirmation of the experiences of the early exporting of newly industrializing countries as shown by the stylized facts in the context of Andhra Pradesh.

IV

Gender Differential in Wage Rates

However, it will be too hasty to conclude that the decrease in the female intensity in the sample firms is the result of technological modernization since we have not looked at the distribution of men and women workers in different categories in the sample firms. Before turning to the issue of categorical divides (which we attempt to do in the next section), let us observe the management's attitude towards their female employees in the two groups of firms, catering to different markets. Change in management attitudes in general can be a proximate cause for a decline in the female percentage share.

When we asked the management 'do you have any gender preference for recruitment in all categories?' The answer was a universal 'Yes' irrespective of categories in our sample. There are mainly two reasons behind this choice behaviour. The management claim that their experience with both male and female workers tells them that women workers are more efficient and sincere in their work. The second reason is broadly related to the 'characteristic docility' of women as a result of which it is less likely for them (women) to be involved in trade union activities. The management reiterate that any kind of unionism which can lead to a strike especially in an export firm, can be extremely costly as the production is highly time bound. These reasons for employing women in the labour intensive industries of the developing countries are often cited in the existing literature (for example, Edgren: 1984).

However, the management never talked about the lower wage cost involved in employing women workers, which is the most important reason behind heavy recruitment of women in the export manufacturing of East and South-East Asian countries. We asked the question: do the rates of wage and other terms and conditions for different categories of work vary across gender? In every case, the management claimed that they did not practice any differential in terms and conditions for workers on the basis of gender?

In order to verify the management's answer, we crosschecked the wage details given by the management with the workers (preferably female) from different categories. The workers were asked how much salary a male worker earned with the same level of formal education and experience for the same category of work as she did. Interestingly, the answer, almost in every case confirmed that the same amount was paid both to the male and the female incumbents, irrespective of the firm's market orientation and other specificities such as level of technological modernization and female intensity. Table 5 gives a summary description of the wage rates for different categories of firms in our sample.

Table 5
Wage Rate for Different Categories (Rs. Per Month)
(Weekly or Daily Wages are Converted into Monthly Wage Rate)

Firms	*Supervisors*	*Tailors*	*Helpers*
A	5300/-	1700 to 2300 depends on the grades of tailoring.	1500/-
B		Completely piece rate approximately 2500 on an average	1200/-
C	4800/-	1600 to 2000 + piece rate	1200/-
D	4000/-	1600 to 2000 + piece rate	1300/-
E	5000/-	1700 to 2200	1500/-
F	4800/-	1800 to 2200 + piece rate	1300/-
G	Not available	Not available	Not available

Note: 1. As firm H does not produce ready-made garments as such and produces garment accessories, the work categories are different.
2. There are generally two to three grades under the tailor category. In each case we have given the range of wage rates for each firm.

Table 6
Earnings of Male and Female Workers in Firms C, D, F.
(Rs. Per Month)

Firms	*TailorFirst Grade*		*TailorSecond Grade*	
	Male	*Female*	*Male*	*Female*
C	2600	2100	1800	1600
D	2000	1800	1600	1600
F	2500	2200	2000	1800

Note: The wage earning figures are collected from the workers and they are based on their previous month's earnings. Workers themselves said that these were approximate figures because piece rate earnings were given as soon as the work was done and not together with the basic wage.

However, a close look at the earnings of the workers segmented by gender reveals a different fact in some cases. We find that the firms which can be considered as practicing continuous process production or which employ three shifts for production, the total earnings and the monthly wage rates for male and female workers, for each category of work, do not differ, ceteris paribus, irrespective of market orientation. This is the case for firm A in the domestic market and firm E in the export market. In the cases of all other firms except firm B and H irrespective of market orientation and technological status, male workers' monthly earnings are more than that of the female workers' (Table 6). In these 4 firms, however, in some cases, monthly earnings exceed the monthly wage rates even for the female workers. These inconsistencies made us go back again to the respondents both at the level of management and the workers. We find that the differences in earnings and wage rates occur because of the existence of piece rate work at times of necessity. The firms that work for three shifts in a day do not practice the piece rate system.

From the detailed discussions with both the male and female workers and with the management we found that in every case male workers did much more piece rate work than did the female workers. In response to the question why this was so, the management said:

> *"We have no problems if women work after the usual working hours, in fact we prefer that, as generally a woman is more sincere in her work; but stringent labour laws do not permit employment of women workers late in the night, as we do not have transport facilities. Given the risks involved for a woman to move alone late at night it may not be advisable also."*

Incidentally, both firms A and E have their own transport system and women workers work in all shifts in those two firms. Moreover, by the management view, because of different household responsibilities women workers prefer not to take a heavy load at the work place. Female workers, in their turn, confirm this fact and mention that it becomes a tremendous pressure, both physical and mental, if they work beyond the usual hours. The family and husbands are ready to let them go for work but not at the cost of their own comfort. This issue of women's constrained utility maximization from her outside job has been extensively dealt with in the context of Bangladesh garment manufacturing sector in Kabeer (2001). Thus, the difference between earnings and wage rates emerges out of the fact that men earn more by doing the piece rate work, confirming Krishnaraj's (1987) finding in the factories of Mumbai.

Does this finding contradict the argument of women's cheap labour that has been considered as the supreme source of the East Asian export performance? In fact, it does not. When East Asian export industrialization started, those countries were not as poor as India. Wage rates were already quite high (Song: 2002).[7] At the same time an educated 'reserve army' of women labour seeking employment in the industrial sector was present, ready to work at a lower wage rate. On the contrary, the Indian condition is quite different even today. The wage rates in the unorganized sector are very low, there is no employment security, and rarely any social security benefits either. It is often found that both men and women are ready to work at a very low wage (Krishnaraj: 1987). In spite of there being a few big firms, much of the garment activities in India are still carried in the unorganized sector. Moreover, in India it is still quite difficult to find educated women ready to join the industrial workforce. Women who usually work for paid employment are mostly poor. Education for a girl child in that economic category is still not common. More on this, later.

This is a point that has to be emphasized, not to contest the usual feminist understanding but to *highlight the importance of contextuality*. Incidentally,

Appleton, et al (1990) find no evidence of gender biases in wage determination in the context of Ivorian labour markets in Africa.[8] This study points out that Ivorian labour markets were in fact more equitable in comparison with labour markets in developed countries. Moreover, Susan Joekes (1995) reports some supporting anecdotal evidence relevant to pay relativities in trade related employment in Bangladesh garment manufacturing. The economic and social conditions of Bangladesh are quite similar to those of India, if not worse. She reports that the wage gap by gender being extremely small in this case with the female: male ratio of wages being almost unity (0.97). She argues:

> *"One interpretation of the situation is that in order to create the kind of (female) workforce that experience in other countries suggests they will find most satisfactory, employers have offered women high start-up wages, on a par with male wages... If this 'kick-start' hypothesis is correct, employers may begin to exploit women's vulnerable labour market position once a female labour supply is established..." (Joekes: 1995: 28).*

But our perception is different. We believe that *for the greater part the reason lies in the generally low economic conditions of the country where men are also ready to work at very low wages.* In this context it becomes irrelevant to imagine lower efficiency and aspiration wages for women alone. Increasing the demand for industrial labour in the economy may be a proximate way to increase the wages in the unorganized sector in general and garment manufacturing in particular. The case of Singapore can be considered as an example in this regard (Yue: 1984).

Let us now turn to the two firms, B and H that need a special consideration. We start with Firm B that caters to the domestic market only. This firm concentrates only on the embroidery work on women's dress materials. The entrepreneur runs the system purely on the piece rate basis. As no machine is involved in the production process, and the designs are often quite varied, it is extremely difficult to standardize the earnings of the male and female workers. Moreover, most of these piece rate workers work for other boutiques in the city as well. Firm H, on the contrary, is mainly an exporting firm. This firm does not produce garments but garment accessories. Therefore the work categories and wage rates are not comparable with those in the other firms in our sample. This firm, as reported earlier, does not have a single woman worker in the year 2002-03, although it had a few initially. In the context of the international experience and, moreover, the experience of the other firms in our sample, we find this fact to be a crucial one.

In response to our question regarding gender preference in recruitment, the management said: 'we do prefer women workers as well. In fact, our own experience with the women we have had is much better than with males'. When asked about the apparent contradiction between preference and practice, the management gave the following reason:

> *"Our firm is a very small one and primarily caters to the export market. Around six to eight months a year we mainly produce for the export market alone. In those months we prefer overtime work. After shipment for the foreign market, we*

> *do not need more than a shift of regular work for catering only to the domestic market. Women cannot work during the night shifts, as we do not have any transport arrangement of our own. So, if we employ women for the day shifts, we need male workers for the night shifts. Considering the size of the total production, it actually becomes more costly. So we have decided to employ only male workers, but a very small number, who will be with the firm as permanent workers and will take care of the extra production at the time of need. In future we have a plan to increase the scale of production and diversify to manufacturing garments. Then we will employ women workers again."*

The above discussion suggests that it is not the labour market discrimination that leads to lower earnings for the female workers. On the contrary, *it is the general social constraints (sometimes in the form of legal constraints), which prohibit women to work and earn at par with their male counterparts in the labour market.*

V

Do Women Concentrate in Lower Categories Only?

We now turn to the distribution of female employment in different categories in the sample firms. It has often been claimed that as a result of 'labour market discrimination', women are found to be working at the lowest categories in all industrial activities. In the Indian context, studies have pointed out women's domination in the low skilled jobs of the garment–manufacturing units of Thiruppur in Tamil Nadu (Cawthorne: 1995; Swaminathan, et al: 1999).[9] Moreover, if the reason behind the decline in the female percentage share in the sample firms is technological modernization, then it is expected that concentration of women in the lower categories increases with an increase in the male concentration in the higher categories.

Table 7 gives the occupational distribution of female workers in the sample firms. This table clearly reveals two important facts. First, while women workers are concentrated in the lower categories such as helpers and grade C tailors, they are also present in the higher categories such as Designers and Supervisors, in all the firms except Firm E irrespective of market orientation, technological modernization and degree of female intensity. Secondly, again while it is true that the higher posts go mostly to the male workers, the latter can also be found in the lower categories such as helpers. The percentage of male helpers varies between 30 and 50 in different firms.

Table 8, however, has something more important to say. Here, we consider only firms A, C and E, because the detailed employment data on the basis of different categories for two points of time are not available for the other firms. Let us start with firm A. In the year 1999-00, i.e., the inception year of this firm, there were no women in the categories of floor-in-charge or designer. The year 2002-03, however, shows the presence of one woman among the 4 employees in this category. The percentage of women in the category of supervisor has also improved to 10 over 0. Now, there are 3 women line supervisors. Two of them have been promoted (from Grade A tailor category) on the basis of their efficient performance, and one has joined with experience of working in some garment-manufacturing unit in Mumbai. In the case of Tailor category also, there is a notable change.

Table 7
Number and Percentages of Women Workers in Different Categories of the Sample Firms as on April 2003

Firms	*Floor Incharge/Designer*	*Line Supervisor*	*Tailor*	*Helper*
A	One (25%)	Three (10%)	210 (70%)	200 (70%)
B	One (100%)	Nil	17 (80%)	4 (100%)
C	One (100%)	Two (50%)	60 (75%)	38 (63%)
D	No females. This firm has only one male incharge	One (100%)	6 (67%)	2 (50%)
E	This category does not exist	No female supervisor. One male supervisor	40 (73%)	14 (70%)
			Trainees30 (100%)	
F	One designer (100%)	One (33%)	65 (75%)	35 (70%)
G	One Designer (50%)	One (33%)	38 (58%)	21 (52%)
H	Nil	Nil	Nil	Nil

Note: Firm H produces garment accessories and not garments, so the categories of work are different from the others. However this is the only firm that employs male workers.

Table 8
Percentage of Women Workers in Selected Firms at Two Different Time Points

Work Categories	*Firm A*		*Firm C*		*Firm E*	
	1999-01	*2002-03*	*1995-96*	*2002-03*	*2000-01*	*2002-03*
Floor-in-charge/Designer	Nil	25 (1/4)	Nil	100(1/1)	This category does not exist	
Line supervisor	Nil	10 (3/30)	Nil	50 (2/4)	Nil	Nil
Tailor			69	63		
Grade A	Nil	60	NA	NA	Nil	35
Grade B	70	79	NA	NA	78	75
Grade C	85	70	NA	NA	Not applicable	Not applicable
Helper	86	72	71	63	74	71

While the year 2002-03 marks a significant improvement in the percentage share of women in the upper categories of tailoring, only the lowest category shows a 15 per cent decline. The same is true for the case of category 'helper' where the female percentage has gone down to 72 in the year 2002-03 from 86 at inception. The picture is not different in the other two firms.

In reaction to the question: do you prefer women workers in the higher categories as well, such as supervisor, the management reiterated that if they got an adequately educated young woman with experience they would definitely prefer the woman to a male candidate with similar background. Here, an obvious question comes to mind: why is the number of women supervisors so low, especially in the case of Firm A, where the total number of supervisors is 30? The management responds:

> *"We are searching for women who have the basic qualifications for a supervisor. But it is extremely difficult to find that kind of women, having experience in a garment unit as well. Because of this specific reason, we have decided to give training to the most efficient women workers, so that in future we can replace at least some of the male supervisors with female ones. In fact, we have already started the process as a test case and the two female supervisors are working quite efficiently in their respective departments."*

This suggests, in the context of our sample, that the *discrimination against women is not taking place within the labour market. It is the lack of education in general and lack of technical education in particular which makes a woman less endowed and bars her entry into the industrial labour market as such.* A similar situation of difficulty in getting female supervisors is reported in Paul-Majumder, et al (1993) in the case of Bangladesh garment manufacturing industry.[10]

"The differential initial endowment of education and access to information and credit emerging out of different social constructs affect women's labour market participation in several ways" (Collier: 1994). In the Andhra Pradesh context, at inception, the management found it very difficult to get the required workforce, as the state was a newcomer in the area of garment manufacturing activities. The management of firm A decided to train the available workforce from the nearby villages, employing more women than men. However, the management emphasized –in our interviews-the fact that they made it a point to employ some male workers in every category together with female workers. This is very significant, and similar to the experiences of other firms as well. Initially, entry qualification for training was basic education and age below 30 years. However, the educational qualifications were generally much better in the case of male workers. The management asserts that the years of schooling attained by a worker plays a very important role in the learning ability. Therefore, even if the machineries are not very complicated and jobs not quite difficult, a strong sense of co-ordination and alertness about things one is doing are essential for getting trained quickly, especially when one is totally unexposed. Theoretically this particular issue of education's overall role in increasing productivity has been substantially dealt with in the literature of industrial organization.

As a result, *the more educated workers were performing better in acquiring skills compared to the less educated ones.* Because almost all the male workers have passed the tenth standard (or, the school leaving examination), most of them managed to get positions in different grades at tailoring. This is more or less true for the better-educated female workers as well. However, within a year, the better-educated women in the lower categories of tailoring started performing more efficiently than better qualified males and started moving up. Table 8 corroborates this experience of the management. It is important to note here that while market orientation has nothing to do with this experience, the level of technology might have played an important role, as all the firms are not only technologically advanced but also operating within the process of continuous modernization. However, this can be confirmed with a more intensive investigation, especially of the non-modernized units.

Let us now turn to another important issue. We have already noticed that there is a general decline in the percentage of women workers in the total workforce of the sample firms, while in almost every case total employment has increased. In the context of strong preferences for female workers, this is apparently contradictory. However, the management say that the shortage of educated female workers is the main reason behind this, apart from social constraints we discussed earlier. Women face many types of constraints, which originate mainly within the household arising from the burden of reproduction and family care. Even though the level of fertility has declined in A.P considerably during the 1990s, families do not allow a woman to go for work during the first 3 or 4 years of marriage. This is mainly because of child bearing and rearing, and related issues. So, the available women workforce for the firms falls either in the age group of 18 to 22 or above 27 or so.

The incidence of education is considerably higher between the first age group women than among the second age group especially if it is after 5th standard. This is also the general trend in rural Andhra Pradesh according to the statistics reported by the Commissioner and Director of School Education, Andhra Pradesh (1999-00). However, according to the management, because of the lack of industrial culture in Andhra Pradesh, especially in rural areas, young unmarried women do not want to work. Working outside home can reduce chances of a good marriage. Therefore, the women who are available for work are in the age group 27 to 35. The comparatively lower educational attainments of these women are a hindrance to their competing for jobs.

This argument is strictly true when the category of work needs some type of skill, especially associated with handling of the machines. But the argument does not hold much water for a category like 'helpers', where uneducated or barely educated women dominate in a major way. However, Table 8 shows a considerable decline in the percentage points of women workers in the lower categories. On the other hand, while moving around inside the villages, we found a number of women workers having been retrenched from the lower categories of work after a year or so, and some more women who were ready to accept any job in the garment factory to get some additional income to support their families. (Moreover, usually a helper is not promoted to the category of tailor, while a tailor can be promoted to the supervisory category).

These facts together can mean that it is a conscious management policy to employ some male workers in every category. When we put forward this question to the management, our hunch came true. The management of firm E (the parent firm of which is in Coimbatore) said:

> *In Tamil Nadu, the garment industry is female dominated. There are certain unskilled and semi–skilled job categories that are specifically ear–marked for women. We found that if there is a temporary shortage of women workers, available male workers with similar background demand a higher wage. And once you give a higher wage for a specific category of work, it is quite difficult to reduce it. Considering the lower female participation in the industrial work in Andhra Pradesh, we purposefully decided not to encourage any kind of stereotyping of job categories whenever it is possible.*

In the context of limited labour supply any kind of stereotyping of job categories leads to labour market distortion and increases inefficiency in terms of increase in costs. The presence of male workers in every category of work in the sample firms is therefore not because of 'breaking women's solidarity' as found by Joekes (1982) in another context. In our case, this situation is better explained as the management's conscious choice to reduce the labour cost arising out of labour market distortion.

To conclude, a major shortcoming of this study is its smallness of the sample size. However, it does open up a set of new questions that can be verified by proper secondary data and through appropriately constructed samples.

Notes

1. However, there are some exceptions such as Dev (2000).
2. Let us assume that the economy is divided into three broad macro economic sectors of "non-tradables, import substitutables and exportables."
3. Import liberalization leading to fall in the relative prices of import substitutables leading to a crunch in production and thereby a crunch in employment.
4. Although in recent years some technological modernization has taken place in this industry. We will come back to this issue as we go along.
5. We were requested by the management not to use the names of the specific firms.
6. Actually, there is no export-oriented firm that can be called technologically backward.
7. "As economic success reduced absolute poverty in the 1970s,the focus of discontent shifted to the relative deprivation that most workers thought was result of government reluctance to distribute equally".
8. As Collier noted in 1994.
9. '...the classic argument that men attend skilled jobs and women to the unskilled ones' [Swaminathan :1999:110].
10. As Kabeer noted in 2001.

References

Cawthorne, P. 1995. 'Of Networks and Markets: The Rise and rise of a South Indian Town', *World Development*: 23:1: 43-56.

Chakravarty, D. 1999. 'Labour Market under Trade Liberalization: Issues Concerning Re-allocation', *Economic and Political Weekly*: 34:48: M163-M168.

Chakravarty D. 2002. 'Work Organization and Employment Contracts: Technological Modernization in Textile Firms', *Economic and Political Weekly*: 37:8: 743-749.

Collier, P. 1994. 'Gender Aspects of Labour Allocation during Structural Adjustment', pp. 279-307 in Susan Horton, Ravi Kanbur, and Dipak Mazumdar (eds) *Labour Markets in an Era of Adjustment*, Volume 1. Washington DC: Economic Development Organization of The World Bank, The World Bank.

Dev, S. Mahendra. 2000. 'Economic Liberalization and Employment in South Asia', *Economic and Political Weekly*: 35: 1, 2 and 3: 41-51 and 135-146.

Edgren, Gus. 1984. 'Spearheads of Industrialization or Sweatshops in the Sun?', pp. 27-52 in Eddy Lee (ed) *Export Processing Zones and Industrial Employment in Asia,*. Bangkok: Asian Employment Programme (ARTEP), International Labour Organization.

Goldar, Bishwanath. 2002. 'Trade Liberalization and Manufacturing Employment: The Case of India', ILO Employment Paper No. 34. Geneva: International Labour Organization.

Jhabvala, R. and S. Sinha. 2002. 'Liberalization and the Women Workers', *Economic and Political Weekly* 37(21): 2037-2044.

Joekes, S. 1982. 'Female-Led Industrialization: Women's Jobs in Third World Export Manufacturing: The Case of the Moroccan Clothing Industry', Institute of Development Studies Research Report No. 15. Brighton: Institute of Development Studies.

Joekes, S. 1995. 'Trade Related Employment for Women in Industry and Services in Developing Countries', UNRISD Occasional Paper No. 5. Geneva: United Nations Research Institute for Social Development, United Nations Development Programme.

Kabeer, N. 2001. *Bangladesh Women Workers and Labour Market Decisions: The Power to Choose.* New Delhi: Vistaar Publications.

Koshy, Darlie O. 1997. *Garment Exports Winning Strategies*. New Delhi: Prentice Hall of India.

Krishnaraj, Maithreyi. 1987. 'New Opportunities on Old Terms: The Garment Industry in India', *Social Scientist:* 15 (6): 45-54.

Lim, Linda Y.C. 1984. 'Labour and Employment Issues in Export Processing Zones in Developing Countries', pp. 53-67 in Eddy Lee (ed) *Export Processing Zones and Industrial Employment in Asia.* Bangkok: Asian Employment Programme (ARTEP), International Labour Organization.

Neetha, N. 2002. 'Flexible Production, Feminization and Disorganization, Evidence from Tiruppur Knitwear Industry', *Economic and Political Weekly:* 37(21): 2045-2057.

Song, Keun Ho. 2002. 'Labour Unions in the Republic of Korea: Challenge and Choice', pp. 199-237 in A.V. Jose (ed) *Organized Labour in the 21st Century.* Geneva: Labour and Society Programme, International Institute for Labour Studies, International Labour Organization.

Standing, G. 1989. 'Global Feminization Through Flexible Labour', *World Development:* 17 (7): 1077-1095.

Swaminathan, P. and J. Jeyarajan. 1999. 'The Knitwear Cluster in Tiruppur: An Indian Industrial District in the Making?', pp. 94-121 in A. Bagchi (ed) *Economy and Organization: Indian Institutions under the Neoliberal Regime.* New Delhi: Sage Publications India Pvt. Limited.

United Nations. 1995. *Women in a Changing Global Economy: 1994 World Survey on Role of Women in Development*. New York: United Nations Department for Policy Coordination and Sustainable Development.

Yue, Chia Siow. 1984. 'Export Processing and Industrialization: The Case of Singapore', pp. 95-156 in Eddy Lee (ed), *Export Processing Zones and Industrial Employment in Asia*. Bangkok: Asian Employment Programme (ARTEP), International Labour Organization.

The paper is based on parts of a project report submitted to the United Nations Development Fund for Women (UNIFEM) in December 2003. The author is grateful to N Krishnaji, discussions with whom at different stages of this work made this paper possible. Thanks are also due to S. Mahendra Dev, Maithreyi Krishnaraj, Jos Mooji and Tirthankar Roy for their comments on an earlier draft of this paper. The paper was first published in the *Economic and Political Weekly*: 39:45:2004:49 10-4916. It is included here with the permission of the author and the Editor, *Economic and Political Weekly*. Address for email correspondence: deepcv@yahoo.com

PART - V

SPACE, VOICE AND TURBULENCE IN THE NEWER SECTORS OF ECONOMY

CHAPTER - TWENTY THREE

Women Engineers in India

P.P. Parikh and S.P. Sukhatme

I

Introduction

All modern societies recognize that education and a career are not only the right of a woman, but key factor that contribute to the economic and social development of a nation. In spite of this recognition, the participation and contribution of women in many professions is insignificant. This is most evident in the field of engineering, where women represent a large untapped source of talent.

In India, the participation of women in engineering was negligible till the early 1980s. It is only in the past 15 years that their enrolment has shown an increasing trend. This movement began first in the southern states and has gradually spread to other parts of the country. However, with the increase in numbers, women engineers are facing many problems in their careers. These problems need to be understood and analyzed.

Keeping these issues in view, two extensive studies on women engineers were taken up at IIT Bombay. The department of science and technology sponsored both studies. This paper presents the salient findings of the two studies. The first study [Parikh and Sukhatme: 1992, 1994, 1997] was conducted about 10 years ago and was concerned with collecting, compiling and analyzing information about women who obtained their bachelor's degree in engineering (BE, B.Tech, BSc (Engg) from all over the country during the period 1975 to 1990. The study focused on the following issues:

1. Data on enrolment and out-turn, statewise and disciplinewise;
2. Job opportunities, job status, nature of work, career profiles and career problems of women engineers.

The second study [Parikh and Sukhatme: 2002] was conducted recently. The sample studied consisted of women who obtained a bachelor's degree in engineering during 1994-98. In contrast to the first study, which was more general in its scope, the second focused on women who had obtained degrees in civil engineering, computer science/engineering, electrical engineering, electronics engineering and mechanical engineering and were located in the states of Andhra Pradesh, Delhi, Gujarat, Karnataka, Kerala, Maharashtra and Tamil Nadu. This was done because Study I had shown that 80 per cent of the stock of women engineers belonged to the above-mentioned states and disciplines. One of the objectives of Study II was to establish the current job and career status of the women engineers and compare it with the picture that had emerged from Study 1. A second objective of the study was to obtain the viewpoint of employers and understand more fully the reasons for the difficulties encountered by women.

Carefully designed questionnaires were used in both studies for obtaining the information from women engineers and from employers. A total of 2,753 responses were received from women engineers in the first study, and 1,020 responses were received in the second study. Care was taken to ensure that these responses were reasonably representative of the total population under study. As far as the employers were concerned, a total of 129 responses from 104 organizations were received in the second study. Of the 129 respondents, 112 were men and 17 were women executives. All the responses were entered in suitable databases and analyzed. They form the basis for the results and views presented and for the recommendations made. It may be mentioned that the two studies conducted are the largest studies on women engineers in India.

In the following sections, the data on enrolment and out-turn of women engineers over the years has been presented to evolve a feel for the numbers involved. This is followed by analysis of the data obtained through the two studies in regards to job status, nature of work and career problems of women engineers. Following this, a summary of the reactions obtained from employers and then some recommendations for action based on the results of both studies are presented.

II

Out-Turn of Women Engineers

It is necessary to take note of the growth in intake capacity for bachelor's degree programmes in engineering in the country. Table 1 presents data for the six-year period 1996 to 2001 for some major disciplines [AICTE: 2002]. The total intake capacity for these years as well as for some earlier years is also given. It is to be noted that over 50 years from 1951 to 2001, there has been nearly a 50-fold increase in intake capacity. The growth in capacity has been particularly large in the past 20 years. This is mainly due to the large number of private institutions started in this period. It should also be noted that the growth in the last 3-4 years is because of the capacity created in the engineering branches of information technology, computer science/engineering and electronics.

Table 1
Intake Capacity for Bachelor's Degree Programmes in Engineering

Year	*1951*	*1961*	*1971*	*1981*	*1991*
Intake capacity	*4778*	*15497*	*18207*	*34835*	*70481*

Discipline	*Intake Capacity*		
	1996	*1998*	*2001*
Mechanical engineering and Production engineering	25704	33160	40044
Electrical engineering	12495	18961	24498
Civil engineering	13706	13852	13806
Chemical engineering	5520	6472	7552
Electronics	20847	26707	49448
Computer Sc/engineering	14853	21383	46418
Information technology	-	1240	27079
Others	8326	12920	17639
Total	101451	134695	226484

Source: AICTE (2002).

Corresponding admission figures are not readily available. However it would be safe to assume that the actual intake was close to 100 per cent of the intake capacity up to 1971, when there was a shortage of capacity. It is likely to have decreased as a percentage of intake capacity since then. We will assume reasonable values of 90 per cent for 1981, 80 per cent for 1991, 75 per cent for 1996, 73 per cent for 1998, and 70 per cent for 2001. The actual annual intake with these assumptions is given in Table 2. The numbers obtained are in good agreement with corresponding enrolment data compiled by UGC (1999).

Table 2
Estimates of Actual Intake for Bachelor's Degree Programme

Year	*1951*	*1961*	*1971*	*1981*	*1991*	*1996*	*1998*	*2001*
Intake Capacity	4778	15497	18207	34835	70481	101451	134695	226484
Per cent filled	100	100	100	90	80	75	73	70
Actual Intake	4778	15497	18207	31352	56385	76088	98327	158539

Table 3
Yearwise Distribution of Women Graduates from Some Institutions

Year	*1975*	*1976*	*1977*	*1978*	*1979*	*1980*	*1981*	*1982*	*1983*	*1984*	*1985*	*1986*	*1987*	*1988*
No of women	13	27	23	30	38	41	90	87	147	165	187	205	184	298
Total no of graduates	1914	2124	2303	2500	2897	2818	3084	2981	3246	3339	3601	3419	3156	3271
Per cent of women	0.68	1.27	0.99	1.20	1.31	1.45	2.91	2.92	4.53	4.94	5.19	6.00	5.83	8.74

Source: Parikh and Sukhatme (1992).

Data obtained in Study I on the number and percentage of women who obtained bachelor's degrees from 13 institutions is given in Table 3. This data is for the period 1975 to 1988 and is reasonably representative of the national picture.

Similar data obtained in Study II for the period 1994 to 1998 from 31 representative institutions is given in Table 4.

Table 4
Yearwise Distribution of Women Graduates from Some Institutions

Year	1994	1995	1996	1997	1998
No of women	454	500	542	703	814
Total no of graduates	4641	4865	5111	5037	5276
Per cent of women	9.78	10.28	10.60	13.96	15.43

Source: Parikh and Sukhatme (2002).

The reliability of this data can be checked by comparing it with enrolment data published by UGC. The yearwise variation of the number of women enrolled in engineering in the country and women as a percentage of total enrolment is given in Table 5.

Table 5
Enrolment of Women in Engineering

Year	*1974-75*	*1979-80*	*1985-86*	*1989-90*	*1994-95*	*1999-2000*
No of women enrolled	1300	4400	12200	15800	24900	63100
Women as a percentage of total enrolment	1.5	3.7	6.9	7.6	8.3	16.2

Source: UGC (1999).

An year-to-year comparison between Tables 3 and 4 and Table 5 is not possible because enrolment is the sum of four years of intake. However, it will be seen that the percentages for all years are in good agreement.

An examination of Tables 3 and Table 4 shows the spectacular increase in enrolment and out-turn of women engineers over the years. In the 1970s, the percentage increased slowly from less than 1 per cent to about 1.5 per cent. Thereafter the percentage has been increasing almost every year, crossing 15 per cent in 1998.

Tables 2, 3 and 4 form the basis for estimating the number of women graduating with degrees in engineering in the country as a whole in recent years. As an example, we take the year 2000. Students passing in 2000 would have been admitted in 1996. From Table 2, the actual intake in 1996 is 76,088. We assume that the percentage passing out is 70 per cent of the actual intake. This is a good assumption based on actual figures for out-turn for earlier years. Assume that women constitute 17 per cent of the out-turn. We obtain the number of women passing out in 2000 as 76,088 x 0.7 x 0.17 = 9050.

In contrast, the number of women passing out in the 1970s ranged only between 100 and 200 every year.

Finally, it is of interest to study data on out-turn of women engineering graduates as a percentage of the total passing out of various types of educational institutes. This is presented in the Table 6. The percentages are compiled from the detailed records of the 12 institutions in Study I and 31 institutions in Study II. The increase in out-turn during the 10 year period from Study I to Study II is clearly seen with regard to government engineering colleges and private engineering colleges. However, it is disappointing to note that the increase in IITs is insignificant and that even in RECs, it is rather small.

Table 6
Women Engineering Graduates as a Percentage of Out-Turn

Type of Institutions	*Study I (Per cent)*	*Study II (Per cent)*
IITs	1.2	3.2
Regional engineering colleges	4.1	9.2
Government engineering colleges	4.4	17.2
Private engineering colleges	1.5	13.1

Statewise and Disciplinewise Distribution

Study I showed that in 1990, Kerala had the largest number of women engineers in the country, followed by Tamil Nadu, Karnataka and Maharashtra, the numbers being about 20, 18, 16 and 12 per cent of the total respectively. Disciplinewise, electrical engineering and electronics were the most preferred branches followed by civil engineering. There was also some indication that although the computer science/engineering population was low, it had started to grow rapidly.

Study II showed that for the years 1994 to 1998, these four states still produced the largest number of women engineers. Disciplinewise, electronics was the most preferred branch for the five years of Study II, with about 37 per cent of the graduates. Electronics was followed by civil engineering, computer science/ engineering and electrical engineering, each being about 16-20 per cent of the total (Table 7). A significant drop in preference for civil engineering and electrical engineering and spectacular increase of preference for electronics engineering and computer science/engineering needs to be underlined.

Table 7
Branchwise Distribution of Women Engineers

Branch	*Study I (Per cent)*	*Study II (Per cent)*
Civil engineering	26.4	19.7
Computer science/engineering	602	17.8
Electrical engineering	32.5	16.1
Electronics engineering	30.4	37.1
Mechanical engineering	4.5	9.3

III

Job Status and Career Profile

The data, analysis and comments presented in this section are based on the responses obtained from women engineers in two studies.

The questionnaires in both studies requested some general background data about the respondents and their perceptions on certain career goals and statements. Analysis of this data showed that the majority of respondents had their schooling in a city or town (Study I: 84.2 per cent; Study II: 85.7 per cent) and that most of them had attended government, missionary or private schools (Study I: 84.2 per cent; Study II: 82.3 per cent). The medium of instruction in school was English for 47.4 per cent of the respondents in Study I and 60.5 per cent in Study II.

Most had planned to take up an engineering career at the higher secondary school stage (Study I: 57.4 per cent; Study II: 59.3 per cent) and came from educated families. The fathers of the respondents generally possessed a graduate or postgraduate degree (Study I:67.0 per cent; Study II: 71.5 per cent). While the mothers had slightly lower qualifications (graduates and post graduates–Study I: 30.2 per cent; Study II: 43.1 per cent; High School-Study I: 47.8 per cent; Study II: 35.0 per cent). Almost all the husbands of married respondents possessed a graduate degree or had a higher qualification (Study I: 99.4 per cent; Study II: 98.5 per cent).

The respondents of both studies considered 'opportunity for personal growth and development of independent thought and action' to be the most desirable career goal and felt that this goal was fully realized by taking up engineering. Women respondents of the two studies ranked 'A feeling of security by being self-supporting and opportunity for financial growth' as the next most desirable career goal. The extent of realization of this goal was also stated to be high. A majority of the respondents (Study I: 66.4 per cent, Study II: 70.5 per cent) perceived that 'women have to do better than men to get equal professional recognition'. About 60 per cent also agreed with the statement that 'even today professional women end up in secondary roles doing routine jobs'.

Both studies showed that a fair number of respondents had obtained a postgraduate qualification or were studying for a postgraduate degree (Study I: 19.4 per cent; Study II: 21.8 per cent). Many of those taking up higher studies have stated to be doing so for want of a job.

Job status: Employment status, sector of employment and nature of work are various aspects of interest in the context of job status. Data on the employment status of the respondents is given in Table 8.

The data in Table 8 is quite disturbing. The percentage of employed women engineers is only 68.7 per cent in Study I and 54.9 per cent in Study II. In fact, out of the 54.9 per cent, only 44.7 per cent have been continuously employed, the remaining 9.3 per cent being intermittently employed. Thus from Study I to Study II, the employed percentage has decreased by 13.8 per cent, while the unemployed percentage has increased from 26.1 per cent to 30.6 per cent. This is not a happy situation. Although comparable data for men is not readily available, it is likely that the unemployment percentage is much less. A good guess would be 15-20 per cent.

Table 8
Employment Status

Status	*Study I*	*Study II*
Employed	1892 (68.7)	560 (54.9)
Unemployed	719 (26.1)	312 (30.6)
Postgraduate student	142 (5.2)	148 (14.5)
Total	2753 (100.0)	1020 (100.0)

Notes: 1. Employed includes self-employed respondents.
2. Numbers in parentheses represent percentage.

Finding the first job after graduation is a major hurdle in the career path of women engineers. This is duly reflected by a higher percentage of unemployment amongst younger members and the fact that the unemployed were without a job for over a year at the time of data collection. Resistance to entry in the job market seems to be the issue. This is supported by the fact that participants report having faced difficulties in being called for campus interviews and getting a job through campus recruitment. It is further corroborated by the fact that 28.4 per cent in Study II did not get their first job in their area of specialization. To a question as to what factors governed their accepting the first job, a significant number have responded with phrases like 'something better than nothing' or 'for experience'.

An important facet that emerged from Study I was that unemployment among women engineers was highest in Kerala, that too among those having a degree in civil engineering. Overall unemployment among women engineers in the state was found to be 36 per cent, but unemployment among women civil engineers was 50 per cent.

The scenario presented by Study II is not very different in regard to Kerala, which continues to have a high unemployment rate of 41.5 per cent. However, the highest percentage of unemployment is now in Andhra Pradesh, where 45.7 per cent of the women engineers are unemployed. Unemployment in Karnataka and Tamil Nadu is 33.5 per cent and 31.9 per cent respectively.

On a branch wise basis, the percentage unemployment amongst electronics (37.3 per cent) and electrical (36.4 per cent) engineering graduates has increased significantly, surpassing the unemployment amongst civil engineers, which is 30.9 per cent. This scenario is not quite in tune with the general belief that electronics is a good area for women engineers. It seems that there is now a big imbalance between the demand and supply of graduates in electronics engineering. It is necessary to verify whether the increased unemployment is generally applicable to all the graduates in electronics engineering, both men and women, or is true only for women engineers.

Table 9 contains data on the sector of employment of respondents. The data pertains to those employed at the time of data collection.

Table 9
Sector of Employment

Sector	*Study-I (Per cent)*	*Study-II (Per cent)*
Technical educational institutions	26.9	29.8
Government/civil service	22.0	4.6
Rand D organisations (government and private)	8.9	4.3
Public sector units	18.9	5.7
Private industry (large-scale)	12.7	18.4
Private industry (small-scale)	9.1	28.8
Others	1.5	8.4
Total	100.0	100.0

It can be seen from the table that technical educational institutions (TEIs) provide the largest avenue for employment of women engineers. Out of the employed respondents, 26.9 per cent in Study I and 29.8 per cent in Study II are employed in TEIs. Government, civil services, R and D organizations (government or private) and PSUs were other places, where 49.8 per cent of the respondents were employed at the time of Study I. The scenario has changed since then and this fraction has dropped to only 14.6 per cent in Study II. The closure of PSUs is one of the likely reasons for this change.

Employment in the large-scale private sector industry has increased from 12.7 per cent in Study 1 to 18.4 per cent in Study II. The growth of the IT industry and significant employment of women engineers as software professionals is the reason for this increase. Diminished percentage employment in civil services and other government/private R and D organizations could also be related to the same phenomenon.

An increase in the employment fractions from 9.1 per cent to 28.8 per cent in the small-scale industrial sector is also to be noted. Whereas increased employment in large-scale private sector industry is a welcome trend and can be considered as an improvement over the earlier scenario, the same does not necessarily apply to employment in the small-scale sector. A job in a small-scale industry is very often a temporary one with low salary. This is amply evinced by responses like 'salary too low' and 'ad hoc temporary job'. For this reason, some women engineers refuse such jobs at the beginning of their career, thinking that they will eventually get a better job offer. However, when that does not happen, they accept a job in a small-scale industry, a typical response being 'something is better than nothing'.

In an overall sense, limited job opportunities in terms of sector of employment are reflected by the data of both studies. Although some changes have taken place since the first study, the situation is still far from satisfactory. What the data does not reflect is that even today there are industrial organizations that have policies against hiring women engineers and that they have no hesitation in making statements to such an effect.

Data on 'nature of work' matches with the data on the 'sector of employment'. Teaching tops the list in both studies (Table 10).

Table 10
Nature of Work

Nature of Work	*Study I (Per cent) (Rank)*	*Study II (Per cent) (Rank)*
Teaching	28.2 (1)	31.8 (1)
R and D	16.2 (2)	8.5 (4)
Design	16.1 (3)	17.7 (3)
Production	4.1 (7)	1.8 (9)
Maintenance/troubleshooting	8.0 (5)	5.5 (5)
Construction/erection	3.7 (9)	3.7 (8)
EDP/computer	9.2 (4)	18.4 (2)
Consultancy	3.7 (9)	4.6 (7)
Project planning	4.8 (6)	4.8 (6)
Marketing	2.0 (11)	0.9 (11)
Finance	0.4 (12)	0.5 (12)
Management	3.8 (8)	1.6 (10)
Total	100.0	100.0

During the period between the two studies, 'R and D' and 'EDP/ Computer' have inter-changed places. Whereas 'R and D' stood only next to 'Teaching' in the Study I, it ranks fourth in Study II. On the other hand, 'EDP/Computer' has risen from 4th to 2nd rank. This is expected because of the growth of the software industry. Design ranks third in both studies. 'Project planning' follows 'Maintenance and troubleshooting'. The comparatively small numbers involved in 'Production', 'Construction/Erection/ Commissioning', 'Consultancy', and 'Management' need to be noted. Insignificant involvement in marketing and finance jobs and the unchanged status of these over the last decade also need to be noted. On the whole, therefore, as far as nature of work is concerned, the picture has remained essentially unchanged excepting for a significant increase in software and computer related jobs.

Career profile: Pace of career growth and career problems are two important aspects of the career profile. The extent of management responsibilities is considered as an indicator of the hierarchical position of a person in an organization. In Study I, where the sample consisted of graduates of over a 15-year time span, such data was collected and analyzed in an attempt to assess the career growth pattern of women engineers. The data of employed respondents presented in Table 11 was received in response to a question asking them whether or not they had management and/or administrative responsibilities. Corroborative data was obtained through another question seeking information about the level of management to which the respondents belonged.

Table 11
Management/Administrative Responsibilities (Study I)

Year of Graduation	*Extent of Management Responsibility (Per cent)*				*Total*
	Nil	*Lower Level*	*Middle Level*	*Upper Level*	
1975–1976	25.0	5.0	50.0	20.0	100
1977–1978	41.2	17.7	32.4	8.8	100
1979–1980	47.5	10.0	38.8	3.8	100
1981–1982	36.7	20.3	34.8	8.2	100
1983–1984	41.5	21.6	34.5	2.4	100
1985–1986	50.0	21.7	23.8	4.6	100
1987–1988	55.2	20.8	20.0	3.9	100

It is interesting to note that only 20 per cent of the graduates of 1975 and 1976 belonged to the upper management and that this figure fell to less than 5 per cent for graduates of later years. This can be referred to as the 'glass ceiling' that women rarely cross. It is even more disheartening to note that a quarter of those who passed in 1975 and 1976 had 'no management responsibilities' at all, even after 15 years. Increase of 'no management responsibilities' fraction among the graduates of later years is to be expected. All the same, the value of this fraction being 41.2 per cent for the graduates of 1979 and 1980 certainly is a cause for concern and indicates the slow pace of career growth of women engineers.

Career Problems: Career-related problems start right from the student stage. A large number of women state that they failed to get a placement of their choice for practical training. Then follow the difficulties in getting a call for a campus interview and a job through campus recruitment. This is compounded by the fact that there are no campus interviews in some of the new colleges. In fact, getting the first job after graduation emerges as the major hurdle women engineers face during their professional career. A significant number of those who opt for further studies do so for want of a job. Lack of opportunities, reluctance of the employers and requirement of experience figure prominently as the factors resulting in such a situation. In certain states and locations, the need to have contacts to get a job has been clearly expressed by the respondents. An overall scarcity of jobs and abundance of engineers is reflected in the responses through expressions like 'too many applicants for a job', 'too many competitors'. Some personal and family factors also restrict job opportunities for women engineers, particularly at the entry level. These include hesitation of parents in letting the girls travel long distances for interviews and a job and reluctance towards letting them stay alone. Married women necessarily look for a job in the vicinity of the place of their stay, at least in the same city. This constrains their job prospects.

Respondents have mentioned 'language difficulty during interviews' as one of the reasons for not getting a job. Lack of confidence and a feeling of not being competent enough have also been mentioned. The emergence of numerous private engineering colleges with insufficient facilities and faculty are responsible for this. New names used for branch specializations and lack of awareness of employers about the same has also been mentioned as an issue. Although some of these factors may equally hold for men, they seem to be affecting women more severely.

Women engineers have strongly expressed the view that they do not get what they deserve in terms of jobs, promotions, salaries as well as professional recognition. 'Unsatisfactory work opportunities and environment' is the most frequently stated factor affecting their career. 'Low financial incentives' has also figured as a career problem. The job and career problems faced by women engineers are reflected in the typical quotations given below. Each of these is one of many expressions of frustration received as a response to certain questions wherein space for free expression was provided. The number in the parentheses at the end of each quote is the year of graduation of the respondent.

> *What will you do when you get married? This question is asked only to female candidates despite the fact that men tend to change jobs more often (as I have seen). A question about your future is quite hard to answer and I have felt this has been a major reason for rejection. A few companies that came to college also clearly stated that they did not require female engineers (1998).*

> *In some states, like in our Gujarat, ladies' seats (15 per cent) are reserved. But if after completion of BE there is no scope to work as an engineer then what is the use of reserving these seats for women (1998).*

> *I consider myself to be a thoroughly professional worker. I valued my company's goals and made sure that my goals were a mirror image of my company's future plans and aspirations. However, my disappointment is evident. After 1 and 1/2 years of service to my company, I find that there is no 'up' for me. I can only move 'down' or 'sideways'. As a female, I will always have to settle for a dull mediocre desk job. It stifles my productivity, I don't get to learn as much as I would like, on-site (1997).*

> *You have to really work hard to convince others that you are the same person with same efficiency and sincerity even though now you are married (1995).*

IV

Employers' Viewpoint

The data presented in this section is based on the responses obtained in Study II.

Responding organizations: The organizations that responded covered a wide spectrum. Responses were received from private industries, public sector units, technical education institutions (TEI), R and D organizations and government and semi-government organizations. Details are given in Table 12. Responses to the questionnaire were obtained from a total of 104 organizations. Of these, 41 were from Gujarat and 31 from Maharashtra. The largest responses were received from TEIs and industries. TEIs responded to the mailings whereas industries had to be persuaded through a personal approach.

The organizations were requested to provide data on the number of employees with an engineering degree and a break-up in terms of men and women. Eighty-two organizations provided the data. Details are given in Table 13.

Table 12
Type of Responding Organisation/Institution

Type	*No. of Organizations*	
	Contacted	*Responded*
Private industry	81	34
Public sector units	17	10
R and D organizations	12	8
Technical education institutions	105	34
Consultancy organizations	5	5
Govt., Semi-govt. and other organizations	20	13
Total	240	104

Table 13
Number of Employees with a Degree in Engineering

Organisation Type	*No of Employees with Engineering Degree*				*Women as Per cent of Total*
	Number	*Men*	*Women*	*Total*	
Industry (private and public sector)	38	11010	395	11405	3.5
Rand D organisations	7	587	67	654	10.2
Technical education institutions	25	986	258	1244	20.7
Consultancy organisations	4	28	8	36	22.2
Govt, semi-govt andother organisations	8	4354	365	4719	7.7
Total	82	16965	1093	18058	6.1

The employment data shows that women engineers constitute about 21 per cent of the engineering staff of TEIs, whereas in industries, the percentage is only 3.5 per cent. On the whole, the percentage of women engineers works out to 6.1 per cent.

Participation of women engineers in management is low. It decreases with increase in the level of management. Among all types of organizations, industries rank the lowest as far as participation of women engineers in management is concerned. It is only 7.6 per cent at the lower management level and falls to 2.4 per cent at the upper level. In contrast, in TEIs the participation of women in management is relatively good. It is 22.9 per cent at the lower management level and 5.7 per cent at the upper level.

The organizations were asked a number of questions regarding the formation of work groups, the rating system for promotion and personnel policies specific to women. Some of the replies were as follows:

1. As far as formation of working groups is concerned, 85.6 per cent of the organizations report that they have mixed working groups. Only nine out of 104 organizations state that they have 'all men' working groups.
2. In all 71.1 per cent of the responding organizations have a rating system for promotion. Of these, 85.1 per cent have a formal rating system. Almost all

organizations have the same rating system for men and women engineers irrespective of the level of management.

3. Most organizations (90 out of 104) have a provision for maternity leave. Only three have no provision and 11 have not responded to this question. The most frequent maternity leave provision ranges between 90 and 135 days. Re-entry/reinduction programmes for women after maternity leave are non-existent.
4. Special provisions for women, such as flexible time slots, option of working from home, part-time job option and availability of crèche, exist in a very limited number of organizations. Apparently the employers do not feel the need for such provisions.
5. Only 20 out of 104 organizations have a policy regarding employment of both husband and wife. Of these, three organizations discourage employment of husband and wife, while 13 encourage it.
6. As regards a special policy for encouraging women engineers, 88 out of 104 organizations state that they have no special policy. Others have not responded.

Responding executives: A total of 129 executives responded to the questionnaire, of which 17 were women. Eighty-two of the respondents belonged to the upper management level, and 43 were from the middle management level; 112 were engineers. Of these, over 60 per cent had a postgraduate qualification. Most had long working experience.

The questionnaire requested the executives to give their views on certain statements posed to them with regard to women in the engineering profession and the barriers faced by them. The respondents were asked whether they 'agreed fully', 'agreed somewhat' or 'did not agree' with the statements. The numbers in parentheses indicate the extent.

Most of the respondents 'agreed fully' with the statements that women are competent enough to be successful in the engineering field (83 per cent), that it is acceptable for them to assume leadership roles (92 per cent), that they possess the self-confidence required of a competent engineer (89 per cent) and that a woman does not have to sacrifice her femininity in order to be a successful engineer (72 per cent).

Most of the respondents 'did not agree' with the statements that women engineers cannot supervise male subordinates (84 per cent) and that they cannot handle tough negotiations (77 per cent). However, for some statements, some respondents 'agreed fully' and some 'agreed somewhat' indicating that a few had reservations. These statements were:

1. There is no difference in experience, knowledge and interaction styles between men and women engineers. (Agreed fully: 48 per cent: agreed somewhat: 36 per cent).
2. The possibility of pregnancy does not make women less acceptable as employees. (Agreed fully: 45 per cent; agreed somewhat: 37 per cent).

3. A full-time employed mother of pre-school children can be just as good as any other employee. (Agreed fully: 38 per 'cent; agreed somewhat: 42 per cent.)
4. It is equally important for a wife to have a career so as to help her husband with his career. (Agreed fully: 57 per cent; agreed somewhat: 29 per cent.)

In contrast, for some statements some respondents 'did not agree' and some 'agreed somewhat' indicating that opposition to the statement was not total. These statements were:

1. Women engineers cannot work on the shop floor. (Did not agree: 41 per cent; agreed somewhat: 43 per cent.)
2. Women cannot take up jobs involving travel. (Did not agree: 51 per cent; agreed somewhat: 36 per cent.)
3. Women engineers do not and cannot join male colleagues in informal groups and there is a certain amount of self-exclusion. (Did not agree: 57 per cent; agreed somewhat: 37 per cent.)
4. Women cannot balance their work with their family, as they would have to give priority to the children. (Did not agree: 39 per cent; agreed somewhat: 43 per cent.)

Opinions on the statement, 'Women engineers cannot work beyond office hours and on weekends' were divided. A more or less equal number 'agreed fully', 'agreed somewhat', or 'did not agree' with the statement.

Information on the performance of women engineers in comparison to men engineers with regard to a number of attributes was sought from the respondents. The data obtained is compiled in Table 14. In terms of 'technical skills, 87 per cent felt that women engineers were the same as men engineers. As regards 'interpersonal skills', 56 per cent felt that women engineers were the same. However a significant number (33 per cent) also thought that they were better than men engineers. The situation with regard to 'confidence' was different. Sixty six per cent felt they were the same. However a significant number (21 per cent) thought that their level of performance was lesser than men engineers. In an overall sense, 81 per cent of the responding executives felt that women engineers were the same as men engineers in terms of performance.

The responding executives felt that on the job women engineers are treated as equal to men and are accepted as equals. There were only a few responses that mentioned discriminatory or preferential treatment.

The statement 'women engineers have to work harder to prove themselves to earn the same credibility as male engineers in similar positions' received a different response from men and women executive respondents. The details are given in Table 15. Whereas a small number of men executives (22 per cent) found the statement to be correct, the same was not the case with the women executives, of whom 53 per cent felt it was true. The response of women engineers to a similar question matched the response of women executives. About 70 per cent of the women engineer respondents agreed with the statement. Overall, there does seem to be some truth in the statement and women perceive it to a much greater extent. This is also reflected in the comments of some women executives; such as 'Women professionals have to work twice as hard......'. 'She has to constantly prove herself'.

Table 14
Performance of Women Engineers in Comparison with Men Engineers as Seen by Executives

Level of Performance	*Attribute*			
	Technical skills	*Interpersonal skills*	*Confidence*	*Overall*
Lesser than men engineers	6	9	21	12
Same as men engineers	87	56	66	81
Better than men engineers	5	33	11	5
No response	2	2	2	2
Total (per cent)	100	100	100	100

Table 15
Views of Executives on the Statement 'Women Engineers have to Work Harder to Prove Themselves'

Response	*Men Executives (Per cent)*	*Women Executives (Per cent)*
Yes	22	53
No	69	35
Uncertain/no response	9	12
Total	100	100

A majority of the responding executives felt that opportunity for advancement of women engineers was the same as for men engineers at the middle and lower management levels. However, at the upper management level, they felt that the opportunity for advancement was less.

The executives were also requested to give their opinions on certain concerns that come up while interviewing women engineers for a job.

1. Nearly 60 per cent of the executives said that they were concerned that a woman engineer would get married and leave her job.
2. In contrast, over 70 per cent did not express concern about the fact that women engineers may need to go on maternity leave.
3. A majority of the executives (over 60 per cent) involved in the recruitment process did not seem to be aware of the legal implications of women being questioned differently during an interview.

Special provisions like 'flexible time slots' for young mothers and 'availability of creches' were widely supported by a majority of the respondents. On the other hand, their views regarding provisions like 'working from home' and 'part-time job option' were divided.

The executives were asked to name the specialization and the type of job that suited women engineers best. They felt that computer science/engineering was the best specialisation and that teaching was the most suitable job.

Finally the executives were asked to comment on the need for having special measures and policies that would benefit women engineers. The following points emerged:

1. Opinions regarding the need for having a company directive to avoid gender bias in the process of selection of engineering staff were equally divided. Opposition is based on the premise that selection has to be merit-based. On the other hand, advocates of a company directive stress the need for the same so that any discrimination against women engineers can be avoided. Among several suggestions given by the respondents, two important ones are to have a woman member in the selection committee and to mention in the advertisement that the company is an equal opportunity employer.
2. A majority of the respondents did not feel that it was necessary to identify women engineers with managerial potential and to create a fast track for them, the premise being that equal opportunity and not special treatment would bring the best out of them.
3. A majority of the respondents felt that it is possible to correct the present scenario of low visibility of women in the engineering job market. In order to do so, inputs have to come from the family, from women themselves and also from the employers. The family has to provide support, women engineers have to perform and the employers have to formulate policies to avoid any bias against women.
4. Regarding the possibility of giving preference in selection to a woman in the event of having an equally qualified and experienced man and woman, a larger number of respondents have expressed their preference fora woman engineer. Discipline, punctuality, hard work and obedience are stated to be the qualities of women engineers, because of which respondents would like to exercise a preference in their favour.

V

Recommendations for Action

Based on the results and viewpoints presented, it seems appropriate to make a number of suggestions in the form of recommendations for action. Implementation of these recommendations should alleviate existing problems and smoothen the entry of women engineers into the mainstream.

The suggestions are made under four broad headings: (1) organizational provisions and policies; (2) physical facilities; (3) awareness programmes; and (4) miscellaneous suggestions.

Organizational Provisions and Policies

Formulation of positive steps to encourage women engineers has to receive attention from many quarters. At present, the work format is so designed that a person works for 30 or more years, five or six days a week in an office or a factory, the domestic needs being taken care of by another individual, the wife. This work format applies to all engineers, a person working on the shop floor or a university professor. It does not accommodate the needs of a woman professional. The following organizational provisions would help women professionals.

Leave and flexible working hours: Modifications in certain rules will greatly help women professionals to cope with the dual responsibility of a home and their profession. Sanctioning of a long leave (twice in the professional career) and flexible working hours are recommended on this count. These facilities are relevant to the child bearing and rearing period.

Part-time job and working from home option: For some years of her life, a woman engineer needs to be provided with the option of a part-time job. With the upsurge of IT, working from home is an accepted practice in many countries. It is non-existent in India so far. The culture of working from home must also be brought in and practiced at least by the relevant sectors of employment.

Employment and transfers of husband and wife: Organizational policies should support employment of both husband and wife and their transfers together. Such policies would enable married couples in transferable jobs to live together. In this regard, it would be useful for the government to enact regulations for those in government service.

Equal opportunity: Every employer should have an organizational directive to avoid gender bias in the process of selection and promotion of engineering staff. The directive should stress the need for avoiding any discrimination against women engineers. In the advertisement for jobs, a mention that the organization is an 'equal opportunity employer' should become mandatory.

Questions asked at interviews: Executives, both men and women, involved in the interviewing and recruitment process should be made aware of the legal implications of women being questioned differently during interviews. In this context, the presence of a woman member in interview boards can prove beneficial. It is a practice adopted by some organizations and should be made mandatory, particularly for situations involving large-scale recruitment.

Shop floor and field jobs: Working on the shop floor and in the field implies exposure to real life situations. No amount of training can substitute this kind of job experience. Debarring women engineers from such work under the presumption that they are not suitable for such assignments amounts to denying them a basic professional foundation. This is harmful for their career development. Women engineers who opt for such jobs must be considered and offered the same, subject to their merits. A programme of sensitization of employers on such professional and career issues is strongly recommended.

Physical Facilities

Accommodation: Many women engineers remain unemployed due to lack of suitable and safe accommodation near the place of work. This view has been expressed by a large number of participants in the studies. Provision of accommodation near the workplace would improve the employment opportunities for women engineers from distant places, small towns and villages. Setting up a chain of working women's hostels is an essential requirement in this regard.

Childcare facilities and crèches: Another problem often faced by married women engineers is the lack of professional childcare facilities. These facilities include crèches for small children as well as places where school-age children are looked after in the early morning, late afternoon or on school holidays. Adequate facilities are not available in this regard. This aspect needs immediate attention.

Awareness Programmes

For employers: Education of employers and creation of awareness among them about the capabilities of women engineers is an important aspect. Such awareness programmes should be in the form of campaigns conducted through popular media channels. Publicizing the success stories of women engineers through the media will help the situation with regard to women securing jobs and will smoothen the path of their career advancement.

For parents and society: Among the reasons for women engineers not being able to get a job, parental constraints figure quite prominently. In fact, this is mentioned much more frequently than other problems. Many parents equip their daughters with an engineering degree only to make them eligible for a good match. They are not interested in the girls getting a job and do not even permit them to apply for one. Such girls can seek a job only after marriage. Many parents are also reluctant to send their daughter alone for interviews. The father or the brother has to accompany her. This makes it expensive and unfeasible due to several reasons including financial constraints. If the girl somehow does manage to secure a job, the parents are not willing to let her stay alone in a distant unknown place. The only corrective action that can be recommended in all such cases is to conduct education and awareness programmes for parents. The media can be the only route through which this can be accomplished, again through publicizing of success stories.

For women engineers: Many women engineers belong to small towns and have little access to information about jobs and the process of getting a job. Career guidance is rarely available from the family. Thus, they do not know where to apply, how to apply and how to perform in an interview. Professional help in this regard is a necessity. Respondents have stressed the need for active career guidance centres on campuses. Special cells could also be established in cities external to the teaching institutions.

It has been found that most women engineers are unaware of the existence of professional bodies and their activities at the time of graduation. This is true for men engineers too. Professional bodies provide a congenial atmosphere for networking and are potential contributors to career growth and advancement. Participation in the activities of such bodies also helps in keeping abreast with technological developments. Colleges need to make deliberate efforts to create awareness among students about the important role professional bodies can play in helping them in the advancement of their careers. Having student chapters of reputed bodies on the campus is one measure recommended in this respect.

Miscellaneous Suggestions

Awareness about opportunities at IITs: Enrolment of girls in engineering courses has remained particularly low in the IITs. The joint entrance examination (IEE) data shows that a small number of girls take up this examination. As a result, the number admitted to IITs has remained low. Institutions like IITs owe it to themselves to take special measures to attract more girls. Girls must get the benefit of an IIT education, which is a type by itself. The corrective measures in this context could include organization of awareness programmes on a continuing basis by IITs. Special mention in the information brochure of opportunities and on-campus facilities for girls at IITs would also help.

Campus interviews: Many of the participants of the study report that they did not attend a campus interview because their college did not have campus selections. This situation needs to be remedied. Women engineers residing in small towns and distant places are unable to reach venues of interviews. Once they get their degree and leave the college, they practically leave the profession. Such women could be really helped if there are campus interviews and they are given the opportunity to attend them. Colleges must make a deliberate effort to get as many employers as possible to come for campus interviews. A regulatory requirement may need to be imposed on colleges to have a certain minimum number of campus interviews and to make sure that girls are not denied an opportunity to appear. As a matter of requirement the institutions may be directed to submit an annual record of such activities to an appropriate office.

Interviews and examinations for jobs: Examination centres and interviews for government jobs are usually located in cities. The same is true for venues of tests and group discussions for jobs in big companies. Women candidates from far-off places are not able to reach these locations. Expenses involved in travel and stay proves to be a serious constraint. Parents are also reluctant to send a girl alone and want to accompany her. This adds to the expense. Thus a distant place of stay becomes a real hindrance in getting a job. Many girls remain without a job due to this reason. It is suggested that the number of centres for examinations and interviews be increased, at least in the case of government jobs.

Compulsory appremiceship for experience: Numerous respondents have expressed the view that the present curriculum and course contents are nowhere near real-life situations. They suggest that either a very strong industrial training programme should constitute a part of the curriculum, or the degree programme should be followed by a compulsory apprenticeship period similar to that in medical sciences to help them prepare for a job.

Experience has become a prerequisite for getting a job. This issue could be partially resolved through having the suggested apprenticeship period. It could help women engineers gain experience and exposure to real-life situations. This may or may not fetch them a job but will surely prepare them for one. Implementation of such a scheme will mean involvement of all categories of employing organizations through regulatory requirements that would require the organisation to take a specified minimum number for training.

Adequate representation for women: Certain regulatory approaches need to be adopted to ensure that an adequate number of women engineers are employed. A mandatory annual statement of employment of engineering staff with a specific mention of the number and percentage of women engineers employed could help. This is a passive approach that would make the existence of women engineers known to the employer.

An active regulatory control could consist in instituting a requirement that a certain number of engineering staff has to be women. This does not seem to be a desirable approach. However, many respondents have expressed the view that reservation at the college level should be followed by job reservation.

Institution of prizes and awards: It is important that women engineers are encouraged by society and helped to establish themselves as professionals. They need to be given opportunities to enhance their professional image through institution of prizes and awards for their contributions. This will contribute to creating awareness among employers, parents, teachers and the women themselves.

VI

Concluding Remarks

The results of the two studies presented would at first sight be a cause for cheer. Engineering has traditionally been looked upon as a profession only for men. Yet from a very low enrolment of one per cent or so in the 1970s, the enrolment of women for the country as a whole is now more than 15 per cent. From a situation where the annual out-turn was a few hundred, today the out-turn is around 10,000.

However, the increase in out-turn has created many problems. There is considerable unemployment and underemployment of women graduates. They have difficulty in being accepted as equals in a male-dominated profession and they have difficulty in rising to the top.

There are no easy solutions to these problems. A number of approaches have to be tried and many recommendations have been made in this regard. The recommendations are largely based on the suggestions of the respondents-the women graduates and their employers. Their implementation will help in alleviating the situation.

As far as the employers are concerned, their viewpoints are generally positive. Replies to the formal questions suggest a positive attitude towards hiring of women engineers. Women engineers are perceived as capable professionals with high potential. Such a response could be because of the general acceptance of 'women in engineering' as a ground reality. It could also be due to the anxiety of the executive respondents to be correct in responding to the questions. The opinions coming through the replies to certain other questions, however, indicate that many employers have some reservations about the concept of women participating in the engineering profession. This is to be expected. Any change in social values is a complex phenomenon and takes time. The studies show that changes are in the offing. It is now a matter of time.

Note

1. Women who had obtained their bachelor's degree in architecture over the same period were also included in the study.

References

AICTE. 2002. 'Background Document, National Consultation on the Future of Technical Education in India', New Delhi, p. 51.

UGC. 1999. *Research and Development Statistics,* New Delh: Department of Science and Technology, Ministry of Science and Technology, Government of India.

Parikh, P.P. and S.P. Sukhatme. 1992. 'Women Engineers in India', final report, Sponsored Project No DST/RD/05/5 1/88, Department of Science and Technology.

Parikh, P.P. and S.P. Sukhatme. 1994. 'Women Engineers in India-Present Scenario and Current Trends', *Journal of Scientific and Industrial Research:* 53:233-47.

Parikh, P.P. and S.P. Sukhatme.1997. 'Job Status, Nature of Work and Career Problems of Women Engineers in India'. Proc Seminar on Engineering Education for the 21st Century, Indian National Academy of Engineering, IIT Madras. pp. 41-67.

Parikh, P.P. and S.P. Sukhatme. 2002. 'Women in the Engineering Profession in India-The Millennium Scenario', final report, Sponsored Project No DST/NSTMIS/05/05/97, Department of Sdence and Technology.

Conducting the studies was a rewarding and revealing experience. The response from women engineers all over the country has been overwhelming. The authors are grateful to all of them. We are indebted to the Department of Science and Technology for sponsoring the studies. In particular, we would like to thank A.R. Rajeswari, joint adviser, DST, for Study I and Parveen Arora, PSO, DST for Study II. Our thanks are also due to our colleague, Indira Mahadevan, for her help in preparing the questionnaires in both projects. They are grateful to the project staff that helped us. Special mention needs to be made of the hard work put in by Ragamayi and Guljeet Kaur for Study I and by R. Bindu, S. Yughabala and Sheeba Menon for Study II. Finally, the authors acknowledge the extensive help received from IIT Bombay throughout the tenure of the projects. The paper was first published in the *Economic and Political Weekly*: 39:2:2004:193-201.It is included here with the prior permission of the authors and the Editor, *Economic and Political Weekly*. Address for email correspondence is: parikh@me.iitb.ac.in

CHAPTER - TWENTY FOUR

Barriers in Careers: Uphill Struggles for Women Scientists in India

Vineeta Bal

Women scientists form not only a very small proportion of women in India, but also a minor proportion of all Indian workingwomen. Despite education and class advantages, prevalent patriarchal notions affect the work and career of women scientists as much as of women from unorganized sectors, or indeed of other professionals such as doctors or lawyers, since a woman is looked at primarily in the family context-a daughter, a wife, a mother. However, perhaps unlike women who have to work hard only to make ends meet in their daily lives, women from the middle classes have begun to have aspirations to *career development*. Whatever little data are available in India today indicate that women who choose careers as scientists tend to come mainly from this class of society. It is therefore instructive to look at the situation of women scientists in the country from the perspective of *career development.*

Women entrants to natural sciences

Higher education in the natural sciences involves long hours of college because of theory and practical classes. Higher studies in humanities or social sciences, on the contrary, can involve fewer hours of mandatory college attendance every day. Despite this difference, in urban middle class India families have now begun expecting women not only to continue with higher education but also to pursue any interests they may have in the natural sciences. In this context, some studies from the West indicate that during their school days girl students make up their minds not to continue studying mathematics or other natural science subjects[1,2]. Various social reasons including discouragement by teachers have been cited for the decision to opt out of natural sciences despite being good at them. But there are hardly any surveys from India which have tried to look at the mentality of girl students regarding their interests and the decision making process for choice of specific areas of higher education. On the other hand, there is evidence of an absence of role models for women in scientific careers. Analysis of illustrations drawn in the latest high school text books of 'science and technology' show that men are portrayed as engineers, doctors, scientists and other professionals, whereas women's roles are only as housekeepers and nurturers-mothers and nurses[3]. Data available from 1981 onwards show that, of the total enrolment for undergraduate studies, women constituted about 28 per cent in 1981 and between 34-37 per cent from 1991 to 2000. Interestingly, at the post-graduate level, the enrolment proportions were no different–29 per cent in 1981 to 38 per cent in 2000[4]. There are no specific data available on the numbers of women obtaining PhD degrees in the natural sciences for recent years, but based on data for Ph Ds in general and trends for post-graduate enrolment for sciences in particular[4], it can be estimated that women may constitute about a third of the total national enrolment for the doctoral studies as well. These frequencies are somewhat lower than, say, in the United Kingdom. In the UK, women constituted 40 and 60 per cent of the graduates in chemistry and biology respectively in the year 2000[5]. At the doctoral levels, the UK proportions are 30 per cent and 48 per cent for the same year. However, even from the Indian data, it can still be expected that after spending some two decades of their lives in studying and in obtaining the highest degrees in the field of natural sciences, these women would be interested in using the knowledge productively, and that therefore women should show a substantial presence in the scientific profession. Here is an informal attempt to take a look at what the reality is.

Most of the data and information collected to make an argument here are based on the broad field of biological sciences, for two reasons. Firstly, as a working biologist in India, I am more familiar with the area of biological research. Secondly, many more women are found in the field of biological sciences than in physics, chemistry or mathematics the other major branches of natural sciences, providing a somewhat larger sample. These comments take into account women as scientists rather than college teachers and therefore, I am looking at information about the national laboratories and the central universities. Also, while the biotechnology and the pharmaceutical industries certainly form a part of the research arena in biological sciences, their research output is measured in terms of product development and is seen in the context of the marketplace, with different parameters being involved in career development in such situations.

What are the perceived goals in careers as academic research biologists?

In pursuing a career in academic research in the biological sciences, certain specific steps and goals are essential for career advancement. Obtaining a stable job is obviously a basic prerequisite for having a career. An appointment as a post-doctoral scientist may provide a 3-5 year working period, but a 'permanent' job is necessary for a stable career. The qualifications needed for getting a permanent job are different from those needed for a post-doctoral position. A proven record of achievements in the form of publications in highly reputed journals is one major criterion for getting even short-listed for biologist faculty positions in India today. In contrast, while a publication record is an advantage for obtaining a post-doctoral position, it is by no means mandatory.

The ability to do and to direct research depends on the ability to think of a research project, to obtain the facilities needed to carry out such a research endeavour and the wherewithal to execute the research programme. In some cases adequate institutional infrastructure makes the beginnings easy, but more commonly competition with peers begins at this stage itself for national and/or international funding. Once a research programme is in place and running, the next step is to seek peer approval in the form of publishing results in professional peer-reviewed journals (and/or, more rarely, filing patents). Actually, peer acceptance begins even earlier, at the level of sanctioning of funds to carry out research, although it does not end there. Peer opinion also influences the future course of the career positively or negatively in a variety of ways. For example, peer recommendation, formal or informal, is necessary for promotions in the job, for nominations to various reviewing bodies and committees making funding decisions, for being appointed on the editorial boards of professional journals, for getting elected to prestigious institutions and clubs such as the science academies or the Guha Research Conference, and for bagging awards. Many of these 'achievements' pave the way for climbing to further echelons such as vice-chancellorships of universities, directorships of institutions, for 'founding' new institutions and possibly even higher targets. How do women biologists in India fare in comparison with men in achieving these kinds of career targets?

How do women biologists fare vis-à-vis men biologists in getting an academic research position?

The baseline for comparison here is the data on science education mentioned earlier. Since there is no gender-based positive discrimination for employment, women would be expected to compete with men for post-doctoral appointments and further for the faculty appointments. Since women constitute a third of all doctoral degree holders over the past decade, the expectation would be that women would constitute about a third of all the junior faculty members in national laboratories and universities where academic biology research is carried out. What is the reality?

In order to get a feel for the numbers and the proportions of women scientists in permanent employment in biology research organizations, let us look at data from a few representative national laboratories and central universities. While selecting examples funded by various government departments, the emphasis here has been on selecting those biology research institutes with largest numbers of faculty members from among those supported by each funding agency. This has meant including some of the oldest institutions in the country, such as the National Institute of Nutrition [NIN] and ACTREC (known until recently as the Cancer Research Institute), as well as some new institutions, such as the National Centre for Cell Sciences [NCCS], Pune. This might help in looking at changes in hiring practices, if any, over a period of years. The numbers and proportions in Table 1 show that women form between 20-31 per cent of the total faculty (with the exception of ACTREC with 55 per cent women faculty). There is no correlation between the age of the Institute and the proportion of women employed in it.

Table 1
Proportions of senior and junior women faculty members in some national institutions funded by various government departments

*Name of the funding agency**	*Name of the Institute***	*Total number of faculty*	*Total*		*Senior faculty#*			*Junior faculty##*		
			Men [%]	*Women [%]*	*Total*	*Men [%]*	*Women*	*Total*	*Men [%]*	*Women [%]*
CSIR	CDRI	193	147 [76.2]	46 [23.8]	67	50	17 [25.3]	126	97	29 [23.0]
CSIR	CCMB	70	48 [68.6]	22 [31.4]	13	12	1 [7.7]	57	36	21 [36.8]
DAE	ACTREC	33	15 [45.5]	18 [54.5]	8	4	4 [50.0]	25	11	14 [56.0]
DBT	NII	38	29 [76.3]	9 [23.7]	22	18	4 [18.2]	16	11	5 [31.2]
DBT	NCCS	25	20 [80.0]	5 [20.0]	5	4	1 [20.0]	20	16	4 [20.0]
DST	Bose Institute	61	47 [77.0]	14 [23.0]	25	21	4 [16.0]	36	26	10 [27.8]
DST	Agharkar Institute$	39	27 [69.2]	12 [30.8]	—	—	—	—	—	—
ICMR	NIN	48	33 [68.8]	15 [31.2]	13	10	3 [23.1]	35	23	12 [34.3]
ICMR	NICED	33	26 [78.8]	7 [21.2]	13	11	2 [15.4]	20	15	5 [25.0]

* CSIR, Council for Scientific and Industrial Research, DAE, Department of Atomic Energy, DBT, Department of Biotechnology, DST, Department of Science and Technology, ICMR, Indian Council for Medical Research.

** CDRI, Central Drug Research Institute, Lucknow; CCMB, Centre for Cellular and Molecular Biology, Hyderabad; ACTREC, Advanced Centre for Treatment, Research and Education in Cancer, Navi Mumbai; NII, National Institute of Immunology, New Delhi; NCCS, National Centre for Cell Sciences, Pune; NIN, National Institute of Nutrition, Hyderabad; NICED, National Institute for Cholera and Enteric Diseases, Kolkata.

\# Faculty are counted as 'senior' if the employment is at E2 or higher levels as per CSIR rules, or Deputy director or above in ICMR rules, or equivalent.

\## Those not fitting in the 'senior' faculty category but listed as 'scientists' (excluding post-doctoral scientists) are included as 'junior' faculty.

$ Details of seniority could not be ascertained.

So it appears that women's representation as permanent faculty members is somewhat less than their presence at the point of obtaining doctoral degrees. What could be the reasons for this? People are about 22-23 years old at the time of obtaining a masters degree and at least 26-27 years of age by the time their PhD is completed. Most biology researchers who have been appointed as permanent faculty in the past 10-15 years in India have had a brief to prolonged [2 to 10 years] experience as post-doctoral scientists in the West, most commonly in the United States. Thus individuals in their thirties join as junior faculty members in biological sciences in national institutions and central universities in India. Most men and women are married by the time they are in their thirties. Decisions about child bearing and child rearing inevitably affect women far more severely than men in conventional households with patriarchal cultures. It is quite plausible that women's ambitions to pursue careers take a backseat at this point, with women taking short or long breaks at this time of their lives for the 'family's needs'. In subsequent years this would translate into having poorer professional achievements than men of the same age and basic qualification. So, when it comes to finding a permanent job after finishing post-doctoral training, fewer women scientists may try, and fewer may be able to compete successfully with men for the same post.

The overall percentage of women faculty in the national laboratories is less than might be expected (20-31 per cent excluding ACTREC). The next point was to look at the relative proportions of women at senior and junior positions within a set-up. The criteria used for counting faculty members as 'senior' are listed in the footnote of Table 1. Except in the case of ACTREC, the proportion of senior women faculty members is uniformly less than 30 per cent, ranging from 7.7 to 25.3. However, women constitute a larger proportion at the junior faculty level in three out of eight national laboratories -34, 37 and 56 per cent respectively. These data may reflect some interesting possibilities. Firstly, on a positive note, many more of those young qualified women mentioned in the preceding section may actually be seeking jobs and getting them without any gender based discrimination, thus resulting in their proportionate representation. Secondly, women who were employed as junior faculty may not be getting promoted at the same speed as their men colleagues may be. Thus, higher numbers of women at junior level may result from a combination of such factors.

Representative data for some central universities are shown in Table 2. Only biology-related departments from these universities are taken into account. The proportions of women faculty range from 10-22 per cent here. Similar to the picture seen in national laboratories, there are proportionately more women at the junior level than at the senior level. In Delhi University, women's representation is poorest [at 10 per cent] among all the national laboratories and university departments included for analysis here and there are no women professors at all. In contrast, in JNU 20 per cent of the professors are women. However, 18 to 33 per cent of junior faculty are women in these universities. The same arguments as made for their numerically larger presence at the junior level in the national laboratories may be applicable here.

Together, these data suggest that fewer women seem to be getting permanent jobs even at the lowest rung than the proportions of potential educationally qualified candidates would lead one to expect. It is possible that their 'experience' and 'achievements' may not be commensurate with their age due to layoff years, but there appears to be no proposal to consider their 'academic age' rather than actual age for employment.

Productivity of women biologists

The next question is how well women scientists compare with men in terms of their scientific output. As mentioned earlier, researchers in biology normally publish their work in professional peer-reviewed journals. If peers approve of the work done, the standing of the scientist goes up in the community. In biological sciences, most work is done as a team and the convention is that the senior investigator/s as the originator/s and developer/s of the idea will be the 'corresponding' author/s of

Table 2
Proportions of senior and junior women faculty members in some central universities

University	*Departments and division included**	*Total number of faculty*	*Total*		*Professors*			*Others*		
			Men [%]	*Women [%]*	*Total*	*Men*	*Women [%]*		*Men Women [%]*	*Total*
Indian Institute of Science#	Division of Biology	63	51 [81.0]	12 [19.0]	31	26	5 [16.1]	32	25	7 [21.8]
Jawaharlal Nehru University [JNU]	SLS, SES, CBT	50	39 [78.0]	11 [22.0]	30	24	6 [20.0]	20	15	5 [25.0]
Delhi University [DU]	Bt, Zo, Bc, Gn, PMB, Micro, Env	63	57 [90.5]	6 [9.5]	31	31	0 [0.0]	32	26	6 [18.8]
University of Hyderabad	Bc, PlSc, AnSc	29	24 [82.8]	5 [17.2]	17	16	1 [5.9]	12	8	4 [33.3]

* SLS, School of Life Sciences; SES, School of Environmental Sciences; CBT, Centre for Biotechnology; Bt, Botany; Zo, Zoology; Bc, Biochemistry; Gn, Genetics; PMB, Plant Molecular Biology; Micro, Microbiology; Env, Environmental Sciences; PlSc, Plant Sciences; AnSc, Animal Sciences.

A deemed university.

the paper, while the person/s contributing the actual hands-on experimentation is/ are normally the first author/s. Thus, the interest here would be to look at women biologists as corresponding authors.

The second relevant issue is which publications should be used for estimating the standing of the scientists in their peer community. In the field of biological sciences, one way to estimate the extent of peer approval is by looking at where a scientist is able to publish her/his papers. Since publishing in prestigious journals is competitive, papers published in such journals become a measure of peer approval. For this, journal Impact Factor [IF] is used as a criterion and it estimates the reputation of the journal based on a variety of parameters. Papers published in journals with higher IF by and large indicate more credit and peer approval than papers published in journals with low IF. IFs for journals are calculated and published for every year by the Institute for Scientific Information. Thus, for the year 2002, the journal with maximum IF in the field of biological sciences was Nature Genetics [IF 29.6]. IF values for many journals published from India are also available, and the topmost journal in biological sciences in this category is the Indian Journal of Biochemistry and Biophysics [IF 0.294]. The list of journals considered for the present analysis excludes purely review journals such as Annual Review of Immunology, and it excludes journals primarily publishing data from clinical work and case reports such as the New England Journal of Medicine. The final criterion of exclusion is to omit any journal with an IF of less than 5 [with 2002 as the reference year]. This means that publications in only the 'top' 5 per cent or so of the total journals published worldwide are being considered. Use of these criteria means that only original experimental biological research work [as against reviews or case reports] published by Indian corresponding authors in journals considered 'respectable' by their global peers is included.

The freely accessible database PubMed was used. In all, 56 journals were included in the search, out of which Indian authors had published papers in only 41 journals. Work of authors of Indian origin but not working in India was not included. In the search, papers published between January 1994 and April 2004 were analyzed. There were two reasons for restricting the analysis to the past ten years. Firstly, publication records over the last ten years would provide the means to judge most recent performances of those scientists who are highly productive today, excluding performances of the older generation of biologists who, however good they were in their more active days should not be considered active researchers if they have not published well in recent years. The second consideration was practical, - the ease of identification of gender of authors. Since many publications do not write complete names of the authors but only the initials and a family name, it was necessary to identify the person before including her or him as the corresponding author. This could be done only for currently working and easily identifiable biologists with certainty.

Table 3 lists the journals considered and the summary of productivity of Indian biologists. Over the period examined, Indian biologists have published a total of 669 papers in journals with IF >5. Only 14.5 per cent of these papers can be credited to women biologists, indicating that the high-quality productivity of women scientists is not commensurate with their proportion of representation in employment. Why is this so?

Table 3
Research output of high quality from Indian women scientists over the past decade

Publications in journals* with IF > 5 from India between Jan-1994 to Apr-2004	Publications by men scientists	Publications by women scientists	
669	572	97	Total numbers
100%	85.5%	14.5%	Proportions

* The following journals were considered for the analysis in the decreasing order of IF : (Nature Genetics#), Cell, Nature, Nature Medicine, Science, (Genes and Development), Immunity, Nature Immunology, (Behavioral and Brain Sciences), (Molecular Cell), (Nature Neuroscience), Journal of Experimental Medicine, (Nature Cell Biology), (Journal of the National Cancer Institute), Neuron, Journal of Clinical Investigation, Journal of Cell Biology, EMBO Journal, (Nature Biotechnology), (Plant Cell), Proceedings of National Academy of Sciences USA, American Journal of Human Genetics, (Nature Structural Biology), Molecular and Cellular Biology, Human Molecular Genetics, Blood, (Antiviral Therapy), (Circulation Research), FASEB Journal, Development, Genome Research, Cancer Research, Journal of Neurosciences, Cell Death and Differentiation, Molecular Biology of the Cell, Current Biology, Journal of Biological Chemistry, American Journal of Pathology, Journal of Immunology, Oncogene, (Journal of Cognitive Neurosciences), (Molecular Endocrinology), Molecular Microbiology, Nucleic Acids Research, Journal of Cell Sciences, Chemistry and Biology, Gene Therapy, Journal of Molecular Biology, Plant Journal, Natural Products Reports, Journal of Virology, Developmental Biology, (Journal of Neuropathology and Experimental Neurology), Journal of Allergy and Clinical Immunology, Molecular Pharmacology, Plant Physiology.

Journals in the bracket are the ones in which no papers were published from India in the period mentioned.

Web address for PubMed: http://www.ncbi.nlm.nih.gov/entrez/query.fcgi?db=PubMed]

One possibility is that the women scientists that are being hired are not as 'good', in terms of ability to formulate and execute research programmes, than their male counterparts. It would be interesting to examine the records of men and women recently hired as faculty in these institutions to see if this was so. However, if this were to be the case, it would be expected that such hiring would be driven by a 'positive discrimination' in favour of women scientists. This would have led to a major increase in their proportions among junior faculty, which does not appear to be the case.

Other factors could be related to woman-specific environmental issues. High-quality output can be hampered by infrastructure facility-related factors such as small lab spaces, lack of necessary equipment and lack of supporting human-power. While Indian data are not available, in case studies of women from the Massachusetts Institute of Technology published many years ago it was documented that women of comparable seniority and productivity as their men colleagues were provided with poorer facilities[6]. There is also the issue of getting extramural funding for research activities. Whether women and men of comparable records and/or seniority are likely to get comparable funding will depend on many factors. For example, whether they submit comparable numbers of grants for funding to begin with, whether the success rate of these grants is different and if gender plays any role in this. These, too, would be issues worth exploring in the Indian context. In an elegant study on the role of peer review in the advancement of the career of post-doctoral scientists in Sweden, Wenneras and Wold argue that 'peer reviewers cannot judge scientific merit independent of gender' [7]. Anecdotally, conversations with women biologist colleagues certainly do give the frequent impression that they tend to underestimate their abilities, which may be related to their social upbringing and context. Such a diffidence, a factor that can contribute to lesser productivity, can manifest itself in many ways-not applying for extramural funding as frequently, asking for less funding than a male colleague would ask for the same work, not sending out research work in journals with higher IF, and not arguing the case for revisions in case of apparently critical reviews from the referees on submitted manuscripts.

Women as members of prestigious academic groups

Even for those women who may be as productive as their male colleagues, there are likely to be hurdles at another level of seeking peer approval from immediate colleagues. Achievements have to be publicized for peers, and the ability [or not] to do so can affect career prospects. This is because there are other areas in the career of a scientist where her/his colleagues have a very significant impact on her/his progress and achievements. Becoming a fellow of national science academies in India is considered a stepping-stone to further achievements. These academies are located in Delhi, Bangalore, Allahabad and becoming a fellow of each of them is a highly desired goal in this context. The procedure of becoming a fellow involves first getting nominated and then elected. Though academic merit is supposed to be an important factor making a person eligible for nomination as a fellow of the society, many unwritten considerations operate and knowing the members of the decision making bodies personally is one such factor. When personal connections matter for achieving targets, women scientists can easily lose out, since personal interactions of women scientists with male colleagues would be deeply constrained by standard patriarchal cultural barriers of so-called morality. Thus, it would not be surprising to find that women are awarded academy memberships far less frequently. Is this indeed the case?

Membership of any of these academies is for life. Thus, once elected, one remains a fellow until one dies. As a result, there are many fellows of the academies who are retired and not working today. In order to get a true picture of active members of the academies, let us look at fellows who were elected in one representative national science academy over the past decade. This election should, in principle, correlate with the quality and the quantity of research output of scientists, since research performance is supposed to be the main criterion for these academy fellowships. Table 4 shows numbers from the membership list of the Indian Academy of Sciences, Bangalore, a representative national science academy. In all disciplines of natural sciences, medicine and engineering taken together, a very small share has come women's way in the past ten years. The situation in biological sciences-which include plant, animal and general biology here-is somewhat better for women. While they are still substantially underrepresented in comparison with their presence in the faculty, their under representation with regard to the performance index as measured by publications is less glaring.

Table 4
Under-representation of women as fellows of national science academies*

Members appointed between 1994-2004	*Male members*	*Female members*	*% male members*	*% female members*
Members in all the disciplines	236	17	93.3%	6.7%
Members in plant, animal and general biology section	57	8	87.7%	12.3%

* Data are collected from the website of Indian Academy of Sciences, Bangalore. http://www.ias.ac.in/php/fell_all.php3?alpha=A.

Table 5
Presence of women scientists in research advisory committees of various research institutions in the country

Agency	*Institution*	*Male members*	*Female members*	*% male members*	*% female members*
DBT	DBT	23	2	92%	8%
DBT	NII	18	1	95%	5%
CSIR	CDRI	11	1	92%	8%
CSIR	CCMB	10	0	100%	0%
ICMR	NIN	20	3	87%	13%
ICMR	NICED	15	4	79%	21%

Another indicator of the rising status of a scientist in the community is getting nominated on government-constituted advisory bodies. This may mean being a part of the committees that make decisions about accepting or rejecting projects for the extramural funding from CSIR, DAE, DBT, DST or ICMR. It can also mean being a member of the research advisory board, scientific advisory committee or research council for various national institutions. There are no defined criteria for achieving such a status. If influential peers consider somebody 'good' s/he gets nominated on a committee. How frequently do women biologists seem to possess this nebulous desirable attribute? Table 5 shows the proportion of women members of advisory bodies of five institutions out of the nine listed in Table 1. Women's representation ranges over 0-21 per cent, and for many other institutions for which data are not shown, the percentages fall in the same range. In addition, DBT as a funding agency has its own advisory board, where there are only 2 women in a group of 25 [8 per cent]. Thus, women's representation appears to be poorer in committee membership, where personal rapport with peers and their recommendations are useful for nomination.

Women are worse off as prizewinners

A further laurel for anyone who claims to be an achiever in biological sciences is bagging prestigious prizes. Only two prizes are considered here which are awarded to mid-career biologists, i.e. those who have not crossed 45 years of age, the Bhatnagar awards and the National Bioscience awards. The age-limit means only actively working scientists will get the prizes for their ongoing performance. Significant contributions to science are measured in terms of research output while working in a laboratory based in India. This way, scientists of Indian origin working primarily outside India are not entitled to compete for the prize. Young faculty rather than full professors and senior scientists as listed in Tables 1 and 2 will thus be eligible in principle for these prizes. The Bhatnagar awards were instituted by CSIR in 1957 and by 2004, there are a total of 387 winners in subjects as varied as biology, chemistry, earth sciences, engineering, mathematics, medicine and physics. The National Bioscience awards were instituted by DBT in 1999, and by 2003 a total of 24 scientists have received these awards. The gender distribution of the recipients of these awards is shown in Table 6. In the entire history of the Bhatnagar awards, very few women have been considered worthy of the award in any field of science, given the sorry figure of 2 per cent. In the areas of biology, the figure creeps up to 3 per cent. Even more striking are the data over the past ten years. There is only one woman recipient of the Bhatnagar award in medicine over the past ten years and none in biology.

Table 6
Women biologists do not receive prestigious awards!

Award [subject]	*Years under consideration*	*Total no. of prizes*	*For men*	*% men*	*For women*	*% women*
Bhatnagar [all subjects]	1958-2004	387	379	97.93%	8	2.07%
Bhatnagar [all subjects]	1994-2004	107	106	99.06%	1	0.94%
Bhatnagar [biology alone]	1958-2004	68	66	97.06%	2	2.94%
Bhatnagar [biology alone]	1994-2004	19	19	100%	0	0%
National Bioscience	1999-2003	24	22	91.67%	2	8.33%

The data provide basis for some speculation. It appears that few women were working as research biologists in India in the early post-independence period and that their numbers have increased only very slowly over the years. If there were proportionately fewer women present in the field it is only to be expected that their representation in the award-winners' list would be low. This may also be reflected as a cumulative phenomenon when the list of all Bhatnagar prizewinners is viewed as is done here. However, the proportion of women scientists has gone up in all fields in natural sciences for which these prizes are awarded, and yet the percentage of women prize-winners is, in fact, worse in the last decade than earlier years. This is true whether all fields of natural sciences are taken together or only the narrower areas of life sciences are looked at. The percentage of women scientists working in biology is the second highest, second only to the medical sciences. Based on the data mentioned above, there are at least 6 per cent of women in senior faculty position, and another 14-15 per cent at more junior levels in biology in India today. A reasonable guess would be that these 6 per cent of the women are mostly in the 45+ age group and obviously none of them were considered worthy of Bhatnagar awards in the past decade [in fact, the institutions to which the two women who have received Bhatnagar awards in biology belong are not included in the present analysis]. The record of the National Bioscience award looks somewhat less gender-biased, but the awards have only a five-year history so far and hence it may be premature to talk about trends.

What do these analyses indicate? Clearly, despite increases in the number of women scientists in biology, *gender-based disadvantages continue to be the order of the day, even in academic performance-based competition. In this connection, the establishment of gender-unbiased, transparent criteria for approval of project proposals, selection of candidates for job appointments, and nomination to the decision-making positions might go some way towards reducing the burden of the problem.*

This is made even more pressing an issue by the fact that academic research in the basic natural sciences, while considered respectable, is not thought of as a high-paying profession. This is likely to result in fewer and fewer young men entering the field, preferring to become IT or management professionals instead. On the other hand, since women's incomes are still seen as 'second' incomes in the family, women are likely to become more and more prominent in academic scientific research, and it may be beneficial to start treating women as professional colleagues with somewhat less of gender biases than appear to be currently operating.

Is the situation of women biologists different from other professional women?

Are there any unique circumstances in this context in the workplace situation of women biologists? Being experimentalists, biologists work as part of a team in their professional careers. They may be leaders, or junior or not-so-junior partners in the team. For optimal work output it is necessary for experimentalists to form a team with overlapping interests and individual specialised skills. Both for getting adequate funding to carry out the research and publishing in reputed journals, it is necessary that the teamwork be optimal. Cultural upbringing often makes it difficult for a man to work under a woman or take orders from a woman, causing problems. Such a situation for women biologists may thus be different from, say, that of theoretical physicists or mathematicians who can work as individuals and achieve professional stature. Even women science teachers or doctors may have to depend less on their colleagues in this sense for survival in their fields.

A factor common to many professions affecting women adversely is long working hours. While keeping strictly to standard working hours is possible in some kinds of jobs, academic research in biology needs longer hours beyond 9 to 5 if success is to be achieved. With family responsibilities being culturally their burden, it becomes very difficult for women faculty to spend such long hours at work. In fact, this issue affects the ability of women both to find and keep faculty positions. Women who complete their Ph D in their late twenties are usually likely to be under pressure to get married during the course of their doctoral work, or immediately after. They also end up taking career breaks of a few months to a few years for childbearing and child rearing. Taking time off always affects careers adversely, but even more so where the work needs a lot of infrastructure and teamwork, as for biologists. If a working scientist loses touch completely for a couple of years, coming back becomes that much more difficult. Employment rules frequently tend to have upper age limits for positions. Many institutions have a convention of not offering jobs to husbands and wives together, and inevitably, women suffer more from these practices than men do. Gaps in careers can haunt women for the rest of their professional lives even if they manage to make a comeback into their careers.

Thus, in a patriarchal culture, even those women who try to break weak gender barriers in order to provide better living conditions for their families while pursuing their interest in the field are faced with many career difficulties. Many of them lose out in the pursuit of their profession in the early phases. Even for those who cross this hurdle successfully, the profession can make them invisible, - not rising far enough to step into leadership roles, and not getting recognition. Rumbler strips on the road function as more efficient controllers of speed than a single speed breaker bump, a situation depressingly familiar to women biologists.

Notes and References

1. AWSEM (Advocates for women in science, engineering and mathematics). In their nature: compelling reasons to engage girls in science. Published in association with Portland State University and Oregon Health and Science University, USA. Web address: www.saturdayacademy.pdx.edu/awsem/Articles/ AWSEM_In_Their_ Nature.pdf-
2. AAUW (American Association of University Women Educational Foundation). How schools shortchange girls: An executive summary of the study. 1992. Web address: www.aauw.org/research/girls_education/hssg.cfm
3. Mehrotra, Swati and Chunawala Sugra. 2004. State of the art: gender illustrations in the new science and technology textbooks. Paper presented at a meeting '*Women in Science: is the glass ceiling disappearing*' at NISTADS, New Delhi.
4. Manpower profile: *India Yearbook 2000 and 2001*. New Delhi: Institute of Applied Manpower Research.
5. Greenfield Susan, Peters Jan, Lane Nancy, Rees Teresa and Samuel Gills. 2002. *Set fair: a report on women in science, engineering, and technology*: 84, Web address: www.set4women.gov.uk/set4women/ research/greenfield-report.pdf -

6. Members of the First and Second Committees on Women Faculty in the School of Science, Massachusetts Institute of Technology, USA. A Study on the Status of Women Faculty in Science at MIT. *The MIT Faculty Newsletter*: 11:4, March 1999. Web address: web.mit.edu/fnl/women/women.html

7. Wenneras, Christine and Wold Agnes. 1997. Nepotism and Sexism in peer-review. *Nature*: 387: 341-343.

The paper was first published in the *Economic and Political Weekly*: 39:32: 2004: 3647-3653. It is included here with the prior permission of author and the Editor, *Economic and Political Weekly*. Address for email correspondence: vineetabal@yahoo.com; vineeta@nii.eres.in

CHAPTER - TWENTY FIVE

Women in Call Centres

Preeti Singh and Anu Pandey

The telecommunications industry has created numerous opportunities of employment in India. One such source of employment has been the emergence of 'call centres', which today form a vital link between a company and its customers. The growth of call centres and the number of people employed there has been phenomenal and has been estimated at an annual rate of 15-20 per cent. This growth will continue as corporate organizations all over the world recognize the strategic value of call centres in an e-commerce world. A call centre acts as a focal point for web-based customer transactions, e-mail management and traditional phone calls.

In developing countries, such new business is considered a good source of employment and looked at only in terms of how well paid it is. India has been selected as a base for call centres because it lies in a time zone that makes it the preferred area for the US, UK, south-east Asia and Australia. Low salaries for services rendered have made call centres in India extremely cost-effective. The advantage of the time factor has provided employment but is also the source of most of women's family problems. It is expected that such employment would have an effect on her physical and mental health as well. This study deals with the problems occurring due to the unusual hours of work. It looks into the changes in the urban outlook, where it was once taboo for girls to travel alone out of the house after dark, and where now they are encouraged to work and do night shifts at call centres. In the present transitional developmental state of the economy, such changes are expected to have a profound influence upon different dimensions of the family system.

Women working in shifts at odd hours are a relatively new phenomenon in the socio-economic scenario in India.[1] The psychological and sociological barriers for working people needs to be well understood. In addition, such work has an impact on the safety, physical and mental health of employees as the time required for sleep and rest is converted into the work hours. Thus, when energy levels are low, people are working and when the body system has high energy they are required to sleep. This adjustment process is not acceptable and the physical balance and well being of workers is thrown out of gear.

Call centres are concerned with e-business, which is expected to grow further and bring in more employment opportunities. Do graduates continue to work in call centres as a career option, or do they use it to gain a foothold in the job arena? What would be the future benefits? Will the monetary rewards compensate for the adjustment in the socialization process of women working at odd hours in this non-traditional industry? These are some queries that need to be answered. This paper is an attempt to explore the value of women at work and home. It analyses their perceptions and constraints and how they balance their family life with their work.

Study Background

The Eighth Five-Year Plan (1992-1997) highlighted the biases regarding the value of women's work, changes in the attitudes of the society, and perceptions in regard to the role of women that are mentioned as essential for empowennent.[2] The Tenth Plan's approach towards the empowerment of women is very distinct from that of the earlier plans, as it now stands as a strong platform for action with definite goals, targets and a time frame. It ensures provision of training, employment and income generation activities with both forward and backward linkages to make women economically independent and self-reliant.

As per the 2001 Census, as an independent target group women account for 495.74 million, or 48.3 per cent of the country's total population. Empowering women as a process demands a life cycle approach. Therefore, every stage of their life counts as a priority in the planning process.[3]

This study has in a small measure conducted an analysis of women from middle class families in their new area of employment. Indian women have taken up professional roles to create an identity for themselves or out of economic necessity. Women have risen above socio-cultural traditions to exploit their potential of employment. Some of the factors responsible for this change are better education and changing socio-cultural values. It has been observed that women in India were accepted in traditional profiles like teachers, nurses, secretaries or clerks. Against this background, it would be useful to look at the new image of women in India- 'breaking barriers of the stereotype' and working in non-traditional employment sectors.

The study is mainly at an exploratory level to determine the quantum and quality of women employed in call centres in India. It throws light on issues such as family background, education, job level, motivation and commitment, attitudes, decision-making power and health.

This study is an empirical one. A questionnaire was circulated at random to women working in call centres in Delhi, Gurgaon and Noida. Personal interviews of a large number of respondents were also conducted. The study is based on primary data covering 100 female employees, to provide an insight into their work and home life. Since call centres are relatively new and employ young graduates, it is useful to enquire into the problems of employees aged 18-24, 24-35 and 35-45 years.

We wanted to obtain information from both married and unmarried women at different levels of managerial hierarchy. We were able to get a fairly representative sample, from women working in 12 call centres. As information with the call centres is very personal and confidential, these centres were reluctant to allow their executives to give out any information without prior permission. The names of the companies giving information and those of the respondents have been kept confidential. Our interviews showed that there are a large number of issues with regard to women working in call centres that need to be addressed. The limitation of our research is that it is exploratory in nature and covers only 100 women selected randomly. Further research could be undertaken to study women working at different levels with a good sample selection at every level and also comparisons with men working in call centres.

The study findings are divided into five sections. The first section describes the work environment of a call centre. Section II depicts the career graph of the employees, where we discuss issues pertaining to the job requirements. The third section provides the family background of employees. Section IV discusses the issue of balancing work with family life. Section V presents the main conclusions.

I

Work Environment in a Call Centre

A call centre has a very pleasant working environment. It is open round the clock as calls keep coming from different parts of the world. Most call centres offer e-customer related marketing services. There are two types of calls-'inbound calling' and 'outbound calling'. Inbound calling is for customer support, where the customer calls in for queries. Outbound calling is related to telesales, where the operators themselves contact the clients. There are two kinds of call centres operating in India, namely, 'process based' and 'client based'. Process-based call centres are those that service the clients of their own parent company. They are at lesser risk of closing down as clients are assured on a regular basis. Client-based call centres, on the other hand, have to look for their own clients. As they are dependent on business conditions, companies in this category are at higher risk. There are two types of job requirements in a call centre: operational and technical. The employees in the operational area cater to the needs of the clients and those in the technical area assist and support the people working in the operational area.

A call centre may be engaged in many different processes in various shifts. The shift system coincides with the timings of the country for whose processes they are working. The employees have to answer a phone call within a set number of rings. Failure to do so will result in an error. The team leaders and managers monitor the calls of the employees and if there are errors, marks are deducted from the employee's performance. If the calls are taken perfectly according to schedule, they get incentives. Generally, the clients would be from the US, Europe and Australia. To make them feel comfortable the employees are given special training on pronunciation and accent. Some call centres also change the name of the employee. Thus Ramesh becomes Robert, Jaspreet becomes Janet and Babita becomes Betty.

Employees in the 'call centres' work on a five-day schedule. This is done to ensure rest and relaxation to help the normal functioning of the human body after continuously working in night shifts. In addition to the weekly off every employee gets 2-3 days' of casual leave per month. This casual leave can be carried forward up to six months. This means that an employee cannot stretch her leave to more than 18 days at a time. If the casual leave is not availed in a month, extra points are added to the employee's performance and incentives are given. In addition, if an employee works on a public holiday positive points are added to her performance and incentives are given. If the performance of an employee is rated as A++ in a month he/she can earn up to Rs. 3,000 extra. The call centres follow a carrot-and-stick approach to motivate their employees. They penalize employees for taking leave without prior permission. The permission has to be taken in advance, via email, before the duty shift begins.

Call centres are increasingly interested in keeping their employees fit, relaxed and less stressed, by providing gyms and yoga classes. The company canteen provides tea, coffee, refreshments and meals. Recreational facilities such as 'carrom boards' and table tennis are available in large call centres that have many employees. The environment is a positive aspect of the job in a call centre, a view that was supported by the employees. One of the questions in our questionnaires was: 'What do you like about your job?' Seventy-five per cent of the respondents answered 'Good Environment'. With this background of the working environment of a call centre, we now discuss aspects of our respondents' at work.

II

Women and Work

This section looks at the career graph of women, their qualifications, age, marital status, position in the organization, the positive and negative aspects of the organization, risks associated with working in call centres, and the effect on health of the respondents.

Age of respondents: In our study of 100 women, our findings showed that the women were generally in the age group of 18-25 years. This industry is relatively new and it has encouraged people to join at a young age. As Table 1 shows, there were 14 women below the age of 20, and 67 respondents were in the 20-25 groups. Three women were in the age group 40-45 and one was above 45. Could this also have some relevance to the qualifications and attrition rate? Our inquiries with the call centres showed that they did not require any major degrees for the jobs. A graduate with good communication skills was acceptable. Undergraduates and housewives were also attracted to such jobs. Table I also shows that the number of women in the 30-40 age group do not take up these jobs because women's careers do not fit into the same framework as men. A wife's career is considered secondary to that of her husband. If someone must stay with a sick child or if one person must relocate due to job demands the husband's career nearly always takes precedence and the wife must accommodate her schedule and employment. These expectations tend to result in interruptions in the career of women who may take years away from employment to care for children or to support a husband's career before rejoining the workforce.[4] Since call centre jobs have night duties and long hours of work, few women in the reproductive age are employed here.

Table 1
Age Group of Women Working In Call Centres

Age	*Number*
Below 20	14
21-25	67
26-30	15
31-35	NIL
36-40	NIL
41-45	03
Above 45	01
Total	100

Table 2
Marital Status of Women Employees

Status	*Number*
Married	08
Unmarried	92
Total	100

Marital status: Table 1 showed that out of 100 respondents, 86 fall in the age group of 18-30 years. Table 2 shows that 92 per cent of the respondents are unmarried. This clearly shows that most workingwomen prefer to remain unmarried for a longer time as they want to be economically independent before marriage. The tables show that women in the age group of 30-40 are not found in call centres, indicating that married women with small children find it inconvenient to pursue a career in such places. Table 2 shows that four respondents who were above 40 years of age, and were housewives, decided to take up employment in a call centre because it did not interfere any more with household duties. We found one example where due to the financial needs of family the woman had to continue with her job even though she found it very inconvenient because of odd and long working hours. In India, married working women find it difficult to continue with their careers because they attach primacy to their domestic roles, except those workingwomen who come from financially weaker families.[5]

Level of education: Table 3 shows that 22 respondents were educated only up to the school level. Also a number of graduates and postgraduates were working in the call centres as process associates/customer care executives at the lowest level.

Table 3
Level of Education of Respondents

Educational Level	*Number*
School Pass	22
Bachelor's degree	60
Master's degree	18
Total	100

Job level: Table 4 shows that there are 89 women in lower level management, consisting of senior and junior customer care executives/process associates. Only 11 women work in the upper level management as team leaders/assistant managers and managers. This shows that there is no discrimination in male or female jobs at the lower levels. Female executives say that being a woman is their major career obstacle because they have multiple roles to play. Women occupy mid-level positions and men tend to move into higher positions.[6]

Table 4
Job Level of Respondents

Job Level	*Number*
Customer care Executive	79
Senior Executive	10
Team Leader	08
Assistant Manager	01
Manager	02
Total	100

This inhibited rise of women in the corporate ladder in call centres is largely due to the fact that they move out of the employment structure due to the demands of marriage, children and household responsibilities. There are a large number of process associates, but as the level goes up fewer women get promotions.

Salary: Table 5 shows that 73 respondents have a salary of less than Rs. 10,000 per month, 23 earn Rs. 10,000-20,000 per month. Only four have a monthly salary above Rs. 20,000. This clearly shows that women are represented more in the lower paid jobs. There is apparently no discrimination in jobs at the entry level. It appears that it is a self-imposed decision of women not to continue with their jobs due to their dualistic role of work at home and at the workplace. Moreover this industry employs both people in the morning and evening shifts, which acts as a barrier for women to continue in employment.[7]

Table 5
Salary Earned by Respondents

Salary (Rs.)	*Number*
Below 10,000	73
10,000-15,000	16
15,000-20,000	07
Above 20,000	04
Total	100

Positive and Negative Aspects of Call Centres

We now turn to the positive and negative aspects of jobs in call centres. The positive aspect may be related to the number of years of experience, age and qualifications of the respondent with that of her salary. There appears to be no other area of employment in India that gives its employees an attractive pay package at such a young age and with minimum qualifications.

There are also some negative aspects about this job, which includes risks such as the difficulty of travelling at night, health hazards and social stigma. But the major problem is the health hazard from doing night duty. Some respondents felt they were like security guards who stayed awake all night to attend to their duties and slept the whole day through, and in doing so they suffer from problems like sleep disorder and indigestion. In order to keep awake against the body clock, they start smoking and drink innumerable cups of tea and coffee. This gets them addicted to tea, coffee and cigarettes, which subsequently becomes the cause of their bad health.

Table 6 shows the types of health problems that employee suffers, including backache, spondylitis, eyestrain, headache and pressure because of the headsets and constant calls.

Table 6
Health Hazards

Problems	*Number*
Backache	43
Earache	12
Leg cramps	11
Spondylitis	31
Sleep Disorder	05
Indigestion	50
Eye strain and headache	40

Our study had 43 responses from people with backaches, 40 with eyestrain and headache, and 50 with indigestion. The respondents also had earache and leg cramps and many of them complained of weight gain. Twenty-five respondents had either mild or no complaints.

III

Family Status

Table 7 shows that out of the 100 respondents 87 women were from nuclear families and only 13 were from joint families. This tallies with our assertion that in the changing socio-economic scenario a large number of families have started accepting the idea of women working in non-traditional spheres like call centres. In the nuclear family system many of our respondents were young girls of the 18-25 age group. Their families did not consider it objectionable to allow women into such professions. However, in lower income families, such jobs were actually required for sustenance and families were very supportive of girls in such jobs even if it meant doing night duties.

Table 7
Family Status of the Respondents

Joint Family	13
Nuclear Family	87
Total	100

Family background: Table 8 shows that 65 respondents come from a service background, which was expected in the changing economic scenario in India. There are also 30 respondents from business families. This was unexpected because business families in India are more conservative and generally don't allow girls to work, especially where night duties are involved.

Table 8
Family Background of Respondents

Background	*Number*
Business	30
Service	65
Professional	05
Total	100

Family income: Our findings show that 47 respondents were in the income group Rs. 20,000-50,000 per month. This was expected because in this sample group people require to upgrade their standard of living and the contribution of the female was considered important for stablizing the family finances. These respondents said that family requirements brought them into this job. Twenty respondents had a family income of below Rs. 20,000 per month. Such families were totally dependent on the respondent's income from the call centre. There were 17 women whose family income was more than Rs. 1,00,000 per month.

These women were working in call centres as a pastime. These aspects of family life of the respondents show that there has been some acceptability of women working in non-traditional areas.

IV

Balancing Work and Family Life

We found from our study that 90 per cent of the respondents did not balance work and family life. The respondents had no social life or interaction with people in the family. This job restricted their social life. Most unmarried respondents left major household chores to their parents. Their main hobby was to sleep for as long as they were at home because the fatigue level was very high with night duties. Parents took care of all the domestic work giving time for rest and relaxation to their working daughters. Among married women, some were stressed because husbands did not alter their domestic roles.[8]

Other married women who shared the provider's role negotiated for a greater share in family power and authority. Such women were able to alter attitudes of their families and the men did an equal amount of work at home to allow them to continue working in call centres. This is shown in Table 9 through the decision-making powers of employed women, both married and unmarried.

Table 9
Respondents' Family Income

Below 20,000	20
20,000-50,000	47
50,000-80,000	13
80,000-1,00,000	03
Above 1,00,000	17
Total	100

Table 10 shows that certain changes are evident even in India's patriarchal society. In balancing work and family life, 11 respondents stated that they took decisions on their work and home themselves. Although 43 respondents said their father or husband were responsible for taking major decisions, 41 also said that one person did not take the decisions but that they were made mutually on matters regarding the family and by themselves, at work.

V

Conclusions

Call centres are one of the most sought after workplaces for young graduates and undergraduates as it provides them with a good environment to work in, decent emoluments and financial incentives, transportation both during day and night, and meals and refreshments. No other job allows the entry of employees with minimum education (school pass) at such attractive perks.

Our research shows that there is a change in the acceptability of women working in call centres having night duties, both in nuclear and joint families. Moreover, in the lower income groups, the woman's salary is very important and the families look up to their daughter's work in improving their economic status. Such jobs are also acceptable in higher income groups, where women are working in the call centres as a pastime.

Table 10
Decision-maker in the Family

Decision Maker	*Number*
Self	11
Father/husband	43
Mutual	41
Mother	05
Total	100

Call centres follow strict rules in granting leave to their employees. The nature of the work is such that the process breaks if the customer care executive/process associate is not present. Hence call centres penalize their workers by deducting salary and reducing leave period if the employees do not apply for leave before the scheduled shift through email to their superiors.

Women in call centres are generally in process jobs and not in technical ones. They work at the lowest level of process associates/customer care executives. Their salary is below Rs. 10,000 but even so they play a meaningful role in their family structures by contributing to the family income.

Women working in call centres are generally in the age group 18-30, indicating that it is mostly unmarried women who take up these jobs. Though in India the age of marriage of a girl is generally the early 20s, we found that women working in call centres delay marriage to their late 20s and early 30s, as they want to be economically independent. This is because they cannot balance their family lives with their jobs in the call centre.

There was no discrimination against women at the entry level. But very few women attain managerial positions, as they dropped out of their jobs to get married and bear children.

Call centre jobs have a direct influence on health, because the women work against the biological clock while on night duty. Women in call centres suffer from stomach-related problems, eye and head strain, backache and spondylities; they also get addicted to smoking and having endless cups of tea and coffee to keep awake at night. Seventy-five per cent of the women respondents reported that call centre job is a health hazard.

There is no balancing at all between work and family life. The families are accepting the work role of the woman as a priority and the people at home make adjustments. Also the decision making power of such women is enhanced.

Notes

1. The literature on status of women shows references to sex role stereotyping as a constraint to entry of women in non-traditional jobs [Desai: 1977, Jain: 1975].
2. Speech by Vina Mazumdar at the national seminar on women's studies:network, issues and agenda, March 16, 2001.
3. Source: Census of India. 1991. Census of India, 2001 Draft Tenth. Plan (2000-2001) page-237. For further information, see Linda Brannon (1999).
4. Chakrabortty's work highlights that Indian society is in a transition, hence the problems of social values, norms and cultural standards are to be expected. Due to this there is a likelihood of conflicts and dilemmas that women experience because of their employment. see also Kariekar (1982).
5. This stereotyping of women's jobs in lower levels is also shown by a study of women in the hospitality industry in India [Singh: 2001, Gulati: 1990].
6. Preeti Singh did a study on women in the corporate world in India. Seventy per cent of women respondents in this study showed that there were social constraints in a woman's life. Teaching jobs, part time jobs or jobs with flexible timings were found to be more suitable in the present Indian scenario because of their conditioning towards family cpmmitments even though society had begun to accept women working in the managerial cadre in the corporate sector [Singh: 2002].
7. For further reading on women's marital adjustment, see Ramu (1989:16).

References

Aries, Elizabeth. 1987. 'Gender and Communication', pp. 149-176 in Phillip Shaver and Clyde Hendrick (ed), *Sex and Gender,* Newbury Park, CA.

Aries, Elizabeth. 1996. 'Men and Women in Interaction', New York: Oxford University Press.

Bleier, Ruth. 1984. Science and Gender-A Critique of Biology and Its Theories on Women. Pergamon Press Inc.

Brannon, Linda. 1999. *Gender Psychological Persectives,* Allyn and Bacon, US.

Breedlove, S. Marc. 1994. 'Sexual Diffemtiation of the Human Nervous System', *Annual Review of Psychology:* 45: 389-4,18.

Chakrabortty, Krishna. 1978. *The Conflicting Worlds of Working Mothers,* Calcutta: Progressive Publisher.

Desai, Neera. 1977. *Women in Modern India,* Bombay: Vora and Co.

Farmer, Helen S. and Sidney, Joan Sliger. 1985. 'Sex Equity in Career and Vocational Education' pp. 338-59 in Susan S Klein (ed), Handbook for Achieving Sex Equity through Education, John Hopkins University Press, Baltimore.

Gulhati, Kaval. 1990. 'Attitudes Towards Women Managers', *Economic and Political Weekly,* February 17-24.

Hahn, William Kerr. 1987. 'Cerebral Lateralisation of Function: From Infancy through childhood', *Psychological Bulletin:* 101: 376-92.

Jain, D. 1975. *Indian Women,* Ministry of Information and Broadcasting, Publication Division, New Delhi.

Janeway, Elizabeth. 1974. Between Myth and Morning: Women Awakening, New York: William Morrow and Company.

Karlekar, M. 1982. *Povery and Women's Work:* A *Study of Sweeper Women in Delhi,* Delhi: Vikas Publishing House.

Mazumdar, Vina. 2001. 'Note on Women through the Plans for Discussion on the Ninth Five Year-Plan 1997', National Seminar, Women's Studies Network Issues and Agenda (Document) March 16-17.

Mitra, Jyoti. 1974. *Women and Society, Equality and Environment,* New Delhi: Kanishka Publishers, Distributors.

Ramu, G.N. 1989. *Women, Work and Marriage in Urban India,* New Delhi: Sage Publications,

Singh, Preeti. 2001. 'Status of Women in the Hospitality Industry in India', paper presented at the conference on women socialization and communication, San Deigo University.

Singh, Preeti. 2002. 'Women in the Corporate World In India: Balancing, Work and Family Life', paper presented and published as conference proceedings, Uppsala University, Sweden, March.

The paper was first published in the *Economic and Political Weekly*: 40:7: 2005:684-88. It is included here with the prior permission of the authors and the Editor, *Economic and Political Weekly*. Address for email correspondence is: anupandey@hotmail.com>

Chapter - Twenty Six

The Globalized Woman in Indian Society: A Case Study of Women Executives in Contemporary Era

Mala Bhandari

The era of economic reforms in India began in the year 1990 as a strategy to become part of the global economy. The corresponding programme of structural liberalization brought about change in the labour market dynamics and caused an upward trend in female waged work and employment. In 2001 the employment of women in the organized sector, both private and public, was 17.8 per cent of the total organized sector employment in the country, which was comparatively higher than in the proceeding years (Census of India: 2001). Much of the increase in employment arising out of globalization resulted in the movement of female labour from the household and subsistence (agriculture) sector, to paid employment. The globalization of trade and economy opened up economic and income opportunities for women in the manufacturing and service sectors and the high-valued industries, causing a new phenomena called, "feminization of labour force".

The distribution in major industries reveal that the community, social and personal services sectors absorbed the majority (2754.5 thousands) of women employees (Census of India: 2001). Due to the inherent nature and requirements of these areas, women with specialized skills and technical know-how are today employed in large numbers, causing a dramatic shift in the demography of the workforce particularly among the upper-middle classes of the society. This category of women workers forms a class of professionals and technical executives, which constitutes about 20 per cent of the total female work force in India (Human Development Report: 2002).

In case of married women from the upper and middle socio-economic strata, the resultant labour force shift shows the following trends:

- Continuing increase of dual-earner couples;

- An increase in the percentage of mothers with young children in the workforce;
- A growing similarity in the labor force patterns of men and women with steady and uninterrupted work profiles; and
- Proliferation of new family forms–nuclear households with dependence upon institutionalized means for child-care.

The present paper aims to analyze the contemporary demographic changes in the labor force within the context of work-life balance and other issues related to women working at executive positions in the corporate sector.

Women and work: Some empirical issues in the era of globalization

The process of globalization has had far reaching effects on issues of gender and society. Through process of adjustment, it has affected the households in a number of basic ways:

- Changes in income, through changes in wages and levels of employment, product prices and product demand;
- Changes in the price of essential purchases like food;
- Changes in the allocation of public expenditure—especially with regard to social or welfare policy, including the introduction or increase of user chargers for services like education and health; and
- Changes in working conditions through changes in hours of work, intensity of work, job security and fringe benefits (this applies to unpaid as well as paid work).

Some empirical studies on women and waged work began with the theory of two distinct roles of women: home and work. These opposing roles presumably led to the double burden and role-conflict for middle class working women (Myrdral and Klein: 1956). A number of scholarly studies (Pleck: 1977; Bailyn: 1978; Gothaskar: 1992; Mathur: 1992) reiterated the dichotomy between women's work role (employment) and traditionally given social roles, i.e., the duties and expectations enjoined on them as caretakers of the family. The nature of conflict between these varied and depended on factors such as access to paid domestic help, higher earnings than husband, structural constraints and demands of job, extended households and child-care (Maria Mies: 1980). In this context, a substantially different set of social values for women exacerbated the double burden of women's responsibilities at home and in the market (Blau and Ferber: 1986:30). These conflicts have become more overt and obvious in case of women's professional and social roles (Fatima: 1993).

The role conflict theory rested on asymmetrical boundaries between the work roles and family roles (Pleck: 1977). For women, while family roles may constrict their work roles, it is seen to be the opposite in the case of men. This observation has been supported by the view that women have two simultaneous roles while men have sequential roles, i.e., while the men can defer their familial roles after work, the women's family responsibilities continue throughout the workday (Hall quoted in Nieva: 1985: 176). The basic assumption of these studies sees a separation between family and work as two distinctive institutions posing competing demands on women, while completely ignoring the possible linkages or interdependence between the two spheres, which is taking place due to demographic changes in women's employment (Nieva: 1985: 163).

Studies that see a 'triple overlap' between gender stratification, economy and family indicate an inflexible and very resistant aspect of family life, which is the nature of housework (Blumberg: 1991). There is a lack of reorganization and negotiation in the division of labour within the household that comprises a limiting factor for women to meet professional demands and expectations with a particular focus on individual goal attainment (Bernhardt: 1993). In addition, socio-cultural reasons and gender-based discriminatory practices at the workplace are subtle and not so subtle factors impeding women's growth to the top positions in the occupational hierarchy as indicated through a study of women biologists in India (Bal: 2004: 3650). Institutional sex-stereotyping regarding women's ability and willingness to accept positions of responsibility and their placement in less strategic areas of activity deprives them of varied and challenging assignments and exposure to the full range of operations and activities in enterprises or organizations. This also leads to women's concentration at the lower levels of the occupational hierarchy (Wirth:1998: 98). Regardless of such constraints and limitations, married women professionals are often assumed to lack professionalism and commitment to work and career as compared to their male counterparts (Rotolo, Thomas and Amy: 2003: 80).

Women perform their roles in varied cultural and socio-political contexts. Their multiplicity of roles requires coping mechanisms for handling work and family concerns at the individual, household and organizational levels. Common strategies at the household front are role sequencing and differential role allocation between family members (Bailyn: 1978; Yoydanoff:1987). These strategies aim to change the environment and work characteristics of family in favour of women's job/ work satisfaction and occupational role stresses (Lakshmirani and Mishra: 2000: 50). Many women even eliminate roles and make choices not traditionally required of men (Nieva: 1985: 176). Division of domestic tasks among female household members, employment of paid help and prioritization of tasks are common coping strategies adopted by working women (Bhandari: 2004: 267). At the occupational front, institutional adjustments help in achieving a work-life balance for women. Many opt to work as part time professionals, which helps them harmonize their responsibilities as a worker and mother while staying in touch with the work place (Waren: 2004: 110).

The Conceptual Framework of the Study

In cognizance of the observation that the role conflict theory cannot adequately explain all the intricate social realities in a woman's life (Krishnaraj: 1991:10), the present study was undertaken with an alternate approach, the quality of life

(QOL) approach. This emphasizes that work and family are two interacting structures or social systems that most profoundly impact women's lives (Sticher: 1990: 62). Therefore, this study focuses on inter-linkages between family/household and women's work life as it has altered with macro-economic changes and analyzes all aspects of women's lives, viewing home, work and family as one integrated whole with relations of interdependence and inter-reliance.

The concept of QOL grew out of the social indicators movement of the 1960s. A social indicators approach was used to define QOL in response to the excessive focus on economic indicators as measures of development and well being. This approach focused on external factors and objective information (Day and Jankey: 1996: 42). The QOL gradually developed as an inclusive concept, which covered all aspects of living including material satisfaction of vital needs and other aspects of life such as personal development, self-realization and a healthy eco-system. It encompasses all the material aspects of human life including the physical and psychological dimensions. This concept may be defined in terms of an aggregate of a number of social and economic outputs received by groups or individuals or as subjective evaluation of satisfaction or well being (Miles: 1985: 152). On the basis of the concept of QOL, the home and office lives of women executives were studied through following indicators:

- Economic autonomy and empowerment through achieved status of an earner;
- Intra-household decision-making through management and control over money resources; and
- The traditional division of labour within the household.

These indicators included the objective conditions of life as well as subjective interpretations by women of their lives that were influenced by social and cultural forces affecting the household.

The Sample and Methodology of the Study

This paper is based on an empirical study of women executives, undertaken by the author with support from the University Grants Commission. This was an in-depth study of the home and office lives of women working in corporate executive positions in Pune city in Maharashtra, India. The sample of the study comprised 40 married women executives in the age group of 30 to 40 years. They worked at executive positions in the manufacturing, information technology, and banking and hospitality areas of the service sector. They held independent charge of operations, marketing, management, sales and public relations departments of their respective industrial units and companies. They lived in nuclear and extended households and were selected through a random sampling procedure. The information was collected by the standard interview method using an interview guide.

A preliminary survey among women executives in the city showed their preference for working in the corporate sector for higher monetary gains and perks, greater opportunities for professional growth, a competitive work environment and respect for acquired status in the society. They emerged as a common group with similarities in socio-economic backgrounds, educational qualifications, familial and household patterns and work and family related stresses and anxieties.

The QOL indicators

Autonomy and Intra-household Decision-making

Management and control are two aspects of handling money. The first is seen as akin to the implementation functions performed within any enterprise; the carrying out of decisions which have already been made. Control, akin to policy-making functions, refers to the decision-making aspect of a family's finances (Edwards: 1981: 4). A spouse may take decisions on major purchases but may only be acting as an agent of his/her partner for trust between them, defined as shared values whereby one person acts in the interest of the other and may speak on behalf of the other.(Blumstein and Schwartg: 1983:63).

Within the household, there are four main types of money management and control:

- *Whole wage system*: the husband hands over his entire pay packet to the wife to manage and provide for the family;
- *Household allowance system*: the husband gives a set amount to the wife to cover the household expenses;
- *Shared management system*: both the partners pool money and have equal access to all the household income. However, one partner may have a greater control and influence over the way money is spent and budgeted;
- *Independent management system*: both the partners have their own money and are responsible for different categories of expenditure.

The concept of control is complex and goes much beyond decision-making. There are four systems of control: predominantly by husband, by wife, shared control and independent control (Singh: 1993). The respondents' salaries comprise the domestic pool once they are brought home. Domestic money is a meaningful socially constructed currency, shaped by the domestic sphere where it circulates and moves according to the gender and social class of the predominant money handlers (Zelizer: 1989: 369). It is either collectivized or trivialized, merged into the housekeeping fund and is thus undifferentiated from collective income or else treated as supplementary earnings, earmarked either for family expenses (child's education or vacation) or for frivolous purposes (clothes, etc.). The most obvious effect of a woman's employment is an increase in the family income (Lazear and Micheal: 1980 in Mclaughlin and Melbere: 1988: 115). The respondents' contribution to the household economy varied between 45 to 55 per cent of the total household income. This proportion was important for bringing these households within the 'higher income' bracket. With the monthly total household incomes of up to Rs. 60,000, the contributions from the respondents and their husbands were almost comparable. Households with total incomes of above Rs. 60,000 received larger contributions from the husbands, a majority of whom were self-employed. The respondents' contributions were not restricted to the regular cash expenses of the household. If their salaries were not directly used for the day-to-day household expenses, these were used for asset building through savings for the future, investment in property or stocks and purchase of expensive household electronics. For instance, in a respondent's words, "my salary is not used for the day to day expenses. My husband wants it to be saved for property and investments."

The respondents' salaries had three components: a certain fixed amount called the basic salary, allowances for lunch and fuel, either in cash or kind, and outstation allowances for official tours and travel. Therefore, the total salaries drawn by them varied by the company they worked in. The purpose of their salaries in the household was classified into four main categories–supplementary, selective payments, given to husband and common pool. The data showed that there was no clear-cut distinction among these categories. The money was for the home but used in different modes, the most common being the supplementary role of the respondents' salaries as seen in 45 per cent of the households. In this, the husbands' salaries primarily managed the household expenses, while those of the respondents were used or withdrawn only when required. Their salaries would be otherwise used for paying loan installments or for investment purposes. For instance, in Case 21, whose husband withdrew his salary from the bank for the running expenses of the household, while she withdrew hers only in case of a family requirement. The other mode was the common pool, used by about 25 per cent of the cases. The respondents pooled their salaries with those of their husbands, either in proportion or the entire amount and deposited the remaining money in their bank account. The common fund was either kept at home or deposited in a joint bank account for subsequent withdrawal. A larger number of respondents pooled in their entire salaries rather than those who pooled only a part. In Case 11, the respondent and her husband deposited their salaries in their joint bank account as a common fund, to be subsequently withdrawn for household expenses. In case of total household incomes exceeding Rs. 40,000 per month, the common modes of household expenditure were the pooling of salaries (common fund) and the supplementary mode for the respondents' incomes. Other modes of expenditure were not very common in the sample households. In one case, the respondent explicitly handed over her salary to the husband and then received pocket money for her personal expenses. This was an extended household where the husband and his parents managed the finances. My data on how the husband's salaries were used showed that most of them withdrew their salaries for household expenses. Those with varying monthly incomes differentiated their incomes into money into a common fund and for business purposes. In such cases, the respondents did not know their husband's salaries.

An important aspect of independence and autonomy over money matters is evident from control over banking, which implies privacy and personal discretion in money transactions. Since respondents had an income of their own, it was important to know the extent of their participation in banking activities, i.e., how many had their own accounts and who decided on the inflow and outflow of money in these accounts? The data showed that around 70 per cent of the respondents had personal bank accounts compared to 74 per cent of their spouses. However, the number of respondents with personal accounts was more than those with joint accounts. As regards managing the accounts, there was greater involvement of husbands in their personal accounts. Those respondents who managed their bank affairs secretly from their spouses, were more in number than those who consulted them. In contrast, around 55 per cent of the respondents managed their own personal accounts, but their husbands either had full or partial knowledge of the transactions; they either told them about all the details of their accounts to their husbands or informed them about only the transactions that involved big amounts of money. For instance, in Case 6, the respondent maintained complete transparency in the management of her bank account. In contrast, her husband did not divulge any personal account details nor did she ask him, reportedly due to their hectic daily routine. In about 25 per cent of the cases, neither the respondents nor their husbands had accounts in their personal names, but had only joint accounts. Interestingly, these accounts were managed by the husbands and very often, the respondents did not even ask for the details. In Case 31, the respondent and her husband transferred their salary amounts into their joint account, which was used by the husband for running the household and the former never interfered in how he managed the funds.

Decision-making is an important area for the dynamics of 'power' attached with it. The one, who decides about what, where and how financial resources are assimilated, compounded and distributed, enjoys greater power than others in the family. The study investigated the respondents' role in intra-household decision-making in the areas that require short and long-term perspective such as food, entertainment, travel and savings for the household. The married couples decide about allocation and expenditure of money in the household in four major possible ways: wife decides what is appropriate or necessary for the household; resources limit the expenditure according to a budget as essential payments are made first while the remaining money is kept for miscellaneous items; husband decides; and husband and wife negotiate and decide together (Pahl: 1989: 139). Due to traditional role expectations by the husband and members of the wider community and segregation of the husband's task allocation patterns, it is often argued that wives are restrained from joint decision-making (Szinovacz: 1977: 789).

With respect to expenses on food, there are two main aspects of decisions made: the extent of money to be spent and kitchen management, which includes selection of food items to be brought and prepared. The data showed that participation of the husband was limited to expenditure related decisions, which, however, reduced with an increase in the total household income. In 35 to 50 per cent of the cases, the respondents made expenditure related decisions about food. In Case 1, the respondent decided and managed the kitchen expenses with the money given to her by her husband for household expenses. She ascertained these expenses according to the money brought home every month. In extended households, the greater role of husband's parents was evidently seen in managing the kitchen expenses. In Case 18, the parents managed the kitchen expenses with the money provided by the spouse. The respondent had no role in it.

In case of entertainment and travel, joint decision-making was evident in more than 50 per cent of the cases. However, the respondents' participation was, by and large, limited to the selection of venue and time for such outings. For instance, in Case 22, while the respondent planned outings, her husband decided about the money aspect. Many a times, their planned trips were cancelled or postponed due to disagreement over the expenditure involved. However, in Case 22, since the respondent and her husband pooled their money, they jointly budgeted their outings.

In the area of savings, decisions were made at two levels: personal and household. Household savings were almost entirely the complete responsibility of the respondents' husbands. At a personal level, the behaviour of the respondents pertaining to savings differed from that of their husbands. While the former preferred the short term, secure savings schemes, husbands were more inclined towards investing in stock markets and real estate. However, the respondents' indulgence in personal savings was almost negligible. In Case 38, the respondent felt no need for personal savings as her husband managed the household money and made stocks and property investments in her name. Such arrangements were evident in the cases of many other respondents in the sample.

The Work Routines and Division of Labour within the Household

A woman's employment may not provide the sufficient context for renegotiation of a domestic division of labour (Gregson and Lowe: 1993: 484). Research shows the lack of sharing in household activities between husbands and working wives (Pleck: 1977; Lopata, Barnewolt and Norr: 1980). This may clearly mean that women's economic status may not be necessarily accompanied by the increasing willingness of male partners to take on domestic labour. This observation has another dimension that emerged from a study of women professionals, which showed that women who felt equal to their husbands in ability and intelligence, still perceived housework and child care as their responsibilities and spent much more time in doing these tasks than did their husbands. This may suggest that egalitarian concepts about the self with unequal division of labour may be a temporary compromise in the process of role definition for both spouses (Yogev: 1981).

An analysis of time-use data of the respondents and their husbands in their daily routines indicated compatibility between their work and rest times. The respondents' day was distinctly compartmentalized into two separate spheres of activity–home and office. As they worked in office, they worked at home. The data on division of labour within the sample households showed that the respondents, paid domestic help and other family members undertook various household tasks. The paid help was employed for four main tasks at home: sweeping the floors, washing dishes and washing and ironing clothes. While the task of cooking was shared with other female family members, the task of dusting was shared with the husband or grown up children. Work patterns showed that respondents with more responsibilities at home than their husbands, prioritized domestic tasks on different days of the week. Their work routine analysis showed that prioritization of tasks was done on the basis of time and requirement for the household. For instance, while some cleaning deemed to be essential was done everyday, it was performed more thoroughly over the weekends. Cooking was the main task of the respondents on a daily basis. Only in 20 per cent of the cases, full-time paid help was hired for all the household tasks, including cooking. The outside household tasks such as fetching vegetables, provisions and other essentials and payment of water and electricity bills were divided between husbands and other members of the household.

The patterns of daily routine were distinct to respondents and their husbands in both the nuclear and extended households. A comparative analysis of respondents' and their husbands' work routines showed considerable difference with regard to the number and type of tasks performed by them at home. On working days, the time spent by them at home and in the office was almost the same. During the hours spent at home, they were involved in different types of tasks. While the respondents cooked or monitored domestic tasks, the husbands either rested or played with the children. Holidays had different connotations for them. While the respondents caught up with household tasks that they were unable to do during the week, their husbands made up for lost sleep and relaxation. The husbands' involvement in household tasks was negligible on holidays.

The work routines of the respondents varied according to the availability of paid help and help from other family members, including husbands. The availability of paid domestic help was an essential feature of the sample households, comprising the backbone of these households. Help from other family members was limited to certain tasks such as cooking, dusting and monitoring the children.The households were marked by the traditional division of labour, as observed in the following aspects:

- Responsibility for performing inside-the-household tasks was, by and large, divided between the respondents and the paid domestic helpers. The husband had a negligible role in such tasks.
- Help from other family members was available only on working days. Their cooperation in domestic tasks was minimal on holidays.
- Husbands' participation in inside-the-household tasks was neither voluntary nor regular. They had no responsibility for any particular task as such. If at all, they extended partial help to respondents at some stage, for instance, they would mind the children for some time but were not responsible for the task of child-care as such.
- Households with full-time paid help provided a more relaxed routine to the respondents than those with the part-time domestic help, easing the drudgery

of household work for the respondents, and facilitating their mobility outside the home.

Conclusion

Women's work profiles are affected by the following stages in their life cycles: marriage, childbirth and re-entry (Aggassi in Jewell: 1977: 38). However, the present study showed that the pattern of the respondents' labour force participation was indistinguishable from that of their husbands. They had continuous uninterrupted work profiles. The processes of reproduction interrupted their work profiles but it was neither unprecedented in duration nor permanent in nature.

The respondents' contribution to the household economy was in the form of:

- Raising the total cash inflow in the household
- Asset-making (movable and immovable) with a long-term perspective
- Savings for future needs of the family through investments
- Helping in occupational mobility of husbands by shouldering the burden of the household economy.

The respondents' incomes contributed significantly to the upward mobility of the sample households. The findings reaffirmed that financial resources contributed by women enhanced their familial living standards and social class position (Scanzoni: 1978). However, potent ideological forces downgrade women's financial role and reaffirm their domesticity (Jackson: 1993). One such attempt is cultural definitions of the man as a 'breadwinner' (Pahl: 1989; Branner and Moss: 1977, 1991). The present study observes the 'supplementary' nature of respondents' salaries as these amounts were used for certain extras, while the basic necessities of the household were born out of the husbands' salaries. This connotes an unequally gendered form or differentiated nature of the husbands and wives' earnings within their households. This defines the man as the 'primary breadwinner' and the woman as the supplementary earner, completely ignoring the fact that both contributed fairly comparable incomes to their households. Related to the gender differentiation in incomes in the households was the issue of control over income and autonomy in spending it. In the light of these gender differences regarding their incomes, evidently women worked for their families rather than themselves, more so than their husbands (Sharma: 1980; Standing: 1985).

The data on intra-household decision-making illustrated the dominant role of husbands. While the respondents played an important role in deciding about the basic issues relating to expenditure, the final say and decisions remained with their husbands. The respondents' participation was more evident in decisions relating to food and entertainment than to savings for the household. In traditional setups, women were considered weak in money matters, therefore, the men as breadwinners of the family held the reins over their monetary resources. In the contemporary setup, although the economic meaning of breadwinner has changed, particularly in dual earner households, the socio-cultural locus of control over money management and related decision-making remains unchanged. The men still control the reins over the cash flow and resource disbursement in the household. This is evident from the fact that my respondents' salary details and personal bank accounts were clearly known to their husbands, but not vice versa. The practice of maintaining common funds or joint accounts was adopted more for reasons of convenience and other benefits, rather than to facilitate and encourage joint decision-making. The respondents did reportedly feel the stranglehold of socio-cultural factors with respect to money matters but called it a voluntary give up in the name of 'trust' or 'faith' in husbands. These observations may be well understood in the context of patriarchy: historical, material and psychoanalytic (Stacey: 1993).

The emergence of patriarchy may be traced in the Engel's work, whereby women lost power during the shift in importance of reproduction to production (Mies 1980). It was a shift of patriarchal structures in the 19th century from the private forms 'based upon household production' to their more public forms in the 20th century, 'employment and state' (Walby: 1986). In material sense, patriarchy originated and practiced by means of control over modes of production; by means of which men exploited the productive and reproductive activities of women in the context of family relations. In psychoanalytic sense, patriarchy formed sexual identities, which were internalized by individual psyche through conscious and unconscious processes (Delphy: 1992:74).

With regard to household work routines, there was no change in the division of labour among the family members. The respondents were responsible for work at home and the household tasks were gendered (Oakley: 1974). While they added work role demands to their traditional family roles and responsibilities, their husbands had not been quick to add new family tasks to their traditional work responsibilities. The lack of interchangeability between the respondents and their husbands for household and work roles led to a 'double burden' for respondents who were trying to simultaneously perform home and market work (Blau: 1986: 29). The husbands' participation in household tasks was not only selective and occasional but was often extended in the way of doing a 'favour' to their wives. These women's work at home created their husbands' leisure (Jackson: 1993:185). At home, the respondents not only had less leisure time than their husbands but also were constantly 'on call' by other family members (Richardson 1993: 185). Their time was a resource, which could be drawn anytime by the family members. This was due to an asymmetrically permeable boundary between work roles and family roles for men and women. While the demands of the family role restricted my respondents' work roles, the men's demands and work roles could intrude into family time (Pleck: 1977).

Economic changes at a global level have had their impact upon the institutions of social system. However, this study indicates that micro-level institutions such as family and household have not shown much change in their traditional orientations in the Indian context. As discussed before, women's role in the workforce has changed but no corresponding change has taken place in the home.

The dominant role of husbands in controlling the household resources remains the same. The norms of patriarchy over economic resources and division of labour among the household members are still predominantly evident. These women's status in the workplace has not changed the traditional orientation of the family.

In today's globalised world, women's liberation and equality require a radical transformation of imperialism, capitalism and patriarchy. A beginning has to be made at the household level, whereby a more egalitarian one replaces a gendered division of labour so that men take up a larger share of responsibilities (Sundaram and Geethakrishnan: 1999: 107). These changes would be possible only when women's work issues are considered as family issues, which would imply an approach based on an equitable distribution of work between the spheres of home and office. Another important approach in this context is the renegotiation of the gendered division of labour by both men and women in the private as well as public spheres, and reassessment of the relative worth of women's and men's work in both (Richardson: 1993: 300). The social connotations of money, income, roles and work require restructuring in line with contemporary economic changes. The study of quality of life of women executives cannot remain independent of such issues, as they reflect the social conditions under which women work in their professional careers.

References

Agassi, Judith, B. 1977. 'The quality of women's working life', pp. 33-57 in Jewell, Donald. O. (ed.). *Women and Management: an expanding role.* Atlanta: Georgia State University.

Bailyn, L. 1977. "Accommodation of work to family', pp. 159-74 in R.R. Rapoport (ed.) *Working Couples.* New York: Harper.

Bal,Vineeta. 2004. Women scientists in India: Nowhere near the glass ceiling". *Economic and Political Weekly*: 2004: 3647-3652.

Bernhardt, E.M. 1993. "Changing family ties women's position and low fertility', pp. 80-103 in Federici, N. Mason, K.O. and Sognar,S.(eds.). *Women's position and demographic change.* Oxford: Clarandon Press.

Bhandari, M. 2004. *Quality of life of urban workingwomen,* New Delhi: Abhijeet Publications.

Blau, F.D., Ferber and Anne. 1986. 'Women and Men: changing roles in a changing society' in Boyd, J. (ed.). *The Economics of women, men and work,* Prentice-Hall,Inc.

Blumberg, R.L. (ed). 1991. *Gender, Family and Economy: The triple overlap,* California: Sage.

Blumstein, P. & S. Pepper. 1983. *American Couples: Money, Work, Sex.* New York: Pocket Books.

Day, H. and S.G. Jankey. 1996. "Lessons from the literature: Towards a holistic model of QOL" in Renwick, et al eds. *QOL in health promotion and rehabilitation: conceptual approaches, issues and applications,* London: Sage.

Delphy C. and D. Leonard. 1992. *Familiar Exploitation: A new analysis of marriage in contemporary western societies.* Cambridge: Polity Press.

D. Lakshmi Rani and P.K. Mishra. 2000. 'Coping behaviour among working women in emergency services'. *Social Science International*: 16:1 and 2: 34-51.

Edwards, M. 1998. *Financial arrangements within families:* National Women's Advisory Council.

Fatima, A.N. 1993. *Women Physicians: A study in roles and role conflicts.* Delhi: Manak Publications.

Gothaskar, S. (ed.). 1992. *Struggles of women at work*. Delhi: Vikas Publishing House.

Gregson, N. and L. Michelle. 1993. Renegotiating the domestic division of labour: A study of dual career households in North East and South East England, *The Sociological Review*: 41: 3: 475–505.

Jackson, Stevi. 1993. 'Women and the family'. pp. 177–200 in Richardson, D. & Victoria. R. (eds). *Introducing Women's studies.* London: Macmillan.

Krishnaraj, M. 1991. *Women and Science–Selected Essays.* Delhi: Himalaya Publishing House.

Mathur, D. 1992. *Women, Family and Work.* Jaipur: Rawat Publications.

Mclaughin, D.S. and M.D. Barbara (eds.). 1998. *The changing lives of American women.* Chapel Hill & London: The University of North Carolina Press.

Mies, M. 1980. *Indian women and Patriarchy: Conflicts and Dilemmas of students and working women.* New Delhi: Concept Publishing House.

Miles, I. 1985. *Social Indicators for Human Devlopment.* London: Frances Printer Publishers.

Myrdal. A. and Klien. V. 1956. *Women's two roles: home and work.* London: Routledge and Kegan Paul.

Nieva, V.F. 1985. 'Work and Family linkages', in I., Larwood, L., Sromberg & Barbara (eds.). *Women and Work: An annual review,* London: Sage Publications,Inc.

Oakley, A. 1974. *Housewife:* New York: Allen Lane.

Pahl, J. 1989. *Money and Marriage.* London: Macmillan.

Pleck, J.H. 1977. 'The Work–Family System'. *Social Problems*: 24: 417- 427.

Richardson, D. and V. Robinson. 1993. *Introducing Women's Studies.* London: Macmillan.

Rotolo, Thomas & Wharton, Amy. 2003. "Living across institutions: exploring sex-based homophily in occupations and voluntary groups" ,*Sociological Perspectives*: 46: 1, Spring 2003: 59-82.

Scanzoni, J. 1978. *Sex roles, women's work and marital conflicts: A study of family change,* Lexington, MA; D.C. Heath.

Sharma, U. 1980. *Women, Work and Property in North West India.* London: Tevistock.

Singh, Supriya. 1993. 'Information, money management and marriage'. Paper presented at the Fourth Australian Family Research Conference. Manly Pacific Parkroyal: 17-19 February.

Stacey, J. 1993. 'Untangling Feminist Theory'. pp. 49-73 in Richardson, D. and V. Robinson. (eds.) *Introducing Women's Studies.* London: Macmillan.

Standing, H. 1985. 'Women's employment and the household: Some findings from Calcutta'. *Economic and Political Weekly*: 20:17: 23-28.

Stitcher, S. & Parpart, J.L. 1990. (eds.) *Women employment and the family in the intrahousehold division of labour:* London: Sage Publications.

Sundaram. D. and K.C. Geethakrishnan. 1999. 'Labour Market Transformation: Issues in Women's Devlopment'. pp. 93-109. in Sethi, R.M. *Globalization, Culture and Women's Devlopment.* New Delhi: Rawat Publications.

Szinovacz, M.E. 1977. 'Role allocation, family structure and female employment'. *Journal of Marriage and Family:* 39: 781-91.

Walby, S. 1986. *Patriarchy at work.* Cambridge: Polity Press.

Wirth, Linda. 1998. Women in management: close to breaking through the glass ceiling?*International Labour Review*: 137:1: 93-102.

Yogev, S. 1981. Work sequences of women during the family life cycle. *Journal of Marriage and the family:* 40:2: 401-411.

Yoydanoff, P. 1987. *Work and Family Life. Family Study,* Text Series 6: London: Sage Publications.

Zelizer, V. 1989. 'The social meaning of money: special monies'. *American Journal of Sociology*: 95:2: 342-377.

This paper is based on a three years' study undertaken by the author at Department of Sociology, University of Pune, Maharashtra, India under the Special Assistance Programme of the University Grants Commission. The author is associated with the Social and Development Research and Action Group Network of Professional Women in Delhi. Address for email correspondence is Email: mala@sadrag.org

Index